Employment Law

Employment Law

Fourth edition

John Bowers, Barrister

BLACKSTONE
PRESS LIMITED

First published in Great Britain 1990 by Blackstone Press Limited,
9-15 Aldine Street, London W12 8AW. Telephone 0181-740 2277

© John Bowers, 1990

ISBN: 1 85431 289 8

First edition 1982
Second edition 1986
Third edition 1990
Fourth edition 1997

British Library Cataloguing in Publication Data
A CIP catalogue record for this book is available from the British Library

Typeset by Style Photosetting Limited, Mayfield, East Sussex
Printed by Ashford Colour Press, Gosport, Hampshire

Contents

Preface

This edition has been much delayed by reason of the much delayed Employment Rights and Industrial Tribunal Acts which finally came into force on 22 August 1996. I have taken these consolidating measures into account as well as the major amendments ushered in by the Sunday Trading Act 1994 and the Disability Discrimination Act 1995, as well as important Regulations such as the Industrial Tribunal (Extension of Jurisdiction) Regulations 1994 and the Collective Redundancies and Transfer of Undertakings (Protection of Employment) (Amendment) Regulations 1995. There have also been very important case law developments since the last edition, not least in the discrimination field where cases such as *EOC, Webb* v *EMO Air Cargo, P* v *S, Seymour-Smith* and *Burton* v *De Vere Hotels* have revolutionised our understanding of discrimination concepts. Discrimination is clearly the most dynamic area at present for employment law.

The challenge for the coming years is to maintain the tripartite structure of industrial tribunals and the Employment Appeal Tribunal which has in my view served the public well. A unibual (a lawyer sitting alone) may be cheaper to run but it is unlikely to provide the same sense of industrial justice for those appearing before it.

There are too many people who have assisted in this edition to mention them all personally but I must single out for praise Elizabeth Stern, Nicholas Chronias, Damian McCarthy, Gary Morton, Geoffrey Mead, Sally Cowen, Janet Simpson and Julia Palca. All but the last two had the misfortune to be my pupils from time to time. Other members of my own Chambers, in particular Michael Burton QC, Daniel Serota QC, Michel Kallipetis QC, Andrew Clarke and Selwyn Bloch, are always generous with their time and many of the ideas in this book owe much to their assistance.

I pay tribute to Blackstone Press for whose excellent staff my handwritten manuscript always provides a particular challenge! The book contains the law up to 15 December 1996.

Two weeks before the edition was due to be published, Suzanne and I had a baby boy, Benjamin. The Government then decided to postpone the Employment Rights Act, and Benjamin is now a hearty 20 months old, who provides a daily challenge and delight to his sisters Emma and Hannah and his parents. I thank my parents for developing my interest in work and the law in Cleethorpes many years ago.

John Bowers
Littleton Chambers
3 King's Bench Walk North
London EC4

List of Abbreviations

All ER	All England Law Reports
ACAS	Advisory Conciliation and Arbitration Service
CA	Court of Appeal
CAC	Central Arbitration Committee
CO	Certification Officer
COIT	Central Office of Industrial Tribunals
CLP	Current Legal Problems
CRE	Commission for Racial Equality
DC	Divisional Court of Queen's Bench Division
EA	Employment Act 1980/1982
EEC	European Economic Community
EPA	Employment Protection Act 1975
EPCA	Employment Protection (Consolidation) Act 1978
ERA	Employment Rights Act 1996
EAT	Employment Appeal Tribunal
EOC	Equal Opportunities Commission
ECJ	European Court of Justice
HMSO	Her Majesty's Stationery Office
HC	High Court
IRLR	Industrial Relations Law Reports
ILJ	Industrial Law Journal
IRC	Independent Review Committee of TUC
IT	Industrial Tribunal
ICR	Industrial Cases Reports
ITR	Industrial Tribunal Reports
KIR	Knight's Industrial Report
LQR	Law Quarterly Review
LSG	Law Society Gazette
MLR	Modern Law Review
NIRC	National Industrial Relations Court
NLJ	New Law Journal
ROIT	Regional Office of Industrial Tribunals
RRA	Race Relations Act 1976
SDA	Sex Discrimination Act 1975
SJ	Solicitors Journal

TUA	Trade Union Act 1913
TUC	Trades Union Congress
TULRA	Trade Union and Labour Relations Act 1974
TULR(A)A	Trade Union and Labour Relations (Amendment) Act 1976
TULR(C)A	Trade Union and Labour Relations (Consolidation) Act 1992
TURERA	Trade Union Reform and Employment Rights Act 1993
UMA	Union Membership Agreement
WCA	Wages Councils Act 1979

Table of Cases

Table of Statutes

Table of Statutory Instruments

1 History

I do not think that you will find any other country in which, in important sections of the economy, the trade unions had attained a considerable bargaining strength long before their members had obtained the franchise — no country, in other words, in which, through their own early history, the unions got so much used to the reliance on industrial rather than on political pressure, on collective bargaining outside the law rather than on legislation.

(Professor O. Kahn-Freund, 7 BJIR 3.)

Employment law and trade union law must be viewed against a long historical perspective in order to understand its modern context.

1.1 ORDINANCE OF LABOURERS

The first recognisable labour legislation, the Ordinance of Labourers, was passed in 1349, following the Black Death, and was concerned with maintaining wages at rates to be fixed from time to time by justices of the peace. To support the maintenance of wages this ordinance, and later the Statute of Artificers 1562, prohibited conspiracies to raise wages, and prosecutions for criminal conspiracy at common law also became more frequent as the first workers' associations were formed. These normally grew out of workmates meeting at a public house and their main activity was the provision of friendly society benefits such as sick and funeral money and a tramping grant to unemployed workers willing to move. They also sought to limit the number of apprentices entering their trades, because of the inevitable consequence of depressing wage rates; this has remained a feature of craft unions to this day.

1.2 COMBINATION ACTS AND THEIR REPEAL

The dominant *laissez-faire* economics of the eighteenth and early nineteenth centuries saw interference in wage levels (whether by government or groups of workers) as anathema. Accordingly Parliament supplemented the common law by banning groupings of workers in particular industries (e.g. wool, silk, and leather), and these were generalised in the notorious Combination Act 1799. This was an immediate reaction to a widespread strike by millwrights, but passed against the background of fear of radicalism as embodied in the French Revolution. It was, however, soon amended by the 1800 statute of the same name, which enacted two further specific offences:

(a)   agreeing for the purposes of improving conditions of employment or calling or attending a meeting for such a purpose; and

(b)   attempting to persuade another person not to work or to refuse to work with another worker.

Jurisdiction was given to justices of the peace who could order up to three months imprisonment, and, since the magistrates came from the same class as the masters, frequently did so. The similar prohibition on masters combining was enforced with much less enthusiasm. The Masters and Servants Act 1823 was another powerful weapon in the hands of the employers, since thereby an employee who was absent from service before his contract expired was punishable by up to three months' hard labour. There were some 10,000 prosecutions per year between 1858 and 1875 under this provision according to K. Coates and T. Topham (*Trade Unions in Britain*, Spokesman University Paperbacks, 1981, p. 267).

A campaign masterminded by such articulate exponents of the unions' liberties as Francis Place and Joseph Hume led to the passage of the Combination Laws Repeal Act 1824. This removed 35 prohibitions on combinations in various sectors of the economy, and repealed most of the 1800 Act. Moreover, union combination ceased to be *per se* criminal at common law. The immediate aftermath was, however, a series of violent and damaging strikes. This caused Parliament to think again the next year and the Combination Act 1825 revived the common law offence, save where the only object of the union collectivity was the determination of wages and hours. It also strengthened the law on the specific crimes of intimidation, violence, molestation and obstruction, which the courts soon applied to persuading a fellow worker to join a strike (*R* v *Rowlands* (1851) 5 Cox CC 436) and inducing a worker to leave in breach of contract (*R* v *Druitt* (1867) 10 Cox CC 592). The former decision was, however, modified by the Combination of Workmen Act 1859 which rendered it lawful to attempt, with the aim of securing changes in wages or hours, 'peaceably and in a reasonable manner, and without threat or intimidation to persuade others to cease or abstain from work'.

Other less obvious provisions were pressed into service against the early trade unions. The famous prosecution of five Dorset farm labourers, known to history as the 'Tolpuddle Martyrs', still lives on in union folklore. Their crime was that they used an oath as a sign of allegiance to their new society because they could not read or write. For this they were sentenced to transportation to Australia under the provisions of the Unlawful Societies Act 1799 and Unlawful Oaths Act 1797 (the latter apparently passed to quell naval mutinies).

1.3   THE NEW MODEL UNIONS AND THE TRADE UNION ACT 1871

The most ambitious nineteenth century union, Robert Owen's Grand National Consolidated Trade Union, collapsed in 1834, barely a year after its foundation, but the mid-nineteenth century saw the first great expansion of trade unionism with the creation of federations of previously localised organisations. The new model unions, as they were later to be called, consisted primarily of skilled craftsmen, and combined efficient internal organisation and a sound financial base with a cautious approach to industrial action. Typified by the Amalgamated Society of Engineers, they began to build a nascent structure of collective bargaining with the masters, some of whom were keen to talk to one single spokesman rather than hundreds of individuals. An agreed list of wage rates was thus determined in the brushmaking trade, for example, as early as 1805.

Soon the courts turned their attention to the new unions' legal status. The first blow came in *Hornby* v *Close* (1867) LR 2 QB 153, when the House of Lords held them illegal as a restraint of trade. In a pattern often to be repeated in later years, down to the present day, this judgment adverse to the workers' interests was soon redressed by legislation. For Gladstone's Trade Union Act 1871 adopted the liberalising minority recommendations of the recent Royal Commission on Trade Unions under Chief Justice Erle, rather than the majority views which sought yet more restrictions of workers' rights. The Act thus accorded the unions the power to enforce certain contracts and to hold property, and provided for their voluntary registration with the Registrar of Friendly Societies.

1.4 RETREAT OF THE CRIMINAL LAW

Soon the Criminal Law Amendment Act 1871 somewhat cut down the scope of the offences of intimidation, molestation and obstruction, but its effect was limited by the continued extent of the common law crime of conspiracy as revealed by the conviction of striking gas stokers in *R* v *Bunn* (1872) 12 Cox CC 316.

Effective trade union pressure led to the passage of the Conspiracy and Protection of Property Act 1875, and it is significant that the Government chose to heed the views of the workers at this time, since many urban workers had just been given the franchise in the Representation of the People Act 1867. Their political potential was seen in the first meeting in 1871 of the Parliamentary Committee of the Trades Union Congress, itself established by 34 delegates in Manchester in 1868. One of the proffered explanations for the course which labour law has taken in Britain in contrast to the Continent, where more workers' rights are guaranteed by statute, is that the Industrial Revolution and the birth of trade unionism preceded the advent of democracy for the industrial worker. The unions thus grew accustomed to look to industrial rather than Parliamentary strength to achieve their ends.

Statute, however, was useful in some areas. The 1875 Act gave immunity from criminal conspiracy where the defendant was acting in furtherance of a trade dispute, and the act would not have been criminal if done by one person alone. It also recognised some legitimate forms of picketing by providing that mere attendance at a place for the purpose of peacefully communicating information would not amount to the crime of 'watching and besetting'. Such immunities became characteristic of the English approach to strikes and picketing.

With the repeal also of the Master and Servant Act 1867 (which had replaced the 1823 statute), the criminal law was largely withdrawn from the regulation of labour relations. The next decades saw the widespread organisation into general unions of low-paid and unskilled workers. This trend was sparked off by the famous strike of match girls at Bryant and Mays London factory, fortified by the formation of the Gasworkers and General Labourers Union, and achieved its greatest success in the securing by the Port of London dockers of their 'tanner' a week after a long and bitter strike in 1889. These new organisations were not usually concerned with the provision of friendly society benefits, which had been a hallmark of the older craft unions. Instead they injected a new spirit of militancy into the movement and were less restrictive in their membership policy; as a result membership increased from 1,576,000 in 1892 to 2,022,000 eight years later.

1.5 CIVIL LAW, *TAFF VALE* AND THE TRADE DISPUTES ACT 1906

With the criminal law largely excluded, the attention of the employers turned to restraint of strikes by means of the civil law, especially the use of injunctions. The law of tort was pressed into service, in particular that of inducing breach of contract, which had been generalised by *Lumley* v *Gye* (1853) 2 E & B 216, and applied to unions' collective action in *Temperton* v *Russell* [1893] 1 QB 715. Although the House of Lords in *Allen* v *Flood* [1898] AC 1 rejected any extension to the tort to include action in which no contract was breached, this victory for the unions was short-lived because, three years later in *Quinn* v *Leathem* [1901] AC 495, the same body held that there was a tortious *conspiracy* where two or more persons combine without justification to injure another. This threat to the freedom to strike might be withstood on the generally held assumption that only individuals, and not the unions themselves, could be sued. Soon, however, the famous *Taff Vale Railway* case [1901] AC 426, directly threatened union funds with bankruptcy, for the House of Lords held that they could not shelter behind their unincorporated status because the Trade Union Act 1871 had enabled them to be sued in their own name. The Amalgamated Society of Railway Servants thus had to pay damages of £23,000 to the Taff Vale Railway Company for striking, together with costs of £19,000. Professor Jenks said of this and the earlier *Quinn* v *Leathem* decision: 'The House of Lords first invented a new civil offence and then created a new kind of defendant against whom it could be alleged.' (Jenks, *History of English Law*.)

The unions reacted by redoubling their support for the newly formed Labour Party, which appeared to be the institution which could relieve them from this threat to their freedom to strike. Under the prompting of increased Labour representation, the new Liberal Government passed the Trade Disputes Act 1906. The statute made union funds themselves altogether immune from any action in tort. It also relieved individual members of liability for conspiracy and inducing breach of contract, whether of employment or commercial agreements, but only if they were acting in contemplation or furtherance of a trade dispute as defined. Other provisions substantially liberalised the law on picketing and, in many respects, this Act did for civil law what the 1875 Act had for criminal law.

The next judicial onslaught on the unions was not long in coming, however, and this time challenged their new found political strength. The House of Lords judgment in *Amalgamated Society of Railway Servants* v *Osborne* [1910] AC 87, held that a union could not spend its funds on political purposes, since they were *ultra vires* the purposes laid down in the Trade Union Act 1871. This was, however, soon reversed by the Trade Union Act 1913, which regulated expenditure on political purposes by the unions until the Trade Union Act 1984 made sweeping amendments to it.

1.6 FIRST WORLD WAR AND THE INTER-WAR YEARS

The pre-First World War period saw several bitter disputes and stoppages in manufacturing industry, partly encouraged by the first traces of the shop steward movement. Unrest continued into the War years themselves, notwithstanding the prohibition of strikes in the Munitions of War Act 1915. The Government reacted by setting up a committee under J. H. Whitley, then Deputy Speaker of the House of Commons. Its report in 1917 recommended the strengthening of collective bargaining and the establishment of joint industrial councils to act as a forum for annual discussions. Several were soon set up and are still known as Whitley Councils. The Industrial Courts Act 1919 was another consequence. It established (despite its rather misleading name) a permanent government arbitration service for industrial disputes to operate with the assent of parties.

The ensuing period saw little judicial intervention. The failure of the General Strike in 1926 demoralised the unions, and the Government reacted with the Trade Disputes and Trade Union Act 1927. This Act made illegal strikes which had any object other than the furtherance of a purely trade dispute, especially if it was a sympathy strike by workers in a different industry, or designed to coerce the Government by inflicting harm on the wider community. The closed shop was outlawed in local and public employment, and public employees were restricted in the unions they could join. These measures had little effect, due to the relative quiescence of the unions in the subsequent 20 years. More important was the accompanying requirement that union members had to actively 'contract in' to pay the union political levy, and this considerably reduced union funds available to the Labour Party. Not surprisingly the newly elected 1945 Labour Government proceeded to reverse this provision in the Trade Disputes and Trade Union Act 1946.

Another significant feature of the inter-war years was the process of mergers of unions to produce the giants of today; the Transport and General Workers Union, Iron and Steel Trades Confederation and General and Municipal Workers Union were formed in this period. Moreover the *range* of unionised workers grew markedly, taking in teachers, and civil servants, and expanding for the first time among other white collar workers, although the boom in their membership came in the 1960s. The Second World War Government resorted to similar measures to those adopted in the First War to prevent industrial disruption; strikes were outlawed with the *quid pro quo* for the unions of binding dispute arbitration.

1.7 THE 1960s AND THE DONOVAN REPORT

It was in the 1960s that for the first time employment protection legislation was passed on a large scale to improve the lot of individual workers. The Contracts of Employment Act 1963 decreed the provision by the employer to each employee of a written statement of contractual terms; the Industrial Training Act 1964 sought better training provisions and set up Industrial Tribunals to adjudicate on its levy provisions; and the Redundancy Payments Act 1965 for the first time provided statutory compensation on dismissal.

The main focus of union fears was on the collective side with the unexpected decision in *Rookes* v *Barnard* [1964] AC 1129. For the House of Lords applied the tort of intimidation away from its traditional ground of threats of assault to include threats of breach of contract. This threatened a return to the law contended for by the employers in *Allen* v *Flood* [1898] AC 1, rendering virtually every strike illegal, and there was no trade dispute immunity covering it. This latter feature was quickly redressed by the Trade Disputes Act 1965 but the furore surrounding this *cause célèbre* was one of the reasons for the appointment in 1965 of the Royal Commission on Trade Unions and Employers' Associations under the chairmanship of Lord Donovan, a law lord. It was 'to consider relations between management and employees and the role of trade unions and employers' associations in promoting the interests of their members and in accelerating the social and economic advance of the nation. . .'. From the beginning it was expected that the main focus would be on the role of the unions, especially because of the widely held view that Britain's continuing industrial decline could be ascribed at least in part to their maintenance of restrictive practices and the large number of unofficial, 'wildcat' strikes.

The report of this high powered investigation was published in 1968, and detected a major industrial problem in the 'irreversible shift' from formal industry-wide collective bargaining to informal and often chaotic arrangements led by increasingly powerful shop stewards. It thus prescribed formal written agreements at plant level and called for union rules to indicate clearly the powers and duties of shop stewards. While it was not wholly opposed to legal enactment (and indeed one dissentient member thought there was no other way) it generally favoured machinery based on consensus. For it thought that 'the shortcomings of our existing industrial relations are . . . primarily due to widespread ignorance about the most sensible and effective methods of conducting industrial relations'.

The detailed analysis contained in the Donovan Report provided the background to the subsequent feverish legislative activity. But the immediate response of the Labour Government, which received the report, did not reach the statute book. Its controversial White Paper, 'In Place of Strife', published in January 1969, split the Labour and trade union movements, especially because of its 'penal clauses' which, in aiming to stamp out unofficial strikes by criminal sanctions, went beyond the Donovan recommendations. The proposed legislation was withdrawn in return for rather nebulous undertakings by the TUC which led to some changes to its Bridlington Rules for inter-union disputes. The Government did, however, set up a Commission on Industrial Relations — the voluntary body recommended in the report.

1.8 THE INDUSTRIAL RELATIONS ACT 1971 AND INDUSTRIAL STRIFE

The new Conservative Government elected in 1970 had no qualms about reform, nor internal dissension. Their Industrial Relations Act 1971 was more radical than the Donovan Report, and, based in large measure on a Conservative Party pamphlet 'Fair Deal at Work', it sought to translate several concepts from Continental and American labour law. The Act put the law at the centre stage in collective bargaining. The Act thus:

(a) *Controlled the closed shop* by outlawing any obligation of trade union membership as a condition for job applicants (the so called pre-entry closed shop) and allowed other forms of 100 per cent unionism only with the approval of the Commission on Industrial Relations and a ballot of affected workers (ss. 6–18).

(b) Accorded rights to employees not to be excluded or expelled from a union by *arbitrary or unreasonable discrimination* and not to be subjected to unreasonable disciplinary action. These were supplemented by a provision that members should not be penalised for refusing to take part in unlawful industrial action and ensuring natural justice for union members by 'guiding principles' (s. 65).

(c) Established the National Industrial Relations Court (NIRC) as a specialist branch of the High Court to hear individual and collective labour law cases (ss. 99–105).

(d) Provided that the NIRC could order a *cooling off period and ballot* for those strikes which would be gravely injurious to the national economy, create a risk of disorder, or endanger lives (ss. 138–145). These provisions, borrowed from the American Taft-Hartley legislation, were in fact used only once, in the 1972 railway dispute, when they resulted in overwhelming support for the trade union leadership continuing the stoppage, by 90 per cent of the union members and 66 per cent of non-unionists.

(e) Gave power to the *Commission on Industrial Relations* to investigate where no procedure agreement existed or where the union sought to be bargaining agent for the workers (ss. 37–43).

(f) Made collective bargains for the first time *legally enforceable* (ss. 34–36) although there was an exception by the will of both parties, and most bargains negotiated in the period of the Act contained the phrase 'This is not a legally enforceable agreement' (the TINALEA clause).

(g) Introduced the right not to be *unfairly dismissed* (ss. 27–32), which still exists in similar form today, and also accorded the cognate right to trade union members not to be discriminated against.

(h) Replaced common law economic torts with a series of *unfair industrial practices* and removed trade union immunity for sympathy and secondary strikes aimed at parties other than those in dispute about wages, conditions, etc.

It also became illegal for any person to call a strike without proper notice unless he was an official of a registered trade union. This sought to prevent unofficial disputes, and of most concern to trade union leaders was the provision in s. 96 that *unregistered* unions would be liable to have their funds sequestered if sued for such 'unfair industrial practices'. This effectively re-enacted the House of Lords decision in *Taff Vale*. Because of their bitter opposition to this and other provisions of the Act, which was shown in mass demonstrations and a one-day general strike called by the Amalgamated Union of Engineering Workers, few unions registered under its provisions (ss. 61–64 and 67–70). They were thus denied most of the benefits open to them, and were liable to have their funds seized. The most threatening event was the imprisonment of docker shop stewards who became known as the 'Pentonville Five', after the prison where they were sent for failing to obey an order prohibiting a strike over containerisation. A planned general strike in their support was only called off after the intervention of the Official Solicitor. Moreover, the scope of s. 96 was apparently widened by the decision of the Court of Appeal in *Heaton's Transport Ltd* v *TGWU* [1973] AC 15, which held the unions vicariously liable for the actions of their shop stewards even when they were engaged on *unofficial* action not authorised by the union leadership. This was overturned by the House of Lords in due course, but the bitterness it engendered continued, and in the last year of the Government the Act was virtually a dead letter.

1.9 THE 'SOCIAL CONTRACT': TRADE UNION AND LABOUR RELATIONS ACT 1974 AND THE EMPLOYMENT PROTECTION ACT 1975

The Labour Government was returned to power in 1974, following a damaging national miners' strike; it proceeded to dismantle the edifice of the Industrial Relations Act which had proved unable to control mounting unrest. Thus s. 1 of the quickly enacted Trade Union and Labour Relations Act 1974 wholly repealed the 1971 Act, although the rest of the statute proceeded to re-enact many of its features, albeit with modifications. The unfair dismissal provisions were strengthened, and listing of unions continued, although no longer providing the gateway to any significant union rights. The immunity of trade unions and individuals in trade dispute cases broadly returned to the position in 1906, although there was a new restriction on the use by employers of injunctions, and the efficacy of no-strike agreements was limited. The minority Government did not quite get the statute it sought through Parliament, so that, on the re-election of the administration with a larger majority, the Trade Union and Labour Relations (Amendment) Act 1976 proceeded to abolish the right to refuse to join a closed shop union on conscientious grounds, which was inserted by the Conservative opposition, and also broadened the protection for trade disputes.

This legislation was part of the Labour Government's 'social contract' with the unions, its *quid pro quo* for wage restraint. This agreement was advanced by the many new employment protection rights accorded by the Employment Protection Act 1975. On the collective level the Act gave statutory powers to the new Advisory Conciliation and Arbitration Service (ACAS), which had already taken over from the Commission on Industrial Relations, and transferred the jurisdiction of the Industrial Court (renamed the Industrial Arbitration Board in 1971) to the Central Arbitration Committee. Industrial tribunals were given several new jurisdictions, and a new appeal body was created — the

Employment Appeal Tribunal (EAT), which differed from the NIRC in that it had neither a primary jurisdiction nor dealt with collective disputes. The Act also:

(a)   Introduced *guarantee payments* for lay-off and short time, and enforced payment during medical suspension from work (para. 10.3).

(b)   Strengthened the provisions for extension of collectively agreed or general level terms and conditions (para. 1.6.3).

(c)   Enacted the right to *maternity pay* and the right to return after maternity (Chapter 9).

(d)   Protected wages and other payments on the *insolvency* of the employer (para. 14.8).

(e)   Provided a new statutory procedure for *recognition* of trade unions after the intervention of ACAS, going much further than the Industrial Relations Act provisions which were only open to registered organisations (para. 19.4).

(f)   Compelled employers to provide *information* for collective bargaining purposes to recognised unions (para. 19.5).

(g)   Gave recognised unions the right to be *consulted about redundancies* (Chapter 15).

(h)   Accorded shop stewards and trade union members the right to *time off* for duties and activities respectively (paras 20.6–20.8).

(i)   Strengthened the right to a *written statement* of contractual terms, and added a regular itemised pay statement (para. 3.10).

The Equal Pay Act, actually passed in 1970, was brought into force in 1975 along with the Sex Discrimination Act (Chapter 7), which sought to supplement it by prohibiting discrimination against job applicants and employees on the grounds of sex and/or marital status. A new Race Relations Act 1976 widened the scope of the similar enactments of 1965 and 1968, in particular giving the individual employee the right to complain to Industrial Tribunals. The late 1960s and the 1970s also experienced a major growth in trade unionism, especially in local government and the health service among white collar and professional employees.

1.10   CONSERVATIVE TRADE UNION LEGISLATION 1980–89

The next three years saw mounting criticism by employers and various pressure groups of the 1974–76 legislation. It was claimed that they greatly increased wage costs at a time of recession, and discouraged employers from taking on more employees, thus defeating their own ostensible objects. Many people reacted sharply against the actions of the unions in the so called 'winter of discontent' of 1978–79, when whole series of strikes (especially in the public sector) paralysed the nation, and were accompanied by widespread secondary picketing — that is, against employers not directly involved in the relevant dispute.

After the election of a new Conservative Government, the Employment Act 1980 thus sought to restrict the powers of the unions and the ambit of individual rights but without mounting the headlong assault on the unions seen in the 1971 legislation. The 1980 Act:

(a)   Enabled the Secretary of State for Employment to give public funds to unions for the holding of secret *ballots,* and to issue Employment Codes of Practice (para. 18.3.1).

(b)   Limited the effectiveness of the *closed shop* by enlarging those situations in which dismissal for failure to join a specified union is unfair, granting the employer the right in this situation to reclaim whatever compensation he may have to pay out from the union signatory of the agreement, and issuing a restrictive Code of Practice.

(c)   Gave individuals the right to complain of *unreasonable exclusion or expulsion* from a union in a closed shop (para. 18.4.2).

(d)   Limited the effectiveness of *unfair dismissal* (the qualifying period already having been increased by statutory order) and maternity rights, although it gave a new right to women workers to time off for ante-natal care.

(e)   Made illegal *secondary industrial action* and secondary picketing directed at an employer not in dispute with the union (para. 21.9).

(f)   Abolished statutory recognition procedures and Schedule II of the Employment Protection Act 1975 with its provision for extension of collectively bargained and general level terms.

Many considered that the Employment Act 1980 did not go far enough to restrain the unions and redress the industrial balance which they thought had been tilted in the unions' favour between 1974 and 1979. Following a Green Paper on 'Trade Union Immunities' in December 1980, the Government announced its intention to introduce further measures of industrial law reform in a statement by the new Secretary of State for Employment, Mr Norman Tebbit, on 23 November 1981. Its stated aim was to 'improve the operation of the labour market by providing a fairer and more balanced framework of industrial relations law and to curb a number of continuing abuses of trade union power'. The main features of the Employment Act 1982 concerned:

(a)   removing immunity from trade union funds;

(b)   subjecting closed shops to periodic review, and prohibiting union membership only clauses in contracts and tender documents; and

(c)   increasing compensation for employees unfairly dismissed in consequence of a closed shop.

The Trade Union Act 1984 was intended by the Government to 'give unions back to their members' and was foreshadowed by the White Paper 'Democracy in Trade Unions' (Cmnd 8878). The statute provided for ballots for the election of the principal executive committee, before industrial action, and to maintain the union's political fund. The effect was to take the courts further into the internal affairs of trade unions.

The Thatcher Government was, however, impelled by European Directives to implement two pieces of legislation which were not to its liking. Both were introduced by statutory instrument: the Transfer of Undertakings (Protection of Employment) Regulations 1981 (SI 1981 No. 1794) which gives employees various rights on takeovers, and the Equal Pay (Amendment) Regulations 1983 (SI 1983 No. 1794) which gives women the right to claim equal pay when their work is of equal value to a man's instead of merely when he and she perform like work. The Government Minister introducing the former measure to the House of Commons said that he did so without any enthusiasm.

More in keeping with the Government's overall strategy was the revoking of the Fair Wages Resolution in 1983, and the Wages Act 1986 which repealed the Truck Acts, abolished the Wages Council protection for those over 21 and removed redundancy rebates save for employers of less than 10 employees.

After 10 years of Conservative Government, the trade unions appeared to be weaker than at any point since the war. They had lost some two million members, been buffeted by the courts and were uncertain of their strategy to fight back. The wounds opened by the year-long miners' strike, which ended with defeat for Arthur Scargill's National Union of

Mineworkers took long to heal. The Trades Union Congress was split with the expulsion of the Electrical, Electronic, Telecommunication and Plumbing Union which had already earned the opprobium of many trade unionists by its willingness to enter into single union deals with employers, most controversially (it was alleged) with News International plc, publishers of *The Times* and the *Sun*.

The Government's continuing ideological approach to employment law may be seen in the statement in their Green Paper 'Lifting the Burden' (Cm 9571, 1985, at p. 29): 'priority should be given to action to reduce the administrative and legislative burdens on business, particularly on small and medium-sized enterprises'. They also indicated their aim to 'free the labour market from any unnecessary and artificial restraints which may affect business performance, competitiveness and jobs'.

The next piece of employment legislation following this pronouncement, however, dealt with other Government preoccupations. The Employment Act 1988 gave further rights to trade union members over union funds and to prevent strikes not supported by a valid ballot, altered the rules on election and political fund ballots, tightened the provisions on the closed shop and introduced the Commissioner for the Rights of Trade Union Members (for full discussion, see J. Bowers and S. Auerbach, *Guide to the Employment Act 1988,* Blackstone Press, 1988). This statute provided the backdrop to increased litigation on the wording and scope of ballots, including major litigation in 1989 concerning the dock and railways strikes, both of which resulted in court victories for the unions. The dock strike was spurred by the fact that the Government abolished, as from 3 July 1989, the National Dock Labour Scheme, which had given special protection to registered dock workers since 1947.

The Employment Act 1989 followed relentlessly on the heels of the 1988 statute, but notwithstanding its title, dealt mainly with amendments to the Sex Discrimination Act 1975. It also restricted the right of trade union officials to have time off for trade union duties, limited the scope of the written statement of terms and removed the right to redundancy rebates even for small businesses. The Social Security Act 1989 introduced the principle of equal treatment in relation to occupational pension schemes.

The Employment Act 1990 was a further move from the consensus view of industrial relations. The Bill was introduced following the Green Paper 'Removing Barriers to Employment' (Cm 655, March 1989). The Act included the abolition of the pre-entry closed shop, further restriction on secondary action, and widening the powers of the Commissioner for the Rights of Trade Union Members. The liability of trade unions was also extended to cover the acts of their committees and officials, including shop stewards, unless disowned by the union, and employees lost the right to claim unfair dismissal if at the time they are engaged in unofficial industrial action.

A further item of legislation, which unusually received cross-party support, is the Trade Union and Labour Relations (Consolidation) Act 1992 consolidating statutory collective labour law. This Act partnered the Employment Protection (Consolidation) Act 1978 which consolidated the law on individual employment rights, particularly with regard to unfair dismissal and redundancy.

The next piece of industrial legislation was clearly controversial and constituted a return by the Major Government to the attack on trade unionism which characterised the Thatcher years. The Trade Union Reform and Employment Rights Act 1993 received its Royal Assent on 1 July 1993, and placed further restrictions on the rights of employees to strike and strictly regulated the financial affairs of trade unions. Although it contained some provisions to extend workers' rights, these derived almost entirely from the impulse of European Directives. Indeed this was the first general piece of primary industrial legislation which derived a majority of its provisions from European Community law, in particular on maternity rights, transfer of undertakings, and proof of employment relationship. (For full details see Bowers, Brown and Gibbons, *A Guide to the Trade Union Reform and Employment Rights Act 1993,* Longmans, 1993.)

Michael Portillo in early 1995 issued a Green Paper which proposed radical reform of industrial tribunal procedure ('Resolving Employment Rights Disputes: Options for Reform' December 1994) and announced that all minimum hours thresholds were to be abolished. The Government had to introduce legislation to ensure that consultation takes place over redundancies and transfer of undertakings whether or not a union is recognised by the employer. This was in order to implement the ECJ decision in *Commission of European Communities* v *UK* [1994] IRLR 412, and regulations were introduced in 1995.

A new consolidation measure, the Employment Rights Act 1996, has brought together the provisions of the Employment Protection (Consolidation) Act 1978, the Wages Act 1986, the Employment Acts 1980 and 1982 and parts of several other statutes. It came into force on 22 August 1996.

The Government has also published a Green Paper 'Industrial action and Trade Unions' (Cm 3470) which countenances more restrictions on strikes, in particular the removal of immunities from 'industrial action which has disproportionate or excessive effects', and extending the strike notice period from one to two weeks.

2 The Status of Employee

It is often easy to recognise a contract of service when you see it but difficult to say wherein the difference [between it and a contract for services] lies.

(Denning LJ in *Stevenson, Jordan and Harrison Ltd* v *Macdonald and Evans* [1952] 1 TLR 101.)

2.1 THE PURPOSE OF DEFINING THE EMPLOYEE

Most working people have a contract of employment and are employees or, in the old-fashioned word, servants. A builder building an extension to a house, a watchmaker repairing a watch or a plumber mending a tap is, however, more likely to be engaged on a contract for services, an independent contractor. He labours for a short time and the hirer is interested not in controlling what he does while he does it but only in the finished product or service.

It is fundamental to employment law to identify who is an employee and who is an independent contractor, yet statute provides only an outline distinction between these two modes in which a man may sell his labour (Trade Union and Labour Relations (Consolidation) Act (TULR(C)A) 1992, s. 295). The Employment Rights Act 1996, s. 230(1) defines an 'employee' as 'an individual who has entered into or works under (or, where the employment has ceased, worked under) a contract of employment'. The question largely depends on conflicting tests established at common law over several decades. They were first formulated to decide on vicarious liability, that is, when an employer is liable to a third party for the torts of his employees. The distinction is now vital more generally, since only employees qualify for:

(a) social security payments such as unemployment benefit, industrial injuries benefits and sickness benefits;

(b) employment protection rights such as guaranteed pay, unfair dismissal, redundancy payments, rights to notice, and time off;

(c) health and safety provisions, including the Factories Acts;

(d) protection of wages on insolvency of the employer;

(e) the benefit of the employer's common law duty of care.

The distinction is most important on a day to day basis for taxation, since while employees are taxed under Schedule E of the Income and Corporation Taxes Act 1988, the self-employed enjoy generally more favourable treatment by Schedule D.

A person may qualify as an employee even though he provides services through the medium of a limited company (*Catamaran Cruisers Ltd* v *Williams* [1994] IRLR 386). While the formation of such a company may be strong evidence of a change of status away from employment, that fact has to be evaluated in the context of all the other facts found.

The common law tests of employee are the same for this multiplicity of purposes. Yet the policy considerations behind a decision under each heading are rather different. Thus, in determining vicarious liability, the court will be most concerned with adequate protection of third parties and the nature of control retained by the putative employer; while in respect of national insurance contributions and tax the policy uppermost in the court's mind may be the prevention of avoidance.

2.2   THE TESTS OF EMPLOYEE STATUS

2.2.1   The control test

Since it was in the context of vicarious liability that the courts first considered who was an employee, it was natural that they saw its touchstone as whether the master controlled or had the right to control not only what the worker did but also the manner in which he did it (*Yewens* v *Noakes* (1880) 6 QBD 530, *Performing Right Society* v *Mitchell and Booker (Palais de Danse) Ltd* [1924] 1 KB 762). An independent contractor, on the other hand, was hired to achieve a certain result but had complete discretion as to how to effect it. This control test also served to differentiate the servant from an agent, who similarly can choose exactly how he goes about tasks given to him by his principal. Thus, while a domestic servant was an employee, a blacksmith was an independent contractor.

The control test was taken to its logical conclusion when a court held that nurses were not employees of a hospital when carrying out duties in the operating theatre (*Hillyer* v *Governors of St Bartholomews Hospital* [1909] 2 KB 820). This rigidity soon led to criticism (e.g. *Walker* v *Crystal Palace FC* [1910] 1 KB 87). As the pace of technological change hastened, it became increasingly unrealistic to conceive of the employer having the knowledge to control many of his increasingly highly skilled employees. One only has to consider as examples a surgeon, a research chemist or an airline pilot, since all will have know-how far beyond that possessed by their employers. It is public policy that someone should normally assume vicarious liability for the worker's negligence to others to ensure a claimworthy defendant. The breakthrough towards a more realistic approach came in a series of cases in the late 1940s in which hospitals were held vicariously liable for the acts of surgeons, radiographers and other specialists (e.g. *Cassidy* v *Ministry of Health* [1951] 2 KB 343), and this was followed by a landmark article by Professor Kahn-Freund (1951) 11 MLR 504; see also *Lane* v *Shire Roofing Company (Oxford) Ltd* [1995] IRLR 493).

The single control test was thus variegated to a series of indications of control. Lord Thankerton in *Short* v *J. & W. Henderson Ltd* (1946) 62 TLR 427, looked at whether the putative master had:

(a)   power of selection of his servant;
(b)   right to control the method of doing the work; and
(c)   right of *suspension* and dismissal.

Only if these questions were answered in the affirmative, and the worker received wages or other remuneration, would a contract of employment exist (see also *Sime* v *Sutcliffe*

Catering Scotland Ltd [1990] IRLR 228). As this notion has developed the two general criteria now in use are: (a) the integration test, and (b) the economic reality test.

2.2.2 The integration test

Denning LJ considered that the decisive question was whether the person under consideration was *fully integrated* into the employer's organisation. (*Stevenson, Jordan and Harrison Ltd* v *Macdonald and Evans* [1952] 1 TLR 101). A ship's master, a chauffeur and a reporter on the staff of a newspaper are thus all employed under a contract *of* service; but a ship's pilot, a taxi driver and a newspaper contributor are hired under contract *for* services. His Lordship detected that: 'one feature which seems to run through the instances is that, under a contract of service a man is employed as part of the business and his work is done as an integral part of the business but under a contract for services his work, although done for the business is not integrated into it but only accessory to it.' In a later case (*Bank voor Handel en Scheepvaart NV* v *Slatford* [1953] 1 QB 248), Lord Denning reformulated the question as whether the worker was 'part and parcel' of the employer's organisation (see also *Beloff* v *Pressdram Ltd* [1973] 1 All ER 241). The great drawback of this approach lies in its failure to define exactly what is meant by 'integration' and 'organisation'.

2.2.3 The economic reality test

More recently the courts have recognised that no one test or series of criteria can be decisive. Instead they have adopted something like the American notion of an 'economic reality' composite test (see *USA* v *Silk* (1946) 331 US 704) and the clearest illustration is the very full judgment in *Ready Mixed Concrete (South East) Ltd* v *Minister of Pensions and National Insurance* [1968] 2 QB 497. The case concerned the appellant company's liability for social security contributions of their workers for which they were responsible only if they had contracts of service. The workers drove ready mixed concrete lorries which they were buying on hire purchase agreement from the appellant company, which required in a detailed contract of 30 pages that they must, *inter alia:*

(a)   use the lorry only on company business;
(b)   maintain it in accordance with their instructions; and
(c)   obey all reasonable orders.

Although this suggested a measure of close control, there were no requirements about hours of work and the times at which the drivers took holidays. Moreover, they could generally hire out the driving of their vehicle to another, and were paid, subject to a yearly minimum, according to the amount of concrete they transported. McKenna J identified three conditions for a contract *of* service:

(a)   The servant agrees that in consideration of a wage or other remuneration he will provide his own work and skill in performing some service for his master.
(b)   He agrees expressly or impliedly that in performance of that service he will be subject to the other's control in a sufficient degree to make that other master.
(c)   The other provisions of the contract are consistent with it being a contract of service.

On the facts, his Lordship decided that the workers were independent contractors, most particularly because the third test (c) was not satisfied since most of the terms pointed to a contract *for* services.

It is the meaning of (c) which has, indeed, caused most difficulty in the subsequent case law. In *Market Investigations Ltd* v *Minister of Social Security* [1969] 2 WLR 1, recently approved by the Privy Council in *Lee Ting Sang* v *Chung Chi-Keung* [1990] ICR 409, Cooke J paraphrased the fundamental test as whether the person performing services is in business on his own account. If the answer was yes, the contract was *for* services; but it was not so in the instant case, where the respondents engaged interviewers for a short time during which they were free to work when they wished, and were permitted to perform tasks for other companies. The learned judge said that:

> No exhaustive list has been compiled and perhaps no exhaustive list can be compiled of considerations which are relevant in determining [the] question, nor can strict rules be laid down as to the relative weight which the various considerations may carry in particular cases.

Indeed, in some cases it has been recognised that the only sure test is to ask whether an ordinary person would think there was a contract of service (see also *Withers* v *Flackwell Heath Football Supporters Club* [1981] IRLR 307). In *WHPT Housing Association Ltd* v *Secretary of State for Social Services* [1981] ICR 737, Webster J saw the essence of the distinction as the fact that the employee provided himself to serve, while the independent contractor only provides his services. See also *Lee Ting Sang* v *Chung Chi-Keung* [1990] ICR 409.

These sorts of instinctive jury-based approaches which derive initially from Somervell J in *Cassidy* v *Ministry of Health* [1951] 2 KB 343, may easily devolve into casuistry *(Thames Television Ltd* v *Wallis* [1979] IRLR 136, *Challinor* v *Taylor* [1972] ICR 129, *Argent* v *Ministry of Social Services* [1968] 3 All ER 208, *Warner Holidays Ltd* v *Secretary of State for Social Services* [1983] ICR 440), and the Court of Appeal did not find the test especially helpful in *Nethermere (St Neots) Ltd* v *Taverna & Gardiner* [1984] IRLR 240. They emphasised that a contract of service required an irreducible minimum of obligation on each side of the bargain. There was, however, no reason why well-founded expectations of continuing home work could not be hardened or reinforced into enforceable contracts by the regular giving and taking of work over periods of a year.

There is no single path to determining whether or not contracts are of service or for services. In *Hall* v *Lorimer* [1994] IRLR 171, the Court of Appeal agreed with Mummery J (who decided the case in the Chancery Division) that

> It is not a mechanical exercise of running through items on a check list to see whether they are present in, or absent from, a given situation. The object of the exercise is to paint a picture from the accumulation of detail. The overall effect can only be appreciated by standing back from the detailed picture which has been painted, by viewing it from a distance and making an informed, considered, qualitative appreciation of the whole.

2.2.3.1 The factors indicating status   McNeill J in *Warner Holidays Ltd* v *Secretary of State for Social Services* (supra) was not 'persuaded that a check-list of criteria is the proper guide or that the court ought to be required to tick off or negative point by point the items on such a list. Essentially, all the relevant facts have to be looked at in the aggregate, to determine, in the absence of an unambiguous or unequivocal written contract, what it was that the parties intended'. The following list provides, however, some indication of the factors considered by the courts as attributes of employees and independent contractors (see e.g. *Market Investigations Ltd* v *Minister of Social Security* [1969] 2 QB 173 at 185):

(a)   *Ownership of tools* and instruments by the worker points in the direction of self-employment.

(b)   Payment of *wages and sick pay* indicates that the person under consideration is an employee, since the independent contractor usually receives a lump sum for the job and bears any risk of ill health himself. As Lord Widgery put it in *Global Plant Ltd* v *Secretary of State for Social Services* [1972] QB 139:

> If a man agrees to perform an operation for a fixed sum and thus stands to lose if the work is delayed and to profit if it is done quickly, that is the man who on the face of it appears to be an independent contractor working under a contract for services.

This factor was of some importance in the case of *Hitchcock* v *Post Office* [1980] ICR 100, where a sub-postmaster who provided the shop for his sub-post office was held to be self-employed even though he had to carry out Post Office instructions and had to advise the head postmaster if absent for three days. The decision was supported by the facts that he could delegate his duties to others, and bore the risk of profit or loss (see the same result in *Tanna* v *Post Office* [1981] ICR 374).

(c)   The presence or absence of *residual control* 'is still an important factor but it is not the only one' (Slynn J in *Hitchcock,* supra). In *Addison* v *London Philharmonic Orchestra* [1981] ICR 261, orchestral musicians were held to be independent contractors since 'the obligations imposed on them were the very minimum to ensure that the work is done. Personal attendance at rehearsals and self-discipline were "simply prerequisites of a concert artist's work and did not decisively point to a contract of service" '. (See also *Midland Sinfonia Concert Society* v *Secretary of State for Social Services* [1981] ICR 454.) While hospital administrators cannot tell the surgeon how he should perform his operations, they can ensure that serious consequences follow if he were to decide to perform them in the middle of a field and they thus maintain some degree of control. As Cooke J said in *Market Investigations Ltd* v *Minister of Social Security* [1969] 2 WLR 1: 'The most that can be said is that control will no doubt always have to be considered, although it can no longer be regarded as the sole decisive factor.' The more *discretion* accorded to *when* his work will be performed, the more likely it is that the worker is under a contract for services (*Willy Scheidegger Swiss Typewriting School (London) Ltd* v *Ministry of Social Security* (1968) 5 KIR 65, also *WHPT Housing Association* v *Secretary of State for Social Services* [1981] ICR 737, *Narich Pty Ltd* v *Commissioner of Pay-roll Tax* [1984] ICR 286).

(d)   Deduction of *PAYE and national insurance contributions* point to employment, but this is not decisive (*Davis* v *New England College of Arundel* [1977] ICR 6, *Airfix Footwear Ltd* v *Cope* [1978] ICR 1210).

(e)   A casual and short-term engagement suggests the status of independent contractor, especially when the worker retains the right to, or actually does, work elsewhere (*Argent* v *Minister of Social Security* [1968] 3 All ER 208). In *Hall* v *Lorimer* [1994] IRLR 171, the most outstanding feature of the facts was that the respondent, a vision-mixer, customarily worked for 20 or more different companies and the vast majority of his assignments lasted for only a single day. Moreover he ran the risk of bad debts and incurred very substantial expenditure in carrying out his engagements. It was thus held that he was self-employed and not an employee.

(f)   The fact that an individual works at his own premises indicates self-employment.

2.2.3.2   Self-description   Often the parties to a contract describe themselves as hirer and independent contractor or employer and employee. This is in no way decisive in determining the true characterisation in law, since the courts consider the substance of the relationship and not its form (*Davis* v *New England College of Arundel* [1977] ICR 6). This is especially true where there are public obligations involved, such as social security contributions (*Warner Holidays Ltd* v *Secretary of State for Social Services* [1983] ICR 440). The description may, however, have persuasive value. The issue most commonly comes before the court where the parties have (a) chosen a self-employed relationship for reasons of tax or national insurance, but (b) the worker later seeks the benefits of employee status in order to gain statutory employment protection rights. This often happens in the building trade where the self-employed 'lump' is a well-developed institution. The cases are by no means easy to reconcile.

In *Ferguson* v *John Dawson and Partners (Contractors) Ltd* [1976] 3 All ER 817, the worker was told on his very informal hiring as a 'general labourer' that he would become part of a 'lump' labour force. There were no 'cards' and no deductions were to be made for tax and national insurance. He nevertheless had to obey the company's instructions concerning what to do and when to do it. When he was seriously injured in the course of his work, the success of his claim for industrial injuries benefit, and damages for breach of statutory duty, depended solely on whether he was an employee, all other criteria being fulfilled. Megaw and Browne LJJ decided that he *was* so entitled, notwithstanding the arrangements voluntarily entered into. The self-description of the parties was only one factor to be taken into account. Lawton LJ dissented and took a more stringent view. It was, he thought, open to anyone to decide how he was to sell his labour and 'contrary to public policy to allow a man to say that he was self-employed for the purposes of avoiding the incidence of tax, then a servant for the purpose of claiming compensation'. He thought that the parties were estopped from reneging on the agreement made.

Two later cases followed the majority approach rather than that adopted by Lawton LJ: *Davis* v *New England College* (supra) and *Tyne and Clyde Warehouses Ltd* v *Hamerton* [1978] ICR 661. The Court of Appeal has, however, since drawn a distinction between the *Ferguson* case and situations where there is an actual and considered, albeit agreed, change in status. Thus in *Massey* v *Crown Life Insurance Company* [1978] IRLR 31 the applicant had been employed for two years by the respondents as a branch manager. He then entered into a new arrangement with them whereby he registered himself as John L Massey and Associates with the Registry of Business Names (although he did not in fact form a company), and his one-man business was appointed manager. The main effect was that the respondents no longer made tax or other deductions from fees paid to Mr Massey. The Inland Revenue agreed to treat him as self-employed, notwithstanding that his duties largely remained the same. When he was removed with one month's notice, he was held not entitled to bring a claim for unfair dismissal, since he was self-employed.

Lord Denning MR distinguished *Ferguson*'s case on its facts because 'there is a perfectly genuine agreement entered into at the instance of Mr Massey on the footing that he is "self-employed". He gets the benefit of it by avoiding tax deductions and getting his pension contributions returned. I do not see that he can come along afterwards and say it is something else in order to claim that has been unfairly dismissed. Having made his bed as being "self-employed" he must lie on it.' The written contract here 'becomes the best material from which to gather the true relationship between the parties'. On the other hand, 'the parties cannot alter the truth of [the] relationship by putting a different label on it and use it as a dishonest device to deceive the Revenue'.

Lawton LJ thought that the existence of the written contract distinguished the case from the majority decision in *Ferguson,* and he agreed with Lord Denning's public policy reasoning. Although *Massey* has been followed by the Privy Council in *Australian Mutual Provident Society* v *Allan* (1978) 52 ALJR 407, little has been done to clarify the exact distinction between the facts in *Ferguson* and *Massey*. In *BSM 1257* v *Secretary of State for Social Services* [1978] ICR 894, the High Court held that effect should be given to the intentions of the parties unless the terms of the contract or the circumstances were inconsistent with those intentions.

However, the Court of Appeal decision in *Young and Woods Ltd* v *West* [1980] IRLR 201, suggests that *Massey* should be confined to its facts. The respondent, a skilled sheet metal worker chose self-employment, again for tax reasons, but since he was paid on an hourly rate, had normal working hours and use of respondent's equipment, he was classified as an employee by the Court of Appeal so that he was eligible to claim unfair dismissal. The important feature for Stephenson LJ was that the applicant was not 'in business on his own account'. He distinguished *Massey* on two grounds, firstly that the applicant in that case had two contracts, one of service as manager of the branch office and the other for services under a general agency agreement; and secondly that the self-employment resulted from a deliberate change of relationship. He concurred with the other members of the Court of Appeal in disapproving of the general operation of the doctrine of estoppel in this area, saying, 'I am satisfied that the parties can resile from the position which they have deliberately and openly chosen to take up and . . . to reach any other conclusion would be in effect to permit the parties to contract out of the Act.' In any case he trusted the Revenue would review Mr West's tax arrangements in the light of the judgment! In *Narich Pty Ltd* v *Commissioner of Pay-roll Tax* [1984] ICR 286, the Privy Council looked behind the terms of an agreement between a weight-watching franchise company and their lecturers. It claimed to create independent contractors, but the court decided that the relationship was one of employment. In reality the company was entitled to control and direct not only the nature and scope of the task allotted to the lecturer but also the precise manner in which it was performed.

2.3 OTHER WORK RELATIONSHIPS

There are several special work situations to consider.

2.3.1 Office holders

The most widely cited general definition of an office is that formulated by Rowlatt J in *Great Western Railway* v *Bater* [1920] 3 KB 266 (a taxation case), that it is 'a subsisting, permanent, substantive position which had its existence independently from the person who filled it, which went on and was filled in succession by successive holders'. Clearest examples are trustees (e.g. *A-G for NSW* v *Perpetual Trustee Co. Ltd* [1955] AC 457); bailiffs; trade union officers (*Stevenson* v *URTU* [1977] ICR 893); officers of the Salvation Army (*Rogers* v *Booth* [1935] 2 All ER 751); company directors (*Ellis* v *Lucas* [1967] Ch 858); police officers (*Fisher* v *Oldham Corporation* [1930] 2 KB 364); prison officers (*Home Office* v *Robinson* [1982] ICR 31); and company registrars (*IRC* v *Brander & Cruikshank* [1971] 1 All ER 36). Clergymen, of whatever religion, are usually classified as holding an office (*Santokh Singh* v *Guru Nanak Gurdwara* [1990] ICR 309) and not as being employees (see also *Birmingham Mosque Trust Ltd* v *Alavi* [1992] ICR 435). In *President of the Methodist Conference* v *Parfitt* [1984] ICR 176, the Court of Appeal emphasised the spiritual nature of the relationship between the applicant Methodist Minister and the

Methodist Conference. There was no contract of any sort between them. In *Davies v Presbyterian Church of Wales* [1986] IRLR 194, the appellant was a pastor of the Presbyterian Church of Wales until his dismissal in May 1981. A tribunal held that he was entitled to bring a claim of unfair dismissal but the House of Lords ultimately allowed the Church's appeal. Here there was no contract between the appellant and the Church. The Book of Rules which governed the pastor did not contain terms of employment, and his duties were not contractual or enforceable, being dictated by conscience and not law (see also para. 2.5, and ECJ decision in *Van Roosmalen v Bestuur, The Times*, 29 October 1986).

The courts have decided that JPs and rent officers fall within the definition of office holder (*Knight v Att-Gen* [1979] ICR 194, *Department of the Environment v Fox* [1979] ICR 736) but not a civil engineer who conducted public enquiries on behalf of the Department of Environment because of the lack of continuity and permanence of his position (*Edwards v Clinch* [1981] 3 WLR 707, nor a senior barristers clerk (*McMenamin (Inspector of Taxes) v Diggles* [1991] ICR 641). In the case of policemen, in *Dale v IRC* [1954] AC 11, Lord Simonds said: 'His authority is original not delegated and is exercised at his own discretion by virtue of the office; he is a ministerial officer exercising statutory rights independent of contract.' In *R v Hertfordshire County Council ex parte National Union of Public Employees* [1985] IRLR 258, Sir John Donaldson MR rejected the decision of the judge below that each local authority employee was an 'officer' within s. 112, Local Government Act 1972. It was at least arguable that only a person who filled a position which had an existence independent to the person who for the time being occupied it, merited such description (see also *102 Social Club and Institute Ltd v Bickerton* [1977] ICR 911).

2.3.2   Crown servants

Crown servants are engaged under or for the purposes of a government department and this makes it a wider category than civil servants alone (*Wood v Leeds AHA* [1974] ICR 535, applied in *Marshall v Southampton and South West Hampshire HA* [1986] ICR 335 by the European Court of Justice). The main reason for distinguishing a separate category of such workers is that it is still undecided whether they have a contract at all (see *Malins v Post Office* [1975] ICR 60), because, at common law, the Crown is thus able to dismiss at pleasure unless it is expressly otherwise provided by statute (*Gould v Stuart* [1896] AC 575).

Thus in *IRC v Hambrook* [1956] 2 QB 641, Lord Goddard CJ said:

An established civil servant is appointed to an office and is a public officer, remunerated by moneys provided by Parliament so that his employment depends not on a contract with the Crown but on appointment by the Crown.

However, in *Reilly v R* [1934] AC 176, Lord Atkin could see no reason why the Crown could not be bound if it expressly contracted for a fixed period. Indeed, most recent cases suggest that a contract of some sort exists (*Kodeeswaran v Att-Gen for Ceylon* [1970] 2 WLR 456, *Att-Gen for Guyana v Nobrega* [1969] 3 All ER 1604, cf. *Gallagher v Post Office* [1970] 3 All ER 712; see also *Council of Civil Service Unions v Minister for the Civil Service* [1985] IRLR 28, discussed at para. 19.11, and *R v Civil Service Appeal Board ex parte Bruce* [1988] ICR 649 approved by the Court of Appeal [1989] ICR 171 and applied in *McLaren v Home Office* [1990] IRLR 338).

The issue arose again in *R v Lord Chancellor's Department ex parte Nangle* [1991] ICR 743, when an executive grade civil servant sought judicial review of decisions that complaints of sexual harassment against him were well founded. The application was dismissed on the bases that:

(a)   the proper question on whether the parties had entered into legal relations was not what the parties themselves believed but an objective construction of the documents by which the applicant was appointed, and the Civil Service Pay and Conditions of Service Code showed that the parties had entered into obligations, rights and entitlements consistent with a contract of employment;

(b)   therefore the documents were to be construed as creating a contract of employment; and

(c)   even if there were no legal relationship the mere absence of a private law remedy did not give rise to public law relief.

The Divisional Court thus declined to follow its previous decision in *R* v *Civil Service Appeal Board ex parte Bruce,* and decided that civil servants do work under contracts of employment. (On the public/private distinction, see *Roy* v *Kensington & Chelsea and Westminster Family Practitioner Committee* [1992] IRLR 233.)

The question is, in any event, less important now that most Crown Servants are expressly included in the unfair dismissal legislation (ERA 1996, s. 191), although in defining them for this purpose the statute talks of their terms of employment, thus studiously avoiding any assumption of contract.

The position of Crown servants has received specific treatment since 1988. The root of most legal proceedings to restrain industrial action is a breach of the contract of employment. It was not clear whether Crown servants had contracts of employment of which a breach might be induced, but s. 245 of TULR(C)A 1992 now deems Crown servants to have such contracts but only for the purpose of the economic torts.

2.3.3   Apprentices

Apprenticeship is not only a relationship of employment, for the apprentice agrees to serve his master for the purpose also of learning and the master agrees to teach the apprentice. Many old rules, such as the master's duty to provide medical care and right to chastise, apply to the institution which is less widely adopted now than in former years. It is now included in most statutory definitions of employment (ERA 1996, s. 230(2)) and has the same consequences for vicarious liability.

2.3.4   Students, cadets and youth opportunity schemes

Some people provide services only to a limited degree *ancillary* to their main role of learning and are distinct from apprentices. Thus a student's essays for his tutor are not services however hard he labours on them, and even though he has some sort of contract with the university it is not one of service. The same applies to a research student engaged on a specific project (*Hugh-Jones* v *St John's College, Cambridge* [1979] ICR 848), and apparently a police cadet. In *Wiltshire Police Authority* v *Wynn* [1980] ICR 649, the applicant cadet sought to claim unfair dismissal, since although police are expressly excluded from this statutory jurisdiction, the Act makes no mention of cadets. She argued that she was an ordinary employee, and the issue before the Court of Appeal turned not, as normally, on the third requirement of *Ready Mixed Concrete* (that is, those factors pointing for and against a contract of employment), but squarely on whether the applicant performed *any services* at all (the first question). The evidence showed that the cadet was allocated to various police departments primarily to gain experience, and that any work was 'in a minor way', for example, placing warning cones at the scene of an accident. Yet several of her rights and duties were characteristic of employment: she was paid a wage, could engage in no other work without permission, and was required to be available for 40 hours per week. While the declaration by the police authority that she was appointed only 'to undergo training with a view to becoming a member of the police force' could not be decisive, the Court of Appeal found it to be borne out by the realities of her position. Their Lordships thus disagreed with the EAT which had decided that a contract of service existed. Dunn LJ thought 'the fact that the conditions of engagement are consistent with a contract of service is not decisive if the primary object of the relationship is teaching and learning'. Police cadets were thus in a class by themselves and could not be fitted into the straitjacket of an employee/independent contractor dichotomy. (On special constables, see *Sheikh* v *Chief Constable of Greater Manchester Police* [1989] 2 All ER 684.)

A similar result was reached in *Daley* v *Allied Suppliers* [1983] IRLR 14, in which it was held that a person taking part in a work experience scheme as part of the Youth Opportunities Programme was not a person employed within the meaning of the Race Relations Act 1976. There was no contract binding the applicants and respondents together notwithstanding that they owed *some* obligations towards each other. If there were a contract it was one of training, enabling the applicant to acquire certain skills and experience (see to the same effect *Hawley* v *Fieldcastle & Co. Ltd* [1982] IRLR 223).

There is as yet no binding authority as to whether persons engaged on Employment Training are employees.

An articled clerk in a solicitor's office was held to be employed by the firm and not merely by the partner to whom she was articled. There is a dual system of a training contract with the partnership (*Oliver* v *J.P. Malnick & Co.* [1983] IRLR 456).

2.3.5 Labour only sub-contractors

Especially common in the building industry is the practice of the 'lump', whereby an individual contractor supplies his labour to complete a job and is paid in a lump sum. Such workers often move on and off the 'cards' (that is, from employment to this form of self-employment and back again), with regularity, performing the same work in both capacities. This is done with the acquiescence of the 'hirers', the main contractors, who thereby have less administrative paperwork and do not pay secondary national insurance contributions or industrial training levies. One drawback is that it retards effective trade unions in the building industry and this received the critical attention of the Phelps Brown Committee of Inquiry into Labour in Building and Civil Engineering (Cmnd 3714). Moreover, such labourers cannot claim employment protection rights. There has been no legislative intervention on this score, but the widespread avoidance of tax has received specific attention in that such independent lump contractors are now treated as though employed under ss. 559–567 of the Income and Corporation Taxes Act 1988. Payments made by a main contractor to a sub-contractor accordingly must have tax deducted at source, save where the sub-contractor has obtained a certificate that he is running a *bona fide* business covered by adequate insurance, and that he has complied with tax requirements over a three-year period. Further, the contractor is responsible for Class 1 national insurance contributions.

2.3.6 Outworkers

Those who work at home (a practice especially common in the garment industry), generally suffer low pay, and if, as is often the case, the outworker can refuse to do work if asked, it is more likely that the relationship is that of independent contractor. On the other hand, in *Nethermere (St Neots) Ltd* v *Taverna & Gardiner* [1984] IRLR 240, the two applicants were found to be employees notwithstanding that they had no fixed hours for doing work brought to their homes by the company and for a number of weeks did no work at all. There was an irreducible minimum of service sufficient for the contract to be one of service, and there was 'a picture of the applicants doing the same work for the same rate as the employees in the factory but in their own homes — and in their own time — for the convenience of the worker and the company', per Stephenson LJ (see also *Airfix Footwear Ltd* v *Cope* [1978] ICR 1210).

2.3.7 Casual workers

The most detailed discussion of the position of casual workers is found in the Court of Appeal's judgment in *O'Kelly* v *Trusthouse Forte plc* [1983] 3 WLR 605. The appellants worked as wine butlers at the Grosvenor House Hotel. They were known as 'regular casuals' and were given preference in the work rotas over other casual staff. They had no other employment. The industrial tribunal found that many factors were consistent with a contract of service but one thing was missing, mutuality of obligation. The respondent had no obligation to provide work, and if the workers could obtain alternative work, they were free to take it. The preferential rota position was not a contractual promise. Their Lordships were not attracted by the proposition that there was in fact a series of short contracts of service.

In *McLeod* v *Hellyer Brothers Ltd* [1987] IRLR 232, the Court of Appeal gave detailed attention to the concept of an 'umbrella' or 'global' contract of employment. The five appellants in the two consolidated appeals were all Hull trawlermen. Prior to January 1984, they had each worked exclusively for the respective respondents over a long period. They had served on the terms of a series of 'crew agreements' which were signed on each engagement on board a fishing vessel. In between sailings, they had registered as unemployed and received social security benefits. In January 1984 the vessels were taken out of commission and the employees each claimed a redundancy payment. The Court of Appeal rejected the employees' contention that they were throughout employed under a global contract of employment which spanned the intervening periods between crew agreements. It was not possible to infer from the parties' conduct the existence in between crew agreements of a trawlerman's obligation 'to serve'. There would have to be mutually legally binding obligations on each side to constitute such a contract of service. It was not possible merely to count the heads of a series of individual contracts. Here the men had not placed themselves under any legally binding obligation either to make themselves available for the respective respondents in between crew agreements or not to accept employment from another trawler owner during such periods. The evidence was that they actually did sign on for other trawler owners in these periods.

2.3.8 Agency workers

A growing sector of the economy is manned by agency workers. They are unlikely to be employees of the agency especially when they work on a temporary basis. In *Wickens* v

Champion Employment [1984] ICR 365 (a case concerning whether the respondent had more than 20 employees), the main considerations militating against employee status of agency workers were that the agency had no obligation to find work for its workers and the contracts did not create a relationship with the necessary elements of continuity and care (see also *Ironmonger* v *Movefield Ltd t/a Deering Appointments* [1988] IRLR 461). This is not, however, an immutable rule (see *McMeechan* v *Secretary of State for Employment* [1995] IRLR 461).

2.3.9 Workers' cooperatives

The Employment Appeal Tribunal (EAT) in *Drym Fabricators Ltd* v *Johnson* [1981] ICR 274, considered that workers involved in a cooperative which is registered as a limited company are likely to be employees. A different result was, however, reached in the case of orchestras which functioned as musical cooperatives, since the musicians were entitled to do other work and effectively provided services in business on their own account. They were subjecting themselves to self-discipline in the orchestra rather than control in the recognised sense of employer direction (*Addison* v *London Philharmonic Orchestra Ltd* [1981] ICR 261).

2.3.10 Directors

A director is an officer of his company but may also have a contract of service, whether an express service agreement or one implied at law. In *Albert J. Parsons & Sons Ltd* v *Parsons* [1979] ICR 271, the Court of Appeal held that there was no contract of employment in the case of a full-time working director who was paid by director's fees only and had not been treated as employed for national insurance. In *Eaton* v *Robert Eaton Ltd and Secretary of State for Employment* [1988] IRLR 83, in which the EAT held that the applicant director was not an employee of the respondent, Kilner Brown J said that the main factors in determining the question were:

(a) the use of any descriptive term such as managing director;
(b) whether there was an express contract of employment or a board minute constituting an agreement to employ;
(c) whether remuneration was by way of salary as opposed to director's fee;
(d) whether that remuneration was fixed in advance rather than paid on an *ad hoc* basis;
(e) whether remuneration was by way of entitlement rather than gratuitous; and
(f) the function actually performed by the director.

Whilst a director may be removed from his office by a simple majority at a general meeting of his company, this is expressly without prejudice to any rights he may have by contract. The following special provisions relate to his contract:

(a) By s. 318, Companies Act 1985, the company must keep a copy of every written service agreement and a written memorandum of every oral contract.
(b) By s. 319, Companies Act 1985 a company may not give its directors a contract of employment for more than five years unless the company approves it by resolution in general meeting. If no such resolution is passed, any contract must be terminable on reasonable notice by the company. If a new contract is made more than six months before

the expiry of the old agreement, the extra period under the new contract is added to the
unexpired period under the old contract (s. 319(2)).

There are restrictions on loans by the company to directors and their associates (ss. 330–346,
Companies Act 1985) and substantial property transactions involving directors (ss. 320–322,
Companies Act 1985).

The term 'director' includes 'anybody who occupies the position of a director regardless
of his title' (s. 741(1), Companies Act 1985) and includes 'shadow directors', that is those
individuals 'in accordance with whose directions or instructions the directors of the
company are accustomed to act' (s. 741(2)).

The general scope of directors' duties is outside the scope of this book, but it should be
noted that a director:

(a)   owes a fiduciary duty to the company;

(b)   must not use his position in the company to further his own personal interests and,
if he does so, must account to the company for any resulting profit;

(c)   owes to his company a duty to exercise proper care and skill (e.g. *Dorchester
Finance Co.* v *Stebbings* [1989] BCLC 498). The court has power to relieve directors of
liability for breach of trust, default, breach of duty or negligence if they have acted honestly
and reasonably (Companies Act 1985, s. 727);

(d)   may claim no remuneration for work done save in accordance with the articles of
association (*Guinness plc* v *Saunders* [1990] 2 WLR 324).

A partner is not an employee of his firm (*Palumbo* v *Stylianou* (1966) 1 ITR 407 and *Cowell*
v *Quilter Goodison Ltd* [1989] IRLR 392).

2.3.11   Merchant seamen

Merchant seamen used to be governed by a totally different regime from other workers. The
antique procedures of the Merchant Shipping Act 1894 have been partially reformed by the
Merchant Shipping Acts 1970 and 1988, but these differences remain:

(a)   Seamen must normally be engaged by a crew agreement approved by the Secretary
of State for Trade, and signed in writing by each crew member on the voyage.

(b)   If the contract is frustrated by wreck or a ship registered in the UK is sold outside,
a maximum of two months' wages is payable unless the seaman unreasonably refuses to
obtain available alternative employment.

(c)   A seaman must be given an account of wages due 24 hours before discharge at port,
and the pay settled within seven days after discharge.

(d)   If the seaman fails in his duties, his contract may be terminated or he can be fined.

On the rights to claim unfair dismissal, see *Wood* v *Cunard Line Ltd* [1990] IRLR 281, para.
11.4.2, infra.

2.4   DEFINITION OF WORKERS

In recent years some statutory provisions have extended to employed and self-employed
alike but this is still relatively rare. Examples include the Health and Safety at Work etc.

Act 1974, and taxation provisions to prevent abuse by lump labour. Moreover, the Sex Discrimination Act 1975 and Race Relations Act 1976 prohibit discrimination against those employed 'under a contract of service or of apprenticeship or personally to execute any work or labour' (see *Mirror Group Newspapers Ltd* v *Gunning* [1986] IRLR 27).

Section 26(1), Social Security and Housing Benefits Act 1982 defines employee for the purposes of statutory sick pay rather differently. An employee is a person over the age of 16 who is gainfully employed under a contract of service or in an office and who is liable to be taxed under Schedule E for income tax purposes.

The former Wages Act 1986 (now ERA 1996, Part II) applies to contracts of service, apprenticeships or 'any other contract . . . whereby the individual undertakes to do or perform personally any work or services for another party to the contract whose status is not by virtue of the contract that of a client or customer of any profession or business undertaking carried on by the individual' (ERA 1996, s. 230(3); see also TULR(C)A 1992, s. 296(1); *Carter* v *Law Society* [1973] ICR 113). Workers who provide general medical, pharmaceutical, dental or opthalmic services under the NHS are expressly included in TULR(C)A 1992, s. 279, as are those in employment under or for the purposes of a government department. Since a worker must 'perform personally' his services, the definition has been held to exclude:

(a)   anyone who agrees to perform a task but can then delegate it to another (*Broadbent* v *Crisp* [1974] ICR 248); and

(b)   persons like writers who undertake no obligation to produce any work (*Writers' Guild of Great Britain* v *BBC* [1974] ICR 234).

The armed forces and police are expressly excluded.

2.5   QUESTION OF LAW OR FACT?

There was for a considerable period controversy as to whether the instant question was one of fact or law. Browne LJ in *Ferguson* v *John Dawson & Partners (Contractors) Ltd* [1976] 1 WLR 1213 was firmly of the view that it was an issue of fact and thus not open to challenge on appeal. The Court of Appeal authority suggests that the question is one of law but that it involves matters of degree and fact which are essentially for the industrial tribunal to determine (*O'Kelly* v *Trusthouse Forte plc* [1983] 3 WLR 605; *Clifford* v *Union of Democratic Mineworkers* [1991] IRLR 518). In *Nethermere (St Neots) Ltd* v *Taverna & Gardiner* [1984] IRLR 240, the Court of Appeal applied the administrative law authority of *Edwards* v *Bairstow* [1956] AC 14 to the effect that the EAT could not interfere with a tribunal's decision unless it had misdirected itself in law or its decision was one which no industrial tribunal properly directing itself on the relevant facts could have reached (also *Warner Holidays Ltd* v *Secretary of State for Social Services* [1983] ICR 440).

The House of Lords in *Davies* v *Presbyterian Church of Wales* [1986] IRLR 194, however, considered that the *Edwards* v *Bairstow* principle was irrelevant. Lord Templeman (at para. 18) said that 'if the industrial tribunal erred in deciding that question [whether the applicant was an employee], the decision must be reversed and it matters not that other industrial tribunals might have reached a similar erroneous conclusion in the absence of an authoritative decision by a higher court'.

This was, however, narrowly confined in *Lee Ting Sang* v *Chung Chi-Keung* [1990] ICR 409, where the Privy Council decided that *Davies* was concerned only with the situation in which the relationship was dependent solely upon the true construction of a legal document. (See also *Andrews* v *King* [1991] ICR 846.)

In *McLeod* v *Hellyer Brothers Ltd* [1987] IRLR 232 (for the facts see para. 2.3.7, supra), the question of whether the appellants were employees depended partly on the interpretation of various written documents and partly on inferences to be drawn from the parties' conduct. The appellate court was thus held to be entitled to interfere with the decision of the industrial tribunal only if the tribunal had misdirected itself in law or the decision was one which no tribunal properly instructed could have reached. The Court of Appeal did not consider the reasoning of the majority in *O'Kelly*'s case to be overruled by the House of Lords in the *Davies* case, which applied where the case turned entirely on the construction of a document and as a matter of law there was only one correct answer. (See also *Santokh Singh* v *Guru Nanak Gurdwara* [1990] ICR 309.)

2.6 SPECIAL STATUTORY REGIMES

2.6.1 School staff

One of the wide-ranging series of reforms ushered in by the Education Reform Act 1988 was the local management of schools, whereby school governors would have power over the budgets for their school. Section 44 and Sch. 3 make special provision for the appointment, suspension and dismissal of staff, the determination of the duties, grading and remuneration of staff, and for disciplinary and grievance procedures to be under the control of the governing body. The general effect is that while the staff remain employed by the local education authority, the most important decisions relating to that employment are taken by the governing body. This has been criticised as according power without responsibility. There are also provisions in s. 149 for the apportionment of costs of dismissal, premature retirement or voluntary severance. Terms in a contract preventing redundancy are rendered void (s. 221).

The Education (Modification of Enactments Relating to Employment) Order 1989 (SI 1989 No. 901) does just what its title states. The most important modifications are that:

(a) for purposes of unfair dismissal, the reason for dismissal is to be that of the governing body (reg. 4), and claims in the tribunal are to be made against the governing body and not the local education authority, though it remains the nominal employer; and

(b) there is no immunity from actions in tort when 'the inducement, interference or threat . . . relates to a contract the performance of which does not affect directly or indirectly the school or institution over which the governing body in question exercises its functions' (reg. 5). This makes most national industrial action by teachers unlawful.

2.6.2 Academic staff

In *R* v *Visitor of the University of Hull ex parte Page* [1992] ICR 67, Mr Edgar Page was a philosophy lecturer from Hull University who was dismissed in effect for redundancy. The matter fell within the jurisdiction of the University Visitor, who decided that the university could dismiss Mr Page because of a provision in his letter of appointment which stated that three months' notice could be given on either side and that this overrode his right under the tenure clause of the university statutes, by which he could be dismissed only for 'good cause'. The Divisional Court held that decisions of the University Visitor were amenable to judicial review, and that on a true construction of the university statutes the normal tenure provisions were not overridden by the notice provisions. That term was only a procedural matter so that three months' notice had to be given if the university had good cause to dismiss (see also *Pearce* v *University of Aston (No. 1)* [1991] 2 All ER 461; *(No. 2)* [1991] 2 All ER 469).

The Education Reform Act 1988 established the new body of University Commissioners, who are like 'academic guardian angels'. They are charged with having regard to the need, *inter alia,* for academic staff to have 'freedom within the law to question and test received wisdom and to put forward new ideas and controversial or unpopular opinions, without placing themselves in jeopardy of losing their jobs or privileges' (s. 202(2)). They must secure that each qualifying institution (broadly speaking, universities and colleges) includes in its statutes provision for dismissal by reason of redundancy or just cause (s. 203(1)). The reason for dismissal must be such as 'may in the circumstances (including the size and administrative resources of the institution) reasonably be treated as a sufficient reason for dismissal' (s. 203(2)). The University Visitor is not to have jurisdiction over any dispute which concerns the 'appointment or employment or termination of appointment or employment' of any member of academic staff (s. 206(1)).

3 The Individual Contract of Employment and its Sources

The modern model of the employment contract, as a voluntary consensual relationship sanctioned by the civil law, is suffused with an individualism that ignores the economic reality behind the bargain.

(K. W. Wedderburn, *The Worker and the Law,* 3rd ed, Penguin, 1986, p. 142.)

The contract of employment, although one of the most important of all legal agreements, is also one of the most informal and formless. This is partly because it is impossible to cover all issues which may arise at work, and partly derives from the trade union movement's suspicion of legally drawn express bargains and the continuation of 'factory gate' employment, where a foreman simply says to a worker 'start on Monday' (e.g. *Ferguson* v *John Dawson & Partners (Contractors) Ltd* [1976] 1 WLR 213).

Most workers do not bargain individually at all; they take what terms are offered to them. The relationship is one of subordination, partially or wholly — forced acceptance of the employer's terms if the employee wants the job, except where he has a strong bargaining position due to high status or qualifications. Then detailed service agreements are the norm. Otherwise the employee is unlikely to receive more than a tawdry piece of paper or letter setting out his terms and conditions. Most contracts are standard in form and in effect, but may derive from several other documents and sources. Further, the courts have formulated many implied terms to supplement the express terms of the employment relationship, and statute has enacted laws protective of employees which operate by incorporating terms into the contract of employment (e.g. guarantee pay, equal pay).

In this chapter, we examine the several sources of its terms, which, besides those expressly agreed, derive from at least some of the following:

(a) collective bargaining;
(b) implied terms;
(c) work rules;
(d) custom and practice;
(e) statute;
(f) awards under statutory provisions.

We will then consider:

(g) capacity to make the contract;

(h) formation of the contract;

(i) the effect of a takeover;

(j) the written statement of terms.

3.1 THE COLLECTIVE BARGAIN

A collective agreement is a treaty between social powers. It is . . . a peace treaty and at the same time a normative treaty.

(O. Kahn-Freund, *Labour and the Law,* 3rd ed, Sweet & Maxwell, 1983, p. 123.)

The most important terms in the employee's contract derive for the majority of workers not from an individual bargain with his employer but from a collective agreement entered into by a union recognised for this purpose at his place of work, although the importance of this element has declined in recent years.

Very often an individual's statement of terms will do no more than refer him to the relevant collective agreement which is likely to deal with, in particular, wages, hours, holidays and the guaranteed week, as its most important substantive rules. This is its legislative or normative function, but it also has another side concerning relations between the union and the employer, including negotiating rights, grievance procedures and also a means for renegotiating the agreement at fixed intervals. Its judicial function and industrial relations implications will be considered later (para. 19.2), since we are here concerned only with its effect on the employee's contractual terms.

3.1.1 The effect of the collective bargain on the individual contract of employment

The unions and employers cannot sue each other on the collective bargain save in the rare cases in which the parties agree that the terms are enforceable at law. In any event, the terms may still be legally binding between employer and employee on an individual basis although the law is somewhat pragmatic as to how and why such incorporation is achieved. There must be some sort of 'bridge' between the collective bargain and individual contract for its incorporation and this is often by way of express reference in the actual contract or in the written statement of terms. Thus in *National Coal Board* v *Galley* [1958] 1 WLR 16, the individual contract fairly typically provided 'wages shall be regulated by such national agreement and the county wages agreement for the time being in force and this agreement shall be subject to these agreements and to any other agreements relating to or in connection with or subsidiary to the wages agreement'. This also means that the contract need not be amended every time such negotiations take place.

Incorporation will be readily implied from the universal observance of the collective bargain in the employee's work place, even though the individual employee may neither know of the pact, nor be a member of the union which negotiates it. There will frequently be no other basis for the employment, but regular observance by itself is not always decisive. Knowledge of the terms is usually not necessary. See *Marley* v *Forward Trust Group Ltd* [1986] IRLR 369.

The impact of consideration has not been much discussed. There was sufficient consideration for the introduction of an enhanced severance package in that thereafter the employee continued in the employment of the employer, thereby abandoning any argument that the increase should have been greater and removing a potential area of dispute between employer and employee (*Lee* v *GEC Plessey Telecommunications* [1993] IRLR 383).

3.1.2   The basis of incorporation

The general legal explanation for incorporation has, in fact, been rarely considered by the courts. While it is prima facie attractive to view the union bargaining as an agent for its members, the problem is that this would restrict the union to acting only on behalf of employees for the time being, implying that a later hired worker was not so bound. There would also be a serious difficulty if a union member as a principal purported to withdraw his authority from the union to act as his agent (see generally *Heaton's Transport Ltd* v *TGWU* [1972] ICR 308, *Singh* v *British Steel Corporation* [1974] IRLR 131). The courts have thus been reluctant to find an agency relationship except when the numbers involved are small. In *Holland* v *London Society of Compositors* (1924) 40 TLR 440, Lush J held that the union acts as a principal and not its members' agent in bargaining. But Arnold J voiced the most widespread view when he said in *Burton Group Ltd* v *Smith* [1977] IRLR 351 at para. 21:

> There is no reason at all why, in a particular case, union representatives should not be the agent of an employee to make a contract, or to receive a notice, or otherwise effect a binding transaction on his behalf. But that agency does not stem from the mere fact that they are union representatives and that he is a member of the union; it must be supported in the particular case by the creation of some specific agency.

(See e.g. *Deane* v *Craik, The Times,* 16 March 1962.) It is generally recognised that non-unionists as well as union members are covered by an effective collective bargain, unlike the United States. The most pragmatic approach is that collective bargains are implied into individual contracts by way of conduct (*Hill* v *Levey* (1858) 157 ER 366, Watson B), or as Professor Kahn-Freund has put it, they become 'crystallised custom'. In the case of factory gate hiring, there may be no other possible terms (see *Kenny* v *Vauxhall Motors Ltd* [1985] ICR 535 on interpretation of collective bargains; *National Coal Board* v *National Union of Mineworkers* [1986] IRLR 439).

Collective bargains are not, however, automatically incorporated into the individual contract because the employer is a member of an employers' association which is party to the collective agreement in the absence of a custom in the trade that such terms would be observed (*Hamilton* v *Futura Floors* [1990] IRLR 478).

An indirect effect of the collective bargain is illustrated by *Gray Dunn and Co. Ltd* v *Edwards* [1980] IRLR 23, where it was held that where employers negotiate a detailed agreement with a recognised union (here concerning a disciplinary code), they are entitled to assume that all unionised employees know of and are bound by its provisions. The Court of Appeal thought that 'there could be no stability in industrial relations if this were not so'. British collective bargains do not, however, operate as a code, as do most Continental systems, so that it is possible for individual employees to have terms less favourable to the employee than those provided for in the agreement between union and management.

3.1.3   Termination of collective agreement

Where a collectively bargained bonus scheme (or any other provision) has been incorporated into the individual contract of employment, the employer cannot unilaterally determine that scheme (*Robertson* v *British Gas Corporation* [1983] ICR 351). On the other hand, in *Gibbons* v *Associated British Ports* [1985] IRLR 376, termination of a collective agreement had no effect on terms of remuneration incorporated into an individual's contract of employment. The inescapable conclusion was that the collectively agreed six-day guarantee, designed to compensate dock workers for loss of profitable shift work, was an integral part of the term of remuneration.

In *Cadoux* v *Central Regional Council* [1986] IRLR 131, however, the Court of Session reached a somewhat surprising decision that a provision for a non-contributory life assurance scheme was not a contractual right. The employee's letter of appointment recorded that 'the post is subject to the Conditions of Service laid down by the National Joint Council for Local Authorities Administrative, Professional, Technical and Clerical Services (Scottish Council) and as supplemented by the Authorities' Rules and as amended from time to time'. When the Council unilaterally withdrew the scheme, the plaintiff sought a declaration that he was contractually entitled to it. This was refused since the local authority's rules were made unilaterally and could be changed at will (*Airlie* v *City of Edinburgh District Council* [1996] IRLR 516).

On a transfer of an undertaking, whether by sale or some other disposition or by operation of law, the transferee company is obliged to observe the terms of any collective bargain negotiated by the transferor (Transfer of Undertakings (Protection of Employment) Regulations 1981 (SI 1981 No. 1794)) (see Chapter 16, although the remedial mechanism by which this aim is to be achieved remains obscure).

3.1.4 Inappropriate terms for incorporation

Some terms of the collective bargain are, moreover, not susceptible to 'translation' into the individual contract, because they relate to obligations entered into by the union collectively, such as union recognition (*Gallagher* v *Post Office* [1970] 3 All ER 714), or redundancy procedure. Thus in *British Leyland UK Ltd* v *McQuilken* [1978] IRLR 245, the appellant company agreed with the union representing the majority of its workers on a phased discontinuance of its experimental department in Glasgow. Skilled employees would have a choice of retraining or redundancy. Some workers who had chosen the latter later changed their minds, and the employees claimed that the employers were breaking their contracts by infringing the collective bargain. Lord McDonald held, however, that the collective agreement 'was a long-term plan dealing with policy rather than the rights of individual employees under their contract of employment'. The court looked for authority to a 1930s Privy Council decision that an agreement between a Canadian railway company and a trade union providing, in a redundancy situation, for staff with the shortest service to be dismissed first, was not part of the individual contract (*Young* v *Canadian Northern Railway Co.* [1931] AC 83), since '[this agreement] does not appear to be a document adapted for conversion into or incorporation with a service agreement'. Further, a term of a bargain conferring rights or imposing duties on a person other than employer and employee cannot be incorporated into an individual contract of employment because of the constraints of the doctrine of privity. The distinction is between terms in a collective agreement which are designed and intended to govern the relationship between the employer and the union which are not incorporated, and those designed and intended to benefit individuals which may be incorporated (*NCB* v *NUM*, supra; *Alexander* v *STC plc* [1990] ICR 291). The following cases illustrate the principle:

(a) A collective agreement between the *Daily Telegraph* and the Institute of Journalists which established a disputes procedure and provided that it should be the only means of resolving a dispute between the parties was also held not incorporated into the individual contract of employment (*Tadd* v *Eastwood* [1983] IRLR 320).

(b)   In *City and Hackney Health Authority* v *National Union of Public Employees* [1985] IRLR 252, the Court of Appeal thought it certainly arguable that an agreement with the union providing facilities for officials was incorporated into the contract of employment of the accredited shop steward. See also *Griffiths* v *Buckinghamshire CC* [1994] IRLR 265.

(c)   In *Alexander* v *STC plc* [1990] ICR 291, Aldous J held that last in first out redundancy selection procedures were arguably incorporated into the individual contract of employment.

3.1.5   Incorporation of non-strike clauses

The only statutory modification of the rules of incorporation is s. 18(4) of the Trade Union and Labour Relations Act 1974, which severely restricts the binding inclusion in a collective agreement of clauses which inhibit the taking of industrial action, or have the effect of doing so. Such a provision may only be incorporated in the individual contract if the following stringent conditions are satisfied:

(a)   The collective agreement is in writing.

(b)   It contains an express statement that such a clause is incorporated into the individual contract.

(c)   It is reasonably accessible at the workplace and available during working hours.

(d)   Each trade union party to the agreement is independent (see para. 17.8 for definition).

(e)   The individual contract expressly or impliedly incorporates such a term.

3.1.6   Levels of bargaining

Where there are different levels of collective bargaining, the courts have tended to look at the national agreement for incorporation into the individual contract. The courts take this view probably because the national agreement is the more legal-appearing document. Thus in *Loman and Henderson* v *Merseyside Transport Services Ltd* (1967) 3 KIR 726, the road haulage national agreement provided guaranteed weekly pay on the foundation of a 40-hour week, yet at the Barking depot of the respondent warehousing company a local agreement offered 68 hours. The Divisional Court, however, held that the latter was 'in the nature of gentleman's agreement for ironing out local difficulties and providing an incentive for cooperation . . .'. This was notwithstanding that the local agreement was much more directly effective, on the ground that employees who refused overtime would have been removed (but cf. *Barrett* v *National Coal Board* [1978] ICR 1102 and *Saxton* v *National Coal Board* [1970] ITR 196). In recent years many industries have witnessed a movement towards plant and local bargaining and away from major national agreements (see para. 19.1).

3.2   IMPLIED TERMS

The classic exposition of the process of implication of contractual terms in all contracts was given by MacKinnon LJ in *Shirlaw* v *Southern Foundries (1926) Ltd* [1939] 2 KB 206 at 227:

Prima facie that which in any contract is left to be implied and need not be expressed is something so obvious that it goes without saying; so that, if, while the parties were making their bargain, an officious bystander were to suggest some express provision for it in their agreement, they would testily suppress him with a common 'Oh, of course!'.

This is in line with Bowen LJ's oft quoted dictum in *The Moorcock* (1889) 14 PD 64, that an implied term must be 'founded on presumed intention and upon reason'. An alternative test provides for implication of terms which are 'necessary in the business sense to give efficacy to the contract' (*Reigate* v *Union Manufacturing Co Ltd* [1918] 1 KB 592 per Scrutton LJ). In any case, the term must also be precise enough to be enforced by the courts (*Lister* v *Romford Ice and Cold Storage Co. Ltd* [1957] AC 555; *Liverpool CC* v *Irwin* [1977] AC 239; *Courtaulds Northern Spinning Ltd* v *Sibson and TGWU* [1988] IRLR 305).

Although there is no difference in principle between the test for implying terms into a contract for employment and other agreements, the courts have had particular experience in exercising their power in this area. Certain standard implied terms have emerged, because of the essentially similar nature of all relationships between employer and employee. Whether the courts always concentrate on the intention of the parties as they profess is rather dubious, especially as the interests of employer and employee so widely and obviously diverge. The judges have also made certain social assumptions about the labour relationship.

Professor O. Kahn-Freund has said 'It is however sheer utopia to postulate a common interest in the substance of labour relations' (*Labour and the Law,* 3rd ed, Sweet & Maxwell, 1983, p. 28). Thus the employee's implied duty of care, fidelity and cooperation may not, in fact, be expressly desired at all, but they are considered necessary by the courts (see *Howman & Son* v *Blyth* [1983] IRLR 139 on implication of reasonable terms, and *Liverpool CC* v *Irwin,* supra). Indeed, in the case of the established terms to be discussed later there is little reference back in the judgments to the business efficacy, and the *Moorcock* tests, or the intention of the parties. The wide scope of implication may be gauged from the following decisions of high authority in favour of implied terms that:

(a)   Teachers have an implied duty to act professionally, which includes covering for absent colleagues (*Sim* v *Rotherham Metropolitan Borough Council* [1986] ICR 897).

(b)   The employer would notify employees of their rights under a complex pension scheme which had been negotiated between the relevant representative bodies when there was a valuable right contingent on action being taken by the employee to avail himself of that benefit (*Scally* v *Southern Health and Social Services Board* [1991] ICR 771, [1991] IRLR 522).

(c)   The employer will reasonably and promptly afford a reasonable opportunity to obtain redress of grievances (*Goold Ltd* v *McConnell* [1995] IRLR 516).

(d)   In the case of an employee on annualised hours, if an employee left early he would be entitled to the standard rate of pay for any hours he had worked in excess of the 40-hour week; 'The employee may be requested to work in excess of the notional 40-hour week, but will not be paid for the excess until the end of the year and then at the higher rate' (*Ali* v *Christian Salvesen Ltd* [1995] IRLR 625 at para. 28).

It is arguable that there is an implied term that the employer would not require employees to carry out so much overtime in any week that it was reasonably foreseeable it would damage the health of the employee, notwithstanding the presence of express terms in the contract of employment that employees should carry out extensive amounts of overtime

(*Johnstone* v *Bloomsbury Health Authority* [1991] IRLR 118, [1991] ICR 269, the case of the junior hospital doctors). Stuart-Smith LJ said that the express obligation to work the additional hours was subject to the implied term that the employer had an obligation to take care of its employees. This was because such an implied term was necessary in order to give efficacy to the contract. However, the other judge in the majority, Sir Nicolas Browne-Wilkinson V-C, thought that the implied term took effect as to the additional hours because there was no absolute obligation to work the overtime. Therefore there was no conflict between the express and the implied term. However, this may not be the meaning of 'absolute' here. It was not that there was no absolute obligation to work, for whether the doctor did so or not was at the hospital's option and therefore when it required him to work he had an absolute obligation to do so. It was, however, not absolutely clear that the hospital would call upon him to work the extra hours.

There was, moreover, until recently, little authority on some of the most important implied terms because litigation in the civil courts on the contract of employment was relatively rare. The adoption of the breach of contract test for constructive unfair dismissal has, however, stimulated the growth of important implied terms based on reasonable industrial practice in the industrial tribunals, which will be considered later under that rubric (para. 13.3.3). The extension of the jurisdiction of industrial tribunals to consider breach of contract claims on dismissal is likely to lead to a greater development of the use of implied terms.

The courts have, however, refused to imply terms (either on the grounds of unreasonableness or lack of common intention) that:

(a)   The employer will indemnify the employee against liability in negligence (*Lister* v *Romford Ice and Cold Storage Co. Ltd* [1957] AC 515).

(b)   The employer will recognise a trade union for the purposes of collective bargaining (*Gallagher* v *Post Office* [1970] 2 All ER 712).

(c)   The employee will work overtime because he has done so for the previous ten years (*Horrigan* v *Lewisham LBC* [1978] ICR 15).

(d)   The employee has a right to strike (*Simmons* v *Hoover Ltd* [1977] ICR 61).

(e)   The employee has a generalised 'right to work' (see para. 4.10.1).

(f)   An employee who used the disputes procedure negotiated between his union and employers would not sue any person who took part in those proceedings for defamation (*Tadd* v *Eastwood* [1983] IRLR 320).

(g)   An employee must undergo a psychiatric examination (*Bliss* v *South East Thames Regional Health Authority* [1985] IRLR 308).

(h)   An articled clerk's contract could be terminated if he did not pass the Law Society examination (*Stubbes* v *Trower, Still & Keeling* [1987] IRLR 321). In order to establish such a term, the employers had to show that the implication was *necessary,* that the contract would have made no sense without it, and that the term was omitted from the written and oral negotiations because it was so obvious that there was no need to make it explicit. The respondents could easily have introduced such a term by expressly adopting regulation 48 of the Law Society's Qualifying Regulations.

(i)   Suspension could take place only after the employer provided the employee with full information as to the reason for the suspension or the full rules of natural justice (*McClory* v *Post Office* [1993] IRLR 159). There was, however, an implied term that the employer's right to suspend would not be exercised on unreasonable grounds and that the suspension would continue only for so long as there were reasonable grounds for its so doing.

(j) The employer would not conduct its business in such a way as to risk putting the employees at a disadvantage in the labour market after termination of employment (*Re BCCI* [1994] IRLR 282).

(k) That if employment terminated without the employee having taken any part of his holiday entitlement, the company would pay in lieu (*Morley* v *Heritage plc* [1993] IRLR 400).

Express and implied terms must be capable of coexistence in the contract without conflict (*Johnstone* v *Bloomsbury Health Authority* [1991] IRLR 118, [1991] ICR 269, *Aspden* v *Webbs Poultry & Meat Group (Holdings) Ltd* [1996] IRLR 521 and *R* v *Secretary of State for Health and Trent Regional Health Authority ex parte Guirguis* [1990] IRLR 30 in the case of termination of employment of a doctor). Implied terms may always be excluded or modified by express agreement.

There is a difference (although it may be a subtle distinction) between implying a term into a contract which negatives an express clause (which is not permitted) and implying one which controls the exercise of the employer's otherwise unfettered discretion. An example in the latter category would be the court controlling the express power of the employer to insist upon a move of the place of work by ensuring that the employer gives reasonable notice of any such change (*United Bank Ltd* v *Akhtar* [1989] IRLR 507; *Prestwick Circuits Ltd* v *McAndrew* [1990] IRLR 191). In *Akhtar* it was put thus (at para. 44): 'There is a clear distinction between implying a term which negatives a provision which is expressly stated in the contract and implying a term which controls the exercise of a discretion which is expressly conferred in a contract.'

3.3 WORK RULES

Many companies lay down detailed 'work rules', which include disciplinary provisions but may also take in sickness, safety provisions, employee sports facilities and holidays. They are given contractual effect by way of express or implied incorporation or custom and practice, and may be communicated by notice board, special handbook, sheet of paper or even word of mouth. A typical format is where the employee signs a declaration that he accepts the conditions of employment as set out in the Works Rules, and such acceptance may be implied if the employee has reasonable notice of them. However, this depends on:

(a) the nature of the document, if any, in which the rules are communicated;
(b) the methods used to bring such document to the employees' attention;
(c) whether notice was given before or at the time of the formation of the contract.

Works rules are not, however, all to be treated as contractual terms — some because, being uncertain and ambiguous like many collective bargains, they are not appropriate for incorporation, or otherwise because they are inherently variable, and solely within the prerogative of the employer.

In the leading case, *Secretary of State for Employment* v *ASLEF (No. 2)* [1972] 2 QB 455, the Court of Appeal had to determine whether the respondent union's 'work to rule' was in breach of contract. In disputing this, the union claimed that it was merely following the employer's rule book to the letter. The Court of Appeal held, however, that the rules of BR, which contained a mass of detailed instructions in 239 rules on 280 pages, were not all contractually binding. Some were clearly out of date, others trivial. Generally, Lord Denning MR said:

Each man signs a form saying that he will abide by the rules, but these rules are in no way terms of the contract of employment. They are only instructions to a man as to how he is to do his work.

The employer might thus alter the rules at will and the boundaries of his prerogative are thereby increased. If the employee refuses to obey a changed rule he might still, however, be lawfully dismissed at common law and (depending on all the circumstances) probably fairly dismissed by statute. The employee must obey lawful and reasonable orders (see para. 4.7).

It may confidently be assumed, however, that those sections of work rule books which deal with particulars required in the statutory statement of terms will be part of the contract. Otherwise the test is what the parties intend to be contractual terms. In *Petrie* v *MacFisheries* [1940] 1 KB 258, a notice about sick pay posted on the factory notice board was held to have contractual effect, even though the employees had never had their attention specifically drawn to it; while in *Dal* v *A.S. Orr* [1980] IRLR 413, the EAT found contractual a statement in the employees' handbook that 'the Company reserves the right to alter the shift system together with the hours of work to meet production requirements'.

3.4   CUSTOM AND PRACTICE

Many day-to-day features of employment, and the way things are done at shop floor level, are governed as much by long-held custom and practice as by express contractual terms. Indeed, most terms were reached in this way in the nineteenth century before collective bargaining took over. One reason for its wide extent today is that industry-wide collective agreements tend to be too remote and vague for application by themselves in the realities of particular factories. Demarcation lines and piece work rates commonly grow up in this way.

To be legally recognised by the courts, a custom must be 'reasonable, certain and notorious'. In the leading case of *Sagar* v *Ridehalgh & Son Ltd* [1931] 1 Ch 310, the Court of Appeal decided that customary deductions from a weaver's wages which had been made in the same way for 30 years were contractual terms. The process of incorporation, according to Romer LJ, was that the employee 'entering the Appellant's service upon the same terms as the other weavers employed by them, . . . must be deemed to have subjected himself to those terms whatever those terms might turn out to be'. See also *Duke* v *Reliance Systems* [1982] ICR 449. Knowledge of the practice by each worker was not necessary. However, in *Meek* v *Port of London Authority* [1918] 1 Ch 415, the long established deduction of income tax was not incorporated into the employee's contract because employees did not know of it. The latter would appear to be the better approach as it seems unfair to impose terms on employees of which they are ignorant. Custom and practice may also be the basis for the incorporation of a collective agreement. Thus in *MacLea* v *Essex Lines Ltd* (1933) 45 L1 LR 254 Acton J said:

In the shipping industry, when people are engaged in this way simply by being told to join a ship without more ado, it is always assumed on both sides, that the engagement is on the terms and conditions of the National Maritime Board.

Indeed, many collective agreements, particularly at local level, are simply a distillation of established custom and practice.

The EAT emphasised recently that the real question is not the number of occasions on which an employer has adopted a particular practice or calculation, but whether an intention to be bound contractually could be discerned from the policy as communicated by the employer (*Quinn* v *Calder Industrial Materials* [1996] IRLR 126; see to the same effect *Baldwin* v *British Coal Corporation* [1995] IRLR 139, esp. para. 30).

A term will be implied by custom only if there is nothing in the express or necessarily implied terms of the contract to prevent such inclusion (*London Export Corp.* v *Jubilee Coffee Roasting Co.* [1958] 2 All ER 411).

3.5 STATUTE

In recent years, statute has often protected the employee by means of implication of terms into the contract of employment, usually by generalising what is already best practice in collective agreements or individual bargains. Thus the rights to guarantee pay, equal pay, notice and maximum hours in factories (infra) are effected in this way. This means that the employee may enforce the contract by action for breach of contract, or, if the claim is current on the termination of the contract, in the industrial tribunal. Conversely some contractual terms are rendered void by statute, for example, a clause excluding rights to claim unfair dismissal or redundancy pay or, at common law, a term ousting the jurisdiction of the courts.

3.6 AWARDS

Some employees' terms derive from an award of an arbitration panel or some other third party. Thus the Central Arbitration Committee, for breach of the duty to disclose information to trade unions, may determine fair terms which are thereby automatically incorporated into the individual contracts of employment of affected workers (para. 19.5). A similar process of implication arises where an *ad hoc* arbitrator or the CAC itself acts under a voluntary reference of a dispute made by ACAS.

3.7 CAPACITY

Rules of capacity to make contracts of employment are much less significant today than in former times. There are, however, some residual matters of importance relating to infants under 18, which are found in the Infants Relief Act 1874, and are most important in relation to apprentices. An infant generally can be sued on an agreement only in respect of necessary goods or a contract for the benefit of the infant. The proper question in relation to a contract of employment is not whether any one stipulation is for his benefit. Instead, the court must look at the whole contract having regard to the circumstances of the case (*De Francesco* v *Barnum* (1890) 43 ChD 165). The contract of employment by its nature contains some terms which are disadvantageous to the employee. The court takes an objective approach, and asks whether, if an offending clause were not in the contract, the minor would be able to enter into a contract of equal or greater benefit. Moreover, an unfavourable clause may be severed from the rest of the contract (*Bromley* v *Smith* [1909] 2 KB 235). There are also particular statutory restrictions on the employment of some children. Thus a child under 14 may not be employed at all (Children and Young Persons Act 1963, s. 18(1)); and those up to 16 may not work for more than 44 hours per week in any factory, mine or transport (Factories Act 1961, Part VI; Mines and Quarries Act 1954, s. 124; Employment of Women, Young

Persons and Children Act 1920, Schedule Part II). Further restrictions are placed on the employment of the young in entertainment (Children and Young Persons Act 1963, ss. 37 and 44), while more broadly, local authorities have powers to gain information about employment of children within their jurisdiction and prevent their taking unsuitable jobs and employment at unsuitable times.

3.8 FORMATION AND VARIATION OF CONTRACT

3.8.1 Formation of contract of employment

Like all other contracts, the contract of employment is constituted by offer and acceptance supported by consideration. The offer in the great majority of cases comes from the employer, and is accepted in writing, or simply by the conduct of the employee in actually turning up for work. There are few analogous restrictions on the prerogative of management to hire workers, as exist in respect of dismissal. The exceptions relate to race or sex discrimination (para. 8.2) and the Rehabilitation of Offenders Act 1974 (para. 13.13).

There are also some unusual situations in which persons may sue another even though no contract of employment as such has been entered into. Where employees were enticed to leave one job on the promise that they would be offered other highly paid positions, which did not materialise, they were entitled to damages for breach of warranty or a collateral contract (*Gill* v *Cape Contracts* [1985] IRLR 499).

Although terms must be relatively certain to be enforced, the courts will go some way in construing ambiguity. The courts may look at an advertisement and letter of appointment to spell out terms or to construe ambiguities in the terms agreed (*Deeley* v *British Rail Engineering Ltd* [1979] IRLR 5, *Pedersen* v *Camden London Borough* [1981] IRLR 173). Thus a judge upheld a promise to work 'such days or part days in each week as may reasonably be required by the management', defining it as demanding work for a reasonable number of days (*National Coal Board* v *Galley* [1958] 1 WLR 16). However, in a case in 1902 the court refused to enforce a contract for services in return for 'a West End salary to be actually agreed between us' (Wedderburn, *The Worker and the Law,* op. cit., p. 194).

Contracts of employment need not themselves be in writing unless, very unusually, there is no consideration provided; a deed is then necessary. Form is important also in the cases of apprentices and merchant seamen. More generally, there must always exist by statute a written statement of the most important terms of the contract of employment (para. 3.10).

3.8.2 Intention to create legal relations

The parties must intend the agreement and individual terms thereof to create legal relations. In *Financial Techniques (Planning Services) Ltd* v *Hughes* [1981] IRLR 32, the question arose as to whether that which was advertised as a 'sophisticated remuneration package' for a tax consultant was enforceable as part of the contract, or payable only at the discretion of the employers. The Court of Appeal tended to the former view because of the terms of the advertisement which attracted the applicant to take up the position, and because he was at no time informed that it was *not* to form part of the contract. In *Edwards* v *Skyways Ltd* [1964] 1 WLR 349 a pension clause was held to be enforceable even though stated to be *ex gratia* (see also *McLaren* v *Home Office* [1990] IRLR 338 in the case of prison officers).

3.8.3 Variation

The contract of employment is one of the most dynamic agreements, changing frequently during its course as circumstances alter. Even so, any variation in contractual terms still requires the assent, express or tacit, of both parties and should be supported by consideration. This may be represented by the employee simply carrying on working under altered conditions. If, however, the employer unilaterally enforces a variation, he repudiates the contract of employment and the employee is put to his election whether to accept the fundamental breach, and resign, or to carry on working and seek damages (*Burdett-Coutts* v *Hertfordshire CC* [1984] IRLR 91; *Rigby* v *Ferodo Ltd* [1987] IRLR 516). Many contracts contain wide flexibility clauses so that a change of actual duties performed may lie within the four corners of the contractual job description, for example that the employee will perform such duties as are from time to time assigned to him by the board of directors or managing director. If not, it is important to have in mind Donaldson LJ's remark in *Janata Bank Ltd* v *Ahmed* [1981] IRLR 457 at para. 50, that 'the continuously changing contract is unknown to law' (see also *Parry* v *Holst & Co. Ltd* [1968] ITR 317, *Dal* v *A. S. Orr* [1980] IRLR 413).

It is necessary to distinguish between a mere variation and a wholly new contract by reason of breach of the old one; thus a unilateral deduction by the management from the employee's pay and/or hours usually amounts to a fundamental breach of contract and its termination (cf. *Hogg* v *Dover College* [1990] ICR 39), while on an agreed variation the contract continues. Often the employee proceeds to work perhaps oblivious of the breach or under undue influence to ignore it. Judges have, however, been vigilant not to spell out agreements to apparent new terms in these circumstances. For example, in *Horrigan* v *Lewisham London Borough Council* [1978] ICR 15 EAT, notwithstanding that the employee had worked overtime for ten years, Arnold J commented:

> It is fairly difficult, in the ordinary way, to imply a variation of contract, and it is very necessary, if one is to do so, to have very solid facts which demonstrate that it was necessary to give business efficacy to the contract, that the contract should come to contain a new term implied by way of variation.

This is a particularly live issue in changes of job duties, the contractual scope of which is vital to decisions on redundancy payments. In *Marriott* v *Oxford and District Cooperative Society (No. 2)* [1970] 1 QB 186, the appellant had been employed by the respondents as an electrical supervisor for two years when they found that there was insufficient work for him. They were prepared to offer him another post at £3 less per week and he took this under protest, worked for three or four weeks but then terminated his contract by notice. In defence to his claim for a redundancy payment, the respondents claimed that they had *not* terminated the agreement by insisting on his taking the new job (as was necessary for him to claim his statutory rights), but had merely varied it. Lord Denning was insistent that (at p. 191C):

> He never agreed to the dictated terms. He protested against them. He submitted to them because he did not want to be out of employment. By insisting on new terms to which he never agreed, the employer did, I think, terminate the old contract of employment.

The issue is also important in relation to the introduction of new technology and the extent to which employees can be expected to adapt to new techniques within their contractual terms. In *Cresswell* v *Board of Inland Revenue* [1984] ICR 508, the defendants' introduction of computers did not change the nature of the job done by PAYE staff. The Revenue were entitled to withhold pay for employees who refused to cooperate with the new system. Walton J thought that employees had no right to preserve their working conditions unchanged throughout the course of their employment. They could reasonably be expected, after proper training, to adapt to new techniques especially where, as here, there was no evidence of real difficulty. He thought that the jobs would remain 'recognisably the same job but done in a different way'.

In *Shields Furniture Ltd* v *Goff* [1973] ICR 187, the National Industrial Relations Court reiterated that work under an alternative offer for a trial period does not constitute acceptance, and in *Sheet Metal Components Ltd* v *Plumridge* [1974] ICR 373, Sir John Donaldson said: 'the courts have rightly been slow to find that there has been a consensual variation where an employee has been faced with the alternative of dismissal and where the variation has been adverse to his interests' (see also *Norwest Holst Group Administration Ltd* v *Harrison* [1984] IRLR 419).

3.8.3.1 Attempts to vary the contract unilaterally   Employers frequently seek unilaterally to vary terms by giving to the employee the notice to which he is entitled under his contract. Recent case law suggests that the employer must make it clear that he is terminating one contract and offering another.

In *Burdett-Coutts* v *Hertfordshire County Council* (supra) the employers sought to change the hours of six dinner ladies by means of a circular letter. The plaintiffs, who were entitled to 12 weeks' notice of termination, sought a declaration that the purported variation was invalid, to which the defendants responded that the letter should be read as a termination of the employment coupled with an offer of new terms. Kenneth Jones J could not so read the letter which referred to 'detailed notice of variations in your contract of service'. The employees had elected not to accept the repudiation and could now claim the total wages to which they were entitled under the contract. The House of Lords confirmed in *Rigby* v *Ferodo Ltd* [1987] IRLR 516 that an employer's unilateral reduction of an employee's wages does not automatically bring the contract to an end. Where the employee had not accepted such a repudiation as terminating the contract, the damages recoverable were not limited to the amount of shortfall from the contractual wage over the employee's notice period, but the whole period to trial (see also *Miller* v *Hamworthy Engineering Ltd* [1986] ICR 846).

It thus behoves employers who wish to change terms and conditions to give proper notice to terminate one contract and offer another, although this carries with it the risk that the employee may claim unfair dismissal.

3.9   EFFECT ON CONTRACT OF TRANSFER OF UNDERTAKING

The common law doctrine that contracts of employment do not continue on a takeover, sought to recognise that 'employees are not serfs and cannot be transferred as though they were property' (*Nokes* v *Doncaster Amalgamated Collieries Ltd* [1940] AC 1014). Although this was designed to protect the employee, it could act as a boomerang in the context of modern employment protection rights, but until 1 May 1982 the only modification was in the context of statutory continuity. Now under the impact of the EEC Directive on Acquired Rights 77/187, the Transfer of Undertakings (Protection of Employment) Regulations 1981, SI 1981 No. 1794, alter the position in the case of a transfer of undertaking, 'whether by sale or some other disposition or operation of law'. This is fully considered in Chapter 16.

3.10 WRITTEN STATEMENT OF TERMS

3.10.1 The details

Most employees have the important right to receive a written statement of some of the most important terms of their contracts of employment. This is vital as the foundation on which employment protection rights may be built and was first introduced, in a limited form, in the Contracts of Employment Act 1963. The detail to be included was substantially increased by the Contracts of Employment Act 1973 and the Employment Protection Act 1975, the Employment Act 1989 and TURERA 1993 and is now found in the Employment Rights Act 1996, ss. 1–12.

The statement must be given within two months of starting work and must include the following details (ERA 1996, s. 1(3) and (4)):

(a) The *names of employer and employee.*

(b) The *date when employment began* and whether any previous service counts as continuous with the present contract. This has important implications for such rights as redundancy payment and unfair dismissal (see Chapters 13 and 14).

(c) A *brief description of the work* for which the employee is employed (ERA 1996, s. 1(4)(f)), which may state simply 'administrative officer' or 'typist'. It is, however, in the interests of the employee not to allow undue width since he might then be dismissed for refusing to perform duties within the title. Further, he will not be redundant if his duties are changed considerably but remain within the job title. The job title is also important when considering constructive dismissal and equal pay claims. In some senses it is the most important element in the written statement.

(d) The *scale or rate of remuneration* or the method of calculating it. This includes fringe benefits which are an increasingly important element of payment. The employee is also entitled to an itemised pay statement every time he is paid (para. 5.5).

(e) Whether remuneration is to be *paid weekly,* monthly or at some other interval.

(f) Normal *hours of work* (see para. 10.2.1).

(g) Entitlement to public and other *holidays* and holiday pay (see *Morley* v *Heritage plc* [1993] IRLR 400).

(h) Provision for *sickness* and injury, and, in particular, sick pay.

(i) *Pension rights,* especially whether a contracting out certificate has been given under the Social Security Pensions Act 1975.

(j) The *length of notice* the employer and employee must give to terminate the contract of employment (ERA 1996, s. 1(4)(e)); but the employee may be referred to 'the law [that is in the case of minimum periods of notice] or to the provisions of any collective agreement directly affecting the terms and conditions of the employment . . .' (ERA 1996, s. 2(3)).

(k) If the contract is for a *fixed period* the date of the end of the period must be stated (ERA 1996, s. 1(4)(g)).

(l) In the case of *non permanent employment,* 'the period for which it is expected to continue' (ERA 1996, s. 1(4)(g)).

(m) Either *the place of work* or, where the employee is required or permitted to work at various places, an indication of that fact and the address of the employer (ERA 1996, s. 1(4)(h)).

(n) '[A]ny *collective agreements* which directly affect the terms and conditions of the employment including, where the employer is not a party, the persons by whom they were made' (ERA 1996, s. 1(4)(j)).

(o)   In the case of an employee *required to work outside the UK for a period of more than a month,* the period of such work, the currency of remuneration, any additional remuneration or benefit by reason of the requirement to work outside the UK, and 'any terms and conditions relating to his return to the UK' (ERA 1996, s. 1(4)(k)).

Where before the end of two months after the start of employment, the employee 'is to begin work outside the UK for more than one month' the statement must be given to him before he leaves the UK to begin so to work (ERA 1996, s. 2(5)) and such a statement must be given notwithstanding that the employment ends before the period in which the statement was to be given (ERA 1996, s. 2(6)).

The Employment Protection Act 1975 sought particularly to give a clearer indication of *disciplinary* procedures to the employee, so that the statement must contain a note specifying any such rules applicable to him or refer him to a reasonably accessible document setting them out. The employee must also be notified of a person to whom he can apply if he is dissatisfied with any disciplinary decision, and how such application should be made (ERA 1996, s. 3). Any further steps are to be specified, and the employer is well advised to include as much detail as possible as protection against unfair dismissal claims.

Consistent with its avowed aim to lessen the burdens on small businesses the Government introduced s. 13 of the Employment Act 1989 to exempt companies with fewer than 20 employees from the obligation to include a note of disciplinary procedures in the written statement of terms. The calculation of 20 involves aggregating the number of employees of the employer concerned and any associated employer of his.

Unusually for an employment protection right, the right to a written statement is extended to temporary employees supplied by an employment agency (reg. 9(6) of the Conduct of Employment Agencies and Employment Businesses Regulations 1976 made under the Employment Agencies Act 1973); but in common with most others it excludes seamen, overseas employment, and employments excluded by order of the Secretary of State.

3.10.2   Supplementary provisions

There are several important aspects to note about the written statement. The employer satisfies the provision by offering the employee a *copy* of the whole contract or providing reasonable access to one while at work (s. 6). A notice on the well-viewed staff notice board referring to a collective agreement would be sufficient.

It must be clearly stated if there are *no relevant particulars* under any of the above headings (s. 2(1)). This is to encourage employers to develop proper and clear terms and procedures. The Secretary of State has power to specify additional matters to be included, and all the terms must be correct not more than one week before the statement is given (s. 7). Only matters relating to sickness and most pension schemes may now be contained in 'some other document which is reasonably accessible to the employee', (ERA 1996, s. 2(2)). The following particulars conversely must be given in a single document (ERA 1996, s. 2(4)):

(a)   the names of employer and employee;
(b)   the date when employment began;
(c)   the date on which the employee's period of continuous employment began;
(d)   the scale of remuneration or the method of calculating remuneration;
(e)   the intervals at which remuneration is to be paid;

(f)   any terms and conditions relating to hours of work;

(g)   entitlement to holidays and details about accrued holiday pay;

(h)   the title of the job which the employee is employed to do or a brief description of the work for which the employee is employed;

(i)   either the place of work or, where the employee is required or permitted to work at various places, an indication of that fact and the address of the employer.

Any *changes* in terms must be communicated in the same manner as the original statement at the earliest opportunity, and in any event within a month of the alteration or, where the change arises from the requirement to work outside the UK for more than a month, the time when the employee leaves the UK (ERA 1996, s. 4(3)). This may be either by a new statement or in a collective bargain, provided that it is reasonably accessible (s. 4(4) and (5)), in respect of sickness, pensions, disciplinary rules and notice provisions. In one case the medium of the company journal (*King* v *Post Office* [1973] ICR 120) was acceptable. A total failure to notify does not, however, render any changes ineffective, and where the employer changes in name only, or where the identity changes but continuity is preserved by statute, this may be stated as a change in particulars, rather than necessitating a whole new statement (s. 4(7)).

New particulars need not be given when an employee is re-employed within six months of ending an earlier employment if he comes back on the same terms and conditions and he had already been given particulars.

3.10.3   The statement is not to be treated as the contract itself

The general aim of the provision is to encourage the development of explicit and clear terms about the most important elements of the employee's contract. It is intended to be a mirror of that agreement but it is *not* the contract itself. This is reflected in the right of either employer or employee to complain to an industrial tribunal in case of dispute as to whether the correct particulars together with any changes have been communicated. Lord Parker CJ said in *Turriff Construction Ltd* v *Bryant* (1967) 2 ITR 292: 'It is of course quite clear that the statement . . . is not the contract; it is not even conclusive evidence of the contract.' However, since very often there will be precious little other information, especially in writing, about the agreement, it is quite natural that the statement is frequently treated as the contract itself. This is particularly so where the employee has signed a receipt for the document: in *Gascol Conversions Ltd* v *Mercer* [1974] ICR 420, Lord Denning went so far as to state that by reason of the parole evidence rule, ' "the statutory statement" being reduced to writing is the *sole evidence* that it is permissible of contract and its terms.' It is not, however, clear from the report of the case whether the document in question was just a written statement or purported to be the contract itself. If the former, it is submitted that the decision is not to be followed.

The most widely cited statement of the effect of the written statement is found in *System Floors (UK) Ltd* v *Daniel* [1982] ICR 54 where Browne-Wilkinson J said that it

provides very strong prima facie evidence of what were the terms of the contract between the parties but does not constitute a written contract between the parties. Nor are the statements of the terms finally conclusive; at most they place a heavy burden on the employer to show that the actual terms of the contract are different from those which he has set out in the statutory statement.

(Approved in *Robertson* v *British Gas Corporation* [1983] ICR 351; *Lee* v *GEC Plessey Telecommunications* [1993] IRLR 383.) The particulars may not, however, be used as evidence about the meaning of a written term.

It was thought at one time that the written statement had legal effect in giving rise to an estoppel if an employee relied on it to his detriment. For example, in *Evenden* v *Guildford City Association Football Club* [1975] ICR 367, the employer stated that employment with a previous employer counted towards continuous service and he was not permitted to renege on that assurance. This case was, however, overruled by the House of Lords in *Secretary of State for Employment* v *Globe Elastic Thread Co. Ltd* [1979] ICR 706, a case with similar facts, on the grounds that estoppel could not confer on a statutory tribunal a jurisdiction beyond that given by the empowering Act in respect of continuity of employment. The facts of the case concerned the giving of a *redundancy rebate* under statute by the Secretary of State who was not privy to the contract, and it may still be argued that an estoppel may arise between employer and employee when there is no third party involved. For the decision was that, in the words of Lord Wilberforce, 'a personal estoppel between employer and employee which is the most that this could be, could not bind the Secretary of State'. (See para. 14.7.)

A failure to object to erroneous statements of terms is not to be taken as acceptance at least where the terms are of no immediate practical importance (*Jones* v *Associated Tunnelling Co. Ltd* [1981] IRLR 477; see also *Courtaulds Northern Spinning Ltd* v *Sibson and TGWU* [1988] IRLR 305; *Aparau* v *Iceland Frozen Foods plc* [1996] IRLR 119).

3.10.4 Remedy for failure to supply written statement of terms

An employee who is dissatisfied because no written particulars have been supplied to him has always been able to refer the matter to an industrial tribunal, which has power to determine what particulars the statement *should* have contained (ERA 1996, s. 11(1)). The EAT at first decided that this gave no power to rectify an error or to construe a misunderstanding between the parties (see *Construction Industry Training Board* v *Leighton* [1978] IRLR 60).

This unsatisfactory position was reversed by the Court of Appeal in *Mears* v *Safecar Security Ltd* [1982] IRLR 183. They held that what was then EPCA 1978, s. 11 gave jurisdiction to the tribunal to confirm the facts already given, amend or replace them by substituted particulars if they did not reflect the contract as agreed. The tribunal could add those particulars not given which *should* have been given. To decide what to so add, it must first decide whether the term in question has been expressly agreed by word of mouth or by necessary implication. If it has not been so agreed, the tribunal must imply and insert the missing term, and in doing so, should consider all the facts and circumstances of the relationship between employer and employee including the way in which they had worked the contract since it commenced.

However, the industrial tribunal had no power to include terms as to holidays, holiday pay, sick pay, pensions or disciplinary rules where none existed by agreement between the parties since the contract was not required to contain such terms (*Eagland* v *British Telecommunications plc* [1993] ICR 644). This is not to say, though, that the tribunal may not identify a term by reference to an agreement evidenced by the conduct of the parties. The Court of Appeal also diverged from the suggestion that in some cases it was open for the industrial tribunal to 'invent terms' where none had been agreed.

There still is no sanction to back the provision of particulars and there are arguments for reverting to the position between 1963 and 1965 when it was enforced by fine. Further, a union cannot bring a test case on behalf of its members. Many employees are too scared to apply or not aware of its importance. As a result very many employers ignore the provisions and in particular changes in terms are not in fact communicated.

4 Rights and Obligations of Employer and Employee

There can be no employment relationship without a power to command and a duty to obey, that is, without this element of subordination in which lawyers rightly see the hallmark of the contract of employment.

(Professor O. Kahn-Freund, *Labour and the Law,* op. cit. para. 3.1, p. 17.)

We now turn to examine the most important terms in the contract of employment, looking in particular at what would be implied in the absence of detailed agreement:

(a) pay (the Wages Act 1986, now the ERA 1996, Part II, see Chapter 5);
(b) cooperation;
(c) care and safety;
(d) Sunday trading;
(e) service, subject to time off and holidays;
(f) competence of employee;
(g) obedience to orders;
(h) fidelity (see Chapter 6);
(i) restraint of trade clauses (see Chapter 6);
(j) right to enter the employer's premises;
(k) references;
(l) access to medical reports.

We then consider disciplinary provisions and lay-off.

4.1 PAY

4.1.1 *Quantum meruit*

We start with the most essential element for the employee — pay for hours worked. Generally, remuneration is negotiated expressly by way of collective or individual bargain on a yearly basis, but so essential is it to the contract, that in the absence of express agreement there is still a right to reasonable remuneration. The court will assess what the employee's labours are reasonably worth by way of a quasi-contractual action for *quantum meruit.* In *Way* v *Latilla* [1937] 3 All ER 759, the statement of the defendants that they 'would look after his interests' was enough to support such an action. (See also *Powell* v *Braun* [1954] 1 WLR 401.) The implied term is, however, excluded if there is any contractual term on the subject, even if it is merely an article of association giving entitlement to 'such amount as the directors may determine' (*Re Richmond Gate Property Co. Ltd* [1965] 1 WLR 335).

4.1.2 Express and implied terms as to payment

There are more generally implied terms and statutory provisions governing:

(a) the manner of payment;
(b) pay when only part of the contract is completed;
(c) payment during illness;
(d) medical suspension;
(e) payment during lay-off (para. 4.10);
(f) maternity pay (para. 9.3);
(g) paid time off for trade union duties (para. 20.6);
(h) low pay (para. 19.8).

We will here consider the first four items, the others being treated under their appropriate subject headings. The itemised pay statement is considered at para. 5.5.

There is, it should be noted, a multiplicity of modern payment systems. Their detail is beyond the scope of this book, but they include:

(a) fixed salary contracts;
(b) hourly/daily pay;
(c) payment by results, whereby the amount of payment is sensitive to output or profits in some way, e.g. piece work or commission payment;
(d) measured day work, where pay is fixed by reference to overall production targets;
(e) overtime.

(See Davies and Freedland, *Labour Law: Text and Materials,* op. cit., p. 318ff. for full treatment.)

4.1.2.1 Payment when only part completed   Considerable problems surround the right to payment of an employee who completes only part of his contract. Confusion primarily derives from the eighteenth-century case of *Cutter* v *Powell* (1795) 101 ER 573. A second mate on a voyage from Jamaica to Liverpool was to be paid 30 guineas, provided he completed the voyage, but instead he died three weeks before the end of the two-month journey. The Court of King's Bench held that his widow was not entitled to any payment on a *quantum meruit* action or otherwise in respect of the part he had completed. Although the decision might have been different had there not been an express term for completion included on a promissory note, the statement of law was generalised in later cases. Thus in *Boston Deep Sea Fishing and Ice Co.* v *Ansell* (1888) 39 ChD 339, it was held that, at common law, an employee was not entitled to pro rata payment in respect of any uncompleted period of service. This means that, if X is employed and paid Monday to Friday, and leaves on the Wednesday, he can recover no wages for days worked. An exception has, however, developed where the employer has received substantial performance even though not all the services bargained for are completed (*Hoenig* v *Isaacs* [1952] 2 All ER 176 CA, *Bolton* v *Mahadeva* [1972] 2 All ER 1322; cf. *Wiluszynski* v *London Borough of Tower Hamlets* [1989] IRLR 259, CA, para. 4.1.2.4).

Further, the injustice of the general rule has been mitigated somewhat by the Apportionment Act 1870, s. 2, which provides that 'all annuities (which includes salaries and pensions) . . . and other periodical payments in the nature of income . . . shall . . . be considered as accruing from day to day, and should be apportioned in respect of time accordingly'. Thus, generally, a proportion of the contractual amount can now be gained. Judicial interpretation has not conclusively decided that 'salaries' mentioned in the statute includes wages.

4.1.2.2 Sick pay The implied right to sick pay was reviewed by the EAT in *Mears* v *Safecar Security Ltd* [1981] IRLR 99, an important decision which for the first time set out detailed criteria for implication of such terms. Nothing was said about sick pay on the appellant's engagement as a security guard, and when he had been away ill in the past no money was provided. The industrial tribunal thought that there was a presumption in favour of payment, but that this was subject to deduction of all sickness benefit received under the Social Security Act 1975. Slynn J repudiated any such presumption. It was thus necessary to look at all the facts and circumstances. Whether payment was to be implied depended on:

(a) the *knowledge* of the parties on making the contract;

(b) whether the contract is one where payment is due if the employee is ready and *willing to work;*

(c) whether payment of wages is consideration for *faithful service* at other times;

(d) the *nature* of the contract;

(e) whether employment is on a *short term* basis or for a fixed term of years;

(f) what the parties did during the *currency* of the contract.

Here, the appellant had been told by his workmates that he would not be paid during sickness, and he had never before sent in sick notes so that a right to payment could not be implied.

On different facts, in *Howman & Son* v *Blyth* [1983] IRLR 139, Kilner Brown J decided that the employee was entitled to sick pay at the rate appropriate to a 40-hour week (less state sickness benefits) payable for such period as is reasonable. This approach was approved by the Court of Appeal which invited industrial tribunals to approach the matter with an open mind unprejudiced by any preconception, presumption or assumption.

The common law position is of somewhat less consequence since the introduction of statutory sick pay. The Regulations effectively render the employer an agent of the Department of Social Security to administer the sickness pay rights of his employees. In outline, the scheme provides that the employer must pay sick pay for the first 28 weeks of illness and only after that is the employee entitled to state sickness benefit.

The employee may not claim statutory sick pay for the first three days of any period of sickness, and the following employees are excluded altogether from claiming it: pensioners, employees for less than three months, those who earn too little to pay national insurance contributions and a person not employed by reason of a stoppage of work due to a trade dispute at his workplace unless the employee had not participated in the dispute and had no irect interest in its outcome. Paragraph 14 of Sch. 8 to the Social Security Act 1989 provides that employees will be entitled to statutory sick pay even if they cannot show that they have not participated in a trade dispute provided that they did not have a direct interest in it.

To claim, the employee must be suffering from some disease or physical or mental disablement rendering him incapable of performing any work which he can reasonably be expected to do under his contract. Two periods of incapacity are treated as one if they are separated by not more than two weeks. Where an employee's contract is terminated in order to evade the employer's liability for sick pay, the entitlement continues as long as the sickness. Although most workers labour from Monday to Friday, there are many variations to this theme, and the employer and employee are to agree what are qualifying days for sick pay. In the absence of agreement, the Regulations lay down the agreed normal working days as qualifying days.

The amount payable is a daily rate but depends on normal weekly earnings. The general rule takes the last normal pay day before the entitlement to statutory sick pay arises and then averages the weekly earnings over the period of at least eight weeks before that date. By s. 23 of the 1982 Act, the rates are reviewed annually. The payment is taxable and the claimant must pay national insurance contributions on it.

To claim statutory sick pay, the employee or his agent has to inform the employer that he is unfit for work. The employer can fix a time-limit for notification, but must give reasonable publicity to it. If he says nothing, the notice must be in writing. It is treated as given if duly posted. In the absence of a published time-limit, the employee has seven days in which to give notice, with a discretionary extension for good cause up to 90 days (reg. 7(1)(a) of the Statutory Sick Pay (General) Regulations 1982 (SI 1982 No. 894) as amended by the Statutory Sick Pay (General) Amendment Regulations 1984). Although the employer cannot require that the sick employee notifies him in person of his illness, the employer may otherwise lay down the mode of notification. He cannot, however, require medical evidence or notification on a special form (reg. 7 of the 1982 General Regulations). In due course, the employer may seek other relevant information, such as medical evidence, from the employee. The employee may conversely ask for a statement of his entitlement to statutory sick pay. Most issues of contributions are ruled on by the DSS in the first instance with a question of law referred to the High Court by way of case stated. In other cases, entitlement is decided by an adjudication officer with appeal to the Social Security Appeal Tribunal and then to a Commissioner.

The Statutory Sick Pay Act 1991 made important changes to statutory sick pay in order to reduce government expenditure. In particular, s. 1 required regulations to be made limiting the amount which could be recouped by an employer from national insurance contributions to 80 per cent of SSP paid out. There was an exception for small firms, that is a company whose contributions for the qualifying tax year did not exceed £20,000 (Statutory Sick Pay (Small Employers Relief) Regulations 1991). When such a small firm had made payments of SSP to an employee totalling in aggregate more than four weeks, the employer might recoup the whole amount. The reimbursement was abolished altogether by the Statutory Sick Pay Act 1994. The employer can now recoup SSP if and to the extent that it exceeds 13 per cent of his liability to pay national insurance contributions in the income tax month in question (Statutory Sick Pay Percentage Threshold Order 1995 (SI 1995 No. 512); see also the Social Security, Statutory Maternity Pay and Statutory Sick Pay (Miscellaneous Amendments) Regulations 1996 (SI 1996 No. 777).

4.1.2.3 Medical suspension pay As part of its policy of preserving income during difficult periods for employees, the Employment Protection Act 1975 (now ERA 1996, ss. 64–68), gave the right to payment to an employee who is suspended by his employer on medical grounds.

The reason for suspension may be statutory requirements or any Code of Practice issued under s. 16 of the Health and Safety at Work etc. Act 1974. These demand suspension in the event of certain dangers arising from, for example, the handling of tin, enamel, chemicals, etc. The employee must then be paid while suspended for a period up to 26 weeks (ERA 1996, s. 64(1)) 'only if and so long as he . . . continues to be employed by his employer, but is . . . not provided with work or does not perform the work he normally performed before the suspension' (s. 64(5)).

The right is excluded where the employee:

(a)   is incapable by reason of disease or bodily or mental impairment, since he can then gain state sickness benefit (s. 65(3));

(b)   unreasonably refuses a suitable offer of alternative work (s. 65(4)(a));

(c)   does not comply with reasonable requirements laid down by his employer to ensure that his services are available (s. 65(4)(b)).

The appropriate week's pay is calculated in accordance with ss. 221–227 of ERA 1996 like the other major employment protection rights (see para. 14.5) and if the employer does not pay what he owes, the employee can complain to an industrial tribunal within three months (s. 70). Moreover, the section is without prejudice to the case of the employee whose employer has suspended him without having any legal contractual right to do so. He has the usual contractual remedies, including a claim of constructive dismissal.

4.1.2.4 *Overpayment by mistake*   Difficulties arise where an employee has been overpaid by mistake and the employer seeks to reclaim these sums. In *Avon County Council v Howlett* [1983] IRLR 171, Mr Howlett, a teacher, was regularly overpaid whilst off work following an accident, to the total of £1,007. When this was discovered, the county council sought recovery of the money in the High Court. The Court of Appeal synthesised legal and equitable considerations in the principle that the employer is estopped from claiming restitution where the payment was accompanied by an express or implicit representation leading the recipient to believe that he was entitled to treat the money as his own. Here the defendant was permitted to retain the overpayment since after such intimation and without notice of claim, he had so changed his position that it would be inequitable to require him to make the repayment. The mistake of the Authority was a mistake of *fact*, namely that the relevant pay clerks were unaware of the fact that or had forgotten that more than six months had elapsed, rather than misinterpretations of the relevant regulations. The result would have been different if the defendant still retained the sum paid by the employer, he had spent it on an obvious change in his style of living, or overpayment was due substantially to the payee's own fault.

4.1.2.5 *Deductions from pay for industrial action*   When an employer is faced with disruption by his workforce short of a strike, he may withhold a proportion or all of the pay for the period of disruption. This was held invalid in an *obiter* dictum in *Miles v Wakefield Metropolitan District Council* [1985] IRLR 108 in the Court of Appeal but it was later reinstated by the House of Lords. The case concerned a superintendent registrar of births, marriages and deaths whose conditions were governed by statute. He normally worked 37 hours per week, three of them on Saturday mornings. Between August 1981 and October

1982, on the instructions of his union as part of industrial action, he refused to carry out marriages on Saturday mornings and the council accordingly withheld 3/37ths of his pay. The Court of Appeal decided that the council was not entitled to withhold the money. Whether office-holders were liable to have salary withheld for breach of statutory obligations was a question of the true construction of the relevant statute. The statutory obligation on local authorities to pay his salary was unqualified. The remedy for a breach lay only in the power to dismiss.

There is Court of Appeal authority of the opposite tenor since Lord Denning MR said in *Secretary of State for Employment* v *ASLEF (No. 2)* [1972] 2 QB 443:

> Is a man entitled to wages for his work when he, with others, is doing his best to make it useless? Surely not. Wages are to be paid for services rendered, not for producing deliberate chaos. The breach goes to the whole of the consideration as it was put by Lord Campbell CJ in *Cuckson* v *Stones* (1858) 1 E & E 248 at 255 . . . .

On further appeal in *Miles* ([1987] IRLR 193), the House of Lords emphasised that an office-holder who had not performed certain of his duties during a period of industrial action was not entitled to remuneration in respect of that period in the absence of proof that he was ready to work in accordance with his contract. The principle is further illustrated in the following cases:

(a)   In *Cresswell* v *Board of Inland Revenue* [1984] ICR 508, Walton J decided that a person who was refusing to accept the new computerised PAYE system had no right to be paid. (See also *Royle* v *Trafford Borough Council* [1984] IRLR 184.)

(b)   In *Sim* v *Rotherham Metropolitan Borough Council* [1987] Ch 216, Scott J decided that teachers were under a contractual duty to comply with cover arrangements for absent colleagues, and the defendant local authorities could justify deductions of £2.00 to £3.37 made from the teachers' salaries during the teachers' industrial action as an equitable setoff arising from their breaches of contract.

(c)   In *Wiluszynski* v *London Borough of Tower Hamlets* [1989] IRLR 259, however, the local authority was held not entitled to withhold pay from an estates officer in the Housing Directorate who was merely boycotting inquiries from council members. This was a small part of his job description. Michael Davies J held that the breach was minimal. Moreover, the council had allowed him to perform the substantial part of his services, so that they were not entitled later to withhold his salary for such period. The Court of Appeal overturned this decision of the High Court on the basis that the council could not physically prevent the plaintiff from attending work and performing his duties, and the doctrine of substantial performance was inapplicable (see also *MacPherson* v *London Borough of Lambeth* [1988] IRLR 470; *Home Office* v *Ayres* [1992] ICR 175, [1992] IRLR 59).

(d)   In an interesting case, but one devoid of any binding authority, a District Judge sitting at Dartford County Court decided that lecturers engaged on terms that they had a 190-day working year should suffer a deduction of 1/190th of their year's salary for each day on strike even though they in fact worked longer than those 190 days per year (*Smith and Others* v *London Borough of Bexley*, unreported, 5 April 1991). The lecturers had contended that the proper deduction was 1/365th of a year's pay (see also *Thames Water Utilities Ltd* v *Reynolds* [1996] IRLR 186).

(e)   The court will not grant an interlocutory order requiring employers to pay to employees engaged in strike action wages and overtime payments which the employers were holding in respect of those periods in which the employers had refused to accept partial performance of the contractual duties of the employees (*Jakeman* v *South West Thames RHA and London Ambulance Service* [1990] IRLR 62, arising out of the 1989 ambulancemen's dispute).

If a refusal to work continues for only part of a day the Apportionment Act 1870 has no application; it apportions wages for a week or more only. The protection given to employees by s.13 of the ERA 1996 (see para. 5.1) is rendered inapplicable in the case of deductions from a worker's wage for taking part in a strike or other industrial action (s. 13(5)).

4.1.2.6 Taxation The subject of taxation of salary or wages is outside the scope of this book but the following should be noted:

(a) The expense incurred in providing a benefit must be treated as the total cost to the employer, including where appropriate an element for overheads and not only the extra expense directly incurred in providing that benefit to the individual taxpayer (*Pepper* v *Hart* [1991] IRLR 126, [1991] ICR 681).

(b) The following benefits are free of tax–

(i)   child care for children under 18 provided by the employer alone, or with other employers or local authorities or other similar bodies;

(ii)   use of employer's assets unless the employee is a director or paid over £8,500 per year;

(iii)   contributions by the employer to an approved superannuation or pension scheme;

(iv)   luncheon vouchers to the value of 15 pence per day;

(v)   canteen meals, save that meals provided for employees who are directors or paid over £8,500 per year but not generally are taxable;

(vi)   medical insurance premiums unless the employee is a director or paid over £8,500 per year.

4.2 COOPERATION

The courts have frequently implied a duty of cooperation between employer and employee, notwithstanding the potential for conflict between their interests. Most of the authorities deal with the obligation this imposes on an employee, and a general statement is to be found in *Secretary of State for Employment* v *ASLEF (No. 2)* [1972] 2 QB 455. The issue arose because under the Industrial Relations Act 1971 then in force the Secretary of State for Employment could order a cooling-off period of a strike where, *inter alia*, employees were acting 'in breach of contract'. The union claimed that their work to rule was not a breach but instead entailed meticulous *observance* of British Rail's own rule book; they claimed they were following their agreement to the letter. Lord Denning, however, identified a breach 'if the employee, with others, takes steps wilfully to disrupt the undertaking, to produce chaos so that it will not run as it should, then each one who is a party to those steps is guilty of a breach of contract.' He gave 'a homely instance' of what he had in mind as a breach (at 491F):

Suppose I employ a man to drive me to the station. I know there is sufficient time, so that I do not tell him to hurry. He drives me at a slower speed than he need, with the deliberate object of making me lose the train, and I do lose it. He may say that he has performed the letter of the contract; he has driven me to the station; but he has wilfully made me lose the train, and that is a breach of contract beyond all doubt.

Lord Denning disapproved of the term suggested by Donaldson P at first instance that the employee should *actively* assist the employer to operate his organisation. It was going too far to suggest 'a duty to behave fairly to his employer and do a fair day's work'. Although far reaching, the Master of the Rolls' was not a positive doctrine: 'A man is not bound positively to do more for his employer than his contract requires. He can withdraw his goodwill if he pleases.' Buckley LJ implied a term that 'an employee must serve the employer faithfully with a view to promoting those commercial interests for which he is employed'.

The general principle is that the employee must serve the employer and his interests faithfully. The Court of Appeal held in *British Telecommunications plc* v *Ticehurst* [1992] ICR 383, that it was necessary to imply such a term 'in the case of a manager who is given charge of the work of other employees and who therefore must necessarily be entrusted to exercise her judgment and discretion in giving instructions to others and in supervising their work. Such a discretion, if the contract is to work properly must be exercised faithfully in the interests of the employers' (at 398e).

More recent authorities, primarily under the impulse of finding a breach of contract for constructive dismissal, have emphasised the mirror-image obligation of the employer to cooperate with the employee, and not to make his task in any way more difficult. Thus, a breach has been identified when employers have criticised managers in front of subordinates; used foul language; made groundless accusations of theft; and failed to show proper respect for a senior employee (see *Associated Tyre Specialists (Eastern) Ltd* v *Waterhouse* [1976] IRLR 386, *Palmanor Ltd* v *Cedron* [1978] IRLR 303, *Robinson* v *Crompton Parkinson Ltd* [1978] ICR 401, and *Garner* v *Grange Furnishings Ltd* [1977] IRLR 206, respectively). As Phillips J stated *obiter* in *BAC Ltd* v *Austin* [1978] IRLR 322 at 334:

It must ordinarily be an implied term of the contract of employment that employers do not behave in a way which is intolerable or in a way which employees cannot be expected to put up with any longer.

(See also para. 13.3.3.)

Another aspect of this rubric of cooperation is that the employer must not put it out of his power to comply with a contract of employment he has entered into. Thus, in *Shindler* v *Northern Raincoat Co. Ltd* [1960] 1 WLR 1038, the plaintiff was managing director of the respondents until their shares were acquired by another company which removed him as a director. His employment as managing director was thus automatically terminated, and notwithstanding that the articles of association of the company clearly permitted this, Diplock J thought that they were in breach of an implied term that they would not deprive themselves of the opportunity of using the employee's services. A similar duty rests on the employee.

4.3 CARE AND SAFETY

Every employer must take reasonable care for the safety of his employees. This is a specialised application of the law of negligence set out generally in *Donoghue* v *Stevenson* [1932] AC 562, but also takes effect as an implied term of the contract for employment.

The consequence may be a different measure of damages (*Wright* v *Dunlop Rubber Co. Ltd* (1971) 11 KIR 311). The House of Lords in *Wilson & Clyde Coal Co.* v *English* [1938] AC 57, categorised three aspects of the generalised duty:

(a) to select proper staff;
(b) to provide adequate material;
(c) to provide a safe system of working.

Moreover, s. 2(2) of the Unfair Contract Terms Act 1977 prohibits exclusion or restriction of liability for negligence in the case of loss or damage unless reasonable in favour of the employee. Detailed provisions are also contained in the Factories Act 1961 and the Offices, Shops and Railway Premises Act 1963, which are beyond the scope of this book. There is, however, no specific implied term that an employee should not be transferred to work involving a serious risk to her health in addition to the general contractual duties already discussed (*Jagdeo* v *Smiths Industries Ltd* [1982] ICR 47; cf. *Johnstone* v *Bloomsbury Health Authority* [1991] IRLR 118, the case of the junior hospital doctors). An employer is not obliged to insure the employee against the effects of unusual or dangerous work (*Reid* v *Rush & Tompkins Group plc* [1989] IRLR 265; cf. *Cook* v *Square D Ltd* [1992] ICR 263).

In return, generally the employee must exercise reasonable care in carrying out his duties (see originally *Harmer* v *Cornelius* (1858) 5 CBNS 236) but the court seeks 'the standards of men and not those of angels' (*Jupiter General Insurance Co.* v *Shroff* [1937] 3 All ER 67).

If the employee is sued in tort and the employer is vicariously liable they are treated as joint tortfeasors under the Civil Liability (Contribution) Act 1978, and the court may thus award such contribution between them as it finds 'just and equitable having regard to the extent of their responsibility for the damage'. The consequence of the contractual duty of care of the employee was controversially demonstrated in the House of Lords case of *Lister* v *Romford Ice and Cold Storage Co.* [1957] AC 555 (see also *Morris* v *Ford Motor Co. Ltd* [1973] QB 792). The appellant, a driver with the respondent company ran over a co-employee, who happened to be his father. The company were vicariously liable to the father but successfully recouped the damages they had to pay by suing the appellant on his contract of employment. The employee's defensive attempt to imply a term of indemnity, i.e. that he would be covered by the employer's insurance, failed by a three to two majority. Viscount Simonds magisterially urged that any such indemnity would 'tend to create a feeling of irresponsibility in a class of persons from whom, perhaps more than any other, constant vigilance is owed to the community'. This might have led to hardship if employers and insurance companies standing behind them regularly used this right to sue their employees, even though later cases held that it did not apply to driving on a special occasion involving unusual tasks (*Harvey* v *O'Dell Ltd* [1958] 2 QB 78), nor if the employer was at all at fault (*Jones* v *Manchester Corporation* [1952] 2 QB 852).

The position is now academic since the fears raised were soon obviated by a gentlemen's agreement among insurance companies not to enforce their rights of subrogation in this respect in the absence of fraud. This was reached in the face of the threat of legislation on the subject and is now adhered to by members of the British Insurance Association and of Lloyd's.

The employer must now be covered by insurance pursuant to the Employers Liability (Compulsory Insurance) Act 1969, and further cannot hide behind a supplier of defective equipment (Employers Liability (Defective Equipment) Act 1969).

The employee also has a cognate duty to take care of such of the employer's property as is entrusted to him. Thus in *Superlux* v *Plaisted* [1958] CLY 195, the defendant was held in breach of contract when 14 vacuum cleaners for which he was responsible went missing or were stolen and this would not have occurred but for his negligence (cf. *Deyong* v *Shenburn* [1946] 1 KB 227). The employee's implied duty of care was considered fully by the Court of Appeal in *Janata Bank* v *Ahmed* [1981] IRLR 457.

The employee is by a general implied term entitled to an indemnity for costs, claims and expenses incurred in carrying out his duties (*Re Famatina Development Corp. Ltd* [1914] 2 Ch 271).

4.4 SUNDAY TRADING

The Sunday Trading Act 1994, which came into force on 26 August 1994, contained important protections for those who do not wish to work on Sundays; it is now the ERA 1996, Part IV to which all statutory provisions here refer. There are two categories of such employees, 'protected shop workers' and 'opted out shop workers'. 'Shop work' means work in a shop in England or Wales on a day on which the shop is open for the serving of customers (s. 232(2)). Retail trade or business includes a barber or hairdresser, hiring goods otherwise than for use in the course of a trade or business and retail sales by auction, but does not include catering businesses or the sale at theatres and places of amusement of programmes, catalogues and similar items.

By s. 36(2) and (3), a 'protected shop worker' must have been in employment as a shop worker on 25 August 1994, must not have been employed to work only on a Sunday and have been a shop worker throughout the period of continuous employment between the coming into force of the Act and the termination of the employment. Alternatively, the employee will fall within this rubric if he is not and cannot be required to work on Sundays pursuant to his contract of employment.

By s. 41, an 'opted out shop worker' is one who under his contract of employment is or may be required to work on Sunday but is not employed to work only on Sunday and who has given to the employer a signed opted out notice stating that he objects to working on Sunday.

By s. 36(5), such a protected worker loses that status if after the commencement date he gives an opting in notice and makes an agreement with the employer to work on Sundays or a particular Sunday.

'Protected shop workers' and 'opted out shop workers' who are dismissed for refusing to work on Sundays have protection from dismissal (s. 101) and selection for redundancy on that ground (s. 105(4)), and must not be put under a detriment by action short of dismissal (s. 45(1)). Detriment may include a failure by the employer to promote the shop worker, or a denial of overtime or training opportunities, but does not extend to the failure to give remuneration or other contractual benefits for Sunday shop work which other shop workers have done but this employee has not (s. 45(5)).

There is no qualifying period to gain this right and the dismissal is automatically unfair (s. 101). An employer must give employees taken on to work *inter alia* on Sundays a written statement in a prescribed form to tell them of their statutory rights (s. 42(4)). Contracting out is prohibited subject to the normal exceptional cases (s. 43). Rights under this Act are statutory rights for the purposes of unfair dismissal by reason of the assertion of statutory rights (ERA 1996, s. 104).

4.5 HOURS OF WORK, TIME OFF AND HOLIDAYS

The central obligation of the employee is to work. He cannot delegate this duty to another, and he must not deliberately disable himself from performance. The most important consequence of the term is that a strike is prima facie a breach of contract (*Simmons* v *Hoover Ltd* [1977] QB 284, *Haddow* v *ILEA* [1979] ICR 202). It is only saved from such fate if the employees give due notice of their intention to terminate their contracts, which rarely happens (*Morgan* v *Fry* [1968] 2 QB 710; cf. *Boxfoldia Ltd* v *NGA (1982)* [1988] IRLR 383) (see para. 21.2).

In examining the employee's service we will consider

(a)   hours of work;
(b)   statutory rights to time off work;
(c)   holidays.

4.5.1 Hours of work

There is no general restriction on the number of hours of work in Britain but the following statutory provisions do exist for children and women in particular:

(a)   Children under 16 must not work for more than 44 hours per week, nor labour in industrial undertakings between 10 p.m. and 5 a.m. (Employment of Women, Young Persons and Children Act 1920 and Hours of Employment (Conventions) Act 1936).

(b)   The Mines and Quarries Act 1954, ss. 125–8 bans altogether employment of children in mines below ground, and severely restricts it above surface too.

There are some scattered restrictions on adult males who must not work more than seven hours a day underground in a mine (Coal Mine Regulation Act 1908, s.1 as amended by Coal Mines Act 1919, s. 1 and Mines and Quarries Act 1954, s. 189). Those employed in bakeries have their night work limited (Bakery Industry (Hours of Work) Act 1954) while lorry drivers can only drive eight hours per day and up to 48 per week and continuous driving is limited (Drivers' Hours (Harmonisation with Community Rules) Order 1978 (SI 1978 No. 1157), and Road Traffic (Drivers' Ages and Hours of Work) Act 1976, Transport Act 1968, Part VI). (See also Shops Early Closing Days Act 1965, Shops Act 1950, Hours of Employment Conventions Act 1936.) In a unique case on doctors' working hours, the Court of Appeal decided (on a summons to strike out the pleadings) that it was arguable that it was not lawful for an employer to require employees to carry out so much overtime in any week that it was reasonably foreseeable that such overtime would damage the health of the employee, notwithstanding the presence of express terms in the contract of employment (*Johnstone* v *Bloomsbury Health Authority* [1991] IRLR 118, [1991] ICR 269).

4.5.2 Time off

Statute provides certain rights for employees to take time off. Two of these rights, of trade unions officials to carry out their duties with pay and of trade union members to participate in trade union activities without the right to be paid, are more appropriately considered as examples of the legal encouragement to collective bargaining (paras 20.6, 20.7). Another permits time off for ante-natal care, and is dealt with under maternity provision (para. 9.5).

Two others are more widely available. Section 52 of the Employment Rights Act 1996 accords an employee who has served over two years and who is dismissed for redundancy, reasonable time off at the normal hourly rate to look for other work or make arrangements for training. What is 'reasonable' depends on the prospects of getting other work, but it is not essential for the employee to give details of his proposed interviews as a precondition of being released (*Dutton* v *Hawker Siddeley Aviation Ltd* [1978] ICR 1057).

Section 50 of the ERA 1996 permits reasonable time off to an employee who is a member of the local authority, magistracy, statutory tribunal, police authority, a board of prison visitors or a prison visiting committee, a relevant health or education body, or a relevant environment agency. This provision is designed to encourage a broader cross-section of society to serve on such bodies, beyond the usual lists of the great and the good, who generally belong to the leisured classes. The criteria for determining the *reasonable* amount of time off include: how much time off is required for the performance of the relevant office; how much the employee has already been permitted; the circumstances of the employer's business; and the effect of the employee's absence. There is no obligation on the employer to pay for such time off since most of these public bodies provide loss of earnings allowances. It is not enough, on the other hand, for the employer merely to alter the times of work so that, for example, lecturer's times of lectures do not clash with council meetings — the employee must actually have *time off* (*Ratcliffe* v *Dorset CC* [1978] IRLR 191; see also *Borders Regional Council* v *Maule* [1993] IRLR 199).

A complaint must be made to an industrial tribunal within three months of default of time off, so that it can award just and equitable compensation for such failure (s. 51). It may not, however, impose conditions of leave; a tribunal which declared that in future all days of absence over ten should be unpaid leave was rebuked by the EAT (*Corner* v *Buckinghamshire CC* [1978] IRLR 320).

4.5.3 Holidays

There is no general right to a holiday in English law. Holidays are generally dealt with in collective agreements, while custom and practice and statute have a subordinate role. The only general statutory provision concerns Bank Holidays, which are regulated by the Banking and Financial Dealings Act 1971. Additionally, the Factories Act 1961 gives the right to take off Christmas Day, Good Friday and Bank Holiday to workers within its scope. The employer may substitute another weekday for those holidays, provided he gives at least three weeks' notice. The Agricultural Wages Board may direct that certain holidays be permitted and the pay to be given therefor (Agricultural Wages Act 1948, s. 3). Further, in *Tucker* v *British Leyland Motor Corporation* [1978] IRLR 493, a county court judge held that, in the absence of express provision or regular usage to the contrary, an hourly paid employee is entitled to a day's holiday on recognised public holidays without fear of dismissal as an absentee. In *Morley* v *Heritage plc* [1993] IRLR 400, the Court of Appeal determined that it was not an implied term of a contract of employment that if the employee's employment terminated without his having taken any part of his holiday entitlement the company would pay him in lieu thereof.

4.6 COMPETENCE

The employee impliedly represents that he is reasonably competent to do his job (*Harmer* v *Cornelius* (1858) 5 CBNS 236). He can thus be lawfully dismissed instantly if in breach.

This harsh common law position is, however, mitigated by the statutory unfair dismissal jurisdiction which affords various procedural safeguards to an incompetent employee as well as to others (see para. 13.7.1), and is now of much more consequence.

4.7 OBEDIENCE TO ORDERS

At common law the employee is, in general, obliged to obey all lawful orders of the employer. That he might be summarily dismissed if he did not comply is a great bulwark of managerial prerogative. In the modern law, the unfair dismissal jurisdiction has established procedural safeguards for the employee, and even at common law some of the harshest early decisions (e.g. in *Turner* v *Mason* (1845) 14 M&W 112) would not be reached today, since they reflect a very different view of the rights of employers.

Now orders must be tempered by reasonableness to be effective. *Ottoman Bank Ltd* v *Chakarian* [1930] AC 277 was a particularly strong case since the employers ordered the plaintiff, an Armenian, to stay in Constantinople where he had previously been sentenced to death and it was held that he was within his rights in refusing. On the other hand, *Bouzourou* v *Ottoman Bank* [1930] AC 271, a Christian employee was obliged to obey an order to work at a branch in Asia Minor, notwithstanding the well-known hostility of the Turkish Government to his religion. It has also been held a breach of contract to refuse an order to visit Ireland because of general fear of IRA activity (*Walmsley* v *UDEC Refrigeration Ltd* [1972] IRLR 80). An employee is also obliged to adapt reasonably to new work methods (*Cresswell* v *Board of Inland Revenue* [1984] ICR 508). In *Dryden* v *Greater Glasgow Health Board* [1992] IRLR 469, the introduction of a non smoking policy did not constitute a breach of contract; the employer is entitled to introduce reasonable rules for regulating his work place.

A dismissal for failure to obey an illegal order is always unlawful, so that in *Morrish* v *Henlys (Folkestone) Ltd* [1973] ICR 482, where an employee was ordered to falsify the account books at the garage where he worked, his refusal was not in breach of contract. The same result was reached in *Gregory* v *Ford* [1951] 1 All ER 121, where the employee said he would not take on the road a vehicle not covered by third party insurance. A sick employee is only excused from performing orders rendered impossible by the illness. His illness does not act as a general solvent or suspension, so that a commercial traveller was in breach in failing to remove merchandise from her car during a period of illness (*Marshall* v *Alexander Sloan and Co. Ltd* [1981] IRLR 264).

4.8 BREACH OF CONTRACT

Broadly, the consequences of a breach of contract by the employee are that:

(a) He may be *disciplined* in accordance with contractual procedures (para. 4.9).

(b) The employer may *sue for damages* in county or High Court (or if the breach is current on termination of employment in the industrial tribunal), but this is rarely done because the amount of damages recoverable is usually minimal (but see *Janata Bank Ltd* v *Ahmed* [1981] IRLR 457 and *Miller* v *Hamworthy Engineering Ltd* [1986] IRLR 461, an imposed salary cut for short-time working) (para. 12.5.4).

(c) The employer may apply for an *injunction* to prevent the employee's breach. This is most common where the employee is infringing restrictive covenants or using trade secrets, but the courts must not make an order the effect of which is that the employee must continue to work for the employer against his will (para. 12.5.1).

(d) If the breach is very serious the employer may *summarily dismiss the employee,* although this may make him liable for an action for damages if such dismissal is wrongful or unfair.

4.9 DISCIPLINE

Disciplinary procedures should not be viewed primarily as a means of imposing sanctions. They should also be designed to emphasise and encourage improvements in individual conduct.

(ACAS Code No. 1: Disciplinary Practice and Procedures in Employment.)

The major means of maintaining discipline amongst employees, of course, is dismissal (which will be considered in Chapter 12), but lesser sanctions are adopted for less serious breaches of work rules. These include reprimands, suspension, demotion, transfer and the temporary withdrawal of privileges. Such disciplinary actions are only lawful so long as they are expressly or impliedly incorporated into the individual's contract of employment. Moreover, there are additional provisions striking down and modifying agreed terms at common law. The ACAS Code of Practice and Procedure also lays down detailed guidance primarily for the unfair dismissal jurisdiction.
For deductions from wages, see para. 5.1.

4.9.1 Common law

Terms are unlawful at common law which:

(a) contain servile incidents, rendering the employee no better than a slave (*Horwood* v *Millar's Timber & Trading Co. Ltd* [1917] 1 KB 305; *Davies* v *Davies* (1887) 36 ChD 359); or
(b) provide for imposition of a penalty, that is a compulsory payment of money in the event of a breach of contract which does not represent a genuine pre-estimate of the damage likely to result from that breach (*Dunlop Pneumatic Tyre Co. Ltd* v *New Garage & Motor Co. Ltd* [1915] AC 79). This rule is common to all contracts.

An employer may take disciplinary proceedings against an employee in respect of an alleged assault notwithstanding that the employee has been acquitted of a criminal offence in respect of precisely the same charge. There was no question of double jeopardy, nor were such proceedings 'other civil proceedings' within the meaning of s. 45 of the Offences against the Person Act 1861, which would have otherwise prevented a civil claim after a criminal conviction (*Saeed* v *Greater London Council (Inner London Education Authority)* [1986] IRLR 23).

4.9.2 ACAS Code of Practice No. 1: Disciplinary Practice and Procedures in Employment

The formulation of detailed disciplinary rules is encouraged by the Employment Rights Act 1996, s. 3, which requires employers to specify them in the written particulars and to indicate a person to whom the employee can apply if dissatisfied with a particular disciplinary decision. Further, the 1977 Code (para. 10) calls on the employer to ensure that his disciplinary procedures:

(a)   are in *writing;*
(b)   specify *to whom* they apply;
(c)   provide for matters to be dealt with *quickly;*
(d)   indicate the *disciplinary action* which may be taken;
(e)   specify the *level of management* which has authority to take the various forms of disciplinary action possible;
(f)   ensure that, except for gross misconduct, no employees are dismissed for *a first breach* of discipline;
(g)   ensure that individuals are given *an explanation* for any penalty imposed;
(h)   provide a right of *appeal* and specify the procedure to be followed (see paras 13.9.4–13.9.5 of this book).

The Code recommends (para. 12) that the following steps should be taken in all cases of misconduct except those for which the rules allow instant dismissal:

(a)   formal oral warning, or, for 'more serious issues' —
(b)   written warning, setting out the nature of the offence and the likely consequences of further offences;
(c)   final written warning saying further misconduct will lead to suspension, or dismissal, or some other penalty;
(d)   transfer, suspension (if allowed by contract) or dismissal.

The Code is supplemented by the ACAS Advisory Handbook: Discipline at Work published in 1987.

4.10   LAY-OFF AND SHORT-TIME WORKING

Everyone has the right to work, to free choice of employment, to just and favourable conditions of work and to protection against unemployment.

(Article 23i, Universal Declaration of Human Rights, 1948.)

It is a common industrial phenomenon that employees are placed on short time with reduced or no pay, due to lack of orders, depression, or natural breaks in production. This practice is particularly widespread in the older industries like shipbuilding and construction, where the legacy of casual working is still most apparent. The practice raises important legal problems in respect of the employer's contractual right to lay off workers, and employees' maintenance of income during such periods. We first examine the complications of the common law and then several statutory interventions, as follows:

(a)   contractual rights to payment;
(b)   guaranteed pay from the employer backed by statute;
(c)   unemployment benefit;
(d)   redundancy payment;
(e)   income support.

4.10.1 Lay-off at common law

At common law, the employer is in breach of contract if he lays off an employee without pay, unless there is an express or implied term permitting lay-off (*Warburton v Taff Vale Railway Co.* (1902) 18 TLR 420, *Hanley v Pease & Partners* [1915] 1 KB 698). A lay-off with pay is normally lawful since the employer is under no duty to provide work, but he must continue to pay employees even in the absence of their actually working. As A.L. Smith MR put it in *Turner v Sawdon* [1901] 2 KB 653: 'It is within the province of the (employer) to say that he will go on paying wages, but that he is under no obligation to provide work.' In *Browning v Crumlin Valley Collieries Ltd* [1926] 1 KB 522, a mine owner was held not to be in breach of contract in laying off his colliery workers when repair work had to be done to return the mine to a safe condition.

In *Miller v Hamworthy Engineering Ltd* [1986] IRLR 461, the employers relied on a provision in the staff terms and conditions for 'adjustments' to monthly salary for 'overtime, lost time or other alterations' to defend a claim for full wages when the employer did not provide work. The Court of Appeal held that this did not apply to an employee who was willing and able to work but not working merely because of the company's inability to provide him with work.

The courts have, however, gone some way to imply a duty on the employer to provide work in three broad categories:

(a)   Where the consideration for the employee's work is 'a salary plus the opportunity of becoming better known', as in the case of an actor (*Herbert Clayton & Jack Waller Ltd v Oliver* [1930] AC 209).

(b)   Where the employee is engaged on skilled work, such as a chief engineer, and his skills may only be maintained with a reasonable amount of work (*Breach v Epsylon Industries Ltd* [1976] IRLR 180, also *Bosworth v Angus Jowett and Co. Ltd* [1977] IRLR 374, sales director). In *Provident Financial Group plc and Whitegates Estate Agency v Hayward* [1989] IRLR 84, Dillon LJ said that the principle would apply to, for example, chartered accountants (see para. 6.4).

(c)   Where remuneration is partly by way of commission, so that the deprival of work reduces the amount earned, e.g. a commercial traveller (*Turner v Goldsmith* [1891] 1 QB 544), or journalist (*Bauman v Hulton Press Ltd* [1952] WN 556). In the Court of Appeal decision, *Devonald v Rosser and Sons* [1906] 2 KB 708, the employee's wages fluctuated with the number of items she completed, and when the employer refused to let her work during the period of notice to which she was entitled, she succeeded in an action for breach of contract. Although decided before *Browning*, this exception is more attune with modern ideas on lay-offs than is the general principle. Thus in *Jones v H. Sherman Ltd* [1969] 4 ITR 63, the court held that the employer had no right at common law to lay off a bookmaker manager when there was no racing.

An obligation not to put workers on short time has also been held to arise in other cases by way of: trade custom, *Bird v British Celanese Ltd* [1945] KB 336; collective agreements, *O'Reilly v Hotpoint Ltd* (1970) 5 ITR 68; or statute, *Wallwork v Fielding* [1922] KB 66, cf. *Waine v R. Oliver (Plant Hire) Ltd* [1977] IRLR 434. An express contractual right to lay off is likely to be restricted to lay-off for a reasonable time (*A. Dakri & Co. Ltd v Tiffen* [1981] IRLR 57). If the employee is appointed expressly to a particular position, it may be a constructive dismissal to remove the employee's duties of that engagement.

There have also been in recent years various generalised dicta about an implied 'right to work' in cases concerning entry to trade unions and professional bodies. It was in this context that Lord Denning in *Langston* v *AUEW* [1974] 1 All ER 980 tentatively suggested that in the case of skilled workers there is an obligation to provide a reasonable amount of work:

> We have repeatedly said in this court that a man has a right to work which the courts will protect . . . I would not wish to express any decided view but simply state the argument . . . In these days an employer when employing a skilled man is bound to provide him with work. By which I mean that the man should be given the opportunity of doing his work when it is available and he is ready and willing to do so . . .

When the case was remitted to the NIRC, Donaldson P declined to implement this tentative but radical essay of the law, and instead decided the case in favour of the plaintiff on the narrower ground that Mr Langston must be given an opportunity to work since he was paid by the piece ([1974] ICR 510). Professor Hepple has convincingly shown that there are insuperable problems involved in implying a general right to work (1981 10 ILJ 65) and there has been no case in which an employee has succeeded in demonstrating breach of contract on that basis.

4.10.2 Income maintenance at common law

Even where lay-off is lawful, payment must normally continue throughout a workless period. In *Devonald*'s case (supra) an attempt to establish 'custom and practice' to the contrary failed, significantly on the ground that it would be 'unreasonable' for the employer to close his factory down at any time without pay while the employees remained obliged to work if called upon to do so. Moreover, where there is an express term withholding pay, the courts have generally construed it restrictively, e.g. *Minnevitch* v *Café de Paris* [1936] 1 All ER 884, and for a temporary period (*Millbrook Furnishing Ltd* v *McIntosh* [1981] IRLR 309). There are, however, two exceptions to this approach:

(a)   where the lay-off is for reasons wholly *beyond the control* of the employer, such as lack of materials, a power breakdown or mechanical mishap (see *Devonald*'s case), when the law impliedly *excludes* a right to payment; and
(b)   where there is an *express term* permitting lay-off without pay.

4.10.3 Guarantee pay by statute

The uncertainty of these rights at common law, and the difficulty of enforcing them in the county court and High Court, stimulated the development in collective agreements of a guaranteed week securing payment during short time. The EPA 1975 thus stepped in to imply a restricted right to guarantee payments in every contract of employment, and in doing this the Government had the secondary aim of transferring some of the liability for loss due to intermittent work from the State to employers (the same policy as is apparent in statutory sick pay and statutory maternity pay).

4.10.3.1   Conditions of entitlement   Now contained in ss. 28–35 of the Employment Rights Act 1996, the guarantee payment is in a sense a temporary daily redundancy payment.

The claim must be made in respect of a 'workless day', i.e. a period of 24 hours from midnight to midnight (s. 28(1) and (3)), when the employee would have normally worked, so that like unemployment benefit it does not apply to a normal idle day or holiday. To qualify the reason for the lack of work must be:

(a) the diminution of the employer's need for the kind of work the employee does; or
(b) any other occurrence which affects the normal working of the business.

The latter rather vague phrase has been little elucidated by litigation, but appears to comprise at least a fall in orders, lack of raw materials, power failure, bad weather and the bankruptcy of a major customer. It does not, according to the industrial tribunal in *North* v *Pavleigh Ltd* [1978] IRLR 461, extend to the lay-off without pay because of the employer's desire to comply with Jewish holidays.

4.10.3.2 Exclusions The right to payment is forfeited if:

(a) The workless day is due to a *strike, lock-out or other industrial action* affecting any employee of the employer or an associated employer (s. 29(3)) and this exception is now wider than the exclusions for unemployment and income support.

(b) The employer has offered *suitable alternative employment* and the employee has unreasonably refused it (s. 29(4)). It is irrelevant that the employee is not contractually obliged to perform the tasks, and a job may be suitable for a short time but not permanently (see *Purdy* v *Willowbank International Ltd* [1977] IRLR 388), otherwise the principles are similar to those applied in the defence to redundancy payment (para. 14.3).

(c) The employee does not comply with *reasonable requirements* imposed by the employer such as that he telephone the employer each day at 10 a.m. to enquire whether work will be available (s. 29(5)).

(d) The employee has been engaged for a period of *three months* or less (s. 29(2)).

A gap in the legislative framework appears to be revealed in relation to casual workers by the difficult decision in *Mailway (Southern) Ltd* v *Willsher* [1978] ICR 511. The female applicant was registered as a part-time packer with the respondent company and worked in accordance with their needs while she was having a baby. Although she otherwise fulfilled all the requirements for guaranteed pay during lay-off, she was not able to claim because she was not 'required to work in accordance with (her) contract of employment' as necessary under what is now s. 28. Rather, according to Kilner Brown J, she was '*invited* to work', being 'told that work was available if she presented herself'.

Where a contract is varied in connection with short-time working, by s. 31(6), the number of days' payment is still to be controlled by the original contract notwithstanding supervening idle days (see *Trevethian* v *Stirling Metals Ltd* [1977] IRLR 416, cf. permanent alteration in *Daley* v *Strathclyde Regional Council* [1977] IRLR 414).

The following categories of workers are excluded: share fishermen (s. 199(2)), employees normally working outside Great Britain (s. 196(2) and (3)), and employees spending less than 12 weeks in employment on specific tasks (s. 29(2)(b)). The Act also makes an exemption for collective agreement guarantee provisions more favourable than its own scheme by order of the Secretary of State.

4.10.3.3 Amount of payment The employee is entitled, where none of the above exclusions apply, in any period of three months, to as many days guaranteed payments as he usually works in a week, subject to a maximum of five (s. 31). Thus if he normally has Friday, Saturday and Sundays off work, he would be entitled to up to four days in any quarter, but if he normally worked a six-day week, his entitlement would still be five.

The appropriate amount of payment is calculated by multiplying the employee's normal working hours by the 'guaranteed hourly rate' (s. 30(1). For those who work regular hours each week, one divides the basic rate of pay, plus bonus, commission and contractual overtime, by the hours worked (s. 30(2)). If, on the other hand, he is on shift work, or works different hours each week, a 12-week average is taken (s. 30(3)). The figures thus produced are subject to a daily maximum payment reviewed annually (ss. 31, 208). Thus if the employee normally works seven hours a day and earns £4 an hour, he is entitled at most to the maximum guarantee per day. Should he labour seven hours a day at £1 per hour his entitlement would be £7 per day. From this must always be deducted any contractual entitlement, whether by guarantee week agreement or otherwise, but only a payment which derives from the employer and not, say, a trade union or sickness benefit (s. 32) (see *Cartwright* v *G. Clancey Ltd* [1983] ICR 552). The statutory payment is also subject to income tax.

If an employer does not comply with his obligations under these provisions, the employee may present a complaint to an industrial tribunal within three months of his default, and the tribunal may then order the employer to pay the amount due (s. 34). If, in the meantime, the employee has claimed jobseeker's allowance the sum so paid out may be recouped. Since it may be a considerable time before the guarantee payment complaint is adjudicated, the worker can claim benefit and then pay back the State from the money he eventually receives as guarantee pay (Employment Protection (Recoupment of Unemployment Benefit and Supplementary Benefit) Regulations 1977 (SI 1977 No. 674), replaced from 7 October 1996 by the Employment Protection (Recoupment of Jobseeker's Allowance and Income Support) Regulations 1996 (SI 1996 No. 2349)).

4.10.4 Jobseeker's allowance

The Jobseekers Act 1995 and the Jobseeker's Allowance Regulations 1996 (SI 1996 No. 207) (in force in their entirety from 7 October 1996) have had the effect of abolishing unemployment benefit and of replacing it with the less generous, 'contribution-based' jobseeker's allowance. Income support for unemployed persons has likewise been subsumed into the new scheme as 'income-based' jobseeker's allowance. A claimant's entitlement to jobseeker's allowance is subject to the conditions set out in the legislation (see ss. 1–25 of the Act and the whole of the Regulations). The principal characteristics of the 'contribution-based' jobseeker's allowance, distinguishing it from unemployment benefit, are as follows:

(a)   Jobseeker's allowance is payable on a weekly rather than a daily basis (s. 1(3)). However, where a claimant is entitled to the benefit only for part of a week, the amount which he or she receives will be calculated in accordance with the 'part-week' provisions contained in reg. 150 of the 1996 Regulations.

(b)   An essential precondition for entitlement to jobseeker's allowance is that the claimant 'has entered into a jobseeker's agreement which remains in force' (s. 1(2)(b)). The detailed legislative provisions concerning this significant innovation appear in ss. 9–11 of the Act and regs 31–45 of the Regulations.

(c)   A claimant loses entitlement for any week in which his or her income exceeds the 'prescribed amount' calculated in accordance with reg. 56 of the Regulations (s. 2(1)(c) of the Act; see also the legislative provisions cited at (d) below.

(d) The amount of jobseeker's allowance which a claimant receives in any week depends on:

(i) his or her age, i.e. whether he or she is under 18, 18–24 years of age, or 25 and over (s. 4(1)(a) and (2) of the Act and reg. 79 of the Regulations);

(ii) any deductions in respect of earnings and pension payments received (s. 4(1)(b) of the Act and regs 80 and 81 of the Regulations).

(e) A claimant's entitlement to 'contribution-based' jobseeker's allowance ends after 182 days (i.e. six months), as opposed to 12 months under the former system of unemployment benefit (s. 5(1)). If necessary, he or she will then be assessed under the provisions relating to 'income-based' jobseeker's allowance, similar in most respects to those previously governing income support for the unemployed.

Like unemployment benefit, entitlement to jobseeker's allowance begins only after three workless days ('waiting days') have passed (see Sch. 1, para. 4 of the Act and reg. 46 of the Regulations). This rule is modified where an employee is subject to a pattern of intermittent working, such as lay-off or short-time; otherwise, such an employee might wait three days each time and never gain entitlement. The period may be aggregated by taking any two days in one week and adding them to any other day within the next 12 weeks. Such an employee can put the two days in the bank or 'deep freeze', taking them out when on the third necessary day work is unavailable. After this, jobseeker's allowance is claimable, and the worker does not then have to wait a further three days if he or she is laid off again, provided those are days on which the employee would normally work. Thus if Iago is laid off every Monday and Friday, days when he is accustomed to work, he will be entitled to unemployment benefit from the Friday of the second week, because the first two days are treated as one jobseeking period and the next two are linked thereto, thus making up three waiting days. On the other hand, if an employee is laid off for only one day a week, and always on the same day, he will not be able to add them together (see Sch. 1, paras 3 and 4 of the Act and regs 46–48 of the Regulations).

4.10.5 Redundancy payment

Normally a dismissal is a prerequisite for claiming a redundancy payment (Chapter 13). An employee sacked with the expectation that he will be re-employed if and when work picks up is still dismissed and there is no problem about claiming a redundancy payment. Further, where a lay-off is in breach of contract, the employee is entitled to react to the employer's breach by resigning and claiming constructive dismissal (e.g. *Puttick* v *John Wright & Sons (Blackwall) Ltd* [1972] ICR 457, *Jewell* v *Neptune Concrete Ltd* [1975] IRLR 147). Where the employer is in breach of contract in that he has laid off the employee for more than a reasonable period, the employee may claim a redundancy payment even though he has not complied with the elaborate statutory procedure (*A. Dakri & Co. Ltd* v *Tiffen* [1981] IRLR 57).

The legislators went further since they considered that even without a statutory dismissal a time must come when the employee can say 'enough is enough' and claim a redundancy payment. Otherwise the employer might effectively exclude his liability — by waiting for employees to resign due to long periods of intermittent work — rather than sacking them. The legislative extension provides the only circumstance where an employee can simply resign, not reacting to his employer's contractual breach, and still claim his statutory right to a redundancy payment.

By s. 147 of ERA 1996, an employee may mount the first hurdle towards a redundancy payment (a dismissal) when there has been a stipulated period of short-time and/or lay-off. The statute provides that an employee is *laid off* if in any week he is entitled to no pay and on *short-time* when he earns less than half his normal week's pay. The provisions relate solely to an employee who is paid only for work he does and depend on *pay* rather than hours worked; thus if an employee is entitled to three-quarters of his normal weekly remuneration even though he works only one day in the week (perhaps by reason of a collective agreement), he is not treated as on short time. This applies only to contractual remuneration and not what he might receive by way of guarantee payment, unemployment or income support (see also para. 13.3.4). *Continuity* of employment is also preserved during short time and lay-off since they will be periods of 'temporary absences from work' although absence caused wholly or mainly by a *strike or lock out* is disregarded (para. 10.3).

The employee can commence this long route to a redundancy payment after: (i) four or more consecutive weeks of short time or lay-off; or (ii) six or more such weeks in any period of 13 weeks. The weeks may consist partly of lay-off, partly of short time, and he must then give notice to his employer within four weeks of the end of these respective periods that he *intends to claim* a redundancy payment (s. 148). An employee's claim will be rejected if he has been laid off for less, even one day less, than four weeks at the time he presents his claim (*Allinson v Drew Simmons Engineering Ltd* [1985] ICR 488; see also *Spinpress Ltd v Turner* [1986] ICR 433). The notice acts as conditional resignation, but to actually gain payment he must give one week's notice of actual termination of his contract of employment or such longer period as is expressly required in the contract of employment. The employee is able to see whether his claim to payment will be disputed before taking the drastic step of resigning, for the employer may serve, within seven days of the employee's communication, a counter-notice that he will contest liability to payment. For full-time work may soon resume again and as part of the statutory compromise the employer may resist payment if it is reasonably to be expected that the employee will, within four weeks, enter into 13 consecutive weeks' employment without either short-time or lay-off (s. 152(1)) (see *Neepsend Steel Ltd v Vaughan* [1972] 3 All ER 725). He may expect new orders to come in, or that the business will be taken over. However, if the employee for the next four weeks is laid off or on short time at all, he is conclusively presumed to be entitled to a redundancy payment. Few tribunals will convene to decide the issue before this period has elapsed, so that the matter may be reviewed *ex post facto*.

Example   Othello was employed by Shakespeare Enterprises for five days a week at eight hours per day at an hourly rate of £1.50. His contract stated that he was to be paid only for hours worked and that the employer had the right to lay him off. Due to lack of orders for his employer, his record of service over a 15-week period was (and this is by no means atypical in some trades):

Week	Time worked (days)	Week	Time worked (days)	Week	Time worked (days)
1	3	6	2	11	5
2	5	7	nil	12	5
3	2	8	5	13	½
4	5	9	1	14	2
5	3	10	4	15	1

His rights are as follows:

(a) *Guarantee payment.* He may claim for two workless days in week 1 and three in week 3, and then not until week 14, when he is entitled to three days in that week and two in week 15. The amount to be paid is the maximum of £14.50 per workless day, since his actual pay would be £12 per day, above the maximum (see *Cartwright* v *G. Clancey Ltd* [1983] ICR 552).

(b) *Jobseeker's allowance.* Othello may claim the allowance from the fourth day of week 6. He cannot claim in weeks 1 and 3 because he receives guarantee payments; and he cannot claim in weeks 2 and 4 because he is then engaged in remunerative work five days per week. In week 5 he is unemployed for two days and he can carry those forward for the next 12 weeks to link in with a further two days in order to fulfil the three waiting days. In fact, he is unemployed for three days in week 6 and can claim from the second of those days. Except for week 7, the amount of Othello's jobseeker's allowance will be calculated on a part-week basis.

(c) *Redundancy payment.* Othello may claim a redundancy payment in week 14 since he has been on short time or lay-off for six out of the preceding 12 weeks; there is no consecutive four-week period. Since he is on short time for the next four weeks the employer cannot argue with his entitlement unless for one of those weeks the short time was as the result of a strike.

4.11 MOBILITY CLAUSES

In some cases the description of job and place of work does not tell anything like the whole contractual story because of express or implied terms for flexibility. It is not unusual to find a works rule book containing a provision for the working of 40 hours per week or such time as may be communicated to employees by notice from time to time. The employee who works in Land's End may be surprised to find a clause in small print that he is expected to work anywhere in Great Britain, but he would still be expected to transfer to John O'Groats. Thus the Barclays Bank contract contains the clause that: 'Every member of the staff must be willing to serve at any office of the Bank as may be required and will serve the bank faithfully, diligently and to the best of his or her ability.' (See *The Employment Acts 1974–80*, eds C.D. Drake and B. Bercusson, Sweet & Maxwell, 1981, Introduction.) Where there is any doubt in the language, however, the courts in construing such provisions adopt a test of reasonableness, so that in *Briggs* v *ICI* (1968) 3 ITR 276, a provision that 'you will accept the right of management to transfer you to another job with a higher or lower rate of pay whether day work, night work or shift work', was held by Lord Parker CJ to 'only entitle management to transfer the process worker to another job within the Billingham factory and only as a process worker'.

The issue most often arises in relation to redundancy payments which are made only if there is no longer a requirement for work of the particular kind carried on by the applicant; it is thus necessary to specify carefully what bundle of duties is comprised in the particular job (para. 14.2.4), and where it is located.

In *Jones* v *Associated Tunnelling Co. Ltd* [1981] IRLR 477, the EAT pointed out that a contract of employment could not be silent on the place of work. The following considerations were relevant in implying such a term: the nature of the employer's business; whether or not the employee has, in fact, been moved during his employment; what he was told when engaged; and whether there is any provision to cover the employee's expenses when he was working out of daily reach of home. This was approved by the Court of Appeal in *Courtaulds Northern Spinning Ltd* v *Sibson and TGWU* [1988] IRLR 305, where it was held that in the case of a HGV driver it was implied that he would work at any depot within reasonable daily reach of his home (see also *Rank Xerox* v *Churchill* [1988] IRLR 280; *United Bank Ltd* v *Akhtar* [1989] IRLR 507; *Bass Leisure Ltd* v *Thomas* [1994] IRLR 104).

4.12   LICENCE TO ENTER THE EMPLOYER'S PREMISES

An employee clearly has a licence to enter his employer's premises but this will normally be determined on suspension or dismissal. (There may be unusual situations where this is not so.) In *City and Hackney Health Authority* v *National Union of Public Employees* [1985] IRLR 252, the plaintiffs' decision to close Shoreditch Hospital led to a sit-in which they believed had been organised by Mr Craig, a NUPE shop steward. He was therefore suspended from work on full pay and told not to enter the hospital premises. He was granted an interlocutory injunction to restrain the ban on him at first instance, but the Court of Appeal thought that this was an error. Although it was arguable that the Whitley Council agreement provided a right to stay on the premises so that the shop steward could exercise his functions, this could not survive the suspension of the contract. The continuance of such right depended on mutual confidence and it was clear that the appellants had lost all confidence in Mr Craig.

4.13   REFERENCES

An employer has a right to refuse a reference for an employee. Where an employer gives a reference, he owes a duty of care to those persons (prospective employers) whom he can reasonably foresee may rely on such reference. In *Spring* v *Guardian Assurance plc* [1994] ICR 596, the House of Lords decided that an employer who gave a reference in respect of a former employee owed to that employee a duty to take reasonable care in its preparation and would be liable to him in negligence if he failed to do so and the employee thereby suffered damage. It was not (as had been argued by the employer) contrary to public policy to impose liability in this area on the ground that it might inhibit the giving of full and frank references. Lords Slynn and Woolf also found that this would be a breach of an implied term in the contract. See also *Lawton* v *BOC Transhield Ltd* [1987] ICR 7.

4.14   MEDICAL REPORTS

By s. 1 of the Access to Medical Reports Act 1988, the employee has a right of access 'to any medical report relating to the individual which is to be, or has been, supplied by a medical practitioner for employment purposes or insurance purposes'. There are various exemptions, the most important of which is when the disclosure of any part of the report 'would in the opinion of the practitioner be likely to cause serious harm to the physical or mental health of the individual or others or would indicate the intentions of the practitioner in respect of the individual'.

5 Wages

5.1 THE POLICY

The Truck Act 1896 sought to protect vulnerable employees and prevent deductions from wages to take account of defective workmanship save where the following conditions were satisfied (s. 1):

(a) The terms of the contract were exhibited in a *notice* constantly affixed at a place open to the worker, or alternatively he had signed the contract.

(b) The deduction did not exceed the actual or estimated damage or loss occasioned to the employer by the act or omission.

(c) The amount of the deduction or payment was *fair and reasonable* having regard to all the circumstances of the case.

These provisions were repealed by the Wages Act 1986 which is now consolidated as Part II of the ERA 1996. The main reforms ushered in by the Wages Act in respect of deductions were to remove the requirements that fines should be fair and reasonable, expand the coverage to all workers whether or not engaged on manual labour, and make the industrial tribunals the forum for complaint. By s. 13 of the ERA 1996, an employer may not make any deduction from any wages of any worker unless the deduction is required or authorised by statute (e.g. PAYE and national insurance contributions) or by contract or unless the worker has previously signified in writing his agreement or consent to making it.

5.2 DEDUCTIONS

In order to be effective to permit the deduction, the agreement must be made before the event giving rise to the deduction rather than the date when the deduction is taken. In *Discount Tobacco & Confectionery Ltd* v *Williamson* [1993] ICR 371, where the EAT laid down this principle, the employee was manager of a store in which, in December 1988 and February 1989, there were large stock deficiencies. In March 1989 he signed a document giving the employers the right to deduct £3,500 from his pay at £20 per week. In May 1989 there was a further deficiency. It was held that the employers could deduct only in relation to the last event. (See *Potter* v *Hunt Contractors Ltd* [1992] ICR 337; *Fairfield Ltd* v *Skinner* [1992] ICR 836 to the effect that it is possible to challenge the justifiability of the deduction made.) Similar provisions apply to the employer's right to receive payments from his employee, but not to agreements that the employer is to pay over a certain amount to a third party such as a trade union under the check off procedure.

A variation to an employee's contract to enable to employer to make a deduction from his wages must have been agreed before the conduct or events on account of which the deduction is made and must have been notified to the employee in writing before the date of deduction, but the variation itself may be oral (*York City & District Travel Ltd* v *Smith* [1990] IRLR 213).

As part of its decision on deductions, the industrial tribunal may indeed have to answer complex questions about the assessment of wages. In *Thames Water Utilities* v *Reynolds* [1996] IRLR 186, for example, when the employee was made redundant he was owed eight days' holiday pay. He had been on an annual salary, and the employers paid him $^8/_{365}$ ths of that salary. The employee brought a Wages Act claim before the tribunal, arguing that the apportionment should have been made on the basis of the number of *working* days in a year (not calendar days), which would have meant that he should have been paid $^8/_{260}$ ths of his salary. The tribunal, applying the Apportionment Act 1870, s. 2, upheld his claim, but the EAT allowed the employers' appeal. The correct interpretation of the section (which states that, unless the contrary is intended, money due is to be 'considered as accruing from day to day') is that applies to calendar days, not working days.

Section 27 of the ERA 1996 defines 'wages' as any sums payable by the employer to the worker in connection with the employment including 'any fee, bonus, commission, holiday pay or other emolument referable to his employment, whether payable under his contract or otherwise'. This includes commission expressed to be discretionary and non-contractual (*Kent Management Services* v *Butterfield* [1992] ICR 272). A failure to pay even a disputed amount is a deduction according to the Court of Appeal in *Delaney* v *Staples* [1991] IRLR 112, [1993] ICR 331, settling a conflict between several EAT decisions in England and Scotland.

The House of Lords in *Delaney* v *Staples* [1992] ICR 483, decided that payment in lieu of notice is not included. The essential characteristic of the concept of wages is that wages are consideration for work done or to be done under a contract of employment, whereas 'if a payment is not referable to an obligation on the employee under a subsisting contract of employment to render his services' it does not qualify (at p. 488d–e). The primary consequence of this important ruling was that claims for payment in lieu of notice had to continue to be brought in the county court or High Court, but this anomalous position was modified by the Industrial Tribunals (Extension of Jurisdiction) Order 1994 (SI 1994 No. 1623), which (subject to certain exceptions) extends the jurisdiction of industrial tribunals to contractual claims existing at the time of termination of employment (for full treatment, see Bowers *et al, Industrial Tribunal Practice and Procedure* (FT Law & Tax, 1996)).

In the event of dispute between employer and employee, the industrial tribunal must determine what amount is properly payable and so whether the sum actually paid is a deduction therefrom (e.g. *Greg May (CF&C) Ltd* v *Dring* [1990] IRLR 19; see also *Bruce* v *Wiggins Teape (Stationery) Ltd* [1994] IRLR 536; *Davies* v *Hotpoint Ltd* [1994] IRLR 538).

5.3 RETAIL EMPLOYMENT

Special rules apply to the employer of a worker in *retail* employment, defined as involving the supply of goods and services directly to members of the public. Such an employer must not deduct in respect of cash shortages or stock deficiencies more than one tenth of the gross amount payable to the worker on a particular pay day (save on the final pay day of the employment or payment in lieu of notice) (ERA 1996, s. 18(1)), and must make a written demand for payment. Any complaint about unauthorised deductions must be made to an industrial tribunal within three months of the incident in question (ERA 1996, s. 23). No contracting out of the provisions is permitted save by an agreement reached after action has been taken by an ACAS conciliation officer.

5.4 EXCEPTIONS

These provisions do not apply to:

(a) overpayment of wages or expenses, but to be effective the deduction must be permissible under the common law. In *Home Office* v *Ayres* [1992] ICR 175, [1992] IRLR 59, the Home Office overpaid a prison officer £830 over two months. There was, however, no explanation given by the employer for the changing rate of pay, and the employee assumed that the money had been paid correctly and spent it on normal living expenses. The employers deducted the moneys in future wage payments and the employee successfully challenged this under the Wages Act 1986, relying on *Avon CC* v *Howlett* [1983] IRLR 171.

There was no requirement, however, that the word 'lawful' be implied before 'deductions' in s. 1(1) of the Wages Act 1986 (now ERA 1996, s. 13) according to the EAT in *Sunderland Polytechnic* v *Evans* [1993] IRLR 196, reconsidering its own decision in *Home Office* v *Ayres* (supra). There it had held that a sum could be claimed only if lawful, and in the case of overpayments by the Home Office which had been accepted without the means of knowing that the prison officer was not entitled to the moneys paid, there was no entitlement in the Home Office to reclaim the money, so that the recovery was by way of unlawful deduction (*SIP Products Ltd* v *Swinn* [1994] ICR 473). It is a breach unilaterally to abolish a wages supplement, so that in *McCree* v *Tower Hamlets London Borough Council* [1992] ICR 99, the employer was not able to avoid the effect of the Act by absorbing a sum into pay increases with a view to showing that there was no deduction at all;

(b) deductions in consequence of statutory disciplinary proceedings (not applying in the main to private employers but to services such as the police or fire service: *Chiltern House Ltd* v *Chambers* [1990] IRLR 88);

(c) a statutory requirement on the employer to pay over specified sums to a statutory authority (*McCree* v *Tower Hamlets London Borough Council* [1992] ICR 99, [1992] IRLR 56);

(d) any arrangement agreed to by the employee whereby the employer is to pay over amounts notified to a third party;

(e) any payment on account of the worker taking part in a strike or other industrial action; or

(f) any payment to satisfy a court or tribunal decision (ERA 1996, s. 14(6));

(g) errors in computation (but this does not include a conscious decision not to make a payment: cf *Yemm* v *British Steel plc* [1994] IRLR 117, *Morgan* v *West Glamorgan CC* [1995] IRLR 68).

There is no restriction on making claims in the civil court for unpaid wages even though a claim could be brought under Part II of the ERA 1996 on the same facts (*Rickard* v *P.B. Glass Supplies* [1990] ICR 150).

5.5 ITEMISED PAY STATEMENT

Section 8 of the EPCA 1978 gives every employee the right to a written pay statement at or before every payment of wages or salary. It must distinguish:

(a)   the gross amount of wages or salary;
(b)   the net amount payable;
(c)   where different parts of the net amount are paid in different ways, the amount and method of each part payment;
(d)   any variable or fixed deductions therefrom.

In the case of fixed deductions (for example, union contributions, or payments in respect of fines or maintenance), a new statement need not be given at each time of payment. Instead a single communication may cover a maximum of 12 months, but should always be specific, the label 'miscellaneous deductions' being inadequate (*Milsom* v *Leicestershire County Council* [1978] IRLR 433; see ERA 1996, s. 9(2)). It should include the amount of the deduction, the intervals at which it is to be made and its purpose. This necessitates some definition of wages and it has been held that waiters' tips are not wages, so that the taking of sums by the employers in accordance with an internal company agreement is not a deduction which has to be notified (*Cofone* v *Spaghetti House Ltd* [1980] ICR 155).

In *Coales* v *John Wood & Co.* [1986] IRLR 129, the industrial tribunal held that the right was not infringed because the employee had not *asked* for such a statement. The EAT held that this was incorrect, as the employee had an inherent right to such a statement and did not need to make any request.

If the statement is not produced or there is a dispute over the terms it contains, an industrial tribunal may: (a) declare the particulars which should have been included; and (b) order the employer to make up the unnotified deductions which have been made up to a period of 13 weeks immediately preceding the application (ERA 1996, s. 12). The courts have recognised this to be a penal provision and thus to be construed restrictively. In *Scott* v *Creager* [1979] IRLR 162, the industrial tribunal took into account that the respondent was a dentist with a busy professional practice, short of time to fulfil his statutory duty, that the requirement was then new and that he had to pay the solicitors for the costs of defending the claim.

The following are excluded from entitlement: share fishermen ERA 1996, s. 199(2) and merchant seamen (ERA 1996, s. 199(4)) (see paras 11.5, 11.6).

6 The Duty of Fidelity and Restraint of Trade Clauses

Several duties owed by the employee may be comprised under the general rubric of fidelity. What they have in common is that, without them, the employee's use to the employer would be limited, but their precise character differs according to the status and position of the employee, and is much influenced by principles of equity. There have been significant developments in this field in recent years, impelled by competition by employers to recruit highly skilled employees, especially in the financial services sector. Moreover, the basic obligations are often taken further by express agreement. If there is a fundamental rule, it is honesty in the service of the employer; and its subdivisions relate to:

(a) the duty of the employee to account for secret profits;
(b) the duty to disclose misdeeds;
(c) restraining an employee working in competition with his employer;
(d) injunctions to restrain employees from resigning without due notice;
(e) non-solicitation of customers or clients when an employee leaves;
(f) non-disclosure of employer's confidential information;
(g) ownership of patents.

The area is difficult to expound because few cases proceed to a full trial but rather are disposed of on applications for interlocutory injunctions when the employer need show only, in most cases, that he has an arguable case, and often the judge proceeds to consider only the balance of convenience until trial.

An employee on secondment owes the same duties of obedience and good faith to the employer to whom he is seconded as to his contractual employer (*Macmillan Inc.* v *Bishopsgate Investment Trust plc* [1993] IRLR 793).

6.1 DUTY TO ACCOUNT

The employee must account to his employer for all money and property received during the course of his employment, and can be disciplined in the event of any dishonesty. A blatant example is illicit borrowing from the till (*Sinclair* v *Neighbour* [1967] 2 QB 279). In *Boston Deep Sea Fishing & Ice Co.* v *Ansell* (1888) 39 ChD 339, the principle was taken somewhat further. The defendant, who was managing director of the plaintiff company A, also owned shares in company B, which supplied ice to A, and received a bonus on these shares for all sales gained. Such secret profits were in breach of his duty to account to the plaintiffs and he was held lawfully dismissed. The case might, however, be narrowly distinguished since Ansell was a director and under strict fiduciary duties, as well as an employee (see also *Reading* v *AG* [1951] AC 507). There is also a nascent duty of good faith of the employer towards the employee. The Court of Appeal in *Newns* v *British Airways plc* [1992] IRLR 575, stated that this duty conveys the notion of fair dealing, and if a particular proposal entertained by an employer was a breach of that obligation, it might be that an employee who would be adversely affected thereby could apply to the court for an injunction, although no breach had been made out on the facts of that case.

6.2 DUTY TO DISCLOSE MISDEEDS

In *Healey* v *Société Anonyme Française Rubastic* [1917] 1 KB 946, Avory J said: 'I cannot accept the view that an omission to confess or disclose his own misdoing was in itself a breach of the contract on the part of the plaintiff.' The duty to disclose misconduct was most fully considered in *Sybron Corporation* v *Rochem Ltd* [1983] IRLR 253. At issue was the occupational pension of the chief manager who was discovered after his retirement to have been involved in a directly competing company while still employed. The plaintiff claimed that the pension had been given as a result of a mistake of fact and sought restitution. The Court of Appeal decided that the company was indeed entitled to recover the money. Stephenson LJ distinguished the House of Lords decision in *Bell* v *Lever Brothers* [1932] AC 161 on the grounds that whilst there might be no duty on the employee to disclose *his own* misconduct, he had a duty to report the misdeeds of *others* especially where he was senior enough to realise that what they were doing was wrong and he was responsible for reporting on their activities each month.

The case may be usefully contrasted with *Horcal Ltd* v *Gatland* [1983] IRLR 459. The defendant, the managing director of the plaintiff building contractors, was negotiating to purchase the shares of the company when a Mrs Kingsbury telephoned him asking that work be done on her home. He gave an estimate on the company's notepaper but kept the proceeds of the contract for himself. When the company found this out they sought recovery of £5,000 paid to him in respect of his past services. The Court of Appeal did not consider that the failure to disclose the incident was sufficient to avoid the termination payment, but he was not entitled to his last salary cheque because during that period he had not served the company honestly and faithfully.

6.3 COMPETITION WITH THE EMPLOYER WHILE EMPLOYED BY HIM

The courts are vigilant to protect an employer whose employee acts part-time in competition with him, but on the other hand, they will not prohibit the individual's legitimate spare time activities (see *Mansard Precision Engineering Co. Ltd* v *Taylor* [1978] ICR 44). Lord Greene MR indicated how far the courts would intervene to protect this delicate balance in *Hivac Ltd* v *Park Royal Scientific Instruments Ltd* [1946] Ch 169:

> It would be deplorable if it were laid down that an employee could consistently with his duty to his employer, knowingly deliberately and secretly set himself to do in his spare time something which would inflict great harm on his employer's business.

In the instant case, two weekday employees of the plaintiff company spent their Sundays working on highly specialised tasks for the defendant firm which also manufactured midget valves and was in direct competition with the plaintiff. An injunction was granted against continuing this arrangement, notwithstanding that there was no evidence of actual misuse of confidential information, because their actions infringed the general duty of fidelity. Lord Greene MR and Morton LJ referred to the danger of future transfer of information, and emphasised the secret nature of their work.

In *Sanders v Parry* [1967] 2 All ER 803, a solicitor employed as an assistant by another, made an agreement with an important client of the latter's to work for him, and Havers J restrained this as a breach of the employee's duty of fidelity. There are, however, some contracts of a routine nature in which there is no question of exclusive services being required. Many employees moonlight, i.e. work for one employer in the morning and for another by night, with the full acquiescence of the employers. In *Nova Plastics Ltd v Froggatt* [1982] IRLR 146 an odd-job man was held not to be in breach of contract when he worked for a competitor of his employer in his spare time. (see also *Laughton and Hawley v Bapp Industrial Supplies Ltd* [1986] IRLR 245.

There is no prohibition on preparing to leave, or even setting up a company to compete with the employer after leaving, but there is a prohibition on actual competition while still employed (*Balston Ltd v Headline Filters Ltd* [1987] FSR 330; *Framlington Group plc v Anderson and Others*, unreported, 9 July 1990; *Saatchi and Saatchi v Saatchi and Saatchi and Others*, unreported (ChD), 13 February 1995). In *Adamson v B & L Cleaning Services Ltd* [1995] IRLR 193, competing for a tender against the employer while still employed was held to be in breach of contract.

This doctrine cannot, however, be applied after the contract has terminated (*J.A. Mont (UK) Ltd v Mills* [1993] IRLR 172). At that point there is no continuing duty of good faith, and the fact that the former employee is remunerated during the period of restraint makes no difference.

6.4 INJUNCTIONS TO RESTRAIN AN EMPLOYEE RESIGNING WITHOUT DUE NOTICE

There is a fast growing jurisdiction to grant injunctions to prevent employees taking up employment with another company before their notice periods have expired.

In *Evening Standard Co. v Henderson* [1978] IRLR 64, a senior production manager on the *Evening Standard* was restrained from working for the short-lived London evening newspaper rival, Mr Maxwell's *London Daily News,* after he had purported to resign on less than his contractual period of notice. The court received an undertaking from the plaintiff that it would continue to provide the employee with his full remuneration and other contractual benefits without insisting that he should actually work. The injunction was granted because there was still trust and confidence between employer and employee. The case was distinguished in *Provident Financial Group plc and Whitegates Estate Agency Ltd v Hayward* [1989] IRLR 84: the employee who gave short notice was going to work for a company which did not directly compete with the plaintiff although it was in an associated field. Whether an injunction should be granted in such a case was a matter for the court's discretion, and it was refused on these facts. This was notwithstanding a contractual term that the employer could suspend the employee from performing work on condition that he received full pay and benefit. Whether relief should be granted in a particular case depended on the *detriment* which the employer would suffer if the clause was not enforced by an injunction. There must also be a real risk that the employee would foster the prospects of a rival (see *Marshall v Industrial Systems & Control Ltd* [1992] IRLR 294). The court must examine whether the new employment proposed by the employee would materially and adversely affect the old employer's business. Dillon LJ expressed the fear that 'the practice of long periods of garden leave is obviously capable of abuse'.

In *GFI Group Inc.* v *Eaglestone* [1994] IRLR 119, the contract of employment of an options broker restrained the employee from engaging in any business other than that of the employer during the 20-week period of notice. The court recognised that his customer connection had been expensively created at the employer's expense and that there would be a substantial loss of goodwill if the employee left. Holland J was not, however, prepared to grant an injunction for the whole period sought by the employer since two other employees on shorter notice periods had already left to join the competitor to whom this employee was bound and substantial damage had already been done to the employer's connections. Therefore the order would be for only 13 weeks.

There is no general principle that time spent on garden leave should be credited against the duration of restrictive covenants, but the existence of such a clause may be a factor in determining the validity of a restraint clause, and there may be an exceptional case where a long garden leave period already served by the time that an attempt is made to enforce a restrictive covenant could provide a good reason for the court not to enforce a restraint clause at all (*Crédit Suisse Asset Management Ltd* v *Armstrong* [1996] IRLR 450).

6.5   RESTRAINING THE EX-EMPLOYEE

The duty of fidelity is broken where an employee leaves a job and then uses his ex-employer's resources or confidential information to assist him to set up in competition with him. Thus in *Wessex Dairies Ltd* v *Smith* [1935] 2 KB 80, a milk roundsman who canvassed his employer's customers on his last day to give their business to him thereafter was held to have broken his contract (see *Marshall* v *Industrial Systems & Control,* supra). To copy out a list of customers will almost always be a breach. Building up goodwill with customers which may incidentally be valuable if the employee were to set up a business himself on his own account, is, on the other hand, quite lawful. In order to prevent even the possibility of such occurring, employers should insert express restrictive clauses (para. 6.8). In the absence of such express restrictive covenant there is no implied restriction on soliciting former customers (e.g. *Horcal Ltd* v *Gatland* [1983] IRLR 459).

6.6   CONFIDENTIAL INFORMATION

If an employee uses information confidential to his employer, both he and the recipients of the details may be liable in damages, and restrained by an injunction. Some employees are also at risk of criminal liability for breach of of the Official Secrets Act 1989.

6.6.1   What is confidential information?

The main problem lies in identifying the perimeters of confidential information and distinguishing it from the employee's 'individual skill and experience', acquired in the course of employment, which he may legitimately put to use in future. In *Printers & Finishers Ltd* v *Holloway* [1965] 1 WLR 1 Cross J stated that an injunction would be appropriate 'if the information in question can fairly be regarded as a separate part of the employee's stock of knowledge which a man of ordinary honesty and intelligence would recognise to be the property of his old employer and not his own to do as he liked with' (see also *G.D. Searle & Co. Ltd* v *Celltech Ltd* [1982] FSR 92, *Fraser* v *Thames TV Ltd* [1983] 2 WLR 917).

In *Thomas Marshall (Exports) Ltd* v *Guinle* [1978] ICR 905, at 926 D–G, Megarry V-C developed criteria including whether the owner reasonably believes the release of the information will be injurious to him or advantageous to his rivals and whether the owner reasonably believes that the information is not already public. The information was to be judged in the light of the usage and practices of the industry involved. The secret need not in any way be unique or complicated, and it is no defence for an employee to contend that a third party has already made it public. He held that the following matters were confidential: prices paid, details of manufacturers and suppliers, customer requirements, contract negotiations and details of fast moving lines.

The employee was not enjoined when the information in question was the paper used by the employer (*Worsley* v *Cooper* [1939] 1 All ER 290), but the following have been considered trade secrets and their passing on restrained:

(a)   the correct type of plastic clamp strip designed to hold together the inner and outer walls of a swimming pool (*Cranleigh Precision Engineering Ltd* v *Bryant* [1965] 1 WLR 1293);

(b)   drawings of a machine tool which, although readily available, required the use of specialist know-how (*Saltman Engineering Co.* v *Campbell Engineering Co.* [1963] 2 All ER 413);

(c)   customer lists (e.g. *Roger Bullivant Ltd* v *Ellis* [1987] IRLR 491).

The leading case is now *Faccenda Chicken Ltd* v *Fowler* [1986] IRLR 69, although its scope is controversial. Mr Fowler had been employed by Faccenda Ltd as its sales manager until he resigned along with several other employees, and set up a business competing with the plaintiff selling fresh chickens from refrigerated vehicles. The employees who left had no express restrictive clauses in their contracts, but the plaintiff claimed that they had broken the duty of confidentiality by using its sales information to its disadvantage. Goulding J thought that there were three classes of case to be distinguished:

(a)   Information which because of its trivial character and/or easy accessibility from public sources of information could not be regarded by reasonable people as confidential, such as a published patent specification.

(b)   Information which an employee was to treat as confidential because he was expressly told to do so or because, from its character, it was obviously confidential but which once learned necessarily remained in his head and became part of his own skill and knowledge. As long as his employment continued, he could not otherwise use or disclose such information without breach of contract, but when he left such employment he could use it in competition with his former employer. It could, however, be protected by an express restrictive clause.

(c)   Information so secret that even though it might be learned by heart, it could not be used for the benefit of anyone but the employer.

The information in the instant case, the prices that customers were paying and the routes by which they could be visited, fell into the second category so that an injunction was inappropriate.

Whilst agreeing with the result, the Court of Appeal differed from Goulding J in that they thought that in determining whether any information fell within the implied term of confidentiality, it was necessary to consider all the circumstances of the case and in particular:

(a)   the nature of the employment;
(b)   the nature of the information: it could only be protected if it could be classed as a trade secret or as material which was in all the circumstances of such highly confidential nature as to require the same protection as a trade secret;
(c)   whether the employer impressed upon the employee the confidentiality of the information;
(d)   whether the information could be easily isolated from other information which the employee was free to use or disclose.

Neill LJ gave as examples of truly confidential information the price to be charged for a new model of car or the prices negotiated for various grades of oil in a highly competitive market. Other truly confidential information was at issue in *Johnson & Bloy (Holdings) Ltd* v *Wolstenholme Rink plc and Fallon* [1987] IRLR 499. The plaintiff obtained an injunction to prevent a former director from using or disclosing details of the secret formula it used to manufacture gold ink in its printing process. Even though Mr Fallon could no doubt remember the process, it did not for that reason form part of his ordinary skill and knowledge.

In *Bjorlow Ltd* v *Minter* (1954) 71 RPC 321 at 322, emphasis was placed on the fact that the employee was at once told that the process was secret. Other criteria to be taken into account are that the information is likely to be held to be confidential only in the circumstances that:

(a)   if it were disclosed to a competitor it would be likely to cause real or significant damage to the employer; and
(b)   'the owner must limit the dissemination of it' (*Lansing Linde* v *Kerr* [1991] 1 All ER 251 at 260);
(c)   the confidentiality (or otherwise) of the information must be judged in the light of the particular *trade and industry usage and practice* (*Thomas Marshall* v *Guinle* [1979] Ch 227 at 248e–g);
(d)   there must be a high degree of specificity of the information sought to be restrained (*Ixora Trading Inc.* v *Jones* [1990] FSR 251). This case also warns against use of confidential information cases as a back-door restrictive covenant, or to harass leaving employees (esp. at 261).

6.6.2   Express restraints

In *Faccenda* the Court of Appeal appeared to think that information in the second category that the employee carried in his head could not be protected by a restrictive covenant unless there was a trade secret to protect (but this was doubted in *Balston* v *Headline Filters Ltd* [1987] FSR 330 and *Norbrook Laboratories* v *Smyth*, unreported, 30 September 1986 (Northern Ireland High Court)).

In *Johnson & Bloy (Holdings) Ltd and Johnson & Bloy Ltd* v *Wolstenholme Rink plc and Fallon* [1987] IRLR 499 CA, Parker LJ said that, in so far as it might be thought that Scott J in *Balston* might have appeared to be laying down as a proposition of law that anything which is inevitably in somebody's head when they leave employment is something which they are free to use, that was wrong. There must be a 'sufficiently high degree of confidentiality to amount to a trade secret' (*Lansing Linde Ltd* v *Kerr* [1991] IRLR 80,

[1991] ICR 428). In *Lansing Linde* v *Kerr* Staughton LJ required that the information, to pass as confidential, be used in a trade or business, and secondly that the owner must limit the dissemination of it or at least not encourage or permit widespread publication. It can thus include not only secret formulae for the manufacturers of products but also, in an appropriate case, the names of customers and the goods which they buy.

There is a countervailing obligation on employers not to reveal confidential information about their employees to third parties otherwise than as required by statute. This received expression in *Dalgleish* v *Lothian and Borders Police Board* [1991] IRLR 422, where the employers were held to be under a duty not to disclose details of the contents of staff records to the local authority in respect of 'poll tax' payments.

6.6.3 Springboard injunctions

In *Roger Bullivant Ltd* v *Ellis* [1987] IRLR 491, the Court of Appeal determined that an injunction restraining former employees from entering into contracts with persons whose names and addresses formed part of information gained in breach of the duty of confidence should last only as long as the employees had an unfair advantage arising out of the breach of confidence. The advantage gained by use of the names and addresses could not last for ever. Their Lordships emphasised that an interim injunction should be granted to prevent defendants from obtaining an unjust headstart in or as a springboard for activities detrimental to the provider of the confidential information.

6.6.4 Exceptions

Information, whether confidential or not, may always be revealed by the employee if it discloses 'iniquity or misconduct on the part of his employer'. Thus in *Initial Services Ltd* v *Putterill* [1968] 1 QB 396, a sales manager was held entitled to disclose an agreement to maintain prices which was contrary to Restrictive Trade Practices Act 1965. Ungoed Thomas J has more broadly defined the circumstances when public interest demands disclosure as 'matters carried out or contemplated in breach of the country's security or in breach of law, including statutory duty, fraud or otherwise destructive of the country or its people, including matters medically dangerous to the public' (*Beloff* v *Pressdram Ltd* [1973] 1 All ER 241 at 260; see also *Speed Seal Products Ltd* v *Paddington* [1985] 1 WLR 1327). It is also not a breach of duty to disclose matters of wrongdoing to City regulatory bodies such as FIMBRA, or the Inland Revenue (*Re a Company's Application* [1989] 3 WLR 265) but information may be confidential even though it shows that a crime has been committed (*Francome* v *Mirror Group Newspapers* [1984] 2 All ER 408).

Information ceases to be confidential when it becomes widely known to the public. This was the essence of the 'Spycatcher' decision (*Att Gen* v *The Observer* [1988] 2 WLR 8057).

One of the most effective remedies in confidentiality cases is an *Anton Piller* order, but the courts have indicated that they should be used sparingly in employment cases (*Lock International plc* v *Beswick* [1989] IRLR 481). (See also *PSM International* v *Whitehouse* [1992] IRLR 279.)

6.7 PATENTS

The common law duty of fidelity used to provide the legal basis of the ownership of inventions made by the employee in his employer's time. The courts emphasised that the employer had first call on the employee's time and any designs made during working hours thus belonged to the employer (*British Reinforced Concrete Co. Ltd* v *Lind* (1917) 116 LT 243, *British Syphon Co. Ltd* v *Homewood* [1956] 1 WLR 1190). Often collective agreements and individual bargaining modified its scope and now the Patents Act 1977 covers the field and greatly improves the position of the employee.

Section 39 provides that an invention made by an employee shall between him and his employer be taken to belong to the employer only if:

(a) the invention was made in the course of the normal duties of the employee and the circumstances were such that an invention might reasonably be expected to result from the carrying out of his duty; and

(b) the employee has a special obligation to further the interests of the employer's undertaking because of his duties and particular responsibility arising therefrom; or

(c) although the invention was not made in the normal course of duties it was made in the course of duty specifically assigned to the employee such that an invention would be expected to result.

In all other cases the patent vests in the employee.

In *Reiss Engineering Co. Ltd* v *Harrison* [1985] IRLR 232, Falconer J decided that an employee's normal duties under the Act are those which he is actually employed to carry out. The plaintiff, a manager of a valve department, was not employed to design or invent. He had no special obligation within the statute to further the interests of the employer's undertaking. The extent of the latter depended on the status of the employee and his attendant responsibilities and duties. The plaintiff's invention accordingly belonged to him.

Even where it is lawfully patented by the employer, a worker may apply to a court or the Comptroller of Patents on the grounds that the patent is of 'outstanding benefit' to the employer and for that reason the employee deserves compensation for his effort (s. 40). He is then entitled, by s. 41(1), to a 'fair share having regard to all the circumstances of the benefit which the employer has derived, or may be reasonably expected to derive, from the patent'.

The criteria for 'fair share' are:

(a) the nature of the employee's duties, his remuneration and other advantages from his employer or the invention;

(b) the employee's effort and skill in making the invention;

(c) the effort and skill of any third party involved;

(d) the significance of any contributions of the employer towards the invention (s. 41(4)).

Since the coming into force of the 1977 Act, compensation may be awarded more generally where the employee has assigned to the employer for inadequate return any of the employee's rights in the invention belonging to himself (s. 40). Again, the appropriate compensation is such as will secure for the employee a 'fair share' of the benefit the employer has derived or may reasonably be expected to derive from the patent. The one exception to the above rules is where there is a relevant collective agreement in force concerning the issue, and there is no requirement that this arrangement be more favourable to the employee than statute. On the other hand, an employee may not validly contract out of the rights conferred by the Act.

Where original works are the subject of copyright, s. 11 of the Copyright, Designs and Patents Act 1988 provides that the employer is first owner of it if the maker was employed by him under a contract of service, the work was made in the course of employment, and the employee was employed for the purpose of making such a work. Outside of employment hours, copyright remains in the employee. (See W.A. Copinger and E.P. Skone James, *Copyright*, 13th edn, Sweet & Maxwell, 1991; Registered Designs Act 1949, s. 2(1B); Copyright, Designs and Patents Act 1988, s. 215.)

Employees have a right to see information held on computer under the Data Protection Act 1984 and to be provided with copies of information maintained about themselves. (See also the Access to Medical Reports Act 1988.)

6.8 RESTRAINT OF TRADE CLAUSES

Many employers, especially in the professions, further protect themselves against damaging competition and misuse of confidential information by an express restrictive covenant. A typical situation would be an accountancy practice including a contractual clause that assistant accountants will not work for another practice within five miles during the first two years of leaving. This also facilitates proof of breach of the implied duties already considered, which otherwise is difficult. The general common law rule against restraint of trade operates in this area just as in contracts between vendor and purchaser of a business (*Esso Petroleum Co. Ltd v Harper's Garage (Stourport) Ltd* [1968] AC 269). A covenant in a sale agreement is, however, more likely to be upheld than one in a contract of employment (*Allied Dunbar (Frank Weisinger) Ltd v Frank Weisinger* [1988] IRLR 60; *Systems Reliability Holdings plc v Smith* [1990] IRLR 377). The court would review the covenants of the defendant, who was the managing director of the plaintiff's company and was negotiating the sale of the business, in a different light to those of a mere employee (*Alliance Paper Group plc v Prestwich* [1996] IRLR 25). The restraint of trade doctrine may also apply to a clause prohibiting a self-employed financial consultant from receiving commission after termination of his agency agreement if he competed with his employer within one year (*Marshall v NM Financial Management Ltd* [1996] IRLR 20). If the covenant is itself an unreasonable restraint of trade, the court will not approve a refusal of commission on that basis.

In employment cases, the court attempts to hold the ring between the interest of the employee to be employed in the future as he wishes, and the employer's interest to preserve his business from disclosures by an ex-employee. Thus restrictive clauses must go no further than is reasonable for the protection of the employer's business interests and serve the public interest. Otherwise, as the House of Lords put it, 'the employee is entitled to use to the full any personal skill or experience even if this has been acquired in the service of his employer. . .' (*Stenhouse Australia Ltd v Phillips* [1974] AC 391 at 400D; see also *Cantor Fitzgerald (UK) Ltd v Wallace* [1992] IRLR 215). The court should review the covenants of the defendant, who was the managing director of the plaintiff company and was negotiating the sale of the business, in a different light to those of a mere employee (*Alliance Paper Group plc v Prestwich*, supra).

To be upheld by the courts a restrictive covenant must, in most cases, prevent the employee from actually soliciting former customers, rather than stopping the employee from working at all. Most generally Stephenson LJ concluded in *Spafax Ltd v Harrison* [1980] IRLR 442, para. 25:

An employer is entitled to take and enforce promises from an employee which the employer can prove are reasonably necessary to protect him, the employer, his trade connection, trade interests and goodwill, not from competition by the employee if he leaves his employment, or from his then using the skill and knowledge with which his employment had equipped him to compete, but from his then using his personal knowledge of his employer's customers or his personal influence over them, or his knowledge of his employer's trade secrets, or advantages acquired from his employment, to his employer's disadvantage.

Moreover, where the true skills and art of a job lie in the make-up of the person performing it (the employee's personality, temperament and ability to get on with people) the employer will not be able to establish a proprietary right by way of customer connections built up during the course of employment where this is the result of the personal qualities of the employee (*Cantor Fitzgerald (UK) Ltd* v *Wallace* [1992] IRLR 215, although the scope of this exception is open to considerable doubt).

6.8.1   Area of restraint

In reviewing what follows, it should be emphasised that each case depends on its own facts and one case should not be treated as decisive of another even though the terms of the covenant are similar (*Dairy Crest Ltd* v *Pigott* [1989] ICR 92).

The area of restraint placed on the employee must be reasonable; a world-wide restraint may be valid only where the employer's business was of a similar extent, as in the leading case of *Nordenfelt* v *Maxim Nordenfelt Guns and Ammunition Ltd* [1894] AC 535. Whether covenants against taking employment in a particular area are valid depends on the size of the area and its relationship to the employer's connections (*Gledhow Autoparts Ltd* v *Delaney* [1965] 1 WLR 1366, *T. Lucas & Co.* v *Mitchell* [1972] 3 All ER 689). In *Spencer* v *Marchington* [1988] IRLR 392, for example, a covenant restraining a former employee from engaging in an employment agency business within a radius of 25 miles from her previous employer's premises was held to be too wide (see also *Rex Stewart Jefferies Parker Ginsberg Ltd* v *Parker* [1988] IRLR 483).

The relevant scope of such clauses can be illustrated by contrasting the Court of Appeal decisions in *Greer* v *Sketchley Ltd* [1979] IRLR 445 and *Littlewoods Organisation Ltd* v *Harris* [1977] 1 WLR 1472. In *Greer,* the plaintiff had been employed for 20 years by the defendants whose branches covered the Midlands and London areas, rising ultimately to become a director of their dry cleaning business with special responsibility for the Midlands. His contract provided that he must not within 12 months of its termination directly or indirectly engage in the United Kingdom in any similar business but this was held too wide since he had only had responsibility for a part of that area. On the other hand, in the *Littlewoods* case, a nationwide restrictive covenant was held to be legal since it was the only way to protect the respondent's mail order business when the ex-employee went to work for their direct national competitor, Great Universal Stores Ltd. (See *Marley Tile Co. Ltd* v *Johnson* [1982] IRLR 75; *G. W. Plowman & Son Ltd* v *Ash* [1964] 1 WLR 568, sales representative; *S.W. Strange Ltd* v *Mann* [1965] 1 WLR 629, credit bookmaker.)

The following have been struck down as unreasonable restraints:

(a)   A covenant not to engage in a similar business in any part of the UK when the company manufactured travelling cranes, pulley blocks and other lifting machinery (*Herbert Morris and Co. Ltd* v *Saxelby* [1916] 1 AC 688).

(b)   A covenant 'not to seek employment with any of our competitors in the PVC calendering field for at least one year after leaving our employ' since:

(i)   it covered the whole world; and

(ii)   the plaintiffs only required protection against competition in PVC calendered sheeting for adhesive tape. Pearson LJ said that by the width of the restraint, 'he would be barred from making use of his skill and aptitude and general knowledge in that field, and that would be detrimental both to his interests and to the public interest' (*Commercial Plastics Ltd v Vincent* [1965] 1 QB 623; cf. *Empire Meat Co. Ltd v Patrick* [1939] 2 All ER 85, butchers; on solicitors see *Fitch v Dewes* [1921] 2 AC 158, *Oswald Hickson Collier & Co. v Carter-Ruck* [1984] 2 WLR 847, *Edwards v Worboys* [1984] 2 WLR 850, *Bridge v Deacons* [1984] 2 WLR 837).

(c)   A covenant which prevented former employees of an employment agency for six months from engaging in the trade or business of an employment agency within a radius of one kilometre of the employer's branch where he or she had previously worked (*Office Angels Ltd v Rainer-Thomas & O'Connor* [1991] IRLR 214). This would do little to protect the employer's connections with its clients since much of the work was conducted by telephone and did not depend on physical proximity. It thus amounted simply to a covenant against competition. In the instant case, the connection which the employer was entitled to protect was its connection with client firms and with the pool of workers available for temporary employment. It would have been adequate for the employer to have a covenant preventing the employees soliciting or dealing with clients with whom they dealt during their employment.

(d)   On the other hand, a covenant of two miles imposed on a doctor was upheld by the Court of Appeal in *Kerr v Morris, The Times,* 21 May 1986.

6.8.2   The construction of covenants

The courts will consider the nature of the market in which the employee was engaged. The narrower and more specialist the market, the more likely it is that a non-dealing covenant will be upheld, given that clients will in those circumstances naturally gravitate to the ex-employee who opens a new, competing company in such a case (*London and Solent Ltd v Brooks, Daily Telegraph,* 27 October 1988; see also *Bennett v Bennett* [1952] 1 KB 249 at 260).

Lord Denning MR said that the courts will not strain to hold a restraint invalid; if it is reasonable in concept, the courts will construe it in a reasonable manner (see *Marion White Ltd v Francis* [1972] 3 All ER 22), and this led in some cases to a narrow reading of restrictive clauses. Thus in *Home Counties Dairies Ltd v Shilton* [1970] 1 WLR 526, an agreement not 'to serve or sell milk or dairy produce' was limited to the defendant's former employment as a milkman. Courts should not too diligently strive to find within restrictive covenants *ex facie* too wide implicit limitations such as would justify their imposition (*J.A. Mont (UK) Ltd v Mills* [1993] IRLR 172).

It clearly is not the role of the courts to correct errors or supply omissions in restrictive covenants (*WAC Ltd v Whillock* [1990] IRLR 22). Thus where a person was restrained from personally carrying on business in competition with the ex-employing company but there was no restriction on his right to be a director or shareholder of another company which carried on such business, the court would not enforce the covenant as though it did include the latter restriction.

6.8.3 Severance

The courts may also sever a part of the restraint and uphold only the remaining part, but only if 'the severed parts are independent of one another and can be severed without the severance affecting the meaning of the part remaining '(Lord Sterndale in *Attwood* v *Lamont* [1920] 3 KB 571; see also *Putsman* v *Taylor* [1920] 3 KB 637, *Rex Stewart Jeffries Parker Ginsberg Ltd* v *Parker* [1988] IRLR 483).

In *Sadler* v *Imperial Life of Canada Ltd* [1988] IRLR 388, the court held that severance would be permitted if three conditions were satisfied: (i) the unenforceable provision was capable of being removed without the necessity of adding to or modifying the wording of what remained; (ii) the remaining terms continued to be supported by adequate consideration; (iii) the removal of the unenforceable provision did not so change the character of the contract that it became 'not the sort of contract that the parties entered into at all'. See also *Business Seating (Renovations) Ltd* v *Broad* [1989] ICR 729; *Marshall* v *NM Financial Management Ltd* [1996] IRLR 20.

6.8.4 Restraint in the public interest

The restraint must generally be in the public interest, which effectively depends on the exercise of the judge's discretion in each case. Slade J in *Greig* v *Insole* [1978] 3 All ER 449 thus held that a ban by the Test and County Cricket Board on cricketers who played in a rival series organised in Australia by Kerry Packer, could not be enforced because its benefits at most were speculative and would deprive the public of watching first class cricket players. For another example from an area other than employment, see *Watson* v *Prager* [1991] ICR 603 on restrictions imposed on licensed boxers.

It was also on this ground that in *Wyatt* v *Kreglinger and Ferneau* [1933] 1 KB 793, the Court of Appeal decided that a pension agreement was void because of a condition that the defendant should not again take a job in the wool trade (see also *Bull* v *Pitney-Bowes Ltd* [1967] 1 WLR 273). Lord Atkinson said in *Herbert Morris* v *Saxelby* [1916] 1 AC 688 at 699: 'It is in the public interest that a man should be free to exercise his skill and experience to the best advantage for the benefit of himself and of all others who desire to employ him.'

6.8.5 Repudiatory breaches

(a)   An employer who has breached the employee's contract, perhaps by failing to give proper notice of termination, or, it seems in breach of a procedural provision in the contract (*Geo Moore & Co. Ltd* v *Menzies* (1989) 386 IRLIB 21) is not able to enforce a restraint clause (*General Billposting Co. Ltd* v *Atkinson* [1909] AC 118; *Briggs* v *Oates* [1990] IRLR 472, [1990] ICR 473, in the case of premature termination by reason of a change in partners in a solicitors' firm).

(b)   The same applies when an employee is given pay in lieu of notice when there is no provision in his contract that he must accept the same as opposed to being given the opportunity to work out his notice (*Rex Stewart Jeffries Parker Ginsberg Ltd* v *Parker* [1988] IRLR 483.

(c)   A clause is often inserted to the effect that the parties consider the clause as drawn to be reasonable, but if the court does not so find it reasonable the parties agree that it be modified so as to render it enforceable. This clause has not been tested in a reported case as part of the *ratio* of a decision, but in *Systems Reliability Holdings plc* v *Smith* [1990]

IRLR 377, Harman J doubted the willingness of the courts to enforce such a clause. This is consistent with the general principle that the court will not draft a clause for the parties (*Davies* v *Davies* (1887) 36 Ch D 357).

(d)   In *Living Design (Home Improvements) Ltd* v *Davidson* [1994] IRLR 69 the Court of Session had occasion to consider a clause commonly found in restrictive covenants that 'In the event that any such restriction should be found to be void but would be valid if some part thereof could be deleted or the period or area of application reduced, such restriction shall apply with such modification as may be necessary to make it valid and effective'. Lord Coulsfield held that this did not permit the rewriting of a covenant which was otherwise too wide to be valid. Pursuant to that clause there could be severance only on orthodox principles, and even then only where what was struck out was of trivial importance or technical and not part of the main import or substance of the provision. Further, the court held that a covenant which was designed to operate whether or not the contract was lawfully terminated was invalid even if in the particular case the contract was lawfully terminated. The law was thrown into some disarray by the decision in *D* v *M* [1996] IRLR 291, to the effect that a clause was invalid in so far as it purported to apply after termination 'for whatever reason whatsoever'.

This was itself overruled by the Court of Appeal in *Rock Refrigeration Ltd* v *Jones* [1996] IRLR 675, where Phillips LJ also suggested that *General Billposting* itself might be ripe for reconsideration.

6.8.6   Restraint on solicitation of employees

A restraint on solicitation of employees will be enforceable if reasonable within the general doctrine of restraint of trade (*Kores Manufacturing Ltd* v *Kolok Manufacturing Ltd* [1959] 1 Ch 108; *Cantor Fitzgerald (UK) Ltd* v *Wallace* [1992] IRLR 215; *Ingham* v *ABC Contract Services Ltd*, unreported, 12 November 1993, CA; *Alliance Paper Group plc* v *Prestwich* [1996] IRLR 25.

6.8.7   Injunctive relief

The normal remedy for restraining breaches of a restrictive covenant is an injunction, but as usual a court will not grant an injunction where this is in effect an order for specific performance (*Whitwood Chemical Co.* v *Hardman* [1891] 2 Ch 416, see para. 12.5.1).

The Court of Appeal in *Lawrence David Ltd* v *Ashton* [1989] IRLR 22 decided that the general test in *American Cyanamid* applies to interlocutory injunctions in restraint of trade cases so that the question of an injunction should normally be decided solely on the basis of whether the plaintiff has a serious issue to be tried, and then whether the balance of convenience or justice is in favour of the grant of an interlocutory order. Only if the case could not be brought to trial before the expiry of the covenant should the exception to *American Cyanamid* be adopted and the court consider the likelihood of success (e.g. *Lansing Linde Ltd* v *Kerr* [1991] IRLR 80, [1991] IRLR 428). Normally a speedy trial should be ordered in such cases (on the general application of *American Cyanamid*, see para. 21.14.2).

In *John Michael Design plc* v *Cooke* [1987] ICR 445, the Court of Appeal decided that once the court had decided that a covenant was prima facie binding, it was not then proper to pick and choose the clients named in that covenant to which the injunction should or should not relate and it was proper to restrain an ex-employee from doing business with an ex-customer of his employer even though that customer had made it plain that he would not deal again with the ex-employer (see, on the scope of injunctions, *PSM International plc* v *Whitehouse* [1992] IRLR 279; see *Warren* v *Mendy* [1989] ICR 525 and generally Mehigen and Griffiths, *Restraint of Trade and Business Secrets: Law and Practice*, Longman, 1992, also Brearley and Bloch, *Employment Covenants and Confidential Information*, Butterworths, 1993).

6.8.8 Repayment clauses

Novel points arose in *Strathclyde Regional Council* v *Neil* [1984] IRLR 11, where the employee raised a series of objections to a contractual provision that she had to return to the employer for at least two years after a paid training leave. If she did not do so she would have to 'refund . . . an amount proportionate to the unexpired portion of the contracted minimum period of service'. The Scottish Court rejected each objection in turn:

(a)   This was not an unlawful restrictive clause since the employee was not restrained from using her skills after leaving the Council.

(b)   There was no restraint on her liberty beyond that normally involved in a contract of service.

(c)   There was no evidence of such compulsion as would invalidate her contractual consent.

(d)   The terms of repayment were not a penalty.

The refusal to pay commission to an ex-employee or agent because of his new employer or principal may be invalid by reason of the restraint of trade doctrine (*Wyatt* v *Kreglinger and Fernau* [1933] 1 KB 793).

7 Equal Pay

It is desirable that the Sex Discrimination Act 1975 and the Equal Pay Act 1970 should be construed and applied in harmony as together they constitute a single code.

(Phillips J in *McCarthys Ltd* v *Smith* [1978] ICR 500.)

7.1 EQUAL PAY: INTRODUCTION

The aim of the Equal Pay Act 1970, as stated in its preamble, is to 'prevent discrimination as regards terms and conditions of employment between men and women'. It is mainly intended to eliminate the clearly lower pay which has been given to women for centuries, and is the first legal embodiment of the equal pay principle which became TUC policy in 1888, was the subject of a Royal Commission in 1944–46, and has been ILO policy for decades. In the 1970s this became more pressing; nearly 40 per cent of the labour force was female and more than half the women between the ages of 16 and 59 were at work.

The statute also represents Britain's enactment of the directly enforceable obligation contained in Article 119 of the Treaty of Rome, equal pay for equal work. The English courts have on several occasions referred cases to the European Court of Justice for interpretation of the principle in the European legislation. These aspects will be dealt with later in this chapter (para. 7.7.1) although the dominance of European law in the area of equal pay and sex discrimination is reflected by the fact that the early part of this chapter contains extensive reference to cases decided by the European Court of Justice or by English courts and tribunals implementing principles laid down by the European Court. Closely allied with this principle are various maternity rights for pregnant employees (Chapter 9).

The Equal Pay Act was brought into force on 29 December 1975 (giving employers a five-year transitional period), having already been amended by the Sex Discrimination Act 1975. Together these two statutes are intended to form one code (see e.g. *Shields* v *E. Coomes (Holdings) Ltd* [1978] ICR 1159, *Jenkins* v *Kingsgate (Clothing Productions) Ltd (No. 2)* [1981] IRLR 388). The borderline between the two Acts is, however, a potent cause of confusion and some injustice, and in many respects it would have been more efficient to have but one enactment (see also *Oliver* v *J.P. Malnick & Co. (No. 2)* [1984] ICR 458).

Promotion, transfer and non-contractual benefits come within the Sex Discrimination Act while the Equal Pay Act relates solely to what is gained by way of contract, although this extends beyond pay mentioned in its title to such elements as bonuses, concessionary coal and mortgage repayment allowances (see *NCB* v *Sherwin* [1978] ICR 700, and *Sun Alliance* v *Dudman* [1978] IRLR 169). The terms of the earlier statute are somewhat narrower than the Sex Discrimination Act since the Equal Pay Act does not prohibit discrimination against married persons, or indirect discrimination. Although primarily introduced to promote equality for women, both Acts are open to applicants of either sex. For the sake of convenience, the applicant will be here assumed to be female.

The Equal Pay Act was amended from 1 January 1984 by the Equal Pay (Amendment) Regulations 1983 (SI 1983 No. 1794). They purport to implement in English law the European Communities Directive 75/117 on Equal Pay by enabling an employee to insist that a job evaluation study be carried out. The Regulations were introduced after the European Court of Justice ruled that the 1970 Act did not satisfy the requirement that 'the principle of equal pay for men and women . . . means for the same work and for work to which equal value is attributed, the elimination of all discrimination on grounds of sex with regard to all aspects and conditions of remuneration' (*Commission of the European Communities* v *United Kingdom* [1984] IRLR 29). The important procedural consequences of the Regulations are now found in Sch. 2 to the Industrial Tribunals Rules of Procedure 1993, SI No. 2687, entitled Complementary Rules (on which see Bowers, Brown and Mead, *Industrial Tribunal Practice and Procedure,* FT Law & Tax, 1996). The Social Security Act 1989 introduces the principle of equal treatment between men and women in occupational pension schemes (see para. 8.2.9).

The scope of the Equal Pay Act extends not only to employees but also to all who are 'employed under a contract of apprenticeship or a contract personally to execute any work or labour' (s. 1(6)(a)), and specifically covers crown service (s. 1(8)). There is no qualifying period or minimum number of hours. The Act and Regulations are complex, now surrounded by much difficult case law, and operate on four levels, which will be considered in turn:

(a)   the implication of an 'equality clause' into the contract of employment;
(b)   the application of job evaluation studies;
(c)   equal value claims; and
(d)   the amendment of discriminatory collective agreements.

7.2   THE EQUALITY CLAUSE AND LIKE WORK

By s. 1(1) of the Equal Pay Act, an 'equality clause' is implied into the contract of every woman who is employed on 'like work' with a man, at the same establishment, or at an establishment where similar terms and conditions are applied. This means that if any aspect of the woman's conditions is or becomes less favourable to the woman than a term of a similar kind in the man's contract, the term is modified so as to be as favourable; if there is no corresponding term, the contract is deemed to include one. Thus, if men have a right to four weeks' holiday and women to three, and the women are found to be engaged on like work, their entitlement must be increased to four. If women have no right to holidays at all, a term to that effect must be inserted at once.

The defining concept of 'like work' is stated by s. 1(4) as where 'her work and theirs (the men) is of the same or a broadly similar nature, and the difference (if any) between the things she does and the things they do are not of practical importance in relation to the terms and conditions of employment'.

7.2.1   The same establishment

The comparators must be employed at the same establishment or at an establishment where common terms or conditions are observed either generally or for employees of the relevant class (s. 1(6)). The word 'establishment' has caused problems of definition here as in redundancy procedures (para. 15.4). (See *Rice* v *Scottish Legal Life Assurance Society* [1976] IRLR 330.)

Example Crest Department Stores Ltd has two branches. All the check out assistants at Branch A are women but at Branch B some are male — the males receive a higher rate of pay: a women at Branch A may compare herself to a man at Branch B if, but only if, the same general terms, possibly because of a collective agreement, apply to both places.

It is thus not a fatal objection to the bringing of an equal pay claim that none of the comparators was employed at the same establishment as the applicant. Those employed at other establishments must, however, be engaged on the same 'terms and conditions of service' or broadly similar terms as the comparator pursuant to s. 1(6) of the Act, and this includes contractual obligations such as hours worked and length of holidays. In *Leverton* v *Clwyd CC* [1989] IRLR 28, the House of Lords determined that a nursery nurse was engaged on similar terms to 11 male clerical officers notwithstanding that their hours and holidays were different. It was a question of fact whether there were common terms and conditions at two establishments. Terms covered by the same collective agreement are the paradigm but not the only case. (See also *Lawson* v *Britfish Ltd* [1987] ICR 726.) The applicant in *Leverton* failed in her claim, however, because her hourly rate was not significantly different to the man's and the tribunal could thus infer that the difference in annual salary was 'genuinely due to a material factor which was not the difference of sex' under s. 1(3) of the Equal Pay Act 1970 (see para. 7.2.4).

The definition of 'common terms and conditions' within s. 1(6) of the Act, has recently engaged the attention of the House of Lords. In *British Coal Corporation* v *Smith* [1996] IRLR 404, canteen workers employed by British Coal who were predominantly women sought to compare their pay and conditions with surface mineworkers who were men. They were faced by the defence that they were not employed in the same employment. The House of Lords upheld the commonsense approach taken by the industrial tribunal: 'common terms and conditions' within s. 1(6) means terms and conditions which are substantially comparable on a broad basis, rather than the same terms and conditions subject only to differences which are *de minimis*. The terms must be sufficiently similar for a fair comparison. There was sufficient material for the industrial tribunal to determine that the facts satisfied the statutory test since the two groups of employees were both governed by national agreements even though there were local variations relating to an incentive bonus and concessionary coal.

7.2.2 The comparator

The applicant for equal pay may normally choose with whom she is to be compared for the purposes of like work (*Ainsworth* v *Glass Tubes and Components Ltd* [1977] IRLR 74. The Northern Ireland Court of Appeal in *McPherson* v *Rathgael Centre for Children and Young People and Northern Ireland Office (Training Schools Branch)* [1991] IRLR 206, however, left open the important question whether an applicant could select an anomalous comparator (see also *Dance* v *Dorothy Perkins* [1978] ICR 760). The search for a precise comparator proved very difficult in those areas where women are generally underpaid, and for which the statute was most needed. In particular, employment in many offices, textile, catering and retail businesses is the preserve of women, so that no man is employed on like work. This was the rationale for the Equal Pay (Amendment) Regulations 1983 which introduced the equal value claim.

This problem also led to women comparing their wages with a man who was no longer employed at the time of a tribunal application, and this important issue was resolved eventually by the European Court of Justice in *McCarthys Ltd* v *Smith* [1980] IRLR 210. The woman applicant was a stockroom manageress who sought to compare her wages with her predecessor in the post. The Court of Appeal interpreted restrictively the English statute: its use of the present tense in their view precluded the applicant's desired comparison. The European Court, however, decided that the applicant *could* compare herself with the predecessor under the Treaty of Rome. It stated that 'the concept (of equal pay) . . . is not exclusively concerned with the nature of the service in question and may not be restricted by requirements of contemporaneity'. However, it fell short of permitting comparison with a hypothetical male, as is possible under the Sex Discrimination Act, since this would be to extend the principle to 'indirect and disguised discrimination' and the leading European case of *Defrenne* v *Sabena* [1976] 2 CMLR 98, had stated that this did not come within the directly applicable aspects of Article 119. It is also possible to compare with a successor (*Diocese of Hallam Trustee* v *Connaughton* [1996] IRLR 505).

Article 119 is wider than the Equal Pay Act 1970, s. 1(6) in that it allows a comparison where the applicant and her comparator(s) are employed 'in the same establishment or service, where private or public' as *Defrenne* v *Sabena* [1976] ECR 455 held. Thus, in *Scullard* v *Knowles* [1996] ICR 399, the applicant, Mrs Scullard, was employed by the Southern Regional Council for Education and Training ('SCRET') as manager and director of a further education unit. There were 12 such units, and all the other managers were men and received higher salaries. The units were supported and funded by the Training and Education Directorate (TEED) of the Department of Employment. The Training and Education Directorate monitored the performance of the contract in respect of each unit but did not employ any of the unit managers. The industrial tribunal dismissed Mrs Scullard's claim under the Equal Pay Act 1970 on the basis that neither SCRET nor the other regional councils were companies within the meaning of s. 1(6) and could not therefore be 'associate companies'. The EAT overturned this decision on the basis that Article 119 was not confined to employment in undertakings which had a particular legal form such as a limited company. The crucial question was indeed whether Mrs Scullard and the unit managers of the other Councils were employed 'in the same same establishment or service'. In so far as this is a wider class of comparators, s. 1(6) 'is displaced and must yield to the paramount force of Article 119'. The industrial tribunal would have to consider upon remission the extent to which Regional Councils were directly or indirectly controlled by TEED as a third party, the extent and nature of control and whether they constituted the same establishment or service.

7.2.3   What is 'like work'

The definition of 'like work' is generally a matter of degree (e.g. *Durrant* v *North Yorkshire AHA* [1979] IRLR 401), and it was suggested in early cases, such as *Capper Pass Ltd* v *Lawton* [1976] IRLR 366, that the words should be interpreted broadly in order to make the Act workable. Industrial tribunals were advised not to undertake too minute an examination, or be constrained to find work to be dissimilar because of insubstantial differences. Thus, there was like work between a female cook who made 10 to 20 lunches for directors in their dining room, and two assistant male chefs who provided rather more meals in the works canteen. The crucial point was that the basic processes were the same. In *Thomas* v *National Coal Board* [1987] ICR 757, the Employment Appeal Tribunal held that women canteen assistants could not claim to be on 'like work' with a male canteen worker who worked permanently at night and alone. The tribunal had decided that the added responsibility of night work was a difference of practical importance, and the EAT would not interfere with that finding of fact. The Court of Appeal gave general guidance in *Shields* v *E. Coomes (Holdings) Ltd* [1978] IRLR 263, where the applicant was employed as a counterhand in the respondent's betting shop. She was paid 62p per hour, while the men received £1.06, but the employers alleged that there was a difference in duties which justified the large variation in pay, for by contract the men were expected to help in case of trouble. This was not enough. The industrial tribunal should first ask whether the work was the same or broadly similar, then, using its industrial experience, examine the nature and extent of any differences, and especial emphasis should be placed on the frequency or otherwise with which differences occurred in practice. In fact, there was no evidence here that a man ever had to deal with a disturbance or incidents of violence, and every indication that the women had their own ways of dealing with difficult customers. Indeed, Lord Denning said (at p. 267): 'He may have been a small nervous man who would not say "boo to a goose". She may have been as fierce and formidable as a battle axe.'

In *British Leyland Ltd* v *Powell* [1978] IRLR 57, the EAT formulated the proper test as 'whether the two employments would have been placed into the same category on an evaluation exercise', and Phillips J took a similar approach in the complex case of *Electrolux Ltd* v *Hutchinson* [1976] IRLR 410. Men and women worked on the same track in the manufacture of refrigerators and freezers, but while all the men were paid on grade 10 rates, 599 out of the 600 women received rather lower wages in class 01. The company argued that the men had additional contractual obligations: they had to transfer to totally different tasks on demand, and work overtime as and when required. The EAT focused on how frequently the men in fact *did* other work; how often they were required to work on Sunday; and what kind of work they did in these unsocial hours. They came to the conclusion that in reality the work was like work. In *Eaton Ltd* v *Nuttall* [1977] IRLR 71, however, a male production scheduler handling 1,200 items worth between £5 and £1,000 each and a women scheduler handling 2,400 items below £2.50 were not engaged on broadly similar work — for an error on the part of the man would be of much greater consequence. Handling substantial sums of money may prevent work being like, as may involvement on heavier work.

The following have been held insufficient to make two jobs dissimilar for the purposes of 'like work':

(a) that the work is performed at different times or in different places although this may constitute a genuine material difference (para. 7.2.4) (*Dugdale* v *Kraft Foods Ltd* [1977] 1 All ER 454);

(b) that two canteen ladies served breakfast to patrons at their tables, while the comparator male did not (*NCB* v *Sherwin & Spruce* [1978] IRLR 122);

(c) that a male driver sometimes drove outside the precincts of the appellant's factory whereas the female applicant did not.

Difference in responsibility may be sufficient (*De Brito* v *Standard Chartered Bank Ltd* [1978] ICR 650, *Waddington* v *Leicester Council for Voluntary Service* [1977] 2 All ER 633).

7.2.4   'Genuine material difference'

Even if the comparative job is like work, the employer has a defence if he can prove that a pay differential was 'due to a genuine material difference (other than sex) between her case and his' (s. 1(3)). This demonstrates that the Act is aimed at differences in terms due to sex alone, for it would be a strange result if there was no possibility of different wages to recognise that a man (although employed on a similar job) in fact deserved more than the woman because of personal qualities or qualifications. Thus, while the like work concept focuses on the make up of the job, the defence of genuine material difference looks to the person filling it. The so-called 'personal equation', as Lawton LJ put it in *Clay Cross (Quarry Services) Ltd* v *Fletcher* [1979] ICR 1, at 9:

> . . . embraces what appertains to her in her job, such as the qualifications she brought to it, the length of time she has been in it, the skill she has acquired, the responsibilities she has undertaken, and where and under what conditions she has to do it.

The courts ask two basic questions:

(a)   Has the employer shown that any variation was genuinely due to (i.e. caused by) a material difference between the two?

(b)   Is that material difference genuinely owing to a reason other than sex?

The burden of proof throughout rests on the employer (*Byrne* v *Financial Times Ltd* [1991] IRLR 417). At first it was thought that a heavier burden than usually demanded in civil cases here rested on the employer, but this heresy was scotched in *National Vulcan Engineering Insurance Group Ltd* v *Wade* [1978] IRLR 225. It is not, however, enough that the employers did not intend to discriminate (*Jenkins* v *Kingsgate Ltd (No. 2)* [1981] IRLR 388).

The cause must *justify* the disparate impact to qualify under this rubric. In *Barber* v *NCR (Manufacturing) Ltd* [1993] ICR 95, the evidence showed the historical process by which the difference in hourly rates between two groups had been arrived at but did not show any objective factor which justified or even supported the result which had been produced, and thus did not suffice as a genuine material difference.

The Court of Appeal placed a vital restriction on the concept of genuine material difference in *Clay Cross (Quarry Services)* v *Fletcher* (supra). The applicant, Mrs Fletcher, was a clerk earning £35 per week, but since the comparator male had received £43 per week in his existing job, Clay Cross Ltd paid him more in order to attract his services. They claimed the previous pay constituted a genuine material difference, but the Lord Justices held that only 'the personal equation' might justify such discrimination, since the subsection went on to say that the distinction was 'between her case and his'. Here extrinsic market forces were in effect determining the rate for the job, and Lord Denning remarked that, 'an employer cannot avoid his obligations under the Act by saying: "I paid him more because he asked for more", or "I paid her less because she was willing to come for less".' To do so would render the statute virtually impotent. He went on: 'These are the very reasons why there was unequal pay before the statute.' This decision does not apply where comparisons are made between employees working at different times (*Albion Shipping* v *Arnold* [1981] IRLR 525). Then the economic circumstances of the business are relevant.

The *Fletcher* case was distinguished on narrow grounds, however, in *Rainey* v *Greater Glasgow Health Board Eastern District* [1985] IRLR 414 and its authority should no longer be relied on. When a prosthetic fitting service was set up within the Scottish NHS, it was agreed that the prosthetists would be paid on the Medical Physics and Technicians pay scale, but in order to attract a sufficient number of experienced prosthetists from the private sector, they were offered the same pay as they had been receiving. Further, a different structure of increase was adopted. A woman complained that a man who had joined from the private sector was paid £2,790 more than she was for the same work. The Court of Session, with one dissentient, thought that the circumstances of the higher pay were sufficiently 'personal' to fall within s. 1(3), and were similar to the 'red circle' cases (para. 7.2.4.2). The circumstances in which the man attained the higher pay were curious, exceptional and unique. The question whether it was material was a matter for the industrial tribunal. The House of Lords agreed in the result ([1986] 3 WLR 1017). Lord Keith of Kinkel considered that the decision of the Court of Appeal in *Fletcher* was 'unduly restrictive of the proper interpretation of s. 1(3)'. The difference had to be 'material', which His Lordship would construe as meaning 'significant and relevant'. This required consideration of all the circumstances of the case. In the light of the decision of the ECJ in *Bilka-Kaufhaus GmBH v Karin Weber von Hartz* [1986] IRLR 317, it was not necessary to construe s. 1(3) as conferring greater rights on a worker than does Article 119 of the Treaty of Rome. Thus 'the relevant difference for purposes of s. 1(3) may relate to circumstances other than the personal qualifications or merits of the male and female workers who are the subject of comparison'. In *Rainey* the difference between the case of the appellant and the comparator was that 'the former is a person who entered the National Health Service . . . directly while the latter is a person who entered it from employment with a private contractor. The fact that one is a woman and the other a man is an accident' (at p. 1027A). (See also *Davies* v *McCartneys* [1989] IRLR 439.)

This defence was satisfied in *Leverton* v *Clwyd County Council* [1989] IRLR 28 (see para. 7.2.1) by the fact that Mrs Leverton worked a 32½ hour week and had school holidays whereas her comparator worked a 37-hour week and had only 20 days' annual holiday entitlement. Lord Bridge said that 'where a man and a woman whose regular annual working hours . . . can be translated into a national hourly rate which yields no significant difference it is surely a legitimate if not a necessary inference that the difference in their annual salaries is both due to and justified by the difference in hours they work in the course of a year and has nothing to do with the difference in sex'.

The EAT held in *Tyldesley* v *TML Plastics Ltd* [1996] ICR 356, that objective justification is required under s. 1(3) only where there is a disparate impact such that a factor relied on was one which affected a considerably higher proportion of women than men. In *Tyldesley* itself, the factor distinguishing the pay of men and women, namely experience of total quality management, did not require such objective justification. The factor relied upon must either have caused the difference or have been a sufficient influence upon that difference to be significant and relevant. The EAT said (at 362g) that 'even if a differential is explained by a careless mistake which could not possibly be objectively justified that would amount to a defence under s. 1(3) and for the purpose of Article 119 provided the tribunal is satisfied that mistake was either the sole reason for it or sufficient influence to be significant or relevant. If a genuine mistake suffices so must a genuine perception whether reasonable or not about the need to engage an individual with particular experience, commitment and skills' (see also *Yorkshire Blood Transfusion Service* v *Plaskitt* [1994] ICR 74 and *Strathclyde Regional Council* v *Wallace* [1996] IRLR 670).

There is no right to require further and better particulars of the part of pay which relates to each factor (*Byrne* v *Financial Times Ltd*, supra).

There are several distinct 'differences' which the courts have considered on many occasions. Greater length of service is as clearly a material difference (*Capper Pass* v *Lawton* [1977] ICR 83), as working at different times of the day is not (*Dugdale* v *Kraft Foods* [1977] ICR 48). In *Navy, Army and Air Force Institutes* v *Varley* [1976] IRLR 408, a distinction in hourly pay between workers based in London and the rather cheaper Nottingham area was held to be a genuine and material difference. A wrong grading which arose because of an initial mistake as to the male comparator's qualifications could not amount to a material factor. The grounds for the variation must be objectively justified (*McPherson* v *Rathgael Centre*, supra). Most controversy has surrounded treatment of part-time workers (para. 7.2.4.1), protected earnings called 'red circles' (para. 7.2.4.2), and grading systems (para. 7.2.4.3).

7.2.4.1 Part-time workers The treatment of part-timers is in the nature of a test case for the Act because of the predominance of women in the part-time labour market, and some of the early cases did much to retard their progress towards equal pay. In *Handley* v *H. Mono Ltd* [1979] ICR 147, for example, a female machinist, who worked a basic 26-hour week, claimed an equal hourly rate with a man who worked 40 hours. It was conceded that they were engaged on like work, but the fact that the woman worked substantially fewer hours, was entitled to overtime rates earlier, and that all '26-hour workers' were paid at the same rate, together established a genuine material difference. Slynn J also referred to the different value of their contribution to the productivity of the company. In the case of part-time employees, machinery in the respondent's clothing factory laid idle. It was thus a less efficient method of business. In *Jenkins* v *Kingsgate Ltd (No. 2)* [1981] IRLR 388, however, the EAT took a more radical view. The employer had to show that the difference in pay between full-time male workers and part-time women is reasonably necessary in order to obtain some result which the employer desires for economic or other reasons. A bare statement to this effect by the employer was not enough, and the case was remitted to the industrial tribunal to determine whether the difference in pay was indeed necessary in order to enable the employers to reduce absenteeism and to obtain maximum utilisation of their plant as claimed. Browne-Wilkinson J said:

> The Equal Pay Act is an integral part of one code against sex discrimination and the rest of the code plainly rendered unlawful indirect discrimination even if unintentional.

In the European Court of Justice ([1981] ICR 592) the prohibition of differences in rates of pay related to differences based exclusively on the sex of the employee. Thus a difference in rates of remuneration between full-time and part-time employees did not offend Article 119 provided that the difference was attributable to factors which were objectively justified and did not relate directly or indirectly to discrimination based on sex. On remission to the Employment Appeal Tribunal ([1981] 1 WLR 1485) Browne-Wilkinson J decided that even if the employer satisfied Article 119, s. 1(3) went further. It must show that the 'difference was reasonably necessary in order to obtain some result (other than cheap female labour) which the employer desires for economic or other reasons'.

In *Calder* v *Rowntree Mackintosh Confectionery Ltd* [1993] ICR 811, women workers were engaged on a regular part-time shift from 5.30pm to 10.30pm while men were employed full-time on a rotating two shift cycle, one from 8am to 4pm and the next from 4pm to midnight. Those on rotating shift received an additional shift premium. There was a genuine material difference since the material factor was the inconvenience of working rotating shifts. This was a valid conclusion notwithstanding the fact that there was an element in the premium the man received which was compensation for working unsocial hours, which the woman also worked.

See paras 7.9 and 8.1.6 on the *EOC* case.

7.2.4.2 'Red circles' In industrial relations jargon earnings are said to be 'red-circled' when jobs are regraded, or a long-serving employee is moved, and his pay protected at the previous rate in order to avoid breach of his contract, or perhaps industrial unrest. New employees performing the same function will, however, receive the normal lower rate for the grade. Very often the long-serving or sick employee is a man, and the grade in which he is placed is solely or mainly female.

A good example of the phenomenon is *Snoxell* v *Vauxhall Motors Ltd* [1977] IRLR 123. As part of a major company pay restructuring in 1970, designed partly to facilitate equal pay, the position of quality controller was downgraded but the males then in post had their wages protected in their inferior jobs. The claimant women who had been employed for many years as inspectors of machine parts sought equal pay with these men who were now doing a similar job. The EAT stated that the red circle was not a decisive defence: the correct approach entailed eliciting and analysing all the circumstances of the case, including the situation prior to the formation of the protected class. An employer could never establish a genuine material difference if past discrimination blatantly contributed to the now protected differential, as indeed it had in *Snoxell*'s case. Phillips J, moreover, thought it desirable 'whenever possible for "red circles" to be phased out and eliminated'.

Other relevant factors included 'whether (the red circle) group . . . is a closed group; whether the red circling has been the subject of negotiations with the representatives of the work people, and the views of the women taken into account; or whether the women are able equally with the men to transfer between the grades'. It is legitimate for a higher rate to continue to be paid where a man is transferred for reasons of illness or age. In *Methven* v *Cow Industrial Polymers Ltd* [1980] IRLR 289, Dunn LJ emphasised that the issue was one of fact for the industrial tribunals who should not be mesmerised by the label 'red circle' (also *Outlook Supplies Ltd* v *Penny* [1978] IRLR 12, *Avon and Somerset Police* v *Emery* [1981] ICR 229, *Forex Neptune (Overseas) Ltd* v *Miller* [1987] ICR 170). Once the reason which led to a woman being paid less than a man has been removed, it is no longer possible for the employer to justify the difference in pay on that ground. When the employee in *Benveniste* v *University of Southampton* [1989] IRLR 122 was appointed a lecturer, the University was subject to financial restraint and it was agreed that she would be offered a salary well below the level normally paid. When those financial constraints came to an end she was still not paid equally with men employed on like work. The Court of Appeal determined that it was 'not right that the appellant should continue to be paid on a lower scale once the reason for payment at the lower scale has been removed. . . . The material difference between the appellant's case and the case of the comparator's evaporated when the financial constraints were removed.'

7.2.4.3 Grading systems The courts have also experienced some difficulty in dealing with grading systems in a series of cases starting with *Waddington* v *Leicester Council for Voluntary Service* [1977] IRLR 32. The applicant there was a female community worker who had responsibility for a male play leader. She was, however, paid some £400 less than him because she was on a different local authority pay scale. Phillips J stated: 'Where men and women are employed on like work, and the variation is in the rate of remuneration and the remuneration is fixed in accordance with a nationally or widely negotiated wage scale ... there will usually be a strong case for saying that the case falls within s. 1(3).' While the scales are not conclusive, 'when one is dealing with nationally negotiated scales, in general use by local authorities, it seems unlikely that a problem caused by grading is very likely to give rise to a remedy under the Equal Pay Act'.

This case was approved by the Court of Appeal in *National Vulcan Ltd* v *Wade* [1978] IRLR 225. The EAT had found fatal in the appellant's grading scheme the fact that 'the assignment of a particular individual, and therefore his remuneration, depended upon the personal assessment of the individual, which was of necessity a subjective judgment'. Lord Denning, however, overruling this decision took a much less interventionist stance; employers will have a defence under s. 1(3) providing only that any scheme is 'genuinely operated'. It was a matter of policy, since 'a grading scheme according to skill, ability and experience is an integral part of good business management . . . If it were to go forth that these grading systems are inoperative and operate against the Equal Pay Act, it would, I think, be disastrous for the ordinary running of efficient business'.

7.2.4.4   Not by reason of sex   To be a valid defence, the relevant difference must not, however, be by reason of sex (see consideration by the Court of Appeal in *Farthing* v *Ministry of Defence* [1980] IRLR 402, and generally para. 7.4.3). In *Bilka-Kaufhaus GmbH* v *Weber von Hartz* [1986] ICR 110 at p. 126, the ECJ decided that 'If the national court finds that the measures chosen by Bilka correspond to a real need on the part of the undertaking, are appropriate with a view to achieving the objectives pursued and are necessary to that end, the fact that the measures affect a far greater number of women than men is not sufficient to show that they constitute an infringement of Article 119'. There is a two-fold test: does the applicant show that a group which is predominantly female is treated less favourably than a group doing like work or work of equal value of whom a majority are men? If so, the burden shifts to the employer to show that the difference is 'objectively justified' on a non-discriminatory basis. If market forces are relied upon the employer must show that these are gender neutral if he is to succeed in establishing the defence.

In the important case of *Enderby* v *Frenchay Health Authority* [1993] IRLR 591, the ECJ decided that there is a prima facie case of sex discrimination where valid statistics disclose an appreciable difference in pay between two jobs of equal value, one of which is carried out almost exclusively by women and the other predominantly by men. It is for the national court to assess whether the statistics appear to be significant in that they cover enough individuals and do not illustrate purely fortuitous and short-term phenomena. Article 119 then requires the employer to show that the difference in pay is based on objectively justified factors unrelated to discrimination on grounds of sex. Further the genuine material difference must justify the whole difference in pay.

The House of Lords in *Ratcliffe* v *North Yorkshire County Council* [1995] ICR 833 made it clear that this provision in the 1970 Act is not to be interpreted as including the distinction between direct and indirect discrimination. In so doing, it narrowed significantly the scope of the s. 1(3) defence. Lord Slynn said that the fact that the employers paid women employees less than their male comparators because they were women constituted direct discrimination and *ex hypothesi* could not be shown to be justified on grounds 'irrespective of sex'. This is particularly important here because a male employee doing the same work would also have been paid the lower rate, but the employees as a whole were women and that meant that they were as a group paid less than if they had been men. Even in this situation, the House of Lords held, there was necessarily direct discrimination.

7.2.5 Terms not included in equality clause

There are several terms on which the equality clause contained in the Equal Pay Act 1970 does not operate:

(a) Terms affected by *compliance with the law* relating to women's employment.

(b) Terms affording special treatment to women for *pregnancy or childbirth*; this does not extend to a sick pay scheme which granted entitlement to maternity leave only for absences not connected with confinement, although there was no restriction on men's illnesses covered. The industrial tribunal held that the difference related to sick pay and not to maternity provision (*Coyne* v *Export Credits Guarantee Department* [1981] IRLR 51).

(c) Terms related to *death or retirement,* or to any provision in connection therewith. There is again a coincident exception in the Sex Discrimination Act, but a later amendment renders it unlawful to deny either sex equal access to an occupational pension scheme contrary to the Social Security Pensions Act 1975 (s. 6(1A)). 'Retirement' is widely defined as 'retirement' on grounds of age, length of service or incapacity including voluntary retirement. This defence will be considered in detail under the Sex Discrimination Act (para. 8.6.3).

7.3 JOB EVALUATION

Section 1(5) of the Equal Pay Act 1970 permits comparison between different jobs. It states:

A woman is to be regarded as employed on work rated as equivalent with that of any men if, but only if, her job and their job have been given an equal value, in terms of the demand made on the worker under various headings (for instance effort, skill, decision) on a study undertaken with a view to evaluating in those terms the jobs to be done by all or any of the employees in the undertaking, or group of undertakings . . .

Example Alan and Betty work for Crest Stores as a travel agent and butcher respectively. A job evaluation study awards both 30 points, but the employers still pay Alan £3 more per week. An industrial tribunal must accept that the two are employed on like work, so that Alan may only be paid more if there is a genuine material difference in the personal equation, e.g. as a result of his longer experience in the store.

A job evaluation scheme is thus an alternative route to equal pay and attempts to be as scientific and objective as possible. Its criteria are commonly agreed between management and unions and are of particular application to white collar staff. Yet its limitations must be appreciated, since it classifies jobs not the people who fill them. It must be followed by a subjective merit assessment of the individual's qualities. A job evaluation study merely provides a building block to indicate the underlying structure of wages on which individual variations may then be built. It is necessary to have regard to the full results of the scheme, including final allocation of grades at the foot of score sheets (*Springboard Sunderland Trust* v *Robson* [1992] ICR 554).

The chief types of job evaluation schemes generally in use are:

(a) Job ranking where 'each job is considered as a whole and is then given a ranking in relation to all other jobs'.

(b)   Paired comparisons, where points are awarded on a comparison between pairs of jobs and then a rank order produced.

(c)   Job classification, whereby all other jobs are compared with benchmark grades.

(d)   Points assessment, 'the most common system' which 'breaks down each job into a number of factors — for example, skills, responsibility, physical and mental requirements and working conditions'.

(e)   Factor comparison, which differs from points assessment only in that it uses a limited number of factors based on key jobs with fair wages (see discussion in *Eaton Ltd* v *Nuttall* [1977] 3 All ER 1131, and ACAS Job Evaluation booklet).

The main legal questions concern the meaning of, and the challenges to, job evaluation study, and the necessity of putting schemes into effect when completed.

7.3.1   Meaning of job evaluation

According to *Eaton Ltd* v *Nuttall* (supra), the subsection requires a study 'thorough in analysis and capable of impartial application'. Further, 'it should be possible by applying the study to arrive at the position of a particular employee at a particular point in a particular salary grade without taking other matters into account'. It must not require management to take a subjective view as to the grading of an employee (see also *McAuley* v *Eastern Health & Social Services Board* [1991] IRLR 467).

The Court of Appeal in *Bromley* v *H. & J. Quick Ltd* [1988] ICR 623 decided that an analytical method must be applied in carrying out the job evaluation scheme. This means that the jobs of the applicants must be valued with those of comparators in terms of various demands on the workers under the various headings set out in s. 1(5) of the Equal Pay Act 1970. Thus assessments made on a 'whole job' basis which do not involve individual comparisons under those headings do not amount to a valid job evaluation study for s. 1(5).

7.3.2   Challenges to job evaluation study

Where there is a valid and proper study, it is impermissible for the industrial tribunal or an employer to override it, or implement only part of it. The study can be challenged only if there is 'a fundamental error in it . . . or a plain error on the face of the record'. A broad attack was attempted in *England* v *Bromley LBC* [1978] ICR 1, where the widely used 'London Scheme' was adopted to grade the respondent council's employees, but it was adjusted for 'special factors'. The male applicant clerks received the same number of points in the main scheme as their female comparators, but were awarded less for 'special factors'. Phillips J closed the door to challenge thus: 'What the claimant cannot do is to base his claim on the footing that if the evaluation study had been carried out differently . . . he would be entitled to the relief claimed. He must take the study as it is.' (See also *Arnold* v *Beecham Group Ltd* [1982] IRLR 307.) The single exception is where the factors used in making the evaluation are in themselves discriminatory.

7.3.3   Putting schemes into effect

In *O'Brien* v *Sim-Chem Ltd* [1980] IRLR 151 CA, [1980] IRLR 373 HL, the courts had to determine whether, once a study had been carried out, it *must* be implemented. This depended on the meaning and effect of the appropriate enforcement provision which modifies the contract of employment where 'any term . . . *determined* by the rating of the work' becomes less favourable. The appellants, all women employees of the respondent company, had been informed of a new grading and appropriate salary range as a result of a job evaluation study carried out by awarding points for each element of their job. All that remained was to complete a merit assessment of each individual after which their exact pay would be decided. Before this could be done, however, the Government announced a 'voluntary incomes policy' which discouraged such increases, and the appellants were never actually paid in accordance with the new structure. The question for the court was thus whether any 'term' had indeed been 'determined by the rating of the work', as required by s. 1(5) for the implementation of the job evaluation scheme.

Cumming Bruce LJ in the Court of Appeal, thought that the word 'determined' must be given its 'normal causative meaning', and since here there was no contractual condition actually *brought about or effected* by the study, it was not compulsory. The House of Lords, however, overturned this decision. Examining the structure of the Act, Lord Russell of Killowen said (para. 16):

> Once a job evaluation study has been undertaken and has resulted in a conclusion that the job of the woman has been evaluated under s. 1(5) as of equal value with the job of the man, then the comparison of the respective terms of their contracts of employment is made feasible and a decision can be made . . .

This is much more in line with the European principle of 'equal pay for work of equal value' than the approach taken by the Court of Appeal, which would also make a job evaluation study defeasible on the whim of management.

According to *Arnold* v *Beecham Group Ltd* [1982] IRLR 307, however, a job evaluation study is not completed unless and until the parties who agreed to carry out the study have accepted its validity.

A job evaluation study is admissible before an industrial tribunal even though it was carried out after the complaints to the tribunal had been presented, provided that the comparison is made between jobs which were carried out by the applicant and the comparator at the date of commencement of the proceedings (*Dibro* v *Hore* [1990] IRLR 129, [1990] ICR 370).

7.4 EQUAL VALUE CLAIMS

Between the coming into force of the 1983 Regulations which amended the 1970 Act and 1996, an applicant could require a job study to be carried out by an independent expert appointed from a panel nominated by ACAS, provided that the claim overcame some preliminary hurdles before an expert was appointed. This was amended by the Sex Discrimination and Equal Pay (Miscellaneous Amendments) Regulations 1996 (SI 1996 No. 438), which in some circumstances gave the industrial tribunal power to decide equal value cases itself, to place time limits on the expert and to replace him if he did not perform to the standards laid down (for full consideration of the procedural aspects see Bowers, Gibbons and Mead, *Industrial Tribunal Practice and Procedure*, FT Law and Tax, 1996).

7.4.1 What is work of equal value

The EAT in *Pickstone* v *Freemans plc* [1986] IRLR 335 reached the somewhat surprising decision that if a woman is employed on like work with *one* man, she may not bring an equal *value* claim with a person employed in a different position. This was a narrow reading of the Equal Pay (Amendment) Regulations 1983, which apply the equal value procedures 'where a woman is employed on work which, not being work in relation to which paragraph (a) or (b) above applies, is . . . of equal value to that of a man in the same employment'. The EAT thought that the contention of the employees would require writing in words to the Regulations and that this was impossible. Community law was ambiguous and in any event 'cannot be applied where the issue can be determined by national law which is in accordance with Community law or by a combination of both'. The Court of Appeal ([1987] IRLR 218) reached the same conclusion on the interpretation of the English statute but determined that under the European Community provisions, the expression 'equal work' had a wide interpretation, and the concepts of 'the same work' and 'work to which equal value is attributed' were not mutually exclusive. Thus, by European law, there was no justification for the UK statute. To hold as the EAT had done would make the presence of one man doing the same work decisive, which in some cases might be wholly fortuitous or even a situation contrived by an unscrupulous employer to defeat legitimate claims of equal value. The House of Lords ([1988] ICR 697) dismissed the appeal and applied a purposive construction of the English statute rather than relying on the European material. The exclusionary words in paragraph (c) 'not being work in relation to which paragraph (a) or (b) above applies' were limited to the situation where the male comparator selected by a female complainant was one in relation to whose work paragraph (a) or (b) applied. It was, moreover, acceptable for the court to take into account the words used by the Government Minister in introducing the Regulations since they had not been subject to parliamentary scrutiny, as statutes would be. Thus the fact that one or more men are engaged on 'like work' with the applicant woman does not prevent an equal value claim.

7.4.2 The preliminary hurdles

The tribunal need not pass the case on to an expert if there are 'no reasonable grounds for determining that the work is of equal value'. This is a matter for the discretion of the tribunal which must hold a preliminary hearing on the point if one side requests that it should. In *Forex Neptune (Overseas) Ltd* v *Miller* [1987] ICR 170, the EAT decided that an industrial tribunal was entitled to consider a defence that the difference in pay was due to a material factor other than sex before referring the matter to an independent expert for a report. This arose from their general discretion under the Industrial Tribunal Rules to conduct a hearing in such manner as they considered most suitable in the circumstances.

The complaint must be stopped in its tracks where there has already been a job evaluation study which has accorded different values to the work of the applicant and comparator and there are no reasonable grounds for determining that the study discriminated on the grounds of sex. The burden of proof that there has been discrimination in the study lies on the employee, and the test is whether there is good reason to suppose that any comparative value set by the system on any demand or characteristic ought to have been given a more favourable value if those determining the values had not consciously or unconsciously been influenced by consideration of the sex of those on whom the demands would chiefly be made. There would, for example, be sufficient reason to doubt a job evaluation study if a traditionally female attribute was undervalued (*Neil* v *Ford Motor Co. Ltd* [1984] IRLR 339).

An industrial tribunal is not entitled to require an expert's report before deciding whether there were no reasonable grounds for determining that the work was of equal value (*Sheffield*

Metropolitan District Council v *Siberry* [1989] ICR 208). Moreover, at the preliminary stage, the industrial tribunal is not confined to the contentions set out in the originating application. In *Dennehy* v *Sealink UK Ltd* [1987] IRLR 120, the EAT said that it was permissible also to consider expert evidence at this early stage. Further, a tribunal should not adjourn an equal value claim to allow the employer to carry out a job evaluation study (*Avon CC* v *Foxall* [1989] ICR 407).

In *McGregor* v *General Municipal Boilermakers and Allied Trades Union* [1987] ICR 505, the EAT held that an industrial tribunal could take a broad approach and acknowledge that a particular employer might lay greater stress on particular factors and thus be prepared to pay a higher wage to the comparator than to the complainant. The defence of genuine material factor under s. 1(3) was available to the employer at the first hearing when the tribunal was considering whether to send the case to an expert, or at any subsequent hearing when the expert's report was received by the tribunal.

In *R* v *Secretary of State for Social Services ex parte Clarke* [1988] IRLR 22, the applicants were speech therapists who sought to compare their work with that of male clinical psychologists and pharmacists. The employers took the preliminary point that health authorities were statutorily *required* to pay their employees pursuant to an established salary scale agreed by the NHS Whitley Council and approved by the Secretary of State for Social Services under the National Health Service (Remuneration and Conditions of Service) Regulations 1974. The industrial tribunal held that this *did* constitute a genuine material factor but that the proper procedure for the applicants to adopt was an application for judicial review to test whether the 1974 Regulations conflicted with the requirements of EEC law. On the subsequent application for judicial review, the Divisional Court remitted the claim to the industrial tribunal on the ground that the mere fact that the pay had been approved by the Secretary of State did not provide a defence. Evidence was required to decide the point, including the reasons why the rates were decided upon by the Minister and the course of negotiations which led to approval of the agreements.

Provided that the study is not discriminatory, there is no limit on the time that such a study may provide a defence. It would, however, be surprising if the study was based on a set of job duties which had been superseded.

If the case does not fall at this first hurdle, the tribunal must invite the parties to 'apply for an adjournment for the purpose of seeking to reach a settlement of the claim'. Before deciding whether to pass the case to an expert, the industrial tribunal must give the parties an opportunity to make representations.

7.4.3 The report

If the conciliation procedures fail and the tribunal decides that there are reasonable grounds for determining that the work is of equal value, the tribunal must require an expert's report in writing, stating particulars of the precise question on which he is required to report and the persons between whom the question of equal value arises. The applicant is still able to choose her comparator and there is no provision to change this if the expert finds a more appropriate man.

The expert has an inquisitorial function, but must take account of all representations made to him, and 'before drawing up his report, [must] produce and send to the parties a written summary of information supplied and representations made and invite further representation on this basis'. A brief account of such representations must be included in his report together with the reasons for his conclusion. The expert may not concern himself with the material factor defence unless it is specified in the reference. He labours under a general duty to 'act at all times fairly', and should produce the report in 42 days after which time the tribunal (whose proceedings are adjourned in the meantime) may ask for an explanation of delay and information as to progress. His task is facilitated by tribunal rules that the tribunal may require any person whom it believes may have relevant information to furnish it and to produce any documents which are in his possession, custody or power. The tribunal will send such material to the expert. He has no power, however, to require a person to give oral evidence before him, nor to gain access to the work place being evaluated. The latter may prove a significant handicap. There is also no power under the Industrial Tribunals Rules of Procedure to compel an applicant for equal value to be interviewed about her job by an expert appointed by the employer (*Lloyds Bank plc* v *Fox* [1989] IRLR 103).

Copies of the report must be sent to all parties, and before accepting it in evidence, the tribunal must hear representations and decide whether:

(a)   the expert has complied with the procedural requirements;
(b)   'the conclusion contained in the report is one which, taking due account of the information supplied and representations made to the expert, could not reasonably have been reached';
(c)   'for some other material reason . . . the report is unsatisfactory'.

The tribunal can call for a progress report from the expert. The report must not be excluded merely because of 'disagreement with a conclusion that the applicant's work is or is not of equal value or the reasoning leading to that conclusion'. If the report is excluded for one or more of these three valid reasons, the tribunal should appoint another expert. In deciding this preliminary issue of admissibility, the tribunal may 'permit any person to give evidence upon, to call witnesses and to question any witnesses upon any matter relevant thereto' to the Industrial Tribunals (Constitution and Rules of Procedure) Regulations 1993 (SI 1993 No. 2687). The expert is a compellable witness.

If and when the report is accepted in evidence, the tribunal holds a hearing at which the expert may be cross-examined on his conclusions. The Rules allow any party on giving reasonable notice to 'call one witness to give expert evidence on the question on which the tribunal has required the [official] expert to prepare a report', but no other person 'may give evidence upon or question any witness upon any matter of fact upon which a conclusion in the report of the [official] expert is based' save in respect of the genuine material factor defence. The expert's report is not conclusive but it is likely to be rare that a tribunal would reject its conclusions.

The expert is given no specific statutory criteria on which to assess equal value. In *Hayward* v *Cammell Laird Shipbuilders Ltd* [1986] IRLR 287, the expert found that the work of a cook was of equal value to that of a painter, joiner and thermal insulation engineer, and the tribunal made the consequential orders. The industrial tribunal said that it would only interfere if the expert had gone badly wrong. It rejected the employers' attack on the expert's analysis of jobs in terms of demands under five factors which he ranked as low, moderate or high. The employers claimed that this was crude and imprecise and criticised the fact that he had only spent one day in the relevant shipyard and kitchens whilst preparing the report. The tribunal considered that the appropriate provision 'does not appear to look for the question of equal value to be dealt with by way of precise mathematical calculation'. They thought that one of the most effective ways to attack the independent expert's report was to commission and represent an expert's report of one's own.

The expert's report has no special status and the industrial tribunal is not obliged to accept its findings of fact (*Tennants Textile Colours Ltd* v *Todd* [1989] IRLR 3). The industrial tribunal is not entitled to use a broad brush. In order for the work to be of equal value the score on the job evaluation scheme must be precisely the same. The industrial tribunal in *Brown and Royle* v *Cearns & Brown Ltd* 304 IRLIB 10 thus held that an employee who gained 95 per cent of her male comparator's score was not employed on work of equal value.

7.4.4 Material factor defence

The 1983 Regulations (SI 1983 No. 1794) introduced an amended s. 1(3) into the Act. Whilst preserving the genuine material difference defence in like-work claims it added a parallel defence in the case of equal value claims, namely where the difference in pay is based on a 'material factor'. The 'most convenient, proper and appropriate time' for employers to raise this issue is at the outset of proceedings before the expert's report is commissioned (*Hayward* v *Cammell Laird Ltd,* supra). (See also *Davies* v *McCartneys* [1989] IRLR 439.)

7.5 CLAIMING EQUAL PAY

A claim for equal pay under the like-work and job evaluation scheme provisions may be presented to an industrial tribunal by the individual employee affected at any time before the expiration of six months after leaving the relevant employment, and then arrears of remuneration may be awarded for up to two years (s. 2(1)). Since the 'equality clause' acts as an implied term of the contract of employment, an action may also be brought in the county court. Like most discrimination actions, while the proceedings are individual in nature, they are usually in the nature of test cases, the pay of hundreds of other similarly placed employees commonly depending on the outcome. This is reflected in the power accorded to the Secretary of State for Employment to bring a complaint if it appears to him that it is not reasonable to expect individual employees concerned to do so. There are, however, no reported instances of his so doing. Moreover, the Equal Opportunities Commission may also provide general advice and assistance to applicants.

The time limit has given rise to contradictory decisions. In *British Railways Board* v *Paul* [1988] IRLR 20, the EAT held that there was no time limit for bringing an equal pay application before the industrial tribunal, although the claim could result in payment of arrears of salary and benefits for only two years before the application (see also *Stevens* v *Bexley Health Authority* [1989] ICR 224). *British Railways Board* v *Paul* was dissented from, however, in *Etherson* v *Strathclyde Regional Council* [1992] ICR 579, and should no longer be considered as binding, in particular since the EAT preferred the *Etherson* decision in *Fletcher* v *Midland Bank plc* [1996] IRLR 486.

The right conferred by the Act to equal treatment does not require equality in *aggregate* pay and conditions. As Phillips J said in *National Coal Board* v *Sherwin & Spruce* [1978] IRLR 122, the Act:

. . . does not mean that men, or women, cannot be paid extra for working at night or at weekends or at other inconvenient times; if the additional remuneration is justified by the inconvenience of the time at which it is done the claim will not succeed. For while every contract of employment is deemed to include an equality clause, it only has the effect so that the terms of the woman's contract shall be treated as so modified not to be less favourable than the man's . . .

(*Hayward* v *Cammell Laird Shipbuilders* [1986] ICR 862.)

7.6 COLLECTIVE ENFORCEMENT

The 1970 Act more broadly facilitated the amendment of whole collective agreements, pay structures, wages regulation orders and agricultural wages orders where such contained a provision applying specifically to men only or women only (s. 3). Reference could be made by union, management or the Secretary of State for Employment, to the Central Arbitration Committee which could give advice, and ultimately declare what amendments must be made to remove the discriminatory features. The Sex Discrimination Act 1986 repealed this provision and introduced the different, more limited procedure under s. 77 of the Sex Discrimination Act 1975, by which a county court might make an order for removing or modifying a discriminatory term. This has been further amended by TURERA 1993 in response to criticism by the EC that the existing regime was in breach of the Equal Treatment Directive. By the revised s. 77, a term of a contract is void where:

(a)   its inclusion renders the making of the contract unlawful by virtue of the Act:
(b)   it is included in furtherance of an act rendered unlawful by the Act; or
(c)   it provides for the doing of any act which would be rendered unlawful by the Act.

This applies if the term is directly or indirectly discriminatory against men, women or married persons by reason of sex or marital status.

A claim may now be made to an *industrial tribunal* 'if any person has reason to believe that the term or rule prohibited may at some future time have effect in relation to him (SDA 1975, s. 77(4A)). An employee, or a person who is genuinely and actively seeking employment with the particular employer, may complain about a term of a collective agreement made by or on behalf of an employer, an employers' association or 'an association of such organisations one of which an employer is a member' (SDA 1975, s. 77(4B)). The tribunal may make an order declaring the term to be void (SDA 1975, s. 77(4D)).

7.7 EUROPEAN LAW

7.7.1 Direct effect of Article 119

Article 119 of the Treaty of Rome provides that: 'Each Member State shall . . . maintain the application of the principle that men and women should receive equal pay for equal work.' The preamble to the Article aims 'to ensure States with equal pay do not suffer a competitive disadvantage in inter-Community competition as compared with undertakings established in States which have not yet eliminated discrimination'. This is extended in concept by Directive 75/117 which states that 'the principle of equal pay' means for the same work or for work to which *equal value* is attributed, the elimination of all discrimination on the grounds of sex with regard to all aspects and conditions of remuneration. Directive 76/207, which was issued in February 1978, seeks equal treatment and non-discrimination for men and women in regard to employment, promotion, working conditions and vocational training.

The European legislation is important in Britain in two distinct ways — its direct enforceability in British courts, and because those courts might gain assistance from it in interpreting national legislation. The European Court has held Article 119 to be directly effective in national courts in *Defrenne* v *Sabena* [1976] ECR 455, *McCarthys* v *Smith* [1980] IRLR 210, and *Worringham* v *Lloyds Bank Ltd* [1979] IRLR 440, [1981] IRLR 178 ECJ. See also *McKechnie* v *UBM Building Supplies (Southern) Ltd* [1991] ICR 710. This is important because of its wider scope than the present English law, in that, for example, it permits comparison with a man previously employed (*McCarthys Ltd* v *Smith*) and applies to pension fund payments (*Worringham* v *Lloyds Bank Ltd*). A key to the understanding of the impact of European law is an appreciation of the wide scope given to 'pay' which must be equal between men and women. The definition of pay does not relate to a particular time of payment during the course of employment, as contended by the employers, but demands a connection between the payment and the employment (*Hammersmith and Queen Charlotte's Special Health Authority* v *Cato* [1987] IRLR 483). Pay thus includes a severance grant (*Kowalska* v *Freie und Hansestadt Hamburg* [1992] ICR 29). The ECJ in *Gillespie* v *Northern Health and Social Services Board* [1996] ICR 498 decided that neither Article 119 nor the Directive required that women should continue to receive full pay during maternity leave, nor laid down specific criteria for determining the amount of benefit payable to them during that period. That was a matter for national law provided that the amount was not so low as to jeopardise the purpose of maternity leave.

We will review two particular issues which have dominated the case law — the treatment of redundancy and pension payments — and then consider the nature of discrimination under Article 119.

7.7.1.1 Redundancy payments It was originally held that a statutory redundancy payment was not within the meaning of 'pay' according to the EAT in *Secretary of State for Employment* v *Levy* [1989] IRLR 469, but after the decision in *Barber* v *Guardian Royal Exchange Ltd* [1990] ICR 616, the Secretary of State for Employment made payment to Mrs Levy and the appeal which had been launched to the Court of Appeal was accordingly withdrawn.

In *R* v *Secretary of State for Employment ex parte EOC* [1994] IRLR 177, all the members of the House of Lords accepted that a redundancy payment was pay but Lord Keith of Kinkel only went so far as to say (at para. 24) that 'There is much to be said in favour of the view that compensation for unfair dismissal is' pay for the purposes of Article 119. The Southampton Industrial Tribunal held that it was in *Warren* v *Wylie & Wylie* [1994] IRLR 316, and this was upheld by the EAT in *Mediguard Services Ltd* v *Thame* [1994] IRLR 504.

7.7.1.2 Pension payments Article 119 relates to 'consideration' which the worker receives directly or indirectly; there must be a benefit paid to a worker or a contribution paid by the employer to a pension scheme on behalf of the employee. In *Newstead* v *Dept of Transport and HM Treasury* [1988] ICR 332, the ECJ held that a civil servant who under a compulsory pension scheme had to pay 1.5 per cent of his gross salary to a widow's pension fund, whereas a female employee did not have to, did not fall within Article 119. This concerned a deduction of contributions from pay and was not a difference in pay itself within the scope of the Article. There was no breach of the Equal Treatment Directive since this did not apply to social security matters.

In a surprising decision, the EAT in *Griffin* v *London Pension Fund Authority* [1993] IRLR 248 determined that pension payments made to an employee of the Greater London

Council were not pay for the purposes of Article 119 because the appellant's scheme was statutory and governed by exhaustive rules which left the employer no discretion.

The ECJ in *Barber* v *Guardian Royal Exchange Assurance Group* [1990] ICR 616 decided that occupational pension schemes count as 'pay' for the purposes of direct effect (that is to say, applicable to individuals' claims under domestic legislation). The result is that any inequalities with regard to occupational pension schemes that were permitted by virtue of the exception contained in SDA 1975, s. 6 are no longer permitted. In other words, s. 6 is overridden by the decision in *Barber*. The court said that, for the purposes of Article 119, pay comprised any consideration, whether cash or in kind, whether immediate or future, provided that the worker received it, albeit indirectly, under the contract of employment.

The House of Lords confirmed in *Duke* v *GEC Reliance (formerly Reliance Systems Ltd)* [1988] 2 WLR 359 that the European Directive did not require any modification to the true construction of this exception given that the statute was not passed with a view to enacting the Equal Treatment Directive (see also *Porter* v *Cannon Hygiene Ltd* [1993] IRLR 329; *Finnegan* v *Clowney Youth Training Programme* [1990] ICR 462).

By an insertion made by the Social Security Act 1989, s. 6 of SDA 1975 makes it unlawful to discriminate on the grounds of sex:

(a)   in the terms on which employment is offered which relate to how access is given to benefits, facilities or services under an occupational pension scheme;

(b)   in the way an employee is given access to such benefits, facilities or services;

(c)   by refusing or deliberately omitting to afford an employee access to any such benefits, facilities or services; or

(d)   subjecting an employee to any detriment in connection with such a scheme;

but in all cases only in so far as the act relates to a matter in respect of which the scheme has to comply with the principle of equal treatment (on which see para. 8.2.8).

The ECJ decision in *Birds Eye Walls Ltd* v *Roberts* [1994] IRLR 29, concerned bridging pensions, such that from the age of 60 the pension for a woman was reduced by the amount of State pension she received, but no such reduction was made in respect of a man until the age of 65. The financial position of the men and women were held not to be comparable because of the differential ages for State pension and the practice could not be regarded as discriminatory. This was not least because to accede to the applicant's arguments would 'produce unequal treatment to the detriment of men who did not receive the State pension until the age of 65'.

Many of the remaining questions were cleared up in a series of judgments by the ECJ on 28 September 1994 as follows:

(a)   Article 119 may be relied upon by employees and their dependants against trustees of a pension scheme as well as against the employer (*Coloroll Pension Trustees Ltd* v *Russell* [1994] IRLR 586);

(b)   the *Barber* principles apply to contracted out and non-contracted out schemes (*Coloroll; Moroni* v *Firma Collo GmbH* [1994] IRLR 130);

(c)   actuarial factors varying according to sex may be taken into account in final salary schemes in determining the employer's contribution rate, calculating capital lump sums and assessing transfer values (*Coloroll; Neath* v *Hugh Steeper Ltd* [1994] IRLR 91);

(d)   Article 119 applies only in respect of benefits payable for periods of service after 17 May 1990 (*Ten Oever* v *Stichting Bedrijfspensioenfonds* [1993] IRLR 601; *Coloroll*);

(e)   equal treatment applies to all pension benefits whether or not they derive from employers' or employees' contributions, but not to benefits payable from employees' additional voluntary contributions (AVCs) because the pension scheme here was merely providing the administrative framework for employees to pay the AVCs (*Coloroll*);

(f)   in relation to periods of employment after the equalisation of pension benefits, Article 119 does not prohibit raising the female age from 60 to 65, but in relation to the period between the date of *Barber* and equalisation the benefits must be awarded at the more favourable level (*Smith* v *Avdel Systems Ltd* [1994] IRLR 602);

(g)   the equalisation of pension ages upwards may not be accompanied by transitional measures of a discriminatory nature which are designed to soften the blow for the women involved (*Smith; Van den Akker* v *Stichting Shell Pensioenfonds* [1994] IRLR 616);

(h)   excluding part-timers from a pension scheme may constitute indirect discrimination if the exclusion affects (as it normally will) a much greater proportion of women than men, unless the employer can demonstrate objective factors to justify this position (*Vroege* v *NCIV Instituut voor Volkshuisvesting BV and Stichting Pensioenfonds* [1994] IRLR 651; *Fisscher* v *Voorhuis Hengelo BV and Stichting Bedrijfspensioenfonds* [1994] IRLR 662 and see also *Dietz* v *Stichting Thuiszorg Rotterdam* [1996] IRLR 692);

(i)   there is no time limit on the presentation of such claims as are referred to in (h) so that they may date back to 1976 when the Equal Treatment Directive was enacted (*Vroege; Fisscher*); if, however, a worker claims retroactively to join a pension scheme she must pay her employee's contributions for the whole of the period of past service (*Fisscher;* but see now *Preston and Others* v *Wolverhampton Healthcare NHS Trust* [1996] IRLR 484 at para. 7.9, infra);

(j)   survivors' pensions are pay and thus fall within Article 119 (*Ten Oever*);

(k)   a pension scheme which supplements or complements rather than replaces the State scheme is covered by Article 119 (*Moroni* v *Firma Collo GmbH* [1994] IRLR 130);

(l)   employers and trustees cannot rely on the pension scheme rules or terms of the pension trust to evade their obligations under Article 119, and this may require the trustees to apply to the national courts to amend the relevant scheme. The court may have to make orders that the employer pay additional sums into the scheme, or that any sum payable by virtue of Article 119 be first paid out of any surplus funds. Any problems arising from the fact that the funds held by the trustees might be insufficient to equalise benefits have to be resolved on the basis of national law in the light of the overriding principles of equality (*Coloroll*);

(m)   the rights of employees cannot be affected by the fact that they changed jobs and transferred their acquired pension rights to the new employer's scheme; if there was insufficient funding for equality, the paying scheme would have to do everything possible to achieve equality, including where possible making a claim against the first scheme under national laws for the additional sum (*Coloroll*);

(n)   a worker cannot rely on Article 119 in order to claim equality with a hypothetical person of the other sex where there are no workers of that other sex in the undertaking concerned and there have never been any such workers in the past (*Coloroll*);

(o)   Article 119 does not embrace social security schemes or benefits such as retirement pensions which are directly governed by statute without any element of negotiation in the undertaking or occupational sector concerned, but might include a civil service pension (*Bestuur van het Algemeen Burgerlijk Pensioenfonds* v *Beune* [1995] IRLR 103).

7.7.1.3   The nature of discrimination under Article 119   In *Bilka-Kaufhaus GmbH* v *Karin Weber von Hartz* [1987] ICR 110, the ECJ held that it was not sufficient for the employer to show that there was no *intention* to discriminate to defend a claim. It was for the national court to decide whether it was objectively justified on economic grounds, and 'if [it] finds that the measures chosen by Bilka correspond to a real need on the part of the undertaking, are appropriate with a view to achieving the objectives pursued and are necessary to that end, the fact that the measures affect a far greater number of women than men is not sufficient to show that they constitute an infringement of article 119.' (See *Rinner Kuhn* v *FWW Spezial-Gebaudereinigung* [1989] IRLR 493; *Chisholm* v *Kirklees Borough Council* [1993] ICR 826; *Commission of the EC* v *Belgium* [1993] IRLR 404, ECJ.) There was, however, no liability in *Stadt Lengerich* v *Helmig* [1996] ICR 35, where all workers who worked more than the ordinary number of working hours for full-time workers received an overtime supplement but part-time workers did not: the ECJ held that there was no discrimination incompatible with Article 119 or the Equal Treatment Directive because part-time employees received the same overall pay for the same number of hours worked (ECJ judgment, para. 27).

The Article precludes:

(a) the application of a provision of a collective agreement under which part-time workers are excluded from the benefit of a severance payment in the case of termination of the employment relationship when it is clear that in fact a considerably smaller percentage of men than of women worked part-time, unless the employer shows that the provision is justified by objective factors unrelated to any discrimination on the grounds of sex (*Kowalska* v *Freie und Hansestadt Hamburg* [1990] IRLR 447);

(b) a collective agreement under which the seniority of workers performing at least three-quarters of normal working time was to be fully taken into account for reclassification in a higher salary grade, whereas only half of such seniority was to be taken into account for workers whose working hours were between one-half and three-quarters of those normal working hours, where the latter group of employees comprised a considerably smaller percentage of men than women. The only justification would be factors which depend for their objectivity in particular on the relationship between the nature of the duties performed and the experience afforded by the performance of those duties, after a certain number of hours had been worked (*Nimz* v *Freie und Hansestadt Hamburg* [1991] IRLR 222);

(c) the making of a different payment to a female applicant who was made redundant at the age of 61 than to a male (*McKechnie* v *UBM Building Supplies (Southern) Ltd* [1991] ICR 710, [1991] IRLR 283);

(d) piece-work schemes in which pay depended entirely or in large measure on the individual output of each worker. The mere fact that there was a difference of average pay of two groups, one consisting mainly of women and the other mainly of men, however, did not suffice to establish discrimination (*Specialarbejderforbundet i Danmark* v *Dansk Industri* [1996] IRLR 648).

7.7.2 ECJ Construction of the Directive

The ECJ in *Defrenne* v *Sabena* [1976] ECR 455, restricted the general influence of the Directive by holding that its direct effectiveness covers only 'direct and overt discrimination which may be identified solely with the aid of criteria based on equal work and equal pay'. It thus did not automatically prohibit 'indirect or disguised discrimination'. In *Jenkins* v *Kingsgate (Clothing Productions) Ltd* [1981] IRLR 228, the ECJ held that paying an hourly rate to part-time workers which was lower than that accorded to full-timers was not covered. It was not *per se* discriminatory provided that the hourly rate was applied to each category without distinction based on sex. Any further prohibition was a matter for national legislatures and courts and, as we have seen, the EAT held that it was covered by the English Acts. Since there was no specific Directive extending the application of the principle of equal treatment to benefits for surviving spouses, Community law did not prevent an employer from making a deduction from the salaries of male employees only as a contribution to a widow's pension fund.

The EEC Equal Pay Directive does not preclude using as criteria in job evaluation schemes muscular effort or exertion or the degree to which work is physically heavy, if the tasks involved do in fact objectively require a certain level of physical strength. The system must as a whole, however, preclude all discrimination on the grounds of sex by taking into account other criteria. The European Court of Justice so held in *Rummler* v *Dato-Druck GmbH* [1987] IRLR 32, and went on to decide that it was for national courts to determine whether the job classification system in its entirety did meet those criteria. A pay system based on degree of strength may be justified under the Directive, but the scheme should, where the nature of the work permits, take into account criteria for which women workers may have a particular aptitude, such as manual dexterity. Otherwise, the scheme may be found to be discriminatory in its overall effect.

7.7.3 Public authorities

Directives in European law are 'binding as to the result to be achieved' but cede to the national authorities 'the choice of form and methods'. They are capable of direct enforcement in national courts (*Van Duyn* v *Home Office* [1975] Ch 358), at least where they are 'clear, precise and admit of no exceptions and of [their] nature need no intervention by national authorities'. The Court of Appeal in *O'Brien* v *Sim-Chem Ltd* [1980] IRLR 151 thought that the Equal Pay Directive was not directly effective. The European Court of Justice, however, decided (*Marshall* v *Southampton and South West Hampshire Health Authority* [1986] IRLR 140) that Directives are only directly enforceable by individuals against government institutions or emanations thereof. This included an area health authority, as in the instant case. (See the EAT in *Hugh-Jones* v *St John's College, Cambridge* [1979] ICR 848.) The European Court decision does extend to British Gas (*Foster* v *British Gas plc* [1990] IRLR 353, [1991] ICR 463) since before privatisation it was invested by statute with control over the provision of a public utility, but not Rolls-Royce (*Doughty* v *Rolls-Royce plc* [1992] ICR 238) because although the company was ultimately controlled by the State through the Government's majority shareholding, it did not provide a public service, nor did it claim any special powers. The proper test according to the EAT in the latter case was that enunciated for other purposes of 'lifting the corporate veil' on an application for discovery in *Lonrho Ltd* v *Shell Petroleum Co. Ltd (No. 2)* [1980] QB 358: 'whether on the established facts, a company is so utterly subservient or subordinate to the will or wishes of some other person . . . that compliance with that other person's demands can be regarded as assured'.

An industrial tribunal may not award interest on compensation for loss under the discrimination directives *(Southampton and South West Hampshire HA* v *Marshall (No. 2)* [1989] IRLR 459, see also *Handels-Og Kontorfunktionaerernes Forbund I danmark* v *Dansk Arbejdsgiverforening* [1989] IRLR 532).

7.7.4 European impact on construction of English statutes

Even if the Directive is not directly applicable it may have an impact in assisting with the construction of the English statutes. In *Coomes Holdings Ltd* v *Shields* [1978] IRLR 263,

Lord Denning MR sought guidance from the Article and Directives, while in the EAT in *McCarthys Ltd* v *Smith* [1978] ICR 500, Phillips J thought that 'as far as industrial tribunals and the appeal tribunal are concerned, the correct approach is to give effect to the *Defrenne* case by construing and applying the Equal Pay Act 1970 in conformity with Article 119'. Lawton and Cumming Bruce LJJ, however, in *Coomes* took the opposite view, that the English Act should not be construed on European lines. In *Handley* v *H. Mono Ltd* [1978] IRLR 534, Lord Denning MR thought there was no conflict between the Act and the Treaty as regards part-time workers, since it would be necessary for the European Court to work out exceptions on the lines of genuine material difference. (See also *Pickstone* v *Freemans plc* [1986] IRLR 335, fully discussed at para. 7.4.1, and *Webb* v *EMO Air Cargo (UK) Ltd* [1994] IRLR 482.)

7.7.5 The forum for complaints under the Treaty and Directives

There is the further question of the forum in which claims pursuant to the Treaty and Directives might be pursued. In *Amies* v *ILEA* [1977] 2 All ER 100, the EAT held that since the EAT was set up by statute it only had power to hear issues of discrimination arising from the Sex Discrimination Act and not from the EEC Treaty or Directives: 'The proper forum for the assertion of such a right would be the High Court of Justice.' In *McCarthys* v *Smith* (supra), the Court of Appeal seems to have assumed that European rights can be enforced in industrial tribunals although the point was not extensively argued (see also *Albion Shipping Agency* v *Arnold* [1982] ICR 22). This was also assumed in *Pickstone* v *Freemans plc* [1986] IRLR 335 and *Stevens* v *Bexley Health Authority* [1988] ICR 442 and was confirmed in *Secretary of State for Scotland and Greater Glasgow Health Board* v *Wright and Hannah* [1991] IRLR 187, by the Scottish EAT.

7.8 EQUAL PENSIONS

The Pensions Act 1995 requires equal treatment in pensions benefits and uses a similar structure to the Equal Pay Act 1970, so that the provisions apply where a member is employed on similar work to, or work of equal value to that of, a member of the other sex. It applies to the terms on which persons become members of a scheme and how members of the scheme are treated (Pensions Act 1995, s. 62(2)). Unusually, there is a specific direction that the Act should be 'construed as one' with the Equal Pay Act (Pensions Act 1995, s. 63(4)).

The rule will not apply if the difference is due to a factor which is not sex-related but is a difference between the man's and the woman's cases such as a difference in job status. Equal treatment is required for pensionable service only on or after 17 May 1990, the date of the *Barber* decision (see 7.7.1.2).

The Occupational Pension Schemes (Equal Treatment) Regulations 1995 (SI 1995 No. 3183) allow a court or tribunal on a complaint of failure to comply with the equal treatment rule, to grant a declaration and make an order requiring the employer to provide additional resources. There is no power, however, to make a financial award to an individual complainant unless he or she is a pensioner. The Regulations also provide for three exceptions to the equality rule, for bridging pensions, the effects of indexation and the continued use of actuarial factors in relation to contributions and additional benefits (regs 13-15).

For further details, see 'Occupational pension schemes' at para. 8.2.8.

7.9 TIME LIMITS IN EUROPEAN LAW

The approach of the English courts to time limits under European law has gradually hardened. It is necessary, however, to draw a number of distinctions between the cases considered, and in particular whether the right which is sought to be enforced is pursuant to a Directive or Treaty article. There is a general principle of EC law laid down in *Emmott* v *Minister for Social Welfare* [1991] IRLR 387, to the effect that where a Directive has not been implemented in domestic law, any time limit begins to run only when full and proper implementation of the Directive into domestic law has taken place. This is based on the principle that a Member State cannot rely upon its own default in fulfilling its Community obligations.

More controversial has been the approach to be adopted in respect of rights under Article 119, where employees could be justifiably ignorant of their rights. In *Rankin* v *British Coal Corporation* [1993] IRLR 69, the EAT sitting in Edinburgh held that there was no time limit directly applicable under UK law to a free-standing claim under Article 119 (such as this one for discriminatory application of statutory redundancy pay). The principle of legal certainty, however, was held by Lord Coulsfield to require some restriction. General legal policy in this area suggested that a period between three to six months could not be stigmatised as an unreasonable period in which to require complaint to be made. A claim brought within a reasonable period of time after the coming into force of the amending legislation should be regarded as timeous, but crucially time could not run until at least the date on which it could be reasonably clear to the applicant that a claim could properly be made.

The issue was considered in depth in *Biggs* v *Somerset CC* [1996] ICR 364. Mrs Biggs was a part-time employee of Somerset County Council, whose claim for unfair dismissal could not be brought in 1976 (as far as she was aware) because of the statutory provisions limiting continuity of service in respect of such employees. Mrs Biggs worked 14 hours per week. Employees could then claim only if they were employed for more than 21 (later reduced to 16) hours a week for at least 26 weeks (later at least two years), or for five years between 8 and 16 hours weekly. The fact that these provisions were discriminatory was first demonstrated to the world by the House of Lords decision in *R* v *Secretary of State for Employment ex parte EOC* [1994] IRLR 176. The fiction of the common law, however, is that all cases (whether unusually striking down legislation or otherwise) merely declare that fundamental truth that a decision will take effect only from the date of judgment and will not apply to cases arising before that date. The EAT in *Biggs* considered that in the absence of Community rules on the subject, it was for the domestic legal system to designate procedural rules, provided only that any conditions were no less favourable than those relating to similar domestic actions and that they did not render virtually impossible the exercise of rights conferred by EC law. The *Emmott* principle could not apply since the claims were brought on the basis of the Article of the Treaty.

Another centrepiece of the argument for Mrs Biggs was that the claim was under Article 119 and constituted a 'free-standing claim' to which the unfair dismissal provisions did not apply. The EAT emphasised that the right not to be unfairly dismissed was not in itself a Community right, and that the industrial tribunal has 'no general (or inherent) jurisdiction, separate and apart from that conferred by domestic statutes'. The tribunal must enforce Community law and 'has jurisdiction to disapply . . . provisions in UK domestic law, such as those relating to procedure, compensation, time limits and so on if they offend against, and are incompatible with, Community law', but it could not merely do as it wished in relation to time limits applicable to unfair dismissal claims. The industrial tribunal was thus obliged to apply the domestic time limits for unfair dismissal or redundancy (as the case may be) unless they were shown to be less favourable than those of a domestic nature or such as to render it impossible in practice to exercise rights under Article 119.

Adopting what is essentially the fiction that the *ex parte EOC* decision only declared the law, the EAT concluded that Mrs Biggs could have brought her case within three months of her dismissal in 1976. Mummery J emphasised as the policy rationale behind the time limits in particular 'the recognition of evidential, procedural and other practical difficulties in achieving a fair and just solution of a dispute long after the event'. The Court of Appeal agreed with this conclusion, and further that the case could not fall within the reasonably practicable extension because that pointed 'to some temporary impediment' such as illness. It was not correct to say that because most employees would not have appreciated that it was possible to make a claim, that time should be extended. There was a mistake of law and not fact. Indeed, at the relevant time when the claim could be made, there was no legal impediment to an employee making the claim.

The matter was taken further by the EAT in *Preston* v *Wolverhampton Healthcare NHS Trust* and in *Fletcher* v *Midland Bank plc* [1996] IRLR 486, when it in effect disposed of many thousand of claims by part-time workers for equal pensions. All the employees had been excluded from contributory or non-contributory occupational pension schemes with a qualifying condition of membership based on a minimum number of hours of work per week. The claim was brought under Article 119 for access to membership and recovery of contributions from the employers or former employers. The EAT decided that such claims were in time only if commenced within six months of the end of the contract of employment containing the equality clause allegedly breached. In other words, the time scale under the European provisions should be applied by reference to the closest available parallel in UK law, here the terms of the Equal Pay Act 1970. That time limit was held to be reasonable. Further, the time limit ran from the end of each contract under which a part-time employee was employed and not from the end of any employment with the particular employer. The EAT also decided that the time limit set down in s. 2(4) of the Equal Pay Act 1970 was reasonable and stressed that even shorter periods had been found in other cases to be compatible with Community law. Further, 'the decisions in *Vroege* and *Fisscher* were declaratory of the law. The principles of legal knowledge applied. The applicant's subjective understanding of the legal position was irrelevant'.

In *Levez* v *T. H. Jennings (Harlow Pools) Ltd* [1996] IRLR 499, the EAT (with Mummery J dissenting) decided to refer to the ECJ the question whether s. 2(5) of the Equal Pay Act 1970 on the two-year claim period was contrary to Article 119 and the Equal Pay Directive. On the other hand, in *Preston* v *Wolverhampton Healthcare NHS Trust* [1996] IRLR 484, the EAT was positive that this was compatible with EC law.

8 Discrimination

States must take measures against any distinction, exclusion or preference made on the basis of race, sex, religion, political opinion, national extraction or social origin which has the effect of nullifying or impairing equality of opportunity or treatment in employment or occupation.

(ILO Convention Concerning Discrimination in Respect of Employment or Occupation 1958 No. 111.)

The common law does not in itself prohibit discrimination, and while the Sex Disqualification (Removal) Act has been on the statute book since 1919, its coverage is minimal. Thus as Britain became a multi-racial country and the women's movement gained momentum, Parliament belatedly determined to put into municipal law the nation's obligations under ILO Convention No. 111, the UN International Convention on Social and Cultural Rights and the European Convention on the Protection of Human Rights, in respect of anti-discrimination laws.

Race relations legislation dates back to the Race Relations Act 1965. This was modelled on the American Civil Rights Act 1964, and stimulated by a series of reports on the low status of blacks in Britain and the first racial violence. It was, however, mainly concerned with public order and incitement to racial hatred, and outlawed discrimination only in places of public resort. It was extended to employment three years later, and the new Act also introduced the definition of direct discrimination which still exists today. The Race Relations Board, however, was still the sole enforcement mechanism, and it was only in 1976 that an individual right of access to industrial tribunals was introduced. The Race Relations Act 1976, which is still in force, also established the Commission for Racial Equality (CRE) — not only to advise and assist individual complainants, but also to concentrate on a collective, strategic role. The Act followed closely the model of the Sex Discrimination Act, which had been passed the previous year to supplement the Equal Pay Act 1970 outside the area of contractual entitlements. It had a counterpart enforcement agency independent of Government, the Equal Opportunities Commission (EOC), with similar powers. Experience with all three statutes has shown the immense difficulty of attempting to achieve equality by use of law.

Moreover, in *Commission of the European Communities* v *United Kingdom* [1984] IRLR 29, the European Court of Justice declared that Britain had failed to comply with Article 4(b) of the EEC Equal Treatment Directive in that the legislation does not outlaw discriminatory treatment in non-binding collective agreements, internal rules of undertakings and rules governing independent occupations and professions. The exclusion of employment in private households or undertakings where five or fewer people were employed was also unlawful. (See also *Johnston* v *Chief Constable of the Royal Ulster Constabulary* [1986] IRLR 263.)

The Race Relations Act 1976 and the Sex Discrimination Acts 1975 and 1986 (as amended by the Employment Act 1989 and the Sex Discrimination (Amendment) Order 1988 (SI 1988 No. 249)) and the Sex Discrimination and Equal Pay (Miscellaneous Amendments) Regulations 1996 (SI 1996 No. 438) now outlaw discrimination in employment, education, housing or the provision of goods, facilities and services on the grounds of:

(a)   race, colour, nationality, or ethnic or national origins;
(b)   sex; and
(c)   marital status.

The Social Security Act 1989 introduced the principle of equal treatment in occupational pension schemes. However, most of the relevant provisions of the 1989 Act were never brought into force properly, and as from 1 January 1996 they have been superseded by ss. 62–66 of the Pensions Act 1995 (see para. 8.2.8).

The EOC issued a Code of Practice on Discrimination in 1985, and the CRE a Code of Practice in 1984. They both recommend monitoring systems and in larger organisations a formal analysis by sex, grade and payment in each unit. The EOC Code recommends that job age limits should be retained only if they are necessary to the job; applications from men and women should be processed in precisely the same manner; and 'questions about marriage plans or family intentions should not be asked, as they could be construed as showing bias against women'.

This account concentrates solely on discrimination in employment, and examines in turn:

(a)   the forms of discrimination prohibited;
(b)   the scope of prohibited discrimination;
(c)   the grounds of discrimination;
(d)   applicants and respondents;
(e)   reverse discrimination;
(f)   exceptions to the general rules; and
(g)   enforcement mechanisms.

Since the forms of illegal discrimination are common to both the Race Relations and Sex Discrimination Acts, they will be examined together, whilst taking note of differences where they arise. Most recently, the Disability Discrimination Act 1995 has introduced similar restrictions on discrimination against the disabled, although there are numerous exceptions and elaborations. These are considered at para. 8.9.

8.1   FORMS OF DISCRIMINATION

There are four main forms of prohibited discrimination — direct, indirect, victimisation and segregation. Common to all is the factor of comparison, and both statutes decree that like must be compared with like so that the 'relevant circumstances are the same or not materially different' between comparators.

appellant's religion, the appellant had failed to establish that he was treated less favourably than the respondents would have treated someone else on the grounds of his Jewish faith. It was not, however, conclusive that the alleged discriminator did not know of the racial, ethnic or national origin of the person who was making the complaint.

A request by a Superintendent Registrar of Births, Deaths and Marriages to a person born or residing abroad to produce his passport was not race discrimination according to the Court of Appeal in *Tejani* v *Superintendent Registrar for the District of Peterborough* [1986] IRLR 502. The request was not made because of the applicant's racial or national origins within the statute. On the facts found, the Registrar treated alike everyone who came from abroad.

In *Qureshi* v *London Borough of Newham* [1991] IRLR 264, the Court of Appeal held that a mere failure by an employer to follow the terms of its equal opportunities policy did not in itself found a discrimination claim. The defect in reasoning by the tribunal was an assumption that the policy would have been properly applied to persons of different racial origin from the applicant.

In the very important case of *James* v *Eastleigh BC* [1989] 3 WLR 123, the two central concepts of less favourable treatment on the grounds of sex were considered in the context of a rather unusual claim for direct discrimination in relation to the provision of facilities. These points are equally valid in employment claims. The plaintiff male who had retired and his wife both went to a leisure centre run by the defendant local authority. They were both aged 61. The wife was admitted free of charge but the plaintiff had to pay. Free admittance was only available to persons who had reached state pension age. The Court of Appeal held that in a case of direct discrimination, it was necessary to consider *why* the defendant treated the plaintiff less favourably. Here, the aim of the council in giving free admittance was to provide benefits to those with limited resources. Since neither the overt condition imposed nor any covert reason related directly to the sex of the plaintiff it could not be said that the defendant was afforded less favourable treatment 'on the ground of' sex. The House of Lords overturned the decision by a three to two majority. The test was simply 'would the complainant have received the same treatment from the defendant but for his or her sex'. The subjective motive, intention or reason was irrelevant. The use of the statutory pension age as a criterion in this case was thus directly discriminatory, and could not be justified as it would have been open to the defendant to do in the case of indirect discrimination. The issue is further illustrated in the following cases.

In *Berrisford* v *Woodard Schools (Midlands Division) Ltd* [1991] ICR 564 the applicant was an assistant matron at a girls' boarding school who fell pregnant but had no plans to marry the father of the child. She was told that she had to marry or leave and, when she said she had no wish to marry, she would be dismissed. The tribunal accepted that a male teacher known to have engaged in extra-marital sex would also have been dismissed, and thus rejected the complaint, and the EAT by a majority upheld the decision. The fact that the evidence in the case of the woman was visible pregnancy did not affect the validity of the comparison. See also *R* v *Commission for Racial Equality ex parte Westminster City Council* [1985] IRLR 426; *Din* v *Carrington Viyella Ltd* [1982] ICR 256; *R* v *Birmingham City Council ex parte Equal Opportunities Commission* [1989] IRLR 173; *Greig* v *Community Industry* [1979] IRLR 158; *Shomer* v *B&R Residential Lettings Ltd* [1992] IRLR 317.

In *Bain* v *Bowles* [1991] IRLR 356 the Court of Appeal followed *James* in deciding that the defendants, who published *The Lady*, had discriminated against the male plaintiff when they refused to publish his advertisement for a housekeeper in accordance with their policy of only including advertisements for female employees outside the UK when the employer was a woman.

In *Dhatt v McDonalds Hamburgers Ltd* [1991] ICR 238 this provision was adopted to deny a claim by an Indian national who was required to produce evidence of his right to work in the UK, even though a similar request was not made to British and EEC citizens. The proper comparison to be made by the tribunal was not between British and EEC citizens on the one hand and Indian nationals on the other but rather between Mr Dhatt on the one hand and others who were not British and EEC citizens on the other. The relevant circumstances were then the same in that all required either a work permit or indefinite leave to enter and all were treated alike by the employers' question. There was no distinction on grounds of nationality since all persons not British citizens or from the EEC of whatever nationality were treated alike. The applicant's claim thus failed.

There is no restriction on the employer having a variety of retiring ages for different jobs provided that there is no direct or indirect discrimination (*Bullock v Alice Ottley School* [1993] ICR 138). In this case, the differences were caused by differences in recruiting and retaining the group of employees to which most of the men belonged and were not sex specific (see also *McConomy v Croft Inns Ltd* [1992] IRLR 561).

The Court of Appeal was held, in *R v Ministry of Defence ex parte Smith* [1996] IRLR 100, that discrimination on grounds of sexual orientation is not sex discrimination. It is hard to see how this can be the case when a person of one sex is discriminated against for having feelings towards members of his or her own sex, when members of the opposite sex having those same feelings towards those same people would not be discriminated against (for more detail, see para. 8.3.2).

8.1.1.3 Generalised assumptions The words of the statute also cover cases where the reason for discrimination is a *generalised assumption* that people of a particular sex, marital status or race possess or lack certain characteristics. In *Coleman v Skyrail Oceanic Ltd* [1981] IRLR 398, a booking clerk in the respondent's travel agency was dismissed when she married a man employed by a rival tour operator, even though she promised not to divulge confidential information, and there was no evidence that she had done so during her engagement. The EAT found the dismissal unfair because of its abruptness but overturned the decision of the industrial tribunal that her treatment constituted unlawful discrimination, on the grounds both of sex and marital status since Mrs Coleman might have given away information, and was not the breadwinner of the family. Slynn J also thought the treatment was not discriminatory since other employees with close relationships, such as brothers and sisters or engaged couples, might have been treated in the same way (see also *Moberly v Commonwealth Hall* [1977] IRLR 176). The decision was, however, overturned by the Court of Appeal (with Shaw LJ dissenting), on the ground that the *assumption* that the man was the breadwinner without further investigation of the personal situation was, in itself, discriminatory. The husband in fact was earning only a modest wage, and there was no evidence that his employers were reluctant to dismiss *him*. The Court also noted that in 56.2 per cent of households married women contributed to their income.

It was also unlawful for the same reason for the respondents in *Horsey v Dyfed CC* [1982] IRLR 395 to refuse to second the applicant to a training course in the London area where her husband was employed because they assumed that she would remain in London when her course was completed and not return to work for the respondents in Wales. It was an inescapable inference that the respondents would have treated a married *man* differently from the way in which they treated the applicant. The EAT did not, however, say that an employer could never act on the basis that a wife would give up her job to join her husband. What the employer could not do was to *assume* that this was so. He must look at the particular circumstances of each case.

8.1.1.4 Sexual harassment The European Union Code of Practice on 'The Dignity of Men and Women at Work' defines sexual harassment as 'unwanted conduct of a sexual nature or other conduct based on sex affecting the dignity of men and women at work'. It goes on to say that harassment pollutes the working environment and can have a devastating effect upon the health, confidence, morale and performance of those affected by it (see e.g. *Wadman* v *Carpenter Farrer Partnership* [1993] IRLR 374). Sexual harassment comprises unwelcome acts involving physical contact of a sexual nature and conduct falling short of such physical acts. It is a form of sex discrimination (*Porcelli* v *Strathclyde Regional Council* [1986] IRLR 134, *Bracebridge Engineering Ltd* v *Darby* [1990] IRLR 3). Sexual harassment may arise from a single act so long as this is serious enough to cause a detriment (see also *Enterprise Glass Co. Ltd* v *Miles* [1990] ICR 787). The question to be posed must follow the statutory language: 'Was the applicant less favourably treated on the grounds of her sex than a man would have been treated?' Lord Emslie in *Porcelli* stated that sexual harassment was a particularly degrading and unacceptable form of treatment which it must be taken to have been the intention of Parliament to restrain (see *Wileman* v *Minilec Engineering Ltd* [1988] IRLR 144).

8.1.2 Indirect discrimination

The concept of indirect discrimination, which was first introduced in the Sex Discrimination Act 1975 and then included in the Race Relations Act 1976, crucially recognises that inequality does not only result from intentional overt acts, the model of *direct* discrimination. Some of the most insidious institutional discrimination operates at a more subtle level, by way of tests or requirements, which, although applying to both sexes or all races, in effect discriminate against one. This is often the legacy of past discrimination. The United States Supreme Court found the concept implicit in the very fabric of the prohibition against discrimination in the Civil Rights Act 1964. The essence of its leading judgment in *Griggs* v *Duke Power Co.* (1971) 401 US 424, is that 'Practices, procedures, tests . . . neutral on their face . . . cannot be maintained if they operate to freeze the status quo of past discrimination'. Thus a height requirement in a company rule book may indirectly discriminate against women, although those who inserted the provision did not at all advert to its effect on them, and short men would be treated similarly.

The English statutes provide that indirect discrimination occurs when an employer applies a requirement or condition which, even though it applies equally to all persons:

(a)   is such that the proportion of people of one race or sex who *can comply* with it is considerably smaller than the proportion in another;
(b)   the employer cannot show is justifiable on other than racial or sexual grounds; and
(c)   is to the detriment of the complainant because he/she cannot comply with it.

Each element of this concept will be considered here in turn, save for detriment which is fully considered in para. 8.2.10. The effect of introducing the concept here is that the right of action is restricted to individual complainants who have actually been affected by the condition in question. The EOC and CRE, however, have wider power to issue a non-discrimination notice when it is practised on a wider scale or without a victim, and it is these practices into which their formal investigations are directed (para. 8.7.5).

The case of *Steel* v *Union of Post Office Workers* [1977] IRLR 288 demonstrates the importance of such an action in rooting out the effects of past discrimination. Mrs Steel had been employed as a postman since 1961, but until 1975 women could hold only temporary and not permanent positions, and this deprived her of the seniority which would have given her priority in allocation of the best postal rounds. She complained when she was turned down for a particularly favourable 'walk' in favour of a man who had greater seniority as a 'permanent' postman, although he had only joined the service in 1973. The EAT found the Post Office's practice prima facie to amount to indirect discrimination, and remitted the case to the tribunal to 'weigh up in particular the needs of the enterprise against the discriminatory effect of the requirement or condition'.

The complexity of the concept may be seen from *Jones* v *Chief Adjudication Officer* [1990] IRLR 533, a case involving a social security invalidity pension, where the Court of Appeal identified the following process where one qualification was under challenge:

(a)   identify the criterion for selection;

(b)   identify the relevant population, comparing all those who satisfy the other criteria for selection;

(c)   divide the relevant population into groups representing those who satisfy the criterion and those who do not;

(d)   predict statistically what proportion of each group should consist of women;

(e)   ascertain what are the actual male/female balances in the two groups;

(f)   compare the actual with the predicted balances;

(g)   if women are found to be under-represented in the second, it is proved that the criterion is discriminatory.

8.1.2.1   Requirement or condition   In *Price* v *Civil Service Commission* [1978] ICR 27 at 30, the EAT stated 'it is necessary to define with some precision the requirement or condition which is called in question', and this need to identify a requirement or condition is not overriden by the decision of the ECJ in *Enderby* v *Frenchay Health Authority* [1993] IRLR 591 (para. 7.2.4.3) (*Bhudi* v *IMI Refiners Ltd* [1994] IRLR 204). The purpose of the draftsman using both words was to extend the ambit of what is covered so as to include anything which fairly falls within the ordinary meaning of either word. In *Perera* v *Civil Service Commission* and *Department of Customs and Excise (No. 2)* [1983] IRLR 166, however, there was no identifiable 'requirement or condition'. The applicant complained that the respondents took into account practical experience in England and ability to communicate in English in their considerations of applicants as administrative trainees. The EAT rejected the claim that these constituted requirements or conditions on the grounds that these were merely *some* of the plus and minus factors which the respondents took into account and which could offset each other. A requirement or condition was, rather, something which *had to be complied with*, a 'must'. The only relevant condition here was that the applicant was a barrister or solicitor and it was a condition which the applicant fulfilled so it could not be a detriment to him (see also *Francis* v *British Airways Engineering Overhaul Ltd* [1982] IRLR 10; *Watches of Switzerland Ltd* v *Savell* [1983] IRLR 141; *Briggs* v *North Eastern Education and Library Board* [1990] IRLR 181). To fall within the provisions a qualification must thus be an absolute bar and not merely one factor which the alleged discriminator had taken into account in reaching its decision (*Meer* v

London Borough of Tower Hamlets [1988] IRLR 399; see also *Weaver* v *NATFHE* [1988] ICR 599). The following have also been held to be requirements or conditions:

(a) a request that a person return to work full-time (*Home Office* v *Holmes* [1984] IRLR 299; cf. *Clymo* v *London Borough of Wandsworth* [1989] IRLR 241);

(b) that part-time workers should be dismissed first under a redundancy selection agreement (*Clarke* v *Eley (IMI) Kynoch Ltd* [1982] IRLR 482);

(c) that work be allocated by reference to the seniority of employees (*Steel* v *Union of Postal Workers,* supra);

(d) a refusal to employ a person with young children, since this would affect considerably more married than unmarried persons (*Thorndyke* v *Bell Fruit (North Central) Ltd* [1979] IRLR 1, *Hurley* v *Mustoe* [1981] IRLR 208);

(e) a refusal to hire persons resident in Liverpool 8 postal district where 50 per cent of the population were black (*Hussein* v *Saints Complete House Furnishers Ltd* [1979] IRLR 337);

(f) the requirement of the Council of Legal Education that graduates from overseas universities should complete three years' study at its School of Law while those from British and Irish institutions need only serve two (*Bohon-Mitchell* v *Common Professional Examination Board and the Council of Legal Education* [1978] IRLR 525);

(g) language tests which exclude large numbers from ethnic minority groups;

(h) a requirement that applicants for Manpower Services Commission sponsorship have managerial experience, since this was less easy for overseas applicants to comply with (*Ojutiku and Oburani* v *Manpower Services Commission* [1981] IRLR 156);

(i) requiring applicants for the post of telex operator to become competent in the use of a particular British machine within six months and without formal training, which was much more difficult for those not born in England (*Bayoomi* v *British Railways Board* [1981] IRLR 431);

(j) imposing an upper age limit of 32 on administrative trainees for the Civil Service because of the number of people from ethnic minorities who immigrated to Britain when already adult (*Perera* v *Civil Service Commission* and *Department of Customs and Excise (No. 2),* supra; see also *University of Manchester* v *Jones* [1993] ICR 474);

(k) requiring school pupils to conform to uniform regulations which required the applicant to cut his hair and remove his turban (*Mandla* v *Dowell Lee* [1983] 2 AC 548; see also in respect of turbans worn in railway carriage repair shop *Singh* v *British Rail Engineering Ltd* [1986] ICR 22);

(l) a rule of the Community Programme restricting access to those already claiming unemployment or supplementary benefit (*Cobb* v *Secretary of State for Employment* [1989] ICR 506);

(m) dismissal on the ground of redundancy because the appellants were part-time cleaners and not full-time (*Bhudi* v *IMI Refiners Ltd* [1994] IRLR 204).

(n) a rule that holidays were not to be taken during the employer's busiest season, since Muslims were unable to take time off for the important Eid religious festival (*J. H. Walker Ltd* v *Hussain* [1996] IRLR 10).

On indirect discrimination in occupational pension schemes, see para. 8.2.8.

8.1.2.2 Ability to comply with requirement or condition In *Mandla* v *Dowell Lee* (supra) the House of Lords understood 'can comply' as meaning 'can consistently with the customs and cultural conditions of the racial group' rather than the restricted meaning of 'can physically' conform. This is essentially an issue of fact (*University of Manchester* v *Jones* [1993] ICR 474). In *Price* v *Civil Service Commission* [1978] ICR 27 the EAT thought that the phrase was to be interpreted broadly: 'It should not be said that a person "can" do something merely because it is *theoretically possible* for him to do so; it is necessary to see whether he can do so *in practice*'.

The facts of the case provide a good illustration of the mischief at which indirect discrimination is aimed. Mrs Price, who was 36, sought to become an executive officer in the Civil Service but her application was summarily rejected because the employers sought only candidates aged between 17½ and 28. The reason why she had not applied whilst she was within that age range was that she had had two children, and she argued that this was the position of many women, so that considerably fewer could qualify for the job. The industrial tribunal initially rejected her application on the ground that the number of men and women in the relevant age range was about the same, and since no one was obliged to have children, the applicant could comply with the condition. The case was sent back to the tribunal with instructions to examine 'current usual behaviour' and 'general social facts'. In fact the respondents on remission conceded that the number of women who could in this sense comply with the condition was much less than that of men. They failed to justify the practice (*Price* v *CSC* [1978] IRLR 3) since it was too wide and discriminatory a way of achieving the aims which the Civil Service said it sought—a proper career structure (see also *Raval* v *DHSS* [1985] IRLR 370, *Training Commission* v *Jackson* [1990] ICR 222).

8.1.2.3 'Considerably smaller proportion'   The use of the words 'considerably smaller [proportion]' does not rule out the case where no members of a particular sex or race can in fact comply with the condition or requirement rather than there being merely a smaller *proportion* who may (*Greencroft Social Club and Institute* v *Mullen* [1985] ICR 796). The industrial tribunal should identify with clarity the applicant's racial group with which the proportional inability to comply with a condition must be assessed (*London Borough of Tower Hamlets* v *Qayyum* [1987] ICR 729; on sex discrimination see *Turner* v *Labour Party* [1987] IRLR 101).

The need for specific statistical evidence is shown by the surprising decision of the EAT in *Kidd* v *DRG (UK) Ltd* [1985] ICR 405. An industrial tribunal was held to be entitled to decide that in modern times it was not safe to assume that a greater proportion of women than men, or married women than unmarried women, regularly undertook a child-caring role which precluded or greatly restricted their acceptance of full-time employment. Surprisingly, the EAT decided that the choice of an appropriate section of the community for the purpose of comparison was a matter of fact for the industrial tribunal. On the other hand, in *Raval* v *DHSS* (supra), the EAT held that the ability of Indians to pass a particular language examination was bound to be affected if the examination was set in and related to a language which was not the language of the examinee's home or was a second language to him. Such a proposition required no statistical proof.

The comparison must be such that the relevant circumstances in both cases are not materially different (*Orphanos* v *Queen Mary College* [1985] IRLR 349) but a pool for comparison does not have to be shown to be a statistically *perfect* match of the persons who would be capable of filling and interested in the post (*Greater Manchester Police Authority* v *Lea* [1990] IRLR 372, where the EAT felt it was not able to interfere with the tribunal's finding that 95.3 per cent is considerably smaller than 99.4 per cent). For a decision to be overturned on appeal, it must be shown that no reasonable tribunal could have adopted the course the tribunal did (*University of Manchester* v *Jones* [1993] ICR 474).

In *McCausland* v *Dungannon District Council* [1993] IRLR 583, the Northern Ireland Court of Appeal treated it as a matter of fact in each case whether a considerably smaller proportion could comply with a requirement or condition and refused to adopt any rule of thumb, such as the four-fifths rule for establishing adverse impact applied in the United States of America, for measuring what is or is not a significantly disproportionate effect (see also *Jones* v *Chief Adjudication Officer* [1990] IRLR 533). In *R* v *Secretary of State for Education and Science ex parte Schaffter* [1987] IRLR 53, Schiemann J summarised the provision (at p. 56):

what you should do is to establish: first, the proportion of all women who can comply with the requirement — I shall call this X per cent; secondly, the proportion of all men who can comply with the requirement — I shall call this Y per cent; thirdly, compare X and Y and determine whether one is considerably smaller than the other.

In *University of Manchester* v *Jones* (supra) the applicant had obtained a university degree as a mature student and answered an advertisement for the post of careers adviser at Manchester University which stated that the person appointed would be a 'graduate, preferably aged 27–35 years'. She was 46 and was accordingly not selected for interview. She claimed that the contents of the advertisement were indirectly discriminatory. The relevant populations were all men and women graduates with the necessary experience, not those who had undertaken degrees as mature students. Any disproportionate effect would have to be demonstrated in relation to that wider pool. Section 5(3) of the SDA 1975 required a comparison of like with like. Peter Gibson LJ reasoned that:

The section referred not to the number of men and women who could comply with the requirement but to the proportion of men and women. That showed that those men and women who could comply with the requirement were to be considered as a proportion of another number and that number had to be the relevant total of men and women to whom the requirement would be applied.

8.1.2.4 Justification

Some conditions are imposed on quite reasonable grounds, and it is considered unfair and inefficient to completely prohibit them just because they may have an adverse effect on certain groups. The employer may thus impose conditions and requirements which have disproportionate impact on a racial group or sex if he can show that they are 'justifiable'. The House of Lords in *Orphanos* v *Queen Mary College* (supra) said that justifiable meant 'capable of being justified' (*University of Manchester* v *Jones* [1993] ICR 474).

In *Hampson* v *Dept of Education and Science* [1989] IRLR 69, Balcombe LJ stated that it 'requires an objective balance between the discriminatory effect of the condition and the reasonable needs of the party who applies the condition', although this argument was not considered by the House of Lords ([1990] IRLR 302, [1990] ICR 511; see also *Greater Manchester Police Authority* v *Lea* [1990] IRLR 372). It may be possible to justify by reference to grounds other than economic or administrative efficiency. That the efficiency of the employer's operation is to be taken into account in determining this question was confirmed by the EAT in *Greater Glasgow Health Board* v *Carey* [1987] IRLR 484. (See also *Briggs* v *North Eastern Education and Library Board* [1990] IRLR 181.)

The test of justification is generally objective, not resting solely on what the employer considers to be justifiable. The stringency of the standard has varied in different cases. The question is one of fact for the industrial tribunal (*Mandla*'s case (supra), *Greencroft Social Club and Institute* v *Mullen* [1985] ICR 796, *Singh* v *British Rail Engineering Ltd* [1986] ICR 22, *Secretary of State for Employment* v *Chandler* [1986] ICR 436). In *Raval* v *DHSS* [1985] IRLR 370 it was not a ground for interference by the EAT that another industrial tribunal might well have taken the opposite view.

A blanket rule which incorporates discriminatory assumptions may prove very difficult to justify. Thus in *Hurley* v *Mustoe* [1981] IRLR 208, where a restaurant manager sought to uphold a general refusal to employ waitresses with young children, it was not sufficient to claim that it was necessary for his small business that employees be reliable. A condition excluding *all* members of a class from employment cannot be justified on the ground that *some* members of that class are unreliable. The employer must investigate the reliability of each member of that class just like all others on their merits. This does not, however, inflexibly require that there be external or independent evidence of justification.

The following cases illustrate the approach of the EAT, Court of Appeal and House of Lords:

(a) In *Singh* v *Rowntree Mackintosh Ltd* [1979] IRLR 199, where the employer's rule that no beards should be worn in their chocolate factory on the grounds of hygiene, effectively excluded all Sikhs, Lord Macdonald thought the term 'necessary' used in *Steel* v *Union of Post Office Workers* [1977] IRLR 288, must be 'applied reasonably and with common sense'. An employer must be allowed some independence of judgment as to what he deems to be 'commercially expedient'. That the employers, who were in competition with other manufacturers, considered standards of hygiene of the highest importance, and the course of action had been approved by the district health officer, rendered the requirement justifiable even though it was not imposed at six of its eight other plants (see also *Panesar* v *Nestlé Co. Ltd* [1980] ICR 144, *Singh* v *British Rail Engineering Ltd* (supra) on the importance of safety considerations).

(b) In *Mandla* v *Dowell Lee* (supra) the defendant, a school headmaster, sought to justify the school rule against turbans on the ground that he was seeking to run a Christian school and that the turban was a manifestation of a non-Christian faith. The House of Lords did not accept this contention since the requirement in question had to be justifiable *without* regard to the ethnic origins of the applicant. Jusification might be based in a proper case on, for example, public health or the prohibitive cost of alternative arrangements.

(c) In *Ojutiku and Oburoni* v *Manpower Services Commission* [1982] IRLR 418, a requirement that applicants for MSC Training Opportunities Scheme sponsorship for a Management Studies Diploma have managerial experience could be justified even though that prima facie indirectly discriminated against those with foreign origins. It was immaterial that the lack of managerial experience was due to direct racial discrimination by employers in the past. (See also *Chiu* v *British Aerospace Ltd* [1982] IRLR 56.)

(d) In *Kidd* v *DRG (UK) Ltd* [1985] ICR 405, the EAT found (in the alternative to the decision that there was insufficient evidence) that selection for redundancy on the basis of part-time workers first was justifiable since there were marginal advantages in retaining one shift of full-time rather than two shifts of part-time workers. A record had to be maintained of the name of each operative who had handled a package in the factory. Using part-timers involved an increase in the length of staff records; the change-over of shift caused a 'mild degree' of disruption; each shift needed clean overalls; and there was a general increase in administrative and personnel functions. Waite J commended the tribunal for its decision since it reflected a realistic recognition that under the competitive conditions of modern industry small advantages of that kind can cumulatively make a crucial difference between success and failure.

(e)   In *Clarke* v *Eley (IMI) Kynoch Ltd* [1983] ICR 165 a policy of 'last in first out' as selection for redundancy was probably justifiable as a 'necessary means (viewed in a reasonable and common sense way) of achieving a necessary objective, i.e. an agreed criterion for selection'.

(f)   The restriction of unfair dismissal and redundancy rights on the basis of hours of work and basing redundancy payments on final salary were not justifiable according to the House of Lords, although the Government had argued and persuaded the Divisional Court that the former was justifiable on the basis that to reduce thresholds to legal protection would adversely affect the employment opportunities available for part-time work (*R* v *Secretary of State for Employment ex parte EOC* [1991] IRLR 493, [1992] ICR 341, [1994] ICR 317, HL).

(g)   In the case of a voluntary aided Church of England school which advertised for a headteacher who was a 'committed communicant Christian', the industrial tribunal should determine whether the school governors' objective was legitimate and whether the application of the condition was a reasonable means of achieving that objective when balanced on the principles of proportionality between the discriminatory effect of the condition and the reasonable needs of the governors (*Board of Governors of St Matthias Church of England School* v *Crizzle* [1993] ICR 401; see also *University of Manchester* v *Jones* [1993] ICR 474).

(h)   In *Brook* v *London Borough of Haringey* [1992] ICR 478, the EAT held that a LIFO (last-in-first-out) selection criterion for redundancy, whereby short-serving employees are selected before longer-serving employees, was not indirectly discriminatory against women (who tend to belong predominantly to the former group) because historically both sides of industry and ACAS have considered such a criterion to be justified. But it is not clear why the disparate impact this criterion has on women is objectively justified, and in any event the assumption needs explanation, which the EAT did not provide.

(i)   Another far-reaching decision is that in *Home Office* v *Holmes* [1984] IRLR 299, where the applicant successfully challenged the requirement of the respondents' Immigration and Nationality Department that she return to work full-time after pregnancy. It worked to her detriment as a single mother and was not found to be justifiable. The employer could not rely on the argument that because the bulk of industry is organised in a particular way (here by full-time employment), the requirement in a particular case is self-evidently justified. This case was distinguished, however, in *Clymo* v *London Borough of Wandsworth* [1989] ICR 250. Wood J said that provided the employer's decision to permit a 'job share' was made upon adequate grounds, and bearing in mind the need to avoid discrimination, the decision was one for management and was in the instant case justifiable.

(j)   A general requirement that telex operators should within six months of appointment and without any formal training become fully competent in the job was not justifiable (*Bayoomi* v *British Airways Board* [1981] IRLR 431).

(k)   A health authority rule that female nurses must not wear trousers on duty was justifiable (*Kingston & Richmond Area Health Authority* v *Kaur* [1981] ICR 631).

(l)   Insistence on an English language 'O' level or its equivalent as the sole and exclusive criterion of ability to communicate was justifiable (*Raval* v *DHSS* [1985] IRLR 370).

8.1.3   Victimisation

Unlawful victimisation arises where a person is treated less favourably because he:

(a)   brings proceedings;
(b)   gives evidence or information;
(c)   alleges a contravention or otherwise acts under the Equal Pay, Sex Discrimination
or Race Relations Acts; or
(d)   intends to do any of these things (SDA 1975, s. 4(1); RRA 1976, s. 2(1).

This rubric includes reporting facts which ought to be investigated to the local Community Relations Council (*Kirby* v *Manpower Services Commission* [1980] IRLR 229), but an employee is not protected if any such allegation is both *false* and made in *bad faith* (RRA 1976, s. 2(2); SDA 1975, s. 4(2)).

In order to succeed in a claim of victimisation the applicant must show that one of the acts in (a) to (d) above done by the applicant (such as bringing an earlier complaint of discrimination) has influenced the alleged victimiser in his unfavourable treatment of the applicant. In the Court of Appeal decision which formulated this proposition, *Aziz* v *Trinity Taxis Ltd* [1988] ICR 534, the applicant was expelled from a cooperative taxi association because he had made secret tape recordings for use in proposed discrimination proceedings. Since the decision to expel would have been the same even though the recordings had nothing to do with a discrimination claim, the victimisation allegation was not made out. (See also *Cornelius* v *University College of Swansea* [1987] IRLR 141.)

It is also necessary to show that the victimisation is as a result of an allegation of a breach of the SDA or RRA committed *by the victimiser*. It follows that if the victimisation by the employer is consequent upon an allegation of discrimination by a fellow employee of the applicant, for which the employer is not vicariously liable, the claim of victimisation will itself fail, according to the EAT in *Waters* v *Commissioner of Police of the Metropolis* [1995] IRLR 531. This decision, while correct on the wording of both of the Acts, is most unsatisfactory from the point of view of principle.

The Social Security Act 1989 extends these provisions to cover a person who has: (a) brought proceedings under Sch. 5 to that Act that is, to enforce the principle of equal treatment in relation to occupational pension schemes, on which see para. 8.2.9; (b) has given evidence or information in connection with such proceedings; or (c) has otherwise done anything under or by reference to the schedule or has alleged that an act has been committed which would amount to a contravention of the schedule.

8.1.4   Segregation

It is unlawful to maintain separate facilities for members of different races, even though they are equal in quality (RRA 1976, s. 1(2)). There is thus no room for any form of apartheid in English law. The decision in *Pel Ltd* v *Modgill* [1980] IRLR 142, shows that the section does not impose *positive* obligations on the employer to pursue actively integration between racial groups. The employers were thus not at fault in failing to insist that Asians go into the mainly white paint shop of their factory in order to remove *de facto* separation. There is no comparable provision as to the keeping apart of members of different sexes.

8.1.5   'Transferred' discrimination

The general direct discrimination prohibition has been somewhat extended to include sacking an employee for serving a black customer (*Zarczynska* v *Levy* [1979] 1 All ER 814).

This appears to be a sort of *transferred* discrimination — dismissal not because of the employee's colour but rather that of the customer. Further, in *Showboat Entertainment Centre Ltd* v *Owens* [1984] IRLR 7 the applicant, a white man, claimed that he was dismissed as manager of an amusement centre because he refused to carry out the employer's instruction to exclude young black people. The EAT decided that the subsection covered all cases in which an employee was treated less favourably on racial grounds even though the race in question was that of another person than the applicant. One ground for this decision was that it would place the applicant in an impossible position if he had to choose between being party to illegality and losing his job. See also *Smyth* v *Croft Inns Ltd* [1996] IRLR 84.

8.1.6 Sex discrimination and part-time workers

The most significant development in discrimination in the 1990s thus far has been the House of Lords decision in *R* v *Secretary of State for Employment ex parte EOC* (supra) which ruled that the minimum hours provisions in the Employment Protection (Consolidation) Act 1978 were unlawful. The case has an importance which transcends its factual circumstances and has profound constitutional significance. It was a major breakthrough that the House of Lords determined that the EOC had *locus standi* to seek a declaration that UK legislation was in breach of the UK's obligation under the Treaty of Rome. As to the discrimination issues themselves, the House of Lords was unanimous in determining that the Secretary of State for Employment had not demonstrated that the 'threshold' hours provisions were objectively justified because it led to an increase in the availability of part-time work. Lord Keith stated that the same result could be achieved from a situation where the basic rate of pay for part-time workers was less than the basic rate for full-time workers. It was also noted by their Lordships that no other Member State of the European Community apart from the Republic of Ireland had legislation providing for similar thresholds. The House of Lords held that a redundancy payment was clearly 'pay' for the purposes of the Treaty of Rome, but were not definitive as to whether compensation for unfair dismissal was.

The EAT in *Mediguard Services Ltd* v *Thame* [1994] IRLR 504, took the principle in the *EOC* case one stage further in holding that unfair dismissal compensation was pay within Article 119, so that the employee could claim unfair dismissal although she lacked the five years' continuous service required by statute for an employee who had worked between eight and 16 hours per week. This whole issue was, however, thrown into doubt by the decision of the Court of Appeal in *R* v *Secretary of State for Employment ex parte Seymour-Smith* [1995] ICR 889.

In *Freers & Speckmann* v *Deutsche Bundepost*, unreported (ECJ), 7 March 1996, the claim concerned compensation for time spent on a training course which was necessary for the performance of the employees' staff committee functions but which took place outside their individual working hours. They were employed part-time by the defendant for 18 hours a week. They attended a week long training course which lasted approximately $38\frac{1}{2}$ hours, that is the weekly working hours laid down for full-time employees in the relevant collective agreement. The employers paid the employees their normal wages calculated on the basis of their part-time work. The German Government argued before the ECJ that this did not fall within the scope of Article 119 because staff committee functions were performed on an unpaid honorary basis and the compensation received was intended only to make good the loss of earnings suffered by staff committee members when staff representation functions, or information or training courses needed for the proper performance of those functions took place during working hours. The ECJ reiterated that legal concepts laid down by national law could not affect the interpretation of Community law. Although the compensation in issue in this case did not derive as such from the contract of employment, it was paid by the employer 'by virtue of legislative provisions and under a contract of employment' so that it did indeed fall within the scope of Article 119. The ECJ emphasised that exclusion of part-timers might be 'justified by objective factors unrelated to any discrimination based on sex'. The German court making the reference considered that the legislature's wish to place the independence of staff council members above financial inducements for performing staff council functions was an aim of social policy, and the ECJ concluded that such an aim appeared unrelated to discrimination on the grounds of sex, reiterating the principles laid down in *Bestuur van het Algemeen Burgerlijk Pensioenfonds* v *Beune* [1995] IRLR 103. The principle enunciated by the ECJ (at para. 29) was that 'It is for the national court to ascertain, in the light of all the relevant factors and taking into account the possibility of achieving the social policy aims by other means, whether the difference of treatment was suitable and necessary for achieving that aim.

(See also *Kuratorium fur Dialyse und Nierentransplantation EV* v *Lewark* [1996] IRLR 637; cf. *Manor Bakeries Ltd* v *Nazir* [1996] IRLR 604.)

8.1.7   Intentional harassment

The new offence of intentional harassment created by the Criminal Justice and Public Order Act 1994 should be noted in this context. It introduced, as from 3 February 1995, a new s. 4A into the Public Order Act 1986 which, whilst wider in its terms, was intended to respond to concern over the increasing incidence of racial harassment. It renders a person guilty of an offence if he with intent, causes another person harassment, alarm or distress by using threatening, abusive or insulting words or behaviour or disorderly conduct or by displaying any writing, sign or other visible representation which is threatening, abusive or insulting. It is a defence for an accused person to prove that his conduct was reasonable in the circumstances of the case. Incidents in the workplace are included within its scope and the offence carries a maximum penalty of six months' imprisonment or a fine not exceeding £5,000. It is an arrestable offence.

8.2   THE SCOPE OF PROHIBITED DISCRIMINATION

The scope of unlawful discrimination is very widely drawn and encompasses every stage of employment. Thus an employee may complain if he is discriminated against in any of the following ways.

8.2.1   Arrangements for recruitment (RRA 1976, s. 4)

A woman or black person can claim if she or he is put off applying for a job by reason of, for example, the way an interview is set up, the questions asked there, or being left off a short list (*Saunders* v *Richmond LBC* [1977] IRLR 362). It is no defence that the employer has so made arrangements in order to keep an overall balance between the sexes. In *Brennan* v *J.H. Dewhurst Ltd* [1983] IRLR 357 a tribunal found that the conduct by the local manager of a butcher's shop at an interview suggested that he did not want a woman for the job on offer, but that there was no discrimination since no one had ultimately been appointed to the job. The EAT thought differently since the subsection covered the discriminatory operation of *arrangements* for selection as well as discriminatory *selection*.

8.2.2 Advertisements

Discriminatory advertisements may be included under the rubric 'arrangements for recruitment', where they impinge on an individual and deter his application for a job; but the EOC and CRE also have general powers to seek an injunction to restrain 'victimless' advertisements. Proof is facilitated in the Sex Discrimination Act by special rules on the use of words with a sexual connotation: thus the description 'sales girl or waitress' is taken to indicate an intention to discriminate unless it is made clear that the position is open to both sexes. Otherwise the correct test is the likely response of the ordinary reader. In *Commission for Racial Equality* v *Associated Newspapers Group Ltd* [1978] 1 WLR 905 (under the similarly worded s. 6(1) of the Race Relations Act 1968), an advertisement for nurses in South African hospitals included the words 'All white patients', but the Court of Appeal held that that would not reasonably be taken to mean that only white *applicants* would be considered. Moreover, the publisher of any such advertisement escapes liability if he proves that he acted reasonably in reliance on a statement by the person effecting the publication that it would not be unlawful. (See also *London Borough of Lambeth* v *CRE* [1990] IRLR 231.)

8.2.3 Refusal or deliberate omission to offer employment

This is one of the few areas where a *potential* employee can complain.

8.2.4 Terms and conditions of employment

The position with regard to race is here straightforward, but difficulties arise in respect of sex discrimination because of the mismatch between the two statutes in the field. The Equal Pay Act 1970 is relevant when a job has been offered and accepted, but if the prospective employee is deterred from accepting the job at all because of the terms offered, the SDA is the proper statute (SDA 1975, s. 6(6)).

8.2.5 Access to transfer or promotion (SDA 1975, s. 6(2)(a))

Example Harry, a West Indian, proves to be an excellent delicatessen manager but Eric refuses to promote him to be assistant manager of the store because he fears that some employees might object. This is prima facie direct discrimination in access to promotion.

8.2.6 Access to training

Differentiation in this respect is generally unlawful, but there is a defence to an action where the employer is taking steps to train minorities and the racial group favoured has been under-represented in the company during any time in the previous 12 months (SDA 1975, s. 6(2)(a)).

8.2.7 Fringe benefits

This heading covers facilities or services, such as loans, medical care, bonuses, travel, free legal advice or access to sports facilities. Again, there is overlap here between the respective spheres of the Equal Pay Act concerning contractual benefits and the Sex Discrimination Act which covers the remainder.

Example   Crest's contract contains a loan scheme for male employees who get married, and Diana complains that she is discriminated against by being refused a loan. This must be brought under the Equal Pay Act. If the scheme is not mentioned in the contract, the complaint is to be made under the SDA. If no man is employed but Diana claims that if he were to be hired he would be given a loan, the SDA is again the relevant statute. If the scheme applies only to whites, Harry can claim under the Race Relations Act, whether or not it is mentioned in the contract.

8.2.8   Occupational pension schemes

8.2.8.1   Background   Schedule 5 of the Social Security Act 1989 was the UK's first effort to implement EEC Directive 86/378 and the principle of equal treatment into the domestic law governing occupational pension schemes. However, it was overtaken by events, namely the decisions of the ECJ in *Barber* v *Guardian Royal Exchange Assurance Group* [1990] ICR 616 and subsequent cases (see para. 7.7.1.2), and the UK Government never brought most of Sch. 5 properly into force. On 1 January 1996, ss. 62–66 of the Pensions Act 1995 came into force. These supplant most of the provisions of Sch. 5 of the 1989 Act, and are designed to make UK law comply with the *Barber* line of cases. They are supplemented by the Occupational Pension Schemes (Equal Treatment) Regulations 1995 (SI 1995 No. 3183) to which all the regulation numbers in this section relate.

8.2.8.2   Scope   Schedule 5 of the 1989 Act embodied a gradualist approach: had it ever come into force, the Act would have empowered the Occupational Pensions Board to make an order modifying, or authorising the trustees or managers to modify, the rules or terms of any scheme caught by the Act. The Directive instructed all Member States to take all necessary steps to ensure that the provisions of occupational pension schemes contrary to the principle of equal treatment were revised by 1 January 1993. The ECJ's conclusion in *Barber* that the directly effective right to equal pay, contained in Article 119 of the EEC Treaty, applied to benefits under occupational pension schemes, changed all this. In a manner reminiscent of the equality clause in the Equal Pay Act 1970, s. 62 of the Pensions Act 1995 provides that an occupational pension scheme which does not contain an equal treatment rule is to be treated as including one. The term 'occupational pension scheme' has the same meaning in the 1995 Act as in the Pension Schemes Act 1993, namely:

. . . any scheme or arrangement which is comprised in one or more instruments or agreements and which has, or is capable of having, effect in relation to one or more descriptions or categories of employments so as to provide benefits, in the form of pensions or otherwise, payable on termination of service, or on death or retirement, to or in respect of earners with qualifying service in an employment of any such description or category.

8.2.8.3   The equal treatment rule   The equal treatment rule applies both to the terms controlling an employee's access to an occupational pension scheme and to the terms governing the treatment of an employee once he or she is a member. The rule is to have the effect that where an employee of one sex is employed on like work, or on work rated as equivalent, or on work of equal value to that of an employee of the other sex, but (apart from the rule) any of these terms is or becomes less favourable to the former than it is to the latter, the term is to be treated as so modified as not to be less favourable. Likewise, the trustees or managers will be unable to exercise any discretion conferred to them by the scheme in such a way as to treat men and women unequally. In so far as the equal treatment rule has the effect of modifying any term relating to the treatment of an employee once he or she is a member, it is to apply to any pensionable service on or after 17 May 1990 (the date of the *Barber* decision). The equal treatment rule applies as much to terms benefiting dependants of members as to terms benefiting members themselves. Where the effect of any term of a scheme on persons of the same sex differs according to their family or marital status, one must compare the effect of the term on persons of the other sex who have the same status to determine whether it should be modified by application of the equal treatment rule.

8.2.8.4 Exceptions In three instances the equal treatment rule will have no effect. These are identified in s. 64 of the 1995 Act, and are as follows:

(a)   In certain circumstances (see reg. 14), where a man who has not attained pensionable age, but would have done so had he been a woman, receives an additional amount of pension not exceeding the amount of Category A state retirement pension a woman on the same earnings as him would be entitled to (s. 64(2) and reg. 13). This is commonly known as a 'bridging pension'.

(b)   Where the variation in question is due to the application of certain actuarial factors which differ for men and women, and relates to:

(i)   the level of employer's contributions (s. 64(3)(a) and reg. 15(1));
(ii)   certain benefits under the scheme (s. 64(3)(b) and reg. 15(2)).

(c)   Where subsequent regulations so provide (no such regulations at the time of writing) (s. 64(4)).

8.2.8.5 Maternity Most of para. 5 of Sch. 5 of the 1989 Act, dealing with unfair maternity provisions, came into force on 23 June 1994. It is expressly preserved by s. 63(3) of the 1995 Act, and the equal treatment rule takes effect subject to it. A maternity provision is unfair unless it treats a woman during the maternity period as if she were working normally and receiving the remuneration she was likely to be paid for doing so in determining her continuity of membership, accrual of rights and benefits payable to or in respect of her (ERA 1996, s. 79(2)(b)).

8.2.8.6 Family leave Like para. 5, para. 6 of Sch. 5 of the 1989 Act came into force on 23 June 1994, and the equal treatment rule takes effect subject to it. This gives similar protection in respect of periods during which employed earners are absent from work for family reasons (which term is undefined) and are paid any contractual remuneration. A provision is deemed to be an unfair family leave provision if it does not treat such periods as periods throughout which employees worked normally and received the remuneration in fact paid to them for that period in determining continuity of membership, accrual of rights and calculation of benefits payable to or for the employees.

8.2.8.7 Enforcement The Pensions Act 1995 provides that the equal treatment rule 'shall be construed as one' with the equivalent provision in the Equal Pay Act 1970, and that pension complainants are to use the same disputes and enforcement machinery as is provided by ss. 2 and 2A of the earlier Act (s. 63(4)). However, this machinery has been substantially modified in the case of pension claims by the Occupational Pension Schemes (Equal Treatment) Regulations 1995 (SI 1995 No. 3183). Under the Regulations, all successful complainants may be entitled to a declaration of their rights by the court or tribunal and an order that their employer make financial provision within the scheme from its own resources to permit them to enjoy those rights. However, only pensioner members may be entitled to the direct payment of arrears of benefit, damages or some other financial award (regs 3, 7, 9 and 12). This is the case in respect of each of the potential causes of action available under the Regulations, which are:

    (a)   claim of right to admission to an occupational pension scheme (reg. 5);
    (b)   claim of right to equal treatment as a member of a scheme (reg. 6);
    (c)   claims analogous to those referred to at (a) and (b) above, but relating to the modification of the terms in an employee's contract of employment concerning pension scheme membership and benefits (regs 10 and 11).

In addition, s. 65 of the 1995 Act empowers those trustees and managers not otherwise permitted to alter the terms of their scheme to do so in accordance with the equal treatment rule.

8.2.9 Dismissal

If an employee is sacked solely because of his colour, or if two employees have stolen from the employer and one culprit is white and one black, but only the black person is dismissed, the latter may have a claim under the Race Relations Act (s. 6(2)(b)). Normally it would be easier to claim unfair dismissal but an employee might not be qualified to do so because he has not served for a sufficient period of continuous employment or is over the normal retiring age. Further, compensation under the SDA 1975, unlike unfair dismissal, can be awarded for injury to feelings and there is no upper limit on compensation. Recommendations also may be made to prevent such acts in the future in discrimination cases. The fact that an employer has applied an indirectly discriminatory condition of 'last in first out' is likely to render dismissal unfair under s. 57(3) of EPCA 1978 (*Clarke* v *Eley (IMI) Kynoch Ltd* [1982] IRLR 482).

8.2.10 Any other detriment (SDA 1975, s. 6(2)(b))

Although 'detriment' is a word of wide import and this is a residual subsection, some action is clearly too insignificant to fall within its scope. Thus, in *Peake* v *Automotive Products Ltd,* as already mentioned, the Court of Appeal decided that the rule allowing women to leave five minutes early was not serious enough and this ratio survives *Jeremiah* (infra). In *Schmidt* v *Austicks Bookshops Ltd* [1978] ICR 85, Phillips J held that a prohibition on female employees wearing trousers did not constitute a detriment since it must 'have something serious or important about it' (see also to the same effect, *Burrett* v *West Birmingham Health Authority* [1994] IRLR 7, cf *Smith* v *Safeway plc* [1996] IRLR 4, discussed at para. 8.1.1.1 supra). This may be a mere matter of opinion, and in *Ministry of Defence* v *Jeremiah* [1979] IRLR 436, where the requirement that men undertake particularly dirty work was sufficient, Brandon LJ paraphrased the word to mean 'putting under a disadvantage'. It was irrelevant that the employers paid an extra 4p an hour to compensate for the dirty work, since they could not thus buy a right to discriminate. In order for there to be a detriment, a reasonable worker must by reason of the acts complained of take the view that he was thereby disadvantaged thereafter in the way in which he would have to work (*De Souza* v *Automobile Association* [1986] IRLR 103). It does not have to amount to a constructive dismissal. In *Kapur* v *Barclays Bank* [1989] IRLR 57, Wood J restricted the scope of the concept to 'an occasion connected with the dismissal or during disciplinary proceedings', but this interpretation was overturned by the Court of Appeal [1989] IRLR 387 whose conclusion was itself upheld by the House of Lords [1991] ICR 208.

The following have been found to amount to detriments:

(a)   transfer to a less interesting job (*Kirby* v *Manpower Services Commission* [1980] IRLR 229);

(b)   failure to investigate an allegation of discrimination (*Eke* v *Commissioners of Customs and Excise* [1981] IRLR 334);

(c)   a requirement of full-time working (*Home Office* v *Holmes* [1984] IRLR 299);

(d)   a restriction on females standing at the bar of a Fleet Street wine bar (*Gill and Coote* v *El Vinos Co. Ltd* [1983] IRLR 206);

(e)   a requirement imposed by BL that all black workers should be checked as they came through the works security gate *could* constitute a 'detriment' (*BL Cars Ltd* v *Brown* [1983] IRLR 193) but whether it did in a specific case depended on all the facts relating to the issue of the instructions and the particular circumstances of the employee.

On the other hand there was *no* detriment within the Act when:

(a)   a manager said in the hearing of the black applicant 'get this typing done by the wog' (*De Souza* v *Automobile Association* (supra));

(b)   a local authority refused to permit a woman librarian to job share since job sharing was not available to any librarians (*Clymo* v *London Borough of Wandsworth* [1989] ICR 250).

8.3   GROUNDS OF DISCRIMINATION

We all differentiate between things or between people every day. Indeed, to be discriminating in some senses is considered a virtue, and it remains perfectly lawful to reject an applicant for a job because, for example, he cannot spell, is a member of the Labour Party, supports Grimsby Town Football Club, has green hair, or is over 45. Discrimination is only prohibited when the reason is one of the following forbidden grounds: sex; marital status; and race.

8.3.1   Sex

The Sex Discrimination Act applies equally to discrimination against men and against women (SDA 1975, s. 2(1)), and more claims by men have been made than was originally envisaged. One important potential applicant left unprotected was thought to be the *pregnant* woman. For the majority of the EAT in *Turley* v *Allders Department Stores Ltd* [1980] IRLR 4, held that the applicant who was dismissed by the respondents on becoming pregnant, did not suffer unlawful discrimination, because the Act prohibits less favourable treatment as a *woman* and 'a woman with child could not properly be compared with the only available comparison, a man, who is incapable of becoming pregnant'. The EAT subsequently upheld the dissent by the dissenting lay member of the EAT in *Turley*. She focused on the reason *why* pregnancy might present a problem for an employer, that it will lead to a request for time off work for the period of confinement, and thus whether the treatment amounted to discrimination depended on a comparison of the facts of each case with the manner in which the employer would treat a man who by reason of a medical condition, for example, a hernia operation, is incapacitated from work. (See also *Reaney* v *Kanda Jean Products Ltd* [1978] IRLR 427.) *Turley* was not followed in *Hayes* v *Malleable Working Men's Club* [1985] IRLR 367. (See *Berrisford* v *Woodard Schools (Midland Division) Ltd* [1991] IRLR 247; *Dixon* v *Rees* [1994] ICR 39.)

The landmark case is *Webb* v *EMO Air Cargo (UK) Ltd* [1994] IRLR 482. A small company had an import operations clerk who became pregnant and Mrs Webb was taken on to replace her. Several weeks after starting work, however, Mrs Webb discovered that she was pregnant and so informed the employers. EMO decided to dismiss Mrs Webb. Mrs Webb claimed sex discrimination because she did not have the two-year qualifying period to make a complaint of unfair dismissal. The House of Lords referred the case to the ECJ which held that dismissal of a woman on the grounds of pregnancy even in these circumstances was sex discrimination. Since pregnancy is not in any way comparable with a pathological condition, and even less so with unavailability for work on non-medical grounds, there was no question of comparing the situation of a woman who finds herself incapable by reason of pregnancy of performing the task for which she was recruited with that of a man similarly incapable. Nor could dismissal of a pregnant woman recruited for an indefinite period be justified on grounds relating to her inability to fulfil a fundamental condition of her contract of employment.

The House of Lords after the ECJ judgment reconciled this with the British statute by concentrating on the need in the Sex Discrimination Act 1975 for like to be treated with like. Lord Keith held at 1027a–c that 'in a case where a woman is engaged for an indefinite period, the fact that the reason why she will be temporarily unavailable for work at a time when to her knowledge her services will be particularly required is pregnancy is a circumstance relevant to her case, being a circumstance which could not be present in the case of a hypothetical man'.

Essentially the *Webb* case stands as authority for the following principles:

(a)   differentiation by reason of pregnancy constitutes sex discrimination (ECJ at 799c);

(b)   there is a distinction between dismissal for pregnancy *per se* and illness (ECJ at 799c);

(c)   no comparison is appropriate directly with a man's physical condition (HL at 1025h).

The scope of this principle was tested in *O'Neill* v *Governors of St Thomas More RCVA Upper School & Bedfordshire CC* [1996] IRLR 371 which raised the highly unusual case of a teacher of religious education and personal relationships at a Roman Catholic Voluntary Aided School who had a baby with the priest who frequently visited the school. The industrial tribunal found that 'an important motive for the dismissal was not the applicant's pregnancy *per se* but the fact that the pregnancy was by a Roman Catholic priest and that, as a result, the school saw the applicant's position as a teacher of religious education and personal relationships as being untenable'. On the basis of this distinction, the industrial tribunal rejected the application for sex discrimination.

The EAT, however, overturned this conclusion (the respondent having conceded that the dismissal was unfair). The EAT read *Webb* as not permitting any comparison between Mrs O'Neill and the hypothetical male comparator proposed by the Governors as a male teacher of religious education and personal relationships who had fathered a child by a RC nun and where there had also been press publicity about that relationship. The EAT rejected the employer's suggestion that the relationship from which the pregnancy arose was a 'super added ground or condition' which took the case outside the scope of *Webb*, and that it was the relationship and not the pregnancy itself which caused the dismissal. The distinction drawn was, said the EAT, erroneous 'because the concept of "pregnancy *per se*" was misleading' and 'Pregnancy always has surrounding circumstances, some arising prior to the state of pregnancy, some accompanying it, some consequential upon it . . . [The dismissal] need not only be on that ground [of pregnancy]. It need not even be mainly on that ground. Thus, the fact that the employer's ground for dismissal is that the pregnant woman will be unavailable for work because of her pregnancy does not make it any the less a dismissal on the grounds of pregnancy'. Here all the matters relied upon by the employer were causally related to the fact that Mrs O'Neill was pregnant and 'Her pregnancy precipitated and permeated the decision to dismiss her'.

It has also been established in *Caruana* v *Manchester Airport plc* [1996] IRLR 378 that *Webb* may not apply to fixed-term contracts. (See also *Rees* v *Apollo Watches* [1996] ICR 466 and *British Telecommunications plc* v *Roberts* [1996] IRLR 601.)

8.3.2 Marital status

The Sex Discrimination Acts apply to discrimination against married persons, although only in respect of employment (SDA 1975, s. 3(1)). It remains lawful, however, to discriminate against *single* people in any way. In *Bick* v *Royal West of England School for the Deaf* [1976] IRLR 326, the applicant could not claim when she was sacked on 30 January because she intended to marry the next day, for at the appropriate time she was not married. Not only does this detract from the general symmetry of the discrimination statutes, but it may not wholly fulfil Britain's obligations under the 1975 EEC Directive that 'there shall be no discrimination whatsoever on grounds of sex, either directly or indirectly in particular by reference to *marital or family status*'.

> **Example** Fred wishes to appoint a new traveller. He believes that a single man will devote more time to the position than a married man, and refuses to give the job to John. John can complain of direct discrimination on the ground of marital status. If, on the other hand, Fred thought a married man would offer more stability and thus rejects Kevin, a bachelor, for that reason, Kevin can make no complaint under the Sex Discrimination Act or any other statute.

8.3.3 Racial grounds

The Race Relations Act now includes within the definition of racial grounds, differentiation on the grounds of 'colour, race, nationality or ethnic or national origins' (s. 3(1)). Although the meaning of this phrase has been little elaborated by the courts, certain points have been clarified.

8.3.3.1 Religions Although *religions* as such are not covered, discrimination on the ground of ethnic origins may include disparate treatment of Jews (*Seide* v *Gillette Industries*

Ltd [1980] IRLR 427; *Simon* v *Brimham Associates* [1987] IRLR 307) and Sikhs (finally determined by the House of Lords in *Mandla* v *Dowell Lee* [1983] 2 AC 548) as ethnic groups. The House of Lords in the latter case held that the adjective 'ethnic' did not (as the Court of Appeal had thought) require the group to be distinguished by some fixed or inherited racial characteristic. The concept was appreciably wider than the strictly racial or biological divide. The group need only regard itself and be regarded by others as a separate and distinct community by virtue of characteristics commonly associated with a common racial origin. Such a group could include converts to a religion. Gipsies constitute a racial group (*Commission for Racial Equality* v *Dutton* [1989] IRLR 8). Rastafarians are not an ethnic group, however, (*Dawkins* v *Department of the Environment* [1993] IRLR 284). Although they are a separate group with identifiable characteristics, they have not established some separate identity by reference to their ethnic origins. They also do not have a long shared history since it goes back only some 60 years.

8.3.3.2 Language Race is not defined by the characteristic of language alone. Thus there is no racial group of English-speaking Welsh so that a condition requiring that applicants for jobs should be able to speak Welsh could not constitute unlawful indirect discrimination on the grounds of race (*Gwynedd CC* v *Jones* [1986] ICR 833).

8.3.3.3 Nationality and national origins The distinction between nationality and national origins causes some confusion. *Nationality* includes discrimination against Scots or Irish. Although one's nationality and national origins are likely to be the same, a person may have a different nationality to his *national origins,* if, for example, he was born in the West Indies but has now gained British citizenship. Nationality was added to the definition in 1976 because of the narrow interpretation of 'national origins' (which alone had been in the Race Relations Act 1968), in *Ealing LBC* v *Race Relations Board* [1972] AC 342. There the plaintiff was a British citizen but of Polish origin. The defendant Council admitted discriminating against him on the grounds of his *origins* in establishing its house waiting list, but the House of Lords held that this was not illegal since it was not included in the definition of nationality.

Articles 48 to 50 of the Treaty of Rome require Member States of the EC to permit the free movement of workers between Member States. There must be no discrimination against EC nationals in relation to employment, remuneration or other conditions of work.

8.3.4 Transsexuals and homosexuals

The question for the European Court of Justice in *P* v *S* [1996] IRLR 347, was whether a transsexual applicant could rely on the Equal Treatment Directive. The facts were quite stark in that P had been taken on as a manager at an educational establishment operated in 1991 by Cornwall County Council, and there were no problems until P told the Chief Executive of that College that she intended to undergo a sex change operation. The Chief Executive was initially sympathetic, but that view changed and the Governors decided to dismiss P. The Advocate General drew attention to the 'proposition, which has ever stronger support in medical and scentific circles, that it is necessary to go beyond the traditional classification and recognise that in addition to the man/woman dichotomy, there is a range of character-istics, behaviour and roles shared by men and women, so that sex itself ought rather to be thought of as a continuum' (para. 17). He rejected the contention that since male and female transsexuals were dealt with alike there could be no relevant discrimination. Rather, the principle of equality prohibits unequal treatment of individuals based on certain distinguishing factors, and these specifically include sex. This means that importance may not and must not be given to sex as such so as to influence in one way or another the treatment afforded, for example, to workers.

He called for 'a rigorous application of the principle of equality so that therefore any connotations relating to sex and/or sexual identity cannot be in any way relevant' (para. 19). It was also noted that 'the abilities and role of the person in question were adversely affected by her change of sex'. The Advocate General concluded that he was 'asking the Court to make a "courageous" decision' on the ground that the sex of a person should be irrelevant with regard to the rules regulating relations in society (para. 24), although he accepted that 'there is no precise provision specifically and literally intended to regulate the problem'. The ECJ did take the approach suggested by the Advocate General, although it may be that the ECJ's approach can be seen as somewhat narrower in scope. It found that 'such discrimination [was] based, essentially if not exclusively, on the sex of the person concerned'. Further, it was open to the respondent to seek to rely upon Article 2(2) of the Directive.

This case does not address directly the issue of sexual orientation as distinct from transsexuality. The most important recent case is the Armed Forces gay servicemen case which is now being taken before the European Court of Human Rights. In *R* v *Ministry of Defence ex parte Smith* [1996] IRLR 100, the Court of Appeal rejected the proposition that dismissal on the grounds of sexual orientation was a breach of the Equal Treatment Directive because:

(a)   the draughtsmen were not addressing their minds to sexual orientation in drafting the Directive;

(b)   the Code of Practice on Sexual Dignity (see para. 8.1.1.4 supra) (which does refer to harassment against gay employees) is 'directed to banning unacceptable behaviour in the workplace and not to regulating employment policy in relation to sexual orientation' (Sir Thomas Bingham at para. 36);

(c)   'social attitudes and concerns twenty years ago when the Directive was in gestation were not focussing upon sexual orientation discrimination' (Thorpe LJ at para. 107).

In *Smith* v *Gardner Merchant Ltd* [1996] IRLR 342, Mr Smith was a barman who claimed he had been sexually harassed because of his sexual orientation. The EAT, which decided that case before the ECJ gave judgment in *P* v *S* but after the Advocate General had given his opinion, decided that: 'Homosexuality is a form of sexual preference which can apply to either sex. The analogy with pregnancy is mistaken — pregnancy is a unique female condition.' Thus it was held that sexual orientation was not included within the SDA. The EAT declined to refer the matter to the ECJ.

The strongest arguments that sexual orientation discrimination is in breach of the Directive appear to be the following:

(a)   The word used in Article 1 is 'for' and not 'as between' men and women. Further, it can be argued that discrimination on the basis of sexual orientation falls within the phrase 'on grounds of sex either directly or indirectly by reference to marital or family status'.

(b)   The EC Recommendation No. 92/131/EC on the protection of the dignity of women and men at work is persuasive of the fact that incorporated within sex is sexual orientation when it provides:

Research in several Member States which documents the links between the risk of sexual harassment and the recipient's perceived vulnerability suggests that . . . lesbians . . . are disproportionately at risk. *Gay men and young men* are also vulnerable to harassment. [emphasis added.]

There is ECJ authority that Recommendations should be taken into account by national courts even though as a matter of EC law they have no binding force (*Grimaldi* v *Fonds des Maladies Professionnelles* [1990] IRLR 400);

(c)   The concept of transferred discrimination may be called upon, on the basis that if the 'partner' of the gay male employee had been a woman, he would not have been treated in the way he was treated (see e.g. *R* v *Birmingham City Council ex parte EOC* [1989] 1 AC 1155, esp. at 1194; *Showboat Entertainment Centre Ltd* v *Owens* [1984] IRLR 7; *Zarczynska* v *Levy* [1979] ICR 184).

(d)   The gay employee may be in a permanent, stable relationship with a male friend; if he were in a heterosexual family relationship, he would not have been treated as he was treated. Accordingly, he has been discriminated against on the grounds of or by reference to 'family status'.

(e)   It is wrong to view discrimination on grounds of sex merely as a matter of anatomical qualities which determine whether a person is male or female.

(f)   The concept of stereotyping may be called in aid. The man who is discriminated against because his sexual orientation is towards other men is thus seen as discriminated against because he does not conform to the discriminator's stereotype for men, in particular because the man appears 'effeminate'.

Discrimination on grounds of sexual orientation may also breach the European Convention on Human Rights since Article 8 provides: 'Everyone has the right to respect for his private and family life, his home and his correspondence.' The case law of the European Court of Human Rights has recognised that sexual life forms an important part of private life (e.g. *X* v *Germany* Yearbook I 1955–7, p. 228; *Dudgeon* v *UK* Series A No. 45, 22 October 1981, para. 52; *Norris* v *Ireland* Series A No. 142, 26 October 1988, para. 46). In *R* v *Ministry of Defence ex parte Smith* [1996] IRLR 100, Sir Thomas Bingham MR indeed said that:

to dismiss a person from his or her employment on the grounds of a private sexual preference, and to interrogate him or her about private sexual behaviour, would not appear to me to show respect for that person's private and family life.

However, that did not cause the Court of Appeal to find in favour of the applicants since the Convention is not a part of UK law. (See also Henry LJ at 342H, Thorpe LJ at 345H.)

An industrial tribunal has asked the ECJ to determine whether Article 119 applies to sexual orientation discrimination in *Grant* v *South West Trains Ltd*, unreported, Case No. 1784/96.

8.4   APPLICANTS AND RESPONDENTS

8.4.1   Applicants

The anti-discrimination statutes are slightly wider in scope than most employment protection legislation in terms of both potential applicants and respondents. For the Sex Discrimination and Race Relations Acts both protect not only employees but also a person who has a contract to 'personally execute any work or labour' even though as an *independent contractor*. This includes a painter or a plumber; an articled clerk (*Oliver* v *J.P. Malnick & Co.* [1983] IRLR 456); a self-employed salesman of fancy goods on a pitch in a department store remunerated on a commission basis (*Quinnen* v *Hovell* [1984] IRLR 227, see also *BP Chemicals Ltd* v *Gillick* [1995] IRLR 128). It excludes: a postmaster, since he is responsible merely for seeing that the work of the Post Office is carried on and does not have to perform any of the duties himself (*Tanna* v *Post Office* [1981] ICR 374); an independent wholesale newspaper distributor who enjoyed an agency for the Mirror Group (*Mirror Group Newspapers Ltd* v *Gunning* [1986] IRLR 27) and a doctor who was not under a contractual arrangement but rather was linked by the statutory scheme with the Family Practitioner Committee or Medical Practitioners Committee (*Wadi* v *Cornwall & Isles of Scilly Family Practitioner Committee* [1985] ICR 492; see also *Ealing Hammersmith and Hounslow Family Health Services Authority* v *Shukla* [1993] ICR 710).

Contract workers supplied by an agency which employs them (e.g. temporary secretaries, cleaners, building workers) are also expressly included (SDA 1975, s. 9; RRA 1976, s. 7). This is necessary because normally it is the client company for whom the 'temp' works (although he is employed by the agency) which has the scope for discrimination. It is not, however, sufficient under this head that work is done by one person for the benefit of another unless there is an *undertaking* to supply the work. It thus does not include a taxi owners' collective which patrons phone to ask for a taxi (*Rice* v *Fon-a-Car* [1980] ICR 133).

It should be noted that even an employee engaged under an illegal contract may claim sexual discrimination (*Leighton* v *Michael* [1996] IRLR 67).

8.4.2 Respondents

8.4.2.1 Non-employers with primary liability The prohibitions extend beyond *employers* to:

(a) *Trade unions,* employers associations, professional and trade associations (SDA 1975, s. 12; RRA 1976, s. 11) which refuse a woman or black person membership, make it more difficult for such an applicant to join, offer inferior terms of membership, offer less favourable terms on being received into membership, or subject the member to any detriment.

(b) *Qualification bodies* for trades or professions (SDA 1975, s. 13; RRA 1976, s. 12) e.g. Law Society, Licensing Justices, and even the British Judo Association in its capacity of awarding national referee's certificates (*British Judo Association* v *Petty* [1981] ICR 660, but did not extend to the grant of an appointment as a subpostmaster (*Malik* v *Post Office Counters Ltd* [1993] ICR 93). Such bodies must not refuse a woman or black person a licence or make it more difficult to obtain one or grant it on inferior terms or withdraw the licence on discriminatory grounds. Appeals by complainants must be made in this case to the normal appeal body, e.g. the Privy Council in the case of the British Medical Association, and not to tribunals or courts.

(c) *Training bodies:* s. 7(1) of the Employment Act 1989 repealed s. 14 of SDA 1975, which applied specifically to industrial training boards, the Manpower Services Commission, employers' associations and any other person designated by the Secretary of State. There was also no reference to 'detriment'. The new provision instead renders unlawful any discrimination as to terms, omission to afford facilities, terminating or subjecting to detriment within the course of 'training which would help fit [a woman] for any employment'. The Secretary of State for Employment may, however, by order exempt discrimination in favour of lone parents in relation to any employment training (EA 1989, s. 8 and Sex Discrimination Act 1975 (Exemption for Special Treatment for Lone Parents) Order 1989, SI 1989 No. 2140).

(d)   *Employment agencies* (SDA 1975, s. 15; RRA 1976, s. 14); (see *Commission for Racial Equality* v *Imperial Society of Teachers of Dancing* [1983] ICR 473).

(e)   *The Training Commission* (SDA 1975, ss. 14(2), 16; RRA 1976, s. 15).

(f)   *The Crown* (SDA 1975, s. 85; RRA 1976, s. 75): 'Service for the purpose of a Minister of the Crown or Government Department, other than a person holding statutory office', but this does not extend to the selection of justices of the peace (*Knight* v *Att-Gen* [1979] ICR 194), or rent officers (*Dept of the Environment* v *Fox* [1979] ICR 736). A special policeman is covered (*Sheikh* v *Chief Constable of Greater Manchester Police* [1989] 2 All ER 684).

(g)   Partnerships of six or more partners in the treatment of fellow partners (RRA 1976, s. 10). This was repealed in respect of sex discrimination by s. 1(3) of SDA 1986.

(h)   Barristers, by reason of the Courts and Legal Services Act 1990.

8.4.2.2   Secondary liability   One who aids discrimination or pressures another to discriminate may be restrained under the Acts (RRA 1976, s. 33; SDA 1975, s. 42). Section 31 of RRA 1976 renders it unlawful to 'induce, or attempt to induce, a person to do any act which contravenes Part II' of the statute. In *Commission for Racial Equality* v *Imperial Society of Teachers of Dancing* (supra) the EAT decided that the words 'procure' and 'attempt to procure' should be construed widely and included the use of words which brought about a certain course of action. 'Inducement' meant to persuade, or to prevail upon or to bring about. They declared unlawful a request by the respondent's secretary in charge of records to the head of careers of a local school not to send along for an assignment a 'coloured person' since that person 'would feel out of place as there were no black employees'.

An employer is liable if an employee or agent of his *in the course of his employment* has discriminated unless he can prove he did all that was reasonably practicable to prevent it (SDA 1975, s. 41; RRA 1976, s. 32). In *Irving* v *Post Office* [1987] IRLR 289, a postman saw a letter addressed to his black neighbours in the course of sorting the post and wrote a racially abusive remark on it. The neighbour brought a claim of discrimination against the Post Office. The Court of Appeal held that although the employment provided the *opportunity* for the misconduct, the misconduct formed no part of the postman's *performance* of the duties, and was not done for the benefit of the Post Office. Accordingly, the Post Office was not vicariously responsible for the action of its employee. The legal burden is placed on the employers by SDA 1975, s. 41(3) to prove that they had taken such steps as were reasonably practicable to prevent the employee continuing a course of sexual harassment (*Balgobin* v *London Borough of Tower Hamlets* [1987] IRLR 401). The widest arc of liability was demonstrated in *Burton* v *De Vere Hotels* [1996] IRLR 596 in which the issue was whether the hotel employer could be held to have subjected two black waitresses to the detriment of racial abuse when the waitresses were exposed to racist remarks and other offensive conduct by the comedian Bernard Manning who was the guest speaker at a Round Table dinner held at the hotel. Smith J in the EAT held that an employer subjects an employee to the detriment of racial harassment 'if he causes or permits racial harassment to occur in circumstances in which he can control whether it happens or not'.

Following the European Court of Justice ruling in *Commission of the European Communities* v *United Kingdom* [1984] IRLR 29, s. 6 of SDA 1986 renders void discriminatory provision in collective agreements, internal rules of undertakings and rules governing independent occupations and professions.

8.4.3 Territorial limitations

8.4.3.1 Sex discrimination The sex discrimination legislation applies to 'employment at an establishment in Great Britain' (SDA 1975, s. 6) as defined in s. 10 of SDA 1975. This definition is exhaustive and does not merely create certain presumptions. A cashier on a cross channel ferry which was registered in Germany was held not to be employed at an establishment in Great Britain. The ship was in any event an establishment for these purposes (*Haughton* v *Olau Lines (UK) Ltd* [1986] 1 WLR 504). The employers were based in Sheerness. The cashier spent the majority of her working time outside UK territorial waters. She claimed that she was discriminated against when she was dismissed. The Court of Appeal held that s. 6 of SDA 1975 (which confined the statute to 'employment at an establishment in Great Britain') was not satisfied when her work was mainly outside Great Britain on a German-registered ship. Section 10 was of no assistance to the applicant. It provides that 'employment is to be regarded as being at an establishment in Great Britain unless the employee does his work wholly or mainly outside Great Britain'. This was a comprehensive definition of 'employment at an establishment in Great Britain' and was to be applied in all cases except those specifically excluded by subsection 2 thereof which related to employment on British-registered ships, aircraft or hovercraft.

8.4.3.2 Race discrimination The Race Relations Act 1976 permits discrimination by an employer in or in connection with employment by him on any ship in the case of a person who applied or was engaged for that employment outside Great Britain (s. 8). In *Deria* v *General Council of British Shipping* [1985] ICR 847 several Somali seamen complained that they had been refused employment on the *SS Uganda* when she was requisitioned by the Ministry of Defence for the Falklands emergency. They were, however, excluded on the ground that the section must be construed in relation to what was in the parties' contemplation as the area of operation. It was not enough to give the tribunal jurisdiction that the ship sailed from Southampton. (See Race Relations (Offshore Employment) Order 1987 (SI 1987 No. 929); Sex Discrimination and Equal Pay (Offshore Employment) Order 1987 (SI 1987 No. 930).)

8.5 'REVERSE DISCRIMINATION'

Normally, the motive of the respondent for the act of discrimination does not matter, and differentiation on the prohibited grounds is unlawful whatever the underlying reason and however benign the purpose behind it. However, the discrimination legislation was introduced on both sides of the Atlantic to improve the position of minority groups and women. In recognition of this, the United States statutes contain power to decree affirmative action to promote the hiring of a particular under-represented race or sex until a fixed quota is reached. Moreover, private schemes of a similar nature were upheld in the important case of *Regents of the University of California* v *Bakke* 438 US 265 (1978) as long as the quotas were not too rigid.

In *Kalanke* v *Freie Hansestadt Bremen* [1995] IRLR 660, the ECJ held that the Equal Treatment Directive precludes national rules which guarantee women equally qualified with men automatic selection for appointment or promotion to posts in which women are unrepresented. This oversteps the limits of the exception made in the Directive for 'measures to promote equal opportunity for men and women, in particular by removing existing inequalities which affect women's opportunities'. The case arose from a selection issue in the City of Bremen's Park Department when the post of selection manager became available. The male and female candidates were equally qualified, but Mrs Glissman was given the post solely because she was a woman. The ECJ held that the derogation must be strictly applied so that national measures were permitted when they conferred a special advantage to women with a view to improving their ability to compete in the labour market and pursue a career on an equal footing with men.

As a result of this decision the EU amended the Equal Treatment Directive. The amendment makes clear that there will be *no* breach of the Directive if positive action is taken to balance an inequality where one sex is under-represented, such as by giving preference to persons of that sex as regards access to employment or promotion. The amendment is intended to give employers the chance to take into account the particular circumstances of each case; so an absolute rule that a woman will be promoted over a man in a particular instance would still be a breach of the Directive.

In Britain, however, 'reverse discrimination' applies only to training and not job *selection,* and even then there are by statute only limited circumstances in which special treatment may be legally given to members of a particular sex or race, as follows:

(a)   Training boards, employers and trade unions may discriminate in training afforded to members of one sex if during the preceding 12 months there were, in respect of the particular job for which training is given:

(i)   no persons of the favoured sex/race doing the job; or
(ii)   the number was comparatively small (SDA 1975, ss. 47, 48; RRA 1976, ss. 35, 37, 38). Discrimination in appointment after such training, however, remains illegal.

(b)   Training bodies may lean in favour of persons who appear to be in special need of training because of periods for which domestic or family responsibilities have excluded them from regular full-time employment (SDA 1975, s. 47(3)).

(c)   Trade unions and similar bodies may reserve seats on elected bodies to members of one sex (SDA 1975, s. 49), and mount a discriminatory recruitment drive, if, at any time, the organisation has no women members or comparatively few (SDA 1975, s. 48(3)), but the Police Federation rules are excluded (Sex Discrimination Act 1975 (Exemption of Police Federation Constitutional and Electoral Arrangements) Order 1989 (SI 1989 No. 2420)).

8.6   EXCEPTIONS

There are several exceptions to both the Race Relations and Sex Discrimination Acts, so that if an employer falls within one of them he may treat a member of one race or sex less favourably than another whether in the arrangements he makes for filling a job; refusing a job; or denying an employee opportunities for promotion, or transfer to, or training for, the job.

8.6.1   Genuine occupational qualification

The most important exception is where being of one sex or race is a genuine occupational qualification as defined by the Act; then an employee may justifiably be refused a position on grounds of race (RRA 1976, s. 5) or sex (SDA 1975, s. 7). This does not, however, allow discrimination on the ground of sex in the terms and conditions provided when he or she is, in fact, offered employment. The appropriate provisions of the Equal Pay Act 1970 and the Race Relations Act still apply here with full force. Moreover, the qualifications concentrate on the individual who applies for the job rather than the particular job itself. For, even where sex or race is a genuine occupational qualification, the employer must consider whether it would be reasonable for him to use existing employees of the appropriate sex or race to carry out the relevant duties, and thus take on either a woman or member of a minority group.

We deal here with the exceptions under the Race Relations and Sex Discrimination Acts separately, although the provisions overlap to a certain extent and have the same underlying policy.

8.6.1.1 Sex Discrimination Acts By s. 7 of SDA 1975 an employer may discriminate on the grounds of sex, although not marital status, if, but only if, he can prove he did so because of one of the following circumstances:

(a) The essential nature of the job calls for a man because of his *physiology,* for example, to work as a model, although greater strength and stamina *alone* are not enough as qualifications.

(b) A man is required for *authenticity in entertainment:* a casting director need not interview women for the part of Iago.

(c) *Decency or privacy* requires the job to be done by a man because, for example, there are men 'in a state of undress' at the workplace, e.g. a lavatory cleaner. This also applies if customers or other employees might reasonably object to physical contact with a person of the opposite sex as an employee. This exempts, for example, *masseurs,* but would probably not extend to doctors or chiropodists. Discrimination is unlawful, however, where there are enough employees of the other sex to perform these duties. Thus, in *Wylie* v *Dee & Co. (Menswear) Ltd* [1978] IRLR 103, a refusal to employ a female in a menswear shop was not permitted under this rubric since it was not often necessary to measure an inside leg, and then one of the seven male assistants could be summoned. In relation to race discrimination, the similar exception is to be broadly construed so that it may be adopted when the services can be most effectively provided by a person of a particular race, but it is not open to an industrial tribunal to disregard a duty cast on an employee unless it is *de minimis* or a sham duty invented for the purpose of qualifying for the exception (*Tottenham Green Under Fives' Centre* v *Marshall (No. 2)* [1991] IRLR 162). See *Lambeth LBC* v *Commission for Racial Equality* [1989] IRLR 379; *Etam plc* v *Rowan* [1989] IRLR 150).

(d) The job is at a *single sex establishment* where people require special care or supervision, e.g. a prison.

(e) The employee provides *personal services* towards the welfare or education of others and they can be provided 'most effectively' by a man, e.g. a probation officer or member of a social work team; and the use of 'personal' indicates that the identity of the giver and recipient of the services is important. The Act contemplates direct contact (*Lambeth LBC* v *Commission for Racial Equality* [1990] IRLR 231, [1990] ICR 768).

(f) The job involves *work abroad* which can be done only by a man. This means that a recruiting agency for, say, the Middle East can take into account the recipient country's views about the role of women (RRA 1976, s. 6).

(g) The job is one of two which are to be held by a *married couple,* e.g. a pub manager.

(h)   The nature of the establishment makes it impracticable for the holder of the job to *live* elsewhere than in premises provided by the employer and the only such premises available are inhabited by men and it is not reasonable to expect the employer to build other premises for women (see *Timex Corporation* v *Thomson* [1981] IRLR 522). In *Sisley* v *Britannia Security Systems Ltd* [1983] IRLR 404, the respondents ran a security console station where the operators were employed in shifts. The employers foresaw problems arising if both sexes worked together in the confined spaces and so hired only women. The case was held not to fall within the 'live in' exception since this involved residence either temporary or permanent, and not merely serving in the premises for a limited period.

(i)   The job is likely to involve the holder of the job doing his work or living in a private home and needs to be held by a man because objection might reasonably be taken to allowing a woman:

(i)   the degree of physical or social contact with a person living in the home; or

(ii)   the knowledge of intimate details of such a person's private affairs (added by s. 1(2) of SDA 1986).

There were restrictions on women's night work in factories under the Factories Act 1961 and the Mines and Quarries Act 1954, s. 124(1) of which provided that: 'No female shall be employed in a job the duties of which ordinarily require the employee to spend a significant proportion of his time below ground at a mine which is being worked.' The Sex Discrimination Act 1986 removed all restrictions on women working shifts and at night, overtime restrictions and maximum hours limitations laid down in the Factories Act 1961, the Bakery Industry (Hours of Work) Act 1984, the Hours of Employment (Conventions) Act 1936 and the Mines and Quarries Act 1954 for women over 18. The Act, however, provides that the restrictions on working hours and other working conditions removed by the Act, shall continue for employees to whom they apply, at the date of commencement of the Act, unless the employee agrees otherwise in writing. Dismissal of an employee for refusing to agree such a variation is unfair. There is also a statutory duty on the employer to consider employees' health, safety, welfare and interests (particularly domestic and family responsibilities) when proposing to make a substantial change in hours.

There is a further exception for certain provisions connected with protection of women at work set out in Sch. 1 to EA 1989, and in particular s. 205 of the Public Health Act 1936 and ss. 74, 128 and 131 of the Factories Act 1961.

8.6.1.2   Race and genuine occupational qualification   An employer is allowed to differentiate on the grounds of race in fewer situations than in the sex discrimination area. Similar exceptions to categories (b) and (e) above, however, apply, so that it would be lawful to choose an Indian social worker to work in an Indian area or to refuse a white for the part of Othello (RRA 1976, s. 5). In addition, an employer can discriminate where:

(a)   a member of a particular race is required for reasons of *authenticity* in art or photography; or

(b)   a bar or restaurant has a particular ambience; this preserves the prerogative of a Chinese or Indian restaurateur in his choice of 'ethnic' waiters. The defence is not, however, available to an employer if he already has employees of the appropriate race and:

(i)   they are capable of carrying out the duties of the job necessary to be performed by that race;

(ii)　it would be reasonable to employ them; and

(iii)　there were enough to meet the employer's requirements.

8.6.2　Other general exceptions under both the Race Relations and Sex Discrimination Acts

There are also general exceptions under both statutes for:

(a)　Acts done to safeguard *national security* (SDA 1975, s. 52; RRA 1976, s. 42).

(b)　Employment in *private households* (RRA 1976, s. 4(3)) except that this does not apply to the concept of victimisation and to contract workers. There can also be a dispute whether a person is employed on such duties, so that in *Heron Corporation* v *Commis* [1980] ICR 713, the primary duty of the respondent chauffeur who worked for the appellant's company's chairman, was not employment for a household purpose, but rather on the business of the company.

(c)　*Charitable trusts* (RRA 1976, s. 34; SDA 1975, s. 43): in *Hugh-Jones* v *St. John's College* [1979] ICR 848, the EAT held that the respondent college need not open its senior common room doors to women because of its charitable status.

In relation to discrimination in the army, the claim is heard by the commanding officer under s. 181 of the Army Act 1955, but a proper hearing must take place (*R* v *Army Board of the Defence Council ex parte Anderson* [1991] ICR 537). As from 1 February 1995 the 1975 Act applies to the armed forces (and employment in support thereof) by the Sex Discrimination Act 1975 (Application to Armed Forces, etc.) Regulations 1994 (SI 1994 No. 3276). However, by s. 85(4), nothing in the Act is to render unlawful any act done for the purpose of ensuring the combat effectiveness of the armed forces.

8.6.3　Other exceptions to the Sex Discrimination Acts

The Sex Discrimination Act 1975 has further restrictions and does not apply to:

(a)　Ministers of religion, if the tenets of the faith provide that they be all of one sex (s. 19).

(b)　Sports and sports facilities (s. 17).

(c)　Police and police cadets in respect of height, uniform, equipment, pregnancy, and pensions; and prison officers in respect of height (s. 18).

(d)　'Special treatment afforded to women in connection with pregnancy or childbirth', in line with the similar exemption in the Equal Pay Act 1970 (para. 7.2.5).

(e)　The restriction of appointment of head teachers in schools and colleges to members of a religious order where such a restriction is contained in any instrument relating to the establishment concerned.

(f)　The post of university professor where the post-holder is required by law to be a canon.

(g)　Academic appointments to women in a university college or institution where this is required as at the date of the Act by any instrument ((e) to (g) in EA 1989, s. 5).

(h)　Provisions in relation to *death or retirement* (s. 6(4)). In the three consolidated cases of *Roberts* v *Cleveland AHA, Garland* v *British Rail Engineering Ltd, Turton* v *Macgregor Wallcoverings Ltd* [1979] 1 WLR 754, the Court of Appeal held that it excluded from the scope of the Act, respectively:

(i)   differential retiring ages;

(ii)   different travel concessions on retirement, so that a man who retired at 65 was allowed reduced fares for his wife and dependant children, but the husband of a woman who retired at 60 had to pay full fare;

(iii) different *ex gratia* redundancy payments under a company scheme whereby men made redundant over 60 gained an additional ten weeks pay, but women were not eligible as they had to retire at 60. The European Court of Justice on reference in the *Garland* case, however, held that special travel facilities after retirement fell within the meaning of 'pay' in the EEC Treaty so that the employers had unlawfully discriminated by offering different provisions to men and women ([1982] IRLR 111). (See also *Burton* v *British Railways Board (No. 2)* [1982] IRLR 116.)

When the matter returned for consideration by the House of Lords [1982] IRLR 257, their Lordships said that '"provision in relation to retirement" ought not to be so widely interpreted as to include a privilege that has existed during employment and is allowed by the employer to continue after retirement'.

8.6.4   Discrimination deemed lawful pursuant to other statutes

The Sex Discrimination Act 1975 formerly rendered lawful discrimination which was *necessary* to comply with instruments made or confirmed under *previous legislation* including any re-enactment after the Sex Discrimination Act of a provision passed before it (SDA 1975, s. 51; also RRA 1976, s. 41). Acts treating women less favourably which were held lawful included:

(a)   the refusal to license women's wrestling under the London Government Act 1963 (*GLC* v *Farrar* [1980] IRLR 266); and

(b)   a men-only fellowship at a Cambridge College under the statutes of the University (*Hugh-Jones* v *St John's College, Cambridge* [1979] ICR 848).

Section 1 of EA 1989 now overrides provisions of any Act or instrument made under Acts passed before the Sex Discrimination Act 1975 which require persons to discriminate on the grounds of sex or marital status in relation to employment or vocational training.

The Secretary of State for Employment has power by order:

(a)   to make such provision as he considers appropriate to remove, in the field of employment and vocational training, any requirement to discriminate in a provision of an Act passed before the Employment Act 1989 or an instrument made under such an Act. He may amend, repeal or revoke such a provision (EA 1989, s. 2);

(b)   to disapply this in respect of any particular provision (EA 1989, s. 6).

In cases of indirect discrimination, s. 1(3) of EA 1989 provides that the party who claims that there is no discrimination must show that the requirement or condition is justifiable.

8.6.5   Race Relations Act: other exceptions

The Race Relations Act 1976 does not apply to *immigration rules,* or civil service regulations which restrict Crown employment on grounds of birth, nationality, descent or residence. A person is not eligible for the civil service unless he or she is a British subject, a Commonwealth citizen or a citizen of the Irish Republic, and additional restrictions apply to the Cabinet Office, Ministry of Defence and Diplomatic Service.

The Act also fails to protect a person who applies abroad for employment on any ship (s. 9(1)), unless the employment is concerned with the exploration of the seabed or subsoil of the continental shelf. Selection for national and local teams for any game or sport is lawful on the basis of nationality, birthplace or length of residence.

To provide a defence under s. 41 which allows exceptions, the act done must be reasonably necessary in order to comply with any condition or requirement of the statute or order concerned (*General Medical Council* v *Goba* [1988] IRLR 425). *Hampson* v *Dept of Education and Science* [1989] IRLR 69, concerned the defence to a claim by a Hong Kong Chinese trained teacher who had been refused status as a qualified teacher by the Secretary of State on the ground that her training course was not comparable with that provided in the UK as required by the Education (Teachers) Regulations 1982 (SI 1982 No. 106). Any act of discrimination was thus in the course of carrying out a public duty and was in pursuance of the enactment. The defence was confined to acts done in necessary performance of an express obligation, and the test under the 1982 Regulations was not an express requirement contained in the Regulations and thus not in pursuance of the Regulations.

The Employment Act 1989, sections 11 and 12, introduced special principles in relation to Sikhs wearing safety helmets.

Further, the industrial tribunal has (by s. 54(2)) no jurisdiction 'in respect of which an appeal, or proceedings in the nature of an appeal, may be brought under any enactment' (see *Zaidi* v *FIMBRA* [1995] ICR 876).

8.7 ENFORCEMENT MECHANISMS

The Race Relations Act 1965 channelled all complaints of racial discrimination through the Race Relations Board, and it was the unsatisfactory working of this system, particularly the delay and complaints that the Board was not taking up proper grievances, which stimulated the granting of an individual right of action in industrial tribunals under both the Sex Discrimination Act 1975 and the Race Relations Act 1976. Difficulties of proof are, however, formidable and the number of claims under both Acts has not been as great as might have been expected. Besides the individual actions the EOC and CRE retain a strategic enforcement role through formal investigations. The various methods and procedures of enforcement will now be examined.

8.7.1 Individual complaint

An individual's application must be presented within three months of the act complained of to an industrial tribunal, unless the tribunal considers it just and equitable to extend the limit (SDA 1975, s. 76; RRA 1976, s. 68). The industrial tribunal may adjudicate only upon the complaint which is actually made in the originating application (*Chapman* v *Simon* [1994] IRLR 124). The power to extend time is rather different from the analogous provision in respect of unfair dismissal (para. 11.2). In *Hutchison* v *Westward TV Ltd* [1977] ICR 279 the learned judge emphasised the width of discretion and 'deprecated [the] very simple wide words becoming encrusted by barnacles of authority'. The EAT would only interfere if the decision of the industrial tribunal was wrong in law or perverse. In a discriminatory dismissal case, the 'act complained of' (from which point time starts to run) arises when the applicant found himself out of a job rather than the date on which he was given notice

(*Lupetti* v *Wrens Old House Ltd* [1984] ICR 348, *Gloucester Working Men's Club &
Institute* v *James* [1986] ICR 603; see also *Adlam* v *Salisbury and Wells Theological College*
[1985] ICR 786; *Clarke* v *Hampshire Electro-Plating Co. Ltd* [1992] ICR 312).
The following principles have been established in the case law:

(a)   A distinction is drawn between a one-off act of discrimination and a continuing
discriminatory arrangement. The former is an act complained of and sets the time limit
running, whereas in the latter case the complainant is a continuing victim of the practice
and the act is perpetrated until the practice is no longer discriminatory. In *Kapur* v *Barclays
Bank* [1989] IRLR 57, East African Asians who were first employed by Barclays Bank in
1970 alleged that the Bank discriminated against them by refusing to credit their African
service for pension purposes, whereas the past service of those of European origin was so
credited. The Employment Appeal Tribunal, however, held that such discrimination was an
act done in 1970, but this was overturned by the Court of Appeal ([1989] IRLR 387 whose
conclusion was itself upheld by the House of Lords [1991] IRLR 137, [1991] ICR 208).

(b)   Where an employee brings an appeal against dismissal, the act complained of will
be that act not the effective date of termination (*Adekeye* v *Post Office* [1993] IRLR 324).

(c)   When the complaint is based upon omitting to offer to a person employment, the act
complained of cannot arise until the alleged discriminator is in a position to offer such
employment (*Swithland Motors plc* v *Clarke* [1994] ICR 231).

(d)   The most liberal position is to be seen in *Littlewoods Organisation plc* v *Traynor*
[1993] IRLR 154, in which the employee was not out of the time limit when the employer
had promised to take action to remedy the alleged discrimination but that had not occurred
and the employee complained within three months of the failure to take the promised
remedial action.

(e)   *Clarke* v *Hampshire Electro-Plating Co. Ltd* [1992] ICR 312 illustrates a common
scenario in which the employee is aware of the act of which he complains within three
months of it occurring but does not have *evidence* that it was actually discriminatory until
a later date, when a person of another sex or race is appointed to the relevant position. In
such a case, time starts to run from the date of that person's appointment, or whatever else
may be the triggering event.

(f)   It is, however, wrong in principle in assessing whether it is just and equitable to
extend time, to take into account the fact that many persons with a perfectly good claim
arising out of the ECJ decision such as in *Marshall* v *Southampton and South West
Hampshire Health Authority* [1986] ICR 335 would not be able to bring them (*Foster* v
South Glamorgan Health Authority [1988] ICR 526). Each case had to be considered on its
merits.

The individual applicant may be financially assisted by the CRE or EOC when the
appropriate body thinks he has a test case raising a matter of principle or it is 'unreasonable
. . . to expect the applicant to deal with the case unaided or if there is any other special
consideration' (RRA 1976, s. 66; SDA 1975, s. 75). However, there is no appeal if the
Commission refuses its aid, which may take the form of seeking a compromise, settlement,
preliminary advice, or any other assistance it considers appropriate.

An ACAS conciliation officer is involved in attempting to settle all employment
discrimination complaints before a full industrial tribunal hearing, and the rules under which
he operates apply in the same way as to unfair dismissal and redundancy claims (para. 11.8).

8.7.2 Problems of proof

In many ways the applicant is like a fettered runner in discrimination cases. Those most prone to suffer acts of racial discrimination are likely to have language difficulties, and to find the English legal system a hostile maze. Application and success rates compare most unfavourably with the analogous jurisdiction in unfair dismissal cases and American experience of not dissimilar provisions (see Lustgarten 6 ILJ 212).

8.7.2.1 Burden of proof Those charging discrimination may be met by a smoke screen defence and all sorts of alternative and spurious reasons put forward for the less favourable treatment meted out. The very heavy burden on the complainant is, however, lightened in two ways:

(a) Tribunals and courts have recognised that 'where there has been established a distinction in treatment where one party is male and the other female, prima facie, this raises a case for answer' (*Moberly* v *Commonwealth Hall* [1977] IRLR 176, *Oxford* v *DHSS* [1977] IRLR 225, *Humphreys* v *St. George's School* [1978] ICR 546). The *evidential burden of proof* then moves to the employer, and tribunals are in particular reluctant to dismiss cases without hearing the employer, and subjecting him to cross examination (*Wallace* v *S.E. Library and Education Board* [1980] IRLR 193). Browne-Wilkinson J in *Khanna* v *Ministry of Defence* [1981] IRLR 331, sought, however, to cut through any metaphysical discussions about shifting burdens of proof by saying that if the primary facts indicate that there has been discrimination of some kind the employer is called upon to give an explanation and failing a fairly clear and specific explanation, the industrial tribunal may infer unlawful discrimination. If there is a finding of discrimination and of difference in race and then an inadequate or unsatisfactory explanation by the employer for that differentiation, the legitimate inference will be that discrimination was on the grounds of race or sex, as the case may be (*Noone* v *North West Thames Regional Health Authority* [1988] IRLR 195). The burden of proof, however, remains throughout on the applicant and it is a misdirection to suggest to the contrary (*London Borough of Barking and Dagenham* v *Camara* [1988] IRLR 373).

In *British Gas plc* v *Sharma* [1991] IRLR 101, the EAT deprecated the concept of an evidential burden. At the end of the case the tribunal would be involved in a fact-finding and balancing exercise. In determining whether the applicant has proved his case, the tribunal needs to find primary facts and to draw inferences from them. Depending on the strength of the applicant's case, the tribunal may look for a detailed and convincing explanation and defence.

These notions were approved by the Court of Appeal in *Baker* v *Cornwall County Council* [1990] ICR 452 and *Dornan* v *Belfast City Council* [1990] IRLR 179. The most general guidance was given by the Court of Appeal in *King* v *GB-China Centre* [1992] ICR 517 where Neill LJ emphasised the difficulty which applicants have in finding direct evidence of discrimination, and stressed that in some cases the discrimination will not be ill intentioned but merely based on the assumption that 'he or she would not have fitted in'. In some cases a finding of difference in treatment and difference in race will point to the possibility of discrimination. The tribunal will then look to the employer for an explanation. If such an explanation is not put forward or if it is inadequate or unsatisfactory it will be legitimate for the tribunal to infer that it was on racial grounds. This is not a matter of law but 'almost common sense'. It was thus unnecessary and unhelpful to introduce the concept of a shifting burden of proof.

(b)   The complainant may submit a special *questionnaire* to the respondent employer, and if the latter fails to reply or gives an evasive or equivocal response, the tribunal may draw inferences as to the existence of discrimination (see prescribed forms in Sex Discrimination (Questions and Replies) Order 1975 (SI 1975 No. 2048), *Virdee* v *ECC Quarries* [1978] IRLR 295). See also *Kingston* v *BRB* [1984] IRLR 146. (For detailed consideration, see Bowers, Brown and Mead, *Industrial Tribunal Practice and Procedure*, 3rd edn, FT Law & Tax, 1996.)

8.7.2.2   Statistical evidence   In the USA, 'statistics speak loudly, and the courts listen' is an oft-repeated dictum. They are accepted as of great significance in both class and individual actions brought under Title VII of the Civil Rights Act 1964, which is in terms very similar to Britain's race and sex discrimination legislation. The demonstration of a large disparity between the number of females or members of minority groups in a work force and the local or national population, establishes a prima facie case (*Kaplan* v *International Alliance of Theatrical Operatives,* 525 F. (2d) 1354), while in some cases, statistics have been held 'dispositive' of the whole case. The rationale is important; as enunciated in *Hazelwood School District* v *US,* 534 F. (2d) 805, it runs: 'absent explanation, it is ordinarily to be expected that non-discriminatory hiring practices will in time result in a workplace more or less representative of the racial and ethnic population in the community from which the employees are hired'.

The issues of the significant disparity and the relevant comparators are approached with a necessary and informed flexibility. In *Shafer* v *Tannian,* 394 F.Supp. 1128, there was evidence that, although women made up 52 per cent of the general population of the Detroit metropolitan area, and 39 per cent of the work force therein, the percentage in the Police Department stood at a mere 2 per cent. A strong prima facie case of discrimination was thus made out, which other evidence in fact did nothing to rebut. On the other hand, the court refused the invitation to infer discrimination from the fact that only 37 per cent of the respondent's university faculty were female in *Perham* v *Ladd,* 435 F. Supp.1101. The courts refuse to draw inferences from a small pool.

Jalota v *IMI* [1979] IRLR 313 appeared to close the door on the effective use of statistics. The Indian applicant claimed that, although amongst payroll employees in the respondent's rolled mill division, there were a number of coloured employees, only one or two minority workers had succeeded on the staff side for which he was applying. He thus sought, among other things, information on the race, colour and ethnic origins of other applicants for the position in question, and the number of coloured persons employed at the date when he submitted his application. Talbot J thought that such revelation could not be directly relevant; the claim was 'wholly unreasonable, irrelevant and should not be answered'. Instead he commended the respondents for not categorising the colour of their employees. He inquired, 'What could be more undesirable and more divisive than keeping such records?' (cf. *Perera* v *Civil Service Commission* and *Department of Customs and Excise (No. 2)* [1983] IRLR 166).

Jalota was disapproved in *West Midlands Passenger Transport Executive* v *Singh* [1988] ICR 614. The Court of Appeal held that statistical material might establish a discernable pattern of treatment by the employers towards a racial group from which an industrial tribunal could infer that discrimination had been the effective cause of the applicant's failure to (in this case) obtain promotion. It might also assist the applicant to rebut the employer's contention that it *in fact* operated an equal opportunities policy. (See also *Carrington* v *Helix Lighting Ltd* [1990] IRLR 6.)

8.7.2.3 Discovery of documents It may be vital for the applicant to see documents drawn up by the respondent even though of a confidential character; for only then can it be shown whether a black or female had as good reports and references as the successful applicant with whom they were competing. In the leading case of *Science Research Council* v *Nassé* [1979] IRLR 465, the House of Lords heard together Mrs Nassé's complaint of sex discrimination against the SRC and Mr Vyas' application against British Leyland on the grounds of race. Both applicants sought details of employment records of all other persons interviewed for jobs they had sought. These were to include service records, personal history forms, personal assessment records, and details of commendations together with their application forms for the post advertised. This produced a clash of two important principles: facilitating proof of discrimination and preserving the confidentiality of staff reports. Although all members of the House of Lords agreed that there was no principle of law that documents are protected from discovery by reason of confidentiality *alone,* their *relevance,* although a necessary condition, is not by itself sufficient. The test was whether discovery 'is necessary for disposing fairly of the proceedings'. Lords Wilberforce and Edmund Davies go on to say:

The process is to consider fairly the strength and value of the interest in preserving confidentiality and the damage which may be caused by breaking it, then to consider whether the objective to dispose fairly of the case can be achieved without doing so and only in the last resort to order discovery.

In especially sensitive cases, tribunals and courts cover up parts of the relevant documents, insert anonymous references or proceed *in camera* (see also *British Railways Board* v *Natarajan* [1979] ICR 326).

In the first important decision post *Nassé, Perera* v *Civil Service Commission* [1980] IRLR 233, the Employment Appeal Tribunal gave its principle ample scope. In order to prove that he had been turned down several times for jobs with the Civil Service because of his race, the applicant sought discovery of all documents relating to those applications. Notwithstanding that the assembly of the necessary information would be difficult and expensive since there were 1,600 applicants, Slynn J called for sufficient material to be disclosed so that the applicant could pursue his relevant inquiry whether other candidates had as high qualifications as he possessed. In particular, the application forms of 78 candidates interviewed in 1977 should be revealed, together with details of nationality and fathers' nationalities and their final reports and assessment. Any identifying material was to be blacked out.

In *Selvarajan* v *ILEA* [1980] IRLR 313, the applicant sought to refer, in support of his claim of discriminatory promotion, to a series of abortive applications between 1961 and 1976 for jobs with the respondents, since he alleged continuing discrimination. The EAT held that these could be logically probative and disagreed with the industrial tribunal's cut-off point in 1973. Since the request was limited to the application forms of the appointed candidates, minutes of appointment and Selvarajan's own file, no unfairness or oppression would result to the respondents. (See further discussion in Bowers, Brown and Mead, *Industrial Tribunal Practice and Procedure,* supra.)

8.7.2.4 Relevant evidence The applicant may refer to incidents before the coming into force of the Race Relations Act, or before the three months period within which complaints must be brought, in order to establish a consistent course of discriminatory conduct (*Eke* v

Commissioners of Customs and Excise [1981] IRLR 334). At the other end of the scale, the EAT decided in *Chattopadhay* v *Holloway School* [1981] IRLR 487 that evidence of events *subsequent* to the discrimination complained of should be admitted where logically probative. Here it satisfied the test, since the applicant sought to bring evidence of his treatment after he was turned down for the post of Head of History at the respondent school, to prove that his previous treatment was racially motivated, but Browne-Wilkinson J counselled against his judgment being taken as a charter for the wholesale introduction of irrelevant evidence.

8.7.3 Remedies

An industrial tribunal which upholds a complaint under either of the discrimination statutes, may grant three types of remedies. Firstly, it may make a *declaration of the rights* of the parties (SDA 1975, s. 65(1)(b)). The other two remedies are dealt with in paras 8.7.3.1 and 8.7.3.2.

8.7.3.1   Recommendation   The tribunal can make a recommendation (but not order) that the respondent should, within a specified period, take such action as the tribunal deems practicable in order to obviate or reduce the adverse effect of the act complained of. If, without reasonable justification, the respondent fails to comply with this recommendation, the tribunal may increase any compensation awarded. The recommendation is, however, restricted to remedying the specific act of discrimination and cannot be more wide-ranging. Moreover, it cannot be used to 'top up' compensation as the industrial tribunal appeared to suggest in *Irvine* v *Prestcold Ltd* [1981] IRLR 281, when it recommended an increase in wages to the applicant who had been discriminated against by not being promoted. The Court of Appeal thought that: 'The words ''action within a specified period'' are inapt to cover a recommendation as to payment of a particular remuneration during a period which might extend over several years.' The industrial tribunal cannot, moreover, recommend *positive* action. The following cases illustrate the scope of the remedy:

(a)   In *Ministry of Defence* v *Jeremiah* [1980] ICR 13 the suggestion that the employers provide showers for women was overturned.

(b)   In *Bayoomi* v *British Railways Board* [1981] IRLR 431, the industrial tribunal refused to make a general recommendation affecting the employer's recruitment policies on the ground that it could only obviate or reduce the adverse effect on the applicant; instead, it decreed the entry of a reference on the applicant's personal file explaining that his dismissal was due to discrimination.

(c)   An industrial tribunal should not make a recommendation that a health authority seek the authorisation of the Secretary of State for Health to dispense with its statutory obligations to advertise its next vacancy for a consultant in order to accommodate the applicant who was found to have been discriminated against on a previous occasion (*Noone* v *North West Thames Regional Health Authority* [1988] IRLR 530; see analogous situation in *British Gas plc* v *Sharma* [1991] ICR 19).

8.7.3.2   Compensation   Until the Sex Discrimination and Equal Pay (Remedies) Regulations 1993 (SI 1993 No. 2798) came into force on 22 November 1993 compensation could only be ordered up to the maximum laid down from time to time by statutory instrument — £11,000 from 1 April 1993. Now there is no limit. The maximum was also removed for race claims from 3 July 1994 by the Race Relations (Remedies) Act 1994. The measure of compensation is the same as that adopted by the ordinary courts (SDA 1975, s. 65(1)(b)), except that it may expressly include injury to feelings (s. 66(4)), provided that the tribunal considers that it is just and equitable to award compensation. The following principles of calculation are the most important:

(1) The general approach

In general the proper question is what would have happened were it not for the unlawful act, because discrimination is a statutory tort (*Ministry of Defence* v *Sullivan* [1994] ICR 193). The most exhaustive consideration of the approach to compensation is to be found in the decision by the EAT in ten conjoined cases of dismissal from the armed services on the ground of pregnancy in *Ministry of Defence* v *Cannock* [1994] IRLR 509, which were cases brought under the EC Equal Treatment Directive but the same principles would apply under the UK statute. Morison J held that the proper measure of damages under the Directive is tortious rather than contractual. The Ministry of Defence had argued that the service women who became pregnant were entitled to loss only to the end of their fixed-term service engagements. On the contrary, held the EAT, the applicants must be put in the position they would be in but for the unlawful conduct in dismissing them by reason of their pregnancy. The industrial tribunal should crucially assess the chance of the employee returning to work after the birth of the child. It was necessary to consider the length of service she hypothetically lost, including within this calculation the possible extension of period of engagement, her chances of promotion and other relevant contingencies. There should not be any separate award for loss of congenial employment since this overlapped with the award for injury to feelings. There is also no separate head for loss of career prospects.

The following principles also appear from the case law:

(a) The full amount of a deduction for a failure to mitigate should be applied to a compensatory award for loss of earnings, so that a discount of 10 per cent reflecting the chance that the applicant might not have completed her service should have been applied to the award before making the deduction for failure to mitigate (*Ministry of Defence* v *Bristow* [1996] ICR 544).

(b) In referring to the disadvantage of having a baby to care for when seeking work, the tribunal was not making a sex-based assumption but was using its experience to come to a realistic conclusion in measuring compensation (*Ministry of Defence* v *Hunt* [1996] ICR 554).

(c) Exemplary or aggravated damages are not appropriate when there is no evidence that either party knew or believed that the discriminatory policy was unlawful when the events occurred (*Ministry of Defence* v *Mutton* [1996] ICR 590).

(d) Earnings which an applicant would have earned had it not been for a failure to mitigate loss should be deducted before rather than after the percentage chance figure of the prospect that the employee would return to work following pregnancy was applied to the resulting sum (see the *Hunt* case, supra).

(2) Injury to feelings

At first appeal bodies took a hard line to large awards for injury to feelings made by tribunals. In *Skyrail Oceanic Ltd* v *Coleman* [1980] IRLR 226, [1981] IRLR 398, the EAT and Court of Appeal thought that no more should be awarded for injury to feelings than is given in defamation cases, and rejected the industrial tribunal's award of £1,000. Their Lordships thought that there could be no damage to the applicant's reputation on the facts and that £100 was thus suitable. In *Noone* v *North West Thames Regional Health Authority* (supra), an award of £5,000 for injury to feelings was too high even though the applicant, a medical consultant, suffered substantial injury to her feelings. The sum of £3,000 was substituted by the Court of Appeal. Where the defendant had behaved high-handedly, insultingly or oppressively in committing the act of discrimination, however, as it was found that prison officers had in *Alexander* v *Home Office* [1988] ICR 685, there should be awarded an amount of aggravated damages. The sum of £50 awarded by the trial judge was too low.

In making an award for injury to feelings in sexual harassment cases an industrial tribunal is entitled to take into consideration the fact that the applicant wore clothes which were 'scanty and provocative', as it found in *Wileman* v *Minilec Engineering Ltd* [1988] IRLR 144. Its award of only £50 under this head would not be overturned. (See *Sharifi* v *Strathclyde Regional Council* [1992] IRLR 259; *Duffy* v *Eastern Health and Social Services Board* [1992] IRLR 251; *Ministry of Defence* v *Sullivan*, supra; *Murray* v *Powertech (Scotland) Ltd* [1992] IRLR 257.) The amount to be awarded for injury to feelings is not bound to rise because the maximum limit for compensation has been removed (*Orlando* v *Didcot Power Station Sports and Social Club* [1996] IRLR 262).

(3) Perverse awards
The EAT may interfere with an award of compensation on the ground that it is perverse and outside the proper range (*Noone* v *North West Thames Regional Health Authority* (supra), *Wileman* v *Minilec Engineering Ltd* (supra)).

(4) Oppressive, etc. acts of government
Exemplary or aggravated damages may be awarded if the conduct falls within the categories recognised in *Rookes* v *Barnard* and *Cassell* v *Broome* [1972] AC 1027. These include oppressive, arbitrary or unconstitutional acts of government, including organs of local government (*Deane* v *Ealing LBC* [1993] ICR 329; *City of Bradford MBC* v *Arora* [1991] IRLR 165).

(5) Compensation for indirect discrimination
No compensation was awarded in the past for indirect discrimination unless the employer *intended* the discrimination to occur. To found the necessary intention it had to be shown that the employer intended discriminatory consequences to follow from his acts, knowing that those consequences would follow and wanting them to follow, according to the EAT in *J. H. Walker Ltd* v *Hussain* [1996] IRLR 10. This position was changed by the Sex Discrimination and Equal Pay (Miscellaneous Amendments) Regulations 1996 (SI 1996 No. 438) which took effect on 25 March 1996. The industrial tribunal can henceforth award compensation in these circumstances if it thinks it just and equitable to do so.

(6) Contributory fault
There is no provision for reduction of compensation on the ground of contributory fault (see *Gubala* v *Crompton Parkinson Ltd* [1977] IRLR 10, *Roadburg* v *Lothian Regional Council* [1976] IRLR 283, *Thorndyke* v *Bell Fruit (North Central) Ltd* [1979] IRLR 1).

(7) Awards of interest in race discrimination cases
The Race Relations (Interest on Awards) Regulations 1994 (SI 1994 No. 1748) permit the awarding of interest in race discrimination cases heard by an industrial tribunal on or after August 1994.

8.7.3.3 Judicial review An application for judicial review may be made when a public authority proposes to embark on an employment policy in breach of the Sex Discrimination Act or the Race Relations Act. In *R* v *London Borough of Hammersmith and Fulham ex parte NALGO* [1991] IRLR 249, however, such relief was not granted since the challenge was to a policy which merely *might* offend the law in individual cases. Whether it would do so depended on how implementation of the redeployment and redundancy policy was carried out (see also *R* v *Secretary of State for Employment ex parte EOC* [1994] IRLR 176).

8.7.4 Commission enforcement

The CRE and EOC each consists of 14 members appointed by the Home Secretary for up to five years. They gain all their funds from the Government (SDA 1975, s. 53; RRA 1976, s. 43). Their statutory duties are to work towards the elimination of discrimination, to promote equality of opportunities, and to keep the respective statutes under review, and in so doing they are meant to be independent of government. The enforcement of certain provisions of the Acts is within their exclusive jurisdictions, and they have the important additional tool of conducting formal investigations, although these have not been much used in recent years. The common thread which runs through all of their roles is that it would be unreasonable to expect individual litigants to shoulder the widespread investigations necessary before they are exercised. The statutory prohibitions are as follows:

(a) Where *advertisements* indicate or might reasonably be understood to indicate an intention to commit an unlawful act of discrimination (SDA 1975, s. 38; RRA 1976, s. 29). A picture showing only men performing the job on offer may be illegal, unless the employer would have a defence to an action for discrimination if no woman was in fact appointed to the job advertised, whether because being male was a genuine occupational qualification, or the job is one of the exceptional cases outside the scope of the discrimination statutes altogether. The publisher of an advertisement also has a defence if he proves that he reasonably relied on a statement by the advertiser that the advertised act of discrimination would be lawful (SDA 1975, s. 38(4)). The EOC or CRE in the first instance seeks a declaration from an industrial tribunal, but if the advertisement is repeated, its proper recourse is to a county court for an injunction.

(b) In the case of an *instruction to discriminate,* attempt to procure unlawful acts of discrimination and pressure to discriminate, either Commission may apply for an injunction to the appropriate county court. This should be granted if the court is satisfied that a breach has occurred and that further such action will be committed unless the respondent is restrained (SDA 1975, ss. 39, 40; RRA 1976, ss. 30, 31).

(c) *Discriminatory practices* are acts of indirect discrimination without a victim. For example, an employer may apply a requirement of workers with beards which is so well known that no woman ever applies for the job in question. No one is put to a detriment so that no individual claim of indirect discrimination can be brought; the Commission may, however, seek an injunction to end the practice (SDA 1975, s. 37; RRA 1976, s. 28).

8.7.5 Formal investigations

Formal investigations are a vital part of the Commission's 'strategic role' (SDA 1975, s. 57; RRA 1976, s. 48). They go beyond testing individual cases to making an overall examination of the structure of discrimination in entire fields of employment. They resemble in many ways Department of Trade and Industry investigations into companies, and similar rules of natural justice apply. They are thus not treated as fully judicial enquiries, so that it is not fatal that the respondents had no opportunity to cross-examine witnesses (*R* v *CRE ex parte Cottrell & Rothon* [1980] IRLR 279), or that the CRE had delegated the investigation to two Commissioners only. Where the Commission itself initiates an investigation, it is vital that the terms of reference are drawn up, and where the terms are confined to a named person, it is also a condition precedent that the Commission should have formed the belief that the named person has done specified discriminatory acts (*London Borough of Hillingdon* v *CRE* [1982] IRLR 424).

The Commissions have extensive powers to compel the production of documents and require witnesses to give evidence. Indeed a person who wilfully alters, suppresses, causes to be destroyed or destroys a document required by the EOC in pursuance of such an investigation may be fined. (See Sex Discrimination (Formal Investigations) Regulations 1975 (SI 1975 No. 1993), and Race Relations (Formal Investigations) Regulations 1977 (SI 1977 No. 841).) The Commission must give the persons to be investigated an opportunity to make representations even though at the time the investigation was commenced, the Commission did not have a belief that any unlawful act had been committed and that the grounds were tenuous because they had not been tested (*R* v *CRE ex parte Prestige Group Ltd* [1984] 1 WLR 335).

After this process of fact finding is completed, the Commission may serve a nondiscrimination order requiring the recipient to comply with the law (SDA 1975, ss. 60, 67; RRA 1976, ss. 51, 58), and to provide such information as may be reasonable to verify compliance therewith. To do so it must have found: an unlawful act of discrimination; a discriminatory practice contrary to SDA 1975, s. 37 or RRA 1976, s. 28; discriminatory advertisement; instruction to discriminate; pressure to discriminate; or an act in breach of equality clause under the Equal Pay Act 1970. The recipient of a notice must have an opportunity of making representations to the Commission and, even though it has no immediate legal effect, may appeal against any requirement to an industrial tribunal. To facilitate this procedure, the notice must be accompanied by a statement of findings of fact on the basis of which the CRE is satisfied that there has been unlawful discrimination. The notice of appeal should then set out each finding which is challenged and all other grounds on which it is alleged that any requirements of the notice are unreasonable (SDA 1975, s. 68; RRA 1976, s. 59). All issues of facts found are then open for consideration on appeal (*Commission for Racial Equality* v *Amari Plastics Ltd* [1982] IRLR 252; see also *R* v *Commission for Racial Equality ex parte Westminster City Council* [1985] IRLR 426).

The notice can be enforced by a county court injunction if, within five years of its issue, it appears to the relevant Commission that the respondent is likely again to act unlawfully (SDA 1975, s. 71). However, if the employer has not appealed, the responsible Commission must first test the legality of the notice before an industrial tribunal. This very round-about procedure has not so far been used. Moreover, there has been much criticism of the limited use which the CRE, and more particularly the EOC, has made of its extensive powers.

Local authorities are not permitted to have regard to equal opportunities policies in relation to public supply or works contracts. The Local Government Act 1988 states that public authorities within the Act must not have regard to non-commercial matters (s. 17(1)), and these include (s. 17(5)) the terms and conditions offered to their workforces; the use of self-employed labour; 'any involvement of the business activities or interests of contractors with irrelevant fields of Government policy; the conduct of contractors in industrial disputes between other persons and various other matters. Only certain approved questions may be asked of contractors about race relations matters (s. 18).

8.8 DISABILITY DISCRIMINATION

There have been more than a dozen attempts in recent years to introduce legislation addressing discrimination against the disabled, but it was not until the Disability Discrimination Act 1995 (the DDA 1995) was passed that the necessary governmental backing was secured. The DDA 1995 attempts to provide equality to disabled people in a similar way as legislation aimed at providing equality between men and women and between people of all racial origins. Like the associated discrimination legislation, in the employment context, the DDA 1995 will be enforced by individual applicants bringing their complaints to the industrial tribunals. It received its Royal Assent on 8 November 1995. The employment provisions come into force on 2 December 1996. An Employment Code of Practice has also been promulgated.

There was much controversy over the scope of the Act, for example, who would be protected and what defences there should be, which has not been, as yet, completely resolved. This is due to the vagueness of the drafting of the DDA 1995, but has been accounted for by the many provisions which allow for Regulations to be issued by government ministers to give further guidance on the meaning of the DDA provisions. Enlightenment should be forthcoming once Regulations are issued. The Act further provides for the creation of a 'National Disabilities Council'. The Council has no enforcement powers and its functions are to advise and draft Codes of Practice on discrimination issues concentrating on non-employment issues. The 'National Advisory Council on Employment of People with Disabilities' is drafting a Code of Practice for employers in relation to disabled applicants and employees.

The DDA 1995 takes a different approach to the problem of discrimination against disabled people than does the associated sex and race discrimination legislation.

8.8.1 The meaning of 'disability'

Section 1(1) of the DDA 1995 defines 'disability' as a 'physical or mental impairment which has a substantial and long-term adverse effect on . . . [a person's] . . . ability to carry out normal day-to-day activities'.

Schedule 1 of the Act elaborates on the meaning of the term 'physical or mental impairment'. Physical impairment is not given a specific definition, but express mention is made of severe disfigurements which have '. . . a substantial adverse effect on the ability of the person concerned to carry out normal day-to-day activities' (para. 3(1)). This provision protects those with disfigurements which may not affect the ability to work but which would lead employers to discriminate by, for example, refusing to appoint an applicant because the applicant had such a disfigurement. An example of severe disfigure-ment is a 'strawberry' birth mark or scarring from burns. Regulations may be issued to exclude deliberately acquired disfigurements. In the Parliamentary debates on the Bill, the Government made it clear that the protection would not apply to those who voluntarily disfigured themselves by tattoos, piercing or certain forms of dental work. The Disability Discrimination (Meaning of Disability) Regulations 1996 (SI 1996 No. 1455) specifically exclude from the definition of disability alcohol and (non-medical) drug dependency, certain behavioural problems and hay fever. A person also does not fall within the definition if he or she exhibits a tendency to set fires, a tendency to steal, a tendency to physical or sexual abuse of other persons, exhibitionism and voyeurism.

Under Sch. 1, 'mental impairment includes an impairment resulting from or consisting of a mental illness only if the illness is a clinically well-recognised illness'. Again, Regulations may make provision as to which conditions will and will not fall within this definition. The Government intends that the term 'mental impairment' should have a wide scope encompassing, for example, schizophrenia, manic depression and severe depressive psychoses, but, on the other hand, it further intends to exclude antisocial disorders or conditions such as kleptomania and paedophilia.

The intention behind the provision that the adverse effects must be substantial and long-term was to exclude trivial, minor and short-lasting ailments. However, impairments which can be medically treated or corrected may still be treated as having a substantial adverse effect. By Sch. 1, para. 2, the impairment must have lasted or be likely to last at least 12 months, or be likely to recur if the illness, such as multiple sclerosis, is of a recurring nature. The provision is also intended to protect HIV sufferers.

Under Sch. 1, para. 4, an impairment in carrying out normal day-to-day activities occurs if one or more of the following activities are affected: mobility, manual dexterity, physical coordination, continence, ability to lift and carry, speech, hearing or eyesight, memory, perception of the risk of physical danger. This list is exhaustive so the applicant must demonstrate that at least one of the activities is affected. The emphasis is thus on day-to-day activities rather than on specific work related activities although, inevitably, the two may involve the same basic skills and abilities. However, a person who can no longer carry out a work activity but can still continue to carry out day-to-day activities may not be covered by the DDA 1995. An example of this is a professional sportsman who can no longer play due to injuries but who is able to carry out normal activities.

8.8.2   The concept of discrimination under the DDA 1995

There is no concept of indirect discrimination in the 1995 Act. The discrimination must be direct, using a comparative approach in a similar way to the RRA and SDA; but, unlike under the RRA and the SDA, the employer has a general defence of justification.

By s. 5(1) of the DDA 1995, an employer thus discriminates against a disabled person if:

(a)   for a reason which relates to the disabled person's disability, he treats him less favourably than he treats or would treat others to whom that reason does not or would not apply; and

(b)   he cannot show that the treatment in question is justified.

The discrimination must relate specifically to the disability of the disabled person, but it is important to note that there is no absolute prohibition on discrimination. It may be justified, and as there is no concept of indirect discrimination in the 1995 Act, an employer's criteria that employees must have legible hand-writing, for example, although unintentionally excluding those who cannot write legibly due to disability, would not fit within s. 5(1). The DDA 1995 is also unlike the other discrimination statutes in that non-disabled people are not protected under the Act whereas, for example, the SDA applies to both men and women. It is not lawful to discriminate positively in favour of disabled people.

8.8.2.1   What constitutes discrimination against applicants and employees?   Under the DDA 1995, s.4, in common with the SDA 1975, s. 6 and the RRA 1976, s. 4, it is unlawful for an employer to discriminate against a disabled person either in the offering of employment or in the course of that employment. This covers recruitment, terms of employment, promotion, transfers, training and other similar benefits. An area of special interest as far as the disabled are concerned is that of medical examinations before employment. Pressure was put on the Government during the passage of the Bill through Parliament to include provisions specifically related to this subject, but it may be that most instances of concern will be covered by s. 4(1)(a), which makes it unlawful to discriminate against a disabled person in the arrangements the employer makes for the purpose of determining to whom employment should be offered.

Differences in pay may be justified if the 'amount of a person's pay is wholly or partly dependent on that person's performance' and it is applied to all of the employees, or to all of a class of employees which includes the disabled person, but is not defined by reference to any disability (Disability Discrimination (Employment) Regulations 1996 (SI 1996 No. 1456)).

8.8.2.2 Victimisation Again using the same structure as analogous provisions in the SDA 1975 and the RRA 1976, s. 55 of the DDA 1995 provides that discrimination includes the victimisation of a person due to the fact that the person has, for example, brought proceedings in connection with the Act or has testified in such proceedings.

8.8.2.3 The section 6 duty Under s. 5(2) of the DDA 1995, an employer also discriminates if he does not carry out certain adjustments to his arrangements or premises stipulated in s. 6. This is a significant and controversial part of the legislation. It puts employers under a duty to carry out whatever adjustments are reasonable in the circumstances of the case if 'the disabled person is placed at a substantial disadvantage in comparison with persons who are not disabled. Although this provision expressly applies in the offering of employment and to the terms and conditions of employment, it also requires employers to adjust the physical features of workplaces.

Unusually examples of steps which may have to be taken by employers are given in s. 6. These include the alteration of working hours, assigning the disabled person to a different place of work, acquiring or modifying equipment and providing a reader or interpreter.

The reasonableness test is then elaborated in s. 6(4), where it is provided that, when determining whether it is reasonable for an employer to take a particular step, regard shall be had to a number of factors including financial and practicable considerations (see also the Disability Discrimination (Employment) Regulations 1996 (SI 1996 No. 1456).

8.8.3 Defences

The main defence under the DDA 1995 is justification by the employer of the direct discrimination. Further, there is the threshold of reasonableness in taking steps (see para. 8.8.2.3) as well as a defence of lack of knowledge with regard to the s. 6 duty and a general exemption for certain employers under s. 7 of the Act. We will examine these issues in turn.

8.8.3.1 Justification Section 5(3) of the DDA 1995 provides that discriminatory treatment is justified, 'if, but only if, the reason for it is both material to the circumstances of the particular case and substantial'. The term 'material' was construed by the House of Lords in *Rainey* v *Greater Glasgow Health Board* [1987] AC 224 in the context of equal pay as 'significant and relevant', and a similar construction may be expected in this new area.

The fact that the employer's reason should serve to exclude as a defence of justification the imposition by employers of superfluous job requirements in an attempt to prevent a disabled person applying for the post. An example of such a requirement, if it can be shown to be discriminatory under s. 1, is the necessity for all applicants successfully to pass a sight test before being able to take a job. Since a blind person cannot successfully pass the test due to his or her disability, this requirement cannot be seen as an adequate justification if, for example, the responsibilities of the specific post applied for do not require an employee to be able to see to the levels stipulated in order to pass the test. The relevance of the reason as to what is seen as material is important since it will prevent employers using generalisations about disabled people without being able to demonstrate relevance in the particular case.

A substantial reason is one which is not minor or trivial, but if that is all that is meant by the term, employers will not have a difficult task in discharging the burden upon them. 'Substantial' has to be read with 'material' and not in isolation. Again, the DDA 1995 makes provision for Regulations to be issued which will give further guidance as to what treatment will and will not be justified.

8.8.3.2 The section 6 duty   Section 5(5) of the DDA 1995 provides that an employer may not justify discriminating against a disabled person if:

(a)   he is under a s. 6 duty to that disabled person which he does not obey without being able to justify this; and

(b)   he cannot justify his discrimination even if he had complied with the s. 6 duty.

This complicated provision essentially prevents an employer from using the need to take certain steps laid down in s. 6(3) as a justification for discrimination when it was reasonable in all the circumstances of the case for him to take those steps.

Section 6 is not a duty of strict liability since, under s. 6(6), it does not apply to an employer if he did not know, *and could not reasonably be expected to know,* either that the disabled person was an applicant for the employment or that the disabled person had a disability and could be affected by the employer's arrangements and/or premises. By adding a reasonableness threshold, the test is made objective so that an employer is prevented from succeeding in the defence if he deliberately closes his mind to the fact that the person concerned has a disability.

8.8.3.3 Exemption   Employers who employ fewer than 20 employees are exempt from all the provisions of the Act relating to employment (s. 7(1)), although they are not exempt from provisions relating to discrimination in the provision of goods and services. This is a most contentious measure as the vast majority of UK employers are small businesses. While over four-fifths of employees will be covered by the Act in that they work for businesses where the employer has more than 20 employees, over 95 per cent of employers will escape its effect because they employ fewer than 20 employees. Although this is in line with government policy to reduce 'burdens on business', and particularly small businesses, it is difficult to see the justification for it in what is basically a moral-based piece of legislation. Furthermore, there is not the same exemption in other anti-discrimination legislation.

Under s. 7(2) a different number (which cannot be greater than 20) may be substituted by statutory instrument. This allows for the possibility that the exemption is too wide in practice and that the DDA is not having the effect that the Government intended. However, before an order can be made to substitute a different number, the Secretary of State has to conduct a review involving full consultation with the relevant organisations. A review has to be carried out in any event immediately after the fourth anniversary of the coming into force of the exemption, but a review can be begun before this date.

8.8.4 Enforcement

Enforcement of the Act is similar in scope to that in other anti-discrimination legislation. Complaint should be made to an industrial tribunal within three months from the date of the Act complained of, under s. 8. The tribunal may, if it finds the case well-founded, make a declaration, an order for compensation, or a recommendation to the respondent. Compensation, which is calculated in the same way as for damages for breach of statutory duty or, in Scotland, claims in tort, may include compensation for injury to feelings. However, there is no body equivalent to the EOC or CRE under this Act, again giving the impression that the Government is less than fully committed to it. In fact, both the EOC and the CRE have never curried much favour with the present Government, at one time being subject to informed speculation that they would be abolished. The Act does set up the National Disabilities Council (see ss. 50–52), but this does not have a similar role to that of the EOC and CRE, having as its principal function the duty to give advice to the Secretary of State on disability discrimination matters.

Under s. 9, it is not possible for a contract of employment or other agreement to oust the effect of the Act, being void in so far as it purports to do so.

9 Maternity Rights

In *Lavery* v *Plessey Telecommunications Ltd* [1982] ICR 373 the EAT said:

> These statutory provisions [on maternity rights] are of inordinate complexity exceeding the worst excesses of a taxing statute; we find that especially regrettable bearing in mind that they are regulating the everyday rights of ordinary employers and employees. We feel no confidence that, even with the assistance of detailed arguments from skilled advocates, we have now correctly understood them: it is difficult to see how an ordinary employer or employee is expected to do so.

The Employment Protection Act 1975 for the first time recognised the problems of the pregnant employee who wished to return to work after having her baby. The statute thus closely supplemented the protection afforded to women under the Equal Pay and Sex Discrimination Acts, and built on the widespread provisions in collective agreements. It was amended by TURERA 1993. Now consolidated in the Employment Rights Act 1996, it gives most of the women who become pregnant the following rights:

(a) a maternity leave period;

(b) the right to return;

(c) not to be *dismissed* for reasons connected with pregnancy, and to claim compensation if she is;

(d) to receive a *maternity grant* and allowance payable by the Department of Health and Social Security;

(e) to take time off for *ante-natal care;*

(f) not to be suspended on maternity grounds.

A collective agreement or contract of employment may improve on these rights and this may be taken advantage of in preference to the statute (ERA 1996, s. 85(1); e.g. *Kolfor Plant Ltd* v *Wright* [1982] IRLR 311). The substantial amendments introduced by the 1993 Act came into force as from 16 October 1994 and made the pyramid of rights even more complex than before, and they were already a highly complicated maze of provisions.

9.1 THE MATERNITY LEAVE PERIOD

The Trade Union Reform and Employment Rights Act 1993 introduced for the first time the concept of the maternity leave period (MLP) which gives rights to all women employees, but these rights are less advantageous than those available to those employed for over two years. By what is now ERA 1996, s. 71, an employee who is absent from work at any time during her MLP is entitled to the benefit of the terms and conditions of employment which would have been applicable to her if she had not been absent. This equalises the position between pregnant employees and all others but 'does not confer any entitlement to remuneration' (s. 71(2)). The MLP commences:

(a) on the day the woman has notified her employer as the date on which she intends her period of absence to commence, or if earlier the first day she is absent from work (wholly or partly) because of pregnancy or childbirth after the beginning of the sixth week before the expected week of childbirth (EWC) which is

(b) in the normal case the beginning of the 11th week before EWC but

(c) is the date of childbirth where childbirth occurs before the beginning of what would otherwise be the MLP.

The duration of the MLP in the normal case is 14 weeks or until the birth of the child if later, but the period may be longer where any enactment prohibits the woman from being employed for any period after the end of the 14 weeks, and if the employee is dismissed during what would normally be the MLP, the period ends with *the time* of that dismissal. 'The time of that dismissal' is not defined and is a term different to those normally used in the statute, namely, the effective date of termination or the relevant date.

In a case where legislation prohibits the woman working for any period after the end of the 14 weeks her MLP continues until the expiry of that longer period (s. 73(2)). Further, under the Maternity (Compulsory Leave) Regulations 1994 (SI 1994 No. 2479), women are prohibited from working for two weeks beginning with the day they give birth. An employer who breaches this provision is (unusually for employment protection provisions) guilty of an offence punishable by a fine not exceeding level 2 on the standard scale, presently £500. It is also illegal to employ a woman in a factory or workshop within four weeks of her giving birth (Public Health Act 1936, s. 205).

The woman employee must inform her employer in writing at least 21 days before her MLP, or as soon as reasonably practicable thereafter:

(a) that she is pregnant; and

(b) when the EWC is (s. 75(1));

provided that the date is not before the beginning of the 11th week before the EWC, and she must for this purpose produce for inspection a certificate.

Where she is absent from work wholly or mainly because of pregnancy or childbirth before the notified leave date or before she has notified a date and after the beginning of the sixth week before the EWC, she must notify the employer as soon as reasonably practicable thereafter. In the event that childbirth occurs before she has notified such a date, she must notify her employer that she has given birth as soon as reasonably practicable after the birth.

Where during the MLP it is not practicable because of redundancy to continue to employ the woman under her existing contract of employment, she is entitled to be offered a suitable alternative vacancy (s. 77). The new contract to be offered must be such that:

(a) the work is *suitable* in relation to the employee and appropriate for her to do in the circumstances;

(b)   the provisions of the new contract concerning capacity and place of employment and other terms and conditions are *not substantially less favourable* to her than under the previous contract.

An employee who has completed her MLP and is turned down for a job share is not thereby subject to direct discrimination unless a man so requesting would have been treated differently (*British Telecom plc* v *Roberts* [1996] ICR 625).

9.2   RIGHT TO RETURN TO WORK

The most fundamental right of a pregnant employee is that she may return to work within 29 weeks following her confinement. This is a much more fundamental right than the MLP and is available only to those who have two years' service. If the employer refuses to allow her to do so, he is treated as having dismissed her (ERA 1996, s. 96). On return, her pay, seniority and pension rights must be no less favourable than when she left (s. 79). While her duties may be altered, the job package as a whole must be just as favourable (*Edgell* v *Lloyd's Register* [1977] IRLR 463, cf. *McFadden* v *Greater Glasgow Passenger Transport Executive* [1977] IRLR 327). 'Job' itself is defined in ERA 1996, s. 235(1).

9.2.1   Conditions

The efficacy of the right is much reduced by the conditions to be fulfilled. The ERA 1996 provides that:

(a)   The employee must have been engaged under a contract of employment for at least two years at the 11th week before the expected week of confinement even though she may not actually have worked until then (s. 79). The essential requirement is that her contract subsists during this period. The EAT said in *Satchwell Sunvic Ltd* v *Secretary of State for Employment* [1979] IRLR 455, 'so long as her contract subsists it does not matter whether she is in fact at her desk or bench and the statute imposes no limitation on the reason why she may not be at work'. According to the EAT in *Lloyds Bank Ltd* v *Secretary of State for Employment* [1979] IRLR 41, this may be achieved where an employee works one week on and one week off.

In order to claim her rights the employee must not resign before going on maternity leave (*Mitchell* v *Royal British Legion Club* [1980] IRLR 425) but the tribunals are astute not to spell out a resignation if it is in ambiguous terms (see para. 13.3.5.4). A general statement of intention that an employee will not return because of the expected birth does not amount to a resignation (*Hughes* v *Gwynned AHA* [1978] ICR 161, *Secretary of State for Employment* v *Doulton Sanitaryware Ltd* [1981] IRLR 365). Moreover, if the woman is dismissed before the 11th week on the grounds that she is physically or legally incapable of continuing to work, she can still claim if she would have completed the two years but for that dismissal (s. 33(4)). This protects her against obvious possibilities for avoidance by an unscrupulous employer.

(b)   She must inform the employer in writing at least 21 days before her absence that she intends to return to work (s. 80; see *F.W. Woolworths plc* v *Smith* [1990] ICR 45). If it is not reasonably practicable to give a period of notice (for example, because the child was born prematurely) she must notify him of it as soon as she can. This test is interpreted in the same manner as the flexibility clause in the time limit for unfair dismissal applications (*Nu-Swift International Ltd* v *Mallison* [1978] IRLR 537, cf. *J. Williams & Co. Ltd* v

Secretary of State for Employment [1978] IRLR 235). If the employer requests it, the employee must provide a medical certificate indicating the expected week of confinement.

(c)   The employer is entitled to ask the employee to confirm her intention to return after the extended maternity absence after childbirth. Such a request must be in writing and accompanied by a written explanation of the consequences for the woman of non-compliance (s. 80(3)). The woman must reply within two weeks of receipt or as soon as reasonably practicable thereafter, but not earlier than 21 days before the end of the MLP (s. 80(2)).

(d)   She must give further written notice 21 days in advance of her return (called the notified date of return). The full period of absence is 29 *pay* weeks (s. 82(1)).

If the employee does not strictly comply with all these conditions, she cannot in most cases claim to have been dismissed if she is not permitted to return to work after the maternity leave (*Kolfor Plant Ltd* v *Wright* [1982] IRLR 311). The Court of Appeal in *Lavery* v *Plessey Telecommunications Ltd* [1983] ICR 534 went further and said that the right is forfeited whether or not the woman's contract of employment continues during her absence, because a woman relying on such a right is treated by statute as exercising a 'composite right' consisting of contractual and statutory rights subjected to the above conditions (*F.W. Woolworths plc* v *Smith* [1990] ICR 45; *Institute of Motor Industry* v *Harvey* [1992] IRLR 343).

Lavery was distinguished on narrow grounds in *Lucas* v *Norton of London Ltd* [1984] IRLR 86. The employer and employee came to a 'nebulous agreement' that the applicant might return to work after her pregnancy. The EAT accepted that even though she had not followed the prescribed procedure for exercising her maternity leave, she was entitled to return. The case was different from *Lavery* since Mrs Lucas had not sought to exercise the statutory rights at all, but had relied on her contractual claim to return. According to the EAT there was an obligation on the employer to take her back in her previous job at a reasonable time after confinement and upon reasonable notice. The employer's action in refusing her return was consequently a dismissal. In *McKnight* v *Adlestones (Jewellers) Ltd* [1984] IRLR 453 the Northern Ireland Court of Appeal thought that the contract was suspended during the maternity leave, and continued only on the basis that the employee might properly exercise her right to return. If she failed to exercise that right effectively, the contract automatically terminated. The contract may continue, however, depending upon the agreement and actions of the parties, for example by reference to the employer's payment of sick pay and a letter requesting notice from the employee of whether or not she intended to return to work (*Hilton International Hotels (UK) Ltd* v *Kaissi* [1994] IRLR 270). This case appears to be in direct conflict with *McKnight*, is very controversial and its consequences have still to be worked out.

There is no presumption that the contract of employment continues to exist once the right to return to work has been lost, according to the EAT in *Crouch* v *Kidsons Impey* [1996] IRLR 79.

The following persons are excluded from the right to return: share fishermen, police-women, those who work for the armed forces, a woman who works for her husband, and anyone ordinarily working outside Great Britain.

9.2.2   Date of commencement of leave

The exact date of commencing maternity absence is for the pregnant employee herself to decide. The employer's challenge to this view failed in *Inner London Education Authority* v *Nash* [1979] IRLR 29. The applicant was a teacher whose contract provided that she must leave at the beginning of the eleventh week before the expected week of her confinement. The expected date was 23 September but she wished to carry on in employment until 2 September, which was the end of the school summer holidays. The EAT, with Kilner Brown J dissenting, upheld her claim on the ground that the Act gave her a choice when to finish and claim her maternity leave, and the contract would be void if it purported to exclude or vary that right.

9.2.3 Exceptions

There are three general exceptions to the right to return. The first is based on the alleged hardship the provisions were causing to small businesses. Thus, if just before the relevant absence the employer had *five or fewer* employees he need not reinstate the pregnant employee if it is not reasonably practicable for him to do so (ERA 1996, s. 96(2)).

Secondly, the right does not apply where it is not reasonably practicable for an employer to permit the employee to return to work; in this case the employer must still offer employment suitable to the employee and appropriate for her to do in the circumstances, and not substantially less favourable than her old job (s. 96(3) and (4)).

Thirdly, if the pregnant woman's job is made *redundant*, the employer or an associated employer need not take her back but must offer her a suitable vacancy (ERA 1996, s. 8). This means that rather like the redundancy provisions, the work must be 'suitable in relation to the employee' and 'appropriate for her to do in the circumstances', and the terms and conditions of employment must be 'not substantially less favourable' than under the old contract (*Philip Hodges & Co.* v *Kell* [1994] ICR 656). The right to return to work is not affected by a dismissal during the MLP.

If there is an alternative available vacancy, failure to make an offer in such circumstances is automatically an unfair dismissal (ERA 1996, s. 99(4)). In *Community Task Force* v *Rimmer* [1986] IRLR 203, the EAT upheld a tribunal decision that a redundancy dismissal was unfair even though the employer's evidence was that the vacancy, which the applicant alleged was 'available' for her could be filled only by an unemployed person under MSC rules, and that defiance of the rule would lead to a decrease in MSC funding for the appellant organisation. Peter Gibson J thought that 'available' was a matter of fact and was not qualified by what was economic or reasonable.

If there really is no available vacancy, the woman is treated as continuously employed until the notified day of return and is entitled to a redundancy payment in the normal way. In all other cases where the employee is not permitted to return, the tribunal must determine what was the reason in the normal way, but if it was connected with her pregnancy, the dismissal is automatically unfair.

Section 203(1) of ERA 1996 which avoids an agreement to exclude statutory provisions, applies to maternity rights and was given scope in *ILEA* v *Nash* (supra) (see para. 11.8.2). The ILEA Staff Code required women to start maternity leave on the eleventh week before confinement. The two lay members of the EAT, with Kilner Brown J dissenting, held that this requirement was void. It was up to the woman herself when she went on leave.

9.2.4 Postponing the date of return

The employee may suspend her return by up to four weeks on production of medical evidence, but an employer's failure to permit a properly notified return to work after maternity is treated as a dismissal, and the employee may invoke the provisions for unfair dismissal in the usual way. For the dismissal to be fair the employer must show the reason why he refused to permit her to return and that it was within one of the five categories of potentially fair reasons. The tribunal must then decide whether the employer would have been reasonable in treating this as sufficient reason for dismissing the woman if she had not been absent. The normal procedures and remedies for unfair dismissal apply (Chapter 13).

9.2.5 Contractual rights

Where an employee has a contractual right to return to work she may elect between that and the statutory right, choosing whichever is more favourable in her case (ERA 1996, s. 85). She cannot, however, select bits from each, for example attempting to combine the contractual offer of part-time employment with retaining under statute her previous terms and conditions (*Bovey* v *Hospital for Sick Children* [1978] IRLR 241, *Kolfor Plant Ltd* v *Wright* [1982] IRLR 311).

The interconnection between statutory and contractual maternity leave was considered by the Court of Appeal in *Dowuona* v *John Lewis plc* [1987] IRLR 310. It was agreed between the employee and the company that she should take one week of her annual holiday at the end of her maternity leave. Thereafter, she sent a sick note postponing her date of return for four weeks, as she was entitled to do under what is now ERA 1996, s. 82(3). She was, however, still unwell at the end of that time and did not return. The employee argued that the effect of the one week's holiday at the end of the maternity leave was that the employee had failed to return to work from holiday rather than from maternity leave. This was soundly rejected by the Court of Appeal. The employee could not complain of unfair dismissal since by seeking to return to work on a date later than that at which she was entitled to do, she had failed to exercise her right to return. Balcombe LJ also expressed doubt on the correctness of the decision in *Lucas* v *Norton of London Ltd* [1984] IRLR 86.

9.3 STATUTORY MATERNITY PAY

Changes to statutory maternity pay followed in the wake of the need to implement the European Directive on Pregnant Workers (92/85). The governing regulations are the Maternity Allowance and Statutory Maternity Pay Regulations 1994 (SI 1994 No. 1230) and the Social Security Maternity Benefits and Statutory Sick Pay (Amendment) Regulations 1994 (SI 1994 No. 1367), the Social Security Contributions, Statutory Maternity Pay and Statutory Sick Pay (Miscellaneous Amendments) Regulations 1996 (SI 1996 No. 777). (For full treatment, see Susan Cox, *Maternity Rights*, Legal Action Group, 1996.) They derive from the Social Security Contributions and Benefits Act 1992. There are no longer any service qualifications for the right to maternity leave period. After six weeks on earnings related pay, such women receive £54.55 for up to 12 weeks. Backdated pay increases must be taken into account in calculating 'normal weekly earnings' as from 12 June 1996 by reason of the Statutory Maternity Pay (General) Amendment Regulations 1996 (SI 1996 No. 1335) (which were introduced to put into effect the second *ratio* in *Gillespie* v *Northern Health and Social Services Board* [1996] ICR 498 that an employee absent on maternity leave was entitled to any increase in pay awarded to similar employees during her absence (see also para. 7.7.1 supra)).

Statutory maternity pay is payable to any woman who:

(a)   is an employee;

(b)   has been continuously employed by the same employer for at least 26 weeks, continuing into the 15th week before the week when her baby is due;

(c)   has average weekly earnings of not less than the lower earnings limit for national insurance contributions, currently £57, during the eight weeks up to and including the qualifying week;

(d)   is still pregnant at the 11th week before the baby is due or has given birth by this time;

(e)   has given 21 days' notice of the date on which she intends to stop work or as much notice as was reasonably practicable in writing if the employer requests it;

(f)   presents medical evidence of the date on which the baby is expected;

(g)   has stopped working for the employer by reason of pregnancy or childbirth.

It does not apply to overseas employees, share fishermen or the police.

Any woman who satisfies these criteria is entitled to receive statutory maternity pay even if she is not returning to work after her maternity leave has ended.

The statutory maternity pay cannot start earlier than 11 weeks before the expected date of childbirth, but it can be as late as the week immediately following the week in which the woman gives birth. An employer who refuses to pay statutory maternity pay must give written reasons for not doing so.

As is the case with most issues of continuity of employment, the following absences from work and transfers of employment do not break continuity of service for the purposes of statutory maternity pay (Part III of the Statutory Maternity Pay (General) Regulations 1986 (SI 1986 No. 1960)):

(a)   periods of incapacity for work of less than 26 weeks;

(b)   weeks which fall between the date of a woman's dismissal which is found to be unfair and her reinstatement;

(c)   a transfer of business;

(d)   transfer of employment to an associated employer.

The employer is entitled to be reimbursed only 92 per cent of the amount which he pays out, except for 'small employers' who continue to receive full reimbursement.

Where the employee does not accept the employer's decision regarding payment of statutory maternity pay, complaint is addressed to an adjudication officer pursuant to s. 52 of the Social Security Act 1986 within six months of the earliest day in respect of which there is a dispute. Appeal from his decision proceeds to the Social Security Appeal Tribunal and thence to the Social Security Commissioners.

The employee cannot validly sign away her right to statutory maternity pay nor can the employer validly require her to contribute towards the costs incurred by him. Any such agreement to the contrary is void (Social Security Act 1986, s. 46(6)).

9.4   DISMISSAL

A refusal by the employer to permit the employee to exercise her statutory right to return to work is deemed to have been a dismissal on the notified date of return (ERA 1996, s. 96). The reasons for the deemed dismissal are taken as the reasons for which the employer refused to permit the woman to return.

TURERA 1993 introduced a wholly redrafted provision (now ERA 1996, s. 99), which provides for automatically unfair dismissals in pregnancy cases. It is now provided that an employee shall be treated as unfairly dismissed if:

(a)   the reason, or principal reason, for her dismissal is that she is pregnant or any other reason connected with her pregnancy;

(b)   her MLP is ended by the dismissal and the reason, or principal reason, for her dismissal is that she has given birth to a child or any other reason connected with her having given birth to a child;

(c)   the reason, or principal reason, for her dismissal, where her contract was terminated after her MLP ended, is that she took, or availed herself of the benefits of, maternity leave. A woman takes maternity leave for these purposes if she is absent from work during her MLP and 'avails herself of benefits' if she takes advantage of any of her terms and conditions preserved by s. 71;

(d)   the reason, or principal reason, is connected with her having given birth to a child where:

(i)   before the end of her maternity leave, she gave her employer a certificate from a registered medical practitioner stating that she would be incapable of work by reason of disease or bodily or mental disablement after the end of the MLP; and

(ii)   she was dismissed within four weeks after the end of her leave when she continued to be incapable of work and certified as such;

(e)   the reason, or principal reason, for her dismissal is a requirement relating to suspension on maternity grounds (see para. 9.6); or

(f)   the reason for her dismissal is redundancy during maternity leave and s. 77 is not complied with. Section 77 provides that where during an employee's maternity leave period it is not practicable by reason of redundancy for the employer to continue to employ her under her existing contract of employment, she is entitled, where there is a suitable available vacancy, to be offered (before the ending of her employment under that contract) alternative employment with her employer or his successor, or an associated employer, under a new contract of employment which takes effect immediately on the ending of her employment under the previous contract.

If a woman can show that her dismissal fell within one of the above heads, then her dismissal will be unfair regardless of length of service and hours of work. This is separate from the principle in *Webb* v *EMO Air Cargo*, which declares a dismissal on grounds of pregnancy to be automatically sexually discriminatory (see para. 8.3.1).

Where the woman has been selected for redundancy and the principal reason for her selection for redundancy is a reason specified in s. 99, then the woman will be taken to have been unfairly dismissed.

Clearly it would be anomalous to give women a right not to be dismissed on pregnancy related grounds regardless of service and not to give them a right to a written statement of the reasons for dismissal unless they have been employed for two years. This is recognised by ERA 1996, s. 92(4), which provides that:

An employee is entitled a written statement under this section without having to request it and irrespective of whether she has now been continuously employed for any period if she is dismissed—

(a)   at any time while she is pregnant, or
(b)   after childbirth in circumstances in which her maternity leave period ends by reason of the dismissal.

The general nature of an employer's breach of the obligation to provide written reasons is changed from 'an unreasonable refusal' to 'an unreasonable failure' (ERA 1996, s. 93(1)).

9.5   ANTE-NATAL CARE

The right to time off for ante-natal care was introduced by s. 13 of the Employment Act 1980 (now ERA 1996, s. 55), following concern at the extent of perinatal mortality and handicap expressed, in particular, by reports of the House of Commons Select Committee on Social Services. It found the UK figure to be one of the highest in the Western world. The right is available to all women employees irrespective of length of service or hours of work. In order to claim it, the employee may, however, be required to produce a doctor's or midwife's certificate of pregnancy, and appointment card. If she does, she should be paid at the appropriate hourly rate for the time taken off, and if this is unreasonably refused, she may complain to an industrial tribunal within three months. It may be reasonable to refuse such time off if an employee can reasonably make arrangements for an appointment outside normal working hours (*Gregory* v *Tudsbury Ltd* [1982] IRLR 267).

Example   Alexandra expects her baby in the week beginning 16 March 1996. In order to claim maternity pay she must have been employed continuously since 1 January 1994, that is, two years and eleven weeks before confinement, and she must inform the employer at least 21 days before, i.e. 23 February 1996, that she will be absent from that week. She is then entitled to maternity pay for up to six weeks from the start of her absence, the precise date of which is for her to decide. If she formerly earned £100 per week she is entitled to £90, less maternity allowance payable. She has 29 weeks in which to return to work and if the employer refuses to let her, he is taken to have dismissed her. She must, however, write to him 21 days in advance of her return to work. During this time the employer has hired Belinda to take over Alexandra's work; if she has been told of the situation regarding Alexandra's absence he has a substantial reason for dismissing her when Alexandra returns.

9.6   SUSPENSION ON MATERNITY GROUNDS

TURERA 1993 introduced new rights with regard to suspension from work on maternity grounds where the employee is prohibited from continuing working (ERA 1996, ss. 66–68).
If an employee is suspended from work by her employer either because she is pregnant, has recently given birth or is breastfeeding a child, she has a number of rights where the suspension is in consequence of any requirement imposed by or under any relevant provision of any enactment, or of any instrument made under any enactment or any recommendation in any relevant provision of a code of practice issued or approved under s. 16 of the Health and Safety at Work, etc. Act 1974 (ERA 1996, s. 66(1)).
The first right which a woman has where she cannot continue working as a result of any requirement or recommendation is that she should be offered any suitable alternative work which is available before she is suspended (s. 67(1)). The alternative work will be suitable by reference to the same principles as relate to the redundancy provisions in s. 77(3). If the

woman is not offered work, in contravention of s. 67(1), then she may complain to an industrial tribunal, which may make an award of such compensation as it considers just and equitable having regard to the employer's infringement and any loss attributable to that breach (s. 70(4)–(7)). Any complaint must be lodged within three months of the first day of the suspension, unless it is not reasonably practicable to present a complaint within three months (s. 70(5)).

If the employee is actually suspended pursuant to s. 66, then she is entitled to be paid remuneration by her employer while she is suspended (s. 68). The suspension lasts as long as the employee continues to be employed but is not provided with work or — excepting alternative work under s. 67 — does not do the work she did before suspension.

Complaint for breaches of s. 68 is to an industrial tribunal. The complaint must be brought within three months of any day on which remuneration is not paid, unless the industrial tribunal considers that it was not reasonably practicable to complain within this period (s. 70(2)). If the tribunal finds that the complaint is well-founded then it must order the employer to pay the amounts of remuneration which it finds due to the woman (s. 70(3)).

10 Continuity of Employment

10.1 BACKGROUND

Statutory continuity of employment is centrally important to most statutory employment protection rights including redundancy pay, maternity pay and unfair dismissal. It is vital in determining: (a) whether the employee has served the appropriate qualifying period; and (b) if so, what is the appropriate amount of award or payment due.

Continuity is extensively defined in the ERA 1996, Part XIV, Chapter I. The aim of the statute is to overcome the common law rule that every change of terms was a new contract, which would artificially restrict employee rights. There is a special continuity regime for statutory maternity pay (see para. 9.3).

The length of continuous service must be stated in the written statement of terms provided under s. 1 of the 1996 Act. The period of service must, however, be lawful employment so that in *Hyland* v *J.H. Barker (North-West) Ltd* [1985] IRLR 403, the employee was not able to count a vital month in which he received an illegal lodging allowance. Time spent 'in work wholly or mainly outside Great Britain' counts towards continuity save for the purposes of building service for a redundancy payment (ERA 1996, s. 215(1) and (2)).

10.1.1 Change of duties

Continuity is preserved even though, during an employee's service, the duties required by his contract and other incidental terms vary greatly. He may rise in status from cleaner to managing director and fall all the way back again, but he still retains his continuity. In *Wood* v *York City Council* [1978] IRLR 228, for example, the employee worked for York City Council for three years in various capacities, finishing up in the Treasurer's Department. He resigned from this post in order to take up a position with the Council's York Festival office and, on being made redundant a year later, he qualified to receive redundancy payment since his employment in both capacities was continuous, notwithstanding the change of his duties and intermediate resignation (see also *Jennings* v *Salford Community Service Agency* [1981] IRLR 76, *Tipper* v *Roofdec Ltd* [1989] IRLR 419; cf. *Ryan* v *Shipboard Maintenance Ltd* [1980] IRLR 16).

10.1.2 Presumption of continuity

Where an employee works for one employer, there is thus a statutory presumption of continuity and the onus is on the employer to to disprove it (ERA 1996, s. 210(5); *Nicholl* v *Nocorrode Ltd* [1981] IRLR 163). The presumption applies only to employment with one employer; an exceptional case in which continuity bridges service with two or more different employers, such as a transfer of business or between associated employers, must be proved by the employee (*Secretary of State for Employment* v *Cohen* [1987] IRLR 169; see further discussion at para. 10.4.1.1).

10.2 MONTHS AND YEARS OF SERVICE

The units for measuring continuity are calendar months and years. The period of continuity begins on the day the employee 'starts work' (ERA 1996, s. 211(1)(a)). This concept itself is not free from difficulty as shown in *General of the Salvation Army* v *Dewsbury* [1984] ICR 498. The EAT decided that it referred to the beginning of contractual period of employment rather than necessarily the date when the full range of the employee's responsibilities began. Thus, a teacher whose post commenced on 1 May, a Saturday, but who did not begin her full teaching load until 4 May because of the intervening bank holiday, was held to have started work on 1 May. The end of continuous service depends on the employment protection right in question, being the effective date of termination in unfair dismissal and the relevant date for redundancy purposes (see para. 13.4).

In most cases, the employee used to have to actually work for 16 hours or more in order to count a week of service, whatever his contract stipulated (EPCA 1978, Sch. 13, para 3). An employee could count a week in which he did not actually work 16 hours, if he had a subsisting contract of employment which *normally* involved employment for the 16-hour period. This threshold has now been repealed by the Employment Protection (Part-Time Employees) Regulations 1995 (SI 1995 No. 31) after the restriction on part-timers was declared unlawful as a matter of EC law by the House of Lords in *R* v *Secretary of State for Employment ex parte EOC* [1994] IRLR 176. This conclusion was on the basis that there was indirect discrimination because the larger number of part-time workers were women and the provision was not based on objectively justified grounds. The suggestion by the Secretary of State for Employment that the threshold provisions were justified by the fact that more part-time work is available than would be the case if employers were liable for redundancy pay and unfair dismissal compensation in relation to part-timers did not find favour with their Lordships. We consider here the previous law because there will still be cases before tribunals which arose before SI 1995 No. 31 was enacted and because it is relevant in other circumstances in which hours of work must be calculated, for example, in assessing the week's pay.

It does not then matter that the employee actually labours for only three or four hours, or not at all, in a particular week, for example by reason of holiday or illness. Moreover, what the contract normally involves may be somewhat different from what is in reality worked. It is enough if the contract normally requires more than 16 hours even if it occasionally involves less. Thus, in *Dean* v *Eastbourne Fishermen's Club Ltd* [1977] IRLR 143, the employee worked less than 21 hours (then the required level) in 13 weeks, but more in 86 weeks. This sufficed, but in *ITT Components (Europe) Ltd* v *Kolah* [1977] IRLR 53, the applicant was held to be employed for 20 hours a week although in fact she generally laboured 23 hours. This was because the 'normal hours' of her contract as laid down therein were 20. The first priority was to examine the contract, and only if its terms were wholly ambiguous was it legitimate to consider what the parties did in *practice*. The tribunal must look at each contract separately even if the employee has three with the same employer (see *Lewis* v *Surrey CC* [1987] IRLR 509, discussed fully at para. 10.3.1.2).

The following principles emerged from the cases:

(a) In *Harber* v *North London Polytechnic* [1990] IRLR 198, Mr Harber was employed as a part-time lecturer for 14 years with fluctuating hours. When Mr Harber was not engaged for the academic year 1987/88 he complained of unfair dismissal. The Polytechnic defended on the basis that he did not have the requisite period of continuous employment. The primary test under Sch. 13, para. 6 to EPCA 1978 (now ERA 1996, s. 212(1)) was not what hours were *actually* worked but what hours the contract *normally* involved.

(b) Schedule 13, para. 4 of EPCA 1978 provided that any week counts in which 'the employee's relations with the employer are governed by a contract of employment which normally involves employment for 16 hours or more weekly'. This does not, however, apply when an employee left one employer of his own volition and worked for another employer before returning to work for the first employer under a new contract of employment (*Roach* v *CSB (Moulds) Ltd* [1991] ICR 349).

(c) Paragraph 4 is not concerned with cases where there has been a change of employment (cf. in the case of two consecutive employers on a transfer of business, *Gibson* v *Motortune Ltd* [1990] ICR 740).

(d) In *Secretary of State for Employment* v *Deary and Cambridgeshire CC* [1984] ICR 413, the seven applicants were 'dinner ladies' whose contractual hours depended on the number of meals to be served. They had all worked in excess of five years for more than eight hours a week. In 1980, the hours of one of them were reduced below this threshold and in 1981 the working time of the others followed downwards. The EAT decided that the use of the word 'normally' required the tribunal to consider not merely the terms of the contract as varied but also the original agreement. On this view, the ladies normally worked more than the statutory eight hours.

(e) The tribunal must look at what is positively *required by the contract*. A teacher could not include preparation and marking of homework which she did at home. The implied term for which she contended, that she had to do as much outside work as was necessary for the proper performance of her duties and which would take her above the statutory minimum, was rejected as too vague and unpredictable in *Lake* v *Essex CC* [1979] ICR 577. The employee thus did not have sufficient hours to bring her claim (cf. *Society of Licensed Victuallers* v *Chamberlain* [1989] IRLR 421).

(f) Similar issues have arisen in relation to employees who are on long standby duties. The evidence in *Merseyside CC* v *Bullock* [1979] IRLR 33, was that a fireman was on call for 102½ hours a week and had to be available then if summoned by a 'bleeper'. The Court of Appeal decided that although the average rate of call-out was 12 hours per week, he could count the much larger figure since 'he was restricted as if he had been sitting in a recreation room at the fire station' (cf. also *Bromsgrove Casting and Machining Ltd* v *Martin* [1977] 3 All ER 487). The case was, however, overruled in *Suffolk CC* v *Secretary of State for the Environment* [1985] IRLR 24, where the House of Lords thought that it did not take account of the fact that a retained fireman would have another job and was not restricted in any way until there was a fire and he was called in to assist.

(g) There is no general provision that the parties can *average* weekly working hours over the contractual period (*Opie* v *John Gubbins (Insurance Brokers) Ltd* [1978] IRLR 540). Where the contract provides that the employee must work such hours as are reasonably required, the industrial tribunal should consider how many hours were in fact worked in practice (*Green* v *Roberts* [1992] IRLR 499). If an employee is required to live on his work premises, only hours spent on duty are included.

10.3 WEEKS IN WHICH THERE IS NO CONTRACT OF EMPLOYMENT

Generally, if a week is not one of employment, continuity is broken, so that the employee would have to start again to pick up continuity. There are, however, exceptions to this principle, especially where the employee is not working for reasons not of his own making, yet the layman would consider him to be still 'on the books'. Unfortunately, the legislation has been read by the tribunals in a technical and somewhat restrictive manner, although that trend appears to be changing.

It should be stressed that in the following cases the employee is treated as retaining continuous employment notwithstanding that the contract of employment has ceased to exist. By ERA 1996, s. 212(3) the provisions protect the continuity of an employee who is absent from work:

(a) in consequence of sickness or injury up to 26 weeks (see *Scarlett* v *Godfrey Abbot Group Ltd* [1978] IRLR 456);

(b) on account of a temporary cessation of work;

(c) by arrangement or custom;

(d) wholly or partly because of pregnancy or confinement.

'Absent from work' in all these subparagraphs means 'not only that the employee is not doing any actual work for the employer but that there is no contract of employment subsisting between him and his employer that would entitle the latter to require him to do any work' (*Ford* v *Warwickshire County Council* [1983] IRLR 126). Although the heading to what was para. 9 in the schedule read 'Periods in which there is *no* contract of employment', the court held that 'absent from work' meant 'not performing in substance the contract that previously existed between the parties' (*G.W. Stephens & Son* v *Fish* [1989] ICR 324). The reason for termination of a contract, whether dismissal, frustration or agreement is irrelevant to the issue of continuity (*Tipper* v *Roofdec* [1989] IRLR 419). In *Roach* v *CSB (Moulds) Ltd* [1991] ICR 349, the EAT held that an employee's employment was not continuous due to a 10-day break in his employment, even though there was no week in which he did not work.

The vital issue is the *reason* why there is no contract for a particular period. In *Pearson* v *Kent County Council* [1992] ICR 20, the employee worked for the county council from 1955 until he decided to resign on the grounds of ill health on 31 May 1984. He accepted the offer of a less demanding position and commenced that work on 11 June. There had been an agreement that there should be a 10-day gap for the purpose of pension arrangements. When he was declared redundant in 1988, he argued for continuity back to 1984 but the tribunal rejected the claim on the ground that during the 10-day gap he had not been incapable of work in consequence of sickness. The EAT upheld the decision on the ground that during the 10 days, there was no medical reason for absence. Further when the employee was to return in a new position, the industrial tribunal had to be satisfied that he was incapable of carrying out that position as well.

'Incapable of work' in this context does not mean that the employee need be incapable of *any* work at all, but is satisfied if the employee is incapable of doing the work he was engaged to perform (*Donnelly* v *Kelvin International Services* [1992] IRLR 496).

10.3.1 Temporary cessation of work

A temporary cessation of work usually signifies a short-term closure of a factory due to say lack of orders, a fire or explosion (*Newsham* v *Dunlop Textiles Ltd (No. 2)* (1969) 4 ITR 268) or a strike at suppliers (although a dispute at the employee's plant would not fall within this rubric, *Hanson* v *Fashion Industries (Hartlepool) Ltd* [1980] IRLR 393). Another typical sequence occurred in *Hunter* v *Smith's Dock Co. Ltd* [1968] 2 All ER 81. During the applicant's 40 years of working for the respondents, he was accustomed to being laid off for a week or two at various times until trade picked up. These were treated as temporary cessations of work and his continuity maintained.

10.3.1.1 Whose work has ceased temporarily? It is sufficient that the employer's work for the particular employee has ceased even if the other aspects of the business run as normal. The issue received elaborate attention by the House of Lords in *Fitzgerald* v *Hall, Russell & Co. Ltd* [1970] AC 984. There, although the applicant welder was laid off for an extended period, many of his colleague welders were not, and the employers thus argued that there had been no cessation of welding work from their viewpoint. The House of Lords, however, decided the relevant consideration was that there 'was no longer work available for him [the employee] personally' and Lord Upjohn continued, 'The question whether at the same time the whole works would close down or a department was closed down or a large number of other employees were laid off at the same time would seem to be irrelevant in a computation essentially personal to the particular workman.'

Where work was in fact available for an employee to perform but it was not offered to him, there cannot be a cessation of work for statutory purposes (*Byrne* v *City of Birmingham DC* [1988] ICR 480). Three questions may be isolated, and must be posed in each case:

(a)   Was there a *cessation* of the employee's work?
(b)   Was the employee's absence *on account* of that cessation?
(c)   Was the cessation *temporary?*

10.3.1.2 What is temporary?

(1) The nature of the breaks
The temporary issue has received most attention in respect of schoolteachers. In *Rashid* v *ILEA* [1977] ICR 157, the EAT held that the school holidays were not a temporary 'cessation of work' for the applicant, a supply teacher, who was not paid during them since 'at the end of each term that job finished; at the beginning of the next term he started another one'. This was, however, overruled in the important House of Lords decision in *Ford* v *Warwickshire CC* [1983] IRLR 126 (see also *Hellyer Brothers Ltd* v *McLeod* [1987] IRLR 232, CA). The employee in *Ford* had been engaged on eight successive contracts for one academic year each. Their Lordships did not consider that it made any difference that the absences for the holidays were foreseeable, predictable and regular; nor were they attracted by the 'job by job' argument. Whilst it would not be so in every case, here it was conceded that having regard to the length of the total period of employment the holiday absences were temporary. Lord Diplock had in mind also seasonal absences in agriculture and the hotel and catering trade. Furthermore, absence because an employer is short of funds to pay the worker is absence on account of a temporary cessation of work since work in this context means *paid* work, according to the EAT in *University of Aston in Birmingham* v *Malik* [1984] ICR 492.

In *Letheby & Christopher Ltd* v *Bond* [1988] ICR 480, it was held that there cannot be such an absence when the employee was engaged under a series of single separate contracts (see also *G.W. Stephens & Son* v *Fish* [1989] ICR 324).

(2) Reviewing temporary breaks

'Temporary' means in this context transient, i.e. lasting only for a relatively short time in relation to the total employment relationship (*Ford's* case). The temporary nature of the cessation of work is reviewed *ex post facto* and what the parties intended at its inception is only marginally relevant. A projected temporary closure may prove permanent because, say, a drop in orders lasts longer than anyone expected. This is a question of fact in each case, and Phillips J stated in *Bentley Engineering Co. Ltd* v *Crown* [1976] IRLR 146 that, 'The Tribunal is enjoined to look at the matter as the historian of a completed chapter of events and not as a journalist describing events as they occur from day to day'. An employee may during the temporary cessation take a job elsewhere (*Thompson* v *Bristol Channel Ship Repairers* (1969) 4 ITR 262). In *Bentley Engineering Co. Ltd* v *Crown* (supra), a two-year gap was held to be temporary in the circumstances, and Phillips J indicated as some factors to be taken into consideration: the nature of the employment; the length of prior and subsequent service; the duration of the breach; what happened during the breach; and what was said on re-engagement. It did not matter in the instant case that re-employment was with a successor employer which was an associated employer by statute.

(3) Aggregation

In *Lewis* v *Surrey County Council* [1987] IRLR 509, the House of Lords determined that the respondent, a part-time teacher, did not meet the necessary continuous service requirements when she was employed by the appellants on a term-by-term basis under three separate and independent concurrent contracts, none of which by itself normally involved employment for 16 hours. It was not possible to aggregate the contracts to find that the minimum period of 16 hours a week was satisfied. Had Parliament intended the hours under such separate contracts to be aggregated, their Lordships considered that guidance would have been provided on how that was to be done. (The 16-hour threshold has been repealed by the Employment Protection (Part-Time Employees) Regulations 1995 (SI 1995 No. 31).) An interval between separate contracts as opposed to intervals between successor and predecessor contracts could also not amount to a temporary cessation of work. Each series of contracts has to be considered in isolation from any other series. On the other hand, Lord Ackner accepted the EAT's view that where an unscrupulous employer deliberately subjects the employment relationship to a mosaic of separate contracts for the purpose of specifically depriving an employee of the rights to which he would have been entitled had the whole of his engagement been incorporated in a single employment contract, the industrial tribunal could penetrate the superficial disguise, look at the substance of the arrangements and arrive at a conclusion that purported multiple contracts were in reality one single contract. It might suggest that there was also a unifying umbrella contract collateral to those separate contracts under which the minimum hours requirement was satisfied.

(4) The mathematical approach

A strictly mathematical approach to the concept of temporary cessation, however, is not to be applied in all cases. In *Flack* v *Kodak Ltd* [1986] IRLR 255, the Court of Appeal said that in determining this issue in relation to persons who had worked intermittently over a period of years, the tribunal must have regard to all the circumstances and should not confine itself to taking the percentage that the gap of work bore to the periods of work immediately adjoining it. Moreover, the whole period of intermittent employment should be considered, not only those in the two-year period which formed the qualifying time.

The statistical approach may, however, be appropriate in particular cases. 'Temporary' in relation to the cessation of work has to be construed in the sense of a relatively short time compared with the period in work. In *Sillars* v *Charrington Fuels Ltd* [1989] IRLR 152, the employee who drove fuel delivery lorries had, over a total period of 15 years, spent about half of each year in the respondent's employment and the remainder out of it. Thus the finding that there was not a temporary cessation would be upheld. Where seasonal workers had a pattern of work of 23 weeks in work and 29 weeks out of work, there was no continuity; a cessation could not be temporary when it was greater than the period in work (*Berwick Salmon Fisheries Co. Ltd* v *Rutherford* [1991] IRLR 203).

10.3.2   Arrangement or custom

In order to maintain continuity by reason of 'arrangement or custom' there must be an agreement or understanding at the time of departure that the employee will be so absent. The lack of such mutuality was fatal to this claim in *Murphy* v *A. Birrell & Sons Ltd* [1978] IRLR 458. The applicant had worked for the respondents for 19 years before taking another job (although not officially resigning) because of an argument with the manager. When things smoothed over, she returned and the newly appointed managing director told her that 'her old contract stood'. This could not *ex post facto* convert the absence into one by arrangement. As in the case of temporary cessation, an employee may be considered as continuing in the employment of one employer even though he takes a position with another. Rather unusually, in *Ingram* v *Foxon* [1984] ICR 685 a reinstatement agreement made some months after the employment ceased and after tribunal proceedings had been issued, was held to constitute such an arrangement.

Secondment is the best example under this rubric. In *Wishart* v *National Coal Board* [1974] ICR 460, the applicant was employed by the NCB from 1946 to 1973 except for one year when he worked for a company called Cementation Ltd, which carried out development work for the NCB. Since he remained a member of the miners' pension scheme and the two companies worked closely together, the EAT considered that he was working for Cementation by arrangement with the NCB. A similar practice is found among shipyard workers whose contracts lasted only as long as there was work to be done but who would expect to be re-engaged as soon as work picked up (*Puttick* v *John Wright & Sons (Blackwall) Ltd* [1972] ICR 457; see also *Brown* v *Southall and Knight* [1980] IRLR 130, *Duff* v *Evan Thomas Radcliffe & Co. Ltd* [1979] ICR 720). Continuing to pay an employee during a break normally points to such an arrangement.

The EAT somewhat widened the provision in the case of *Lloyds Bank Ltd* v *Secretary of State for Employment* [1979] ICR 258, where the employee, who worked one week on, one week off, was held to be absent from work on her off weeks by arrangement or custom. This was notwithstanding that the cross-heading to the provision indicates that it only applies where there is *no contract*, and here the agreement clearly still subsisted. The case was indeed distinguished in *Corton House Ltd* v *Skipper* [1981] IRLR 78, and its authority must be considered very doubtful in the light of *Ford*'s case in which the House of Lords decided that 'absent from work' meant more than merely not at work; rather it was when there was no contract which could require the employee to work.

10.3.3 Pregnancy

A female employee may count towards her continuity of service any week during which, or during part of which, she was absent because of pregnancy or confinement, whether or not her contract subsists during that period (*Secretary of State for Employment* v *Doulton Sanitaryware Ltd* [1981] ICR 477). Although there is no necessity that she be actually incapable of work at this time, there is a 26 weeks maximum which may be counted under this rubric. Moreover, the employee must show that if she were not pregnant, she would still be working under her contract; absence by reason of her resignation would not count. The employee may also be able to bring herself within one of the other headings preserving continuity which have no maximum of 26 weeks to be counted (see *Mitchell* v *Royal British Legion Club* [1980] IRLR 425). Further, if the employee takes the maternity leave to which she is entitled by statute and complies with all the conditions as to returning to work, the intervening period by special provision in ERA 1996, s. 212(2) goes towards continuity without a 26-week maximum.

10.3.4 Strikes

Special rules apply to the treatment of strikes. Their effect on continuity is a hybrid in that, while a week during which for any part of that week the employee is engaged in a strike does not breach continuity, it is not counted as a week of employment (see *Hanson* v *Fashion Industries (Hartlepool) Ltd* [1980] IRLR 393). Nice questions may arise in this regard as to when a strike begins and ends (e.g. *Winnett* v *Seamarks Brothers Ltd* [1978] IRLR 387). The weeks of a lock-out are deducted in a similar manner. It does not matter that an employee took work elsewhere during the strike or lock-out.

10.3.5 Reinstatement

Where an employee successfully claims to have been unfairly dismissed and is reinstated or re-engaged by his employer, a successor employer or associated employer, his continuity is preserved and he can include the time in between dismissal and reinstatement. This applies where re-employment is as a result of an industrial tribunal order, an agreement made through the good offices of an ACAS conciliation officer or under an approved dismissal procedure agreement, or by a valid compromise contract (Employment Protection (Continuity of Employment) Regulations 1993 (SI 1993 No. 2165)). A similar preservation applies to voluntary reinstatement outside of the ACAS or tribunals systems (*Ingram* v *Foxon*, supra). This does not, however, apply to a redundant employee when the weeks of the interval count only for the purpose of redundancy payment qualification.

10.3.6 Miscellaneous

(a)   In the case of redundancy payments, a week does not count if the employee worked outside Great Britain during the whole or part thereof and no employer's Class 1 national insurance contributions were payable by the employer (ERA 1996, s. 215(2)).

(b)   Periods spent in the armed forces do not break continuity but do not count as periods of employment if the employee is entitled to apply to his former employer under the Reserve Forces (Safeguard of Employment) Act 1985 and he rejoins that employer within six months of leaving (ERA 1996, s. 217(1)). (See also the Employment Protection (National Health Service) Order 1996 (SI No. 638).)

10.4   CHANGE OF EMPLOYER

The common law took the view that every contract of employment was discrete, and for the good reason that if employees might be transferred at will, they would, in the words of Lord Atkin in *Nokes* v *Doncaster Amalgamated Collieries Ltd* [1940] AC 1014, be 'serfs and not servants'. However, this can act as a boomerang against employees in the new circumstances of a statutory floor of employment protection rights. Thus, there are five important rules for maintaining continuity when an employee works in sequence for *different* employers. The periods are considered continuous where:

(a)   'a trade or business, or an undertaking . . . is transferred from one person to another. . .' (s. 218(2));

(b)   'an employee of an employer is taken into the employment of another employer who, at the time when the employee enters the second employer's employment, is an *associated employer* of the first employer. . .' (s. 218(6));

(c)   one *body corporate* is substituted for another body corporate as the employer by or under an Act of Parliament (s. 218(3));

(d)   the employer *dies* and his personal representatives or trustees keep on the employee (s. 218(4)), even where the employee is also the personal representative (*Rowley, Holmes and Co.* v *Barber* [1977] ICR 387);

(e)   there is a *change in the partners,* personal representatives or trustees who employ him (s. 218(5)). This is necessary since the employees of a partnership are employed by the individual partners jointly, so that each time there is a change of partners continuity would be lost if it were not for this provision in ERA 1996, s. 218.

In applying these rules the *capacity* in which the worker is employed with the second company is irrelevant. The House of Lords established this important principle in *Lord Advocate* v *De Rosa* [1974] 2 All ER 849. The majority thought that all that was required was employment continuously first by one employer, and then by another to whom the business had been transferred. It was irrelevant that the first employer had terminated the contract and the second had not continued the employment by a suitable alternative offer. The same rule applied both to initial entitlement to rights and assessment of the value of the rights where this depended on length of service.

The courts originally approached these paragraphs in a somewhat restrictive manner, which may not in all respects have fulfilled the United Kingdom's obligations under the EEC Directive No. 77/187 on Acquired Rights of Workers on Transfers of Undertakings. Moreover, the technical nature of the provisions render unfulfilled the Court of Appeal's declaration in *Gardiner* v *London Borough of Merton* [1980] IRLR 472 that, 'the Act is meant to offer simple justice, easily understood where a litigant in person will be at no disadvantage before the Industrial Tribunal'.

10.4.1   Transfer of business

The Transfer of Undertakings (Protection of Employment) Regulations 1981 (SI 1981 No. 1794) achieve an automatic continuation of the contract of employment on a transfer which falls within its scope. Continuity provisions are probably rights arising 'under or in connection with the contract of employment', which is the bundle of rights transferred under the 1981 Regulations. The result will in any event be the same since the definition under the 1981 Regulations is virtually coincident with that under s. 218(2) (see Chapter 16). That provision applies to the transfer of a 'trade or business, or an undertaking' and the only further definition is that business includes a trade or business or any activity carried on by a body of persons whether corporate or unincorporate. 'Undertaking' includes the functions of a Minister or government department. Although there is no express reference to transfer of *part* of an undertaking, industrial tribunals should read this concept into the statute (e.g. *Gibson* v *Motortune Ltd* [1990] ICR 740).

10.4.1.1 Transfer In *Melon* v *Hector Powe Ltd* [1981] ICR 43 Lord Fraser declared that there was an 'essential distinction between the transfer of a business, or part of a business and a transfer of physical assets . . . in the former case the business is transferred as a going concern so that the business remains the same but it is in different hands . . . whereas in the latter the assets are transferred to the new owner to be used in whatever business he chooses'.

The Court of Appeal decision in *Woodhouse* v *Peter Brotherhood Ltd* [1972] 2 QB 520 was a landmark on the path to this decision. Crossleys Ltd had for many years manufactured diesel engines at their Sandiacre factory. They removed this part of their operation to Manchester and sold to Peter Brotherhood Ltd the factory and much of the plant and machinery therein. The latter company ultimately turned it to the production of spinning machines, compressors and steam turbines. They first completed four large engines on which Crossleys were engaged at the time of the sale. The two employees who claimed redundancy payments had been engaged for the last six months of their service on the same engines as before. The National Industrial Relations Court's test for transfer was whether the 'working environment' had changed, and they decided it had not done so. Thus continuity was preserved. They were particularly impressed by the fact that, the entire workforce taken over, most employees were unlikely to realise that they should at this point claim redundancy payments if continuity was indeed broken.

The Court of Appeal, however, rejected this straightforward approach, and decided that 'the new owner did not take over the business as a going concern, but only the physical assets, using them in a different business'. Although 'the same men are employed using the same tools, the business is different'. The EAT was again overruled by the higher courts in *Melon* v *Hector Powe Ltd* (supra). The respondents were multiple tailors who owned a factory at Blantyre where they had, for many years, manufactured men's suits made to measure. In 1977, due to a fall in demand, Executex Manufacturing Ltd took over the factory, including work in progress which they undertook to complete. One hundred and twenty employees sought redundancy payments on the takeover. Hector Powe Ltd defended these claims on the ground that there was a transfer of business and pointed in particular to the continuation of work in progress. Lord Fraser dismissed this factor as 'merely a temporary expedient to help Executex through the initial stages'. In a *laissez-faire* judgment, the House of Lords decided that the issue was one of fact for the industrial tribunal. They also rejected the contention that this was at least a transfer of *part* of a business since such a change 'will . . . seldom occur except when that part is to some extent separable and severable from the rest of the business either geographically or by reference to products or in some other way'.

In *Gibson* v *Motortune Ltd* [1990] ICR 740, the majority of the EAT (with Wood J dissenting) decided that there must be a transfer of business when the same work was being carried on at the same premises by the same staff so that no one would have known from the outward and visible signs that the business being carried out was any different before and after the transfer.

The distinctions which have to be drawn are often narrow. In *Crompton* v *Truly Fair (International) Ltd* [1975] ICR 359, for example, the EAT decided that since the new employer was manufacturing children's clothing rather than men's trousers, the business was different and had not been transferred (see also *Port Talbot Engineering Co. Ltd* v *Passmore* [1975] IRLR 156, *Dhami* v *Top Spot Night Club* [1977] IRLR 231; cf. *Umar* v *Pliastar Ltd* [1981] ICR 727).

The concept embraces the transfer of goodwill alone of a professional practice where no other assets were sold (*Ward* v *Haines Watts* [1983] ICR 231). There may be a transfer between partners (*Jeetle* v *Elster* [1985] IRLR 227) but there must be an actual transfer of some sort, and it is insufficient that another company may have assumed *de facto* control whilst negotiations for purchase of a business took place (*SI (Systems and Instrumentation) Ltd* v *Grist and Riley* [1983] IRLR 391; cf. *Dabell* v *Vale Industrial Services Ltd* [1988] IRLR 439).

The 'transfer of business' as construed by the appeal courts serves to exclude the transfer of a franchise (an increasingly important aspect of modern economic organisation; *McKinney* v *McCaig, Paisley & Melville* (1966) 1 ITR 240) and a right to sell petrol (*Bumstead* v *John Cars Ltd* (1967) 2 ITR 137) although the result of the cases today would probably be different. It also failed the groundsman in *Evenden* v *Guildford City AFC* [1975] QB 917, who had worked from 1955 to 1968 for the football supporters' club and thereafter for the football club itself. Notwithstanding the close interconnection between the two bodies, he was in no sense carrying on a business and so did not qualify when transferred.

In *Secretary of State for Employment* v *Cohen* [1987] IRLR 169, the EAT recognised that documentary evidence of the true nature of a transaction between the first employer and subsequent employer(s) would not in the ordinary way be available to an employee. It would not thus be essential for an employee to place such evidence before the industrial tribunal although the statutory presumption did not apply. It is sufficient to justify the inference of a transfer if the employee could demonstrate that his employment continued in the same place, under the same directors, with the same customers and the same stock being used, since all these incidents are consistent with a transfer of business. In such circumstances and subject to evidence to the contrary from the purported transferee, this would justify the inference of a transfer.

10.4.1.2   Employment 'at the time of transfer'   There are two possible interpretations of the statutory phrase:

(a)   that the *relationship of employer and employee* must subsist at that time; or
(b)   that the *period of employment* accumulated counts.

Both interpretations require that the concept of 'transfer' has a starting and end point. The most searching, but ultimately unsatisfactory, discussion of the concept is found in the Court of Appeal decision in *Teesside Times Ltd* v *Drury* [1980] IRLR 72. The applicant had been employed by Champion Publications Ltd for six years, when the company ran into financial difficulties and negotiations were opened with the appellants with a view to a takeover. These reached fruition in a general agreement at about 3 p.m. on Friday, 17 November 1975. A few hours later Champion's receiver dismissed all its employees, but this was still some time before the formal contract was signed. Although the appellant's management assured the staff that they would be re-engaged, the applicant was dismissed three days after takeover. He had to establish that there was a transfer of business to claim unfair dismissal.

The appellants argued that he was not employed at *the 'time* of transfer', since he had been dismissed before the formalities of the sale had been completed. All three Lord Justices found for the respondent on the ground that he was, under the then provisions of Sch. 13 to EPCA 1978, to be taken to have been employed the whole of the week, and therefore his continuity was preserved until the following Monday.

On the conceptual issue, Eveleigh LJ adopted the first view set out above so that there was continuity 'so long as the dismissal was a step towards the re-engagement'. Stephenson LJ on the other hand considered that a contract must be in effect during the transfer. This was, however, 'a complex of operations which are part of a continuous process through different stages, including dismissal and re-engagment of staff'. The full extent of the transfer was a 'question of fact and degree in the light of common sense'. Goff LJ defined it more narrowly as 'the moment when the transaction of transferring the business is effected'.

It is submitted that an ample view is most in line with the policy of both the European Directive and the English legislation. This would include at least the stages of general agreement, the dismissal and re-engagment of employees and the entry into possession, and transfer of full legal title. Should the employee be under contract at any of these stages, continuity would be preserved. (See *Litster* v *Forth Dry Dock Engineering Co. Ltd* [1989] ICR 341.)

10.4.2 Associated employer

Unlike the transfer of business provision, this rule has undergone amendment in the course of the legislation. Until 1975 it was akin to the definition of subsidiary company within the Companies Act. Section 231 of ERA 1996 gives 'associated employer' a technical and rather limited meaning:

... any two employers shall be treated as associated if—
   (a) one is a company of which the other (directly or indirectly) has control, or
   (b) both are companies of which a third person (directly or indirectly) has control
...

10.4.2.1 Exhaustive definition The definition of 'associated employer' was previously contained in EPCA 1978, s. 153(4), and the vital question for determination was, and is now, whether the subsection was exhaustive or had merely illustrative status. The Court of Appeal determined in *Gardiner* v *London Borough of Merton* [1980] IRLR 472 that the former was the correct view. In that case the appellant's local government career began in 1965 and he had worked for four different authorities before his dismissal in 1977. He sought to count all 12 years in assessing compensation. The Court of Appeal restricted the definition to limited companies and in any event doubted whether anyone had sufficient control of the various councils to fall within the subsection. Griffiths LJ pointed to the problems which might arise if the section were not construed as exhaustive. It would then be necessary to give some other meaning to 'associated'. There were a myriad of possibilities including 'associated in a common purpose, associated through a common element of control or associated through a common interest or associated through common negotiation with a trade union'. This would necessitate 'far-ranging and complex inquiries into the activities of a complainant's present and previous employers'. To predict the outcome of such litigation would prove hazardous. In his Lordship's view, the change from 'company' to employer in the 1975 Act merely intended to include the case of the sole trader who became a limited company. Further, if the section was not intended to be exhaustive, it would not be appropriate for s. 153(4) to conclude with the phrase 'and the expression "associated employer" shall be construed accordingly' (see to the same effect *Hasley* v *Fair Employment Agency* [1989] IRLR 106 — where it was held that the Northern Ireland Fair Employment Agency and the Equal Opportunities Commission were not associated employers, but a partnership of companies may be associated: *Pinkney* v *Sandpiper Drilling Ltd* [1989] ICR 389).

Since it defeated the reasonable expectations of employees who had spent all their working life in local government, the result in *Gardiner* was altered for the purpose of redundancy payments by the Redundancy Payments (Local Government) (Modification) Order 1983 (SI 1983 No. 1160). This has been amended on four subsequent occasions, primarily in order to extend the number of bodies within the (already extensive) definition of local government employer. The provisions do not apply to water authorities (*Liversidge* v *London Residuary Body; West Midlands Residuary Body* v *Deebank* [1990] ICR 349).

Further, by ERA 1996, s. 218(7), continuity is preserved in the special case of an employee who moves from employment by a local education authority to the service of governors of a local education authority maintained school and vice versa and in certain other narrowly defined circumstances.

In the normal case, for continuity to be preserved the second employer must be an associated employer *at the time when the employee enters his employment* of the second employer. The courts have rejected the proposition that there may be no gap at all between the first and second employment (*Bentley Engineering Co. Ltd* v *Crown* [1976] IRLR 146, *Charnock* v *Barrie Muirhead Ltd* [1984] ICR 641).

10.4.2.2 The meaning of control The concept of control by one company of another was at first flexibly construed. It had regard to the direction of operations not merely the ownership of shares (*Zarb and Samuels* v *British & Brazilian Produce Co. (Sales) Ltd* [1978] IRLR 78). This liberal approach was limited by the EAT in *Secretary of State for Employment* v *Newbold and David Armstrong (Catering Services) Ltd* [1981] IRLR 305, with unfortunate results for the applicant, and possible opportunities for avoidance for employers. David Armstrong Junior owned 46 per cent of the shares of the applicant's first employer, Armstrong Bakers Ltd and 99 per cent of the second employer, David Armstrong (Catering Services) Ltd. They were not, however, associated according to Bristow J, because:

> In the law affecting companies, control is well recognised to mean control by the majority of votes attaching to shares exercised in General Meeting. It is not how or by whom the enterprise is actually run. Control rests in those who by the constitution of the company can say to the management 'Thou shalt do this; thou shalt not do that; thou art no longer the management'.

The applicant lost his valuable continuity rights notwithstanding that: the share ownership was beyond his ken; he had no written contract; and David Armstrong was 'the mainspring of the family business'.

In *Washington Arts Association Ltd* v *Forster* [1983] ICR 346, a transfer between the appellants, a guarantee company, and an Arts Centre which they in effect ran, was held not to be a transfer between associated employers. Further, in *Hair Colour Consultants Ltd* v

Mena [1984] ICR 671, a claim for continuity failed where the applicant had started work as a hair stylist at a salon run by Interhair Ltd which was owned jointly by two brothers, each of whom held 50 per cent of the shares. She then went to the respondents in which one brother owned 85 per cent of the shares, but the other had none. Negative control of just 50 per cent of the shareholding was not enough to satisfy the stringent conditions of the statute (see also *South West Launderettes Ltd* v *Laidler* [1986] ICR 455). *Zarb's* case is, however, still good law for the proposition that the persons who control two companies may be a group acting in concert. They must be the *same* group of individuals in each company (*Poparm Ltd* v *Weekes* [1984] IRLR 388). The approach in *Zarb* was preferred in *Harford* v *Swiftrim Ltd* [1987] ICR 439 (cf. *Strudwick* v *IBL* [1988] ICR 796, *Payne* v *Secretary of State for Employment* [1989] IRLR 352).

A company qualifies for the purposes of being an associated employer even if it is incorporated overseas, provided that it is a body which can be likened in its essentials to a company limited under the Companies Act (*Hancill* v *Marcon Engineering Ltd* [1990] ICR 103).

10.4.3 Change of partners

Where there is a change of the partners who employ the applicant continuity is preserved. In *Harold Fielding Ltd* v *Mansi* [1974] 1 All ER 1035, it was held that this did not apply where employment by a partnership is followed by work for one of the former partners on his own account. It can hardly be supposed that such a technical limitation was intended by Parliament and the case was narrowly distinguished in *Allen & Son* v *Coventry* [1979] IRLR 399 as applying only when different businesses were involved. Moreover, in *Jeetle* v *Elster* [1985] IRLR 227, the transfer from four doctors to one was held to fall within the paragraph, and the *Mansi* case disapproved.

10.5 ESTOPPEL

Continuity is a purely *statutory* concept. A second employer who told an employee that he would recognise 50 years' previous employment as continuous with the new job could not be held to his statement under statutory remedies, although possibly by contract enforceable in the county court. Certainly the Department of Employment would not have had to pay a rebate for such period, as it was not privy to the arrangement.

In *Evenden* v *Guildford AFC* [1975] QB 917, the Court of Appeal had suggested that a statement by the respondent football club that the appellant could carry forward his previous service with the Guildford Supporters Club (which was not associated with the Football Club within the meaning of the Act) operated by way of proprietary estoppel, so that the club could not go back on it. Lord Denning MR further thought that the statutory presumption of continuity of employment applied to employment by successive employers.

The doctrine of *Evenden* was overruled in *Secretary of State for Employment* v *Globe Elastic Thread Co. Ltd* [1979] 2 All ER 1077. The Department of Employment refused to give a redundancy rebate to the respondents in respect of the dismissal of Mr Wyazko. This was calculated to include not only the five years' work for Globe but also 22 years for Heathcotes which was not an associated company. Further, no business had been transferred from one to the other. There had, however, been a statement, on which Mr Wyazko relied, that the service would be treated as continuous. The ratio of the decision was that the redundancy payment had not been 'made under the Act' so that the Department of

Employment were not obliged by statute to pay a rebate, and could not be estopped from denying continuity. Their Lordships stated that any arrangement worked not by estoppel but by contract between Globe and Wyazko, and went on:

> Any employer is perfectly entitled to make his own arrangement with his employees, and no doubt many employers do so, departing in various ways from the terms of the Act. Such arrangements may have the force of a contract, and be enforceable as such, but they cannot commit the Minister to make a rebate. The Minister is only liable to do so in respect of payments made strictly under the Act.

Although this leaves open the possibility of a contractually binding statement by the second employer, this could only at the time have been established in the county court and it might be difficult to prove the employee had provided consideration.

The 'two-way' case of *Smith* v *Blandford Gee Cementation Ltd* [1970] 3 All ER 154, remains good law. The applicant thought he was employed by the respondents as an underground waller on repairs for the National Coal Board. By a Task Work Agreement between the respondents and the NCB, Blandford Gee were agents for the NCB for employment purposes. Since it was Gee which behaved as his employers and gave him his written statement of terms they could not deny they were his employers for the purposes of redundancy payment.

11 The Scope of Statutory Protection

It has already been emphasised that only employees and not independent contractors are eligible for most employment protection rights. Before examining the main such statutory rights of redundancy and unfair dismissal, it must be noted that the employee must also have completed the minimum qualifying period of service which is different for each right (para. 11.1), and make his claim in time (para. 11.2). There are also several exclusions, most of which are common to unfair dismissal, redundancy and other employment protection rights, although any necessary distinctions will be identified. They broadly relate to:

(a) illegality of the employment;
(b) geographical limitations;
(c) the nature of the employment;
(d) the age of the employee;
(e) voluntary exclusion agreements between employer and employee;
(f) miscellaneous disqualifications.

There have been several changes in the scope of exclusions, including the repeal of the exemption of employers of less than five workers which was found in the Industrial Relations Act, and varying the length of qualifying periods on several occasions.

Once it is established that the applicant is an employee of the employer the onus is on the latter to show that the employee was excluded from the statutory entitlements (*Kapur* v *Shields* [1976] ICR 26). Most exclusions, however, go to jurisdiction so that even if neither party raises them, the tribunal itself must enquire (*BMA Ltd* v *Lewis* [1978] ICR 782). It is normally proper for an industrial tribunal to consider the question as a separate preliminary issue.

11.1 QUALIFYING PERIOD

The qualifying period in redundancy payments has always been two years' continuous service but the time for unfair dismissal has varied with the differing policies of different Governments. Between March 1975 and 1 October 1979 the relevant period was 26 weeks. Between 1979 and 1 June 1985 an applicant required one year's continuous service up to the effective date of termination in order to claim. An exception was introduced by the Employment Act 1980, s. 8 in the case of employers who had at no time during the applicant's employment employed more than 20 employees. The section caused great difficulties of construction. These difficulties were laid to rest by the Unfair Dismissal

(Variation of Qualifying Period) Order 1985 (SI 1985 No. 782) which provides that all employees must have two years' service. There are just two modifications:

(a)   Where the dismissal is on the grounds of trade union membership or activities, health and safety activities or assertion of a statutory right, or race or sex discrimination, or the employee is dismissed by reason of pregnancy, or as a protected Sunday worker or as an employee representative, or as an occupational pension fund trustee, there is no qualification period at all (ERA 1996, s. 108).

(b)   Where the dismissal follows refusal by the employer to pay an employee who is suspended from work on medical grounds, there is a one month qualification period (ERA 1996, s. 64(1)).

11.2   CLAIM IN TIME

The intention of the Act is that claims for compensation should be presented promptly.

(*Westward Circuits Ltd* v *Read* [1973] ICR 301 NIRC.)

11.2.1   The normal time limit

The following principles apply:

(a)   The employee has three months from the effective date of termination (defined at para. 13.4) inclusive of the first day in which to present a claim to an industrial tribunal for unfair dismissal, and six months for redundancy and where strikers claim unfair dismissal under TURERA 1993, ss. 237–9. If the effective date of termination is 31 August, the last date for presentation would be 30 November (*Pruden* v *Cunard Ellerman Ltd* [1993] IRLR 317; *University of Cambridge* v *Murray* [1993] IRLR 460; for full discussion see Bowers, Brown and Mead, *Industrial Tribunal Practice and Procedure*, FT Law & Tax, 1996).

(b)   There is no limitation period for references to industrial tribunals of claims under the contractual redundancy pay provisions which used to exist under the Whitley Council Agreement other than the six-year period under the Limitation Act 1980 *(Greenwich Health Authority* v *Skinner and Ward* [1989] ICR 220). In so far as the issue raised was discrimination between men and women under Article 119 of the EEC Treaty and the Council Directive 76/207, the time limit is probably the UK right most closely analogous to it, such as six months for equal pay and three months for sex discrimination (*Etherson* v *Strathclyde Regional Council* [1992] IRLR 392; *Stevens* v *Bexley Health Authority* [1989] ICR 224).

(c)   A claim is presented when it is delivered to the Central Office of Industrial Tribunals (*Hammond* v *Haigh Castle & Co. Ltd* [1973] ICR 148, *Post Office* v *Moore* [1981] ICR 623). This may include a Sunday, at least where the regional tribunal office has a letter box (*Hetton Victory Club Ltd* v *Swainston* [1983] ICR 341).

The EAT in *Birmingham Midshires Building Society* v *Horton* [1991] ICR. 648, counselled, however, that it was no longer reasonable to expect first class post to arrive the following day (see also *St Basil's Centre Ltd* v *McCrossan* [1992] ICR 140). Instead, in the case of first class mail, this is deemed to be on the second working day after posting, and in the case of second class mail, on the fourth working day after posting. For a solicitor to act reasonably and without fault there must be a system in place which enables the solicitor to find out contemporaneously whether the conduct of business is taking a normal course and to check at or near the time that replies which should have been received at a given date have in fact been received. This did not apply where a system involved no more than a check several weeks after the solicitor expected an acknowledgement from the industrial tribunal (*Camden & Islington Community Services NHS Trust* v *Kennedy* [1996] IRLR 381).

(d)   Whether the claim is presented in time goes to the jurisdiction of the tribunal to hear the claim. As Lord Denning MR said in *Dedman* v *British Building & Engineering Appliances Ltd* [1974] ICR 53, 'If [an application] arrives a minute after midnight on the last day the clerks must throw it out; the tribunal is not competent to hear it.' Section 111(3) of ERA 1996, however, permits a premature application, so that where a dismissal takes place with notice, the employee may make an application during that notice period.

11.2.2   The power to extend time: general principles

Although the former time limit has been increased from the original 28 days it often proves inadequate and the industrial tribunal may thus allow a reasonable further period 'in a case where it is satisfied that it was not reasonably practicable for the complaint to be presented before the end of that period of three months' (ERA 1996, s. 111(2)). The Court of Appeal considered that this statutory phrase was 'not really apt in the particular context'. The best approach was to read the word 'practicable' as the equivalent of feasible '. . .and to ask colloquially and untrammelled by too much legal logic — was it reasonably feasible to present the complaint to the industrial tribunal within the relevant three months' (*Palmer* v *Southend-on-Sea BC* [1984] IRLR 119).

The early cases tended to view this as a general equitable principle, to be 'considered in the light of general standards of ordinary people in industry'. More guidance, however, was given in the canonical statement of Lord Denning MR's so-called liberal approach in *Dedman* v *British Building & Engineering Appliances Ltd* [1974] IRLR 379, then construing the 28-day period for unfair dismissal:

If in the circumstances the man knew or was put on inquiry as to his rights, and as to the time limit then it was practicable for him to have presented his complaint within the four weeks, and he ought to have done so. But if he did not know and there was nothing to put him on inquiry, then it was not practicable and he should be excused.

The working out of this principle did not prove so liberal primarily because the Master of the Rolls went on to say:

If a man engages skilled advisers to act for him and they mistake the time limit and present it too late — he is out. His remedy is against them.

This weighs against less well-advised employees and it is indeed often unrealistic to expect an applicant to go through further litigation to bring an action for negligence against his adviser. Moreover, the concept of the 'skilled adviser' was widely interpreted to include not only a solicitor (as in *Dedman*) but also such persons as a trade union official and a Citizens Advice Bureau adviser. In *Riley* v *Tesco Stores Ltd* [1980] IRLR 103, the Court of Appeal, however, disapproved of construction of the title 'skilled adviser' as if it were itself a part of a statute. Stephenson LJ regarded this as 'bewildering and deplorable'. The fault of an adviser is to be treated as the fault of the applicant for these purposes (*Trevelyans*

(Birmingham) Ltd v *Norton* [1991] ICR 488). It has subsequently been held that there is, however, no absolute rule about skilled advisers to the effect that in each case where such an adviser has been consulted, the applicant may not show that it has not been reasonably practicable to present his or her complaint in time (*London International College Ltd* v *Sen* [1993] IRLR 333, see also *Harber* v *North London Polytechnic* [1990] IRLR 198; *Capital Foods Retail Ltd* v *Corrigan* [1993] IRLR 430). The time limit may indeed be extended on the basis that the employee was given erroneous legal advice (*Hawkins* v *Bell* [1996] IRLR 258).

The trend is now towards emphasising that the issue is one of fact and deprecating appeals. Thus in *Walls Meat Co. Ltd* v *Khan* [1979] ICR 52, Shaw LJ stated:

> The test is empirical and involves no legal concept. Practical common sense is the keynote and legalistic footnotes may have no better result than to introduce a lawyer's complication into what should be a layman's pristine province. These considerations prompt me to express the emphatic view that the forum to decide such questions is the Industrial Tribunal and that their decision should prevail unless it is plainly perverse or oppressive.

There are, however, two reasons why the construction of the courts has become ever stricter over time:

(a)   When Lord Denning MR confirmed the *Dedman* approach in *Walls Meat* v *Khan* (supra) he added the rider that now the longer three-month time limit applies 'there is less reason for granting an indulgence to a complainant', and that 'industrial tribunals can and should be strict in enforcing [it]'.

(b)   As public consciousness of unfair dismissal provisions grows, mainly through reports in the daily press and Department of Employment leaflets, there is less likelihood that an applicant can realistically claim complete ignorance.

11.2.3   The power to extend: particular examples

11.2.3.1   Internal proceedings   Some principles have been established for the more common types of valid excuse for delay. One frequently encountered example is that internal proceedings arising out of the dismissal were pending at the same time, and that it was reasonable to delay the application to the industrial tribunal in order not to prejudice them. The EAT said in *Crown Agents* v *Lawal* [1979] ICR 103 at 109:

> Merely as a statement of general principle, it would seem to us that in cases where a person is going through a conciliation process, or is taking up a domestic appeal procedure, whether it be on discipline, or whether it be for medical reasons, that common sense would indicate that while he is going through something which involves him and his employer directly, he should be able to say, 'It is not reasonably practicable for me to lodge my application within the three months.'

This dictum was, however, disapproved of as a general principle in *Bodha* v *Hampshire AHA* [1982] ICR 200 (see also *Croydon Health Authority* v *Jaufurally* [1986] ICR 4). In *Walls Meat* v *Khan* (supra), Shaw and Brandon LJJ gave as examples of valid excuses physical impediment, absence abroad or a postal strike, while in *Dedman* Scarman LJ spoke of 'some untoward and unexpected turn of events'. In *Porter* v *Bandridge* [1978] IRLR 271, Stephenson LJ thought that the tribunal should consider whether the employee 'was discouraged or impeded or misled or deceived'.

11.2.3.2 Discovery of new facts outside the three-month period In *Churchill* v *A. Yeates & Sons Ltd* [1983] IRLR 187, the employee excused his delay by reason of the discovery outside the three-month period that his old job declared redundant had in fact been filled. Although this was only one of the five grounds on which he challenged the fairness of his dismissal, the EAT decided that it was not reasonably practicable to bring a complaint until the applicant knew of a fundamental fact which rendered the dismissal unfair (cf. *Belling & Lee* v *Burford* [1982] ICR 454).

The case is often met in which the employee does not know that he has a viable claim until after the three-month time limit has expired, typically because it is only when the employer appoints another to the position that it gives the lie to the claim that the employee was redundant.

According to the Court of Appeal in *Machine Tool Industry Research Association* v *Simpson* [1988] IRLR 212, it is thus not reasonably practicable to bring a claim if during the period of three months there were crucial or important facts unknown and reasonably unknown to the applicant which later became known to him and which were such facts as to give him a genuine belief that he had a claim before the industrial tribunal. At this stage, it is not necessary for the employee to establish in evidence the veracity of the facts which led him belatedly to make the claim. In the instant case, it was appropriate to extend time where the employee only knew after her dismissal that another employee had been re-engaged. She claimed that this called into question whether the real reason for dismissal was redundancy as the employers claimed. The Court of Appeal held that it was proper to extend time, notwithstanding that she had not as yet proved that anyone had *in fact* been re-engaged.

11.2.3.3 Other examples The following have, however, failed to render it not reasonably practicable to present a complaint in the time stated:

(a) the holding of union negotiations (*Times Newspapers Ltd* v *O'Regan* [1977] IRLR 101);

(b) that criminal proceedings were on foot at the same time (*Norgett* v *Luton Industrial Co-operative Society Ltd* [1976] IRLR 306, *Union Cartage Co. Ltd* v *Blunden* [1977] ICR 420; *Trevelyans (Birmingham) Ltd* v *Norton* [1991] ICR 488);

(c) the claiming of unemployment benefit with a case pending before the national insurance local tribunal (*Walls Meat* v *Khan* (supra), *House of Clydesdale Ltd* v *Foy* [1976] IRLR 391 EAT);

(d) misleading advice from e.g. the Free Representation Unit (*Croydon Health Authority* v *Jaufurally* [1986] ICR 4);

(e) the fact that an ex-employee has entered into a commission arrangement with his employer: this may make it a matter of commercial convenience and interest that he should not issue proceedings against his former employer, but it does not render it not reasonably practicable to do so (*Birmingham Optical plc* v *Johnson* [1996] ICR 459);

(f) the fact that the employee was putting in an application for long-term sickness pay which would conflict with the claim he would be making in the industrial tribunal (*Moore* v *Thrings & Long*, unreported (CA), 15 November 1996).

On the other hand:

(a)   There was no principle that mistaken advice by any third party will prevent an employee establishing that it was not reasonably practicable to make a claim in time. The mistake in *Rybak* v *Jean Sorelle Ltd* [1991] ICR 127 arose from a combination of tribunal staff and CAB.

(b)   In *James W. Cook & Co. (Wivenhoe) Ltd* v *Tipper* [1991] IRLR 386, the Court of Appeal held that it was not reasonably practicable to present applications for redundancy where the employees thought that work would pick up again. The time should run from the moment the business closed down and the dismissals were recognised as irrevocable (see also *Machine Tool Research Association* v *Simpson* [1988] 1 Ch 558; *Marley (UK) Ltd* v *Anderson* [1996] IRLR 163).

11.3   ILLEGALITY

The principle of public policy is this: *ex dolo malo non oritur actio.*

(*Holman* v *Johnson* per Lord Mansfield (1775) 1 Cowp 341, translated by A.P. Herbert as 'The dirty dog gets no dinner here'.)

The general view of the courts is that an employee cannot claim employment protection rights when his contract is tinged by illegality, for as Bristow J has stated 'The rights, though creatures of statute. . . depend on or arise from the contract just as do the common law rights which arise from the contract itself' (*Tomlinson* v *Dick Evans 'U' Drive Ltd* [1978] IRLR 77). Thus, an employee cannot claim for unfair dismissal or redundancy payment if his contract is illegal, nor count a week spent on an illegal contract in determining the length of continuous employment. This denial may, however, be out of all proportion to any wrong committed by the employee. For all sorts of incidental breaches of the law, whether of statutory provisions or at common law on the ground of public policy, have been held to avoid a contract. In *Napier* v *National Business Agency Ltd* [1951] 2 All ER 264 Evershed MR said:

> There is a strong legal obligation placed on all citizens to make true and faithful returns for tax purposes and, if parties make an agreement which is designed to do the contrary, i.e. to mislead and delay, it seems to me impossible for this court to enforce that contract at the suit of one party to it.

(see also *Hyland* v *J.H. Barker (North-West) Ltd* [1985] IRLR 403).

Moreover, there appears to be no *de minimis* rule. In *Hannen* v *Ryman* (1979) EAT 478/79, the tax evaded in four years was just £4, yet the contract was still declared invalid. Fraud of the Inland Revenue is by far the most common vitiating factor in the employment field, and the doctrine operates most harshly when the evasion of statute is not the fault of the employee at all. The fact that he is excluded from claiming may be somewhat fortuitous (cf. *Annandale Engineering* v *Samson* [1994] IRLR 59). The courts have gone some way to mitigate its effect by adopting three doctrines:

(a)   that the employee must *know* of the illegality;

(b)   that an illegal aspect of the contract may be *severed* leaving the rest intact and enforceable;

(c) that *incidental illegality* does not avoid the contract.

The authorities are, however, in a state of some confusion and narrow lines of distinction have been drawn.

11.3.1 Knowledge of illegality

In *Davidson* v *Pillay* [1979] IRLR 275, the EAT stated that the employee must actually participate in the illegality to be fixed with the consequence of it, while in *McConnell* v *Bolik* [1979] IRLR 422, the employer's failure to disclose to the Inland Revenue income derived from the sale of two calves did not automatically make the whole contract illegal, since there was nothing to suggest the employee was privy to the arrangement. *Corby* v *Morrison t/a The Card Shop* [1980] IRLR 218, still reflects orthodoxy, however: the employer paid the applicant £5 a week which was not subject to tax in addition to her basic wages, but she claimed that she did not know the arrangement was illegal. The EAT still rejected her contention that she should be able to claim unfair dismissal. May J said: 'In truth it makes no difference whether or not the parties were ignorant that what they were doing was illegal; ignorance of the law is no excuse.'

The question was exhaustively discussed by the EAT in *Newland* v *Simons & Willer (Hairdressers) Ltd* [1981] ICR 521. The applicant was paid a weekly cash wage which was falsely recorded at lower amounts in the wage books. She received her tax form showing her annual gross wage completed by the employer, but the EAT held that whether this prevented her enforcing her statutory rights depended on whether she knew of the illegality. May J did, however, warn that: 'The incidence of tax frauds both large and small is so rife that they cannot be brushed aside and the blame for them laid only at the feet of the employers.' In a convincing dissent, Mr Goff thought that mere knowledge of the illegality should not be enough since the employee could hardly refuse her wages.

When the party to an illegal contract knew what was being done which was illegal, it did not matter that he did not *know* that the same was illegal (*Salveson* v *Simons* [1994] ICR 409; cf. *Wilkinson* v *Lugg* [1990] ICR 599). A contract was not, however, avoided because an employee in its course was engaged in a fraud on the company by way of an agreement between the employee and his manager that he be given an unofficial pay rise after the managing director decided not to increase his pay (*Broaders* v *Kalkare Property Maintenance Ltd* [1990] IRLR 421). This was held to be quite different from an agreement between employer and employee for an illegal element in the contract such as a fraud on the Revenue.

11.3.2 Severance

The courts have sometimes allowed severance of illegal terms leaving the remainder of the contract valid and enforceable in respect of employment rights. They have also in some cases permitted the less blameworthy party to the contract to enforce it where he has been the victim of fraud, duress or oppression by the other party. Beldam LJ said in *Hewcastle Catering Ltd* v *Ahmed and Elkanah* [1992] ICR 626, in which the employees made no personal gain from the illegality perpetrated by their employer:

the fact that a party has in the course of performing a contract committed an unlawful or immoral act will not by itself prevent him from further enforcing that contract unless the contract was entered into with the purpose of doing that unlawful or immoral act or the contract itself (as opposed to the mode of its performance) is prohibited by law.

11.3.3   Incidental illegality

Incidental illegality during the course of a contract does not necessarily render the contract wholly void. An unfair dismissal action may be brought where contractual obligations are *capable* of being performed lawfully, and were initially intended so to be lawfully performed, but they have in fact been performed by unlawful means. Thus in *Coral Leisure Group Ltd* v *Barnett* [1981] IRLR 204, a public relations officer for the appellant's casino operation who claimed that he regularly obtained prostitutes for gamblers who patronised the company's clubs could bring a claim since the intention of the contract was originally lawful; illegality was later and incidental to its performance. (See C. Mogridge 10 ILJ 32.)

11.4   GEOGRAPHICAL LIMITATIONS

The complicated provisions excluding those working abroad differ between different employment protection rights, and the differences reflect the different history of the rights concerned rather than any clear or apparent differences of policy.

(a)   An employee who under his contract of employment *ordinarily works* outside Great Britain is excluded from rights to unfair dismissal, itemised pay statements, written reasons for dismissal, guarantee payments, medical suspension pay, not to have action short of dismissal taken on the grounds of trade union membership, time off, maternity rights (ERA 1996, s. 196) and rights under the former Wages Act 1986 (now ERA 1996, ss. 13–27). Great Britain means England, Wales and Scotland but excludes Northern Ireland, Channel Isles and the Isle of Man. The question of whether this exclusion applies is to be addressed as at the effective date of termination of the employment. An employee can count service wholly or mainly outside Great Britain towards continuity (see para. 10.1).

(b)   A claim for redundancy payments will be unsuccessful if:

(i)   the employee is abroad at the relevant date of dismissal, unless under his contract he ordinarily works in Great Britain; or

(ii)   he ordinarily works outside Great Britain unless on the relevant date he is in Great Britain in accordance with *instructions* given by his employer. He may however have a claim if he is employed to work aboard a ship registered in the United Kingdom and ordinarily works in Great Britain unless employment is *wholly* outside Great Britain or he is not ordinarily resident in Great Britain (see *Roux International* v *Licudi* [1975] ICR 424).

(c)   Written statements of terms and notice requirements do not apply to an employee engaged in work wholly or mainly outside Great Britain, unless the employee ordinarily works in Great Britain and the work outside is for the same employer (ERA 1996, s. 196(1)).

(d)   The Transfer of Undertakings (Protection of Employment) Regulations 1981 (SI 1981 No. 1794) do not apply to an employee who ordinarily works outside the UK (i.e. including Northern Ireland).

(e)   An employee cannot claim rights against the National Insurance Fund on the insolvency of his employer if he ordinarily works outside the territory of the Member States of the EC (ERA 1996, s. 196(7)).

The rules for discrimination statutes are considered at para. 8.4.3.

The Employment Protection (Offshore Employment) Order 1976 (SI 1976 No. 766) (promulgated under EPCA 1978, s. 137, now ERA 1996, s. 201), extended employment protection to British Territorial Waters (as amended by SI 1977 No. 588, SI 1981 No. 1208 and SI 1984 No. 1149) and designated waters of the Continental Shelf, thus extending to most employees on oil rigs (Employment (Continental Shelf) Act 1978).

The meaning of 'ordinarily works' outside Great Britain is thus common to all these rules, and it has been the subject of various controversial judicial interpretations. Particular difficulties arise in the case of peripatetic employees like airline pilots, whose peregrinations it is probably not apt to describe.

11.4.1 'Ordinarily works'

The word 'ordinarily' has caused most problems of construction. At first, the EAT held that an employee might ordinarily work *both* outside and inside Great Britain, the word serving as an antithesis to 'extraordinary', rather than focusing on the place where the employee spent *most* of his time. This also meant that an employee who went abroad for relatively short periods might be excluded. A change in this approach was heralded by the Court of Appeal which, in *Wilson v Maynard Shipbuilding Consultants AB* [1978] QB 665, favoured a 'base' test. The appellant had been employed from July 1973 until September 1975 under a written contract which contained no terms about his place of work. It was implied, however, that he was to work 'as required in any country in which his employers . . . had contracts'. The evidence indicated that he had worked in the UK for 40 weeks and in Italy for 50 weeks. The Court of Appeal has decided that the important point was the location of his 'base' as defined by his contract, not what actually happened in practice. The most important considerations in its determination were:

(a) express terms which determine his *headquarters* or indicate where the travel involved in his employment begins and ends;
(b) where his private *residence* is or is expected to be;
(c) where, and in what *currency,* he is to be paid;
(d) whether he is subject to *national insurance* contributions in Great Britain.

Megaw LJ said:

An employee may properly be regarded as 'ordinarily working' in a particular place under his contract of employment even though in the event at the end of the employment it shall turn out that he had actually spent more of his working hours or days or weeks or months away from that place; and even though the forecast made at the time when the contract of employment was made would be that he would so spend his time.

He exemplified a meter reader who would spend much time away from the electricity board premises from which he started his round but still have his base there. The same was true of a barrister and his chambers.

In *Todd v British Midland Airways Ltd* [1978] ICR 959, the applicant pilot who worked for a British company, had spent just over half his flying days in Great Britain. The Court of Appeal held that he ordinarily worked in Great Britain but departed somewhat from their earlier analysis in *Wilson*. For Lord Denning MR said that in determining where the base was, contractual terms were often of little help and, 'you have to go by the conduct of the parties in the way they are operating the contract'. The Court disapproved of *Claisse* v *Hostetter, Stewart and Keydril Ltd* [1978] ICR 812, in which it was held that a man who worked on an oil rig was based on that rig and not at Great Yarmouth where the company employing him had their headquarters.

The base test is not a universal solvent of the issue and in *Janata Bank Ltd* v *Ahmed* [1981] IRLR 457, Donaldson LJ was anxious lest this issue became encrusted with legal technicalities. The 'base test merely points the way to a likely, and if I may say so, a common sense inference from the facts and no more. . . The issue . . . should not be allowed to generate a large body of learning. The use of the words "ordinarily" and, by implied contrast, "extraordinarily", points the way inexorably, and rightly in a labour law context, to a broad brush approach under which, on a given set of marginal facts, one tribunal may decide one way and one another'. As general guidance, he distinguished three common situations:

(a)   Where an employee has a two-year contract to work for one month in London and thereafter in Paris: he ordinarily works in Paris even though he may be dismissed whilst still in London.

(b)   Where an employee works in different countries as his employer directs in a series of postings, the base test is most appropriate.

(c)   Where an employee is appointed to a new position involving a fundamental variation so that he is required to work in a particular country until the next variation, that will be the country in which he ordinarily works (cf. *Sonali Bank* v *Rahman* [1989] ICR 314; *Weston* v *Vega Space Systems Engineering Ltd* [1989] IRLR 429).

11.4.2   Ships

Where the applicant was employed on a British-registered ship which never entered UK waters, even for repair or refit, a seaman who was paid in sterling and given a travel allowance (which could, but did not have to, be used to return to the UK on leave), was not entitled to claim unfair dismissal on the true construction of s. 141 of EPCA 1978 (now ERA 1996, s. 196) (*Wood* v *Cunard Line Ltd* [1990] IRLR 281).

11.5   THE NATURE OF THE EMPLOYER

Statutory protection of certain employees is modified as follows:

(a)   *Crown servants*   The definition and coverage of Crown servants has already been considered (para. 2.3.2). Employees of central government and Territorial Army Associations in permanent pensionable posts are not covered by the redundancy payment scheme. They have their own rather better special provisions (*Robinson* v *County of London Territorial and Auxiliary Forces Association* (1967) 2 ITR 652). Section 159 of ERA 1996 also exempts those employed in certain government employment from statutory redundancy payments.

On the other hand, civil servants are specifically *included* within the scope of the unfair dismissal provisions (ERA 1996, s. 191). This is notwithstanding that they hold office at the pleasure of the Crown and cannot claim to have been wrongfully dismissed. The provisions also extend to House of Commons staff (s. 195), although they and other employees may be excluded by reason of national security (s. 193).

(b) *Overseas governments* Redundancy payments legislation does not apply 'to any person in respect of his employment in any capacity under the Government of an overseas territory' (ERA 1996, s. 160(1)). Further, the doctrine of sovereign immunity applied to a clerk at the Indian High Commission in London since the dismissal was an act done in pursuance of the Republic of India's public function (*Sengupta* v *Republic of India* [1983] ICR 221).

11.6 THE NATURE OF THE EMPLOYMENT

The following are excluded from some or all employment protection rights:

(a) *Share fishermen* who are 'remunerated only by a share in the profits or gross earnings of the vessel' (ERA 1996, s. 199(2)), but this does not apply to a person who shares in the profits of a whole *fleet* of vessels (*Goodeve* v *Gilsons* [1985] ICR 401).

(b) *Domestic servants* in a private household where the employer is a close relative cannot claim redundancy payments (ERA 1996, s. 161(1)).

(c) Members of the *armed forces* (ERA 1996, s. 192(1)), i.e. the naval, military and air forces of the Crown.

The old exclusion from most employment protection rights for registered dock workers was removed by s. 6 of the Dock Work Act 1989, when the National Dock Labour Scheme was abolished.

11.7 AGE

The legislators were anxious to prevent a person from claiming unfair dismissal on retirement. On the other hand they recognised that there must be flexibility to take account of widely varying retiring ages in different occupations. Section 109(1) of ERA 1996 is the resulting compromise and excludes an applicant who, on or before the effective date of termination, has attained the 'normal retiring age' for an employee holding the position which he held, or if a man or woman has attained the age of 65, unless dismissal is for a trade union reason. There are certain other claims to which the age limit does not apply, i.e. dismissals by reason of pregnancy or as a protected Sunday worker or as an employee representative, or as an occupational pension fund trustee, or by reason of health and safety activities or by reason of assertion of a statutory right. Before the Sex Discrimination Act 1986, the relevant 'back-stop' ages were 65 for a man and 60 for a woman. Between 1965 and 1989 a woman could not claim redundancy payment if dismissed when she was over 60, whilst a man could claim up to 65 (EPCA 1978, s. 82, now ERA 1996, s. 156). This led to several discrimination claims under the European Directive, culminating in the *Marshall* decision (see para. 7.7.3).

Section 16 of the Employment Act 1989 sought to resolve the continuing controversy about the discrimination between men and women over redundancy payments and retirement by inserting a similar provision for redundancy pay to that which had existed for unfair dismissal since the Sex Discrimination Act 1986. Thus there must be a 'normal retiring age for an employee holding the position which he has held and the age was the same whether the employee holding that position was a man or a woman' or in any other case 65. Consequently, an employee may not receive a redundancy payment if:

(a)   there was a 'normal retiring age of less than 65 for an employee holding the position which he held', and
(b)   the age was the same for men and women, and
(c)   that employee was above that age.

In the absence of any such normal retiring age, the age of 65 applied as a cut-off point for both men and women.

The most vital questions concern:

(a)   whether it provides a *double barrier* (para. 11.7.1);
(b)   whether normal retiring age is a *contractual* or factual test (para. 11.7.2).

11.7.1   The double barrier

Doubts about the first query were silenced by the House of Lords decision in *Nothman* v *Barnet LBC* [1979] IRLR 35, which allowed the applicant, a woman schoolteacher of 61, to present a complaint of unfair dismissal. A tribunal should apply the normal retiring age if there is one; only if there is not, should it consider 65 or 60 as the vital break point. The essence of Lord Salmon's judgment was that:

> [The section] sets up only one barrier to be overcome by the class of employee whose conditions of employment specify a normal retiring age, and another and entirely different barrier to be borne by the class of employee whose conditions do not specify a normal retirement age. The first class of employee deserves the right to claim . . . only if it has been established the dismissal took effect before the normal retirement age specified in the conditions of employment had been reached.

11.7.2   Construction of normal retiring age

In *Ord* v *Maidstone and District Hospital Management Committee* [1974] IRLR 80 Donaldson P thought 'normal retiring age' meant 'the age at which the employee concerned usually retires'. This was challenged in *Nothman* where Lawton LJ stated:

> I construe the word 'retiring'. . . as having gerundive qualities so as to give the sense of must or should. It follows that the normal retiring age of teachers employed by the local authority is the age at which they would have to retire unless their services were extended by mutual agreement.

This approach brings rather unexpected results, and occasional injustice. The Court of Appeal has emphasised that the vital issue, just as for the definition of 'ordinarily works' (para. 11.4.1), is the construction of the *contract,* not what actually happens in practice. These two things may in some cases differ widely, especially where the employer has a discretion whether or not to retain an employee above a certain age. This clause is common in the public sector.

The terms of employment in the Telecommunications Branch of the Post Office, for example, laid down a retiring age of 60, but went on to provide that all fit and willing officers would be kept on as long as possible depending on their efficiency, physical fitness and the best interests of the public service. In *Post Office* v *Wallser* [1981] IRLR 37, the evidence showed that a substantial majority of the employees in the same grade as the applicant were in effect retained after 60. Even so, the normal retiring age in the contract was 60 and this was held to be decisive of the issue. Only if there is evidence that the policy of retiring at a particular age was *generally disregarded* could it be said that there was not a normal retiring age, and that 65 was the appropriate limit for a man and 60 for a woman. Lawton LJ differed from the other Lord Justices in that he thought 'the concept . . . does not depend exclusively or indeed at all on the fixing of a contract', then the issue is a 'matter of evidence'. Lord Denning considered that could only be so where there was no specific term in the contract fixing the time of retirement.

This approach was disapproved of in *Howard* v *Department of National Savings* [1981] IRLR 40 where another division of the Court of Appeal accepted that only if the contract did not make the normal retiring age clear, custom and practice should be looked at. This opens the somewhat alarming possibility that an employer might insert in a contract a retiring age of 40, subject to the exercise of its discretion to extend it. Even though most employees would be kept on until 60 there would (on the strict interpretation of *Howard)* be no opportunity for an unfair dismissal claim over the age of 40.

Ackner and Griffiths LJJ hardly concealed their disapproval of this approach, although feeling bound as to their decision by the House of Lords in *Nothman.* Ackner LJ admitted that the decision means 'perhaps surprisingly that often the normal retiring age is the minimum retiring age in the sense that it is the earliest date at which there is a contractual liability to retire', while Griffiths LJ thought that in the absence of authority it was not the most obvious construction. (See also *DHSS* v *Randalls* [1981] ICR 100.)

The most important statement of principle is to be found in the House of Lords' decision in *Waite* v *Government Communications Headquarters* [1983] IRLR 341. 'Normal retiring age' is the age at which employees in a group can reasonably expect to be compelled to retire unless there is some special reason in a particular case for a different age to apply. This is not conclusively fixed by the contract of each member of the group, although there is a presumption to that effect. This presumption may, however, be rebutted by evidence that there is in practice some higher age at which those employees regularly retire. 'Normal' in this context is not a synonym for usual. The first question to be asked is what are the contractual provisions; then whether that age has been departed from in practice. This requires full consideration of the relevant facts and figures. The fact that retention beyond the age of 60 was at the employers' discretion is irrelevant in this regard (*Whittle* v *Manpower Services Commission* [1987] IRLR 441; see also *Mauldon* v *British Telecom plc* [1987] ICR 450).

The following elaborations are to be found in case law subsequent to *Waite:*

(a) A normal retiring age must be a definite cut-off point and cannot be a band between, say, 62 and 63. The EAT decided this in *Swaine* v *Health and Safety Executive* [1986] IRLR 205. Where employees in fact retired at a variety of ages higher than the contractual retiring age, there is no normal retiring age so that the statutory cut-offs of, at that time, 65 for men and 60 for women applied, and as the male appellant was below 65 he could claim. A change in the age at which an employee could expect to be forced to retire could be made orally at an annual staff meeting, even though that policy had previously been contained in written documents. Whether there was a sufficient change was a question of fact which the industrial tribunal had decided in favour of the employer, and the EAT would not interfere.

(b) The contractual retiring age may cease to be the normal retiring age because it is regularly departed from in practice. In *Secretary of State for Scotland* v *Meikle* [1986] IRLR

208, the Scottish EAT decided that the industrial tribunal could properly decide that the contractual retiring age of 55 had so ceased to be the normal retiring age for prison officers. It was not correct that the presumption that the contractual retiring age was the same as the normal retiring age and could only be rebutted when the contractual retiring age had been *abandoned* altogether. Since there were now a variety of ages for retirement, the tribunal had properly determined that there was no normal retiring age.

   (c)   The question to be asked is: what is the normal retiring age of an employee holding the *position* of the applicant; this need not be the same as the retiring age of the *applicant* himself (*Secretary of State for Trade* v *Douglas* [1983] IRLR 63, *Age Concern Scotland* v *Hines* [1983] IRLR 477). The Court of Session had occasion to consider in *Highlands and Islands Development Board* v *MacGillivray* [1986] IRLR 210 the scope of those in a similar position to the applicant. In 1975 the appellants reduced the normal retiring age for men to 60, subject to the proviso that they would apply a policy of maximum retention up to 65 for existing male staff. The EAT considered the positions of the 16 administrative officers including the respondent who were covered by this policy. Instead, they should have looked at the positions of all 63 administrative officers in employment at the time of the employee's dismissal. The fact that all those within a group do not have the same contractual retiring age does not mean that they did not remain members of the same group. All 63 had the same status, nature of work and terms and conditions save for the retiring age. In *Brooks* v *BT plc* [1992] ICR 414, the Court of Appeal rejected the submission that the proper test of determining the normal retiring age was to ask what members of the relevant group could reasonably expect would happen to those members who were approaching the alleged retirement age. Rather, it was 'what at the effective date of termination of the claimant's employment and on the basis of the facts then known was the age at which employees of all ages in the claimant's position would reasonably regard as normal'. It was not correct to ask what was the expectation of a person of the age of the applicant. To qualify as the normal retiring age, the age need not be that which was the *universal* expectation of each member of the group; rather a small number by way of exception from the norm may have a different expectation to most, yet the age of the vast majority would still constitute the normal retiring age (*Barclays Bank plc* v *O'Brien* [1994] ICR 865).

   (d)   The vital question is the policy in force *at the time when the employee was dismissed* according to the House of Lords in *Hughes* v *DHSS; Coy* v *DHSS; Department of the Environment* v *Jarnell* [1985] IRLR 263. The employees whose expectations are relevant are those in a position similar to that held by the applicant. 'Position' here takes into account the status of the employee, the nature of the work done and the terms and conditions of his employment. The previous history of the employment is left out from the picture so that a change in policy will alter the normal retiring age. Sir John Donaldson MR, however, stressed that such a change will not bind if it is a sham or has been subsequently varied or modified.

   In *Barber* v *Thames Television plc* [1991] ICR 253, the EAT held that in identifying employees holding the same position as the applicant, the tribunal may not found its conclusion on a term which deals only with retirement. In the particular case, the employees in the same position could thus not be limited to those who had received letters which informed them that their retiring ages would be reduced. Knox J said that 'A term, of employment regarding retirement and not linked to or reflecting some other distinguishing feature of the employee's position cannot have been intended by Parliament to be the basis for distinguishing between one group of employees and another because that would negate the purpose behind the legislation' but this was overturned by the Court of Appeal ([1992]

ICR 661). They held that the word 'position' did not include the circumstances by which as a matter of history some employees had different terms and conditions of employment from others, but did include terms, whether contractual or arising by virtue of the expectation of the person concerned, as to retirement. *Barber* was not followed, however in *Bratko* v *Beliot Walmesley Ltd* [1996] ICR 76, which also held that the action of the employers in purporting to reduce the normal retiring age below the contractual retirement age was in breach of contract and was not effective for that purpose.

(e)   The relevant age need not be actually *attained* in the employment from which the employee is claiming to have been dismissed. Thus in *Dixon* v *London Production and Tools Ltd* [1980] IRLR 385, the applicant was only appointed at 65 ½ after having retired from his earlier employment; the Employment Appeal Tribunal rejected his claim that retirement is an historical event which occurs only once.

An announcement may be made as to a different age provided that the policy was genuine and clearly stated (*Barclays Bank plc* v *O'Brien,* supra).

11.8   EXCLUSION BY AGREEMENT

It might render the unfair dismissal provisions virtually meaningless if employers and employees could agree between themselves to exclude their operation, particularly given the normally greater bargaining power of the employer in this respect. Thus, by s. 203 of ERA 1996, any provision in an agreement is void in so far as it purports to exclude or limit the operation of the unfair dismissal provisions or in so far as it precludes any person from pursuing a claim for unfair dismissal. This has a wide scope especially since it may exclude even accepting a contractual variation. Its aim has been described as to 'protect employees from entering perhaps into misguided bargains before their claim is heard by the industrial tribunal' (*Times Newspapers Ltd* v *Fitt* [1981] ICR 637) or 'hasty and imprudent agreements' (*Council of Engineering Institutions* v *Maddison* [1977] ICR 30).

In *Tocher* v *General Motors (Scotland) Ltd* [1981] IRLR 55 EAT, the employers concluded an agreement with the union to deploy employees made redundant on new work removing other employees whose positions were not redundant (a so-called 'bumping' agreement). The applicant lorry driver volunteered for redundancy, but since the employers wished to keep him they put him in the less skilled position of washer operator for which he received £6 per week less. He tried it but resigned after 10 days. The industrial tribunal said that his taking the job amounted to an agreed variation of contract, so that on his resignation, since there had been no dismissal, he could not claim redundancy payment. The EAT allowed an appeal on the ground that although the agreement was incorporated into the contract of employment, it was rendered void since it purported to exclude or limit the operation of the redundancy payments and deprived the employee of his right to a trial period in the alternative employment (see also on effect on continuity and s. 203, *McCarthy* v *Selflock,* COIT 1411/226, *Hanson* v *Fashion Industries (Hartlepool) Ltd* [1981] ICR 35). Section 203 may apply to a reduction in hours. In *Secretary of State for Employment* v *Deary and Cambridgeshire CC* [1984] IRLR 180, the EAT held that if employees could not meet the service qualification of hours worked for redundancy payments when they were dismissed, whereas prior to the reduction in their hours they would have qualified, it was the reduction in their hours which deprived them of their rights, and an agreement to that effect was rendered void by what is now s. 203 (see *Igbo* v *Johnson Matthey Chemicals Ltd* [1986] IRLR 215; *Barkat Ali* v *Joseph Dawson Ltd,* EAT 43/89 (paras 13.3.5.5 and 13.3.5.6)).

Notwithstanding the amplitude of s. 203, there are certain strictly defined circumstances in which an agreement, whether collective (para. 11.8.1) or individual (para. 11.8.2) might exclude these vital forms of employment protection. Since 1993 there is also provision for compromise agreements (para. 11.8.2.3).

11.8.1 Agreement between management and union

The Secretary of State may by statutory instrument exclude parties to a dismissal procedure agreement or redundancy payments agreement from the scope of the legislation (ERA 1996, s. 110(3)), and similar provisions apply to handling redundancies and guarantee payments. They are all designed to encourage domestic procedures tailored to the particular needs of different industries. The statutory requirements have proved too stringent for their wide-spread development and in 1996 the Government brought forward proposals to extend their scope.

In the case of redundancies, an application must be made by all parties and the agreement must result in submission of disputes to an industrial tribunal.

In the case of unfair dismissal pacts (s. 110(3)):

(a)   Every union party to it must be *independent.*

(b)   Procedures must be available *without discrimination* to all employees of the description covered by it.

(c)   The *remedies* must be on the whole as beneficial as in the statute.

(d)   The final stage must involve recourse to an *independent body* or industrial tribunal.

(e)   It must be possible to determine with *reasonable certainty* whether a particular employee is covered by the agreement.

The Secretary of State may revoke an order if that is the desire of all the parties to it or it has ceased to fulfil all the statutory conditions. The only exclusion order so far approved is that between the Electrical Contractors' Association and the Electrical, Electronic, Telecommunication and Plumbing Union in September 1979.

11.8.2 Individual agreement

11.8.2.1 Fixed term contract   An employee under a contract of employment for a fixed term would normally be entitled to claim unfair dismissal or a redundancy payment on its expiry without being renewed under the same contract (ERA 1996, ss. 95(1)(b), 130(1)(b)), since that is included within the statutory definition of dismissal (para. 13.3.2). The statute goes on to provide an exclusion in respect of 'the expiry of that term without its being renewed' if 'before the term expires, the employee has agreed in writing to exclude' any right to redundancy payment or unfair dismissal in that event (ERA 1996, s. 197(1)). The minimum period was two years for fixed term contracts entered into before 1 October 1980 and since then one year for unfair dismissal but remains at two years for redundancy payments. The Act thus seeks to preserve the flexibility of the employer to take on a worker for a specific project. Typical examples are the short-term hirings of a researcher, a teacher or an oil-rig worker, when it is reasonable for the employer to tailor the length of employment to the expected length of the work. The provision applies only where dismissal is on the 'expiry of the term', not if it occurs beforehand or for some other reason.

Example A is hired for two years as a researcher at Billingsgate College; after one year and six months he is dismissed for theft. An agreement to exclude unfair dismissal does not apply here since the dismissal was not through the expiry of the fixed term.

Further, if a four-year contract is extended for another six months, it appears that the relevant period is the *last engagement* which is for less than the necessary one year. A distinction was drawn in *BBC* v *Ioannou* [1975] ICR 267, between an extension or renewal of an existing fixed term contract which would be one continuous fixed term contract, and re-engagement under a *new* contract which would not. On the facts, the presence of additional terms put this in the latter class. Lord Denning preferred on the other hand always to take as relevant only the final contract, and this view was applied by the EAT in *Open University* v *Triesman* [1978] IRLR 114 (see also *Mulrine* v *University of Ulster* [1993] IRLR 545).

11.8.2.2 Agreement to settle through an ACAS conciliation officer The unfair dismissal legislation seeks to promote conciliation. Even though the statute does not normally countenance such an agreement excluding the right to claim, there must be some restricted circumstances in which they may bind the parties. The compromise reached by the statute is that, to be enforceable, agreements must be made under the guidance of an ACAS conciliation officer. This is insurance against an employer using his extra bargaining power to prevail on an employee. The importance of the conciliation officer's role as a 'sieve', and the utility of conciliated settlements are both shown by the fact that the majority of unfair dismissal applications which go through conciliation officers are settled or withdrawn without hearing. The following principles apply:

(a) By s. 203 (1)(b) of ERA 1996, any agreement which purports to exclude any person from presenting a complaint to an industrial tribunal is void unless a conciliation officer has *'taken action'* under s. 18 of the Industrial Tribunals Act 1996. The general statutory duty of the officer is to endeavour to promote a settlement or where appropriate to seek to promote agreement on a sum in compensation. The conciliator need not do much so as to support the enforceability of a conciliated settlement to have taken action according to the House of Lords. In *Moore* v *Duport Furniture Products Ltd* [1982] ICR 84, the applicant was suspended on suspicion of stealing from his employers. An ACAS conciliation officer was contacted for advice and eventually the employer and employee agreed on the payment of a lump sum for the latter's resignation in return for the employee withdrawing his claim to the industrial tribunal. The officer took no part in these negotiations, but did record the details of the settlement in the standard ACAS form COT3. Later the employee sought to go back on the arrangement and claimed to have been unfairly dismissed. The Court of Appeal and House of Lords held that the minimal 'action' taken here by the conciliation officer was sufficient to make the agreement binding. Moreover, there was no duty on the officer to promote a *fair* settlement (as the applicant had argued). It seemed to Cumming Bruce LJ 'inconceivable or extremely unlikely that Parliament intended to make it impossible for parties who have arrived at a settlement between them before a conciliation officer arrives on the scene to render that settlement valid to exclude a complaint to an industrial tribunal'.

(b) Section 203 does not avoid a genuine agreement to terminate a contract of employment since this is not to exclude but rather to apply the provisions of ERA 1996 (see para. 13.3.5.1; *Logan Salton* v *Durham CC* [1989] IRLR 99).

(c)   An agreement through ACAS need not be in writing, and is enforceable even though the standard ACAS COT3 form is left unsigned (*Gilbert* v *Kembridge Fibres Ltd* [1984] IRLR 52).

(d)   In *Slack* v *Greenham (Plant Hire) Ltd* [1983] IRLR 271, an agreement was not avoided because the conciliation officer did not advise the employee of the possibility that he could claim future loss of earnings. The officer's duty must depend on the circumstances of each case, and here the applicant was an intelligent man keen to have a settlement without delay.

(e)   An agreement might, however, be set aside if the officer were to act in bad faith or adopt unfair methods when promoting the settlement. In *Hennessey* v *Craigmyle & Co. Ltd and ACAS* [1986] ICR 461, the Court of Appeal confirmed that the doctrine of duress could apply to settlements of industrial tribunal proceedings, but this will be established only in the most exceptional circumstances. Here the settlement was not invalidated by the fact that at the date of its signing the applicant had not been dismissed or given notice of dismissal (see also *Courage Take Home Trade Ltd* v *Keys* [1986] IRLR 427).

(f)   A Citizens Advice Bureau officer has ostensible authority to enter into an agreement to settle a claim, as has a counsel, solicitor or law centre member named as a representative by a party to proceedings before industrial tribunals (*Freeman* v *Sovereign Chicken Ltd* [1991] ICR 853).

(g)   In *Livingstone* v *Hepworth Refractories Ltd* [1992] ICR 287, the EAT held that an agreement reached under the auspices of a conciliation officer does not prevent the employee bringing a claim under discrimination legislation. Section 203 applies only to matters within the 1996 Act which have been settled.

(h)   An employee who enters into such a void agreement which involves a payment to him of a sum greater than the statutory maximum may still bring a claim under the Act, on the grounds that the employee has the right to have his compensation assessed by a tribunal, according to the EAT in *NRG Victory Reinsurance Ltd* v *Alexander* [1992] ICR 675.

11.8.2.3 Compromise agreements   Under TURERA 1993, certain agreements not to take proceedings before industrial tribunals were for the first time exempted from the general rule that such agreements are void. Section 39 inserted a new s. 140(3) into EPCA 1978 so that certain compromise agreements became effective. Under ERA 1996, s. 203(3) they must now comply with the following stringent conditions:

(a)   The agreement must be written.

(b)   The agreement must relate to the particular complaint.

(c)   The employee must have 'received independent legal advice from a qualified lawyer [that is, a barrister or a solicitor who holds a practising certificate] as to the terms and effect of the proposed agreement and, in particular, its effect on his ability to pursue his rights before an industrial tribunal.

(d)   There must be in force, when the adviser gives the advice, an insurance policy 'covering the risk of a claim by the employee in respect of loss arising in consequence of the advice'.

(e)   The agreement must identify the adviser.

(f)   The agreement must state that the 'conditions regulating compromise agreements under this Act are satisfied'.

Independent legal advice in relation to the employee means by a 'lawyer who is not acting in the matter for the employer or an associated employer' (new s. 140(4)).

11.9 MISCELLANEOUS

(a) By s. 209(1) of ERA 1996 the Secretary of State has *residuary power:*

(i) to bring specifically excluded employees or holders of certain public offices within the scope of the Act; and

(ii) to exclude employees otherwise included in its coverage.

(b) A person employed in the *police service* is excluded from all rights derived from TULR(C)A 1992 and ERA 1996 but not the right to a written statement of terms, minimum notice or redundancy payments. 'Police service' here means service as a member of a statutory constabulary or in any other capacity by virtue of which the person has the powers and privileges of a constable. It includes prison officers (*Home Office* v *Robinson and Prison Officers' Association* [1981] IRLR 524). A prison officer has in any event a right to complain to the Civil Service Appeal Board, and it must give reasons for its decisions (*R* v *Civil Service Appeal Board ex parte Cunningham* [1990] IRLR 503). For the purpose of the Sex Discrimination and Race Relations Acts, a policeman is deemed to be employed by his Chief Constable or police authority (SDA 1975, s. 17; RRA 1976, s. 16; on the position of special constables see *Sheikh* v *Greater Manchester Police Authority* [1989] 2 All ER 684).

(c) The Redundancy Payments Office Holders Regulations 1965 (SI 1965 No. 2007) extended the scope of redundancy payments to offices such as Clerk of the Peace, airport police, rent officers and registrars of births and deaths.

12 Termination of Contract and Wrongful Dismissal

There are several ways in which the contract of employment may be terminated at common law — that is, by:

(a) supervening event (para. 12.1);
(b) notice given by either party (para. 12.2);
(c) breach (para. 12.3);
(d) dismissal (para. 12.4);
(e) agreement;
(f) performance;
(g) frustration.

The first four will be considered here while the last three are more appropriately covered in Chapter 13 on unfair dismissal, to which the same principles apply.

12.1 AUTOMATIC TERMINATION BY SUPERVENING EVENT

The contract of employment is terminated by automatic operation of law without action by employer or employee in the following circumstances:

(a) A fundamental change in *partners* in a firm where the contract of employment is personal to the partners (*Brace* v *Calder* [1895] 2 QB 253, *Harvey* v *Tivoli (Manchester) Ltd* (1907) 23 TLR 592, *Tunstall* v *Condon* [1980] ICR 786, *Phillips* v *Alhambra Palace Co.* [1901] 1 KB 59, *Briggs* v *Oates* [1990] ICR 473).

(b) Compulsory *winding up* of a company, although there is no termination where a company voluntarily resolves to wind itself up (*Fox Bros (Clothes) Ltd* v *Bryant* [1978] IRLR 485, *Golding and Howard* v *Fire Auto & Marine Insurance Co. Ltd* (1968) 3 ITR 372).

(c) Appointment of a *receiver* (*Hopley-Dodd* v *Highfield Motors (Derby) Ltd* (1969) 4 ITR 289, see *Nicoll* v *Cutts* [1985] BCLC 322 and, for further discussion, para. 14.8).

(d) Permanent *closure* of the employee's place of employment (*Glenboig Union Fireclay Co. Ltd* v *Stewart* (1971) 6 ITR 14).

(e) *Death* of a personal employer (*Farrow* v *Wilson* (1869) LR 4 CP 744).

12.2 TERMINATION BY NOTICE

12.2.1 Notice at common law

Save in the case of a fixed-term contract, an employee is employed for an indefinite period subject to termination by a reasonable period. The length of notice is usually expressly agreed and if so it must now be stated in the written particulars of employment. Otherwise the common law will imply a period of reasonable notice depending on the circumstances of the particular employment. In many cases this is taken to be the same length as the period of payment (e.g. monthly or weekly); it also has regard to differences of worker status. Thus, a year was reasonable notice for a steamer's chief officer and a newspaper editor (*Grundy* v *Sun Printing and Publishing Association* (1916) 33 TLR 77), and six months for a manager of 120 cinemas (*Adams* v *Union Cinemas Ltd* [1939] 3 All ER 136) and a journalist (*Bauman* v *Hulton Press Ltd* [1952] 2 All ER 1121). An airline pilot was entitled to three months (*Nicoll* v *Falcon Airways Ltd* [1962] 1 Lloyd's Rep 245).

12.2.2 Statutory minimum notice

The common law was modified by minima first introduced in the Contracts of Employment Act 1963, later amended and now to be found in the Employment Rights Act 1996 (ss. 86, 87). The statutory rule is that the employer must give one week's notice to an employee who has served him between one month and two years and thereafter one week for each year served up to a maximum of 12 weeks for 12 years. The employee in return must give at least one week's notice of resignation if employed for more than one month (s. 86(2)). This code does not, however, apply to servants of the Crown, those working outside Great Britain and House of Commons staff. Further, the statute does not:

   (a)   prevent either party from *waiving* the right to notice;
   (b)   affect the rights of either party to terminate the contract as a result of the *conduct* of the other (s. 86(6)); or
   (c)   prevent a party from accepting a payment *in lieu of notice* (s. 86(3)). Employers often take the realistic view that an employee under notice is unlikely to be a hard or willing worker. If he has another job to go to the employer may fear that he will abuse confidential information. He may give him money instead, essentially as settlement of damages for breach of contract (on the true nature of payment in lieu of notice, see *Delaney* v *Staples* [1992] ICR 331). It is not clear whether the employer has a right to make such payment in the unlikely event that the employee demands to work out his notice. The general lack of a right to be provided with work suggests a negative answer (*Marshall (Cambridge) Ltd* v *Hamblin* [1994] ICR 363), especially where there is an express term to that effect.

    The Court of Appeal has held, in *Trotter* v *Forth Ports Authority* [1991] IRLR 419, that where the right to waive notice is exercised, the right to payment in lieu is lost (*Baldwin* v *British Coal Corporation* [1995] IRLR 139). Despite the fact that there is nothing in s. 86(3) expressly to this effect, this would appear to be consistent with viewing payments in lieu as damages for breach of contract, for where notice is waived, there is no breach of contract, according to the Court of Appeal in *Rex Stewart Jeffries Parker Ginsberg Ltd* v *Parker* [1988] IRLR 483.

The Employment Rights Act 1996 also lays down the rate of pay which must be maintained during the period of statutory notice (ss. 88–91). The employer must provide a normal week's pay even though his employee does not work, if (s. 88(1)):

(a)   he is ready and willing to work but the employer has no work for him;
(b)   he is incapable of work through sickness or injury;
(c)   the employee is absent from work wholly or partly because of pregnancy or childbirth; or
(d)   he is away on holiday.

Any sickness or industrial injury benefit paid during such period may be deducted from what the employee is entitled to under this provision. There is no right to payment where:

(a)   the employee takes time off (s. 91(1));
(b)   the employee breaks his contract during notice (s. 91(4));
(c)   the employee has given notice and he then goes on strike during the notice period (s. 91(2)).

In the case of an employee without normal working hours, the right to remuneration is conditional upon that employee being 'ready and willing to do work of a reasonable nature and amount to earn a week's pay' (s. 89(2)).

Fringe benefits like holiday stamps are not included in the assessment of holiday pay (*Secretary of State for Employment* v *Haynes* [1980] ICR 371). A remedy for failure to make any payment during notice may be sought in the civil courts or in the industrial tribunals since the Industrial Tribunals (Extension of Jurisdiction) Order 1994 (SI 1994 No. 1623) (see para. 5.1).

12.2.3   Probationary periods

Employees may be given probationary periods and difficulties frequently arise on the construction of the terms relating thereto. In *Dalgleish* v *Kew House Farm Ltd* [1982] IRLR 251, the letter of appointment provided that 'Your position will be probationary for a period of three months at the end of which time your performance will be reviewed and if satisfactory you will be made permanent.' The plaintiff was dismissed after three weeks and was given one week's pay in lieu of notice. The Court of Appeal determined that this was not a breach of contract.

12.3   TERMINATION BY BREACH

As a general approach . . . it is really very desirable that in relations between employers and workmen and the workmen's union there should be so far as can possibly be achieved simplicity: academic discussions as to the operation in certain circumstances in the law of contract of repudiations and acceptances, and acceptances of offers and novations and counter offers and so on should not be allowed to produce a waste of time and energy.

(Per Winn LJ in *Marriott* v *Oxford Co-op* [1970] 1 QB 186 at 193.)

A party to a contract of employment is discharged by a fundamental breach, that is, a breach which:

(a)   the parties regard as vital (*The Mihalis Angelos* [1971] 1 QB 164);
(b)   is so serious in its consequences as effectively to deprive the other party of what he had contracted for (*Hong Kong Fir Shipping* v *Kawasaki Kisen Kaisha* [1962] 2 QB 26); or

(c) shows that the other party no longer intends to be bound by one or more of the essential terms of the contract (*Western Excavating (EEC) Ltd v Sharp* [1978] QB 761).

MacCardie J put it thus in *Re Rubel Bronze & Metal Co.* [1918] 1 KB 315 at 322:

> In every case the question of repudiation must depend on the character of the contract, the number and weight of the wrongful acts or assertions, the intentions indicated by such acts and words, the deliberation or otherwise with which they are committed or uttered and on the general circumstances of the case.

The fundamental breach may be made up of a series of small breaches, the last providing the straw which breaks the camel's back (*Pepper v Webb* [1969] 2 All ER 216, *Garner v Grange Furnishing Ltd* [1977] IRLR 206).

12.3.1 Must a breach be accepted by the innocent party?

One of the great questions of labour law is whether or not a repudiation of a contract of employment, including a dismissal itself, needs to be accepted. This apparently academic issue is practically important when deciding:

(a) the date when termination took place;
(b) whether strikers by the very act of striking, i.e. in fundamental breach of contract, put an end to their contract;
(c) whether a termination/repudiation comes within the definition of direct or constructive dismissal for unfair dismissal (para. 13.3) and redundancy; and
(d) to what date the employee must be paid.

The normal contractual doctrine is that 'an unaccepted repudiation is a thing writ in water', and this was restated in *Photo Production Ltd v Securicor Transport Ltd* [1980] AC 827. Many cases have determined that this holds true for contracts of employment also. There are, however, special difficulties in this area since a contract of service cannot be specifically performed, so that even if a breach is not accepted the court has no mechanism to force the parties to continue in harmony, and employment depends more than most contracts on the existence of mutual trust and cooperation between the parties.

Thus the specialist employment tribunals have often taken the view that such a repudiation operates automatically to determine the contract. In *Sanders v Neale Ltd* [1974] ICR 565, a group of employees went on strike, but after an ultimatum on 11 May presented themselves for work the next day. The question for the NIRC was whether, by their action, the employees could claim that they had refused to accept the employers' repudiation in the ultimatum. Donaldson P thought not, as 'the repudiation of a contract of employment is an exception to the general rule'. It terminates the contract without necessity for acceptance by the injured party. Megarry V-C reviewed an extensive array of cases in *Thomas Marshall (Exports) Ltd v Guinlé* [1979] Ch 227, where the employers were suing the employees. The defendant had been employed as managing director of the plaintiff company under a 10-year service contract, but in 1977 he resigned and the company discovered that during his contract he had been soliciting business for himself away from the employers in breach of his implied duties of good faith to them. In response to the company's application for an interlocutory injunction to prevent the defendant from so acting, the defendant claimed that, with effect from the date of his resignation, the contract had automatically terminated, so that he was no longer bound by its conditions. Megarry V-C rejected this on three grounds:

(a) *Policy:*

Why should a person who makes a contract of service have the right at any moment to put an end to his contractual obligations? No doubt the court will not decree specific performance of the contract, nor will it grant an injunction which will have the effect of an order for specific performance: but why should the limitation of the range of remedies for the breach invade the substance of the contract?

(b) *Authority,* since any other decision was difficult to reconcile with, *inter alia, Lumley* v *Wagner* (1852) 1 De GM & G 604, and *William Robinson & Co. Ltd* v *Heuer* [1898] 2 Ch 451.

(c) *Justice:* 'the courts must be astute to prevent a wrongdoer from profiting too greatly from his wrong' and this is supported by the discussion of the House of Lords on the general law of contract in *Photo Production Ltd* v *Securicor Transport Ltd* [1980] AC 827.

It may be possible to find a *via media* differentiating between the two extremes of *Sanders* and *Guinlé*. Shaw LJ achieved this in *Gunton* v *Richmond-upon-Thames LBC* [1980] ICR 755. The employee, a college registrar, was dismissed for misconduct on one month's notice without adherence to the contractual disciplinary procedure. Automatic termination was raised since it was necessary to decide the correct amount of damages for wrongful dismissal, that is, whether this should run from dismissal or acceptance thereof. The realism of Shaw LJ's approach may be seen in this passage:

The servant who is wrongfully dismissed cannot claim his wage for services he is not given the opportunity of rendering; and the master whose servant refuses to serve him cannot compel that servant to perform his contractual duties.

Thus 'a total repudiation is at once destructive of the contractual relationship'; and a straightforward dismissal would not need to be accepted. But he goes on to suggest that:

There may conceivably be a different legal result where the repudiation is oblique and arises indirectly as for example where the employer seeks to change the nature of the work required to be done or the times of employment.

It should then be in the power of the employee not to accept such a repudiation but instead to go on working.

The majority took the same orthodox view as *Guinlé*. After a thorough analysis of the 'ebb and flow of judicial decisions' on the subject, Buckley and Brightman LJJ were not convinced of the need to differentiate, noting that innumerable other agreements besides those of service could not be ordered to be specifically enforced. Buckley LJ thought it absurd to say that a man could remain an employee after he had been dismissed but not at all absurd to suggest that the contract might nevertheless continue for other purposes. In particular, an employer may want to utilise a restrictive covenant or arbitration clause; the employee may want to rely on a disciplinary procedure and thus delay the effective date of termination in order to qualify for statutory rights. Further, the reality is that damages would be minimal, for as Salmon LJ said in *Decro-Wall International SA* v *Practitioners in Marketing* [1971] 1 WLR 361, where the employee sought to keep the contract alive:

Perhaps a servant could sit still whilst the contract ran its course with the knowledge that the contract was in law alive. But in practice this knowledge could be of little real comfort to him because he would be failing to take reasonable steps to minimise his loss . . . Accordingly he would be far better off accepting the dismissal.

The final conclusion of the *Guinlé* case, concurred in by all their Lordships, was that he could not claim as damages his salary to the end of the contract since the procedural provisions were in no way inconsistent with the power of the employer to dismiss the plaintiff on a month's notice.

In *Dietman* v *London Borough of Brent* [1987] IRLR 259, Hodgson J, who preferred the acceptance theory of termination, said that 'if a plaintiff wishes to contend that a repudiation has not been accepted, it is, in my judgment, essential that he should make the position plain at once and at once bring proceedings and seek interlocutory relief'. There was an acceptance of the repudiation here since the employee never indicated to the defendants that she regarded her employment as a social worker to be continuing. Her industrial tribunal application was not made merely in order to preserve her rights, and she had made vigorous attempts to secure alternative employment. Indeed, she had gained a job which she later turned down. An appeal against dismissal by the employee is not, however, inconsistent with his acceptance of repudiation (*Batchelor* v *British Railways Board* [1987] IRLR 136; see also *Octavius Atkinson & Sons Ltd* v *Morris* [1989] IRLR 158, *Marsh* v *National Autistic Society* [1993] ICR 453, *Rigby* v *Ferodo Ltd* [1988] ICR 29).

12.3.2 Self-dismissal/constructive resignation?

This discussion is closely related to the converse concept of 'self-dismissal'. For the courts at one time threatened to exclude a whole range of terminations from the statutory definition of dismissal, and thus from examination on their merits, by concluding that the employee himself brought the contract to an end when he committed acts of misconduct. The NIRC in *Jones* v *Liverpool Corporation* [1974] IRLR 55, had described the concept as a 'mere novelty'.

The leading case (*Gannon* v *Firth* [1976] IRLR 415) involved a particularly serious breach of contract by a group of eighteen striking employees. Not only did their walking out breach the most fundamental term of their contracts, to provide services, but they also left a high pressure steam system switched on causing severe damage to the factory. Bristow J held that they had thus automatically determined their contracts. Even though in *Trusthouse Forte Leisure* v *Aquilar* [1976] IRLR 251, the EAT concluded that the stealing of liquor from the respondent's hotel was not a serious enough breach, in two later cases Talbot J applied the doctrine to less extreme misconduct. In *Smith* v *Avana Bakeries* [1979] IRLR 423, the employees failed to comply with a company rule that medical certificates were required to cover illness, while in *Kallinos* v *London Electric Wire Co.* [1980] IRLR 11, the applicant was discovered asleep in his employer's rest room when on duty.

In *Rasool* v *Hepworth Pipe Ltd (No. 1)* [1980] IRLR 88, the EAT adopted an alternative approach developed in a series of cases that such repudiatory breaches determined the contracts of employment *de jure* but not *de facto.* Waterhouse J thus found that the attendance by 240 employees at a union meeting which had not been authorised by the management was a repudiation, but that the operative act in terminating the contract was still the acceptance of the repudiation by the employer, which was a dismissal, since it was thus the latter who terminated the contract for the purposes of s. 55(2)(a) of EPCA 1978 (now ERA 1996, s. 95(1). Indeed, this line appears to be assumed by TULR(C)A 1992, ss. 237–239, since if strikers automatically dismissed themselves a provision exempting unfair dismissals during strikes would be unnecessary (para. 13.14).

These questions were canvassed before the Court of Appeal in *London Transport Executive* v *Clarke* [1981] IRLR 166. Mr Clarke was a bus mechanic with London Transport, and when his employers refused him leave to visit his native Jamaica, he just 'took off'. He remained in the sun for seven weeks, sending to London a sick note to cover the exact period of his absence, but was met on his return by the announcement that he was no longer employed by London Transport; he had, they said, dismissed himself. On his complaint of unfair dismissal, the proffered doctrine of 'constructive resignation' was rejected alike by the industrial tribunal, Employment Appeal Tribunal, and a majority of the Court of Appeal. Only the first body, however, thought that the dismissal was unfair. Dunn and Templeman LJJ sought to lay at rest the heresy of automatic termination, seeing it as 'contrary to principle, unsupported by authority binding on this court and undesirable in practice'. It was manifestly unjust to allow a wrongdoer to determine a contract if the innocent party wished to affirm the contract for good reason. Thus if a worker walked out of his job (and did not thereafter claim to be entitled to resume work as did Mr Clarke) it was still the employer who terminated it by accepting the repudiation. Lord Denning MR, dissenting, thought this 'weighs the scales too heavily against the employer'. He stuck to his guns, first trained in his 1929 edition of *Smith's Leading Cases* and still apparently blazing despite the decision of the House of Lords in *Photo Production Ltd* v *Securicor Transport Ltd* [1980] AC 827. For him a fundamental breach or breach going to the root of the contract leads to the discharge of the contract without any need for acceptance. This happens when the misconduct of the employee is such that it is completely inconsistent with continuance of the contract so that the ordinary member of the industrial tribunal would say of the employee 'he sacked himself'. The Master of the Rolls exemplified cases when an employee leaves and gets another job, or absconds with the money from the till or goes off indefinitely without a word to his employer (see also *Rigby* v *Ferodo Ltd* [1988] ICR 29).

Although the orthodox contractual theory has emerged triumphant (see *Norris* v *Southampton City Council* [1982] IRLR 141), one detects in the majority some concern about its effect on situations posited by Lord Denning. This goes back to the problem of remedies, for it is trite law, now confirmed by statute, that a court will not specifically enforce a contract of service. Yet if the employee repudiates and the employer does not accept it, and instead seeks to affirm the contract, what can the courts do? In the converse case of employer repudiation in *Gunton* v *Richmond-upon-Thames LBC* [1980] 3 WLR 714, the Court of Appeal unusually issued a declaration that the contract remained in being, but the consequences of granting such a remedy, outside of statutory offices where it has become established, have still to be worked out.

The courts are likely to avoid such problems by readily finding acceptance of a repudiation. Buckley LJ in *Gunton* thought it could be 'easily inferred' especially where the employee took another job. Traces of this approach, which would make the distinction between orthodox and automatic theory more apparent than real, can be seen in *Clarke*. The court spelt out an acceptance of the breach by omission in that the employer took no action to affirm the contract, and Templeman LJ stated that it 'can take the form of formal writing or can take the form of refusing to allow the worker to resume or continue his work'. Dunn

LJ regarded cases where the employer gives notice and 'the employee has no option but to accept the notice . . . as an exception to the general rule. In these cases the contract is terminated by the notice of the employer'.

Dunn LJ took the decision of the majority in *Clarke* to its logical conclusion by expressly overruling the EAT cases of *Gannon* v *Firth* [1976] IRLR 415, and *Kallinos* v *London Electric Wire Ltd* [1980] IRLR 11. Strangely, he did not think that *Smith* v *Avana Bakeries Ltd* [1979] IRLR 423, should suffer a similar fate 'on the basis that in that case the company's rules were incorporated into the man's contract of service . . . [and] the contract was terminated in accordance with its terms'. The apparent distinction between breaches of express and implied terms is somewhat difficult to understand, all the more so because the breach in *Gannon*, a walk out knowingly leaving machinery in a dangerous condition, would appear to be the gravest breach of all.

The question of when a repudiatory breach has been accepted is one of fact for the industrial tribunal (*F.C. Shepherd & Co. Ltd* v *Jerrom* [1986] IRLR 358). In *Pendlebury* v *Christian Schools North West Ltd* [1985] ICR 174, it occurred, for example, when the employers sent the applicant his final wages and Form P45. The EAT also stressed in *Shook* v *London Borough of Ealing* [1986] IRLR 46, that an employee could not assert that by reason of an agreed breach of the dismissal procedure by her employer, she had never been lawfully dismissed. The acceptance of such repudiation must have occurred at the latest by the end of her case before the industrial tribunal.

12.4 TERMINATION BY DISMISSAL

12.4.1 Ordinary employees

The general view of the common law is that a dismissal with proper notice is lawful, except in the rare event that procedural provisions for termination are built into the contract (e.g. *Tomlinson* v *LM & S Railway* [1944] 1 All ER 537). There is no general implication of the rules of natural justice (e.g. *McClory* v *Post Office* [1992] ICR 758).

12.4.2 Office holders

Hodgson J in *R* v *East Berkshire Health Authority ex parte Walsh* [1984] IRLR 278, thought that judicial review was appropriate to quash a breach of a health authority's procedure since 'the applicant is an officer of a profession recognised as a profession by Parliament'. Judicial review was only unavailable to review activities 'of a purely private or domestic kind'. This was heretical to the Court of Appeal. Employment by a public authority did not *per se* inject any element of public law. The relationship, which incorporated the Whitley Council terms, fell into the category of 'pure master and servant', and the rules of natural justice could not be implied.

The decision was narrowly distinguished by Hodgson J in *R* v *Secretary of State for the Home Department ex parte Benwell* [1985] IRLR 6. The applicant, a prison officer, was charged with disobedience to orders. After an inquiry had recommended a severe reprimand, the Home Office dismissed him after considering notes on his disciplinary file of which he was unaware, and which he had obviously had no opportunity to answer. Hodgson J decided that, if the case were considered on the proper material, no reasonable Home Secretary would have dismissed. Accordingly *certiorari* would issue to quash the decision to dismiss (see also *R* v *Secretary of State for the Home Department ex parte Broom* [1986] QB 198,

McLaren v *Home Office* [1990] IRLR 338, *R* v *Secretary of State for the Home Department ex parte Attard, Independent,* 21 July 1989).

In recent years, the common law, moving in step with the statutory unfair dismissal jurisdiction and modern ideas of personnel management, has indicated a somewhat wider scope to the need for an unbiased hearing. In *Stevenson* v *URTU* [1977] ICR 893, [1977] 2 All ER 941, the plaintiff, a full-time employee of the defendant trade union, was dismissed by its executive after disciplinary proceedings, and the Court of Appeal upheld his claim that this was invalid because he was not given an adequate opportunity to defend himself.

In *R* v *BBC ex parte Lavelle* [1982] IRLR 404, Woolf J went further and indicated, albeit *obiter,* that when there is a procedure for dismissal in an employment not covered by statute at all, employers must comply with that procedure for the dismissal to be valid. If the contractual procedure was infringed, an injuction should issue to prevent the dismissal. This view was partly based on the notion that employment protection legislation had substantially changed the position at common law, so that 'the ordinary contract between master and servant now has many of the attributes of an office'. Judicial review was not the appropriate remedy here because there was no statutory element in the employment but an injunction could issue in an appropriate case.

Office-holders and occupants of statutory positions have a greater security, however, first because the law implies into their office a right to natural justice, and secondly, because a declaration might issue that the dismissal was void. The fact that a decision was taken in the interests of national security, however, precludes any challenge by way of judicial review (*Council of Civil Service Unions* v *Minister for the Civil Service* [1985] ICR 14, *R* v *Director of GCHQ ex parte Hodges, The Times,* 26 July 1988). In *Ridge* v *Baldwin* [1964] AC 40 the dismissal of the Chief Constable of Brighton was declared void because he had not been given an opportunity to give his explanation for alleged misconduct. *Malloch* v *Aberdeen Corporation* [1971] 1 WLR 1578, was an analogous case, the appellant being a Scottish teacher whose terms were set out mainly in statute, and here Lord Wilberforce sought to clarify the relevant distinctions:

> All requirements of the observance of rules of natural justice are excluded [in] . . . what have been called 'pure master and servant' cases which I take to mean cases in which there is no element of public employment or service, no support by statute, nothing in the nature of an office or a status which is capable of protection. If any of these elements exist, then in my opinion, whatever the terminology used and even though in some *inter partes* aspects the relationship may be called that of master and servant, there may be essential procedural requirements to be observed, and failure to observe them may result in a dismissal being declared to be void.

(See also *Chief Constable of North Wales* v *Evans* [1983] 1 WLR 141; *R* v *Chief Constable of Thames Valley Police ex parte Cotton* [1990] IRLR 344.)

The rules of natural justice 'must depend on the circumstances of the case, the nature of the inquiry, the rules under which the tribunal is acting, the subject-matter that is being dealt with and so forth' (*Russell* v *Duke of Norfolk* [1949] 1 All ER 109). In employment cases, the essentials are, as in the concept of fair procedure in unfair dismissal, the rights to be heard by an unbiased tribunal, to have proper notice of charges of misconduct, to be heard in answer to the charges, and to appeal from the initial decision. These have been supplemented by the following principles:

(a)   that the employee should see reports about his dismissal (*Stevenson* v *United Road Transport Union* [1977] 2 All ER 941);

(b)   that the body determining the truth of allegations should adopt a higher standard of proof the more serious the charges are (*R* v *Hampshire CC ex parte Ellerton* [1985] ICR 317);

(c)   that an appeal should be heard by persons who had not been involved in the decision to dismiss (*Re John Snaith* [1982] IRLR 157).

A dismissal has also been held to be invalid at common law in the following circumstances:

(a)   The contract stated that the employee could be dismissed only on a limited number of grounds and that selected did not fall within them (*McClelland* v *Northern Ireland General Health Services Board* [1957] 2 All ER 129).

(b)   A registered dockworker under the former statutory scheme (now abolished by the Dock Work Act 1989) was dismissed by a committee which had no power to take such a decision (*Vine* v *National Dock Labour Board* [1957] 2 AC 488).

(c)   A statutory body dismissed for a *mala fides* reason (*Short* v *Poole Corporation* [1926] Ch 66).

(d)   A Chief Constable failed to realise that under the Police Regulations 1971 he did not have complete discretion whether to dispense with the services of a constable (*Chief Constable of North Wales* v *Evans* (supra)).

(e)   A police authority failed to inform the appellant police officers for two and a half years that complaints had been made against them, since this seriously prejudiced their ability to defend themselves (*Calveley* v *Merseyside Police* [1989] 1 All ER 1025).

(f)   An allegation against a college lecturer could not fall within the terms of the disciplinary procedure (*Jones* v *Gwent CC* [1992] IRLR 521).

A dismissal of a university lecturer does not fall within the jurisdiction of the university visitor (*Thomas* v *University of Bradford* [1986] ICR 87, cf. *Hines* v *Birkbeck College* [1986] 2 WLR 97), so that the ordinary courts have jurisdiction (see also *R* v *Hull University ex parte Page* [1992] ICR 67).

After the decision in *Council of Civil Service Unions* v *Minister for the Civil Service* [1985] ICR 14, a civil servant may have a legitimate expectation to be heard before dismissal (see para. 19.11).

12.4.2   Summary dismissal

The principles [of summary dismissal] are but rarely revealed.

(*Re Rubel Bronze & Metal Co. Ltd* [1918] 1 KB 315.)

There are some cases in which a dismissal without notice may be lawful at common law. The general test of whether summary dismissal is justifiable was stated in *Laws* v *London Chronicle (Indicator Newspapers) Ltd* [1959] 1 WLR 698, as 'whether the conduct complained of is such as to show the servant to have disregarded the essential conditions of the contract of service'. (See also *Freeth* v *Burr* (1874) 9 CP 208 at 213.) Such conduct may be found in just one action by the employee (*Blyth* v *The Scottish Liberal Club* [1983] IRLR 245).

Summary dismissal has thus been held justified in cases of:

(a)   a strike (*Simmons* v *Hoover Ltd* [1977] ICR 61) and probably a work to rule (*Secretary of State for Employment* v *ASLEF (No. 2)* [1972] 2 QB 455);

(b)   dishonesty, e.g. where a betting shop manager took money from the till for his own purposes (*Sinclair* v *Neighbour* [1967] 2 QB 279);

(c)   a series of incidents of intoxication (*Clouston & Co. Ltd* v *Corry* [1906] AC 122 PC);

(d)   the taking of a secret commission in breach of the employee's duty of fidelity (*Boston Deep Sea Fishing & Ice Co.* v *Ansell* (1888) 39 ChD 339);

(e)   gross negligence, e.g. where the manager of the life insurance department of an insurance company negligently recommended the insurance of a life which a few days earlier the managing director had refused to insure (*Jupiter General Insurance Co. Ltd* v *Shroff* [1937] 3 All ER 67);

(f)   wilful disobedience to orders such as refusal to attend meetings (*Blyth* v *The Scottish Liberal Club* (supra)). In *Laws* v *London Chronicle (Indicator Newspapers) Ltd* (supra), however, the fact that a female employee defied the managing director's orders not to leave the room with her superior following a row between the two men, was insufficiently serious since:

one act of disobedience or insubordination or misconduct can justify dismissal only if it is of a nature which goes to show in effect that the servant is repudiating the contract or one of its essential conditions.

The lawfulness of the dismissal depends *inter alia* on:

(i)   the position of the employee;

(ii)   his past record;

(iii)   the social conditions of the time; many old cases are thus unreliable as precedents today, since as Edmund Davies LJ said in *Wilson* v *Racher* [1974] ICR 428 at 430B, they:

date from the last century and may be wholly out of accord with current social conditions. What would today be regarded as almost an attitude of Czar-serf, which is to be found in some of the older cases where a dismissed employee failed to recover damages would, I venture to think, be decided differently today.

In *Wilson*'s case, the employee, a gardener, was dismissed by the defendant following a heated argument about his early departure the previous Friday. This culminated in his saying: 'Get stuffed'. There was no background of inefficiency or insolence as in *Pepper* v *Webb* [1969] 1 WLR 514, an earlier case with otherwise similar facts. The test the Court of Appeal applied was 'whether the plaintiffs conduct was insulting and insubordinate to such a degree as to be incompatible with the continuance of the relation of master and servant'. Here it was not so serious and the dismissal was therefore wrongful. (See also *Hamilton* v *Argyll and Clyde Health Board* [1993] IRLR 99).

The employer may rely on facts discovered *after* the dismissal to justify his action in giving his employee the sack. This is the very opposite of the rule developed in unfair dismissal (*Boston Deep Sea Fishing & Ice Co.* v *Ansell* (1888) 39 ChD 339; cf. *W. Devis & Sons Ltd* v *Atkins* [1977] AC 931).

In the absence of gross misconduct, the employee dismissed without notice may claim for wrongful dismissal and this exists today alongside statutory unfair dismissal. One of the greatest reforms wrought by the introduction of the latter was the new importance of procedure in dismissal, and consequent lessening of the power of summary dismissal. This does not, however, mean that summary dismissal is not still valid in some cases. The Code of Practice and the courts have isolated very serious cases of misconduct and incapability which merit dismissal without any pretence of natural justice for the employee (para. 13.9).

12.5 REMEDIES FOR WRONGFUL DISMISSAL

The potential remedies for wrongful dismissal are: specific performance and injunction; declaration; prerogative orders; and damages.

12.5.1 Specific performance and injunctions

A central defect of the common law of wrongful dismissal from the point of view of employees is that the courts will not enforce a broken contract by specific performance, so that if an employee has been unlawfully sacked, there is no way he can regain his job. Moreover, the courts have in general refused to countenance his regaining his old position by injunction preventing the dismissal taking effect. The following reasons have been advanced for this conclusion:

(a) It would amount to *forced labour*. Thus Fry LJ in *De Francesco v Barnum* (1890) 43 ChD 165, was:

very unwilling to extend decisions the effect of which is to compel persons who are not desirous of maintaining continuous personal relations with one another to continue those personal relations . . . I think the courts are bound to be jealous lest they should turn contracts of service into contracts of slavery.

(b) It would be inconsistent with the *trust and confidence* which must exist between employer and employee, although this is less valid in modern times when the employer is most likely to be a large impersonal corporation.

(c) If the effect of dismissal is to terminate the employment, equity will not act on the basis that it is still alive.

(d) It offends against the doctrine of *mutuality* since to force an employer to reinstate cannot be balanced by forcing an employee to work.

(e) The court cannot *supervise* performance of the contract.

(f) *Damages* are usually an adequate remedy.

Section 236 of TULR(C)A 1992 enacts part of this principle, providing that 'no court shall issue an order compelling an employee to do any work or attend at any place for the doing of any work'.

The courts have long held that these rules do not prevent the court enforcing an agreement not to *compete* with the employer whether during or after employment, even where this may have the indirect effect of pressurising him to carry on working in that employment. Thus in *Warner Bros Pictures Inc. v Nelson* [1937] 1 KB 209, Bette Davis the actress broke her agreement to work solely for the plaintiff and Branson J granted them an injunction by adopting the negative provision that she should work for no other motion picture or stage producer. She could work in other fields and the judge was not impressed by the argument that: 'The difference between what [she] can earn as a film artiste and what she might expect to earn by any other form of activity is so great that she will in effect be driven to perform her contract.' The court will not, however, enforce a provision not to take any employment at all for a period after termination of the contract of service. For this would constitute a thinly disguised form of compelling service. (See *Page One Records Ltd* v *Britton* [1967] 3 All ER 822, *Lumley* v *Wagner* (1852) 1 De GM & G 604, *Evening Standard Co.* v *Henderson* [1987] IRLR 64, discussed at para 6.4). In *Warren* v *Mendy* [1989] IRLR 210, Nourse LJ said that: 'Compulsion is a question to be decided on the facts of each case, with a realistic regard for the probable reaction of an injunction on the psychological and material, and sometimes the physical, need of the servant to maintain the skill or talent.'

12.5.1.1 Exceptions Some exceptions are developing to this general rule. The Court of Appeal in *Hill* v *CA Parsons and Co. Ltd* [1972] 1 Ch 305, went considerably further than precedent, to grant an injunction which had the effect of specific performance although only in very particular circumstances. The plaintiff was dismissed after 35 years working for the defendant company as a chartered engineer because he would not join the union DATA with which the employers had just signed a closed shop agreement. The Court of Appeal, with Stamp LJ dissenting, granted an interim injunction preventing them from implementing the dismissal. Lord Denning MR and Sachs LJ thought that in this case the normal arguments against enforcement did not apply, since:

(a)   there was continued confidence between employer and employee, as it was the union and not the company who sought to remove him; and
(b)   damages would not here be an adequate remedy.

It may also have been significant that at the time of the decision the unfair dismissal provisions were due to take effect in two months' time when the remedy of reinstatement would become available. The case was distinguished in *GKN (Cwmbran) Ltd* v *Lloyd* [1972] ICR 214, *Sanders* v *Ernest A. Neale Ltd* [1974] ICR 565, and *Chappell* v *Times Newspapers Ltd* [1975] ICR 145. It was however followed in:

(a)   *Jones* v *Lee* [1980] ICR 310, where the Court of Appeal issued an injunction to prevent managers of a Roman Catholic primary school from dismissing its headmaster without the consent of the local council and without affording him the opportunity to be heard, both of which were required in his contract.
(b)   *Irani* v *Southampton and South West Hampshire Health Authority* [1985] IRLR 203, where an ophthalmologist was dismissed by the authority without the procedural protection afforded by the Whitley Council. Warner J considered it important that, just as in *Parsons,* damages would not be an adequate remedy since Mr Irani would become virtually unemployable throughout the National Health Service and would lose the right to use NHS facilities to treat his private patients. (See also *Marsh* v *National Autistic Society* [1993] ICR 453.)

An injunction may normally be granted only where there is the necessary trust and confidence remaining between employer and employee as was the case in *Irani* and *Powell* v *London Borough of Brent* [1987] IRLR 466. The courts will scrutinise carefully an employer's assertion that trust and confidence has broken down in order to ensure that there are facts on which that assertion is based. This must be judged by reference to all the circumstances of the case including the nature of the work, the people with whom the work must be done, and the likely effect on the employer and employer's operations if he is required by the injunction to suffer the plaintiff employee to remain in his position (cf. *Ali v Southwark LBC* [1988] ICR 567; see also *Alexander v STC plc* [1990] ICR 291, *Wishart v NACAB* [1990] ICR 794).

In *Wadcock v London Borough of Brent* [1990] IRLR 223, the High Court awarded an injunction even though it was impossible to say that trust and confidence remained. Nevertheless, the judge felt that the employee was competent and would be well able to work in the post to which he had been assigned if he were minded to obey his superiors. There are also cases where the employee seeks an injunction, not to remain in his job, but to treat the original dismissal as *void* in order to recover pay until the proper procedures are gone through. In this event, as the High Court pointed out in *Robb v London Borough of Hammersmith and Fulham* [1991] ICR 514, the retention of trust and confidence is not so material.

12.5.1.2 Licence to enter premises after dismissal   An employee clearly has a licence to enter his employer's premises but this will be determined on suspension or dismissal. In *City and Hackney Health Authority v National Union of Public Employees* [1985] IRLR 252, the plaintiffs' decision to close Shoreditch Hospital led to a sit-in, which they believed had been organised by Mr Craig, a NUPE shop steward. He was suspended from work on full pay and told not to enter the hospital premises. He was granted an interlocutory injunction to restrain the ban at first instance, but the Court of Appeal thought that this was an error. Although it was arguable that the Whitley Council agreement provided a right to stay on the premises so that the shop steward could exercise his functions, this could not survive the suspension of the contract. The continuance of such right depended on mutual confidence and it was clear that the appellants had lost all confidence in the respondent.

12.5.2   Declaration

The declaration is of increasing importance in the area of dismissals. This has been for some time used as a remedy in cases involving statutory status and offices, declaring void the dismissal of a registered dockworker (*Vine v National Dock Labour Board* [1956] 1 QB 658) and of a trade union official (*Stevenson v United Road Transport Union* [1977] ICR 893), but in the past they have been refused in the case of ordinary employees (*Francis v Municipal Councillors of Kuala Lumpur* [1962] 1 WLR 1411).

The Court of Appeal in *Gunton v Richmond-upon-Thames LBC* [1980] ICR 755, countenanced an extension in the use of the declaration to declare that the employee's contract remained in being. They indicated that it was not issued because of any special statutory status of the applicant; it may be particularly appropriate for declaring that a contract still exists and a repudiation has not been accepted by the other party.

There may be a further development of the use of declarations in employment cases using the procedures of determination of a point of law under the Rules of the Supreme Court, ord. 14A, as seen in *Jones v Gwent CC* [1992] IRLR 521 and *Porter and Nanayakkara v Queen's Medical Centre* [1993] IRLR 486.

12.5.3   Judicial review

Where the employer is a statutory authority, the prerogative orders of *certiorari* and mandamus may be sought in the Divisional Court (*University Council of the Vidyodaya*

University v *Silva* [1965] 1 WLR 77), but this does not extend to post office employees (*R* v *Post Office ex parte Byrne* [1975] ICR 221) since this is a public corporation.

In *R* v *East Berkshire Health Authority ex parte Walsh* [1984] IRLR 278, the Court of Appeal stressed that judicial review was only available where an issue of public law was involved. A breach of the contract of employment by a public authority was not a matter of public law. The Master of the Rolls explained that it was the existence of special statutory provisions bearing directly upon the right to dismiss which distinguished this case from the cases of *Vine* (supra), *Ridge* v *Baldwin* [1964] AC 40 and *Malloch* v *Aberdeen Corporation* [1971] ICR 893 where judicial review was granted.

The following have not been held issues of public law so that judicial review is an inappropriate remedy:

(a)   the termination of the contract for services between a deputy police surgeon and a county council (*R* v *Derbyshire CC ex parte Noble* [1990] ICR 808);

(b)   a decision of a Probation Committee to phase out a mileage allowance on financial grounds (*Doyle* v *Northumbria Probation Committee* [1992] ICR 121).

In *R* v *Hertfordshire CC ex parte National Union of Public Employees* [1985] IRLR 258, the applicants failed in their request for *certiorari* to quash the decision of the defendants to terminate the contracts of the school meals service employees and offer them less favourable terms on the grounds that it was unreasonable. Their Lordships refused to accept that the authority took no or insufficient account of the adverse effects of failing to adhere to nationally agreed collective agreements in reaching their decisions.

12.5.4   Damages

Damages are the normal remedy for breach of contract and the usual measure is the wages and benefits the employee would have earned if due notice had been given (*Radford* v *De Froberville* [1977] 1 WLR 1262, *Shove* v *Downs Surgical plc* [1984] IRLR 17). (This is quite different to unfair dismissal compensation.) For that is the only period when he is entitled by contract to continue in employment. If his contract can be determined by three weeks' notice he cannot claim his loss over the next three years even though he is unemployed for that length of time; for at any time within that period he might have been dismissed with three weeks' notice.

12.5.4.1   Treatment of benefits   Contractual fringe benefits are taken into account and an important element for consideration in *Shove* v *Downs Surgical plc* (supra) was the provision of a Daimler motor car. Sheen J rejected the employer's submissions that:

(a)   the correct method of assessment was by reference to the tax charge imposed by the Finance Acts;

(b)   the employee was entitled to compensation only in respect of such vehicle as he could expect to be provided with in his position; and

(c)   the absence of contractual entitlement to petrol meant that it could not be claimed even though it had been provided to him free by the company for many years.

An increasingly common component of remuneration packages, especially for senior executives, is *share options* in the company. Most schemes expressly provide that they are not exercisable after termination of employment save typically in cases of sickness or redundancy (i.e. factors which are not created by employer or employee) and that loss of the options on termination shall give no rights to damages or compensation for wrongful or unfair dismissal. It seems likely that such clauses would be upheld, but it is possible to argue that they were an exclusion clause and unreasonable under the Unfair Contract Terms Act 1977. For this argument to succeed, it would be necessary to show that they were standard terms of a company's business, which would be difficult (e.g. *Micklefield* v *SAC Technology Ltd* [1990] IRLR 218).

12.5.4.2 Damages for distress etc. The amount of damages is limited in that no damages are recoverable for:

(a) the *humiliating* way in which the employee was dismissed;
(b) *loss of reputation* even if it leads to difficulty in getting a job in the future (*Addis* v *Gramophone Co. Ltd* [1909] AC 488, *Shove* v *Downs Surgical plc* (supra)).

There will be no award for:

(c) *bonuses* which are solely within the discretion of the employer (*Lavarack* v *Woods of Colchester Ltd* [1967] 1 QB 278);
(d) share options in the discretion of the employers (*O'Laiore* v *Jackel International Ltd* [1991] ICR 718).

That the approach to items (a) and (b) was changing was suggested by the decision of Lawson J in *Cox* v *Philips Industries Ltd* [1975] IRLR 344. The employee was demoted and resigned as a result; he was granted £500 in damages for distress and depression arising from the breach, because the learned judge found this was a breach of a term to provide job satisfaction. This was, however, overruled by the Court of Appeal in *Bliss* v *South East Thames Health Authority* [1985] IRLR 308. Although *Addis* increasingly appears a case out of keeping with modern ideas, it was recently applied in a claim brought by two employees of BCCI for 'stigma damages' (*Re BCCI* [1994] IRLR 282, now upheld by the Court of Appeal [1995] IRLR 375).

Extra damages may also be available where the parties envisage a greater return from the contract of employment than simply pay for hours worked. Thus an American actress wishing to establish her name in London who contracted to play a part for the defendant was held to have done so in return not only for money but also for full publicity and her damages were thus enhanced (*Marbe* v *George Edwardes (Daly's Theatres) Ltd* [1928] 1 KB 269). There is also an old exception in cases of apprenticeships (e.g. *Dunk* v *George Waller & Sons Ltd* [1970] 2 QB 163).

12.5.4.3 Loss of a chance In *Robert Cort & Son Ltd* v *Charman* [1981] IRLR 437, Browne-Wilkinson J suggested *obiter* that damages might include a sum for the loss of the right to compensation for unfair dismissal which the employee would have successfully claimed had the correct notice been given (see also *Stapp* v *The Shaftesbury Society* [1982] IRLR 326, *Collins* v *Hall Blinds Ltd,* unreported, Clerkenwell County Court, 10 October 1994, *FOCSA Services (UK) Ltd* v *Birkett* [1996] IRLR 325).

Where a dismissal was wrongful on procedural grounds the proper amount of damages is what would have been earned from the date of the unlawful dismissal to the date when the contract could lawfully be terminated, according to Hodgson J in *Dietman* v *London Borough of Brent* [1987] IRLR 259. The plaintiff would not, however, be entitled to a sum to reflect the fact that she had lost the statutory minimum notice period she had built up since she might have been lawfully dismissed in the near future had the proper procedure been followed.

Very large measures of damages are available only where the contract is for a fixed term and cannot be terminated by notice. This is most usually the case in high status occupations like company directors, football club managers and accountants. The measure of damages is then similarly the amount which would have been earned in the unexpired part of the fixed term, but here there might be four or five years to run.

12.5.5 Deductions from damages

From the amount of damages so made up must be deducted sums to take account of: mitigation; taxation; and benefits received.

12.5.5.1 Mitigation   As in every contract, the employee plaintiff must mitigate his loss as a result of its breach. He cannot sit back at home and mount up his losses in the confident expectation that he will be able to claim them from his former employers. In particular he must take reasonable steps to obtain another job, and if he succeeds any wages earned in the new position will be deducted from wages due over the period of notice. If, on the other hand, he does not try to find another post, a sum is taken away to represent his lack of effort (see also *Westwood* v *Secretary of State for Employment* [1984] IRLR 209).

Each case depends on its own facts but the dismissed employee does not normally have to take the first job which comes along. He may also act reasonably in refusing to take another position in the company which has just dismissed him. He is entitled to preserve a skilled job, so that a painter is not necessarily expected to take work as a general labourer (*Edwards* v *SOGAT* [1970] 3 WLR 743) nor a managing director as an assistant manager (*Yetton* v *Eastwoods Froy* [1967] 1 WLR 104). A similar approach is taken to that of suitable alternative employment offers after redundancy (para. 14.3.4).

The employee must also give credit for any opportunities gained as a result of his dismissal, but not where these arise indirectly. Thus in *Lavarack* v *Woods of Colchester Ltd* [1967] 1 QB 278, the plaintiff was after dismissal able to take shares in a competing company, which was profitable, but this was too indirect to be brought into account.

There is no duty to mitigate, however, in a case where the contract of employment provides for a specific period of payment on termination which may be thus recovered as a debt (*Abrahams* v *Performing Rights Society Ltd* [1995] ICR 1028). This controversial decision arose out of an unusual factual situation since the employee's terms included the provision that in the event of termination he 'would be entitled other than in the case of dismissal for gross misconduct, to a period of two years or the equivalent payment in lieu' (see 1030H). The Court of Appeal found that this was not a case in which damages were being awarded for wrongful dismissal but the employer was exercising its entitlement to a debt claim pursuant to the contract. This was a liquidated damages claim.

12.5.5.2 Taxation   Since the relevant damages are based on lost wages, the court deducts from them the amount of tax the employee would have paid if he had received the money week by week or month by month rather than in a lump sum. This is the same rule as applies to damages in tort (*BTC* v *Gourley* [1956] AC 185) and is based on the assumption that damages are not taxable in the hands of the plaintiff, but this is not always the case in all damages claims for wrongful dismissal (Income and Corporation Taxes Act 1988, ss. 148 and 188 and Sch. 11). The Inland Revenue has intervened in respect of termination of employment contracts to prevent 'golden handshakes' being used as tax avoidance devices so that payments of over £30,000 are subject to tax in the plaintiff's hands. The rule in *Gourley*'s case therefore applies only to the first £30,000 of an award or settlement. Section 148(2) applies to 'any payment . . . which is made, whether in pursuance of any legal obligation or not, either directly or indirectly in consideration or in consequence of, or otherwise in connection with, the termination of the holding of the office or employment or any change in its functions or emoluments. . . .'.

In *Shove* v *Downs Surgical plc* [1984] IRLR 17, Sheen J decided that the assessment of the plaintiff's loss should be increased by such amount as was necessary to leave him after deduction of tax with the net compensation due to him, so as properly to put him in the same position as if the contract had been properly performed.

12.5.5.3 Other benefits There may be other sources of assistance during unemployment besides recourse to the courts for damages. These must be balanced against damages so that the dismissed employee does not recover twice. The following rules apply to such other benefits:

(a) *Unemployment benefit* (now the *jobseeker's allowance*) and supplementary benefit received during the period of notice for which damages can be gained are deducted (*Parsons* v *BNM Laboratories Ltd* [1964] 1 QB 95, *Cheeseman* v *Bowater Paper Ltd* [1971] 3 All ER 513, *Nabi* v *British Leyland (UK) Ltd* [1980] 1 All ER 667, *Lincoln* v *Hayman* [1982] 1 WLR 488).

(b) *Redundancy payment* is not deducted since it is not a substitute for wages but a lump sum recognition of past employment (*Yorkshire Engineering & Welding Ltd* v *Burnham* [1974] ICR 77, *Basnett* v *J. & A. Jackson Ltd* [1976] ICR 63, *Stocks* v *Magna Merchants Ltd* [1973] ICR 530, *Wilson* v *National Coal Board* (1980) 130 NLJ 1146).

(c) The sum of social security contributions which the employee has not had to pay while unemployed are deducted (*Cooper* v *Firth Brown Ltd* [1963] 1 WLR 418).

(d) Unfair dismissal compensation is deducted, at least the amount awarded for loss of earnings (*Berry* v *Aynsley Trust Ltd* (1976) 127 NLJ 1052), but the court will not be able to do this if the unfair dismissal award is for the maximum figure then available and the tribunal has not apportioned that amount to any particular period when the employee was out of work (*O'Laiore* v *Jackel International Ltd* [1991] ICR 718).

(e) Occupational pension benefits are not deductible (*Hopkins* v *Norcross plc* [1994] IRLR 18).

Normally unfair dismissal is the more efficacious remedy for dismissal but wrongful dismissal maintains a residual utility where:

(a) The employee is a *higher earner* and may claim the full extent of his loss beyond the artificially low maximum on unfair dismissal claims (para. 13.18).

(b) The employee *cannot claim* the statutory right because he has not applied within three months of dismissal, or he is over retiring age (Chapter 11).

(c) The dismissal is *fair* but in breach of contract.

(d) A declaration or judicial review is required.

13 Unfair Dismissal

The expression 'unfair dismissal' is in no sense a common sense expression capable of being understood by the man in the street.

(Phillips J in *W. Devis & Sons Ltd* v *Atkins* [1976] ICR 196.)

13.1 THE BACKGROUND

Unfair dismissal was a completely new concept when ushered in as a minor part of the controversial Industrial Relations Act 1971. It is different from common law wrongful dismissal since as Phillips J said in *Redbridge LBC* v *Fishman* [1978] ICR 569, many dismissals are unfair although the employer is contractually entitled to dismiss the employee. In contrast, some dismissals are fair even though the employer was not contractually entitled to dismiss as he did dismiss. The new superstructure was, however, built on a common law base in that many of the underlying concepts arose directly from the law of contract. Dismissal, gross misconduct and the failure to obey reasonable orders can hardly be understood apart from these roots.

The statutory jurisdiction seeks to meet the following shortcomings of the common law of wrongful dismissal:

(a)   the low level of damages, generally only compensating for the appropriate notice period;

(b)   the inability of the dismissed employee in most cases to regain his job;

(c)   the artificiality and archaism of the principles of summary dismissal;

(d)   the lack of express procedural protections for most employees.

Unfair dismissal is undoubtedly the most important aspect of employment protection legislation — in volume of case law, in public awareness and in its lasting effect on personnel practices. Indeed, in recent years the civil courts have become more willing to grant injunctions to restrain breaches by employers of contracts of employment (see para. 12.5.1.1). Yet whether it has achieved its central objectives must be questioned. In particular, what was intended as a central remedy of reinstatement, that is, putting an unfairly dismissed employee back in his old job, is granted in only about 1 per cent of cases. It also remains far from the ideal of proponents of establishing a form of 'property interest' in the employee's job. Some suggest that it has inhibited employers from taking on as many workers as they otherwise would. The decision of the House of Lords in *Polkey* v *Dayton*

Services Ltd [1988] ICR 142 reinvigorated unfair dismissal, and tribunals now place much greater stress on procedural requirements.

13.2 OUTLINE

The central provisions have remained remarkably little changed since 1971. The amendments contained in the Trade Union and Labour Relations Act 1974, the Employment Protection Act 1975 and the Employment Acts 1980, 1982 and 1988 concerned, in the main, the way this individual protection affects the trade unions and the closed shop, and the remedies it provides. Further changes were made by TURERA 1993 in respect of dismissal for assertion of statutory rights and on the ground of maternity. The provisions are now consolidated in Part X of the Employment Rights Act 1996.

Section 94 of the ERA 1996 still proclaims, that, subject to exceptions, 'An employee has the right not to be unfairly dismissed by his employer'. The elaboration of this slogan caused Phillips J, after rejecting the idea that it was a commonsense concept, to explain: 'It is narrowly and to some extent arbitrarily defined . . . it is a form of words which could be translated as being equivalent to dismissal ''contrary to statute'' and to which the label unfair dismissal has been given.' (*Devis* v *Atkins* (supra)). Moreover, in some ways the statute does not adopt the most direct approach to the definition of an unfair dismissal.

Once (a) eligibility, and (b) dismissal have been established (themselves very complicated in concept), the necessary determination is twofold:

(a) The employer must prove the reason or *principal reason* for the dismissal. Some reasons are automatically unfair (discrimination, union membership or activity, pregnancy), but the five most important statutory reasons are *potentially* fair. They are: capability or qualifications; conduct; redundancy; statutory prohibition; and some other substantial reason for dismissal.

(b) To be actually fair in any particular case it must be *reasonable* in all the circumstances for the employer to treat the reason he has given as a reason to dismiss (see para. 13.6 for full formula).

This process, according to Viscount Dilhorne in the leading case of *W. Devis & Sons Ltd* v *Atkins* [1977] AC 931, directs the tribunal to focus on the conduct of the employer and not on whether the employee in fact suffered any *injustice*. It involves consideration of substance and procedure, the latter being most clearly set out in the ACAS Codes of Practice which are non-binding but persuasive in industrial tribunals in the same way as the Highway Code (while not having the force of law) receives marked respect from the criminal courts.

13.3 DISMISSAL

At common law there were just two sorts of terminations of employment which might found an action for wrongful dismissal:

(a) a sending away by the employer; and

(b) a radical change of the employee's terms and conditions which amounted to repudiatory breach of his contract (*Marriott* v *Oxford Co-op Society (No. 2)* [1970] 1 QB 186).

An extended definition became necessary as first the Redundancy Payments Act 1965 and later the Industrial Relations Act 1971 with its unfair dismissal provisions, attempted to meet the deficiencies of the common law.

In order to claim either type of remedy, the employee first has to prove he was dismissed, and both statutes adopted virtually the same codification of the concept, which has remained largely intact through several re-enactments. The three main headings are now to be found in s. 95(1) (and repeated in s. 136(1)), of the ERA 1996. An employee shall be treated as dismissed by his employer only in the following circumstances:

(a) *Direct dismissal* — when the contract under which he is employed by the employer is terminated by the employer, whether it is so terminated by notice or without notice.

(b) *Expiry of fixed term* — where under that contract he is employed for a fixed term, that term expires without being renewed under the same contract.

(c) *Constructive dismissal* — when the employee terminates that contract, with or without notice, in circumstances such that he is entitled to terminate it without notice by reason of the employer's conduct.

All three species of dismissal focus on the termination of *the contract* of employment rather than of the *relationship* of the employer and employee. The last remaining doubt concerned constructive dismissal and it was removed by *Western Excavating (ECC) Ltd* v *Sharp* [1978] 1 All ER 713. One consequence is that an employee can claim to have been dismissed even though taken back by the same employer under a different contract, although it is then unlikely that he could prove unfairness (see *Hogg* v *Dover College* [1990] ICR 39, *Alcan Extrusions Ltd* v *Yates* [1996] IRLR 327).

The difficulties under each paragraph will now be examined, and then we turn to those terminations which remain outside their scope. The employee must prove dismissal, so that if there is any dispute on this point he goes first before an industrial tribunal (*Horsell* v *Heath* (1966) 1 ITR 332).

13.3.1 Direct dismissal (s. 95(1)(a))

13.3.1.1 Words of dismissal The concept of direct dismissal appears obvious at first sight. Some cases, however, are not clear-cut, and courts and tribunals have demanded that words of dismissal should be unequivocal and set a date for the end of employment. It is essential to distinguish clearly words of dismissal from words which are equivocal or uttered in the heat of the moment. Where words are not obvious but the employee has interpreted them as amounting to a dismissal, tribunals have been counselled to concentrate on the employer's intention and the employee's reaction to it. The approach of the EAT is revealed in the following cases:

(a) In *Tanner* v *D. T. Kean Ltd* [1978] IRLR 110, the respondent lost his temper on finding that the employee had taken the company's van and he ended his somewhat vitriolic attack by saying, 'You're finished with me.' The EAT decided that these words were spoken in anger, and were not meant to be an effective dismissal.

(b) A worker on Hull docks was so anxious to finish his job for the day quickly that his foreman was moved to comment that if he did not like the job he could 'fuck off'. In interpreting the words in the light of the language normally heard on Hull Docks, the tribunal held that the words were not indicative of dismissal (*Futty* v *D & D Brekkes Ltd* [1974] IRLR 130).

(c)   In *J. & J. Stern* v *Simpson* [1983] IRLR 52, the applicant was told to 'go, get out, get out' by Mrs Stern who was ill at the time and had just overheard a heated discussion between her son and the applicant. Tudor Evans J emphasised the need to consider all the surrounding circumstances. Here it should have been clear that the words were not intended to be a dismissal.

(d)   In *Martin* v *Yeomen Aggregates Ltd* [1983] IRLR 49 the employee was angrily told to leave when he refused to get a spare part for the car of a director. Within five minutes the director had eaten his words and instead suspended the employee without pay so that a more rational decision might be taken about the incident. The employee, however, insisted that he had been dismissed. Kilner Brown J considered that it was a matter of plain common sense vital to industrial relations that an employer and employee should be given the opportunity of recanting from words spoken in the heat of the moment. It was a question of degree for the tribunal in each case to decide whether the change of mind is too late to recover from the unwise and unwonted words.

The dispatch of a Form P45 may be evidence, although not conclusive, that an employee has been dismissed (*Makin* v *Greens Motor (Bridport) Ltd, The Times,* 18 April 1986).

The jurisdiction to make a complaint of unfair dismissal after an employee has been given notice but before that termination takes effect is unaffected by a subsequent summary dismissed (*Patel* v *Nagesan* [1995] IRLR 370).

13.3.1.2   Date of termination must be set   Secondly, to be effective, a dismissal, although it may be with or without notice, must set a date for termination or at least make it possible to ascertain such a date. Thus a dismissal would be valid which was to take effect on the Queen's birthday, since that is easily identifiable, whereas a sacking to take effect when Grimsby Town FC win the FA Cup would not be. A vital distinction is thus drawn between an actual dated dismissal and advance warning thereof (*Hicks* v *Humphrey* (1967) 2 ITR 214). As Lord Parker CJ stated in *Morton Sundour Fabrics Ltd* v *Shaw* (1967) 2 ITR 84: 'As a matter of law you cannot dismiss an employee by saying "I intend to dispense with your services in the coming months".' This is not to deny that a very long period of notice, even a year in length, may be given, but a final date must always be set and communicated to the individual concerned. While in *Shedden* v *Youth Hostel Association (Scotland)* (1966) 1 ITR 327, there *was* a dismissal where the employee was told, 'We are moving in six months' time but you are not coming with us', a mere announcement of factory closure, even fixing a general date, was not sufficient. In *Doble* v *Firestone Tyre Co. Ltd* [1981] IRLR 300, the respondents declared towards the end of 1979 that their Brentford factory would shut on 15 February 1980, and their statement continued with the assurance that: 'Obviously we will be keeping these plans under constant review and any change will be notified to you.' Less comforting was the indication that 'notices of termination will be issued as they become due'. In the atmosphere of insecurity thus engendered, the appellant naturally saw his best course in securing alternative employment as quickly as possible. He took this up on 17 December 1979, and claimed both a redundancy payment and unfair dismissal. The EAT upheld the employer's contention that he had not been dismissed and Waterhouse J echoed Lord Widgery's statement in *Morton* that (at 87):

The employee has the perfectly secure right if he thinks fit to wait until his contract is determined, to take his redundancy payment, and then see what he can do in regard to obtaining other employment. If he does, and one can appreciate that there may be compelling reasons, choose to leave his existing employment before the last minute in order to look for a new job before the rush of others competing with him comes, then it is up to him. The effect of the employer's warning is not in any way to derogate from his statutory rights but to give him an alternative which, if he is so minded, he can accept.

(See also *Tunnel Holdings Ltd* v *Woolf* [1976] ICR 387.)

The rule can work with particular harshness when an aura of uncertainty descends on a factory, yet the employee who leaves has no remedy. An indication that his job is at risk, even that the factory where he works 'will close within a year', is not an anticipatory breach of contract according to the EAT in *Haseltine Lake & Co.* v *Dowler* [1981] IRLR 25. (See also *International Computers* v *Kennedy* [1981] IRLR 28.) This is because for such a breach it must be *inevitable* that an actual breach will occur in due course because the other party to the contract has renounced it whether by showing that he intends not to be bound by it or that he has rendered performance impossible by putting it out of his power to perform it. However, a termination with proper notice cannot constitute a repudiation (*Land and Wilson* v *West Yorkshire MCC* [1981] IRLR 87).

The same rules formulated in *Morton* as to dates of dismissal apply to resignations (*Hughes* v *Gwynedd AHA* [1978] ICR 161), so that a statement that the applicant intended to leave her job to have her baby and would not return was not sufficient since it was merely a statement of present intention. On the other hand, an announcement that 'I am resigning' contains no ambiguity according to the Court of Appeal in *Sothern* v *Franks Charlesly & Co.* [1981] IRLR 278, and is to take effect at once. The matter was to be examined in the context of a senior secretary who had taken a considered decision. There may, however, be circumstances permitting the industrial tribunal to find that words were said in the heat of the moment and thus did *not* amount to a true resignation. In so deciding in *Sovereign House Security Services Ltd* v *Savage* [1989] IRLR 115, the Court of Appeal came down in favour of the objective test. (See also para. 13.3.5.4.)

13.3.1.3   Repudiation as dismissal

(a)   There is a termination by the employer, and thus direct dismissal, when he repudiates the contract of employment. This may be constituted, for example, by his insistence on a change in terms (*Marriott* v *Oxford Co-op Society (No. 2)* [1970] 1 QB 186), or by making it impossible for the employee to continue by closing the factory at which the employee worked (*Maher* v *Fram Gerrard Ltd* [1974] ICR 31). This is more normally treated as a constructive dismissal, but the fact that it is a termination by the employer within s. 55(2)(a) does have some consequences in respect of effective date of termination and the acceptance of breach.

(b)   Termination of one series of tasks where a contract is severable does not amount to a dismissal according to the Court of Appeal in *Land and Wilson* v *West Yorkshire MCC* [1981] IRLR 87. Thus when the respondents terminated the retained part-time duties of the appellant firemen, they were not dismissed.

(c)   The question whether or not there has been a dismissal is one of fact for the industrial tribunal (*Martin* v *MBS Fastenings (Glynwed) Distribution Ltd* [1983] ICR 511).

(d)   Once given, notice of termination may not be retracted without the agreement of the other side (*Harris & Russell Ltd* v *Slingsby* [1973] ICR 454).

13.3.2 Fixed-term contracts (s. 95(1)(b))

13.3.2.1 What is a fixed term? The old presumption of yearly hiring, which was appropriate to a predominantly agricultural community, vanished long ago (e.g. *Richardson* v *Koefod* [1969] 3 All ER 1264), so that most contracts of employment are now of indefinite duration determinable by notice on either side. A significant sector of the workforce are, however, engaged for a fixed term of so many weeks, months or years. This is especially so amongst high status professionals employed for specific tasks, like managers or television researchers. Unlike the normal continuous contracts, those for a fixed term end automatically and the employer need take no active steps to terminate them. At common law they are thus discharged by agreement or performance so there is no remedy for wrongful dismissal. However, in the new statutory jurisdictions it was felt that special rules were essential to assimilate all contracts, so that thousands of workers would not for such rather fortuitous reasons be denied the right to claim a remedy for unfair dismissal or a redundancy payment. Thus the expiry of a fixed-term contract of employment without its being renewed is deemed a dismissal. There is, however, a difference from most contracts of service, in that such workers do at least know what is coming to them at its end, and are in a position to plan ahead. Thus as a compromise, while its expiry counts as a dismissal, employees can validly agree not to pursue their statutory rights. Section 197 of ERA 1996 enacts that where an employee is employed for a fixed term of a year or more he may agree in writing to exclude his rights to unfair dismissal, and if engaged for two years or more, for redundancy payment purposes also (see para. 11.8.2.1).

It was in connection with this exclusion that the phrase 'fixed term' first arose for construction, and the tension between the policies of what is now s. 197 and the dismissal provisions has ever since been apparent. In *BBC* v *Ioannou* [1975] ICR 267, the Court of Appeal were concerned to read it narrowly in relation to the section (then EPCA 1978, s. 142) in order to prevent the exclusion being too widely exploited. The respondent employee's contract was for a fixed term but it could be determined by notice before its expiry, and the Court of Appeal for this reason rejected the argument that it was for a fixed term. Within the statute, Geoffrey Lane LJ stated:

> The word 'fixed' must have been intended to add something to the word 'term' and the only meaning it seems to me which can be applied to it is that the term should not be capable of abbreviation except by one of the reasons imposed by the common law in every contract of employment such as wilful and serious misconduct.

Lord Denning MR summed up this principle in a nutshell — 'a fixed term is one which cannot be unfixed by notice'. There was, however, another ratio of their Lordships' decision, that the employee's last contract was for less than two years, and for that reason, on the wording of the legislation then current (i.e. at least two years), it did not fall within the exclusion clause.

The then Master of the Rolls was also party to the decision in *Dixon* v *BBC* [1978] ICR 357, where the same employers sought to use the *Ioannou* decision to argue that the expiry of a similar contract was not a dismissal at all for the purposes of what was then EPCA 1978, s. 55(2) (now ERA 1996, s. 95), since there was no fixed term to expire. In this context, the Court of Appeal took a different view of the meaning of fixed term. Brandon LJ thought the *Ioannou* principle 'would create an enormous breach in the wall of protection which [unfair dismissal] had built around employees'. It would, according to Lord Denning

MR, be 'an absurd position if a man was employed for four weeks and he can claim for dismissal when the four weeks come to an end. But by inserting a clause for a week's notice, the employer can get rid of any employee when the period of four weeks comes to an end'. They thus held that such a contract subject to notice was for a fixed term, and upheld *Ioannou* only on the second ground, that the contract was to last for less than two years. Indeed Shaw LJ thought the *Ioannou* decision *per incuriam;* Lord Denning MR thought that 'seeing that the second ground was erroneous, I think we can depart from it'; while Brandon LJ commented that there 'the code was not viewed as a whole'. Thus it still remains the position that if a contract for two years is renewed for nine months, even though no other terms are varied, the relevant contract is for nine months.

These two decisions still left unclear the general definition of 'fixed term', but in *Ryan* v *Shipboard Maintenance Ltd* [1980] IRLR 16, the EAT provided some elucidation and restricted the concept. The applicant employee was hired to carry out repairs to ships on a 'job by job' basis, the tasks varying considerably in length, but Kilner Brown J held that this was not a series of fixed-term contracts. Such engagements were of indeterminate duration, there being no fixed date for their end, and each was discharged by performance rather than expiry. There was therefore no dismissal for statutory purposes.

This principle was upheld in *Wiltshire CC* v *NATFHE and Guy* [1978] ICR 998, [1980] ICR 455, although a different view was taken of the facts of the case itself. The applicant, a part-time teacher at Swindon College, received a fresh contract of employment at the beginning of every academic year. Each agreement was subject to early termination if interest in the courses she taught did not remain at a satisfactory level. The employer's argument that this amounted to a contract for a particular purpose, and thus not for a fixed term, was rejected since there *was* a determinable ending point. On the other hand, their Lordships indicated that a seaman engaged for a voyage or a man hired to cut down trees would be employed on a contract terminating by performance. A person employed for 'the duration of the present government' would not have a contract for a *fixed term* (such workers would not be able to claim to have been dismissed). Lawton LJ said: 'A "term" means a period. A "fixed term" means a term with a defined beginning and a defined end.'

Lord Denning MR concurred that: 'If there is a contract by which a man is to do a particular task or carry out a particular purpose then when that task or purpose comes to an end the contract is discharged by performance.' While this cannot be gainsaid on the construction of the Act, the distinction may prove arbitrary in practice. The parties are unlikely to have referred to the issue in deciding whether to give the contract fixed dates. In some cases it may be a mere matter of words.

13.3.2.2 Termination by expiry Even assuming a fixed-term contract, there is a dismissal under s. 95(1(b) only where it *expires* without being renewed under the same contract, and not when it is prematurely terminated or renewed. By s. 235 'renewal' includes extension, and *Ioannou* suggests that it is enough if this is in substantially the same terms. The end of an apprenticeship will amount to a dismissal but there is no dismissal if the complaint is that the apprentice is not re-employed as a journeyman (*North East Coast Shiprepairers* v *Secretary of State for Employment* [1978] IRLR 149).

13.3.3   Constructive dismissal

Section 95(1)(c) of ERA 1996 reflects the common law position that an employee may be entitled to resign in reaction to his employer's behaviour and yet claim to have been dismissed. Otherwise the employer could make life so difficult for the employee that he had to leave, yet escape liability since he had not actually terminated his contract. The most difficult questions raised by the statutory codification of the concept are:

(a) what is the degree of conduct which entitles the employee to leave (paras 13.3.3.1–13.3.3.6); and
(b) whether the particular worker has in fact genuinely *reacted* to that conduct in leaving (para. 13.3.3.7).

13.3.3.1 What conduct entitles the employee to terminate? To claim constructive dismissal, the employee must be *entitled* to terminate his contract by reason of his employer's conduct, and two alternative criteria have struggled for recognition as the proper construction of 'entitled'. The broad view, propounded *inter alia* in *George Wimpey Ltd* v *Cooper* [1977] IRLR 205, was that the statute required only 'conduct of a kind which in accordance with good industrial relations practice no employee could reasonably be expected to accept'. This test, however, received its quietus in *Western Excavating (ECC) Ltd* v *Sharp* [1978] QB 761, where the Court of Appeal held that the employer must be in breach of contract. It was a case with particularly strong facts which left the higher courts with little sympathy for the employee. He was originally suspended from work for taking an afternoon off to play cards and in his consequent self-inflicted financial plight he asked the company for his accrued holiday pay or a loan. When the employers refused, he resigned. The industrial tribunal decided in his favour on the preliminary issue of dismissal, but the Court of Appeal found this to be perverse. The determination of whether the employee was 'entitled to terminate' his contract was in their view, a purely contractual matter. Lord Denning MR said:

If the employer is guilty of conduct which is a significant breach going to the root of the contract of employment or which shows that the employer no longer intends to be bound by one or more of the essential terms then the employee is entitled to treat himself as discharged from any further performance. If he does so, then he terminates the contract by reason of the employer's conduct. He is constructively dismissed. The employee is entitled in those circumstances to leave at the instant without giving any notice at all, or alternatively he may give notice and say he is leaving at the end of his notice. But the conduct in either case must be sufficiently serious to entitle him to leave at once.

The employee could not claim to have been dismissed since the appellants had committed no breach of contract. The Court of Appeal gave several reasons for preferring this more stringent contractual approach:

(a) The statute *distinguished* between dismissal and unfairness and it was anomalous to have the same test of reasonableness applying to both.
(b) The words in paragraph (c), 'terminate' and 'entitled', had a *legal,* and hence *contractual,* connotation.
(c) The test of unreasonableness was *too indefinite* by far, and had, according to Lord Denning MR, led to decisions on 'the most whimsical grounds'.
(d) Any man of *common sense* could apply the contractual test.

The reasonableness test appeared to be subtly reintroduced in *Woods* v *WM Car Services (Peterborough) Ltd* [1982] IRLR 413, when Watkins LJ commented, in determining whether the employee had been constructively dismissed, that:

Employers must not in my opinion be put in a position where, through the wrongful refusal of their employees to accept change, they are prevented from introducing business methods in furtherance of seeking success from their enterprise.

It appears that this *obiter* remark must be confined to the facts of the case since the EAT emphasised in *Wadham Stringer Commercials (London) Ltd* v *Brown* [1983] IRLR 46, that neither the circumstances inducing the fundamental breach by the employer nor the circumstances which led the employee to accept the repudiation were relevant to the question of constructive dismissal (see also *Millbrook Furnishing Industries Ltd* v *McIntosh* [1981] IRLR 309). In an isolated, and certainly unorthodox decision in *Dutton & Clark Ltd* v *Daly* [1985] IRLR 363, Kilner Brown J decided that the tribunal should consider whether the action of the employer which is alleged to found a constructive dismissal was such that no reasonable employee could have taken it.

13.3.3.2   Employer's duty of good faith   One consequence of the *Western Excavating* case has been to encourage the development at common law of manifold implied contractual terms specifically related to dismissal. The courts have taken to heart the words of Bristow J that 'implied terms should reflect the changes in the relationship between employer and employee as social standards change'. Most room for manoeuvre has been found in the developing obligation of the employer to act towards his employee in good faith. The fount of this stream of authority of 'reverse fidelity' is *BAC* v *Austin* [1978] IRLR 332. Mrs Austin was supposed to wear goggles at work, but did not find those provided to be suitable. She accordingly complained bitterly to management about them and when they failed to respond in any meaningful way, she resigned. The EAT found that the employer had indeed been in breach of a contractual obligation to act reasonably in dealing with safety and complaints, and more fundamentally Phillips J uttered the widely quoted (albeit *obiter*) words:

If employers behave in a way which is not in accordance with good industrial practice to such an extent that the situation is intolerable or the situation is such that the employee cannot be expected to put up with it any longer that is a breach of an implied term of the contract.

The distinction between this and the old reasonableness test is wafer thin and it has stimulated a creative approach to implied terms in several cases.

In *Courtaulds Northern Textiles Ltd* v *Andrew* [1979] IRLR 84, Phillips J identified an implied term that the employers would not, 'without reasonable and proper cause conduct themselves in a manner calculated or likely to destroy or seriously damage the relationship of confidence and trust between the parties' (see para. 13.11). Some commentators see this development as heralding a revolution in the very conceptual foundations of the contract of employment, moving from a relationship of subordination to one necessitating trust and cooperation on each side. It appears to impose a 'proper purposes' doctrine on the use by management of its power. The exact extent of this movement is difficult to pinpoint. It is, however, clear that it does apply also to the employer's role in relation to its pension scheme (*Imperial Group Pension Trust Ltd* v *Imperial Tobacco Ltd* [1991] ICR 524).

The various obligations imposed under this rubric include:

(a)   not to treat employees *'arbitrarily,* capriciously or inequitably' with respect to increases in pay (*Gardner (F. C.) Ltd* v *Beresford* [1978] IRLR 63); on the other hand, an employee has no right to an annual pay rise (*Murco Petroleum Ltd* v *Forge* [1987] IRLR 50);

(b)   not to *undermine the authority* of senior staff over subordinates;

(c)   not to *falsely accuse* an employee of theft (*Robinson* v *Crompton Parkinson Ltd* [1978] IRLR 61); nor to threaten to call in the CID if she did not resign (*Allders International Ltd* v *Parkins* [1981] IRLR 68);

(d)   not to expect employees to work in *intolerable conditions* (*Graham Oxley Tool Steels Ltd* v *Firth* [1980] IRLR 135);

(e)   not to persistently attempt to vary the employee's conditions of service. In *Woods* v *WM Car Services (Peterborough)* [1981] IRLR 347, there was a potential repudiation when the new management of the company, which had recently been taken over, within a few months tried to reduce the pay of the long serving applicant, who had been its chief secretary, and also insisted that she work longer hours, gave her unjustified warnings as to conduct, issued new terms and gave her a job specification which was more than one person could handle. In fact, the EAT did not interfere with the industrial tribunal's finding of fact that here there was no fundamental breach. The Court of Appeal upheld this view and Lord Denning MR said that, 'Just as a servant must be good and faithful so an employer must be good and considerate.' (See also *Wadham Stringer Commercials (London) Ltd* v *Brown* [1983] IRLR 46);

(f)   to *positively encourage,* and maintain appraisal of, a probationer during his trial period in particular by giving guidance and advice (*White* v *London Transport Executive* [1981] IRLR 261);

(g)   to treat staff with dignity, being guarded in the use of foul language, particularly where the employee is in a close personal relationship with the employer; thus in *Isle of Wight Tourist Board* v *Coombes* [1976] IRLR 413, a director of the appellants said of his secretary, in front of another employee: 'She is an intolerable bitch on a Monday morning.' This clearly shattered the relationship of complete confidence which must exist in the circumstances so that she could resign and claim constructive dismissal;

(h)   not to require without reasonable cause the applicant to undergo a psychiatric examination (*Bliss* v *South East Thames Regional Health Authority* [1985] IRLR 308);

(i)   not to impose a disciplinary punishment (even though expressly provided for in the contract of employment) if it is out of proportion to the 'offence' committed (*BBC* v *Beckett* [1983] IRLR 43, *Cawley* v *South Wales Electricity Board* [1985] IRLR 89);

(j)   not to seek to change an employee's job specification by underhand means. The employee succeeded in *Chapman, Lowry & Puttick Ltd* v *Cox,* EAT 270/85, even though his job title was unchanged. The company had appointed another man to carry out several parts of his job, and pressure was exerted on him to take an open-ended job with a subsidiary at a less senior position. The industrial tribunal held that no reasonable employee could have been expected to put up with the employer's conduct and that the company was in fundamental breach of its duty of trust and confidence;

(k)   to hear properly an employee's grievance (*Elder* v *Clydebank Co-operative Society Ltd,* EAT 165/87).

The EAT warned of the limits of this general doctrine in *Post Office* v *Roberts* [1980] IRLR 347, although it found a breach of contract on the facts. The employee was a clerical assistant who worked for the respondents in Brighton. She applied to be transferred to a similar position in Croydon but was turned down ostensibly on the ground that there were 'no suitable vacancies' in the area. She soon discovered, however, newspaper advertisements in the Croydon district announcing the availability of the very positions which she was seeking. It was only several weeks later, and after much probing, that she discovered the real reason for her initial 'brush off'; that she had been given a bad report which she had not been shown. In the view of Talbot J, this constituted a breach of the employer's implied duty of trust and confidence. He rejected the respondent's contention that a repudiation must be deliberate and in bad faith, but considered that it was going too far to say that an employee had to be treated in a reasonable manner. The behaviour must be, and here was, 'such that its effect judged reasonably and sensibly is to disable the other party from properly carrying out its obligations'. (See also *Lewis* v *Motorworld Garages Ltd* [1985] IRLR 465.)

13.3.3.3   Other breaches of contract justifying resignation   Other breaches of express and implied terms which have been held sufficient to justify resignation include:

(a)   A deliberate reduction in pay: this is the repudiation *par excellence,* since: 'The basic rate of pay is a fundamental element in any contract of employment and in our opinion it cannot be said that there is no material breach on the part of an employer who proposes to reduce the basic rate even for good reasons and to a relatively small extent.' This was even though in *Industrial Rubber Products* v *Gillon* [1977] IRLR 389 (at 390), from which this quotation derives, the reduction was dictated by government pay policy. It is, however, subject to the *de minimis* rule, so that the sharing out with fellow employees of 1 ½p per hour bonus for lifting crates of empty bottles, which would at most reduce the applicant's wages by £1.50 per week out of a total of £60, was held not to be fundamental. On the other hand, abolition of a 1 per cent commission was held repudiatory, even though the introduction of a new scheme might eventually at least restore that loss. The crucial point was that at the time of resignation this could only be a matter for speculation (*R.F. Hill Ltd* v *Mooney* [1981] IRLR 258). It may be sufficient that the employer fails to increase pay in line with contractual entitlement (*Pepper & Hope* v *Daish* [1980] IRLR 13).

(b)   Change in *job content or status:* in one case an acting manager had his 'most interesting and enjoyable duties' of buying greengroceries removed from him, and this constituted constructive dismissal (*Coleman* v *S & W Baldwin* [1977] IRLR 342). The change is a question of degree and, in assessing the scope of job duties, it is pertinent to examine not only the employee's statement of terms, but also the advertisement by which he was attracted to the post and all surrounding circumstances in order to build up a full picture of what he was employed to do (*Pedersen* v *Camden London Borough* [1981] IRLR 173). Temporary changes are treated less severely than permanent imposed variations and the EAT have held that:

If an employer under the stresses of the requirements of his business directs an employee to transfer to other suitable work on a purely temporary basis and at no diminution in wages that may in the ordinary case not constitute a breach of contract. However, it must be clear that 'temporary' means a period which is either defined as being a short fixed period . . . or which is in its nature of limited duration.

In *Millbrook Furnishing Industries Ltd* v *McIntosh* [1981] IRLR 309, where Browne-Wilkinson P enunciated this principle, a transfer of highly skilled sewing machinists in the respondent company's upholstery department to unskilled work in their bedding section was a breach; for it was to last until work picked up in the former section and this could not be at all accurately estimated at the time of application (see also *McNeill* v *Charles Crimin (Electrical Contractors) Ltd* [1984] IRLR 179).

(c)   Substantial change in the *place of work. (See Hawker Siddeley Power Engineering Ltd* v *Rump* [1979] IRLR 425, and *Little* v *Charterhouse Magna Assurance Co.* [1980] IRLR 19.) Whether a forced move is a fundamental enough breach of contract 'is a question of degree to be determined according to all the circumstances such as the nature of the work, the circumstances in which it is performed and the circumstances of the place to which the work is to be transferred'. Thus neither the move of Times Newspapers from Printing House Square to Grays Inn Road (*Times Newspapers Ltd* v *Bartlett* (1976) 11 ITR 106), nor of a restaurant from Holborn to Regent Street was a *fundamental* breach of contract (*Managers (Holborn) Ltd* v *Hohne* [1977] IRLR 230), but a requirement to move 15 miles from Mosshill Industrial Estate, Ayr to Irvine was a fundamental breach (*McAndrew* v *Prestwick Circuits Ltd* [1988] IRLR 514). In *Courtaulds Northern Spinning Ltd* v *Sibson and TGWU* [1988] IRLR 305, the Court of Appeal decided that it was not a fundamental breach to instruct the respondent HGV driver to transfer to another depot one mile away in order to avoid conflict with the union. It was not correct to postulate that an implied term to transfer from depot to depot was subject to the qualification of reasonableness and had to be for genuine operational reasons. (See also *United Bank Ltd* v *Akhtar* [1989] IRLR 507.) The *Sibson* case was later heard before the European Court of Human Rights on a complaint of breach of Article 11 of the Convention, but this was rejected. There is an implied term that reasonable notice of a transfer should be given (*Prestwick Circuits Ltd* v *McAndrew* [1990] IRLR 191; cf *White* v *Reflecting Roadstuds Ltd* [1991] ICR 733).

Other potentially fundamental breaches include:

(d)   Change in *hours of work* (*Derby CC* v *Marshall* [1979] ICR 731).

(e)   *Suspension* by employer without contractual authority.

(f)   Failure to *provide work* where this is an implied term, e.g. refusal to allow employee to perform his contractual duties while working out his notice.

(g)   Failure to provide such assistance as was customary, for example in a hairdressers (*Seligman & Latz* v *McHugh* [1979] IRLR 130).

(h)   Failure to provide a *safe system of work* (*Keys* v *Shoefayre Ltd* [1978] IRLR 476), including enhanced security after an armed robbery.

(i)   Failure to follow a contractual disciplinary procedure (*Post Office* v *Strange* [1981] IRLR 515).

(j)   Punishment out of all proportion to the offence even though such punishment was expressly provided for in the contract as a penalty for misconduct (*BBC* v *Beckett* [1983] IRLR 43).

(k)   A failure to pay in accordance with relevant Wages Council orders (*Reid* v *Camphill Engravers Ltd* [1990] IRLR 268, [1990] ICR 435).

The following principles apply:

(a)   A constructive dismissal may arise by way of an anticipatory breach. In *Norwest Holst Group Administration Ltd* v *Harrison* [1985] IRLR 240, the Court of Appeal decided that an employer who threatened a breach was entitled to withdraw the threat at any time before the innocent party communicated his unequivocal acceptance of the repudiation. In that case the employee was engaged as director and chief engineer, but was told by letter on 14 June 1982 that he would lose his directorship as from 1 July 1982. The employee replied by letter headed 'Without prejudice' that he was not prepared to accept the loss of the directorship. Faced with this, the company withdrew the threat but later on that day the employee sought to accept the repudiation. The Court of Appeal did not think that this could be a constructive dismissal.

(b)   The employee may complain of conduct such as a reprimand by a member of management even though that person would have no authority actually to dismiss. The proper question is whether that person was acting within the scope of his employment in delivering the reprimand (*Hilton International Hotels (UK) Ltd* v *Protopapa* [1990] IRLR 316).

(c)   There may be a fundamental breach of contract when an employer threatens that unless employees change their hours, the employer will dismiss them with due notice (*Greenaway Harrison Ltd* v *Wiles* [1994] IRLR 380).

(d)   The employee can rely on a matter as giving rise to a constructive dismissal even though the body purporting to carry out the act which amounts to the fundamental breach of contract relied upon had no power to do so on behalf of the respondent (*Warnes* v *Cheriton Oddfellows Social Club* [1993] IRLR 58).

An employee can only claim constructive dismissal on the takeover or merger of his employer if a substantial change is made in his working conditions to his detriment under reg. 5(5) of the Transfer of Undertakings (Protection of Employment) Regulations 1981 (SI 1981 No. 1794) but not simply by reason of the change of employer (see para. 16.4).

13.3.3.4   The breach must be fundamental   In all these cases the breach in question must be fundamental. This means, according to Lord Macdonald, that 'the conduct of the employer would require to be of a fairly serious nature and, in the normal case, over a period of time'. However, what is not normally a fundamental breach in respect of a new employee may be sufficient to justify resignation where the employee has given long and faithful service. A small straw may break this doughty camel's back. The question is always one of degree, but the following are illustrations of cases where the breach was *not* fundamental:

(a)   failure to interview candidates for redundancy in accordance with the appropriate collective bargain (*British Leyland Ltd* v *McQuilken* [1978] IRLR 245);

(b)   failure to pay the employee on the due date because of cash flow problems, since he was assured of full settlement in the near future (*Adams* v *Charles Zub Associates Ltd* [1978] IRLR 551);

(c)   failure by the employers to investigate a complaint against themselves by the employee (*GLC* v *Canning* [1980] IRLR 378);

(d)   absence of consultation over appointment of a subordinate and not telling an employee of pay increases received by subordinates when his own increment was withheld (*Walker* v *Josiah Wedgwood & Sons Ltd* [1978] IRLR 105; see also *Kenneth McRae & Co. Ltd* v *Dawson* [1984] IRLR 5);

(e)   failure to take further measures to limit the risk of criminal attacks at a building society agency (*Dutton & Clark Ltd* v *Daly* [1985] IRLR 363);

(f)   failure to treat an allegation of sexual harassment seriously (*Bracebridge Engineering Ltd* v *Darby* [1990] IRLR 3).

13.3.3.5   Disputed contractual construction   There can be no repudiatory breach and no constructive dismissal where there is a dispute about the construction of the contract of employment. This follows orthodox contractual reasoning, but does not fit well in the employment area. Thus in *Frank Wright & Co. (Holdings) v Punch* [1980] IRLR 217, the employee resigned when he was not paid cost of living increases. His original contract signed in 1973 had indicated that he was entitled to these rises; his statement of terms issued in 1978 did not. The EAT denied that an expression of intention by one party (here the employer) to carry out the contract only in accordance with its own erroneous interpretation was repudiatory, and thought this was especially so where there was a genuine mistake of law and fact. It placed a strict onus on the employee in this case to prove that the mistake was not genuine, and if followed this would be likely to considerably limit the scope of constructive dismissal. It is, moreover, somewhat unrealistic to expect an employee to bring an action in the county court which alone could clear up any misinterpretations.

In *Financial Techniques v Hughes* [1981] IRLR 32, Lawton and Brandon LJJ followed the approach of *Punch,* but Templeman LJ 'desire[d] to guard myself against the implication which might otherwise be read . . . that if any party to a contract has a plausible but mistaken view of his rights under that contract he may insist on that view and his insistence cannot amount to repudiation'.

Punch does not mean that there is no repudiation where the motive for breach was to preserve the employee's job rather than to terminate the contract; for outside of issues of contractual construction, repudiation is judged on the basis of the nature of the breach of contract and its impact on the contractual relationship of the parties and without reference to the subjective intentions in acting as they did. (See *Ready Case Ltd v Jackson* [1981] IRLR 312; cf. *BBC v Beckett* [1983] IRLR 43, *Bliss v South East Thames Regional Health Authority* [1985] IRLR 308).

In *Bridgen v Lancashire CC* [1987] IRLR 58 Sir John Donaldson MR emphasised (at para. 16) that: 'The mere fact that a party to a contract takes a view of its construction which is ultimately found to be wrong, does not of itself constitute repudiatory conduct. It has to be shown that he did not intend to be bound by the contract as properly construed.' In *Brown v JBD Engineering Ltd* [1994] IRLR 568 the EAT held, however, that there is no rule of law that a mistaken belief as to construction of a contract cannot amount to a repudiatory breach, but the fact that the action or omission on the part of the employer arose from mistake rather than deliberate conduct may be a factor in determining whether it does amount to a repudiation.

13.3.3.6 The question is a question of fact The Court of Appeal in *Woods v WM Car Services (Peterborough) Ltd* [1982] IRLR 413 decided that there was no rule of law for determining whether a particular set of facts constitutes a repudiatory breach. The EAT should only interfere with the decision of the industrial tribunal if it is shown that the industrial tribunal misdirected itself in law so that the decision was such that no reasonable tribunal could reach it (see also *Pedersen v Camden London Borough* [1981] IRLR 173; cf. *McNeill v Charles Crimin (Electrical Contractors) Ltd* [1984] IRLR 179, *Scott v Coalite Fuels and Chemicals* [1988] IRLR 131).

13.3.3.7 The resignation must be in reaction to the fundamental breach There must be evidence that an employee's resignation was really in reaction to, and motivated by, a fundamental breach by the employer, and thus an acceptance, in orthodox theory, of his repudiation. While the worker need not use such technical language, he 'must indicate the reason why he is going and must make it plain that he is accepting a breach on the part of his employers' (*Genower v Ealing AHA* [1980] IRLR 297). A long period between breach and resignation will be difficult to explain without good reason, and may amount to waiver of any breach (*Bashir* v *Brillo Manufacturing Co.* [1979] IRLR 295).

Lord Denning MR said in *Western Excavating* v *Sharp* [1978] QB 761, that:

> the employee must make up his mind soon after the conduct of which he complains; for if he continues for any length of time without leaving, he will lose his right to treat himself as discharged.

Thus in *Jeffrey* v *Laurence Scott* [1977] IRLR 466, where the employer's conduct occurred some three and a half months before the resignation, the employee was held not to have been constructively dismissed. On the other hand, a few weeks will probably not amount to waiver, particularly if the applicant is looking for other work in that time, or clearly objects to the breach of contract. (See *W.E. Cox Toner International Ltd* v *Crook* [1981] IRLR 443; *G.W. Stephens & Son* v *Fish* [1989] ICR 324; *Reid* v *Camphill Engravers Ltd* [1990] IRLR 268.)

Even if an employee has not treated a breach of an express contractual term as a wrongful repudiation, he is entitled to add such a breach to other actions which taken together may cumulatively amount to a breach of the implied obligation of trust and confidence (*Lewis* v *Motorworld Garages Ltd* [1985] IRLR 465; cf. *Reid* v *Camphill Engravers* (supra) in which a failure to pay in accordance with relevant Wages Council orders was characterised as a continuing breach).

The latest time for the employee to accept the employer's repudiatory breach is at the close of his unfair dismissal claim before the industrial tribunal (*Shook* v *London Borough of Ealing* [1986] IRLR 46). There is, however, no need for an employee to take the precaution of an express reservation of the right to accept repudiation when the employer had expressly allowed the employee time to make up his mind (*Bliss* v *South East Thames Regional Health Authority* [1985] IRLR 308). (On equivocal conduct in accepting a repudiation, see *Spencer* v *Marchington* [1988] IRLR 392.)

13.3.3.8   Constructive dismissal and fairness   It is a commonly held misconception that a constructive dismissal is necessarily an *unfair* dismissal. The fact that there has been a breach of contract (however fundamental) by the employer means only that the employee has crossed the first hurdle of establishing dismissal. For the employer may still seek to justify the reason for his actions. The proper question was formulated in *Savoia* v *Chiltern Herb Farms Ltd* [1982] IRLR 166, as whether, though in fundamental breach of contract, the employer had in all the circumstances behaved fairly, and the facts of the instant case provide a good example of a positive answer to that question. The employers decided to reorganise their business operation after one of their foremen died. They moved the applicant to the dead man's position because they had certain complaints about his performance in his previous job. He refused what was described by the employers as a 'promotion', claiming that it would expose him to conjunctivitis. The Court of Appeal found that the reorganisation was necessary and that the employers had in the circumstances done all that they could to ease the changeover by offering him a higher salary. On the other hand, he had refused to undergo a medical so that they could judge whether his claims of potential sickness were genuine. Thus the constructive dismissal was fair. (See also *Stephenson & Co. (Oxford) Ltd* v *Austin* [1990] ICR 609.)

The EAT has naturally indicated that cases of this sort will be rare (*F.C. Shepherd & Co. Ltd* v *Jerrom* [1985] IRLR 275, overturned on appeal on other matters). Moreover, it is perverse of an industrial tribunal to decide that an employee has been constructively dismissed because he has received a disciplinary penalty out of all proportion to the offence he had committed and still decide that he has been treated fairly in all the circumstances. Waite J said that, 'Considerations of fairness on the one hand and the considerations affecting constructive dismissal on the other are two sides of the same coin' (*Cawley* v *South Wales Electricity Board* [1985] IRLR 89).

13.3.4 Statutory extensions of dismissal

There are several circumstances in which the notion of an employer termination has been widened beyond the common law, because of potential injustice if these situations lie outside the concept of dismissal. There are four statutory enlargements in favour of the employee, although the first two have some counterpart at common law.

13.3.4.1 Leaving early If the employee is under notice of dismissal but wishes to leave early in order to take another job, it would be unjust to hold that he has thus resigned and lost his rights to claim unfair dismissal and redundancy payments. Section 136(3) of ERA 1996 enacts that there is still a dismissal for redundancy provided that the employee gives notice in writing that he wishes to leave prematurely.

If, on the other hand, the employer does protest, an industrial tribunal must decide, on the justice and equity of the whole case, whether to grant a redundancy payment, and if so, in part or in full. For redundancy this declaration of intention must be given within the 'obligatory period of notice', that is, within the period of notice required to be given either 1by statute or under the employee's contract. The EAT has wavered between applying this requirement strictly and flexibly. It does not apply to unfair dismissal (*Ready Case Ltd* v *Jackson* [1981] IRLR 312; see also *CPS Recruitment* v *Bowen and Secretary of State for Employment* [1982] IRLR 54), but there are similar provisions. By s. 95(2) of ERA 1996:

> (2)   An employee shall be taken to be dismissed by his employer for the purposes of this Part if—
> (a)   the employer gives notice to the employee to terminate his contract of employment, and
> (b)   at a time within the period of that notice the employee gives notice to the employer to terminate the contract of employment on a date earlier than the date on which the employer's notice is due to expire;
> and the reason for the dismissal is to be taken to be the reason for which the employer's notice is given.

The passing on of a copy of an originating application by the industrial tribunal to the employers did not constitute notice by the employee to terminate the contract within the forerunner to s. 95(2) (*Cardinal Vaughan Memorial School Governors* v *Alie* [1987] ICR 406).

Example   Gibbon tells Harvey in week 1 that he will be dismissed in week 14. Harvey has been employed for 10 years, and gives notice that he wishes to leave in week 10. The industrial tribunal then has to decide in its discretion whether he still deserves redundancy pay. There are as yet no reported cases on how the discretion will be exercised. If Harvey seeks to leave in week 2 he forfeits all rights to redundancy pay because this is not within the 'obligatory notice period', i.e. 10 weeks for 10 years (= 14-10) which begins in week 4.

13.3.4.2 Taking a new job for a trial period After dismissal from one position with an employer, the employee may take on another with the same or an associated employer with the aim of trying it out. This is particularly so where the termination is by way of the employer's repudiatory conduct. It would penalise the employee who attempted in this way to make a new start if he were not still entitled to claim the statutory remedies if things did not work and he then resigned. At common law, the courts thus often characterise the employee's acceptance of such new post after a breach of contract by an employer as qualified and conditional. If he leaves after a reasonable period for assessing the new job, the termination relates back to the employer's original action of repudiation and he can claim his rights. This notion of a 'trial period' is found in ERA 1996, s. 138(3). An employee has four weeks to decide whether he accepts the new terms (para. 14.3.2) and this relates to actual weeks and not weeks in which work was carried on (*Benton* v *Sanderson Kayser Ltd* [1989] IRLR 19). This may be extended, although rather restrictively, only for the purposes of retraining (s. 138(6)).

Example Blake worked as a machinist for Coleridge Textiles Ltd for 10 years. The managing director announces that henceforth he must do the work of presser. He is not sure whether to take it; the statute gives him four weeks to make up his mind. If in that time he decides he does not like it, he can still claim unfair dismissal and/or redundancy pay.

The EAT has, however, held that the legislation does not supplant the common law but rather is concurrent with it. This gives the employee a reasonable time to make up his mind before the four weeks begin to run, and may make the statutory provision virtually redundant. Thus, in *Air Canada* v *Lee* [1978] IRLR 392, the airline moved staff including the applicant from one office to another in breach of her contract. She agreed to go on a trial basis, but after two months she decided it was not for her and left. The EAT held that she had never finally and without qualification accepted the proffered new terms and conditions. The statutory trial period had never begun to run, since the termination of her original contract only occurred 'when, before the expiry of the reasonable period of the common law trial period, she made up her mind that she did not wish to continue to be employed'. In *Turvey* v *C. W. Cheyney and Sons Ltd* [1979] IRLR 105, the EAT said that the trial period 'provides an improvement on rather than a restriction of the employee's common law rights'.

13.3.4.3 Lay-off and short-time An employee may be left in a state of limbo by his employer, being given little or no work but not actually dismissed. Again statute protects him, but in this respect only allows him to claim he has been dismissed for the purposes of redundancy payments (see para. 4.10.5). Sections 147–152 of ERA 1996 provide a species of 'implied dismissal' where, for at least four consecutive weeks or at least six weeks spread over not more than 13 weeks, the employee is 'laid off' (no work provided at all for a week — s. 147(1)), or on 'short-time' (i.e. where the employee receives less than half a week's pay, not including bonus — s. 147(2)). The employee may then give notice in writing equivalent to the period of notice required by his contract to his employer, indicating his intention to claim a redundancy payment (see *Walmsley* v *C. & R. Ferguson Ltd* [1989]

IRLR 112). The employer may react by issuing a counter-notice that he will contest the claim, in which case the matter will be referred to an industrial tribunal to decide whether 'it was reasonably to be expected that the employee would . . . not later than four weeks after that date enter on a period of not less than thirteen weeks during which he would not be laid off or kept on short-time for any week' (ERA 1996, s. 152(1)(a)).

13.3.4.4 Implied termination Section 136(5) of ERA 1996, which provides for 'implied termination', is unique to redundancy, and reads:

> (5) Where in accordance with any enactment or rule of law—
>   (a) an act on the part of an employer, or
>   (b) an event affecting an employer (including, in the case of an individual, his death),
> operates to terminate a contract under which an employee is employed by him, the act or event shall be taken for the purposes of this Part to be a termination of the contract by the employer.

Again this is an example of the statute rather obscurely building on the quicksand of the common law. It comprises all the automatic dismissals already discussed in Chapter 12, including death of a personal employee, dissolution of partnership, appointment of a receiver and liquidation of a company, and also a frustrating event affecting the employer such as a fire at his sole place of business, or his imprisonment. This means that even though the employee is not entitled to claim unfair or wrongful dismissal, he may be eligible for redundancy payment, although only if the frustrating event affects the employer.

13.3.5 Terminations which are not dismissals

One of the main aims of the unfair dismissal provisions is to give employees a hearing of their grievances on their merits; to narrow the concept of dismissal nips that policy in the bud. However, although the statutory concept of dismissal is somewhat wider than at common law, many terminations still do not qualify. The common law devices adopted by the employers to exclude dismissal are primarily the following:

(a) termination by agreement or pure resignation;
(b) discharge by performance;
(c) frustration;
(d) self-dismissal (already discussed in para. 9.3.2).

13.3.5.1 Agreement to terminate If there is a genuine agreement between employer and employee that a contract of employment shall terminate, there is no dismissal, either at common law or by statute (*Strange Ltd v Mann* [1965] 1 All ER 1069). The same is true where there is a 'pure' resignation, rather than one in response to a repudiatory breach of the employer, i.e. constructive dismissal. The main problem lies in identifying and construing any purported agreement, and assessing when it is reached under employer pressure, in which case it will be a dismissal. A statement that it was in the mutual interest of both parties to part company after the employers had given notice, is not, however, enough to amount to agreed termination (*Harman v Flexible Lamps Ltd* [1980] IRLR 418). Moreover, tribunals have been astute not to recognise a consensus where the initiative has clearly been taken by the employer. In *McAlwane* v *Boughton Estates Ltd* [1973] 2 All ER 299, Donaldson J said that tribunals 'should not find an agreement to terminate employment unless it is proved that the employee really did agree with full knowledge of the implications it had for him'. Another example is *Hellyer Bros Ltd* v *Atkinson* [1992] IRLR 540, where the applicants had been employed on the respondent's trawlers under crew agreements which provided for termination by mutual consent or notice. At appropriate times, the employees would be asked to sign off. The Court of Appeal upheld the tribunal's decision that there was a dismissal. The employees had been requested to sign off in the particular case on terms which allowed the conclusion that they had not been freely consenting to termination but rather had been signifying their assent to a *fait accompli*, that is termination by the employer.

The following principles apply:

(a)   The claim that the employee agreed to leave has been made in several cases where the applicant was dismissed but wanted to go early to take another job. Donaldson J thought it would 'be a very rare case' where such agreement overrode the dismissal 'when one realises the financial consequences to the employee of such an agreement'. Indeed, the learned judge thought 'the possibility might appeal to a lawyer more than to a personnel manager'.

As already mentioned, this has been codified by statute and the reason why *McAlwane* and *Lee* were decided on the common law rules was that the employees did not satisfy provisions in the legislation then effective which demanded written notice to the employer. These have now been amended for unfair dismissal.

(b)   An agreement to terminate does not fall foul of s. 203 of ERA 1996. In *Logan Salton* v *Durham CC* [1989] IRLR 99 Wood J said:

In our judgment . . . in the resolution of industrial disputes, it is in the best interests of all concerned that a contract made without duress, for good consideration, preferably after proper and sufficient advice, and which has the effect of terminating a contract of employment by mutual agreement (whether at once or on some future date) should be effective between the contracting parties, in which cases there will probably not have been a dismissal within [ERA 1996, s. 95].

13.3.5.2   Discharge by performance   In *Brown* v *Knowsley BC* [1986] IRLR 102, the EAT held that the appellant was not dismissed when her employment as a temporary lecturer came to an end because the course she was teaching at Prescot College of Further Education did not receive further funding. Her contract of employment stated that 'the appointment will last only as long as sufficient funds are provided either by the Manpower Services Commission or by other firms/sponsors to fund it'. The contract thus terminated automatically on the non-happening of the event specified (see *Ironmonger* v *Movefield Ltd t/a Deering Appointments* [1988] IRLR 461, where the applicant was engaged as clerk of works for a specific construction project).

13.3.5.3   Resignation under threat   The courts are understandably reluctant to hold that there has been no dismissal where an employee is prevailed upon to resign under threat that if he does not do so he will be dismissed (*Scott* v *Formica Ltd* [1975] IRLR 104, *East Sussex CC* v *Walker* (1972) 6 ITR 280). However, the fact that disciplinary proceedings are in train does not in itself amount to sufficient pressure (*Staffordshire CC* v *Donovan* [1981] IRLR 108) to avoid an agreed termination.

In *Sheffield* v *Oxford Controls Co.* [1979] IRLR 133, the EAT sought to lay down some principle to be applied in such cases by means of a rule of causation. The applicant had been a director and employee of the respondent company until a boardroom row, when he was threatened that, if he did not resign, he would be dismissed. After negotiations he signed an agreement to leave in return for certain financial benefits, including £10,000, but then claimed to have been unfairly dismissed. The EAT began from the premise that an employee who resigns as a result of a threat is dismissed, but there was in this case an intervening cause: 'He resigns because he is willing to resign as the result of being offered terms which are to him satisfactory terms on which to resign.'

There was, however, held to be a dismissal in *Caledonian Mining Co. Ltd* v *Bassett and Steel* [1987] IRLR 165, where the industrial tribunal found that the employers had falsely inveigled the employees to resign with the express purpose of avoiding liability for redundancy payments.

13.3.5.4 Words of resignation The courts look for unambiguous, unequivocal words to amount to a resignation (*Hughes* v *Gwynedd AHA* [1978] ICR 161) and did not so find, for example, where the employer knew that the employee was a mental defective and that he uttered the words in the heat of the moment after an argument (*Barclay* v *City of Glasgow DC* [1983] IRLR 313). Ordinarily the employer can treat unambiguous words of resignation as a termination of employment, but if there are special circumstances, such as the particular character of the employee, the employer should allow reasonable time for facts to come to light which may cast doubt on the proposition that these were intended to be words of resignation. Should the employer not investigate the matter, he might not be able to rely on those words (*Kwik Fit (GB) Ltd* v *Lineham* [1992] IRLR 156). An employer may not rely on a letter of resignation which the employee is induced by the employer to sign on the basis of a misrepresentation (*Makin* v *Greens Motor (Bridgport) Ltd, The Times*, 18 April 1986).

13.3.5.5 'Voluntary redundancy' It is often difficult to characterise on which side of the line an application for voluntary redundancy falls. In *Birch* v *University of Liverpool* [1985] ICR 470, the applicants wrote to the University making formal application to retire under a premature retirement compensation scheme and received a reply that, 'The University hereby confirms that it is in the managerial interests for you to retire . . . and requests you to do so . . .'. The EAT overturned the industrial tribunal's decision that, since the offer of retirement was subject to the University's approval, it was the giving of that approval which terminated their employments. Instead, both in form and in substance, this was a termination by agreement.

An unusual situation arose in *Morley* v *C. T. Morley Ltd* [1985] ICR 499. The applicants, a father and two sons, were employees and sole directors of a family business. The father volunteered for redundancy and later he and his sons decided that the company should cease trading. Their claims for redundancy payments were rejected by the industrial tribunal on the ground that this was an agreed termination. The EAT pointed out that their status as directors and employees was quite different and that this was a dismissal in the normal way by the company.

In *Scott* v *Coalite Fuels and Chemicals Ltd* [1988] IRLR 131, there was no dismissal when employees who had received notice of redundancy accepted voluntary early retirement as an alternative thereto. It was not the case that once a notice of dismissal has been served to take place on a future date, nothing which occurs in the interim can alter that position.

Section 140 of EPCA 1978 (now ERA 1996, s. 203) was not relevant, since the agreement to resign was only relevant to a consideration whether one of the applicable provisions of the Act had been satisfied, rather than an exclusion or limitation of rights under the Act itself.

There may be a dismissal where an employee agrees to continue working on a temporary basis beyond the date on which his redundancy notice expired pending a permanent position becoming available (*Mowlem Northern Ltd* v *Watson* [1990] IRLR 500).

13.3.5.6   Late return after extended leave   Where an employee signs an undertaking that he will return to work on a stated date in order to gain extended leave of absence from his employment, and he fails to come back at the agreed time, the trend of authority has ebbed and flowed between accepting the undertaking as an agreed termination and viewing it as a dismissal.

In *British Leyland Ltd* v *Ashraf* [1978] ICR 979, the applicant sought five weeks unpaid leave of absence to visit his native Pakistan and this was granted subject to the condition that there be no further holiday. He signed a form stating: 'You have *agreed* to return to work on 21/2/77. If you fail to do this, your contract of employment *will terminate* on that date.' (author's italics). The EAT took this at face value as a subsidiary contract and agreed termination, stressing the employee's full knowledge of its terms and open acceptance. It had in mind the fact that these were conditions attached to a *privilege*, since the applicant had no contractual right to leave of absence; they also pointed out that such failure to return was becoming a widespread problem in British industry. The danger of this approach is that it might be extended to an agreement that the contract would end if the employee was late even once. These draconian implications, which would mean that in such circumstances the employee could not test the fairness of the employers' action since there would be an agreed termination, were indeed spelt out by Phillips J who commented that the employer's argument would prevail even if the return flight 'had been hijacked or diverted because of fog'.

The case was, however, distinguished in *Midland Electric Manufacturing Co. Ltd* v *Kanji* [1980] IRLR 185, on somewhat narrow grounds. Mrs Kanji's leave of absence was conditional on the 'warning that if you fail to return . . . for whatever reason the company will *consider* that you have terminated your employment'. She failed to return on the specified date because of illness, but the EAT found the letter a mere statement of intention by the employer as to what would happen in the event of failure to return, i.e. she would be dismissed. Referring to the more ambiguous wording here than in *Ashraf,* Slynn J was generally mindful 'not to defeat the objects of the employment protection legislation or in particular to fly in the face of the intent of s. 140 of the Employment Protection (Consolidation) Act 1978 [now ERA 1996, s. 203]'.

A return to the *Ashraf* line was signalled by the EAT in *Igbo* v *Johnson Matthey Chemicals Ltd* [1985] IRLR 189. Mrs Igbo was given leave of absence after signing a 'contractual letter for the provision of extended holiday absence'. It stated *inter alia* that 'if you fail [to return on 28 September 1983], your contract of employment will automatically terminate on that date'. She did not report to work on that day but instead sent a medical certificate. This was an agreed termination and Kilner Brown J thought that an employer could rely on automatic termination if:

(a)   he could produce a document in writing to comply with s. 4 of EPCA 1978 (now ERA 1996, s. 203) as a written statement of terms;

(b)   he set out clearly in plain words that failure to attend, for whatever reason, on the appointed day would result in automatic termination;

(c)   he obtained the signature of the employee to words that he or she agreed with and he or she accepted those terms;

(d)   he could produce evidence that the effect of the document and the signature thereto was explained at the time to the employee and that he understood and accepted it. In this respect the learned judge thought that EPCA 1978, s. 140 (now ERA 1996, s. 203) was not a problem since the agreement was in conformity with ss. 1 and 4 of EPCA 1978. The Court of Appeal, however, thought that such an agreement fell foul of s. 140 and was void ([1986] IRLR 215). The effect of the agreement was to 'limit' the operation of ss. 54 and 55 of EPCA 1978 (now ERA 1996, ss. 94 and 95). It was not correct, as was argued by the respondents, that the effect of the arrangement was only to bring the contract to an end by consensual termination, that is, otherwise than by one of the ways which constitute dismissal for the purposes of s. 54 of the Act (now s. 94). If this were so the Act could be circumvented by a term in the contract of employment that if the employee were late for work in any day, no matter for what reason, the contract would automatically terminate. Their Lordships took the opportunity to overrule the *Ashraf* case. (See also *Barkat Ali* v *Joseph Dawson Ltd,* EAT 43/89.)

13.3.6   Frustration

There is no dismissal where the contract of employment is frustrated. The general contractual test is that:

> Frustration occurs whenever the law recognises that without default of either party a contractual obligation had become incapable of being performed because the circumstances in which the performance is called for would render it a thing radically different from that which was undertaken by the contract.

(Lord Radcliffe in *Davis Contractors Ltd* v *Fareham UDC* [1956] AC 696.)

Donaldson J formulated the appropriate test in employment cases in *Marshall* v *Harland & Wolff* [1972] ICR 101, primarily with cases of long sickness or injury in mind, when he asked:

> Was the employee's incapacity to work of such a nature that further performance of his obligations in the future would be either impossible or be something radically different from that which he undertook under the contract?

(See also *Williams* v *Watsons Luxury Coaches Ltd* [1990] IRLR 164.)

13.3.6.1   Frustration and ill health   Donaldson J went on to counsel tribunals to take account of (author's italics):

(a)   *The terms of contract* including the provisions as to sickness pay. The whole basis of weekly employment may be destroyed more quickly than that of monthly employment and that in turn more quickly than annual employment. When the contract provides for sickness pay, it is plain that the contract cannot be frustrated so long as the employee returns to work, or appears likely to return to work, within the period during which such sick pay is payable. But the converse is not necessarily true. The right to sick pay may expire before the incapacity has gone on for so long as to make a return to work impossible or radically different from the obligations undertaken under the contract of employment.

(b) How long the employment was *likely to last* in the absence of sickness. The relationship is less likely to survive if the employment was inherently temporary in its nature or for the duration of a particular job, than if it was expected to be long-term or even life long.

(c) The *nature of the employment* — where the employee is one of many in the same category, the relationship is more likely to survive the period of incapacity than if he occupies a key post which must be filled and filled on a permanent basis if his absence is prolonged.

(d) The *nature of the illness* or injury and how long it has already continued and the prospects of recovery. The greater the degree of incapability and the longer the period over which it has persisted and is likely to persist, the more likely it is that the relationship has been destroyed.

(e) The period of *past employment* — a relationship which is of long standing is not as easily destroyed as one which has but a short history.

(In *Williams* v *Watsons Luxury Coaches Ltd* (supra) Wood J added another consideration, i.e. the terms of the contract as to the provisions for sickness pay, if any, and also a consideration of the prospects of recovery). Donaldson J said that: 'these factors are interrelated and cumulative, but are not necessarily exhaustive of those which have to be taken into account.' In particular they are hardly appropriate to short-term periodic contracts where the more likely event anyway is dismissal on short notice (*Harman* v *Flexible Lamps Ltd* [1980] IRLR 418; cf. *Notcutt* v *Universal Equipment (London) Ltd* [1986] 1 WLR 641).

In *Egg Stores (Stamford Hill) Ltd* v *Leibovici* [1977] ICR 260 Phillips J added four extra considerations in this context:

(a) the *need* of the employer for the work to be done, and the need for a replacement to do it;

(b) the risk to the employer of *acquiring obligations* in respect of redundancy payments or compensation for unfair dismissal to the replacement employee;

(c) whether *wages* have continued to be paid;

(d) the *acts and the statements* of the employer in relation to the employment, including the dismissal of, or failure to dismiss, the employee.

He asked as a matter of common sense: 'Has the time arrived when the employer can no longer be expected to keep the absent employee's place open?' and this was a similar conclusion to that which had to be reached in determining whether a dismissal for sickness was fair.

In *Chakki* v *United Yeast Co. Ltd* [1982] ICR 140, the EAT declared that in order to determine whether an 11-month prison sentence frustrated the contract, it was essential to determine precisely when it had become commercially necessary for the employer to decide whether or not to employ a replacement; to have regard to what, at that time, a reasonable employer would have considered the probable duration of the employee's absence and to consider whether the employers had acted reasonably in employing a permanent rather than a temporary replacement.

It is instructive to distinguish two cases on either side of the thin frustration/dismissal line. In *Hart* v *Marshall* [1977] ICR 539, the employee was a night service fitter, and described by his employer as a 'key worker'. In 1974 he contracted industrial dermatitis which continued for about 20 months, and during this time regularly sent to his employers medical certificates of his unfitness to work, which were received without comment. On his recovery, he was told that he had been permanently replaced. The EAT decided that, because he was such an important employee 'this is one of the comparatively rare cases where it can be said that a short-term period contract of employment has been frustrated'.

On the other side of the line stands *Hebden v Forsey and Son* [1973] ICR 607. The respondents ran a small factory employing two sawyers — Mr Forsey's son, and the applicant, who had worked for the business for many years when he had to undergo an operation on one of his eyes. Since the necessary equipment was not available at the local hospital, it would be two years before he could work again. Mr Forsey, with whom the applicant maintained frequent contact, agreed with him that it would be better if he waited on the sick list, drawing state benefits until his eye was fully recovered. There was insufficient work for him to do when he was completely fit, so that he could not return. On these facts it was held that the employer had not discharged the burden resting on him to prove frustration; he had in fact dismissed him. Frustration cannot occur because of the risk of *future* illness (*Converfoam (Darwen) v Bell* [1981] IRLR 195).

13.3.6.2 Other cases of frustration Although illness is the most common frustrating event, contracts have also been held to be frustrated when the employee was:

(a) called up to the army (*Morgan v Manser* [1948] 1 KB 184);
(b) interned as an enemy alien (*Unger v Preston Corporation* [1942] 1 All ER 200);
(c) suspended from medical practice for 12 months and his name temporarily removed from the register (*Tarnesby v Kensington, Chelsea and Westminster AHA* [1981] IRLR 369).

There have been differing views of the effect of imprisonment. In *Hare v Murphy Brothers* [1974] ICR 603 and *Harrington v Kent CC* [1980] IRLR 353, the contract was held to be frustrated, even though the latter sentence was quashed on appeal. In *Norris v Southampton City Council* [1982] IRLR 141, the EAT held that imprisonment was a self-induced event. The contract was also frustrated when the employers' property was destroyed by fire (*Taylor v Caldwell* (1863) B & S 826).

Frustration must be due to an occurrence 'for which neither contracting party was in any way responsible' (Salmon LJ in *Denmark Productions Ltd v Boscobel Productions Ltd* [1969] 1 QB 699 at 725). In respect of the prison sentence in *Hare's* case, the court addressed the employer's argument that the frustration was self-induced because the employee committed an assault by noting that the actual disabling event was the sentence of the court.

In *F.C. Shepherd & Co. Ltd v Jerrom* [1986] IRLR 358 a four-year apprenticeship was held to be frustrated by a Borstal sentence of six months. The Court of Appeal held that, contrary to the argument on behalf of the employee, what affected performance of the contract was the sentence of borstal training which was the act of the judge, and not of the employee himself. Thus the doctrine of self-induced frustration could not be applied to the case. Moreover, the apprentice should not be allowed to plead his own default in order to establish his right to claim compensation for unfair dismissal. *Hare's* case was not binding authority since the legal basis on which the court decided the case was not clear. Since the borstal sentence was a substantial break in the period of training, the contract was radically different from what had been envisaged and had been frustrated. The employee thus could not make an application for unfair dismissal.

The difficulty found in the decisions on ill health shows the inappropriateness of the concept of frustration in this area. In the sphere of commercial contracts it provides a narrow exception, a defence, to parties who are strictly liable for contracts. It assumes that each side knows its rights and can take advice on major unforeseen circumstances. In unfair dismissal and redundancy, however, it breaks down the statutory definition of fault, and leaves complainants fettered at the starting line for statutory protections.

13.4   EFFECTIVE DATE OF TERMINATION

Where there has been a dismissal, it is necessary to pinpoint the actual date of termination of employment for several statutory purposes:

(a)   the *qualifying period* before a claim may be made, e.g. two years for unfair dismissal (para. 11.1);

(b)   the *date of calculation* of the employee's week's pay for redundancy payment and unfair dismissal basic award (para. 14.5);

(c)   when an employee may seek *written reasons* for his dismissal (para. 13.5.2);

(d)   the *age* for the purposes of exclusion from employment protection (para. 11.7);

(e)   to decide whether the employee has brought his *claim in time*, since the claim must be submitted within three months or six months of that date for unfair dismissal or redundancy respectively (para. 11.2).

This important stage is called the 'effective date of termination' in the unfair dismissal provisions and the 'relevant date' for redundancy payments. In most respects the concepts coincide and the appropriate dates can both best be considered in the following series of nine propositions (ERA 1996, s. 92(6)):

(a)   Where the employee is dismissed *with notice* the effective/relevant date is the date on which the notice expires. Where the employer orally gives the employee 'a week's notice from now', this means seven clear days excluding the day on which the employee started work and was actually given notice (*West* v *Kneels Ltd* [1987] ICR 146).

(b)   Where the dismissal is *lawfully without notice*, that is, summary dismissal for gross misconduct, the effective date of termination is the date on which the termination takes *effect*. It is not sufficient that the employer *characterised* a dismissal as one on the grounds of gross misconduct. According to the Scottish EAT in *Lanton Leisure Ltd* v *White and Gibson* [1987] IRLR 119, it was necessary to inquire into the merits of whether there was *in fact* such misconduct as would enable the employer to terminate without notice.

The date of termination has generally been assumed to be the date when the employer tells the worker he is fired, but there was scope for argument since this implicitly assumes that the dismissal automatically terminates the contract. If, instead, it is brought to an end only on the other party's acceptance of that breach, it may be that the correct effective date is the date of acceptance of the repudiation. In *Robert Cort & Son Ltd* v *Charman* [1981] IRLR 437, the EAT held that, on the authorities, the effective date of termination was that of repudiation. The contract terminated at once for this purpose irrespective of whether, as a matter of contract law, the employer ought to have given notice. The EAT was not attracted to the contention that this was inconsistent with the decision in *London Transport Executive* v *Clarke* [1981] IRLR 166 (see para. 12.3.2). A further recommendation for this decision was that there should be no doubt or uncertainty as to the proper date; if, however, the employee's approach was accepted, it would depend on the 'legal subtleties of the law of repudiation and the employee would not be able to understand the position'. In *Stapp* v *The Shaftesbury Society* [1982] IRLR 326 the EAT held that the effective date of termination was the actual date of termination of the employment whether the employment was lawfully or wrongfully terminated.

The EAT dealt with a situation where communication is not instantaneous in *Brown* v *Southall and Knight* [1980] IRLR 130, and held that the effective date of termination when dismissal was by letter was generally the date when the letter was *received.* Slynn J stated:

> In our judgment the employer who sends a letter terminating a man's employment summarily must show that the employee has actually read the letter or at any rate had a reasonable opportunity of reading it. If the addressee of the letter to the employee does not deliberately open it or goes away to avoid reading it he might well be debarred from saying that notice of his dismissal had not been given to him.

The case was approved in *Hindle Gears Ltd* v *McGinty* [1984] IRLR 477. This still leaves open the question of an employee who is away on holiday abroad when a letter is sent, but does not receive it (*Heera* v *John Laing Services Ltd,* EAT 600/80).

The following principles have been established:

(i)   The situation where the employer dismisses an employee immediately but with a payment to cover the period of notice which should have been given was considered in *Adams* v *GKN Sankey Ltd* [1980] IRLR 416. The EAT considered this payment in effect as damages for instant dismissal, so the effective date was that of dismissal itself.

(ii)   An employee can waive the right to notice so that the contract is brought to an end immediately (*Secretary of State for Employment* v *Staffordshire CC* [1989] IRLR 117).

(iii)   In construing an ambiguous letter of dismissal, the tribunal should adopt the construction which a reasonable employee receiving it would understand (see *Chapman* v *Letherby & Christopher Ltd* [1981] IRLR 440, *TBA Industrial Products* v *Morland* [1982] ICR 686, *Leech* v *Preston BC* [1985] ICR 192, *Stapp* v *The Shaftesbury Society* (supra)).

(iv)   The date on which tax form P45 is sent to the employee has no significance at all for these purposes (*London Borough of Newham* v *Ward* [1985] IRLR 509).

(v)   A clear notice of immediate dismissal takes effect at once, notwithstanding that the employers did not operate the disciplinary procedure properly. The employee may have an action at common law against the employer but that does not affect the effective date of termination (*Batchelor* v *British Railways Board* [1987] IRLR 36).

(vi)   It does not matter that the meeting at which the decision was taken to dismiss was not properly constituted (*Newman* v *Polytechnic of South Wales Students Union* [1995] IRLR 72).

(c)   Where notice *should* have been given longer than that which is given or where no notice is given, the proper *statutory minimum notice* is added to the actual date of the dismissal (ERA 1996, s. 97(2)); (see also *Secretary of State for Employment* v *Staffordshire CC* (supra)). The reasoning behind this general statutory extension is that it is unfair that by the employer's own wrongful act in terminating employment in breach of the statutory notice requirement he might reduce the employee's entitlement, whether the amount of basic award or taking into account a later pay rise in calculating the week's pay.

Moreover, if the employee's contract provides that a period longer than the statutory minimum notice must be given to the particular employee, still only the minimum number of weeks decreed by statute need be added if notice has not in fact been given to the employee.

This does not apply to summary and constructive dismissal nor the determination whether the employee had reached his normal retiring age (*Slater and Secretary for Employment* v *John Swain Ltd* [1981] IRLR 303), nor to:

(i)   the start of the three or six-month period for bringing a complaint to a tribunal;

(ii)   written reasons for dismissal;

(iii)   whether the employee was striking at the material time;

(iv)   the start of the seven-day period for an application to the industrial tribunal for interim relief;

(v)   redundancy consultation;

(vi)   the requirement that an offer of renewal or re-engagement be made before the ending of the employment.

Example   Jack's contract provides for eight weeks' notice. He is dismissed after 100 weeks of employment without notice. He can claim a statutory extension to week 101 because he is entitled by ERA 1996 to one week's minimum notice, but cannot add the eight weeks. If the employer in fact gives eight weeks' notice, the effective date of termination is week 108 and he would be entitled then to claim unfair dismissal.

(d)   Where the contract is for a *fixed term*, the date is when the fixed term expires.

(e)   Where the employee is dismissed by reason of a *strike* or other industrial action even when terminated by notice the effective date is the date on which the notice is given; otherwise the above rules apply, as appropriate.

(f)   Appeals — the courts have generally rejected attempts to extend the effective date of termination to cover periods during which an appeal is being heard under an internal disciplinary procedure. In *J. Sainsbury Ltd* v *Savage* [1980] IRLR 109, this refusal was notwithstanding that the internal disciplinary procedure provided for 'suspension without pay' pending appeal. Brightman LJ stated that: 'If an employee is dismissed . . . on terms that he then ceases to have the right to work under the contract of employment and that the employer ceases likewise to be under an obligation to pay the employee, the contract is at an end' (approved by the House of Lords in *West Midland Co-operative Society Ltd* v *Tipton* [1986] IRLR 112; see also *Crown Agents* v *Lawal* [1978] IRLR 542).

The same result was reached in *Board of Governors, National Heart and Chest Hospital* v *Nambiar* [1981] IRLR 196, even though in that case the employee was paid for a 10-month period while his appeal was pending. The principle was held not to depend on any express term being included in the contract (*Howgate* v *Fane Acoustics Ltd* [1981] IRLR 161), instead resting on the policy reason of the uncertainty of any other course, and the desirability that speed be of the essence in enforcing employment rights.

(g)   Where the employee gives a *counter-notice* to take effect before the employer's notice expires, the effective date of termination is that of the counter-notice (*Thompson* v *GEC Avionics* [1991] IRLR 488).

(h)   Agreement—in special circumstances the parties may agree that a particular date is to be taken as the effective date of termination (*Crank* v *HMSO* [1985] ICR 1) and this may be a date after the notice of redundancy termination was due to expire (*Mowlem Northern Ltd* v *Watson* [1990] ICR 751).

(i)   The effective date for a constructive dismissal is not necessarily the date when the resignation takes effect; rather, it may be when the relationship of employer and employee has ceased. In the case in which this proposition was laid down the facts were such that the effective date was properly when the employee ceased to be director, and thereby chairman, of the company (*BMK* v *Logue* [1993] ICR 601).

13.5 THE REASON FOR DISMISSAL

Several cases have laid down the principles in defining the reason for dismissal:

(a)   The onus of proof is on the employer to establish on the balance of probabilities the reason for dismissal. If the employer cannot prove any reason for dismissal, the dismissal is automatically unfair (*Adams* v *Derby City Council* [1986] IRLR 163).

(b)   The employer's reason for dismissal, of which the industrial tribunal must go on to determine the fairness, is 'the set of facts known to the employer or beliefs held by him which cause him to dismiss the employee' (*Abernethy* v *Mott Hay and Anderson* [1974] ICR 323, as approved in *W. Devis & Sons Ltd* v *Atkins* [1977] AC 931). This does not necessarily imply automatic acceptance by the tribunal of the reason put forward by the employer if there are grounds to think that it was not the real cause. Thus, many employers claim that they are dismissing for reasons of redundancy although this is in reality a cloak of getting rid of particular employees. The 'reason for dismissal' must be that 'uppermost in the mind of the employer at the time of dismissal'.

(c)   The reason may, however, incorporate a series of incidents and not only one event (e.g. *Turner* v *Wadham Stringer Commercials (Portsmouth) Ltd* [1974] ICR 277), and where there is more than one ground the tribunal must establish what was the *principal* factor motivating the dismissal (*Carlin* v *St Cuthberts Co-op Association Ltd* [1974] IRLR 188).

(d)   When the employer mistakenly construes as a resignation an equivocal expression of an intention to resign by the employee, that may constitute a reason for dismissal (*Ely* v *YKK Fasteners (UK) Ltd* [1994] ICR 164).

(e)   A reason cannot be treated as a sufficient reason for dismissal when it has not been established as true or that there were reasonable grounds on which the employer could have concluded that it was true (*Smith* v *City of Glasgow District Council* [1987] IRLR 326).

(f)   To be believed the employer must tell a consistent story, and may not put forward a different reason:

(i)   at the tribunal, from that which he stated in his Notice of Appearance; nor
(ii)   on appeal, from that relied upon before the industrial tribunal (*Nelson* v *BBC* [1977] ICR 694); nor
(iii)   on an internal appeal, from that initially tendered.

In *Monie* v *Coral Racing Ltd* [1981] ICR 109, the applicant was dismissed for dishonesty and he exercised his contractual right of internal appeal. This was heard by the managing director, who confirmed the dismissal, but since he found no evidence of dishonesty against Mr Monie, he gave as the reason that his failure to exercise the authorised cash control procedures justified dismissal. Their Lordships thought that the reason must be that which operated at the time of dismissal. The internal appeal made no difference. If the employer has no reason for dismissal such sacking is automatically unfair.

(g)   Alternative claims as to the reason are tempting but may be dangerous for the employer (*Murphy* v *Epsom College* [1983] IRLR 395). A tribunal is not entitled to find a dismissal fair on a ground not pleaded or argued where the difference in grounds goes to facts and substance of the case and where there would, or might have been, some substantial or significant difference in the way the case was conducted, had another reason been put forward. On the other hand, where the different grounds are different labels for the same facts (such as redundancy or some other substantial reason for dismissal), a tribunal is justified in finding that the true reason for dismissal was one which was not pleaded (*Hannan* v *TNT-IPEC (UK) Ltd* [1986] IRLR 165; *Burkett* v *Pendletons (Sweets) Ltd* [1992] ICR 407).

In *Hotson* v *Wisbech Conservative Club* [1984] IRLR 422 the employers' notice of appearance gave the reason for dismissal as 'inefficiency' but their representative at the tribunal agreed with the chairman's remark that 'in effect what you are claiming is that the [applicant] was dishonest'. The tribunal decided that the employee had been fairly dismissed on the ground of reasonably suspected dishonesty. The EAT would not let the decision stand since the suspicion must be stated at the outset by the employer. Whilst the employer would not be necessarily tied to a 'label' he put on the fact on which he relied, he could not substitute dishonesty for negligence at so late a stage. It did not give the employee sufficient opportunity to meet the challenge. The EAT in *Clarke* v *Trimoco Motor Group Ltd* [1993] ICR 238, said that where it is obvious to the employee what the real reason was for the dismissal, that does not render the dismissal unfair.

(h)   An industrial tribunal cannot pick out and substitute a reason for dismissal which was neither given nor entertained by the employer merely because the tribunal considers that it was a better reason or one which would justify dismissal whereas the employer's stated reason would not. The tribunal can, however, find that the reason proffered by the employer is not the real or principal reason provided that the employee shows that there is a real issue whether that was the true reason. The onus then shifts back to the employer to show his real reason (*Maund* v *Penwith DC* [1984] IRLR 24; see also *McCrory* v *Magee* [1983] IRLR 414).

In *Labour Party* v *Oakley* [1988] IRLR 34, the applicant's fixed-term contract as head of the Labour Party's Sales and Marketing Unit was not renewed, and she complained that her application for a new job was not fairly considered. The EAT allowed an appeal from the tribunal's finding of unfair dismissal on the ground that EPCA 1978, s. 57(3) (now ERA 1996, s. 98(4)) applied to the act of *dismissal* only and not to the manner of selection for a new job, which occurred after the act of dismissal. The Court of Appeal overturned the EAT's views. Since the tribunal had concluded that the Labour Party had 'made up its mind to get rid of the appellant and the restructuring was simply a pretext', a finding of unfair dismissal was appropriate.

13.5.1   Later discovered reason

The employer cannot dismiss for an insubstantial reason and then hunt round for misconduct to justify it. In this there is a vital distinction from wrongful dismissal where this is permissible (*Ridgway* v *Hungerford Market* (1835) 3 Ad & El 173, *Boston Deep Sea Fishing & Ice Co.* v *Ansell* (1888) 39 ChD 339). The rule in the statutory jurisdiction was clearly established by the House of Lords in the leading case of *W. Devis & Sons Ltd* v *Atkins* [1977] AC 931. The respondent, who managed the appellant's abattoir, was dismissed on the ground that he refused to implement his employer's purchasing policy. Later they found evidence of much dishonest conduct while he was employed, and sought to advance that as the reason for dismissal, even though they did not know of it at the time. Their Lordships thought that the statutory language that fairness must be determined 'having regard to the reason shown by the employers' could only mean the set of facts known to him *at the time of dismissal.* The overall effect of this decision is limited because, although they can have no influence on the reason and fairness, subsequently discovered matters may diminish the amount of compensation; in the *Devis* case itself no compensation at all was granted on the grounds that he suffered *no loss* (para. 13.18.4).

Moreover, what happens between the date of notice and expiry of notice, especially of a procedural nature, like hearings and appeals, *is* relevant. In *Rank Xerox (UK) Ltd* v *Goodchild* [1979] IRLR 185, the fact that appeals from employees were heard after the date of termination did not mean that aspects affecting their fairness could not be taken into account in determining reasonableness. Otherwise the procedural provisions at the heart of the unfair dismissal jurisdiction would be rendered unenforceable. The industrial tribunal can also take into account medical information about the employee which comes to light in the course of his appeal against dismissal (*Board of Governors, National Heart and Chest. Hospital* v *Nambiar* [1981] IRLR 196).

In *Stacey* v *Babcock Power Ltd (Construction Division)* [1986] IRLR 3 the EAT accepted that it was proper to consider matters occurring between the communication of dismissal and the effective date of termination, that is, when notice expired. In the instant case, the announcement of new orders during that period converted what would have been a fair dismissal for redundancy into an unfair dismissal. In *West Midlands Co-operative Society Ltd* v *Tipton* [1986] IRLR 112 the House of Lords re-emphasised that this included matters which came to the employer's knowledge on appeal from his initial decision to dismiss. The appeal is inextricably bound up with the employer's action of dismissal. Lord Bridge of Harwich could 'see nothing in the language of the statute to exclude from consideration [of] "equity and the substantial merits of the case" evidence relevant to show the strength or weakness of the real reason for dismissal which the employer had the opportunity to consider in the course of an appeal . . .'. Although the facts of the case concerned a contractually binding appeal, this principle applies also to a non-contractual appeal (*Greenall Whitley plc* v *Carr* [1985] IRLR 289, *Whitbread & Co. plc* v *Mills* [1988] IRLR 501).

13.5.2 Written reasons for dismissal

Statute facilitates the employee's discovery of the reasons for dismissal by according the right to a written statement of them. The employee can now under ERA 1996 request such written reasons if he is given notice of dismissal, is dismissed without notice or the employer does not renew his fixed-term contract (but not if he is constructively dismissed). He must also have completed two years' continuous employment with the employer (ending with the last complete week before the effective date of termination).

The employer must, if reasonably possible, reply to an employee's request for reasons within 14 days and give true and adequate particulars (ERA 1996, s. 92(2)) (on the meaning of 'true' see *Harvard Securities plc* v *Younghusband* [1990] IRLR 17)). This document is available as evidence before an industrial tribunal (s. 92(5)), and an employer may be effectively estopped from denying the accuracy of the particulars given. If the statement as given by the employer is untrue or inadequate, the industrial tribunal may decide what the employer's reasons really were, looking at all the evidence and drawing inferences, and make a declaration as to the true reason.

The following principles have been established by the cases:

(a) The written statement must 'at least contain a simple statement of the essential reasons for the dismissal' (*Horsley Smith and Sherry Ltd* v *Dutton* [1977] IRLR 172), otherwise 'no particular technicalities are involved and no particular form is required. It can be perfectly simple and straightforward'.

(b)   A written statement can refer to letters previously written to an employee, according to the Court of Appeal in *Kent CC* v *Gilham* [1985] IRLR 16. The respondent dinner ladies refused to accept terms put forward by the county council to economise on the school meals service. The council sent out an explanatory letter to the dinner ladies explaining the reasons for the changes and a week later gave them notice of termination referring back to the earlier letter, which was held legitimate. Furthermore, it was adequate compliance with the Act to send the reasons to their representative rather than to the employees personally.

(c)   The employee may complain to an industrial tribunal if there has been: (i) an *unreasonable refusal* by the employer to provide the necessary written statement; or (ii) the statement given is untrue or inadequate. Any claim must be made during notice of dismissal or within three months after the effective date of termination, although the industrial tribunal has the usual discretion to extend the time limit if it was not reasonably practicable to comply.

(d)   A claim may be brought before the tribunal only if a specific request for reasons had been made of the employer (*Catherine Haigh Harlequin Hair Design* v *Seed* [1990] IRLR 175).

(e)   If the employer is found to be in default of his obligations, the tribunal must award two weeks' pay to the employee. The provision is generally strictly construed since according to the EAT in *Charles Lang & Sons Ltd* v *Aubrey* [1977] IRLR 354, 'it is a penal section. Parliament was intending to impose a penalty on a contumacious employer who decides he is not going to give the employee the required statement'. Thus, in *Lowson* v *Percy Main & District Social Club and Institute* [1979] IRLR 227, the employers were not held to have acted unreasonably where the failure was due to a lack of communication with their solicitors and as soon as the solicitors realised that the employee's request had not been complied with, the company gave the reasons.

(f)   A general request to the employer by the police not to communicate with the employee was not a reasonable ground for refusing to provide reasons (*Daynecourt Insurance Brokers Ltd* v *Iles* [1978] IRLR 335); but in *Brown* v *Stuart Scott & Co.* [1981] ICR 166, it was held reasonable not to give reasons where the employer had a conscientiously formed belief that there was no dismissal.

13.5.3   Statutory reasons for dismissal

The statute proceeds to divide reasons for dismissal into three categories.

(a)   *Potentially fair reasons:* these are by far the most important category demanding an analysis of the overall fairness of the dismissal. They are thus necessary but not sufficient conditions for showing a dismissal was fair. Those specified in ERA 1996, s. 98 are:

   (i)   a reason related to the *capability or qualification* of the employee for performing work which he was employed by the employer to do (para. 13.7);
   (ii)   a reason related to the *conduct* of the employee (para. 13.8);
   (iii)   *redundancy* (para. 13.10);
   (iv)   that the employee could not continue to work in his position without contravention by him or his employer of a *duty or restriction* imposed by or under an enactment (para. 13.12);

(v)   some *other substantial reason* of a kind such as to justify the dismissal of an employee holding the position which that employee held (para. 13.11).

(b)   *Automatically fair reasons:*

(i)   where the decision was taken 'for the purpose of safeguarding *national security*', and a certificate signed by or on behalf of a minister is conclusive evidence of this fact (see *Council of Civil Service Unions* v *Minister for the Civil Service* [1985] IRLR 28);

(ii)   dismissal whilst taking part in a *strike* or other industrial action when all strikers are sacked (para. 13.14), or in the case of unofficial action even though there is selection amongst those dismissed and those retained).

(c)   *Automatically unfair reasons since the industrial tribunal has no jurisdiction to consider the issue of fairness:*

(i)   dismissal of a woman because she is *pregnant* or for a reason connected therewith (para. 9.4);

(ii)   dismissal for *trade union membership or activities*, or because of refusal to join a trade union or because the employee was not a member of any trade union or of one of a number of particular trade unions or had refused or proposed to refuse to become or remain a member, or by reason of health and safety activities (para. 20.1);

(iii)   dismissal because of a *conviction* which is spent under the Rehabilitation of Offenders Act 1974 (para. 13.13);

(iv)   where the reason for dismissal was connected with a transfer of undertaking (Regulation 8, Transfer of Undertakings (Protection of Employment) Regulations 1981 (SI 1981 No. 1794)) save where there are 'economic, technical or organisational reasons entailing changes in the workforce' (para. 16.5);

(v)   dismissal of a protected shop worker or an opted-out shop worker in respect of Sunday working;

(vi)   dismissal for assertion of a statutory right (para. 13.16);

(vii)   dismissal of an occupational pension fund trustee because he performed his functions;

(viii)   dismissal of an elected representative because he performed any functions or activities as such.

13.6   FAIRNESS OF DISMISSAL

In all cases which are not rendered automatically unfair or automatically fair, once the tribunal has determined the reason for the dismissal, s. 98(4) of ERA 1996 provides as follows:

(4)   Where the employer has fulfilled the requirements of subsection (1), the determination of the question whether the dismissal is fair or unfair (having regard to the reason shown by the employer)—

(a)   depends on whether in the circumstances (including the size and administrative resources of the employer's undertaking) the employer acted reasonably or unreasonably in treating it as a sufficient reason for dismissing the employee, and

(b)   shall be determined in accordance with equity and the substantial merits of the case.

First, there is no burden of proof of fairness (see *Abbots & Standley* v *Wesson-Glynwed Steels Ltd* [1982] IRLR 51, *Murray MacKinnon* v *Forno* [1983] IRLR 7, *Post Office Counters* v *Heavey* [1990] ICR 1). An appeal is likely to be upheld if the industrial tribunal misdirected itself that the employer must prove fairness (*Howarth Timber (Leeds) Ltd* v *Biscomb* [1986] IRLR 52). Secondly, tribunals must have regard to the size of the respondent employer's undertaking (see e.g. *Henderson* v *Granville Tours Ltd* [1982] IRLR 494), although the small size of an employer cannot excuse it, for example, from making any effort at all to consult over a redundancy (e.g. *De Grasse* v *Stockwell Tools Ltd* [1992] IRLR 269); it may, however, affect the nature or formality of the consultation process.

The following principles apply on appeal as developed in the cases:

(a) The fairness of a dismissal is essentially a question of fact, and the industrial tribunal as an industrial jury is best equipped to deal with it, using its industrial experience and knowledge of local conditions. Tribunals have been directed by appeal bodies to approach the matter with common sense and common fairness, eschewing technicalities. The cases which follow are offered merely as examples of the approach of tribunals, and more particularly the Employment Appeal Tribunal and Court of Appeal, in so far as they have offered guidance. They are not binding precedents (*Jowett* v *Earl of Bradford (No. 2)* [1978] ICR 431).

(b) The Court of Appeal has recognised that two tribunals may on similar facts reach opposite conclusions, yet this does not necessarily amount to an error of law to be corrected by the appeal bodies (*Kent CC* v *Gilham (No. 2)* [1985] ICR 233). The Court of Appeal set the tone for the current orthodox position in *Bailey* v *BP Oil (Kent Refinery) Ltd* [1980] IRLR 287, where Lawton LJ said:

> The wording [of s. 98(4) of ERA 1996], which is clear and unambiguous, requires the tribunal, which is the one which hears the evidence, not the one which hears the legal argument, to look at every aspect of the case . . . .. Each case must depend on its own facts. In our judgment, it is unwise for this court or the Employment Appeal Tribunal to set out guidelines and wrong to make rules and establish presumptions for industrial tribunals to follow or take into account.

(See also *Retarded Children's Aid Society* v *Day* [1978] ICR 437, *Thomas & Betts Manufacturing Co. Ltd* v *Harding* [1980] IRLR 255, *Kingston* v *British Railways Board* [1984] IRLR 146, *Spook Erection* v *Thackray* [1984] IRLR 116.) In *The County Council of Hereford and Worcester* v *Neale* [1986] IRLR 168, the Court of Appeal re-emphasised the narrowness of the perversity jurisdiction. May LJ said (at para. 45) 'Deciding these cases [of unfair dismissal] is the job of industrial tribunals and when they have not erred in law, neither the EAT nor this Court should disturb their decision unless one can say in effect: "My goodness, that was certainly wrong" '. (See also *British Telecommunications plc* v *Sheridan* [1990] IRLR 27.) The Court of Appeal in *Piggott Brothers & Co. Ltd* v *Jackson* [1991] IRLR 309, went even furher and pronounced that the EAT should only interfere with the decision of an industrial tribunal if that conclusion was not a permissible option, that is that it was not supported by *any* evidence. Reasonableness is to be characterised as a mixed issue of fact and law but the factual element predominates (but cf. the powerful *dicta* of the EAT in *East Berkshire HA* v *Matadeen* [1992] IRLR 336).

The approach of the EAT has largely reflected the character of its President for the time being. Browne-Wilkinson J pioneered the use of 'guidelines', concerned as he was that there was little uniformity between different tribunals. Such guidelines were distillations of good industrial practice: 'properly instructed industrial tribunals would know [them] to be the principles which, in current industrial practice, a reasonable employer would be expected to adopt'. In the *locus classicus* of this position, *Williams* v *Compair Maxam Ltd* [1982] IRLR 83, the EAT formulated five guidelines for a redundancy dismissal which it would 'expect . . . to be departed from only where good reason is shown to justify such departure'. It counselled, however, that there should 'be no attempt to say that an industrial tribunal which did not have regard to or give effect to one of these factors has misdirected itself in law. Only in cases where a genuine case for perversity on the grounds that the decision flies in the face of commonly accepted standards of fairness can be made out are these factors directly relevant' (see also *Grundy (Teddington) Ltd* v *Plummer and Salt* [1983] IRLR 98, for a powerful defence of the use of guidelines). In fact, guidelines of this nature have been laid down to cover the most important aspects of misconduct and procedure in *British Home Stores Ltd* v *Burchell* [1978] IRLR 379 and *British Labour Pump Co. Ltd* v *Byrne* [1979] ICR 347, and had been expressly approved by the Court of Appeal in *W. Weddel & Co. Ltd* v *Tepper* [1980] ICR 286 and *W. & J. Wass Ltd* v *Binns* [1982] ICR 486 respectively.

Waite J, however, deprecated the use of guidelines or even citation of previous authorities to tribunals in *Anandarajah* v *Lord Chancellor's Department* [1984] IRLR 130. He said that Court of Appeal decisions had 'upheld the right of industrial tribunals to be their own guides on the issue of reasonableness'. It was not right in the infinite variety of circumstances which might occur to 'constrain the criteria by which a person's conduct is judged'. Past cases could only be of illustrative value, and 'industrial tribunals are not required and should not in our view be invited, to subject the authorities to the same analysis as a court of law searching in a plethora of precedent for binding or persuasive authority'. Indeed, 'it should seldom be necessary (and may sometimes even be unwise) for an industrial tribunal to frame its decision by reference to any direction other than the express terms of the statute'. (See also *Kearney & Trecker Marwin Ltd* v *Varndell* [1983] IRLR 335; *Siggs & Chapman (Contractors) Ltd* v *Knight* [1984] IRLR 83.)

Popplewell J followed very much in the footsteps of Waite J but Wood J was more prepared to give detailed guidance to industrial tribunals, as seen in cases such as *Whitbread & Co. plc* v *Mills* [1988] IRLR 501 on the conduct of appeals and *Linfood Cash & Carry Ltd* v *Thomson* [1989] IRLR 235 on the use of evidence of informers.

(c)   The EAT is reluctant to interfere with the decision of a tribunal provided that the tribunal directed itself by statute, however much the EAT might disagree with the outcome. It is astute not to allow issues of fact to be dressed up as issues of law. Together with the limited role of industrial tribunals as reviewers of the decisions of employers, this has added great strength to managerial prerogative. Tribunals are regarded by appeal bodies not as being in the seat of management but rather as having to decide whether what management did was reasonable. It is for management to lay down the standards, and only if dismissal was not 'within the range of reasonable responses of the reasonable employer' should a tribunal decide that the dismissal is unfair (*British Leyland UK Ltd* v *Swift* [1981] IRLR 91; also *Vickers Ltd* v *Smith* [1977] IRLR 11, *N.C. Watling & Co. Ltd* v *Richardson* [1978] ICR 1049, *Iceland Frozen Foods Ltd* v *Jones* [1982] IRLR 439, reiterated in *Securicor Ltd* v *Smith* [1989] IRLR 356, *Scottish Midland Cooperative Society Ltd* v *Cullion* [1991] IRLR 261, *British Railways Board* v *Jackson* [1994] IRLR 235).

(d)   It is important that the industrial tribunal considers fairness in the light of matters known, or which should have been known, to the employer at the time of dismissal and not on the basis of the evidence which comes out at the industrial tribunal for the first time

(*Linfood Cash & Carry Ltd* v *Thomson* [1989] IRLR 235; *Dick* v *Glasgow University* [1993] IRLR 581).

(e) The appeal body will need to have it clear from the tribunal's decision that they have directed themselves by reference to s. 98(4) of ERA 1996 (*United Distillers* v *Conlin* [1992] IRLR 503).

It is difficult to put each case of dismissal into its proper pigeon hole, but the general approach here followed is to discuss the case law on each of the reasons given for dismissal, and then attempt a general overview of the procedures needed in most cases for a fair dismissal.

13.7 INCAPABILITY

The only guidance to be found in the ERA 1996 in relation to capability as a reason for dismissal is its definition to include 'skill, aptitude, health or any other physical or mental quality' (s. 98(3)(a)). 'Qualifications' means 'any degree, diploma or other academic, technical or professional qualification relevant to the position which [the employee] held' (s. 98(3)(b)). The ground put forward by the employer need only *relate to* capability. It need not prevent the employee performing all work of the kind he was employed to do (*Shook* v *London Borough of Ealing* [1986] IRLR 46). The relevant case law will be considered under the headings of: incompetence; health; and qualifications.

13.7.1 Incompetence

The general principle is that 'the employee's incapacity as it existed at the time of dismissal must be of such a nature and quality as to justify dismissal'. It need not, however, be reflected in any one particular incident but may arise from several indications (*Miller* v *Executors of John Graham* [1978] IRLR 309). Thus, in *Lewis Shops Group Ltd* v *Wiggins* [1973] ICR 335, a shop manageress was fairly dismissed when she left her shop dirty and untidy, cash registers failed to operate properly, and stock was not put away.

13.7.1.1 Evidence of incompetence Industrial tribunals find it difficult to measure intangible examples of poor work performance. In *Taylor* v *Alidair Ltd* [1978] IRLR 82, Lord Denning MR said:

Wherever a man is dismissed for incapacity or incompetence it is sufficient that the employer honestly believes on reasonable grounds that the man is incapable or incompetent. It is not necessary for the employer to prove that he is in fact incapable or incompetent.

The case had particularly strong facts since the applicant was an airline pilot, dismissed because he was thought to be at fault for a bad landing which had caused serious damage to the respondents' aircraft. According to the Court of Appeal, the employers had reasonably demanded a high degree of care and fairly dismissed him when he failed to measure up to it on one occasion. He was engaged in a special category of:

activities in which the degree of professional skill which must be required is so high, that the potential consequence of small departures from that high standard is so serious that the failure to perform in accordance with those standards is sufficient to justify dismissal.

The Court of Appeal specifically approved Bristow J's examples of other such employees as, 'the scientist operating the nuclear reactors, the chemist in charge of research into the possible effects of, for example, thalidomide, the driver of the Manchester to London Express, the driver of an articulated lorry full of sulphuric acid'. Few procedural safeguards were then necessary in relation to such employees, but in *ILEA* v *Lloyd* [1981] IRLR 394, the Court of Appeal restricted this principle to cases where safety was in question.

Most other cases will have less serious consequences, and there should then be some other evidence besides the *ipse dixit,* or opinion of the employer, of the employee's incapacity. The EAT did, however, say in *Cook* v *Thomas Linnell & Sons Ltd* [1977] IRLR 132, that: 'When responsible employers genuinely come to the conclusion that over a reasonable period of time a manager is incompetent, we think that it is some evidence that he is incompetent.' This recognises that although ideally there should be more objective assessments, when one is dealing with such imponderables as quality of management, this may be almost impossible to provide. The tribunal must, however, ensure that the employer's standards are attainable.

In *Gray* v *Grimsby Town FC* [1979] ICR 364, the EAT accepted a football club manager's assessment of a player's capabilities in the first team. The industrial jury were hardly in a position to review his decision. (See also *Hooper* v *Feedex* Ltd [1974] IRLR 99.) Evidence of staff and consumer complaints (*Dunning and Sons (Shopfitters) Ltd* v *Jacomb* [1973] ICR 448), or a fall off in trade, even though not directly attributable to the applicant's failure (*Cook* v *Thomas Linnell and Sons Ltd* (supra)), may assist as evidence.

13.7.1.2 Incompetence and procedure One of the most difficult procedural questions in unfair dismissal is how far the stringent guidance found in the ACAS Code on Disciplinary Practice and Procedure, mainly provided for dealing with conduct cases, should apply to dismissal on the grounds of incapacity. This goes to the heart of the policy behind such procedural requirements; if they are enacted because warnings and hearings might lead the employer to change his mind, they are unlikely to be of much value in relation to those employees who have shown themselves manifestly incapable of doing the job in any event. If, on the other hand, the intention is to give the employee a chance to prove or improve himself there is no reason to distinguish between incompetence and misconduct. It is, in fact, often difficult in practice to draw the line. The result is that, according to the NIRC in *James* v *Waltham Holy Cross UDC* [1973] IRLR 202 (author's italics):

An employer should be very slow to dismiss upon terms that an employee is incapable of performing the works which he is employed to do without first *telling the employee* of the respects in which he is failing to do his job adequately, *warning him* of the possibility or likelihood of dismissal on this ground, and giving him an *opportunity to improve* his performance.

13.7.1.3 Appraisal Without proper appraisal the employer may not be able to prove that he has adequately taken a reasonable view of the employee's incapacity. This is particularly important in cases at opposite ends of the spectrum of experience, that is:

(a) where a long service employee has to adapt to new methods; and

(b) in the case of a probationer who will need to know what standard he is required to meet.

In *Post Office* v *Mughal* [1977] IRLR 178, Cumming Bruce J formulated these tests for industrial tribunals:

Have the employers shown that they took reasonable steps to maintain appraisal of the probationer throughout the period of probation, giving guidance by advice or warning when such was likely to be useful or fair; and that an appropriate officer made an honest effort to determine whether the probationer came up to the required standard having informed himself of the appraisals made by supervising officers and any other facts recorded about probationers?

A dismissal of a probationer was subsequently held unfair where the employing authority did not realise his status for the first 17 months (*ILEA* v *Lloyd* [1981] IRLR 394).

13.7.1.4 Warnings   A warning is less vital in the case of incapability than for misconduct. It is most important where the required level of performance is uncertain, and independent judgment thereof difficult. Sir Hugh Griffiths graphically gave the reason in *Winterhalter Gastronom Ltd* v *Webb* [1973] IRLR 120, thus:

There are many situations in which a man's apparent capabilities may be stretched when he knows what is being demanded of him; many do not know that they are capable of jumping a 5-barred gate until the bull is close behind them.

Where the prospects of an employee improving are next to nil, however, a warning and opportunity of improvement can be of no benefit to the senior employee and may constitute an unfair burden on the business (*James* v *Waltham Holy Cross UDC* (supra); cf. *McPhail* v *Gibson* [1976] IRLR 254). This is also the case in situations with very serious consequences, such as a gaming inspector who failed to notice a serious fraud being conducted under his nose (*Turner* v *Pleasurama Casinos Ltd* [1976] IRLR 151). There is no requirement to offer such an employee an alternative position (*Bevan Harris Ltd* v *Gair* [1981] IRLR 520). However, in other circumstances length of service may have the opposite effect in that dismissal may be too serious a sanction for a single act of negligence by an old employee (*Springbank Sand & Gravel Ltd* v *Craig* [1973] IRLR 278).

13.7.2 Health

Cases on dismissal through ill health demonstrate clearly the role of the unfair dismissal provision in mediating between the economic interest of keeping production moving and maximising profits, on the one hand, and humanitarian requirements on the other. The EAT in *Spencer* v *Paragon Wallpapers Ltd* [1977] ICR 301, most generally reconciled this tension by stating:

The basic question which has to be determined in every case is whether in all the circumstances the employer can be expected to wait any longer and if so how much longer . . .

for an employee to return. This is not so widely different from the test for frustration on account of sickness discussed earlier (para. 13.3.6) (see *Tan* v *Berry Brothers and Rudd Ltd* [1974] ICR 586). In neither case is there a fixed period the employer has to wait, each situation depending on its own facts.

The Court of Appeal in *Hooper* v *British Railways Board* [1988] IRLR 517 decided that if an employee is declared by his doctor to be fit for that work which he can reasonably be expected to do, he is not 'incapable' within the statutory definition even though he is not capable of returning to his own particular job on which he was in fact engaged before his absence through sickness.

13.7.2.1 Medical opinion and consultation with the employee The most important procedural requirement in health cases is that the employer take an informed view on the basis of proper medical information. The best practice includes consultation with the employee, as stressed in the leading case of *East Lindsey DC* v *Daubney* [1977] ICR 566, approved by the Court of Session in *A. Links & Co.* v *Rose* [1991] IRLR 353. There the employer council's own physician asked a doctor to examine the employee and as a result of his short advice recommended retirement. The procedure was inadequate since the employers had not seen the medical report and had not extended to Mr Daubney the opportunity to obtain and present his own version. The EAT thought that such requirements were far from futile since:

> Discussion and consultations will often bring to light facts and circumstances of which the employers were unaware and which will throw new light on the problem, or the employee may wish to seek medical advice which, brought to the notice of the employer's medical advisers, will cause them to change their opinion.

The medical evidence must be more detailed than a mere statement of unfitness if the employer is to take the necessarily 'rational and informed decision'; but dismissal is a personnel and not a medical decision, and in this the employer may have to use his own discretion in choosing between conflicting medical opinions (*BP Tanker Co.* v *Jeffries* [1974] IRLR 260). There is no countervailing duty on the employee to keep the employer informed as to his progress (*Mitchell* v *Arkwood Plastics (Engineering) Ltd* [1993] ICR 471).

It is irrelevant in considering the fairness of a sickness dismissal that the illness was caused by action of the employer (*London Fire & Civil Defence Authority* v *Betty* [1994] IRLR 384). The question is whether the employee at the time of dismissal was incapable of performing his job duties.

13.7.2.2 When discussion and consultation are unnecessary Before *Polkey* v *Dayton Services Ltd* [1988] ICR 142, tribunals had moved away from what they considered excessive requirements for consultation. In the landmark case of *Polkey* v *Dayton Services,* the House of Lords held that the one question which an industrial tribunal may not ask is whether the proper procedural protection would have made any difference to the decision to dismiss. This question may be relevant to a consideration of the amount of compensation to be awarded (see para. 13.18.4).

The Court of Appeal in *Hooper* v *British Railways Board* (supra), moreover, emphasised even after *Polkey* that the lack of consultation in a health case did not necessarily render a dismissal unfair. Tribunals have readily responded to the employer's problems where the contract specifically and reasonably calls for an employee of robust health: in one case the dismissal was fair without consultation because the employee had to labour in the North Sea in the depth of a West Highland winter constructing an oil production platform and working to a strict deadline. Further, the appropriate collective agreement clearly stated that if the employee was absent on two occasions, he would be considered unsuitable for continued employment (*Leonard* v *Fergus and Haynes Civil Engineering Ltd* [1979] IRLR 235).

13.7.2.3 Intermittent absences   The tribunals have also significantly lowered the procedural threshold where a series of *intermittent absences* apparently for illness cause serious hardship to the employer. In *International Sports Co. Ltd* v *Thomson* [1980] IRLR 340, the employee had been away for 25 per cent of her last 18 months' employment. She had submitted various medical certificates to cover these absences, specifying dizzy spells, anxiety and nerves, bronchitis, and virus infection. Four warnings were to no avail, and the company claimed that they were excused from having her examined by their doctor, because none of her illnesses could be subsequently and independently verified. The EAT agreed that this was a dismissal on the grounds of misconduct rather than ill health, and Waterhouse J said:

> What is required . . . is, firstly, that there should be a fair review by the employer of the attendance record and the reasons for it; and, secondly, appropriate warnings after the employee has been given the opportunity to make representation.

The EAT in *Rolls Royce* v *Walpole* [1980] IRLR 343, took a similar line and found the meagre requirements satisfied. The applicant's attendance record was around 50 per cent for the last three years of employment. He received several warnings, and even counselling to discover the reason for his absences, some two years before his actual dismissal, but, on termination, no medical evidence was sought. In an important statement of a principle, the EAT declared that:

> Frequently there is a range of responses to the conduct or capacity of the employee on the part of the employer, from and including summary dismissal downwards to a mere informal warning, which can be said to have been reasonable.

The employer's reaction could not be said to be outside this spectrum, and the dismissal was fair (see also *Lynock* v *Cereal Packaging Ltd* [1988] ICR 670).

A sick note from a doctor may not be conclusive of the genuineness of an employee's illness. In *Hutchinson* v *Enfield Rolling Mills Ltd* [1981] IRLR 318, the employee was held fairly dismissed without any procedure being followed when he was seen at a union demonstration in Brighton on a day when certified as off work by reason of sciatica. (See also *Patterson* v *Messrs Bracketts* [1977] IRLR 137.)

13.7.2.4 Other factors   While a medical opinion is normally necessary for fair dismissal in pure sickness cases, it is not quite sufficient. In determining whether the employer was reasonable, an industrial tribunal can here be expected to have particular regard to 'the size and administrative resources of the employer's undertaking', as directed by s. 98(4) of ERA 1996.

Amongst the several additional factors which the employer must weigh in the balance are:

(a)   The employee's past and likely future *service*.

(b)   The *likely duration* of the illness (*Luckings* v *May and Baker* [1975] IRLR 151), and how far this can be accurately predicted.

(c)   How readily a *temporary replacement* could be trained or recruited if necessary.

(d)   The *status* of the employee, since the more important his position the more likely that his dismissal will be fair (*Spencer* v *Paragon Wallpapers Ltd* [1976] IRLR 373).

(e)   Whether it is possible for the employee to perform some of his *functions from home*.

(f)   Whether the prospect of the job remaining open might be a major *promoter of recovery*.

(g)   Whether the results of the illness and in particular any *lasting disability* will prevent the employee in fact or by law doing his old job.

(h)   Whether reasonable alternative employment is available; if so, it should usually be offered. Thus, an employer was held to have acted unreasonably in not giving consideration to finding the employee a job in circumstances where although he was not fit to do shift work he could do a day job. Slynn P said here: 'Employers cannot be expected to go to unreasonable lengths in seeking to accommodate someone who is not able to carry out his job to the full extent.' (*Garricks Caterers Ltd* v *Nolan* [1980] IRLR 259; see *Hardwick* v *Leeds AHA* [1975] IRLR 319, *Shook* v *London Borough of Ealing* [1986] IRLR 46).

(i)   A contractual clause providing for a certain number of days off (*Smiths Industries Aerospace and Defence Systems* v *Brookes* [1986] IRLR 434). There may be complex collective agreements covering sickness absence which are incorporated into the individual contract of employment, and the industrial tribunal is bound to adopt the ordinary canons of contractual construction of the agreements, including the principle that an agreement cannot be construed in the light of the subsequent actions of the parties (*Hooper* v *British Railways Board* [1988] IRLR 517). The fact that the employee is dismissed while in receipt of his contractual entitlement to sick pay does not, however, make the termination automatically unfair. The only relevance of this right to payment is that its duration may be evidence of the period during which the business could do without the employee.

(j)   While an alternative position should be offered even if it is likely that the employee will refuse, e.g. because it carries a lower rate of pay, the authorities fall short of suggesting that there rests a duty on the employer to 'create a special job for an employee however long serving he may be' (*Merseyside & North Wales Electricity Board* v *Taylor* [1975] IRLR 60; see also *Spencer* (supra)), nor where to propose it would breach an agreement with the unions.

13.7.2.5   Other situations in which the employee's health may be relevant   There are three other situations in which health may be relevant:

(a)   Where health problems are manifested at work to the detriment of *working arrangements*. Thus an epileptic employee was held fairly dismissed by the Scottish EAT for 'some other substantial reason' when, after 20 years without problems, he suffered three fits in two years during which he violently attacked fellow employees (*Harper* v *NCB* [1980] IRLR 260).

(b)   The EAT has held that an employer cannot fairly dismiss an employee on the ground that there is a *risk* of a heart attack unless that risk is of such importance as to make it unsafe for the employee to continue in the job (*Converfoam (Darwen) Ltd* v *Bell* [1981] IRLR 195), which might include a sole wireless operator on a sea-going ship.

(c)   Failure to state illness in an *application* for a job may justify a dismissal if it is serious and job-related, e.g. mental illness (*O'Brien* v *Prudential Assurance Ltd* [1979] IRLR 140).

13.7.3   Qualifications

Although 'qualifications' is widely defined in ERA 1996, s. 98(3)(b), it does not extend to the personal characteristic of trustworthiness (*Singh* v *London Country Bus Services Ltd*

[1976] IRLR 176) and must be related to 'performing work of the kind which he was employed by the employer to do'. Thus in *Blue Star Ship Management Ltd* v *Williams* [1979] IRLR 16, lack of authorisation as a registered seafarer was irrelevant to the employee's position so that this could not be a reason for dismissal. The requirement of a clean driving licence need not be set out in a written contract of employment to be a qualification (*Tayside Regional Council* v *McIntosh* [1982] IRLR 272).

13.8 MISCONDUCT

Dismissals relating to misconduct cover a multitude of sins, and the cases will be discussed under the rubrics: breach of employer's reasonable orders and rules; and commission of criminal offences. Conduct must be action of such a nature, whether done in the course of employment or not, as to reflect in some way on the employer/employee relationship. The fact that an employee had caused damage to the employer's petrol pump did not in any way affect her capacity to perform her duties, and so did not amount to conduct under the Act (*Thomson* v *Alloa Motor Co. Ltd* [1983] IRLR 403; see also *Sonoco Capseals Lines* v *Keshwala*, EAT 580/88 on fighting outside work). The fact that an employee has been dismissed without notice cannot in itself render a dismissal unfair (*BSC Sports & Social Club* v *Morgan* [1987] IRLR 391).

13.8.1 Disobedience to reasonable instructions

There must be considered not only the nature of the order but the circumstances surrounding the giving of the order . . . and also the reason for not carrying out the order.

(Talbot J in *Union of Construction Allied Trades and Technicians* v *Brain* [1980] IRLR 357.)

The unfair dismissal jurisdiction maintains the important principle of the contract of employment that the employee must obey the lawful and reasonable instructions of the employer. There must, however, be a serious breach of the rules to justify dismissal just as at common law, and moreover, the employee must not only be *warned* as to the consequence of a breach of the rule, but also have an *opportunity to state his side of the story*. More generally, the ACAS Code of Practice for Disciplinary Practice and Procedures in Employment provided (1977, para. 5) that, 'if they are to be fully effective rules and procedures need to be accepted as reasonable by those who are to be covered by them and by those who operate them'.

13.8.1.1 Instructions and the contract The scope of lawful instructions must be determined primarily by construing the contract of employment. This may require analysis of the written statement of terms, custom and practice, works rules and collective agreement, particularly with regard to job duties, hours of work and location. Thus in *Deeley* v *BRE Ltd* [1980] IRLR 147, the original engagement gave the right to the respondent company's managing director to transfer the employee to whatever duties he saw fit. Although the advertisement referred to the applicant's post as Sales Engineer Export and he had always been engaged in export sales, a requirement to work on home sales was not in breach of contract. His dismissal for refusal to carry out these duties was thus fair.

If an employee is dismissed for refusing or failing to do something which was not within his contractual duties to do, the dismissal is likely to be unfair, although any compensation may be reduced because of the employee's contributory fault in failing to react reasonably in the circumstances. In *Redbridge LBC v Fishman* [1978] ICR 569, the applicant was appointed to be in charge of the resources centre at a large comprehensive school. At first she did little teaching, but the school's new headmistress informed her that henceforth she would have to take 18 English lessons a week; she refused and was dismissed, in the industrial tribunal's and EAT's view, unfairly, since she had been recruited for special duties which would largely absolve her from general teaching duties. The instruction was not within her contractual duties and she could reasonably refuse it.

Phillips J, however, warned against the imposition of a contractual strait-jacket in approaching this question. In particular, the employee's duties may be considerably wider than what he has actually been accustomed to do on a day to day basis. Flexibility may be called for on the part of the employee, particularly in a small business (*Glitz v Watford Electric Co. Ltd* [1979] IRLR 89, *Coward v John Menzies (Holdings) Ltd* [1977] IRLR 428, *Simmonds v Dowty Seals Ltd* [1978] IRLR 211).

13.8.1.2 Reasonableness of the instruction One important way in which the modern law differs from wrongful dismissal is that it focuses on the reasonableness of the employer's order as well as its legality by contract. In *UCATT v Brain* [1981] IRLR 225, the applicant employee was publications officer of the respondent union when a libel action was brought against him and the union in respect of articles in the union journal. As a part of its settlement, the applicant was required by the union to sign a statement that neither he nor any officers, servants or agents would repeat the defamatory statement, but he refused on the grounds that he would be thereby making himself liable for the acts of others over whom he had no control. His persistence in this stance led to his dismissal and the Court of Appeal upheld a finding of unfairness on the ground that the instruction was manifestly unreasonable. This points the difference from wrongful dismissal where the only question is whether the employer's order was contractual.

Determining the scope of fair dismissal for disobeying instructions is vital in delimiting the bounds of managerial prerogative. For example, *Boychuk v H. J. Symons Holdings Ltd* [1977] IRLR 395 suggests that an employer can still dictate his employee's appearance in the workplace. The applicant, an audit clerk, was held to have been fairly dismissed because of her insistence on wearing badges proclaiming her lesbianism. The EAT considered that: 'a reasonable employer . . . can be allowed to decide what upon reflection and mature consideration, can be offensive to the customers and the fellow employees'. In another case, it was held fair to dismiss a woman school cleaner who insisted on bringing her young child to school even though he distracted her attention from her work and had caused accidents (*Lawrence v Newham LBC* [1978] ICR 10).

As in the common law of wrongful dismissal, it is not fair to dismiss an employee where he refuses to obey an unlawful order. Thus, in *Morrish v Henlys (Folkestone) Ltd* [1973] ICR 482, the appellant was sacked for refusing to acquiesce in the alteration of accounts on drawing diesel oil from petrol pumps; and this was held unfair.

13.8.2 Rules

13.8.2.1 The need for clear rules The employer may codify the instructions and requirements for his employees into a series of disciplinary rules relating to everything from time sheets and attendance, to standards of appearance and rudeness. The employee's written statement of terms must include 'any disciplinary rules that apply' and the Code of

Practice on Disciplinary Practice and Procedure lays down detailed guidance (see para. 6.11.2). This is not to say that every 'i' need be dotted and every 't' crossed.

In *Pringle* v *Lucas Industrial Equipment Ltd* [1975] IRLR 266, the EAT said that 'if employers wish to dismiss automatically for certain misconduct which is short of inherently gross misconduct they must be able to show that management has unequivocally brought to the attention of employees what that conduct is and what its consequences will be'. To cover a series of offences in company rules does not, however, mean that matters falling outside its terms cannot merit dismissal.

It is reasonable for an employer to expect that his workforce are aware of the most obvious prohibitions. This was confirmed with respect to fighting in *C.A. Parsons & Co. Ltd* v *McLoughlin* [1978] IRLR 65. Although it was not included in the respondent company's rules as gross misconduct, Kilner Brown J thought that 'it ought not to be necessary for anybody, let alone a shop steward, to have in black and white in the form of a rule that a fight is something that is going to be regarded very gravely by management'. The effects here of an assault near machinery on the factory floor were obviously serious, but the position may be different when the action is not so grave. Thus in *Meyer Dunmore International Ltd* v *Rogers* [1978] IRLR 167, a summary dismissal for fighting was held to have been unfair and Phillips J declared:

> If employers wish to have a rule that employees engaged in what could properly and sensibly be called 'fighting' are going to be summarily dismissed, as far as we can see there is no reason why they should not have a rule provided — and this is important — that it is plainly adopted, that it is plainly and clearly set out, and that great publicity is given to it so that every employee knows beyond any reasonable doubt whatever that if he gets involved in fighting he will be dismissed.

The distinction between the *Parsons* and *Meyer* cases must be a matter of fact and degree, but at least three cases have emphasised the need for clear rules in regard to overstaying leave and drinking alcohol during working hours (*Hoover Ltd* v *Forde* [1980] ICR 239, *Dairy Produce Packers Ltd* v *Beverstock* [1981] IRLR 265, and *Distillers Co. (Bottling Services) Ltd* v *Gardner* [1982] IRLR 47).

Disciplinary rules are particularly important in emphasising to employees those less serious breaches which the employer is going to visit with the severe sanction of dismissal. In this way the rule acts as a preliminary warning. Instant dismissal has been considered fair following breach of clearly stated rules relating, for example, to clocking on (*Dalton* v *Burton's Gold Medal Biscuits Ltd* [1974] IRLR 45), and working for a competitor (*Golden Cross Hire Co. Ltd* v *Lovell* [1979] IRLR 267).

13.8.2.2   Where dismissal for breach of rules is unfair   Even where there is a disciplinary rule and it is broken, a tribunal is still likely to find a consequent dismissal unfair in the following situations, although each case depends on its own facts:

(a)   Where the rule breached is of *no relevance* to the employment (see *Greenslade* v *Hoveringham Gravels Ltd* [1975] IRLR 114).

(b)   Where the rule is *ambiguous:* thus Kilner Brown J in *Meridian Ltd* v *Gomersall* [1977] IRLR 425, found insufficiently precise a works notice that 'anyone found clocking cards on behalf of other personnel will render themselves *liable* to instant dismissal'. The authority of this decision has, however, been shaken by the opposite result by the EAT on similar facts in *Elliot Brothers (London) Ltd* v *Colverd* [1979] IRLR 92.

(c) Where the 'punishment' of dismissal does *not fit the 'crime'.* Thus in *Ladbroke Racing Ltd* v *Arnott* [1983] IRLR 154, where three betting shop employees were summarily dismissed for placing bets on behalf of relations in breach of a clearly stated rule in the respondent's disciplinary code, the tribunal's determination of unfairness was upheld by the EAT and the Court of Session on the grounds that instant dismissal was an unreasonable response in all the circumstances. The full extent of their misconduct was that one employee had placed just one bet for his brother on one occasion, the second occasionally for two old age pensioners, and the third was the office manager who had apparently condoned the practice. (See also *Richards* v *Bulpitt & Sons Ltd* [1975] IRLR 134.) In *Unkles* v *Milanda Bread Co.* [1973] IRLR 76, although rules existed to restrict smoking, dismissal for breach was too severe since the employee's conduct in breaking the rule was inadvertent not wilful.

Employers should normally take into account length of service when determining on the application of disciplinary rules. In *Johnson Matthey Metals Ltd* v *Harding* [1978] IRLR 248, an employee with 15 years' unblemished service was dismissed when found in possession of a fellow worker's wrist watch six months after it had been lost. The EAT held that the amount of previous years' service was 'plainly a matter to be taken into consideration' and held that the dismissal was unfair. Past work did not, however, weigh against the serious and proved misconduct in *AEI Cables Ltd* v *McLay* [1980] IRLR 84, where the applicant had made false claims for reimbursement for diesel fuels and had been presenting such fraudulent vouchers for the last two years.

(d) Where there is no semblance of *consistency* in application of the rules. It may be that breaches of clear disciplinary rules are waived with such regularity that an employee is lulled into a false sense of security. Employers often acquiesce, for example, in breaches of rules prohibiting drinking in the lunch hour or leaving the night shift early when all allocated work has been completed. Several decisions have stressed that clear warning is necessary if there is to be a 'purge' on a particular breach which has not before been visited with disciplinary sanction:

(i) In *Post Office* v *Fennell* [1981] IRLR 221, the employee was summarily dismissed after assaulting a fellow employee in the works canteen. His case was that many other workers had been guilty of similar offences but were not punished in this way. The Court of Appeal upheld a decision that the dismissal was thus unfair for that reason. The statutory reference to equity and the substantial merits of the case comprehended the concept that employees who behave in much the same way should receive similar punishments. (See also *Parr* v *Whitbread & Co. plc* [1990] ICR 427.)

(ii) In *Hadjioannou* v *Coral Casinos Ltd* [1981] IRLR 352, the EAT limited the applicability of this case by stating that an appeal to consistency was only relevant when:

(1) there was evidence that employees had been led to believe that certain categories of conduct will either be overlooked or at least not dealt with by dismissal;

(2) evidence in relation to other cases supports the inference that the employer's purported reason for dismissal was not the real reason; and

(3) the circumstances in other cases were truly parallel.

Here these conditions were not fulfilled so that the EAT upheld a finding by an industrial tribunal that the appellant's dismissal for socialising with customers was in breach of company rules and was fair (see also *Trusthouse Forte (Catering) Ltd* v *Adonis* [1984] IRLR 382, *Securicor Ltd* v *Smith* [1989] IRLR 356; cf. *W. & J. Wass Ltd* v *Binns* [1982] IRLR 283).

(iii)   It is no answer to a claim on the ground of consistency for the employer merely to assert that the decisions in the cases of other employees were taken by different employees or agents of the employer (*Cain* v *Leeds Western HA* [1990] IRLR 168, [1990] ICR 585). (On the tension between the desirability of consistency and flexibility, see *United Distillers* v *Conlin* [1992] IRLR 503.)

(iv)   The employer should consider truly comparable cases of which he has knowledge, or of which he ought reasonably to have known, but not every case of leniency should be considered a deviation from declared policy (*Procter* v *British Gypsum Ltd* [1992] IRLR 7).

(e)   Where the employer did not consider the facts of the *individual case* but simply dismissed because it was his policy to do so in the class of cases concerned, e.g. assault (*Taylor* v *Parsons Peebles NEI Bruce Peebles* [1981] IRLR 119).

(f)   Where nothing is done for some time and the employee is then suddenly faced with *a stale allegation* (*Allders International Ltd* v *Parkins* [1981] IRLR 68, *Refund Rentals Ltd* v *McDermott* [1977] IRLR 59). In *Marley Homecare Ltd* v *Dutton* [1981] IRLR 380, it was held to be unfair to inform an employee of the result of test purchases which pointed to the applicant cashier's dishonesty seven days after the event. She could not then be expected to remember the particular incident, and the EAT suggested that it would be much fairer to suspend the suspect at the time, so that she could identify the transaction, albeit that a disciplinary hearing might not be effected until some time later. Moreover, a dismissal may be unfair because of delay in bringing disciplinary proceedings even though there was no evidence that delay had prejudiced the employee's position (*RSPCA* v *Cruden* [1986] ICR 205).

13.8.3   Offences

13.8.3.1   Does commission of the offence merit dismissal?   The tribunals and courts draw a distinction between offences committed at work and those committed outside. Whether the commission of a criminal offence outside his job merits an employee's dismissal depends above all on its relevance to the individual's duty as an employee. The tribunal should take into account: the *status* of the employee; the *nature* of the offence; the employee's *past record;* his access to *cash;* and proximity to members of the *public*. Thus in *Rentokil* v *Mackin* [1989] IRLR 286, for example, dismissal for theft of a milkshake from a customer was held to be unfair.

The 1977 Code of Practice provided in para. 15(c) that:

[Criminal offences committed outside employment] should not be treated as automatic reasons for dismissal regardless of whether the offence has any relevance to the duties of the individual as an employee. The main considerations should be whether the offence is one that makes the individual unsuitable for his or her type of work or unacceptable to other employees. Employees should not be dismissed solely because a charge against them is pending or because they are absent through having been remanded in custody.

The EAT has emphasised that in these cases reasonable employers may reach different decisions, and 'it does not necessarily mean if they decide to dismiss they have acted unfairly because there are plenty of situations in which more than one view is possible' (*Trusthouse Forte Leisure Ltd* v *Aquilar* [1976] IRLR 251). It is also not a valid argument for the applicant that he has suffered already in the criminal courts by way of fine (*British Leyland (UK) Ltd* v *Swift* [1981] IRLR 91; see also *British Gas plc* v *McCarrick* [1991] IRLR 305). The EAT has concluded that a second offence of deliberate fraud by an employee on his employers so obviously strikes at the fundamental relationship of trust and confidence between the employer and employee that there would have to be some clear reason to justify a finding that the decision fell outside the range of reasonable responses open to an employer (*United Distillers* v *Conlin* [1992] IRLR 503). The employer is entitled to take into account aggravating factors such as poor disciplinary record (*London Borough of Harrow* v *Cunningham* [1996] IRLR 256).

Tribunals have as examples upheld as fair:

(a)   The dismissal of a film cameraman after a conviction of indecent assault on a young girl, since his employers would henceforth have to be selective in the assignments they might give him (*Creffield* v *BBC* [1975] IRLR 23).

(b)   Dismissal of lecturers who taught students between the ages of 16 and 18 when they were found guilty of gross indecency (*Gardiner* v *Newport County Borough Council* [1974] IRLR 262, and *Nottinghamshire CC* v *Bowly* [1978] IRLR 252). In *Wiseman* v *Salford City Council* [1981] IRLR 202, on similar facts, the EAT rejected the appellant's argument that it was self-evident that an employee who regarded his homosexual behaviour as no more than incautious and foolish could not be a risk to teenage boys in his charge. (See also *Saunders* v *Scottish National Camps Association Ltd* [1980] IRLR 174.)

(c)   Dismissal of a drama teacher for possessing and cultivating cannabis (*Norfolk CC* v *Bernard* [1979] IRLR 220; *Mathewson* v *R. B. Wilson Dental Laboratory Ltd* [1988] IRLR 512).

(d)   Dismissal of a shop assistant who had stolen from a nearby store (*Moore* v *C & A Modes* [1981] IRLR 71).

On the other hand, dismissal following a conviction for incest has been held unfair since it was 'an isolated incident, it had nothing to do with the applicant's work, his work did not bring him into contact with female staff' (*Bradshaw* v *Rugby Portland Cement Co. Ltd* [1972] IRLR 46).

An employee may be fairly dismissed where he conceals from his employer a criminal conviction imposed before his employment began (*Torr* v *British Railways Board* [1977] IRLR 185) or where the employee has been sentenced to three months' imprisonment for a serious offence (*Kingston* v *British Railways Board* [1984] IRLR 146).

13.8.3.2   Degree of proof   Tribunals have steered a middle course in relation to dismissal for offences, both at work and outside, between demanding such proof of guilt as would be necessary in a criminal court and allowing dismissal on suspicion. The crucial question (which applies to all misconduct cases) was formulated by Arnold J in *BHS Ltd* v *Burchell* [1978] IRLR 379, as whether the employer:

entertained a reasonable suspicion amounting to a belief in the guilt of the employee of that misconduct at that time . . . First of all, there must be established by the employer the fact of that belief; that the employer did believe it. Secondly, that the employer had in his mind reasonable grounds upon which to sustain that belief. And thirdly, we think that the employer at the stage at which he formed that belief on those grounds, at any rate at the final stage at which he formed that belief, had carried out as much investigation into the matter as was reasonable in all the circumstances of the case.

(See also *Scottish Special Housing Association* v *Cooke* [1979] IRLR 264, *ILEA* v *Gravett* [1988] IRLR 497.)

In approving this test in *Weddel and Co. Ltd* v *Tepper* [1980] IRLR 96, Stephenson LJ did, however, emphasise that belief on reasonable grounds entailed that employers must not 'form their belief hastily without making the appropriate enquiries' (cf. Griffiths J in *St Annes Board Mills* v *Brien* [1973] IRLR 309; see also *Trusthouse Forte Leisure Ltd* v *Aquilar* [1976] IRLR 251, *Trusthouse Forte Hotels Ltd* v *Murphy* [1977] IRLR 186, *Scottish Midland Cooperative Society Ltd* v *Cullion* [1991] IRLR 261). Similar principles were applied in the case of suspected serious negligence in *McPhie & McDermott* v *Wimpey Waste Management Ltd* [1981] IRLR 316, and generalised in *Distillers Co. (Bottling Services) Ltd* v *Gardner* [1982] IRLR 47, but are not in themselves rules of law. Indeed, *Burchell* should be understood as a 'guideline not a tram-line' (*Boys' and Girls' Welfare Society* v *McDonald* [1996] IRLR 129; *Scottish Daily Record Ltd* v *Laird* [1996] IRLR 665). It is, however, an error of law for an industrial tribunal to substitute its own view of the facts for those in the mind of the employer at the time of the dismissal (*British Gas plc* v *McCarrick* [1991] IRLR 305).

The need for a reasonable belief in the guilt of the employee is illustrated by *Ferodo Ltd* v *Barnes* [1976] IRLR 302. The applicant was dismissed when it was thought that he had committed an act of vandalism in the company's toilets. The fact that the employers could not prove that the employee had committed the offence was not relevant save as evidence that the employer acted reasonably or otherwise in concluding that the employee had so behaved. The vital question was the state of evidence and information known to the employer at the time of dismissal. Thus a dismissal may be fair even though a criminal court decides that the offence was not in fact committed by the applicant (*Harris (Ipswich) Ltd* v *Harrison* [1978] IRLR 382). One reason is that while the criminal court must be convinced of guilt beyond reasonable doubt, the industrial tribunal works on the less exacting standard of balance of probabilities (*Lees* v *The Orchard* [1978] IRLR 20). Conversely:

> If an employer thinks that his accountant may be taking the firm's money but he has no real grounds for so thinking, and dismisses him for that reason, he acts wholly unreasonably notwithstanding that it was later proved that the accountant had been guilty.

(*Earl* v *Slater and Wheeler (Airlyne) Ltd* [1972] ICR 508.)

While the law generally rejects blanket dismissals (*Scottish Special Housing Association* v *Cooke* [1979] IRLR 264, *Gibson* v *British Transport Docks Board* [1982] IRLR 278), there is a difference where the net of reasonable suspicion rests on the heads of *two* employees, and both may be dismissed. This was established in the difficult case of *Monie* v *Coral Racing Ltd* [1980] IRLR 464. The appellant worked for the respondent company as an area manager with control and supervision over 19 betting shops, and only he and his assistant knew the combination for the safe in the area headquarters. While Mr Monie was on holiday, his assistant discovered that £1,750 was missing from this safe. There were no indications that either the premises or the safe had been forcibly entered, and the respondent's security officer thus concluded that one or other, or both, must have been involved in the theft. The two were dismissed, and this decision was confirmed by a director. The ordinary application of the *Burchell/Weddel* test demanding reasonable belief in the applicant's guilt would result in a finding that both dismissals were unfair and the EAT so held.

On appeal, however, all three Lord Justices confined the *Burchell* principle to those cases in which only one employee is under suspicion. Here, 'looking at the matter as an ordinary businessman', Sir David Cairns thought that the industrial tribunal had correctly inquired 'whether there were solid and sensible grounds on which the employer could reasonably *infer or suspect* dishonesty' (author's italics), and had rightly answered in the affirmative. The fact that the two employees would have the right to be acquitted on a criminal charge of theft on this evidence was immaterial. It must be stressed that an employer will need to show that the most careful investigation has been undertaken. Moreover, it should not be forgotten in applying its principle that in *Monie* both suspects were in senior positions and handled money in a business in which security and honesty were obviously vital.

This principle was taken further in *Whitbread & Co. plc* v *Thomas* [1988] ICR 135, where three employees were dismissed who *might* have been responsible for stock losses at an off-licence. The EAT held that where an employer could not identify the individual or individuals responsible for an act or acts of commission or omission, an employer was entitled to dismiss a group of employees on grounds which would justify dismissing an identified individual, provided that the employer had carried out a proper investigation and could show that the acts had been committed by one or more of the group and each member of that group had been individually capable of having committed the acts complained of. (See also *Parr* v *Whitbread & Co. plc* [1990] IRLR 39, *Secretary of State for Scotland* v *Campbell* [1992] IRLR 263 and, in the case of the small employer, *Walker* v *Lakhdari t/a Mayfair Newsagency* [1990] IRLR 469.)

The converse of the principle is that where any one or more of a group of employees could have committed a particular offence or deed of misconduct, the fact that one was not dismissed does not make the dismissals thereby unfair, provided that the employer can demonstrate sensible grounds to differentiate between those dismissed and those not dismissed (although these factors do not have to be related to the relevant offence) (*Frames Snooker Centre* v *Boyce* [1992] IRLR 472).

13.8.3.3 Investigation There are no hard and fast rules governing an employer's investigations of criminal offences. The main principle was enunciated by Viscount Dilhorne in *W. Devis & Sons Ltd* v *Atkins* [1976] IRLR 314: 'It cannot be said that the employer acted reasonably . . . if he only did so in consequence of ignoring matters which he reasonably ought to have known.'

The ACAS Code states:

> When a disciplinary matter arises, the supervisor or manager should first establish the facts promptly before recollections fade, taking into account statements of any available witnesses. In serious cases consideration should be given to a brief period of suspension while the case is investigated, and this suspension should be with pay.

(See also *ILEA* v *Gravett* [1988] IRLR 497.) Often there will be agreed procedures for such fact finding processes and if these are followed the dismissal is likely to be fair (see *Bentley Engineering Co. Ltd* v *Mistry* [1978] IRLR 436).

There is no need for a long inquiry where, for example:

(a) a thief admits guilt or is caught red-handed (*Scottish Special Housing Association* v *Linnen* [1979] IRLR 265, *Parker* v *Clifford Dunn Ltd* [1979] IRLR 56, *Royal Society for the Protection of Birds* v *Croucher* [1984] IRLR 425);

(b) the employee makes a tacit acknowledgement of guilt; in *Parker Bakeries Ltd* v *Palmer* [1977] IRLR 215, a bread salesman was 20 loaves short in deliveries to one customer on four consecutive days and his agreement to pay back some of the money was taken as a tacit admittance of his guilt;

(c)   the employee has pleaded guilty to the criminal offence (in *P* v *Nottinghamshire CC* [1992] IRLR 362, to an offence of indecency).

The following principles apply to an employer's investigation, whether of an offence or breach of the employer's own internal rules:

(a)   Where there has been a confession and then a retraction by the employee, the tribunal should decide whether the employer behaved reasonably in relying on the admission (*University College at Buckingham* v *Phillips* [1982] ICR 318).

(b)   Where there are large numbers of alleged offenders, each case must still be dealt with individually (*Gibson* v *British Transport Docks Board* [1982] IRLR 228).

(c)   The Judge's Rules do not apply (*Morley's of Brixton Ltd* v *Minott* [1982] IRLR 270).

(d)   Where a complaint is received about an employee, the employer should inquire whether there has indeed been any misconduct and its gravity and not merely rely on the integrity of the complainant (*Henderson* v *Granville Tours Ltd* [1982] IRLR 494).

(e)   It is improper for police to be present at an internal inquiry without the foreknowledge and consent of the employee (*Read* v *Phoenix Preservation Ltd* [1985] IRLR 93).

(f)   Police statements may be taken into account even though they would be inadmissible in criminal proceedings; the weight to be attached to them is a matter for the industrial tribunal (*Dhaliwal* v *British Airways Board* [1985] ICR 513).

In *Linfood Cash & Carry Ltd* v *Thomson* [1989] IRLR 235, the EAT gave general guidance on the use of informers and Wood J laid down the following principles:

1.   The information given by the informant should be reduced into writing in one or more statements. Initially these statements should be taken without regard to the fact that in those cases where anonymity is to be preserved, it may subsequently prove to be necessary to omit or erase certain parts of the statements before submission to others — in order to prevent identification.

2.   In taking statements the following seem important:
(a)   date, time and place of each or any observation or incident;
(b)   the opportunity and ability to observe clearly and with accuracy;
(c)   the circumstantial evidence such as knowledge of a system or arrangement, or the reason for the presence of the informer and why certain small details are memorable;
(d)   whether the informant has suffered at the hands of the accused or has any other reason to fabricate, whether from personal grudge or any other reason or principle.

3.   Further investigation can then take place either to confirm or undermine the information given. Corroboration is clearly desirable.

4.   Tactful inquiries may well be thought suitable and advisable into the character and background of the informant or any other information which may tend to add or detract from the value of the information.

5.   If the informant is prepared to attend a disciplinary hearing, no problem will arise, but if, as in the present case, the employer is satisfied that the fear is genuine then a decision will need to be made whether or not to continue with the disciplinary process.

6.   If it is to continue, then it seems to us desirable that at each stage of those procedures the member of management responsible for that hearing should himself interview the informant and satisfy himself what weight is to be given to the information.

7. The written statement of the informant — if necessary with omissions to avoid identification — should be made available to the employee and his representatives.

8. If the employee or his representative raises any particular and relevant issue which should be put to the informant, then it may be desirable to adjourn for the chairman to make further inquiries of that informant.

9. Although it is always desirable for notes to be taken during disciplinary procedures, it seems to us to be particularly important that full and careful notes should be taken in these cases.

10. Although not peculiar to cases where informants have been the cause for the initiation of an investigation, it seems to us important that if evidence from an investigating officer is to be taken at a hearing it should, where poossible, be prepared in a written form.

13.8.3.4 Hearing

(a) At the stage of investigation there is no need to involve the employee, but once the facts are fully gained, they must be put before him at a hearing. The two processes often merge into one, especially when only the employee can give information about the incident; in that case a distinct second stage of hearing is unnecessary.

(b) Some difficulties have arisen when police inquiries and internal procedures are being held simultaneously. Employees have sought to prevent the latter prejudicing them in any criminal charges. Dicta (e.g. Lord Macdonald in *Carr* v *Alexander Russell Ltd* [1976] IRLR 220) that employment procedures should be suspended while a prosecution was pending have been later disapproved. There is also no general rule that employees should be suspended on full pay whilst awaiting the outcome of criminal proceedings, although this commonly happens (*Conway* v *Matthew Wright & Nephew Ltd* [1977] IRLR 89).

(c) The employee should not be left in a state of uncertainty. Thus in *Portsea Island Mutual Co-op Society* v *Rees* [1980] ICR 260, the employers were held to have acted unreasonably when at the date of dismissal the incident relied on was six weeks old and the employee had already been reprimanded for it.

(d) It is not necessarily unfair to fail to disclose to the employee or his representative the witness statements which formed the basis of the decision to dismiss, when the employee knew exactly what was being alleged against him. The question which still remained was always, when there was a procedural defect, whether the employer's procedure constituted a fair procedure (*Fuller* v *Lloyds Bank plc* [1991] IRLR 336).

(e) The tribunal should not second guess the employer's appreciation of a witness (*Linfood Cash & Carry Ltd* v *Thomson* [1989] IRLR 235; *Morgan* v *Electrolux* [1991] IRLR 89).

(f) It was suggested by the Court of Appeal in *P* v *Nottinghamshire CC* (supra) that the fairness of the dismissal may be determined in part by whether or not the employer has considered the issue of suitable alternative employment. The extent of the duty depends upon the size and administrative resources of the undertaking. Although previously this principle had been accepted in ill-health and redundancy cases, the Court of Appeal extended it here to the situation where the employee had been dismissed for misconduct.

13.8.4 Conduct checklist

It is impossible to catalogue all types of misconduct dismissals but the following are further examples, and in most the courts have demanded the same degree of investigation into the facts and fairness in applying the sanction as above:

(a)   failure to cooperate with the employer (e.g. *Retarded Children's Aid Society* v *Day* [1978] ICR 437);

(b)   insubordination (e.g. *Chantrill* v *W. F. Shortland Ltd* [1974] IRLR 333);

(c)   assault (e.g. *Parsons (C.A.) & Co.* v *McLoughlin* [1978] IRLR 65, *Stevenson* v *Golden Wonder Ltd* [1977] IRLR 474);

(d)   breach of hygiene and safety standards (e.g. *Unkles* v *Milanda Bread Co. Ltd* [1973] IRLR 76);

(e)   absenteeism and bad timekeeping (e.g. *City of Edinburgh DC* v *Stephen* [1977] IRLR 135);

(f)   disclosing confidential information (*Archer* v *Cheshire & Northwich Building Society* [1976] IRLR 424);

(g)   disloyalty by entering into competition with the employer (*Golden Cross Hire Co. Ltd* v *Lovell* [1979] IRLR 267), especially where this is accompanied by lies about such action (cf. *Laughton and Hawley* v *Bapp Industrial Supplies Ltd* [1986] IRLR 245; cf. *Marshall* v *Industrial Systems & Control Ltd* [1992] IRLR 294);

(h)   covert deals by a managing director with members of his own family so that his personal interests and the interests of the company might conflict (*Maintenance Co. Ltd* v *Dormer* [1982] IRLR 491);

(i)   taking a holiday without permission (*Brandon and Goold* v *Murphy Bros* [1983] IRLR 54);

(j)   deliberate use of unauthorised password in order to enter a computer known to contain information to which the employee was not entitled (*Denco Ltd* v *Joinson* [1991] IRLR 63, [1991] ICR 172);

(k)   making nuisance telephone calls to other members of staff whilst on duty as a mental health night charge nurse (*East Berkshire HA* v *Matadeen* [1992] IRLR 336).

13.9   PROCEDURE

Good industrial relations depend upon management not only acting fairly but being manifestly seen to act fairly.

(Sir John Donaldson, *Earl* v *Slater & Wheeler Ltd (Airlyne)* [1972] ICR 508.)

In the case of misconduct, the employer will normally not act reasonably unless he investigates the complaint of misconduct fully and fairly and hears whatever the employee wishes to say in his defence or in explanation or mitigation.

(Lord Bridge in *Polkey* v *Dayton Services Ltd* [1988] ICR 142.)

There are two axes to the reasonableness of a dismissal — the substantive merits and procedural fairness — and it is the latter which forms the subject of this section. It focuses on the 'equity' part of the s. 98(4) test and is most conveniently dealt with here because most of the cases in which it is relevant concern capacity or misconduct.

13.9.1   The significance of procedural irregularities

The most important elements of procedure are set down in the 1977 ACAS Code on Disciplinary Practice and Procedures in Employment, which applies expressly only to misconduct cases. The Industrial Relations Code of Practice, first introduced under the Industrial Relations Act 1971, is wide in its scope, but failure to observe a provision of either Code is not in itself actionable (*Neefjes* v *Crystal Products Co. Ltd* [1972] IRLR 118). It is, however, admissible in evidence and any relevant part must be taken into account by the tribunal. It should have been replaced by a more up-to-date code but the Secretary of State for Employment refused to accede to the ACAS draft. This was instead issued in 1987 as a handbook and guide, which may be referred to by tribunals but which has no statutory underpinning.

The central requirements of the codes and case law are:

(a) warnings (para. 13.9.3);
(b) proper investigation (para. 13.8.3.3);
(c) hearings (para. 13.9.4); and
(d) appeals (para. 13.9.5).

In the early case of *Earl* v *Slater and Wheeler (Airlyne) Ltd* [1972] IRLR 115, Sir John Donaldson thought that the only exception to the need to allow the employee to state his case was 'where there *can be no explanation* which could cause the employer to refrain from dismissing the employee'. This must be a very rare situation and here the dismissal was held unfair when the employee was, without more ado, handed letters of dismissal, notwithstanding that missing drawings and contracts for which he was responsible were discovered in his house. Procedure is to be tempered by substantive considerations and the rules of natural justice do not form an independent ground upon which a decision to dismiss may be attacked (*Slater* v *Leicestershire Health Authority* [1989] IRLR 16). For example, in *Bailey* v *BP Oil (Kent Refinery) Ltd* [1979] IRLR 150, where the employee had claimed to be sick while on holiday in Majorca, the failure to inform a full-time union official before the decision to dismiss was taken (as required by a union-negotiated agreement) was held not sufficient to render the dismissal unfair. Their Lordships stressed that each case depended on its merits and that it was unwise for the EAT to set out guidelines, make rules, or establish presumptions. Lawton LJ said in *Parsons (C.A.) Ltd* v *McLoughlin* [1978] IRLR 65, that:

Cases can occur when instant dismissal without any opportunity for explanation being given would be fair, as for example, when on the shop floor a worker is seen by the works manager and others to stab another man in the back with a knife.

From the case of *Dunning (A.J.) & Sons (Shopfitters) Ltd* v *Jacomb* [1973] IRLR 206, the approach developed that a procedural defect would only make the dismissal unfair if the decision might have been different at the end of the day. The trend is to see procedural matters as issues of substance to be weighed in the scales of the overall merits of the case.

In *British Labour Pump Co. Ltd* v *Byrne* [1979] IRLR 94, which is the main authority for this proposition, Slynn J posed two essential questions:

(1) Have the employers shown on the balance of probabilities that they would have taken the same course had they held an inquiry, and had they received the information which that inquiry would have produced?
(2) Have the employers shown — the burden is on them — that in the light of the information which they would have had had they gone through the proper procedure, they would have been behaving reasonably in so deciding to dismiss?

This applied as much to contractual procedural requirements. (See also *Gray Dunn and Co. Ltd* v *Edwards* [1980] IRLR 23.)

The Court of Appeal in *W. & J. Wass Ltd* v *Binns* [1982] IRLR 283 accepted that *British Labour Pump* laid down useful guidelines. More recent authorities, however, deprecated the approach as speculative and as imposing a gloss on the general test of reasonableness. In *Sillifant* v *Powell Duffryn Timber Ltd* [1983] IRLR 91, the EAT thought that it was inconsistent in principle with *Devis* v *Atkins,* and had given rise to practical difficulties since 'tribunals have come to apply the principles to cases where the error though in one sense procedural goes to the very substance of the employer's decision'.

The law on procedural requirements in unfair dismissal has been revolutionised by the House of Lords decision in *Polkey* v *Dayton Services Ltd* [1987] IRLR 503, which exploded the 'heresy' of *British Labour Pump* v *Byrne*. Lord Mackay in the leading judgment in *Polkey* concentrated on the fact that the subject-matter for consideration by the industrial tribunal pursuant to what is now s. 98(4) of ERA 1996 is 'the employer's action in treating the reason for dismissal as a sufficient reason'. He went on to say (at paras 4 and 5):

It is that action and that action only that the tribunal is required to characterise as reasonable or unreasonable. That leaves no scope for the tribunal considering whether, if the employer had acted differently, he might have dismissed the employee. It is what the employer did that is to be judged, not what he might have done. On the other hand, in judging whether what the employer did was reasonable it is right to consider what a reasonable employer would have had in mind at the time he decided to dismiss as the consequence of not consulting or not warning. . . .

Failure to observe the requirement of the code relating to consultation or warning will not necessarily render a dismissal unfair. Whether in any particular case it did so is a matter for the industrial tribunal to consider in the light of the circumstances known to the employer at the time he dismissed the employee.

The House of Lords expressly overruled *British Labour Pump* v *Byrne,* the Court of Appeal decision in *Wass* v *Binns* and all cases following them. There is still, however, an inkling of the *Byrne* test, albeit in more limited circumstances, in *Polkey,* in that Lord Bridge stated that:

It is quite a different matter if the tribunal is able to conclude that the employer himself, at the time of the dismissal, acted reasonably in taking the view that, in the exceptional circumstances of the particular case, the procedural steps normally appropriate would have been futile, could not have altered the decision to dismiss and therefore could be dispensed with. In such a case the test of reasonableness under [s. 94(4)] may be satisfied.

(See also Lord Mackay at para. 5.) Moreover, compensation might be reduced in a case in which 'taking the appropriate steps . . . would not have affected the outcome'. A percentage reduction of compensation may be appropriate. To fall within the exception recognised in *Polkey,* however there need be no conscious decision by the employer to the effect that consultation or some other procedural protection would be utterly senseless (*Duffy* v *Yeomans and Partners Ltd* [1995] ICR 1). Rather, it is relevant to consider whether a reasonable employer *could* have thought that exhaustion of the procedures would have been useless.

Not every defect in procedure will render the dismissal unfair, but only if it is sufficiently serious, as the EAT made clear in *Fuller* v *Lloyds Bank plc* [1991] IRLR 336. The last years have thus seen a reassertion of the importance of procedural correctness by industrial tribunals. The *Polkey* decision is the most important signpost in this direction, but it is also significant that in *West Midlands Cooperative Society Ltd* v *Tipton* [1986] ICR 192, Lord Bridge expressly approved the following passage from the judgment of Viscount Dilhorne in the *Devis* case ([1977] IRLR 314 at 317):

> It does not follow that non-compliance with the code necessarily renders a dismissal unfair, but I agree with the view expressed by Sir John Donaldson in *Earl* v *Slater and Wheeler (Airlyne) Ltd* [1972] IRLR 115, that a failure to follow a procedure prescribed in the Code may lead to the conclusion that a dismissal was unfair, which, if that procedure had been followed, would have been held to have been fair.

After considerable uncertainty about the scope of the exceptional case in *Polkey* v *Dayton*, the Court of Appeal in *Duffy* v *Yeomans and Partners Ltd* [1995] ICR 1 determined that it was not necessary for the employer to apply his mind specifically or consciously to the question whether consultation in the particular case would have been futile; rather the industrial tribunal must decide what the employer *could* have done, and therefore whether the employer acting reasonably could have failed to consult in the given circumstances. This is a question of fact for the industrial tribunal and should not be over-complicated by setting down rules of law.

The employer cannot rely on the exceptional circumstances of an industrial dispute *per se* to justify the withdrawal of procedural protection for employees. Thus, in *McLaren* v *National Coal Board* [1988] IRLR 215, a dismissal of a striking miner who was convicted of assault without any hearing by the employer was held to be unfair. The Court of Appeal considered that 'no amount of heat in industrial warfare can justify failing to give an employee the opportunity of offering an explanation. What industrial warfare may do is to create a situation in which conduct which would not normally justify dismissal becomes conduct which does justify dismissal' (cf. *Lees* v *British Coal*, 363 IRLIB 6, *Dillett* v *National Coal Board* [1988] ICR 218).

13.9.2 Agreed procedures

Tribunals have strained to uphold union agreed procedures in accordance with the legislative policy to promote autonomous bargains between union and management. *East Hertfordshire DC* v *Boyten* [1977] IRLR 347, is the highpoint of that trend, even referring to the agreed code as the 'Bible'. The applicant refuse collector had been dismissed for fighting which was witnessed by two fellow employees who made statements about it. On appeal, the employer did nothing to ensure the presence of the witnesses, as appeared to be necessary to give the appellant a fair hearing. Yet Forbes J overturned the industrial tribunal's determination of unfairness since the employers had followed the agreed code of procedure to the letter, and tribunals should not rush in where management and unions fear to tread. His Lordship said:

> The point is that there is a code, carefully agreed between the parties, and . . . it is not for the Industrial Tribunal, or indeed, this Appeal Tribunal to rewrite an agreed code of that kind which has been hammered out by both sides of industry. No employer, it seems to us, should be accused of acting unreasonably in those circumstances if that employer follows a code which has been arrived at in that way.

Moreover, the EAT in *Stevenson* v *Golden Wonder Ltd* [1977] IRLR 474, said:

> Grievance and other procedures should not be construed with such rigidity that any failure on the part of an employer, however insignificant, to follow the literal letter of the code means it is automatically unfair.

13.9.3 Warnings

It is good sense and reasonable that in the ordinary way for a first offence you should not dismiss a man on the instant without any warning or giving him a further chance.

(*Retarded Children's Aid Society* v *Day* [1978] ICR 437.)

An employee should generally be given a warning about his misconduct or incompetence before being dismissed if that dismissal is to be considered fair. Warning in this context is shorthand for 'efforts to try to make the employee change and (an indication) to him of the consequence if these efforts are unsuccessful' (*Plasticisers Ltd* v *Amos,* EAT 13/76). A warning is intended to deter and reform the employee, and should be administered to the worker individually. Exceptionally a general warning to all staff might be acceptable (*Connely* v *Liverpool Corporation* (1974) 9 ITR 51).

The ACAS Code lays down that in the case of minor offences there should be a formal oral warning followed by a written warning, and then a final written warning which should specify that recurrence of the offence may lead to dismissal. The aim is to put the employee on notice as to further misconduct. Although there is thus no maximum or minimum number of warnings the figure three has entered popular mythology. Where minor misconduct takes place at extended intervals, a series of several warnings without taking the matter further may be the most reasonable course.

Although the latter stage of the process should be in writing, 'there is no special magic' about it (*McCall* v *Castleton Crafts Ltd* [1979] IRLR 218). Its value is that it invests the process with a more official character, and its seriousness is also shown by the supplementary provision that the employee may be represented by a union official or friend before the final warning is administered.

To have its proper effect, the warning must be *sufficiently specific.* An employer's insistence that 'you undertake these responsibilities and duties forthwith if you are to continue as Deputy Head of the Documentary Credit Department', did not suffice in *UBAF Bank Ltd* v *Davis* [1978] IRLR 442. (See also *Littlewoods Organisation Ltd* v *Egenti* [1976] ICR 516.)

In most cases a warning on ground 'A' should not be used as a step in procedure to dismiss on a completely different ground 'B'. Previous warnings may be considered even if the conduct for which the employee is dismissed is different in character (*Auguste Noël Ltd* v *Curtis* [1990] ICR 604, [1990] IRLR 326). Although confidential records should be kept at all stages, if the employee improves, the warning should be removed (para. 19 of the Code of Practice); usually a 12-month period is reasonable and a specific time will be often inserted in disciplinary rules (*Charles* v *SRC* (1977) 12 ITR 208). This brings to the forefront the aim to deter and reform.

Further, a time limit on the currency of a warning is likely to be strictly construed, so that in *Bevan Ashford* v *Malin* [1995] ICR 453, the 12-month currency of the admonition was not effective when the warning was used by the employers, a firm of solicitors, in a dismissal one day after the year had expired.

The general requirement of a warning represents one of the most important improvements in the employee's protection from the law of wrongful dismissal, so that instead of summary dismissal, the employee is to be given a reasonable opportunity to improve. The ACAS Code urges, as we have seen, that disciplinary procedures should ensure that, except for gross misconduct, no employees should be dismissed for a first breach of discipline. This is particularly important where a rule has lain dormant for a considerable time. Thus the EAT said in *Wilcox* v *Humphreys & Glasgow* [1975] ICR 333:

If the requirement had been ignored for ages to everyone's knowledge it would not be right without some kind of warning to dismiss the first person to break it after the employers took it into their heads to enforce it.

This is the explanation for the notorious case of *Ayub* v *Vauxhall Motors Ltd* [1978] IRLR 428, where an industrial tribunal found the dismissal of the applicant for sleeping during night shift at a car factory unfair because of evidence that while many other workers did the same and their conduct in breach of the rules was condoned, the applicant was dismissed without warning. (See also *Hackwood* v *Seal (Marine) Ltd* [1973] IRLR 17.)

Many disciplinary procedures have provisions for appeals against a warning. There is, however, no general rule that an employee may not be dismissed while his final warning is under appeal (*Stein* v *Associated Dairies Ltd* [1982] IRLR 447). The tribunal is not to sit in judgment whether the employee should or should not have received such warning. Rather, it is sufficient that the final warning has been issued in good faith and that there was at least prima facie ground for following the procedure. If there was anything to suggest that the warning had been issued for an oblique motive or that it was manifestly inappropriate, the tribunal could take that into account in reaching its general decision on fairness. (*Tower Hamlets Health Authority* v *Anthony* [1989] IRLR 394).

13.9.3.1 Where a warning is not necessary The Code itself envisages that, just as at common law, there may be some breaches of rules so serious that a warning may be neither appropriate nor necessary. These follow closely the cases on lawful summary dismissal (see Chapter 12). There is no exhaustive definition of gross misconduct in either jurisdiction; rather it depends on the nature of the employer's business, the position held by the employee and all the circumstances of the case. In *Stevenson* v *Golden Wonder Ltd* [1977] IRLR 474, for example, the employee, a technical manager, was dismissed after assaulting a fellow worker. Notwithstanding that the company's procedure was not followed as to warning, the EAT found the dismissal fair.

Many works rules attempt to codify what misdemeanours will be treated as gross misconduct by the employee and thus where warnings will not be given. Even when this happens it still remains for the tribunal ultimately to determine whether the conduct was sufficiently serious in the circumstances. In *Laws Stores Ltd* v *Oliphant* [1978] IRLR 251, the employee was guilty of one lapse in operating the till, and although this fell within the definition of gross misconduct in the rules, and instant dismissal was the penalty laid down, dismissal was held to be unfair. (See also *Ladbroke Racing* v *Arnott* [1979] IRLR 192.)

Other circumstances where a warning may be reasonably dispensed with broadly include:

(a) Where the employee's conduct is likely to endanger the *safety* of others (*Yorkshire Imperial Metals Ltd* v *Martin* [1978] IRLR 440).

(b) Where the disciplinary rules are *so clear* as to constitute a warning of dismissal in themselves. This principle is, however, narrowly circumscribed so that in *Meridian Ltd* v

Gomersall [1977] ICR 597, a notice that 'anyone found clocking cards on behalf of other personnel will render themselves liable to instant dismissal' was held to be insufficiently specific since it did not mean necessarily that the employee would be sacked for one offence.

(c) Where a warning would *not make any difference* to the final outcome. Thus in *Retarded Children's Aid Society* v *Day* [1978] ICR 437, the applicant who worked in a home for mentally subnormal children required one of his charges to perform extra duties knowing that this was wholly against the rules and philosophy of the home. The Court of Appeal determined that his dismissal was fair even in the absence of warning or hearing since 'he showed himself out of sympathy with the society's methods in fundamental respects and so presented the risk of further transgressions'. His constitutional inability to change his ways rendered any warning superfluous.

(d) Where the employee knew, or was in a position to know, that he was putting his *job in jeopardy* by his action or inaction. This may be because of his close relationship with the employer in a small unit (*Brown* v *Hall Advertising Ltd* [1978] IRLR 246 — confidential private secretary and managing director). A diametrically opposite view was, however, taken in the strange decision in *McPhail* v *Gibson* [1977] ICR 42. The applicant farm manager had given a grossly inaccurate reference for an employee to a neighbouring farmer. Kilner Brown J thought that a warning was particularly necessary before the dismissal of a person in such a position of trust and that 'instant dismissal even in a case of grave misconduct is very rarely associated with no preliminary step having taken place'.

(e) Where there is a specific *agreed procedure* and a dismissal has proceeded in accordance therewith, it is very difficult to persuade an industrial tribunal that more in the way of warnings is required (*Donald Cook & Son Ltd* v *Carter* [1977] IRLR 88).

The requirements of procedure often run into one another and, of course, the dismissal must be viewed as a whole.

13.9.4 Hearings

Before a decision is made or penalty imposed the individual should be interviewed and given the opportunity to state his or her case and should be advised of any rights under the procedure including the right to be represented.

(ACAS Code No 1: Disciplinary Practice and Procedures in Employment, para. 11)

In the normal case the following are required:

explain the purpose of the meeting; identify those present; if appropriate, arrange representation; inform the employee of the allegation or allegations being made; indicate the evidence, whether in statement form or by the calling of witnesses; allow the employee and representatives to ask questions; ask whether the employee wishes any witnesses to be called; allow the employee or the representative to explain and argue the case; listen to the argument from both sides upon the allegations and any possible consequences, including any mitigation; ask the employee whether there is any further evidence or enquiry which he considers could help his case.

(*Clark* v *Civil Aviation Authority* [1991] IRLR 412 at para. 20.)

The right for the employee to be heard before dismissal is one of the most important elements in the natural justice which is an inherent part of unfair dismissal. Its remit is to consider whether the allegations of misconduct or incapability are proved, and, if so, what should be the proper penalty.

(a) The hearing should be conducted as fairly as possible in the circumstances, but the EAT has been anxious to guard against the rigid imposition of judicial-style proceedings in inappropriate situtations. The operation of the hearing requirements can be seen in two contrasting cases. In *Bentley Engineering Co.* v *Mistry* [1979] ICR 47, the dismissal was unfair because the employee did not know what evidence the employers had against her when she approached the 'hearing'. On the other hand, in *Khanum* v *Mid-Glamorgan AHA* [1978] IRLR 215, the lack of opportunity to cross-examine and to see statements of witnesses to alleged misconduct did not render the hearing unfair. (On cross-examination of witnesses at internal appeal, see *Ulsterbus Ltd* v *Henderson* [1989] IRLR 251.) The EAT in *Khanum* summarised the three guiding principles:

(i)   that the employee should know of the accusations he has to meet (see also *Greenhalgh* v *James Mills Executors* [1973] IRLR 78, *Bell* v *Devon & Cornwall Police Authority* [1978] IRLR 283);
(ii)   that he should be given an opportunity to state his case; and
(iii)   that the internal tribunal act in good faith.

(b)   A dismissal may be unfair because the hearing of a complaint against the applicant was conducted in breach of the rules of natural justice. In *Moyes* v *Hylton Castle Working Men's Social Club & Institute Ltd* [1986] IRLR 482, two officials of the employers, a working men's club, acted as witnesses of the incidents of sexual harassment and judges of the truth of the allegations by sitting on the committees which took the decision to dismiss. The EAT decided that such a procedure rendered the procedure unfair.

(c)   A hearing is completely useless unless it is held before the final decision to dismiss is taken (*Earl* v *Slater & Wheeler Airlyne) Ltd* [1972] IRLR 115; *Clarke* v *Trimoco Motor Group Ltd* [1993] ICR 238); and before those who will actually take that decision (*Budgen & Co.* v *Thomas* [1976] IRLR 174).

(d)   A hearing should take place as soon as possible after the alleged misdemeanour; thus a delay of nine months was criticised in *Distillers Co. (Bottling Services) Ltd* v *Gardner* [1982] IRLR 47.

(e)   The employee should have the opportunity to present mitigation of penalty as well as arguments on 'liability' (*Siggs & Chapman (Contractors) Ltd* v *Knight* [1984] IRLR 83).

(f)   A hearing may proceed in the absence of the employee provided he or she has been given fair and proper opportunity to attend, especially if he is represented (*Pirelli General Cable Works Ltd* v *Murray* [1979] IRLR 190). It should, however, be adjourned if the employee is not in a fit state to go through with it (*Tesco Group of Companies (Holdings) Ltd* v *Hill* [1977] IRLR 63) although there is no obligation to postpone it until criminal proceedings have ended. If an employee chooses to say nothing because it might prejudice a pending case, the dismissal may still be fair provided he has been given the opportunity to present his case (see *Murray* v *British Rail* [1976] IRLR 382). The roles of prosecutor and jury are often inevitably confused in industrial matters (see *Haddow* v *ILEA* [1979] ICR 202).

(g)   The presence of the police at an internal inquiry without the applicant's foreknowledge and consent would be wholly improper (*Read* v *Phoenix Preservation Ltd* [1985] IRLR 93).

(h)   An employee should always be informed of allegations against him. In *Pritchett & Dyjasek* v *J. McIntyre Ltd* [1987] IRLR 18 the Court of Appeal held that the tribunal's conclusion that the employers had evidence so clear and overwhelming that a reasonable employer could assume that there was no sensible possibility of an explanation or mitigating circumstances being advanced, was perverse. (See *Spink* v *Express Food Group Ltd* [1990] IRLR 320).

(i)   The employee should also see any written statements where an employer intends to rely on the same in disciplinary proceedings, and any other procedure would be prima facie unfair (*Louies* v *Coventry Hood and Seating Co.* [1990] IRLR 324). Where there had been an investigation which had led to a belief that there had been misconduct on the part of the employee, the subsequent dismissal procedure had to be conducted so that the fairness of the procedure balanced the initial belief of misconduct.

(j)   A failure to keep notes at a hearing and to provide them to the employee during the hearing may be a procedural error (*Vauxhall Motors Ltd* v *Ghafoor* [1993] ICR 376).

13.9.4.1   Right to be represented   The employee has a concomitant right, which is the right to be accompanied at a hearing by a trade union representative or fellow employee; and because of the sensitivity of the shop steward's position no disciplinary dismissal should be implemented without the involvement, usually at the hearing stage, of a senior trade union representative or full-time official. Again, the lack of this representation by itself is unlikely to make the dismissal unfair (*Bailey* v *BP Oil Ltd* [1980] IRLR 287).

13.9.4.2   Where a hearing is superfluous   There are some situations in which the courts have found that a hearing itself would be superfluous, although these must be subject to scrutiny in the light of *Polkey* v *Dayton Services Ltd* [1988] ICR 142, which decided that a dismissal will be fair only if the employer reasonably, at the time of dismissal, considered that further procedural steps would be futile. In *Gray Dunn & Co. Ltd* v *Edwards* [1980] IRLR 23, Lord MacDonald commented that: 'It is . . . well settled that common sense places limits on the degree of investigation required of an employer who is seized of information which points strongly towards the commission of a disciplinary offence which merits dismissal.' There the failure to allow the employee to call witnesses at an internal appeal following his dismissal for drunkenness did not render the dismissal unfair since three senior officials had formed the view that he was intoxicated, and he had himself admitted drinking earlier. Tribunals should not, however, speculate about what would have been the result of a hearing had it been held without direct evidence (*Dunn* v *Pochin (Contractors) Ltd* [1982] IRLR 449).

The exceptions to the right to a hearing include cases where:

(a)   'The employee, as part of the conduct complained of, states in terms why he adopted that attitude [and] it is clear that this is the employee's considered view and not merely the result of a passing emotion', or the conduct is of such a nature that whatever his explanation, his continued employment is not in the interests of the employer's business (*James* v *Waltham Holy Cross UDC* [1973] ICR 398).

(b)   A serious theft has been admitted by the employee (*Carr* v *Alexander Russell Ltd* [1976] IRLR 220), or conversely where the employee so strongly denies the matter to the police that an internal opportunity to state his case would not advance matters further (*Conway* v *Matthew Wright & Nephew Ltd* [1977] IRLR 89).

(c)   The circumstances were so grievous (i.e. five serious and costly errors) that although an explanation might conceivably have been produced, it was wildly unlikely that it would be (*Lowndes* v *Specialist Heavy Engineering* [1976] IRLR 246; see also *Cardiff City Council* v *Condé* [1978] IRLR 218.)

(d)   The employee was reasonably required to work overtime and was dismissed on refusal (*Martin* v *Solus Schall* [1979] IRLR 7).

(e)   The relationship between employer and employee is so close (e.g. director and confidential private secretary) that the former already knew what her case would be (*Brown* v *Hall Advertising Ltd* [1978] IRLR 246).

Even in these cases there may be some possibility of mitigation and an opportunity to apologise should be offered. These cases must be read in the light of the *Polkey* decision, so that only if a reasonable employer at the time would determine that a hearing would be *futile* should the tribunal decide that in its absence a dismissal would be fair.

13.9.5   Appeals

The Code of Practice lays great stress on the availability of an appeal from an initial decision to dismiss (para. 16). An appeal procedure should be stated in the written statement of terms (ERA 1996, s. 3(1)(a)). Tribunals have sometimes held a dismissal unfair for the lack of an appeal (*Lloyd* v *Scottish CWS* [1973] IRLR 45). The importance of a properly conducted appeals procedure was emphasised in *Whitbread & Co. plc* v *Mills* [1988] IRLR 501. The EAT held that in certain circumstances, defects in disciplinary and dismissal procedures may be remedied on appeal but whether they are so corrected depends on the degree of unfairness at the original hearing. If it is to remedy procedural defects at that hearing, the appeal must be of a comprehensive nature, in essence a rehearing and not a review. Wood J said that while a minor departure from a contractual appeal process may be ignored, a total failure to comply with it may entitle an industrial tribunal to find the dismissal unfair (see also *Qualcast (Wolverhampton) Ltd* v *Ross* [1979] IRLR 98). In *Sartor* v *P&O European Ferries Ltd* [1992] IRLR 273, it was held that a defect could not be cured if the manager hearing the appeal had already been involved in earlier stages of the disciplinary process. Where the first stage of the disciplinary process is seriously flawed it is essential, if the appellate process is to be treated as establishing fairness, that it should be able to stand on its own merits as conferring on the employee all the rights which should have been accorded at the initial stage, especially proper notice of the complaint and a proper opportunity to state the employee's case. A review would be insufficient (*Byrne* v *BOC Ltd* [1994] IRLR 505).

The following propositions appear from the cases:

(a)   An employee should be *informed* of his right to appeal (*Tesco Group of Companies (Holdings) Ltd* v *Hill* [1977] IRLR 63) and have the right to be *represented* (*Rank Xerox (UK) Ltd* v *Goodchild* [1979] IRLR 185).

(b)   The appeal body should be composed of *different persons* from those who took the original decision to dismiss (para. 17 of the Code; *Johnson Matthey Metals Ltd* v *Harding* [1978] IRLR 248).

(c)   An employer need not grant the applicant's request to be accompanied by his solicitor.

(d)   In small companies, to provide an appeal at all where there is only one level of management may prove an 'Elysian standard' (e.g. *Tiptools Ltd* v *Curtis* [1973] IRLR 276).

(e)   A full judicial hearing is unnecessary. The procedure adopted in *Rowe* v *Radio Rentals Ltd* [1982] IRLR 177 thus did not conflict with the rules of natural justice because the person hearing the appeal had been informed of the decision to dismiss before it took place, and the person who took that decision was also present throughout the appeal hearing. Such procedure should not be cramped by legal requirements imposing impossible burdens on companies in the conduct of their affairs. Nevertheless, in any event, previous dealings with the applicants by those hearing the appeal should be made known to the employee.

(f)   The cutting short of an appellate process by way of a dismissal before a decision is given by the person hearing the appeal is a procedural defect in itself (*Rao* v *Civil Aviation Authority* [1992] IRLR 203). There may be no injustice if there has been a proper and sufficient hearing on appeal even though there were procedural defects in the employer's original decision to dismiss (*Clark* v *Civil Aviation Authority* [1991] IRLR 412, [1992] IRLR 503).

(g)   It is unfair if a trade union convenor has the power to decide whether an appeal should be permitted to be made (*Vauxhall Motors Ltd* v *Ghafoor* [1993] ICR 376).

(h)   Failure by the employee to appeal does not constitute acquiescence in the decision to dismiss (*Chrystie* v *Rolls Royce Ltd* [1976] IRLR 336, overruling *Sutherland* v *National Carriers Ltd* [1975] IRLR 340), although in one case it indicated a failure to mitigate loss (*Hoover Ltd* v *Forde* [1980] ICR 239).

(i)   The employer is expected to comply with the full requirements of an appeal procedure in its own disciplinary code (*Stoker* v *Lancashire County Council* [1992] IRLR 75), but the fact that the appeal procedure provided by the employer's disciplinary code has not been followed to the letter does not mean that the decision to dismiss is necessarily unfair (*Westminster City Council* v *Cabaj* [1996] IRLR 399). The EAT held that, on remission, the industrial tribunal must not consider what would have happened if the proper procedure had been followed, but whether the defect denied to the employee an opportunity of showing that the employer's real reason for dismissing him could not reasonably be treated as sufficient. (See also *Blundell* v *Christie National Hospital NHS Trust* [1996] IRLR 347.)

The fact that the appeal takes place after the effective date of termination does not mean that it should be ignored in relation to the fairness of the dismissal (*Rank Xerox (UK) Ltd* v *Goodchild* [1979] IRLR 185; see also *National Coal Board* v *Nash, The Times,* 7 May 1986).

13.10   REDUNDANCY

The definition of redundancy first laid down by the Redundancy Payments Act 1965, and now to be found in s. 139 of the ERA 1996, serves as the basis for defining redundancy as a reason for dismissal in the unfair dismissal jurisdiction. The presumption that a dismissal is for redundancy unless proved otherwise does not, however, apply, in unfair dismissal cases as it does where a statutory redundancy payment is claimed (para. 14.2.1). There are three ways in which a redundancy dismissal may be unfair:

(a)   Selection for redundancy by reason of membership of, or activities at an appropriate time in, an independent trade union, or because he was not a member of any trade union nor of one of a number of particular trade unions or had refused or proposed to refuse to become or remain a member, is a protected or opted out shop worker, was a trustee of an occupational pension scheme or an employee representative, or has asserted a relevant statutory right (ERA 1996, s. 105). The burden of proof here is heavy on the applicant

(*Taylor* v *Butler Machine Tool Ltd* [1976] IRLR 133), and it is more appropriately discussed in connection with the general question of dismissal for trade union activities (para. 20.2).

(b) The *general reasonableness* test posited by s. 98(4) of ERA 1996, for all cases of unfair dismissal; for the industrial tribunal must still consider, even in the absence of any procedure, whether the employer 'acted reasonably . . . in treating [redundancy] as a sufficient reason for dismissing the employee' (para. 13.10.2).

Selection of a woman for redundancy because she is pregnant and will require maternity leave is dismissal for a 'reason connected with her pregnancy' within s. 99 of ERA 1996 and is automatically unfair (*Brown* v *Stockton on Tees BC* [1988] IRLR 263, discussed at para. 5.8.3).

The employer does not have to justify his declaration of redundancy itself unless it is an obvious sham (*Goodwin Ltd* v *Fitzmaurice* [1977] IRLR 393). Thus in *Moon* v *Homeworthy Furniture (Northern) Ltd* [1977] ICR 117, the employees claimed that there was no true redundancy because the factory from which they were dismissed was still economically viable. Kilner Brown J thought that if the courts were to decide such questions they would be in danger of being utilised as a forum for industrial disputes. Therefore 'there could not . . . be any investigation into the rights and wrongs of the declared redundancy'. (See also *Campbell* v *Dunoon & Cowal Housing Association Ltd* [1993] IRLR 496).

There are, however, some indications of a more interventionist approach by the EAT. In *Ladbroke Courage Holidays Ltd* v *Asten* [1981] IRLR 59, it demanded that if the employer sought to give as a reason for dismissal that he needed to reduce his wage costs he should produce evidence of the need for economy, while Slynn J in *Orr* v *Vaughan* [1981] IRLR 63, thought that the employer must act on reasonable information properly acquired when choosing a method of reorganisation.

An employer formerly was deemed to be acting unfairly if employees were selected for redundancy in breach of a customary arrangement or agreed procedure, where 'the circumstances constituting the redundancy applied equally to one or more employees in the same undertaking who held positions similar to that held by [the applicant]'. This has been abolished by the Deregulation and Contracting Out Act 1994 with effect from 3 January 1995. Tribunals will probably henceforth treat a failure to follow agreed or customary procedure as a factor in establishing unfairness of dismissal pursuant to ERA 1996, s. 98(4).

13.10.1 Reasonableness: the residuary question

In the case of redundancy, the employer will normally not act reasonably unless he warns and consults any employees affected or their representative, adopts a fair basis on which to select for redundancy and takes such steps as may be reasonable to avoid or minimise redundancy by redeployment within his own organisation.

(Lord Bridge in *Polkey* v *Dayton Services Ltd* [1988] ICR 142.)

The manner in which the tribunals should approach the residuary question of reasonableness under s. 98(4) in the case of redundancy has never ceased to be highly controversial. In *Atkinson* v *George Lindsay & Co.* [1980] IRLR 196, the Court of Session thought that it would 'in most cases be extremely difficult for any tribunal to hold' that a dismissal was unfair under this general test if it survived the agreed selection hurdle. These cases have tended to treat the employer as though he were an administrative agency whose decisions in this respect should be challenged only *in extremis*. The same test of perversity has been applied here as to judicial review of administrative action. This is notwithstanding the unambiguously objective terms of the general test of reasonableness in unfair dismissal. It does, however, reflect the limited options open to an employer at a time of crisis. Thus in *Vickers Ltd* v *Smith* [1977] IRLR 11, the EAT thought that the tribunal should have asked 'whether the decision of management was so wrong that no sensible or reasonable management could have arrived at the decision which the employers [reached]'. In *Jackson* v *General Accident, Fire and Life Assurance Co. Ltd* [1977] IRLR 338, Lord Macdonald commented, 'whilst where the ground of dismissal is capability or conduct and there has been some procedural failure . . . it can readily be seen how the employer could be held to have acted unreasonably . . . it is not so easy to envisage this where the ground is redundancy' (see *Valor Newhome Ltd* v *Hampson* [1982] ICR 407).

This trend appeared to be halted in *Williams* v *Compair Maxam Ltd* [1982] IRLR 83, where the EAT laid down guidelines of good industrial practice in redundancies. The tribunal was directed to consider whether objective selection criteria were chosen and fairly applied, whether the possibility of transfer to other work was investigated, whether employees were warned and consulted and whether the union (if there was one) was consulted over the most equitable manner of implementing the redundancies. The background in the *Compair Maxam* case was a major redundancy in an employer with a recognised union.

The EAT in Scotland has scathingly criticised the use of the guidelines in different circumstances. Notwithstanding that the case was approved by the Northern Ireland Court of Appeal in *Robinson* v *Carrickfergus BC* [1983] IRLR 122, Lord Macdonald thought that the guidelines were 'becoming overworked and increasingly misapplied' in cases of small non-unionised employers such as in *Simpson* v *Reid & Findlater* [1983] IRLR 401. The facts of the case concerned the dismissal of two out of three employees. In such a context the EAT felt that the guidelines should not be used by tribunals 'like a shopping list'. Further in *Buchanan* v *Tilcon Ltd* [1983] IRLR 417, the Court of Session reverted to the restrictive approach of the *Jackson* case (see also *Eaton Ltd* v *King* [1995] IRLR 75). These latter cases have questioned the appropriateness of the appeal tribunal's role in offering guidelines at all in the light of certain Court of Appeal dicta. Browne-Wilkinson J, however, defended this role in *Grundy (Teddington) Ltd* v *Plummer and Salt* [1983] ICR 367 on the ground that it was a useful and proper part of the appeal tribunal's function in a limited number of cases to give guidance on the general approach as to what constitutes reasonable conduct. This was especially necessary since the Code of Practice was falling behind the times. In *Gray* v *Shetland Norse Preserving Co. Ltd* [1985] IRLR 53, the Scottish EAT 'welcomed the opportunity of pointing out yet again how very limited the scope of these principles is', and in *Rolls Royce Motors Ltd* v *Dewhurst* [1985] IRLR 184, the EAT sitting in England commented that, 'No decision of this court seems to give greater trouble than the decision in *Williams* v *Compair Maxam*.'

The rest of para. 13.10 discusses the general principles adopted by tribunals to fairness in redundancy cases but must be read in the light of the caveat of the recent authorities just discussed.

13.10.2 Criteria of selection

In an important statement of principle, in *British Aerospace Ltd* v *Green* [1995] IRLR 433, the Court of Appeal said that:

. . . in general the employer who sets up a system of selection which can reasonably be described as fair and applies it without any overt sign of conduct which mars its fairness will have done all that the law requires of him. . . . The tribunal is not entitled to embark upon a re-assessment exercise . . . it is sufficient for the employer to show that he set up a good system of selection and that it was fairly administered, and that ordinarily there is no need for the employer to justify all the assessments on which the selection for redundancy was based.

This demonstrates the generally *laissez-faire* approach taken by appeal courts over many years to employers' decisions on selection.

The employer should, however, have settled criteria for the selection of employees to be dismissed. In *Compair Maxam* the criterion used was those employees 'who in the opinion of the managers concerned would be able to keep the company viable'. This, above all, rendered unfair the dismissals. Browne-Wilkinson J thought that the criteria should be capable of being objectively checked against such matters as attendance record, job efficiency, experience, and/or length of service. In *Cox* v *Wildt Mellor Bromley Ltd* [1978] IRLR 157, the EAT held that the employer must 'show how the employee came to be dismissed for redundancy, upon what basis the selection was made and how it was applied in practice'. (See also *Bristol Channel Ship Repairers Ltd* v *O'Keefe* [1977] IRLR 13, *Greig* v *Sir Alfred McAlpine & Son (Northern) Ltd* [1979] IRLR 372, *Graham* v *ABF Ltd* [1986] IRLR 90.) On the other hand, the question for the tribunal should be whether 'the selection [was] one which a reasonable employer could have made, not would we have made that selection' (*BL Cars* v *Lewis* [1983] IRLR 58).

The pool of selection must be reasonably defined so that in *GEC Machines Ltd* v *Gilford* [1982] ICR 725, selection from a section rather than the whole department was held unfair since the work was interchangeable between employees within the department. The idea that the employer has to produce direct evidence to support his selection was, however, challenged in the *Buchanan* case. In the view of Lord Emslie, the employer had only to establish that the selection was fair 'in general terms'. The following matters have been considered in the cases:

(a) Attendance figures: employers often use comparative attendance figures as a criterion for selection for redundancy but where they do, they must go further and ascertain the *reason* for absence. It is unfair to dismiss without such investigation (*Paine and Moore* v *Grundy (Teddington) Ltd* [1981] IRLR 267). Unlike in a case of dismissal for misconduct or incapability, the employer need not, however, warn an employee that his poor attendance may lead to his being selected for redundancy (*Gray* v *Shetland Norse Preserving Co. Ltd* [1985] IRLR 53).

(b) Bumping: an employer may decide to declare the redundancy not in the section in which the work requirements have diminished but to move employees from other sections to cover that work and make the redundancies elsewhere in the establishment. Thus, in *Thomas & Betts Manufacturing Co. Ltd* v *Harding* [1980] IRLR 255, the Court of Appeal approved a tribunal decision that a woman who was employed making fittings and had two years' employment was unfairly dismissed where a packer who had served for a few weeks was retained. (See also *Forman Construction Ltd* v *Kelly* [1977] IRLR 469.) The Scottish EAT, however, has held that this was not necessarily a general 'hard and fast' principle which must be followed in every case (*Green* v *A & I Fraser (Wholesale Fish Merchants) Ltd* [1985] IRLR 55).

(c)   Participating in a strike: in *Cruikshank* v *Hobbs* [1977] ICR 725 a redundancy arose after a dispute at the employer's Newmarket racing stables. The employer chose five out of the six stable lads who had gone on strike, and the EAT thought that this was a fair reaction, having regard to the loyalty of the other 24 lads during the dispute. The result would have been different, however, if the redundancy had been merely a pretext to remove the strikers.

(d)   Last in first out: this is the criterion most often advocated by trade unions, but employers are sometimes reluctant to accede to it on the ground that after a redundancy, it will leave them with the oldest and least fit workers. The Court of Appeal commented in *Bessenden Properties Ltd* v *Corness* [1977] ICR 821 that, 'it is generally regarded as fair to retain the services of that employee who has been longest in service'. As already mentioned, employers often temper this by the need to maintain a balanced workforce or by taking into account attendance and conduct record, and in recent times tribunals have been reluctant to criticise an employer's selection unless manifestly unfair.

(e)   Discriminatory selection: selection which is unlawful because it is on the grounds of race or sex will probably (but not necessarily always) render the dismissal unfair as well as entitling the dismissed employee to claim under the Race Relations or Sex Discrimination Acts. This applies to indirect as well as direct discrimination, as seen in *Clarke* v *Eley (IMI) Kynoch Ltd* [1982] IRLR 482. The EAT decided that the commonly applied criterion of dismissing part-time workers first was indirectly discriminatory against women since a considerably smaller proportion of women than men could comply. In *Kidd* v *DRG (UK) Ltd* [1985] IRLR 90, however, the EAT decided that dismissal of a part-time employee before full-timers was not discriminatory, and even if it had been it would have been justifiable because of the marginal advantages in cost and efficiency in operating one shift.

(f)   Disabled employees: selection of disabled employees for redundancy is not necessarily unfair if the employer satisfies the tribunal that it was in the interests of the business to retain able-bodied employees (*Seymour* v *British Airways Board* [1983] ICR 148; see also *Hobson* v *GEC Telecommunications Ltd* [1985] ICR 777).

There is no absolute requirement for a right of appeal in a selection case (*Robinson* v *Ulster Carpet Mills Ltd* [1991] IRLR 348).

13.10.3   Consultation

According to the *Compair Maxam* case, the employer must consult the union as to the best means by which the desired management result of redundancies can be achieved with as little hardship to the employees as possible. This principle receives specific statutory embodiment in TULR(C)A 1992 in the case of recognised unions or employers with recognised representatives who must be consulted 30 or 90 days before the dismissals begin. An employee who loses by such failure is entitled to compensation by way of a protective award (Chapter 15).

Consultation with the union does not, however, absolve the employer from consulting each individual employee about his future (*Huddersfield Parcels Ltd* v *Sykes* [1981] IRLR 115; cf. *Pink* v *White and White & Co. (Earls Barton) Ltd* [1985] IRLR 489; cf. *Eclipse Blinds Ltd* v *Wright* [1992] IRLR 133, *Ferguson* v *Prestwick Circuits Ltd* [1992] IRLR 267). Consultation is 'one of the fundamentals of fairness' (*Holden* v *Bradville Ltd* [1985] IRLR 483; cf. *F. Lafferty Construction Ltd* v *Duthie* [1985] IRLR 487). To fail to consult is not a matter of mere discourtesy to the employee, but rather it deprives the employer of the opportunity to consider whether there may be another slot for the worker to fit into (*Abbots & Standley* v *Wesson-Glynwed Steels Ltd* [1982] IRLR 51) and how he might ameliorate the blow for the employee (*Graham* v *ABF Ltd* [1986] IRLR 90, *Freud* v *Bentalls Ltd* [1982] IRLR 443). In the latter case, Browne-Wilkinson J stressed that, 'Consultation is one of the foundation stones of modern industrial relations practice.' (See *Walls Meat Ltd* v *Selby* [1989] ICR 601.) It is not correct for an industrial tribunal to find that since consultation on the choice of criteria to be applied in a redundancy situation had been taken as far as it was practicable to do, there ceased to be any obligation on the employer to consult with the union or with the employees concerned about the application of those criteria to individuals (*Rolls Royce Motor Cars Ltd* v *Price* [1993] IRLR 203). Further, in a very important judgment, the Court of Session, in *King* v *Eaton Ltd* [1996] IRLR 199, ruled that the union should have been consulted at a time when they could have influenced the criteria for selection and not after they have been set in stone.

There was, however, authority that if consultation would have made no difference to the decision to dismiss, there would be no liability in unfair dismissal for failing to consult (*Atkinson* v *George Lindsay & Co.* [1980] IRLR 196, *Ladbroke Courage Holidays Ltd* v *Asten* [1981] IRLR 59). In *Freud*'s case, the EAT recognised that 'there may well be circumstances (for example, a catastrophic cash flow problem making it essential to take immediate steps to reduce the wages bill) which would make consultation impracticable', but the small size of an employer cannot excuse it from making any effort at all to consult over a redundancy (e.g. *De Grasse* v *Stockwell Tools Ltd* [1992] IRLR 269).

Following the decision of the House of Lords in *Polkey* v *Dayton Services Ltd* [1988] ICR 142, this matter may be considered on the assessment of compensation but not in determining liablity (see also *Heron* v *Citylink-Nottingham* [1993] IRLR 372).

13.10.4 Alternative employment

The principle that the employer should take reasonable steps to seek alternative employment for his employees was first enunciated in *Vokes Ltd* v *Bear* [1974] ICR 1. This was a strong case since the respondent company was part of the massive Thomas Tilling group of companies in which there existed several vacancies in the type of senior management positions which the applicant had occupied before his redundancy. The failure to offer such a position rendered the dismissal unfair. In *MDH Ltd* v *Sussex* [1986] IRLR 123, the applicant was employed by Dent & Hellyer Ltd, which was part of the large Tilling Group. Dent & Hellyer was merged with another company to form MDH Ltd. When the applicant was made redundant the tribunal thought that there was an obligation to look for alternative opportunities *throughout* the Tilling Group. The EAT thought that this was an error of law and a misinterpretation of *Vokes Ltd* v *Bear* (supra), which had also dealt with the Tilling Group. The industrial tribunal should not have relied on that case as a binding precedent. In *British United Shoe Machinery Co. Ltd* v *Clarke* [1977] IRLR 297, the EAT counselled against unreal or 'Elysian standards' being expected of an employer, and in *Barratt Construction Ltd* v *Dalrymple* [1984] IRLR 385, the Scottish EAT decided that the appellant employers did not have to look for alternatives in other parts of the Barratt group for junior jobs. Lord Macdonald thought that the change in the onus of proof in s. 57(3) of EPCA 1978 (now ERA 1996, s. 98(4)) had altered the scope of the *Vokes* principle, and:

Without laying down any hard and fast rule we are inclined to think that where an employee at senior management level who is being made redundant is prepared to accept a subordinate position he ought, in fairness, to make it clear at an early stage so as to give his employer an opportunity to see if this is a feasible solution.

(Cf. *Avonmouth Construction Co. Ltd* v *Shipway* [1979] IRLR 14, *Modern Injection Moulds Ltd* v *Price* [1976] ICR 370.) An employer who can offer alternative employment must make such offer sufficiently clear so that an employee may make a decision. In some cases, this obligation to consider offering alternative work has meant that another employee has to be dismissed (*Thomas & Betts Manufacturing Co. Ltd* v *Harding* [1980] IRLR 255).

The Court of Appeal has indicated that an employer only has a duty to provide such alternative employment as is available whilst the employee remains in the employment of the employer. In *Octavius Atkinson & Sons Ltd* v *Morris* [1989] IRLR 158, new employment became available in between the employee leaving work, having been summarily dismissed, and arriving at his home on the same day. Although the EAT had found that the employee remained in employment until he got home, the Court of Appeal could not agree ([1989] ICR 431) and held that the employers had acted reasonably in not offering the employee the alternative employment.

It may be an unfair dismissal for an employer to dismiss even though before the effective date of termination the employers offer to retain an employee on the understanding that another employee will be dismissed in her place. It is unfair to put that onus on the employee and constitutes an abrogation of the employer's responsibility to manage the business (*Boulton & Paul Ltd* v *Arnold* [1994] IRLR 532).

13.10.5 Future needs

There is some industrial tribunal authority that the employer ought to consider the possibility of vacancies in the future. This is probably confined to employers with a large turnover of staff such as in bookmakers' shops (*Allwood* v *William Hill (North East) Ltd* [1974] IRLR 258).

13.11 SOME OTHER SUBSTANTIAL REASON

This provision has been variously described as a 'dustbin category' or 'employer's charter', intended as a safety net to catch substantial reasons for dismissal which did not fall within other potentially fair gateways to dismissal. It has a 'rubber band' quality which arguably has been stretched too far. (See J. Bowers and A. Clarke, 10 ILJ 34.) Its language is indeed rather wider than the provisions of ILO Recommendation Number 119 on which most of the unfair dismissal legislation was based.

The test was explained by the Court of Appeal in *Kent CC* v *Gilham* [1985] IRLR 16 as follows:

> The hurdle over which an employer has to jump at this stage of an enquiry into an unfair dismissal complaint is designed to deter employers from dismissing employees for some trivial or unworthy reason. If he does so, the dismissal is deemed unfair without the need to look further into its merits. But if on the face of it the reason *could* justify the dismissal, then it passes as a substantial reason, and the enquiry moves on to [s. 98(4)] and the question of reasonableness.

According to Sir John Donaldson MR, 'different types of reason could justify the dismissal of the office boy from those which could justify the dismissal of the managing director'. (See also *Harper* v *National Coal Board* [1980] IRLR 260.) Very few reasons have failed because they are not substantial and there is a tendency in this area to conflate the issue of 'other substantial reason' with the question of whether the employer acted reasonably.

These, and other, developments have important implications for the whole policy of unfair dismissal. For the delicate balance at its heart between employer and employee is thus subtly tilted in favour of the employer. Central to this imbalance is the fact that rejection of management-instituted reorganisation is often portrayed as an undesirable curb on employer prerogative.

In three respects, subsequent judgments have not lived up to what general statements there have been in the NIRC and EAT about 'some other substantial reason'. Most importantly, Brightman J in *RS Components Ltd* v *Irwin* [1973] ICR 535, while deciding that the subsection was not to be construed *ejusdem generis* with the other headings, did go on to say that: 'It ought not as a matter of good industrial relations and common fairness to be construed too widely against the employee.' Subsequently, however, a conglomeration of reasons, usually flowing from management-pronounced notions of 'business efficiency', have come through the wide-open door.

Secondly, the NIRC were at pains to keep distinct the employer's reasons for dismissal and the reasonableness thereof. In *Mercia Rubber Mouldings* v *Lingwood* [1974] IRLR 82, Donaldson J commented: 'The reason must be one which can justify dismissal, not one which *does* justify the dismissal.' This has proved rather easier to formulate than apply, as demonstrated by the relative paucity of cases in which 'another substantial reason' has been found, and yet the dismissal has been subsequently held unfair.

Thirdly, although the EAT roundly declared in *Trusthouse Forte Leisure Ltd* v *Aquilar* [1976] IRLR 251, that 'the employer's description of the reason for dismissal is by no means conclusive', this principle has recently been honoured more in the breach than in its observance. The most extreme expression of non-intervention is to be found in the acceptance by tribunals of the employer's policy on reorganisation. As Arnold J formulated it in *Banerjee* v *City and East London AHA* [1979] IRLR 147 (at para. 19):

If an employer comes and says 'we have evolved such and such a policy'. . . it seems to us that it must inevitably follow that this enunciation by the employer of the policy as a matter of importance . . . can be seen to be the subject of a substantial other reason.

It may be challenged only on the basis of a complete lack of evidence. This approach rears its head with devastating effect in other areas of unfair dismissal, most notably selection for redundancy, and it undermines the principle that the statutory procedure should ensure that the dismissed employee receives an objective assessment of the basic factual adequacy of accusations made by the employer.

The reasons laid down by statute as being substantial reasons are dismissals of workers:

(a) taken on temporarily to replace permanent employees who are medically suspended or pregnant (in both cases the replacement must be warned of the temporary nature of the job on engagement (ERA 1996, s. 106));

(b) where there are 'economic, technical or organisational reason[s] entailing [a change] in the workforce of either the transferor or transferee before or after a relevant transfer' on a transfer of undertaking (reg. 8(2) of the Transfer of Undertakings (Protection of Employment) Regulations 1981 (see para. 16.5)). If an employer wishes to rely on this reason for dismissal, he must expressly raise it before the tribunal or at the very least relate the full facts establishing it before the tribunal (*Murphy* v *Epsom College* [1983] IRLR 395).

The five most important categories of cases under this rubric are as follows.

13.11.1   Quasi or reorganisational redundancy

It is in the area of 'quasi redundancies', that is, reorganisations which fail to satisfy the detailed requirements of ss. 135 and 139 of ERA 1996 for redundancy, that the EAT has found most scope for a dynamic interpretation of s. 98(1)(b). They have allowed the undertaking which reorganises or regroups, and finds that it has 'surplus staff', to escape both redundancy payments and unfair dismissal. That there should be some flexibility for employers to reorganise cannot be gainsaid, but the threshold for use of this heading has been lowered.

When this notion crystallised is difficult to pinpoint. Phillips J in *Gorman* v *London Computer Training Centre* [1978] IRLR 22, however, dwelt on the 'clear distinction' recognised between redundancy (s. 98(2)(c)) and quasi 'redundancy' (s. 98(1)(b)). The learned judge said:

> An employer may say 'I was overmanned, so we had to get rid of someone so A and B had to go, they were redundant'. The wording of [now ERA 1996, s. 139] may show he was wrong, but these grounds may well form a substantial reason.

It is difficult to define the criteria of reorganisation beyond the need for a 'policy', and the need to show the solid advantages of that strategy has steadily diminished. As to the existence of a policy, 'this is not an onus which it is at all difficult to discharge'. Only where there is no evidence at all is the claim open to challenge. In *Banerjee* v *City and East London AHA* [1979] IRLR 147, a consultancy had been held jointly by two part-time employees. One left and the authority decided to create a single full-time appointment so that the applicant Dr Banerjee, the other part-timer, was consequently dismissed. The defendants stated that this was determined in accordance with its 'policy of rationalisation, and the custom and practice of amalgamating part-time posts', but the EAT thought that was not enough and called on the Authority to produce relevant minutes of meetings to prove that due consideration had been given to all relevant matters in formulating the policy. There was no evidence of this at all.

Once there is evidence of a policy, however, the next stage which would appear crucial to the substantiality of the reason has been much less strict. In *Ellis* v *Brighton Co-op Society* [1976] IRLR 419, there was a properly consulted-upon and trade union-agreed reorganisation which, if not done, would 'bring the whole business to a standstill'. In *Robinson* v *British Island Airways Ltd* [1978] ICR 304, the EAT required a 'pressing business reason', and in *Hollister* v *NFU* [1979] ICR 542, the Court of Appeal pointed to the necessity for a 'sound good business reason'. After *Banerjee,* however, all that need be shown is that the changes were considered to be 'matters of importance' or to have 'discernible advantages to the organisation'. *Bowater Containers Ltd* v *McCormack* [1980] IRLR 50 demands that the reorganisation be 'beneficial'. (See also *Genower* v *Ealing, Hammersmith & Hounslow AHA* [1980] IRLR 297.)

It was in *Hollister* v *NFU* (supra) that the Court of Appeal formalised the close relation between reorganisation and managerial prerogative. The appellant was one of the respondent union's group secretaries, and received a modest wage and commission on insurance policies sold. The Union reorganised their business in a drastic way, so that insurance was no longer dealt with locally, and the appellant's income was substantially cut as a result. On his refusal to sign a new contract, he was dismissed. Not only was this 'some other substantial reason', but the Court of Appeal, differing in this respect from the EAT, decided that there was no requirement for consultation with the employee.

In this area more than elsewhere, the tribunal has to weigh the economic interests of employer and employee. In *Evans* v *Elemeta Holdings Ltd* [1982] IRLR 143, the EAT suggested that if it was reasonable for an employee to decline new terms offered by the employer, it would be unreasonable to dismiss him for it. In *Chubb Fire Security Ltd* v *Harper* [1983] IRLR 311, the EAT dissented from this view, however, and stressed that the only proper question is the reasonableness of the employer's conduct in dismissing: were the employers reasonable in determining that the advantages to them of implementing the proposed reorganisation of terms outweighed any disadvantage they should have foreseen that the employee might suffer? (See also *Richmond Precision Engineering Ltd* v *Pearce* [1985] IRLR 179.)

The crucial question is not whether the terms offered were those which a reasonable employer could offer, because that blinds the industrial tribunal to the important issue of what happened between the time when the offer was made and the dismissal. The proper question instead is whether the dismissal was reasonable in all the circumstances, and that would be affected by the question of whether only 1 per cent or as many as 99 per cent of the other employees had accepted the offer. The situation may be one in which the employer's legitimate interests and the employee's equally legitimate interests are irreconcilable, but if there is a sound business reason for the particular reorganisation, the reasonableness of the employer's conduct must be considered in the context of that reorganisation (*St John of God (Care Services) Ltd* v *Brooks* [1992] IRLR 546). The tribunal must examine the employer's motive for the changes and satisfy itself that they are not to be imposed for arbitrary reasons (*Catamaran Cruisers Ltd* v *Williams* [1994] IRLR 386). It is also important to bear in mind whether the trade union accepted the changes (*Catamaran Cruisers Ltd*, supra). While the formation of such a company may be strong evidence of a change of status away from employment, that fact has to be evaluated in the context of all the other facts found. The EAT did 'not accept as a valid proposition of law that an employer may only offer terms which are less or much less favourable than those which pre-existed if the very survival of his business depends upon acceptance of the terms' (para. 19).

A review of the reorganisation case law shows that the EAT and the Court of Appeal appear to accept as wholly valid employers' claims that to compete efficiently in a free market they must be allowed latitude to trim and make efficient their workforce and work methods, without being hampered by laws protecting their workers.

In *Orr* v *Vaughan* [1981] IRLR 63, the EAT stressed that the employers must act on reasonable information reasonably acquired as to their business needs. Here, the employers could not be satisfied on the information available that it was at the particular salon where the respondent was employed that the business was losing money. The employer must provide evidence that there was a need for economy there and it is material for the industrial tribunal to know whether the company was at the time making profits or losses (*Ladbroke Courage Holidays Ltd* v *Asten* [1981] IRLR 59).

Where the employer decides to dismiss an employee and uses a reorganisation as a pretext to achieve this covert aim, the dismissal is unfair (*Oakley* v *The Labour Party* [1988] IRLR 34).

13.11.2 Contractual changes: a blow to the sanctity of contract?

Another widespread use of 'other substantial reason' is where an employer insists on a change in the employee's contractual terms and conditions. Thus in *RS Components Ltd* v *Irwin* [1973] ICR 535, the company was losing profits because of the activities of some ex-employees who had set up in competition to them. They thus required their 92 current salesmen to sign a restrictive convenant. Four refused and the NIRC held their consequent dismissal fair. Brightman J posited,

a case where it would be essential for employers embarking, for example, on a new technical process to invite existing employees to agree to some reasonable restriction on their use of the knowledge they acquire of the new technique.

Unfair dismissal provisions have provided no protection against unilateral changes in:

(a)   job content (e.g. *Robinson* v *Flitwick Frames Ltd* [1975] IRLR 261);
(b)   location (e.g. *Farr* v *Hoveringham Gravels Ltd* [1972] IRLR 104);
(c)   pay (*Industrial Rubber Products Ltd* v *Gillon* [1977] IRLR 389);
(d)   night shift working (*Martin* v *Automobile Proprietary Ltd* [1979] IRLR 64).

These cases emphasise that what would be a constructive dismissal is not necessarily unfair (para. 13.3.3.8). Yet it is ironic that the unfair dismissal provisions, which were intended to give employees broader rights than at common law, should recognise as a reason for dismissal a compulsory change in contractual terms which would be unlawful at common law and could lead to a claim for wrongful dismissal.

13.11.3   Temporary workers: a recognition of the dangers

One of the clearest perceptions of British individual employment law is that it provides a form of 'job security' only to employees who have been with the undertaking for more than a minimal amount of time. This principle might be infringed if employees were too readily held to be 'temporary', and thus not deserving of protection. 'Other substantial reason' has been at times adopted to cover dismissals of temporary workers, but the dangers of an over-extended definition have been recognised.

In the leading case, *Terry* v *East Sussex CC* [1976] ICR 536, the EAT stressed that in every instance the tribunal must ensure that the description was 'a genuine one, where an employee has to his knowledge been employed for a particular job on a temporary basis'. In *Cohen* v *London Borough of Barking* [1976] IRLR 416 EAT, Slynn J emphasised that, while the fact that the contract was not assured of continuance beyond a fixed term was a material factor to be considered, it was not at all conclusive. The temporary employee ought to be given the opportunity of being considered if a full-time position becomes available (*Beard* v *St Joseph's School* [1978] ICR 1234), and tribunals must not omit a 'full consideration of the circumstances surrounding a decision to dismiss at the end of a temporary fixed term contract'. In the case of *North Yorkshire CC* v *Fay* [1985] IRLR 247 the Court of Appeal dealing with a teacher's contract decided that there was a fair 'other substantial reason' if it is shown that the fixed term contract was adopted for a genuine purpose and that fact was known to the employee, and that the specific purpose for which the contract was adopted had indeed ceased.

These cases show a welcome recognition of the underlying intentions of the Act, refusing to allow 'some other substantial reason' to deny too easily protection for the temporary employee.

13.11.4   Subverting the other gateways: conduct

The ERA 1996 defines with some particularity conduct, redundancy and contravention of an enactment which may give rise to a fair dismissal, but tribunals have used 'other substantial reason' to extend the concepts. While conduct connotes active behaviour by the employee, 'another substantial reason' includes omissions. In *O'Brien* v *Prudential Assurance Co. Ltd* [1979] IRLR 140, an employee failed to disclose a long period of mental illness when applying for the job and this was some other substantial reason justifying dismissal. The argument that the reason had to be directly referable to the employee's work for the employer failed, as it did in a series of cases in which activities outside and before the job have been included under s. 98(1). These raise philosophical issues about how far the managerial prerogative strays into the employee's private life. The cases include dismissals on the grounds of:

(a) The homosexuality of a maintenance handyman at a children's holiday camp — the Court of Session would not interfere with the determination of fairness once they found the employers held a common and not unreasonable belief that homosexuals were more likely than heterosexuals to interfere with young children (*Saunders* v *Scottish National Camps Association Ltd* [1980] IRLR 174).

(b) The wish of the employer to appoint his son to the employee's job (*Priddle* v *Dibble* [1978] ICR 149).

(c) The employee's epileptic attacks which frightened fellow employees (*Harper* v *National Coal Board* [1980] IRLR 260).

(d) The employee's plan to join another firm (*Davidson and Maillou* v *Comparisons Ltd* [1980] IRLR 360).

(e) A woman employee's plans to marry a man who worked for a rival travel company (*Skyrail Oceanic* v *Coleman* [1980] ICR 596), and this fell within the section notwithstanding that the two clerks had no financial interest in their respective companies. It was found unfair in all the circumstances, however, because the employer had given no warning of dismissal so that there was no opportunity to find alternative employment.

(f) A breakdown in relationships between employees has often been characterised as some other substantial reason, but the EAT in *Turner* v *Vestric Ltd* [1980] ICR 528, counselled that the employer must take reasonable steps to try to improve the relationship and examine all options short of dismissal to obviate the situation (see also *Treganowan* v *Robert Knee* [1975] ICR 405).

(g) A three-month prison sentence for a serious offence (*Kingston* v *British Railways Board* [1984] IRLR 146).

(h) The employee's husband having been dismissed as bar manager and the employers required a husband and wife team (*Kelman* v *G. J. Oram* [1983] IRLR 432).

(i) A refusal by the employee to work at weekends (*Yusuf* v *Aberplace Ltd* [1984] ICR 850).

On the other hand, the following reasons have been held to be insubstantial:

(a) a rumour that the employee would leave to set up a rival business;

(b) a rescinded decision to depart (*Ready Case Ltd* v *Jackson* [1981] IRLR 312);

(c) the employee's age (*Betts* v *Beresford* [1974] IRLR 271);

(d) the fact that the applicant's wife had been convicted of many offences of dishonesty (*Wadley* v *Eager Electrical Ltd* [1986] IRLR 93).

13.11.5 Outside pressure

There are several decisions in which an outside source of pressure on the employer has been seen as some other substantial reason. In *Scott Packing and Warehousing Co. Ltd* v *Paterson*

[1978] IRLR 166, the EAT held that it might be justifiable to dismiss an employee in response to an ultimatum from the company's major customer. The US naval authorities refused the applicant's services because of a suspected theft, of which no evidence was presented. This could hardly be a fair dismissal for misconduct, since the employing company had been fully aware of the facts for a full six weeks before dismissal, but it was some other substantial reason. *Moody* v *Telefusion Ltd* [1978] IRLR 311, takes this further, since the EAT held fair a dismissal because the employee was unable to secure a fidelity bond. In deciding whether the reason was substantial the EAT failed to enquire into the reasonableness of requiring a fidelity bond (see also *Dobie* v *Burns International Security Services (UK) Ltd* [1984] IRLR 329). In *Grootcon (UK) Ltd* v *Keld* [1984] IRLR 302, the EAT stressed that the employer must lead convincing evidence of the outside pressure he was under.

13.12 ILLEGALITY

The employer may prove as a reason for dismissal 'that the employee could not continue to work in the position which he held without contravention (either on his part or on that of his employer) of a duty or restriction imposed by or under an enactment' (ERA 1996, s. 98(2)(d)). The statute to qualify must in any case be related to the work the applicant was actually employed to do, so that a clear example is the determination by the Secretary of State for Employment under his statutory powers that a teacher is unsuitable (*Sandhu* v *Department of Education and Science* [1978] IRLR 208). Dismissal often, for example, follows the disqualification from driving of an employee who must use his car for work.

Even in these cases the resulting dismissal is not automatically fair. In *Sutcliffe & Eaton Ltd* v *Pinney* [1977] IRLR 349, the applicant, a hearing aid dispenser, was sacked when he failed to pass the Hearing Aid Council's examination and was thus removed from the appropriate register of dispensers. It was an offence for him to continue to so act under the Hearing Aid Council Act 1968. Since, however, it was possible for him to obtain an extension of time to take the exam and prosecution was unlikely, his dismissal without the employer inquiring of the likely position was held unfair by the EAT. Reasonableness may also require the employer offering suitable alternative employment if appropriate. Thus the disqualified driver may be transferred to a stationary task (e.g. *Appleyard* v *Smith (Hull) Ltd* [1972] IRLR 19).

Dismissal of an employee because he has not obtained a proper work permit often falls under this head, but if the employer is mistaken as to the legality of the permission the appropriate subsection is 'some other substantial reason' (*Bouchaala* v *Trusthouse Forte Hotels Ltd* [1980] ICR 721).

13.13 SPENT OFFENCES

The aim of the Rehabilitation of Offenders Act 1974 is that a convicted criminal may put his past behind him and make a fresh start. When the rehabilitation period appropriate to his sentence has elapsed, the conviction is 'spent' and should not be taken into account for any purpose including employment. Thus s. 4(3)(b) provides that a spent conviction or the failure to disclose a spent conviction shall be an automatically unfair ground for dismissing someone from any office, profession, occupation or employment, or for prejudicing him in any way. The rehabilitation period depends on the sentence imposed; the most important are as follows:

Sentence	*Rehabilitation period*
Imprisonment between 6 and 30 months	10 years
Imprisonment under 6 months	7 years
Fine	5 years
Borstal	7 years
Detention centre	3 years

By the Criminal Justice and Public Order Act 1994, the rehabilitation period in respect of probation order was increased from one year from the date of conviction or the date the order ceased (whichever was longer) to five years from the date of conviction in the case of an adult, and two and a half years from the date of conviction or the date the order ceased (whichever is longer) in the case of a person aged under 18.

The effect is limited by subsequent regulations (Rehabilitation of Offenders Act 1974 (Exceptions) Order 1975 (SI 1975 No. 1023)), which make exemptions from these provisions in the case of certain sensitive professions including medical practitioners, lawyers, accountants, dentists, nurses, police and social services workers (see *Hendry* v *Scottish Liberal Club* [1977] IRLR 5). By the Rehabilitation of Offenders Act 1974 (Exceptions) (Amendment) Order 1986 (SI 1986 No. 1249), a general exception exists for any office or employment which is concerned in the provision of accommodation, leisure and recreational facilities, schooling, social services, supervision or training to persons under 18 years, where the holder of the office or employment would have access to such minors in the normal course of his duties, or if the duties are carried out wholly or partly on the premises where such provision takes place. There is no exception in respect of security guards (*Property Guards Ltd* v *Taylor and Kershaw* [1982] IRLR 175; see also *Wood* v *Coverage Care Ltd* [1996] IRLR 264).

13.14 DISMISSAL DURING STRIKE OR LOCK-OUT: OFFICIAL ACTION

The provisions of TULR(C)A 1992, ss. 237–239 (previously Employment Protection (Consolidation) Act 1978, ss. 62 and 62A) concerning dismissal during lock-out, strike or other industrial action are a borderline where collective and individual labour law meet. The interconnection is not altogether happy, and the tensions are apparent in the case law. One can see in particular the natural desire of the industrial tribunals to avoid determining the merits of industrial disputes. The section was used by News International plc management in January 1986 to dismiss 5,500 print workers in the 'Wapping dispute' and by P & O in the Dover ferry dispute in 1988. (For fuller consideration, see J. Bowers and M. Duggan, *The Modern Law of Strikes,* Financial Training, 1987, pp. 109–24.)

By s. 238 of the 1992 Act a tribunal has no jurisdiction to determine whether a dismissal is unfair if at the time of the dismissal, the employer was conducting a lock-out or the employee was taking part in a strike or other industrial action and if all so participating are dismissed, and none re-engaged within three months of the dismissal. (There are more stringent provisions against unofficial action, whereby any participants may be dismissed without the industrial tribunal having jurisdiction (see para. 13.15).) The employer does not have to prove that the industrial dispute was the *reason* for the dismissal, merely that such termination coincided with the industrial action. The employer may even deliberately provoke the stoppage to remove his workforce with financial impunity.

In *Hindle Gears Ltd* v *McGinty* [1984] IRLR 477, Waite J said that the general immunity is subject . . . to stringent sanctions, designed to deter employers from abusing the immunity by treating a strike as a pretext for dismissing the unwanted elements in their workforce and retaining the remainder . . . . Motive is irrelevant. Inadvertance makes no difference. The rule is wholly rigid and inflexible. The result (as the authorities show) has been to turn the process of dismissal of a striking workforce into something like a game of hazard in which the winner takes all, in which defeat or victory turns upon the fall of a single card and in which the stakes increase dramatically according to the number involved.

As Browne-Wilkinson J said in *Coates* v *Modern Methods and Materials Ltd* [1982] ICR 763, in these cases 'it is of great importance to employers that they should so far as possible know the consequences of their acts before they decide to dismiss and who to retain or re-engage'. The costs of getting it wrong from the employer's point of view may indeed be colossal, especially if the tribunal were to decide that the employees were not dismissed in the course of a strike and that the reason for dismissal was the trade union activities of the workforce. In such cases the much enhanced special award would be available to dismissed employees (see para. 13.18.5). (On issue estoppel in such cases, see *Munir* v *Jang Publications Ltd* [1989] IRLR 224.)

The judgments do little to clarify the law for employers and employees. Indeed, there have been many decisions that the vital issues which arise are matters of fact for the industrial tribunal sitting as an industrial jury.

13.14.1   The meaning of strike, other industrial action or lock-out

13.14.1.1   What is a strike?   'Strike' is undefined for the purposes of TULR(C)A 1992, ss. 237 to 239. In one case, the Employment Appeal Tribunal incorporated by reference its definition for continuity purposes in Sch. 13 to the EPCA 1978 (now ERA 1996, ss. 210–219 and 235(5)). Lord Denning's definition in the contractual case of *Tramp Shipping Corporation* v *Greenwich Marine Inc.* [1975] ICR 261 has also been applied in this context and this is rather more appropriate. The then Master of the Rolls considered that a strike was 'a concerted stoppage of work by men done with a view to improving their wages or conditions or giving vent to a grievance or making a protest about something or other or sympathising with other workmen in such endeavours'. An individual protest would not qualify (*Bowater Containers Ltd* v *Blake*, EAT 522/81; cf. *Lewis and Britton* v *E. Mason & Sons* [1994] IRLR 4).

13.14.1.2   What is other industrial action?   Tribunals and appeal bodies have been reluctant to place a rigid limit on the activities which might constitute other industrial action for the purposes of TULR(C)A 1992, ss. 237 to 239. They again see it as a question of fact in each case; the categories are certainly not closed. The phrase includes a go-slow, work-to-rule, concerted non-cooperation, and probably a picket of the employer's premises. Most such activity will break the implied contractual duty that an employee shall not disrupt the employer's enterprise (*Secretary of State for Employment* v *ASLEF (No. 2)* [1972] 2 QB 455; see also *Miles* v *Wakefield Metropolitan District Council* [1987] ICR 368).

The phrase is not, however, restricted to such a breach of contract; thus a concerted withdrawal of cooperation over admittedly voluntary overtime constituted 'other industrial action' according to the Court of Appeal in *Faust* v *Power Packing Casemakers Ltd* [1983] IRLR 117. It was sufficient that the action applied pressure against management, and was designed to extract some benefit from management for the workforce. In *Lewis and Britton v E. Mason & Sons* [1994] IRLR 4, this was somewhat surprisingly held to apply to a protest by a lorry driver about driving a particular vehicle from Wales to Edinburgh becuase it did not have an overnight heater, unless he was given an extra £5 for overnight subsistence. It may be doubted whether this will be followed in later cases, and it should be noted that the EAT was concerned to uphold the decision of the industrial tribunal on the ground that it was a matter of fact for it.

Controversy has arisen over participation in unauthorised mass meetings. In some businesses, the disruptive union meeting at the peak point of production is a well-worn union tactic (see also *Rasool* v *Hepworth Pipe Co. Ltd (No. 1)* [1980] ICR 494, *Lookers of Bradford* v *Marvin*, EAT 322/80).

It may be difficult in some cases to distinguish between a strike and other industrial action. In *Thompson* v *Eaton Ltd* [1976] ICR 336, for example, employees stood round a new machine for a short time to prevent their employers from testing its operation. The EAT held that this could qualify under either heading.

13.14.1.3 What is a lock-out? The EPCA 1978, Sch. 13, para. 24(1) defined lock-out for the purposes of continuity of service as 'the closing of a place of employment, suspension of work, refusal by an employer to continue to employ any number of persons employed by him in consequence of a dispute done with a view to compelling those persons to accept terms and conditions of or affecting employment' (see now ERA 1996, s. 235(4)). These words were applied to what was then EPCA 1978, s. 62 in *Fisher* v *York Trailer Co. Ltd* [1979] ICR 834, but the Court of Appeal sought to take a broader view in *Express & Star Ltd* v *Bunday* [1988] ICR 379. In the course of a dispute over the introduction of new technology into a local newspaper, the employers refused the employees access to the premises where they worked, with the exception of one door which was manned by members of management. When employees arrived through this door, they were taken at once to a meeting at which those who refused to work with new machinery were suspended without pay. The issue was whether there was a lock-out for the purposes of the former s. 62.

The Court of Appeal decided that the Sch. 13 definition could not be applied word for word, but May LJ said that 'they may give an indication of the sort of ingredients that one should look for'. May and Croom-Johnson LJJ regarded the question of whether the employers were in breach of contract as a 'material consideration' in determining whether there was a lock-out. Glidewell LJ, dissenting, thought that as a matter of law an employer who refuses to let all employees work unless they undertake to perform the terms of their contract cannot be regarded as conducting a lock-out. In the result, the Court of Appeal decided that the industrial tribunal was correct as a matter of fact in determining that the employees were taking part in industrial action at the date of their dismissals rather than that the employer was conducting a lock-out.

13.14.1.4 Can an employer provoke industrial action and then dismiss those who participate in it? It appears that an employer may deliberately engineer a dispute and then dismiss without compensation those who participate in it. The test is merely whether the employee was dismissed *in the course of the industrial action.* Whether the action was the real *reason* for the sacking is irrelevant to this issue (see *Faust*'s case). This principle has the advantage of keeping the industrial tribunals away from the merits of the dispute. Moreover, as Phillips J said in *Thompson* v *Eaton* (supra): 'It is rare for a strike or other industrial action to be wholly the fault of one side or the other. Almost always there is some blame on each side.' (See also *Marsden* v *Fairey Stainless Ltd* [1979] IRLR 103.)

Employers who follow this strategy must be careful not to repudiate the contracts of employment of their employees since the workforce might accept such a breach as a constructive dismissal, and then claims would be made on grounds not of the employer's choosing. The question for the industrial tribunal would then be whether in breaching the contract, the employer acted reasonably in all the circumstances of the case (the normal s. 98(4) test). The fact of going on strike in itself will probably not, however, be treated as the acceptance by the employee of the employer's repudiation (*Wilkins* v *Cantrell & Cochrane (GB) Ltd* [1978] IRLR 483).

13.14.2 Was the dismissed employee participating in the action?

The section only has effect in giving immunity if the dismissed employee was participating in the strike or other industrial action on the *date of dismissal.* Stephenson LJ in *Coates*'s case considered that this vital issue on which the jurisdiction of the tribunal depended was 'just the sort of question which an industrial jury is best fitted to decide' (see to the same effect *Hindle Gears Ltd* v *McGinty* [1984] IRLR 477). This position was criticised with great force by the EAT in *Naylor* v *Orton & Smith Ltd* [1983] IRLR 233. There, 33 employees were dismissed for participating in an overtime ban. Two others had voted in favour of such action at a meeting but later signed a form sent out by the employers that they would work normally. The industrial tribunal decided that these two were not to be taken as participating in industrial action, and the EAT President considered that the appeal body could not intervene in the light of the Court of Appeal's pronouncements in *Coates*'s case. It is, however, clear that participation must be personal and direct, and not vicariously through the agency of a shop steward (*Dixon* v *Wilson Walton Engineering Ltd* [1979] ICR 438). In *McKenzie* v *Crosville Motor Services Ltd* [1989] IRLR 516, the EAT decided that the employer had immunity if he dismissed all those whom he reasonably *believed* to be participating in the industrial action; but in *Manifold Industries Ltd* v *Sims* [1991] IRLR 242, another division of the EAT preferred the approach taken in *Bolton Roadways Ltd* v *Edwards* [1987] IRLR 392, so that the matter was one of objective fact, not the knowledge of the employer (see also *Jenkins* v *P&O European Ferries (Dover) Ltd* [1991] ICR 652).

Participation in a strike need not necessarily be known to the employer before it can amount to 'taking part in the action' (*Hindle Gears Ltd* v *McGinty* (supra)). Two categories of employee have engaged particular attention.

13.14.2.1 The frightened employee In *Coates*'s case (supra) a Mrs Leith went on strike, not because of her support for the cause in dispute, but because she was frightened that she would be abused by her fellow workers if she did not. The tribunal decided that she was nevertheless participating in the strike, so that it had jurisdiction to hear the claims of other workers who had been dismissed while she had been re-engaged after the end of hostilities. Kerr LJ did not think that the employee's reasons or motives for participating in the strike were of any moment. Such an enquiry would not be 'correct or practicable'. It would not be relevant 'to consider whether [the employee's] utterances or actions, or silence or inaction showed support, opposition or indifference in relation to the strike'. Stephenson LJ took the direct view that: 'In the field of industrial action, those who are not openly against it are presumably for it.' Eveleigh LJ, however, dissented on the ground that an employee must act in concert with the strikers to be participating in the strike, and this Mrs Leith did not do.

13.14.2.2 The sick employee An employee genuinely on sick leave or holiday during a strike could not normally be said to be participating in it, even though he might have spoken to pickets when attending work to present his sickness certificate (*McGinty*'s case (supra)). The position is, however, different if the employee has already taken part in the action before he goes off sick. In *Williams* v *Western Mail and Echo Ltd* [1980] ICR 366, members of the NUJ were given an ultimatum to discontinue industrial sanctions by a certain day or face dismissal. The applicant was away sick at the time but made clear that he would not have submitted to the ultimatum had he been well. Slynn J was not impressed by the argument that he was not to be considered as taking part in industrial action (*McKenzie* v *Crosville Motor Services Ltd* [1989] IRLR 516).

A genuine belief by the employer that the employee took part in a strike is not enough to justify the employer's action in dismissing (*Thompson* v *Woodland Designs Ltd* [1980] IRLR 423). Moreover, the onus is on the employer to prove that the employee took part in the strike, but it is not correct that participation in a strike must be *known* to the employers before it can qualify as conduct taking part in a strike *(McGinty*'s case (supra)).

In a case where there was no clear finding by the industrial tribunal that had the employee not been ill she would have taken part in industrial action, there was insufficient factual foundation for the inference that she took part in strike action (*Rogers* v *Chloride Systems Ltd* [1992] IRLR 198).

13.14.3 The importance of the date of dismissal

The employee must be taking part in the appropriate action on the date of dismissal for the employer to remain immune from an unfair dismissal claim. The 'date of dismissal' has been construed as the actual time of dismissal with important consequences. In *Heath* v *J. F. Longman (Meat Salesmen) Ltd* [1973] ICR 407, a dispute about overtime payments for Saturday working provoked the employer to declare that if the employees did not work on the following Saturday, they would be dismissed. The applicant and two colleagues went out on strike in response to this ultimatum, but after seeing their union representatives, one of them told the employer that the strike of all of them was at an end. Even so, the employer announced that all three were dismissed. The National Industrial Relations Court was of the view that, 'once the men had telephoned and told the employer that they no longer wished to withdraw their labour and wanted to come back to work, they had in our view clearly ceased to be on strike'. The rule that a part equalled the whole day was not appropriate in this context. The essence of the decision was that the return to work had been communicated to the employer.

The employer may not dismiss with impunity those employees who have announced their intention of going on strike but have not yet begun their action (*Midland Plastics* v *Till* [1983] IRLR 9). If, on the other hand, a strike has already begun, and an employee who is off duty states a clear intention to become involved as soon as his shift starts, he is treated as participating from the time at which he makes his intention clear even if his shift has not started at the time of dismissal (*Winnett* v *Seamark Brothers Ltd* [1978] ICR 1240). There are three important questions to be asked:

(a) By what time does the tribunal decide whether all relevant employees have been dismissed? In *P&O European Ferries (Dover) Ltd* v *Byrne* [1989] IRLR 254, the Court of Appeal determined that the question had to be asked at the *conclusion* of the industrial tribunal hearing. If only some have been dismissed by this time, the tribunal must examine whether the employer was fair or unfair in deciding who was to remain and who was to go. This introduces a certain arbitrary element since the length of time between dismissal and hearing can vary greatly. Moreover, the reason for dismissal of the comparative employees need not be by reason of the strike but may be, for example, because of redundancy.

(b) What is the position if participants in action have returned to work by the time of the applicant's dismissal? Following the amendments introduced by the Employment Act 1982, any participant in strike action who has returned to work at the time of the applicant's dismissal does not amount to a 'relevant employee'. Thus, the employer need not dismiss all those on strike at any time, but merely all those participating in the disruptive action at the time of the applicant's dismissal. He may thus issue an ultimatum to his employees on strike to return or else. Moreover, only those participating in the action at the establishment 'at or from which' the complainant worked are to be considered.

(c) Must all the employees be involved in the *same* strike? This issue was considered in *McCormick* v *Horsepower Ltd* [1981] IRLR 217, where the appellant was one of a number of boilermakers who struck for increased pay. A fitter's mate in a different department (this was before the restriction to establishment was introduced) refused to cross the picket lines of the boilermakers. The appellant claimed that the other employee was a relevant employee for the purposes of EPCA 1978, s. 62 who had not been dismissed. The Court of Appeal disagreed on the ground that there was no agreement between the parties to take industrial action.

13.14.4   Relevant employees in a lock-out

A different regime applies to dismissals in a lock-out. A relevant employee is one 'directly interested in the dispute in contemplation or furtherance of which the lock-out occurred'. These words import two concepts familiar in other spheres. The words 'direct interest' were used to define the exception to claim unemployment benefit (Social Security Act 1975, s. 19(1), as amended; see *Presho* v *DHSS* [1984] IRLR 74), whilst contemplation or furtherance is used in strike cases (see para. 21.8.7).

In *Fisher* v *York Trailer Co. Ltd* [1979] ICR 834, the EAT decided that locked out employees who subsequently returned to work were 'relevant employees' if their colleagues were subsequently dismissed. In *H. Campey & Son Ltd* v *Bellwood* [1987] ICR 311, a haulage contractor decided unilaterally to vary the terms and conditions of its employees. The employees gave notice that because of threatened industrial action the operation of the company was to be suspended forthwith. The employers dismissed only those who had failed to return to work, and argued before the EAT that *Fisher* was wrongly decided. The EAT did not accede to this submission and thought that the test was a retrospective one and had to be looked at when the lock-out occurred.

13.14.5   Re-engagement

As already mentioned, a tribunal must consider whether all participating in a strike or other industrial action have been dismissed and whether some have been re-engaged. The re-engagement need not be at the same site as that from which the employee was dismissed, nor need the employer realise that it was re-engaging an employee previously dismissed from one of its sites (*Bigham* v *GKN Kwikform Ltd* [1992] ICR 113, [1992] IRLR 4). There was, however, no offer of re-engagement within the meaning of the statute when the employers placed notices at their bus depot, made press and local radio annoucements that they were recruiting and so advised local job centres (*Crosville Wales Ltd* v *Tracey* [1993]

IRLR 60). What was made available to employees in this case was merely the opportunity of having an offer made to them, not an offer of re-engagement itself. If not all have been dismissed *or* some but not others have been re-engaged the tribunal has jurisdiction to consider the reason for the non-dismissal or re-engagement of some but not others on its merits in each case.

13.14.5.1 The time of re-engagement Before the Employment Act 1982 came into force, the industrial tribunal had to consider whether any employee had been re-engaged by the time of its hearing. That statute limited the tribunal's view to the three months following dismissal of the relevant employee. Thereafter, the employer can re-engage employees without any effect on unfair dismissal claims at all. The Scottish EAT decided in *Highlands Fabricators Ltd* v *McLaughlin* [1985] ICR 183 that the industrial tribunal had no jurisdiction where all the striking employees, including the applicant, had been offered re-engagement before the end of three months even though in an original offer of re-engagement, the applicant was one of 400 employees who did not receive the offer and had gained work elsewhere. Lord McDonald considered that 'it would wreck all chances of negotiations on what is frequently a delicate and tense situation if a limited offer of re-engagement were to confer immediately on employees to whom the offer was not directed a vested right to complain of unfair dismissal'. The three months was in effect a 'cooling off' period.

13.14.5.2 What are suitable terms of re-engagement? An offer of re-engagement is defined as an offer in the same job as that held before dismissal or in a different job which would be reasonably suitable in the case of the employee. This focuses on the nature of the work and the place where it is to be carried on. An offer may so qualify even though it requires that the employee be treated as on the second warning stage of the disciplinary procedure (*Williams* v *National Theatre Board Ltd* [1982] ICR 715.) The question is one of fact and degree for the industrial tribunal.

13.14.6 Discriminatory selection

Where there is a selective dismissal or re-engagement, the employer must reveal the criteria on which he made his choice of who should go and who should stay. He must show that his selection criteria are fair in all the circumstances of the case so that if the reason for picking and choosing between employees would be invalid if there were no strike, it is likely to be invalid in this situation. The fact that the employee was on strike may itself be taken into account. The EAT in *Laffin and Callaghan* v *Fashion Industries (Hartlepool) Ltd* [1978] IRLR 448 said that 'a valid matter to be considered is the loyalty of those who serve during the strike but . . . by the same token to give *carte blanche* to the loyalty of those who did work is likely to cause indignation among those who . . . did not stay loyal to the management'.

13.15 DISMISSAL DURING UNOFFICIAL INDUSTRIAL ACTION

The Conservative Government was apparently spurred into action on dismissals of unofficial strikers by the unofficial strikes which paralysed London Underground over several weeks in the summer of 1989. It introduced what is now s. 237 of TULR(C)A 1992 so that no employee can complain of unfair dismissal if at the time of his dismissal he was taking part in unofficial industrial action. Action will be taken to be unofficial unless the employee is a member of a trade union and the action is authorised or endorsed by that union or 'he is not a member of a trade union but there are among those taking part in the industrial action members of a trade union by which the action has been authorised or endorsed'.

In similar circumstances, there will be no immunity under s. 223 of TULR(C)A 1992 if the act is done because an employee has been dismissed in circumstances such as by virtue of s. 237 he cannot complain of unfair dismissal.

13.16 DISMISSAL FOR ASSERTION OF A STATUTORY RIGHT

Section 29 of TURERA 1993 inserted a new s. 60A into EPCA 1978 (now ERA 1996, s. 104) which renders the dismissal of employees automatically unfair where they assert that their employer has breached a statutory right. The dismissal is unfair if the reason, or the principal reason, was that the employee brought proceedings against his employer to enforce a relevant statutory right (s. 104(1)). No qualifying period of employment is needed in order to claim the right.

In order to exercise the right the employee need not specify the right that he claims has been infringed but need only make it reasonably clear to the employer what the right was that he was alleging had been infringed (s. 104(3)).

The relevant rights are all those under the ERA 1996 and TULR(C)A 1992 for which the remedy is a complaint to an industrial tribunal, in particular the rights to written particulars of employment, guarantee payments, suspension from work for medical grounds, protection against dismissal and other detriments in health and safety cases, time off for public duties and to look for work or to make arrangements for training, time off for ante-natal care, to return to work after pregnancy, to be given written statement of reasons for dismissal, to claim redress for unfair dismissal, redundancy payments, to reclaim unauthorised deduction from wages, require employer to end check-off, object to political fund contribution, protection against action short of dismissal related to union membership or activities, payment for time off for union duties, and time off for trade union activities.

In addition the right in ERA 1996, s. 86, to receive a minimum period of notice is expressly included (s. 104(4)(b)) even though it is not enforceable in an industrial tribunal.

It is immaterial whether the employee actually has the right or whether it has in fact been infringed or not (s. 104(2)). So long as the employee claims in good faith that the right has been infringed the protection of s. 104 applies. The relevant time within which a complaint must be presented is three months (ERA 1996, s. 111).

In the first important case on the provisions, *Mennell* v *Newell & Wright (Transport Contractors) Ltd* [1996] IRLR 384), a clause in a new draft contract provided that the employers would recover certain training costs by a deduction from payment of final salary on termination of employment. The applicant refused to sign the contract and alleged that he was told that if he did not sign he could expect dismissal. He was indeed eventually dismissed. He claimed that the dismissal was automatically unfair because he had been asserting a right then conferred by the Wages Act 1986. The employers contended that there was no infringement of a right under that statute of which complaint could be made, but the EAT decided on the contrary that there need be no actual infringement or claim brought.

13.17 DISMISSAL: PRESSURE ON EMPLOYER TO DISMISS

The employer cannot argue as a defence or in mitigation of compensation that he was forced to dismiss because of the threat of a strike, whether the pressure was implicit or explicit

(ERA 1996, ss. 107 and 123(5)). The former was illustrated in *Colwyn Borough Council* v *Dutton* [1980] IRLR 420 EAT, where the applicant's trade union branch refused to act as crew of the applicant's dustcart because they considered his driving dangerous, and he was dismissed in consequence. The test propounded in *Ford Motor Co. Ltd* v *Hudson* [1978] ICR 482, was whether:

> the pressure exerted on the employers [was] such that it could be foreseen that it would be likely to result in the dismissal of those employees in respect of where the pressure was being brought?

13.18 REMEDIES

The remedies for unfair dismissal are: reinstatement; re-engagement; and compensation. After a finding of unfairness the applicant is put to his election whether or not he wishes to be reinstated, re-engaged or gain only a monetary award, and the industrial tribunal must explain to him the consequences of each course (*Pirelli General Cable Works Ltd* v *Murray* [1979] IRLR 190, although a failure to do so does not render the decision a nullity (*Cowley* v *Manson Timber Ltd* [1994] ICR 252) (see generally A. Korn, *Compensation for Dismissal*, Blackstone Press, 1992).

13.18.1 Reinstatement

Reinstatement is an order that 'the employer shall treat the complainant in all respects as if he had not been dismissed' and must include benefits payable in respect of the period since dismissal and rights and privileges, including seniority and pensions (ERA 1996, s. 114(2)). It was designed to be the primary remedy for unfair dismissal, an order akin to the specific performance which the common law refused to grant. In 1994–95, only 0.6 per cent of cases which went to an industrial tribunal hearing resulted in a reinstatement or re-engagement order (*Labour Market Trends*, July 1996, p. 305). The explanation is partly that applicants do not wish to return to employers who in their view have treated them disgracefully, and partly because tribunals and judges, imprisoned by common law training, have not been adventurous in its application (see Hart *et al.*, 10 ILJ 160). The EPA 1975 sought to increase use of the remedy by converting it from a 'recommendation' into an order, yet ironically its use has actually dropped since then.

13.18.1.1 The principles in awarding reinstatement Reinstatement should not be ordered if it is 'not practicable' for the employer to comply with it or it would be unjust to do so because the employee contributed to the dismissal. This concept is to be applied in the same way as reduction of compensation (see para. 13.18.6). In *Boots Co. plc* v *Lees-Collier* [1986] IRLR 485, the EAT held that it is unnecessary to decide under separate headings contributory fault for the two different purposes. At the first stage of determining whether an order should be made, the decision as to practicability is necessarily provisional; it is not final in the sense that it creates an estoppel or limits the employer at the second stage to relying on facts which occurred after the order for re-engagement was made (*Port of London Authority* v *Payne and Others* [1994] IRLR 9).

'Practicability' is only one of the considerations to be taken into account at the initial stage and the tribunal need not make a definite finding on this aspect (*Timex Corporation* v *Thomson* [1981] IRLR 522; see also *Nairne* v *Highlands and Islands Fire Brigade* [1989]

IRLR 366 and *Motherwell Railway Club* v *McQueen* [1989] ICR 418). The general meaning of practicability was considered by the Court of Appeal in *Coleman* v *Magnet Joinery Ltd* [1974] IRLR 343, where, in rejecting the employee's contention that it depended solely on whether a job was available, Stephenson LJ said:

> The tribunal ought to consider the consequences of re-engagement in the industrial relations scene in which it will take place. If it is obvious as in the present case that re-engagement would only promote further serious industrial relations strife, it will not be practicable to make the recommendation.

(See also *Meridian Ltd* v *Gomersall* [1977] ICR 597.)

The matter is one pre-eminently for the tribunal's independent discretion, and appeals are only reluctantly entertained. The EAT would not order reinstatement where:

(a)   It would *poison the atmosphere* in a factory either generally or among particular workers (*Coleman* v *Toleman's Delivery Service Ltd* [1973] IRLR 67).

(b)   The employee has shown that she distrusts the employers, and has made allegations of a serious nature against them (*Nothman* v *London Borough of Barnet (No. 2)* [1980] IRLR 65).

(c)   A *genuine redundancy* or reorganisation has arisen in the position since dismissal (*Trusler* v *Lummus Co. Ltd* [1972] IRLR 35).

(d)   It would lead to *strike* action (*Langston* v *AUEW (No. 2)* [1974] ICR 510) and this is especially likely in a closed shop where a worker has been dismissed for non-membership on grounds of conscience (*Goodbody* v *British Railways Board* [1977] IRLR 84).

(e)   The employee is *not fit to return* (*McAulay* v *Cementation Chemicals Ltd* [1972] IRLR 71).

(f)   A local education authority had grave doubts as to the abilities of a teacher (*ILEA* v *Gravett* [1988] IRLR 497).

In *Boots* v *Lees-Collier* (supra) the EAT held that the industrial tribunal had not erred in deciding that it was practicable for the appellants to reinstate the respondent even though his ultimate superior was convinced that he was guilty of theft from the company.

The employer does not have to go so far as to require voluntary severances in his workforce before he can demonstrate that it was not practicable to reinstate or re-engage the applicants (*Port of London Authority* v *Payne and Others* [1994] IRLR 9). It was stressed in *Payne* that the test under the statute is the *practicability* of reinstatement or re-engagement, not the *possibility* of reinstatement or re-engagement. Although the industrial tribunal should carefully scrutinise the reasons advanced by the employer for not reinstating or re-engaging, due weight should be given to the commercial judgment of management, and the standard must not be set too high as to the practicability of reinstatement or re-engagement. The employer cannot in particular be expected to explore every possible avenue which ingenuity may suggest. In *Cold Drawn Tubes Ltd* v *Middleton* [1992] ICR 318, the EAT, however, appeared to be laying down a general proposition that the absence of vacancies at the particular time when reinstatement was being considered made re-engagement impracticable.

The most important general restriction was introduced in *Enessy Co. SA* v *Minoprio* [1978] IRLR 489, where Lord McDonald said, *obiter*: 'In our view it was not realistic to make an order of this nature in a case where the parties involved were in close personal relationships with each other such as they were in the present situation. It is one thing to make an order for reinstatement where the employee concerned works in a factory or other substantial organisation. It is another to do so in the case of a small employer with a few staff.'

13.18.1.2 Dismissal of replacement for reinstated employee The fact that the employer has engaged a replacement for the dismissed employee before the tribunal hears the case is irrelevant and does not make it impracticable to reinstate unless the employer shows that:

(a)   it was not practicable for him to arrange for the dismissed employee's work to be done without engaging a permanent replacement for him; and

(b)   he engaged the replacement after the lapse of a reasonable period without having heard from the dismissed employee that he wished to be reinstated or re-engaged and that when the employer engaged the replacement it was no longer reasonable for him to arrange for the dismissed employee's work to be done except by a permanent replacement (ERA 1996, s. 116(5)).

13.18.2   Re-engagement

Re-engagement resembles reinstatement in its effect except that the employee does not necessarily return to the *same* post. The job must still be comparable and suitable, and so far as is reasonably practicable as favourable as the previous position (ERA 1996, s. 115(1)). It may, however, be with an associated or successor employer and the tribunal decides what terms should apply and the date by which compliance must be made. The tribunal has no power to commit to prison for contempt of court, or fine the employer if he ignores an order to reinstate or to re-engage, but the sacked worker may apply for an *'additional award'* — a special form of exemplary or punitive damages — amounting to between 13 weeks' and 26 weeks' gross pay as extra compensation (s. 117(3)(b)) (*George* v *Beecham Group* [1977] IRLR 43). If the dismissal was due to discrimination or trade union membership or activities, the additional award is between 26 and 52 weeks' pay. The week's pay is normally subject, as usual, to a maximum of £210 per week.

The industrial tribunal must properly exercise their discretion in determining where in the range between 13 and 26 weeks the additional award should be fixed (*Morganite Electrical Carbon Ltd* v *Donne* [1987] IRLR 363). The factors to be taken into account include the conduct of the employer in refusing to comply with the order, the extent to which the compensatory award has met the actual loss suffered by the applicant and mitigation (*Mabrizi* v *National Hospital for Nervous Diseases* [1990] IRLR 133).

The employer may avoid an additional award if he 'satisfies the tribunal that it was not practicable to comply with the order' (s. 117(4)). The criteria are different from the determination in respect of the order for reinstatement itself. Then practicability is merely one consideration amongst others, here the onus is on the employer to prove impracticability and if he cannot, the additional award will be made (*Freemans plc* v *Flynn* [1984] IRLR 486). Should the employer not comply with an order for reinstatement or re-engagement, as mentioned above, the only remedy is extra compensation (*O'Laiore* v *Jackel International Ltd* [1990] ICR 197). The actual amount awarded in a particular case is in the discretion of the industrial tribunal, but it is clear that it is not based on loss to the employee (see *Electronic Data Processing Ltd* v *Wright* [1986] IRLR 8). Further, in respect of the amount ordered to be paid by way of salary and benefits between dismissal and reinstatement, there is no statutory maximum on the amount which the employer may be ordered to pay.

Various issues of jurisdiction have arisen under this rubric:

(a)   An industrial tribunal has jurisdiction to interpret its own order for reinstatement. In *Artisan Press* v *Strawley and Parker* [1986] IRLR 126, the applicants had been employed as security staff until they were unfairly dismissed. The employers purportedly complied with a reinstatement order by giving them positions as cleaners with minor security functions. The EAT said that under EPCA 1978, s. 69(2) (now ERA 1996, s. 114(1)) reinstatement meant treating the employee as if he had not been dismissed, and this was not carried out if the employee were given less favourable terms.

(b)   An industrial tribunal may not order that an employee be re-engaged on terms significantly more favourable than those he would enjoy if reinstated (*Rank Xerox (UK) Ltd* v *Skyczek* [1995] IRLR 568).

(c)   There is no jurisdiction to reduce the amount of arrears of pay between the date of termination and the date of re-engagement to reflect a finding that had the appellant pursued her complaint more expeditiously before the industrial tribunal she would have been re-engaged at an earlier date (*City and Hackney Health Authority* v *Crisp* [1990] IRLR 47, [1990] ICR 95; *Conoco (UK) Ltd* v *Neal* [1989] IRLR 51; *O'Laiore* v *Jackel International Ltd* [1991] IRLR 170).

13.18.3   Compensation: basic award

Since EPA 1975 unfair dismissal compensation has in most cases consisted of two components, the basic and compensatory awards (ERA 1996, s. 118) and both may be reduced owing to failure to mitigate the loss or contributory fault. The unfairly dismissed employee claims as basic award so many weeks' pay for each year of continuous employment with his own or any associated or predecessor employer before the effective date of termination, irrespective of whether the unfair dismissal has caused any loss to him. This head was first introduced by EPA 1975 and is intended at the same time to convey disapproval of the employer's action and also to compensate for the loss of job security. It performs a similar function to a redundancy payment and it is appropriate that they should be calculated in almost the same way (ERA 1996, s. 119).

Donaldson J has described it as reflecting the loss of the employee's 'paid-up insurance policy' against redundancy, but the House of Lords in *W. Devis & Sons Ltd* v *Atkins* [1977] AC 931, saw it in a different, negative light. Their remarks were wholly *obiter*, since the case was decided on the law before its introduction in 1975, but Lord Diplock said that: 'The compensation provisions are therefore converted into a veritable rogues' charter, for the tribunal would be bound to award to a fraudulent employee because he had successfully concealed his fraud a basic compensation which might well amount to a substantial sum.'

The amount of basic award depends on the age of the employee in this way:

(a)   each year which consists wholly of weeks in which the employee was over 41, one and half weeks' pay; and

(b)   each year which consists wholly of weeks not within (a) but in which the employee was not below 22, one week's pay;

(c)   any year wholly consisting of weeks under 22, half a week's pay (s. 119(2)).

No account is to be taken of any time employed beyond 20 years (s. 119(3)) or of any week's pay over £210 (Unfair Dismissal (Increase of Basic and Special Awards) Order 1992 (SI 1992 No. 312)) so that the maximum potential award at present is £6,300.

In the 65th year the basic award is reduced by one-twelfth for both men and women (s. 119(4) and (5)).

Example Josephine is unfairly dismissed when aged 64 years and 8 months. Her week's pay is £80 and she has been employed for 10 full years. Her overall entitlement would be, prima facie, (1 ½ weeks × 10 = 15) × 80 = £1,200 and one-twelfth of that is £100. This is multiplied by 8 to make £800, and that £800 is then deducted from the amount of compensation to reduce the basic award to £400.

Before the coming into effect of the Employment Act 1980 the basic award had to consist of at least two weeks' pay. There is now no minimum, except £2,770 in cases of dismissal by reason of carrying out health and safety functions, or acting as an occupational pension fund trustee or employee representative (ERA 1996, s. 120). The amount may be reduced:

(a) if the employee had unreasonably refused an offer of reinstatement (ERA 1996, s. 122(1); and

(b) because of any conduct before the dismissal with the exception of a dismissal for redundancy (ERA 1996, s. 122(2)).

The latter is designed to mitigate the effect of the *Devis* v *Atkins* sort of case where the dismissal is unfair because the employer did not know at the time of the facts for which he could reasonably dismiss. Unlike contributory fault in assessing the compensatory award, it does not matter under this subsection whether there was a causal link between the applicant's conduct and the dismissal.

There is a two weeks' maximum of basic award where the reason for dismissal was redundancy and the employee unreasonably refuses to accept a renewal of the contract or suitable alternative employment or where the employee during a trial period unreasonably terminates the contract (ERA 1996, s. 121). Because the basic award performs the same function and is assessed in a similar way, any redundancy pay is fully deducted from it. However, the EAT in *Chelsea Football Club & Athletic Co. Ltd* v *Heath* [1981] IRLR 73, held that the basic award was not automatically to be reduced by any money paid by the employer *ex gratia* although it was presumed referable expressly or impliedly to the basic and compensatory award. It is a matter of construction of the payment in each case.

Where the employer makes a larger redundancy payment than is required by statute, any excess goes to reduce the compensatory award where the dismissal is found to be by reason of redundancy (s. 122(4)). (See also *Darr* v *LRC Products Ltd* [1993] IRLR 257.) In *Boorman* v *Allmakes Ltd* [1995] IRLR 553, however, an employee was paid an *ex gratia* sum expressed to include statutory redundancy payment, but it was held that it did not fall to be deducted from the basic award when he was ultimately found to have been unfairly dismissed on a ground other than redundancy.

13.18.4 The compensatory award

The compensatory award provides what is just and equitable as compensation having regard to the loss suffered as a result of the dismissal so far as that loss is attributable to action taken by the employer (ERA 1996, s. 123(1)). This is subject to a maximum at present of £11,300, and is varied by order from time to time (s. 124). The test for assessing the award within the maximum has remained consistent since the introduction of unfair dismissal in

1971. In *W. Devis & Sons Ltd* v *Atkins* [1977] ICR 662, Viscount Dilhorne thought that it had two elements:

[Section 123(1)] does not . . . provide that regard should be had only to the *loss* resulting from the dismissal being unfair. Regard must be had to that but the award must be just and equitable in all the circumstances, and it cannot be just and equitable that a sum should be awarded in compensation when in fact the employee has suffered no injustice in being dismissed. (Emphasis added.)

(a) This means that if the employee has suffered *no loss* because, for example, he has immediately gained a better-paid job, he can claim nothing under this head, although he may still be entitled to the basic award. Thus in *BUSM Co. Ltd* v *Clarke* [1978] ICR 70, where a redundancy dismissal was held unfair because there was no consultation, the EAT would not give the employee compensation because he would have been made redundant at a later stage anyway. Phillips J commented:

In some cases it will happen that the industrial tribunal reaches the conclusion that had everything been done which ought to have been done it would not have made the slightest difference . . . where the industrial tribunal finds that the dismissal was unfair it will be necessary for them to proceed to assess compensation and for that purpose to make some estimate of what would have been the likely outcome had that been done which ought to have been done. This is often a difficult question, but one which the industrial tribunal in their capacity as industrial jury are well suited to answer, and in respect of which they will not go wrong if they remember that what they are trying to do is to assess the loss suffered by the claimant and not punish the employer for his failure in industrial relations.

(See also *Winterhalter Gastronom Ltd* v *Webb* [1973] IRLR 120, *Mansfield Hosiery Mills Ltd* v *Bromley* [1977] IRLR 301, *Barley* v *Amey Roadstone Corporation Ltd* [1977] IRLR 299.)

(b) On the other hand, the degree of unfairness of the dismissal is probably not a relevant consideration in the assessment of what award is just and equitable. The tribunal is not entitled at this stage to take into consideration, for example, that the employers had no wish to treat the employee in anything other than a fair manner (*Morris* v *Acco Co. Ltd* [1985] ICR 306; cf. *Townson* v *Northgate Group Ltd* [1981] IRLR 382).

(c) Compensation may be reduced under both the just and equitable rubric and contributory fault head at the same time (*Rao* v *Civil Aviation Authority* [1994] IRLR 240). The reductions should be applied in that order (see also *Campbell* v *Dunoon & Cowal Housing Association Ltd* [1993] IRLR 496). As to the justifiability of a nil award, see *Chaplin* v *Rawlinson* [1991] ICR 553.

(d) An industrial tribunal may take into account in measuring compensation that the employee resigned in a peremptory manner without warning (*TGWU* v *Howard* [1992] IRLR 170).

(e) Conduct after dismissal, such as the applicant selling a story about the case to a national newspaper, is not relevant and cannot be taken into account in reducing an award (*Soros* v *Davison* [1994] IRLR 264).

Tribunals have also been counselled not to act 'in a general benevolent manner according to the conception of what they think will be fair in the circumstances' (*Lifeguard Assurance*

Ltd v *Zadrozny* [1977] IRLR 56). The burden of proving loss is firmly on the complainant, although: 'It is not therefore to be expected that the precise and detailed proof of every item of loss will be presented.' (*Norton Tool Co. Ltd* v *Tewson* [1972] ICR 501 per Donaldson J). The *Norton* case also required industrial tribunals to set out their findings in appropriate subheadings, and these remain generally the same today despite much subsequent elaboration. The EAT has frequently called upon tribunals to take a broad brush approach to compensation questions, and will interfere with a decision on this matter only if it is perverse (*Manpower Ltd* v *Hearne* [1983] IRLR 281). Moreover, in *Courtaulds Northern Spinning Ltd* v *Moosa* [1984] IRLR 43, Browne-Wilkinson J accepted that 'the assessment of compensation in industrial tribunals cannot be as scrupulously accurate as, say, in an action for personal injuries in the High Court'. There may be a nil award of both the basic and compensatory award (*Chaplin* v *Rawlinson* (supra)).

Many of the criteria derive from the principles adopted in awarding damages for personal injuries. The headings include the following: .

    (a)   immediate loss of wages;
    (b)   future loss of wages;
    (c)   loss of benefits;
    (d)   expenses in seeking work;
    (e)   loss of pension;
    (f)   loss of future employment protection;
    (g)   manner of dismissal.

13.18.4.1 Immediate loss of earnings This heading replaces loss of net earnings from the date of dismissal to the hearing, and receipt of unemployment benefit is ignored for this calculation because the Department of Employment can recoup such benefits from the employer of a successful applicant (see para. 13.18.8). It was at one time thought that no deduction was to be made for anything which was or could have been earned during the notice period (*Everwear Candlewick Ltd* v *Isaac* (1974) 8 ITR 334, *Norton Tool Co. Ltd* v *Tewson* [1972] ICR 501), so that where proper notice was not given, payment in lieu thereof was the irreducible minimum to be awarded as compensation. This was, however, doubted in *Tradewinds Airways Ltd* v *Fletcher* [1981] IRLR 272, where the EAT confirmed that compensation is to be awarded for actual financial loss, and if, as in the instant case, the employee proceeds to take another position within the notice period, earnings therefrom must be fully deducted.

In *Babcock FATA Ltd* v *Addison* [1987] IRLR 173, however, the Court of Appeal indicated that this was not a rule of law (see below). Before awarding compensation the industrial tribunal must first determine what salary the employee should have been receiving if there is disagreement on the contractual terms between employer and employee (*Kinzley* v *Minories Finance Ltd* [1988] ICR 113). In *Finnie* v *Top Hat Frozen Foods* [1985] ICR 433, the EAT stressed that the general rule was that *ex gratia* payments on account of wages and other benefits should be deducted from any award. (See also *Roadchef Ltd* v *Hastings* [1988] IRLR 142, *Horizon Holidays Ltd* v *Grassi* [1987] ICR 851.)

It was quite proper to make an award for loss of earnings even though the employee was in receipt of invalidity benefit during the relevant period (*Hilton International Hotels (UK) Ltd* v *Faraji* [1994] IRLR 267).

13.18.4.2 Future loss of earnings This element depends on how long the dismissed worker is likely to be unemployed, and whether he has already or soon will have to take a job at a lower rate than his previous employment. The proper comparison is between net (and not gross) pay in the two positions. Tribunals must:

compare his salary prospects for the future in each job and see as best they could how long it would have been before he reached with [the second employer] the equivalent salary to that which he would have reached if he had remained with his old employers. Then the amount of shortfall during the period before he reached parity would be the amount of his future loss.

(*Tradewinds* v *Fletcher* (supra).)

The following principles have been established in the cases:

(a)   There is a considerable body of conflicting case law on the vital question whether a summarily dismissed employee should lose anything from his compensatory award because he has earned money in the period during which he should have received his period of notice. A strictly compensatory principle suggests the full duty to mitigate loss during that period, so that any earnings in the alternative position *should* indeed be deducted. The counter-argument runs that if the employer had given *proper* notice, the employee would have received full payment of wages. The early authorities took the latter approach (e.g. *Norton Tool Co. Ltd* v *Tewson* [1972] IRLR 86, *Blackwell* v *GEC Elliott Process Automation Ltd* [1976] IRLR 144) but the EAT departed from this practice in *Tradewinds Airways Ltd* v *Fletcher* (supra). Browne-Wilkinson J in *TBA Industrial Products Ltd* v *Locke* [1984] ICR 228 reverted to past practice and took as the proper premise that:

the employer would act . . . in accordance with good industrial practice which would require (in the absence of gross misconduct) that an employee who is summarily dismissed should at the time of his dismissal be paid payment in lieu of notice covering the notice period. If such good industrial practice is adopted there is no right to recover any part of it from the ex-employee if during the notice period he obtains alternative employment.

(See also *Finnie* v *Top Hat Frozen Foods Ltd* [1985] IRLR 365.)

The employer should pay such sums as good industrial practice requires and sums earned by way of mitigation during a period of notice will not normally be taken into account to set off that sum according to the Court of Appeal in *Babcock FATA Ltd* v *Addison* [1987] IRLR 173. Ralph Gibson LJ said that:

circumstances may arise in which, having regard to the length of notice required and the known likelihood of the employee getting new employment within a short period of time, or for other sufficient reason, an employer may show that a payment less than 'the wages due over the full period of notice did not offend good industrial practice . . . . The number of cases in which an employer will be able, in the view of the industrial tribunal, to justify a departure from the general practice will probably be small.

There was no rule of law to either effect (see also *Horizon Holidays Ltd* v *Grassi* [1987] ICR 851).

(b)   Where an employee set up in business immediately after his dismissal and received gross earnings some £10,000 in excess of his previous earnings, the EAT in *Isleworth Studios Ltd* v *Rickard* [1988] IRLR 137 decided that he was to receive no compensatory award. (See also *Trico Folbeith Ltd* v *Devonshire* [1989] IRLR 396.)

(c)   Normally the tribunal then adopts a multiplier and multiplicand, as in tort cases, so that the proper sum is the difference between earnings in the new job and the old multiplied by a reasonable estimate of how long any shortfall will last. In *Cartiers Superfoods Ltd* v *Laws* [1978] IRLR 315, since the shortest period the applicant would work was two to three years and the longest 10, the industrial tribunal were held correct in applying a multiplier of three. (See also *Adda International Ltd* v *Curcio* [1976] ICR 407.) There may be a discount for accelerated receipt of earnings which may as a lump sum be invested and bear interest, and to take account of a whole range of possible future contingencies, although the EAT has criticised over-complicated analysis of this factor. If the employee has not found other employment before the tribunal hearing, the tribunal must consider the local job market and the following circumstances may be relevant:

(i)   If the employee is in poor health or has defective eyesight (*Fougère* v *Phoenix Motor Ltd* [1976] ICR 495, also *Penprase* v *Mander Bros Ltd* [1973] IRLR 167) or was injured in a fight which led to his dismissal (*Brittains Arborfield* v *Van Uden* [1977] ICR 211), it may prove more difficult for him to find other work, so that a higher award is appropriate, and again this resembles a tort principle — of taking the victim as one finds him. It is wrong in principle not to make a compensatory award because the employee was unfit for work ever since dismissal since the tribunal should consider loss of sickness benefits which attach to the former employment (*Slaughter* v *C. Brewer & Sons Ltd* [1990] IRLR 426, [1990] ICR 730).

(ii)   The tribunal may award compensation for a time beyond the *normal retiring age* if it finds that the employee would probably have stayed in a job beyond that time (*Barrel Plating Co. Ltd* v *Danks* [1976] 3 All ER 652).

(iii)   An employee who was engaged in, say, a sophisticated *high technology area* where there are few other jobs may recover a longer period of loss of earnings.

(iv)   If the employee might have been fairly *dismissed in the near future*, the period of future loss will be thereby reduced to last only until the date of fair dismissal. In *Evans* v *George Galloway & Co. Ltd* [1974] IRLR 167, for instance, the applicant was dismissed because of poor productivity. The industrial tribunal thought that the five weeks he had been given to improve his performance was insufficient, but that he was hardly likely to turn the corner given a longer period. They thought six months was a reasonable period to test his capabilities and that he could have been fairly dismissed at the end of it, and they thus limited future loss of earnings to this period. (See also *Winterhalter Gastronom Ltd* v *Webb* [1973] IRLR 120.) In some cases this may mean that no compensation at all is awarded although the practice has proved very controversial, not least because it renders a finding of unfairness virtually useless. Even so, in *Devis & Sons* v *Atkins* (supra), the House of Lords rejected the applicant's argument that the statutory provision that the tribunal 'shall' award compensation precluded a nil award. They did this on the ground that in the circumstances of the subsequently discovered fraud it was neither just nor equitable to award compensation.

(d)   The industrial tribunal is not, however, bound to refuse a compensatory award when it finds that even if consultation over redundancy had taken place, the employee would still have been dismissed (*Mining Supplies (Longwall) Ltd* v *Baker* [1988] ICR 676). Wood J said that the question of loss may depend on whether the period of consultation which is missing could reasonably, and should have, taken place within the period prior to dismissal, or in fact the employee might have been employed longer. In the instant case, the EAT thought the tribunal's award of six weeks' loss of pay was in the circumstances excessive and reduced the compensatory award to two weeks. It is open to the industrial tribunal to award a percentage of what would otherwise have been the compensatory award to reflect the degree of procedural default (see *Polkey* v *Dayton Services Ltd* [1988] ICR 142). This same conclusion is sometimes reached in redundancy selection or reorganisation cases where the tribunal considers that, even if further consultation had taken place, as it should, it would not have made a jot of difference to the final outcome (*Clyde Pipeworks Ltd* v *Foster* [1978] IRLR 313 EAT; e.g. in ill health cases, *Slaughter* v *C. Brewer & Sons* (supra)). When calculating the compensatory award a deduction on the grounds of what is just and equitable is to be deducted *after* reducing the award to reflect payments made to the employee on termination of employment (*Cox* v *London Borough of Camden* [1996] IRLR 389), for example an enhanced severance payment (see also *Digital Equipment Co. Ltd* v *Clements* [1996] IRLR 513).

(e)   At least the evidential onus of proof of this matter is on the employer (*Townson* v *Northgate Group* [1981] IRLR 382; *Forth Estuary Engineering Ltd* v *Litster* [1986] IRLR 59). An industrial tribunal may take into account the fact that the employee would probably have been dismissed anyway, for the same ground as that for which he was dismissed, but not that the employer could dismiss fairly on some other ground, since the employer had chosen not to do so (*Devonshire* v *Trico-Folberth Ltd* [1989] IRLR 396). The fact that the employee has been *accused of* gross misconduct may increase compensation (*Vaughan* v *Weighpack* [1974] ICR 261), while the possibility of *redundancy* in the old and new job may lead to its reduction (*Marcus* v *George Wimpey Co. Ltd* [1974] IRLR 356, *Youngs of Gosport* v *Kendall* [1977] ICR 907).

(f)   It is important to ask when the compensation 'clock' should stop ticking in a case where the employee gets another job and promptly loses it. In *Courtaulds Northern Spinning Ltd* v *Moosa* [1984] ICR 218 the EAT decided that compensation should only be granted up to the time the employee secures alternative employment. The position may be different where the employee takes a temporary job to mitigate his loss (*Ging* v *Ellward Lancashire Ltd* (1978) 13 ITR 265). The application of this principle may also be modified when there is a long gap between dismissal and the hearing of the claim. In *Lytlarch Ltd* v *Reid* [1991] ICR 216, the delay was between 16 June 1989 and 1 May 1990; the employee found new employment on 18 August 1989. The Scottish EAT felt that having regard to the general 'just and equitable' principle adopted by the statute for compensation, the industrial tribunal was correct in restricting the award to the period between the date of dismissal and that of the new employment. In *Fentiman* v *Fluid Engineering Products Ltd* [1991] IRLR 150, the Scottish EAT held that where the employee obtains higher paid work before the date of the hearing and retains that work up to that date and the tribunal is satisfied that the work is permanent, the loss should be calculated only until the date of the new employment. A tribunal was, however, wrong to limit compensation to be paid to school dinner ladies on the basis that without the reduction in numbers the school meals service would have closed in 12 months' time through lack of funds (*Gilham* v *Kent County Council (No. 3)* [1986] IRLR 56). It is an error of law to make a compensatory award for a period beyond the time at which the employers' premises close, even though the employees allege that if the employers had acted reasonably the premises would have continued for a longer period (*James W. Cook & Co. (Wivenhoe) Ltd* v *Tipper* [1991] IRLR 386).

13.18.4.3   Loss of fringe benefits   By s. 123(2) of ERA 1996, recoverable loss includes 'any expenses reasonably incurred by the complainant in consequence of the dismissal, and

. . . loss of any benefit which he might reasonably be expected to have had but for the dismissal'. This has covered, in various cases, a company car (*Mohar* v *Granitstone Galloway Ltd* [1974] ICR 273), commission, free housing, food, special travel allowance, and benefits under a share participation scheme (*Bradshaw* v *Rugby Portland Cement Ltd* [1972] IRLR 46). Non-contractual bonuses, such as Christmas gifts, cannot be claimed; while tronc tips are subject to differing decisions (*Palmanor Ltd* v *Cedron* [1978] ICR 1008).

Where an employee is unfairly made redundant five months before he would have been entitled to over £100,000 under a share option scheme, it was held by a Bedford industrial tribunal that the loss of the benefit might be included in the award of compensation (*Clarke* v *Linfood Cash and Carry Ltd,* COIT 1727/178). There is as yet no appeal authority on this point, which is of increasingly practical importance.

It is not proper to take into account loss of allowances paid free of tax in the former employment since they go to reimburse the employee for expenses necessarily incurred in the course of his job and there is no profit element thereon (*Tradewinds Airways Ltd* v *Fletcher* [1981] IRLR 272). Similarly nothing can be awarded where a company car was only to be used for business purposes. On the other hand, where the employee has lost tied free accommodation, the loss will be the rent which he has to pay on new accommodation (*Scottish Cooperative Wholesale Society Ltd* v *Lloyd* [1973] ICR 137).

13.18.4.4 Expenses in looking for work The sacked employee may have to move to get appropriate work and will inevitably have other expenses such as travel, and buying trade journals to search the appointments vacant columns (*Cooperative Wholesale Society* v *Squirrell* (1974) 9 ITR 191). This is part of his necessary mitigation of loss and he can claim therefor. Legal expenses in fighting a claim are not, however, recoverable under this head, although they may, in certain restricted circumstances, be included in a costs order (see J. Bowers, D. Brown and G. Mead, *Industrial Tribunal Practice and Procedure,* FT Law & Tax, 1996). The tribunal may also in a proper case award expenses incurred in a reasonable attempt to set up a new business (*Gardiner-Hill* v *Roland Berger Technics Ltd* [1982] IRLR 498) or in having to move away for the purposes of a new job.

13.18.4.5 Loss of pension right Loss of pension entitlement can in some cases be a very large sum, and its calculation often proves difficult. Guidance is provided in a paper by the Government's Actuary Department which the EAT judicially approved and stated should be used in preference to the opinion of an actuary called by one of the parties (*Tradewinds Airways Ltd* v *Fletcher* [1981] IRLR 272). This has been replaced by the *Industrial Tribunals Compensation for Loss of Pension Rights,* a guide drawn up by three industrial tribunal chairmen with the assistance of the Government Actuary Department. Its use was approved by the EAT in *Benson* v *Dairy Crest Ltd,* EAT 192/89, but it is only to be treated as guidance not as binding authority (*Bingham* v *Hobourn Engineering Ltd* [1992] IRLR 298). A deduction must, however, be made if there is such a high turnover of the employer's staff that it is in the highest degree unlikely that the employee would have stayed until retirement age even if not dismissed at the time he was dismissed (*Manpower Ltd* v *Hearne* [1983] ICR 567).

There are basically two forms of pension loss which may be suffered, the loss of pension position earned thus far, and loss of future pension opportunity (*Copson* v *Eversure Accessories Ltd* [1974] ICR 636). Usually it is most appropriate to base the sum lost on the amount of employee's and employer's contributions made to a future pension (*Willment Brothers Ltd* v *Oliver* [1979] IRLR 393 EAT), and this is reached by applying the conventional multiplier and multiplicand method. Where, however, the employee is approaching retirement, tribunals may instead determine how much it would cost to purchase an annuity to produce the pension which he has lost and award this amount subject to a discount for accelerated payment (*Smith, Kline & French Laboratories* v *Coates* [1977] IRLR 220). In the leading case, *Powrmatic* v *Bull* [1977] IRLR 144, it was also necessary to take into consideration that the 32-year-old employee was unlikely to remain in the same job for the next 33 years and that he might go on to another job with much better pension prospects, the scheme might be altered or he might die prematurely. A multiplier of 15 was adopted instead of the actual number of years to take account of these contingencies. A withdrawal factor as high as 70 per cent may be justified in recognition of the high probability that an employee's poor performance would sooner or later result in his dismissal (*TBA Industrial Products Ltd* v *Locke* [1984] IRLR 48).

13.18.4.6   Loss of employment protection   It will take a sacked employee two years in a new job to build up continuous employment sufficient to found a claim for unfair dismissal or redundancy payment, and the entitlement to continuous service in both will also be correspondingly lower. A fairly nominal sum is awarded because of loss in respect of unfair dismissal while the basic award is intended to serve this purpose for loss of redundancy payment (*Norton Tool Co. Ltd* v *Tewson* [1972] ICR 501; see generally *Mono Pumps Ltd* v *Froggatt and Radford* [1987] IRLR 368). The tribunal may also take into account the fact that an employee's dismissal may deprive him of his entitlement under the employer's redundancy scheme through lack of service (*Lee* v *IPC Business Press Ltd* [1984] ICR 306). The EAT has declared that an amount to reflect loss of notice entitlement in a new job is *especially* necessary in a time of high unemployment (*Daley* v *A.E. Dorsett* [1981] IRLR 385). Kilner Brown J decided in *S. H. Muffett Ltd* v *Head* [1986] IRLR 488 that the conventional sum awarded by the tribunal under this head should be increased to £100 and now £150 is more usual. The tribunal was right not to make an award covering the respondent's loss of entitlement to eight weeks' notice of termination. This depended on a double contingency that the dismissed employee would gain another job and be dismissed therefrom without building up entitlement to the same period of notice applicable to the first job. The industrial tribunal should consider the remoteness or otherwise of these contingencies using knowledge of local conditions.

13.18.4.7   Manner of dismissal   A sum may be awarded if the way the employee's sacking was handled makes him less acceptable to another employer, but damages cannot be gained solely for the inevitably concomitant distress, frustration and depression (*John Mill and Sons* v *Quinn* [1974] IRLR 107), not even when it amounts to an accusation of gross misconduct (*Brittains Arborfield Ltd* v *Van Uden* [1977] ICR 211). In *Lewis Shops Group* v *Wiggins* [1973] IRLR 205, an award for delay in providing a written reference which might have affected the employee's attempt to secure an alternative employment was quashed by the EAT (see also *Gallear* v *Watson and Son Ltd* [1979] IRLR 306). 'Loss does not include injury to pride or feelings' (Sir John Donaldson in *Norton Tool Co. Ltd* v *Tewson* (supra)), nor the loss of job satisfaction (*Robert Normansell Ltd* v *Barfield* (1973) 8 ITR 171).

13.18.4.8   Deductions

(a)   *Ex gratia* sums: employers should give close attention to how they structure *ex gratia* payments if they envisage the possibility of an unfair dismissal claim. The EAT in

Chelsea Football Club v *Heath* [1981] IRLR 73 held that if an employer admits that he has unfairly dismissed an employee and pays him an amount specifically referable to the basic award the employer may properly contend that he has made a basic award and need not pay again. Whether a general payment covers the basic award is 'a question of construction in each case'. Here the letter was really an offer without prejudice to legal rights.

In an unexpected decision, the Scottish EAT in *Finnie* v *Top Hat Frozen Foods* [1985] ICR 433, declared that whilst *ex gratia* payments should be deducted, contractual or statutory payments should not be offset against the compensatory award. Lord McDonald's reasoning was that: 'Wages in lieu of notice . . . is an independent payment to which an employee has a separate right under statute and, in this case, under contract.'

In *McCarthy* v *British Insulated Callenders Cables plc* [1985] IRLR 94, the EAT decided whether an *ex gratia* payment should be deducted from the amount which would otherwise have been awarded and then the maximum compensatory award applied, or alternatively should merely be deducted from the maximum compensatory award. This may make a major practical difference. Here the employee had been given an *ex gratia* sum of £1,274. Compensation was assessed by the tribunal at £15,820. The tribunal reduced the sum to £7,000, then the maximum award, and deducted £1,274 from that. The EAT thought that this was the wrong approach. The £1,274 should be deducted from the amount which would be awarded irrespective of the maximum. The applicant thus received the then £7,000 maximum. The same process applies to deduction for contributory fault (*Walter Braund (London) Ltd* v *Murray* [1991] IRLR 100).

Where the industrial tribunal has not stated the period for which it is awarding compensation, such sum is not to be deducted from an award for wrongful dismissal on the basis that the plaintiff was unable to point to any double recovery (*O'Laiore* v *Jackel International Ltd* [1991] IRLR 170, CA, [1991] ICR 718). This case, however, was determined before the Industrial Tribunal (Constitution and Rules of Procedure) Regulations 1993 came into force, whereby an industrial tribunal must set out 'either by a table showing how the amount or sum [of compensation] has been calculated or by a description of the manner in which it has been calculated' (reg. 10(3)).

(b)   Discrimination compensation: s. 126 of ERA 1996 states that where compensation falls to be awarded under unfair dismissal and one or both of the discrimination statutes, an industrial tribunal must wholly offset the compensation under one head against the others.

(c)   Tax rebate: a £54 tax rebate need not be deducted (*MBS Ltd* v *Calo* [1983] IRLR 189; cf. *Lucas* v *Lawrence Scott and Electromotors Ltd* [1983] IRLR 61).

(d)   Sickness benefits: where an employee has received after his dismissal statutory sick pay for six months and invalidity benefit for more than three years, it is appropriate to deduct all sums thus received (*Puglia* v *C. James & Sons* [1996] ICR 301).

13.18.5   Special award

Sections 4 and 5 of the Employment Act 1982 greatly increased the amount of compensation to be awarded for unfair dismissal on the grounds of trade union membership and activities or non-membership of a particular union by introducing a special award. This is in addition to the normal basic and compensatory elements, and is calculated as follows (now ERA 1996, s. 125(1), (2)):

(a)   In normal cases, a week's pay multiplied by 104, or £13,775, whichever is the greater, subject to a maximum of £27,500.

(b)   Where an industrial tribunal has made an order for reinstatement or re-engagement of the dismissed employee, and the employer does not comply therewith, a week's pay multiplied by 156 or £20,600, whichever is the greater sum; the only defence is where the employer satisfies an industrial tribunal that it was not practicable to comply.

The award is subject to reduction where the employee:

(a)   is nearing retirement;
(b)   is responsible for conduct which makes a deduction from the special award just and equitable; or
(c)   has unreasonably prevented the reinstatement order being complied with.

13.18.6   Contributory fault

13.18.6.1   Blameworthy and causative   A deduction for contributory fault allows a tribunal a wide discretion to reduce compensation in a case where they find the applicant employee to some degree at fault. By s. 123(6) of ERA 1996, 'Where the tribunal finds that the dismissal was to any extent caused or contributed to by any action of the complainant' compensation may be reduced by 'such amount as it considers just and equitable'. The tribunals possess a slightly differently worded power to deduct for contributory fault from a special award (s. 125(4)) and basic award (s. 122(2)). Viscount Dilhorne called contributory fault an industrial form of contributory negligence in *W. Devis & Sons Ltd* v *Atkins* [1977] AC 931.

Sir Hugh Griffiths said in *Maris* v *Rotherham Corporation* [1974] 2 All ER 776 that the concept 'brings into consideration all the circumstances surrounding the dismissal, requiring the tribunal to take a broad common sense view of the situation, and to decide what, if any, part the applicant's own conduct played in contributing to his dismissal and then in the light of that finding, decide what, if any, reduction should be made in the assessment of this loss'. The onus lies on the employer to prove that the employee contributed to his dismissal by conduct which is 'culpable or blameworthy' and unreasonable in the circumstances. His action need not, however, amount to a breach of contract or tort (*Nelson* v *BBC (No. 2)* [1979] IRLR 346, *Gibson* v *British Transport Docks Board* [1982] IRLR 228). In *Nelson*'s case Brandon LJ thought that it 'includes conduct which is . . . perverse or foolish or, if I may use the colloquialism, bloody-minded. It may also include action which, though not meriting any of those more pejorative epithets, is nevertheless unreasonable in the circumstances'. It is only the complainant's conduct which may be taken into account, not all the circumstances of the case (*Parker Foundry Ltd* v *Slack* [1992] IRLR 11, [1992] ICR 302).

The employee's misdeeds need not relate to the reason given by the employer for the dismissal (*Robert Whiting Designs Ltd* v *Lamb* [1978] ICR 89) but according to the EAT in *Hutchinson* v *Enfield Rolling Mills Ltd* [1981] IRLR 318 there must be 'a causal link between the actions of the employee and the dismissal'. In that case, the employee was dismissed for attending a union demonstration in Brighton, notwithstanding that he had presented a sick note for the day to his employers in which he gave sciatica as the reason for absence. The EAT considered that the tribunal was wrong to take any of the following as contributory fault: that he had been a 'troublemaker' throughout his employment; that he intended to picket his union leaders in Brighton; and that his political views were affecting his work. None of these were causative of the dismissal, but his attendance in Brighton *was* and in itself justified a reduction for contributory fault. The need for causation was re-emphasised in *Tele-Trading Ltd* v *Jenkins* [1990] IRLR 430.

Tribunals must concentrate on the conduct of the employee and not probe his state of mind (*Ladbroke Racing Ltd* v *Mason* [1978] ICR 49).

The following situations raise conceptual difficulties for the issue of contributory fault and have received attention from the EAT:

(a) Incapability cases: in the normal case, fault consists of some misconduct by the employee and there has been much discussion in the case law as to whether it is appropriate to deduct when the complaint is about the employee's incapability. There are many borderline cases between conduct and capability. Kilner Brown J in *Kraft Foods Ltd* v *Fox* [1978] ICR 311 drew this distinction:

> In the case of a man who falls short, he may not try. He may not be doing his best. That is something over which he has control. However, if he is doing his best and his best is not good enough, it does not seem to us to be proper to say that in those circumstances he has contributed.

(See also *Moncur* v *International Paint Co. Ltd* [1978] IRLR 223, *Sutton & Gates (Luton) Ltd* v *Boxall* [1978] IRLR 486.) Lord McDonald went somewhat further than this in *Finnie* v *Top Hat Frozen Foods Ltd* [1985] ICR 433 when he considered that a reduction was appropriate in any incapability case, but this will be unusual (*Slaughter* v *C. Brewer & Sons Ltd* [1990] IRLR 426, [1990] ICR 730). One example would be where the employee blatantly and persistently refuses to obtain appropriate medical reports or attend for medical examination.

(b) Constructive dismissal: a reduction is only exceptionally appropriate in a case of constructive dismissal since the finding involves a fundamental breach by the employer (*Holroyd* v *Gravure Cylinders Ltd* [1984] IRLR 259). One such rare case was *Garner* v *Grange Furnishing Ltd* [1977] IRLR 206, where the EAT criticised the employee's 'oversensitivity and his most unfortunate choice of time for taking the step of walking out' (see now *Morrison* v *ATGWU* [1989] IRLR 361). Further in *Polentarutti* v *Autokraft Ltd* [1991] ICR 757, the EAT held that there need not be found a reason for dismissal to which the employee specifically contributed for contributory fault to be awarded.

(c) Post-dismissal conviction: in *Ladup Ltd* v *Barnes* [1982] IRLR 7, the EAT sanctioned a deduction for contributory fault in the light of a subsequent conviction of the employee for the possession of cannabis, which was promulgated after compensation had been assessed. Bristow J considered the employer's application for a review 'unanswerable' since the conviction made the original award a 'blatant unfairness'.

(d) Selective re-engagement: it had been argued that the general principle should be modified in a case under s. 62 of EPCA 1978 (now ss. 237–239 of TULR(C)A 1992) in that the tribunal should concentrate not on the conduct leading to the dismissal but conduct contributing to the employer's resolve not to take the striker back after the dispute. This contention was, however, firmly rejected in *Courtaulds Northern Spinning Ltd* v *Moosa* [1984] ICR 218.

13.18.6.2 Examples of contributory fault A survey of the case law gives the following examples of contributory fault:

(a) failure to take alternative work offered by the employer (*Nelson* v *BBC (No. 2)* [1979] IRLR 346);

(b) refusal to join a union when the applicant knew that he would not be able to carry out the job without a union card (*Sulemanji* v *Toughened Glass Ltd* [1979] ICR 799);

(c) threats of violence when allegations of financial misdeeds were made (*Munif* v *Cole & Kirby Ltd* [1973] ICR 486);

(d) participation in violence towards work colleagues who ignored an overtime ban,even though it could not be proved precisely what part the applicant played (*Gibson's* case (supra));

(e) setting up a rival business (*Connor* v *Comet Radiovision Services Ltd,* EAT 650/ 81);

(f) placing the wrong body in a coffin (*Coalter* v *Walter Craven* [1980] IRLR 262); and

(g) not returning a cheque to the employer which the employer had mistakenly sent to the applicant (*Allen* v *Hammett* [1982] IRLR 89).

On the other hand, the following matters have been held not to constitute contributory fault:

(a) failure to exercise a right of appeal under the employer's internal procedure (*Hoover Ltd* v *Forde* [1980] ICR 239);

(b) failure by an employee to disclose a criminal conviction which he had no need to reveal by reason of the Rehabilitation of Offenders Act 1974 (*Property Guards Ltd* v *Taylor and Kershaw* [1982] IRLR 175); and

(c) ill health (*Slaughter* v *C. Brewer & Sons Ltd* [1990] ICR 730).

Participation in industrial action was for many years held to fall outside this rubric (*Courtaulds Northern Spinning Ltd* v *Moosa* (supra)) since this would require tribunals to attach blame in industrial disputes, but the EAT departed from this principle in *TNT Express Ltd* v *Downes* [1994] ICR 1, on the basis that it was not warranted by the statutory language.

The broad position in *Moosa* was restored by the Court of Appeal in *Tracey* v *Crossville Wales Ltd* [1996] ICR 237, on the basis that this was the presumed intention of Parliament, especially given that many who had been involved in the same industrial action would have been offered re-engagement. There is, however, important caveat that where complainants have been shown to be responsible for some additional conduct of their own over and above mere participation in the industrial action, the fact that such conduct occurred during and as part of the industrial action does not preclude the industrial tribunal from examining it separately and considering whether it contributed to the dismissal. The case is presently under appeal to the House of Lords.

13.18.6.3 Amount of reduction Once a causal link has been established, the *amount* of deduction is at large for the tribunal. It takes a percentage from such compensation as the employee would otherwise be entitled to. In extreme cases the award may be reduced to nil, but this should only occur where the unfairness is highly technical, perhaps a minor breach of procedure, and the employee's own conduct was highly provocative. There has been a major difference of opinion as to the acceptability of large deductions. Although the English EAT reduced compensation by 100 per cent in *Maris* v *Rotherham Corporation* [1974] IRLR 147, it commented in *Trend* v *Chiltern Hunt Ltd* [1977] ICR 612 that reductions should rarely exceed 80 per cent. Lord McDonald, on the other hand, in the Scottish EAT in *Courtney* v *Babcock & Wilcox (Operations) Ltd* [1977] IRLR 30 could see nothing wrong in principle or practice with a 100 per cent reduction, adding that the English EAT's approach savoured of a tariff. This line was indeed approved in *Devis & Sons* v *Atkins* (supra). The question of what is just and equitable is directed to the proportion of the reduction and not whether there should be any reduction at all, which is simply a question of causation (*Warrilow* v *Robert Walker Ltd* [1984] IRLR 304).

The deduction for contributory fault is made from the losses of the employee as assessed without regard to the statutory maximum award of compensation. Thus if the tribunal computes the potential award as £12,000 but considers a 50 per cent reduction appropriate, £6,000 is deducted from £12,000 notwithstanding that the statutory maximum is presently £11,300. That only operates as a ceiling on the final figure awarded (see *Parker & Farr Ltd* v *Shelvey* [1979] IRLR 435, *UBAF Bank Ltd* v *Davis* [1978] IRLR 442; cf. *Derwent Coachworks* v *Kirby* [1995] ICR 48). The termination payment made should be deducted before making the *Polkey* reduction (*Cox* v *London Borough of Camden*) [1996] IRLR 389). Doubt was cast on the *Derwent Coachworks* decision.

There has been some conflict of authority as to whether a tribunal errs in law in making a reduction for contributory fault from only the compensatory award whilst leaving intact the basic element. The Northern Ireland Court of Appeal in *McFall & Co.* v *Curran* [1981] IRLR 455 thought that this showed unacceptable inconsistency, but the EAT in *Les Ambassadeurs Club* v *Bainda* [1982] IRLR 5 saw no objection. In most cases the same percentage should be deducted from both awards (*RSPCA* v *Cruden* [1986] IRLR 83).

The EAT will generally not intervene in a tribunal's finding of contributory fault, still less in the amount of deduction. In *Hollier* v *Plysu Ltd* [1983] IRLR 260, the Court of Appeal advised industrial tribunals to take a broad common-sense view. It was a matter of 'impression, opinion and discretion'. (See also *Warrilow* v *Robert Walker Ltd* (supra), *Yate Foundry Ltd* v *Walters* [1984] ICR 445, *F. C. Shepherd & Co. Ltd* v *Jerrom* [1986] IRLR 358). A finding of contributory fault for the purposes of not making an order for reinstatement should be reflected in a reduction of the basic and compensatory awards.

13.18.7 Mitigation

Reduction in compensation will be made if the employee failed to take reasonable steps to get another job or otherwise keep down his loss, as at common law (ERA 1996, s. 123(4)). The onus of proof of failure of mitigation rests on the employer (*Sturdy Finance Ltd* v *Bardsley* [1979] IRLR 65 and *Fyfe* v *Scientific Furnishings Ltd* [1989] IRLR 331), and the duty only arises after dismissal, so neither a refusal to accept other employment before that date (*Savoia* v *Chiltern Herb Farms Ltd* [1981] IRLR 65, nor the employee's failure to carry out any internal procedural steps is relevant. Indeed, in general, conduct prior to dismissal cannot feature in an allegation of failure to mitigate loss (*Prestwick Circuits Ltd* v *McAndrew* [1990] IRLR 191).

The employee cannot, however, sit back and mount up his losses in the confident expectation that they will be met by the respondent. The proper test for tribunals to apply was set out by the Court of Appeal in *Bessenden Properties* v *Corness* [1974] IRLR 338, as whether, 'if the complainant had had no hope of recovering compensation from anybody else and if he had consulted merely his own interests and had acted reasonably in all the circumstances, would he have accepted the job in mitigation of the loss which he had suffered'. (See also *Archbold Freightage* v *Wilson* [1974] IRLR 10, *Scottish and Newcastle Breweries Ltd* v *Halliday* [1986] IRLR 291, *Morganite Electrical Carbon Ltd* v *Donne* [1987] IRLR 363; cf. *Fyfe* v *Scientific Furnishings Ltd* [1989] IRLR 331). This is a question of fact in each case, and reference may be made to the authorities on the similar question for wrongful dismissal (Chapter 12). The applicant need not show that he took steps in mitigation *before* he was actually dismissed (*McAndrew* v *Prestwick Circuits Ltd* [1988] IRLR 514).

Broadly, although the employee need not take the first job that comes along (*Gallear* v *Watson* [1979] IRLR 306), it may be reasonable after a period of unemployment to accept a post at a lower rate of pay than he enjoyed before (*Daley* v *A. E. Dorsett* [1981] IRLR 385, *Hardwick* v *Leeds AHA* [1975] IRLR 319). To make one job application in eight weeks has been held to be unreasonable (*O'Reilly* v *Welwyn and Hatfield District Council* [1975] IRLR 334, *Sweetlove* v *Redbridge & Waltham Forest AHA* [1979] IRLR 195). The proper approach involves assessing how long the employee would be out of work if he had properly mitigated his loss, rather than reducing the global sum by a percentage as in contributory fault (*Smith, Kline & French Laboratories Ltd* v *Coates* [1977] IRLR 220). A similar process is to be applied to loss of pension rights.

Tribunals realistically recognise that a former employee who starts a new business after dismissal will probably earn little in the initial period but this does not mean that he is not reasonably mitigating his loss. In *Gardiner-Hill* v *Roland Berger Technics Ltd* [1982] IRLR 498, the applicant was dismissed from his position as managing director of the respondent consultancy service when he was 55 years old and decided then to set up on his own account. In the six and a half months between dismissal and tribunal hearing he had earned only £1,500. The employers argued that this did not reflect a reasonable attempt to mitigate his loss and the tribunal decided that since he was spending some 90 per cent of his time on the new business and not looking for alternative employment his compensation should be reduced by 80 per cent. The EAT thought that the applicant's strategy was a reasonable one and that in any event it was wrong to make a percentage reduction in relation to mitigation. Rather the tribunal should have decided on a date when, if the ex-employee had used reasonable efforts, he would have gained other employment at a similar level. (See also *Lee* v *IPC Business Press Ltd* [1984] ICR 306.) A failure to follow the internal appeals procedure laid down at the place of work is not a failure to mitigate (*William Muir (Bond 9) Ltd* v *Lamb* [1985] IRLR 95). An employee is well advised to keep a list of all jobs he has applied for and the answers he has received in order to demonstrate to a tribunal that he has tried as hard as he can to find alternative work.

13.18.8 Jobseeker's allowance

Jobseeker's allowance and unfair dismissal cover similar types of loss through unemployment. After initial doubts whether they should be set off one against the other, the relationship between them is now governed by two sets of regulations.

By the Employment Protection (Recoupment of Jobseeker's Allowance and Income Support) Regulations 1996 (SI 1996 No. 2349), the Department of Social Security has first claim on the amount of compensation for the days on which the allowance or social security has already been paid out. The employee should not recover twice over. An industrial tribunal thus has to set out a 'prescribed element' of compensation, that is, immediate loss of earnings up to the tribunal hearing, if any, and this must not be paid over by the employer until the Department has determined whether to recoup the allowance paid. If so the Secretary of State must serve a recoupment notice within 21 days after the hearing, or nine days after the decision has been sent to the parties, whichever is later. There is no appeal against the amount of money stated in the notice. As to post-tribunal loss, under the Social Security (Unemployment, Sickness and Invalidity Benefit) Regulations 1983 (SI 1983 No.

1598) reg. 7, an employee is not to be treated as unemployed following an industrial tribunal award for:

(a) reinstatement or re-engagement; or
(b) additional award for non-compliance therewith; or
(c) compensation for unfair dismissal.

The 1996 Regulations merely apply the old recoupment provisions to the new benefits regime.

Where the payment represents remuneration which the industrial tribunal considered the employee might have earned for a particular day, he cannot receive an allowance. This applies even if the former employers are insolvent so that the sum due is *not* in fact paid (*Morton* v *Chief Adjudication Officer* [1988] IRLR 444).

Where the case is settled without a tribunal hearing there is no provision for recoupment, and this has undoubtedly been an additional spur to settlement of claims. Where the employee received sickness benefit between his dismissal and the tribunal hearing, the amount will be deducted from a compensatory award if, had he continued in employment, it would have been an addition to his wages, but not if they would have been reduced accordingly (*Sun and Sand Ltd* v *Fitzjohn* [1979] ICR 268; see also *Homan* v *A1 Bacon Co. Ltd* [1996] ICR 721).

13.18.9 Other issues

(a) There is now no limit on compensation in sex discrimination and race discrimination cases and interest may be awarded for a discriminatory dismissal under both the Sex Discrimination and Race Relations Acts, but there remains a limit the unfair dismissal jurisdiction.

(b) The maximum compensatory award is applied after any deduction for contributory fault has been made.

(c) The tribunal cannot make a general award of *interest* since it is not a court of record (*Nelson* v *BBC (No. 2)* [1979] IRLR 346 and *Southampton and South West Hampshire HA* v *Marshall (No. 2)* [1989] IRLR 459) but the industrial tribunal must make an award of interest even if it is unpaid 42 days after the decision is promulgated (Industrial Tribunals (Interest) Order 1990 (SI 1990 No. 479) and there are special provisions for sex discrimination and equal pay claims (Sex Discrimination and Equal Pay (Remedies) Regulations 1993 (SI 1993 No. 2798) (see Bowers *et al, Industrial Practice and Procedure* (FT Law & Tax, 1996)).

(d) Invalidity benefit is an insurance-type benefit and does not fall to be deducted from unfair dismissal compensation (*Hilton International Hotels (UK) Ltd* v *Faraji* [1994] IRLR 267).

13.19 UNFAIR DISMISSAL: OVERVIEW

The Industrial Relations Act 1971 was a remarkable piece of social legislation. Parliament recognised that even if the employer had the right in strict law to dismiss the employee there were circumstances in which it would be unfair for the employer to exercise that right.

(per Lord Salmon, *Nothman* v *Barnet LBC* [1979] IRLR 35 para. 4.)

Of the whole panoply of employment protection rights which began to be enacted in the mid 1960s, the unfair dismissal provisions have had by far the most effect in changing personnel practices and collective bargaining arrangements. They were intended to accord employees a form of property in their jobs. Such was the employee's compensation for his relative lack of property in the capital that employs him. If taken away unjustly, he should be reinstated in his job, or at the least gain compensation for loss suffered. No longer could an employer autocratically terminate an employee's contract at whim.

On its procedural side it has important implications for the development of rules for industrial justice which go far beyond dismissal alone. Some 85 per cent of industrial tribunal applications concern unfair dismissal and its effect is in inverse proportion to the degree of unionisation in a particular factory or plant, so that in poorly organised industries, like construction and distribution, claims are disproportionately high. Department of Employment figures show that a quarter of all claims are made against firms employing fewer than 20. However, there are disturbing indications that those most at risk from the 'hire and fire' mentality of management are least aware of the legislation, and are often persuaded to become independent contractors and to accept unfavourable settlements. Moreover, in times of high unemployment, many workers feel that to bring an unfair dismissal application will mark them as a 'troublemaker' and, whether they win or lose, render it more difficult to gain another job.

The major criticism of the unfair dismissal jurisdiction has, however, come from those who believe that its restrictions on management have led them to become reluctant to hire staff. Such general claims are difficult to prove or disprove, but such research as has been carried out does not substantiate this widely held view. (See R. Clifton and C. Tatham Browne, *Impact of Employment Legislation in Small Firms,* D of E Research Paper No. 6, 1979, and for an excellent survey, *Dismissed, A Study of Unfair Dismissal and the Industrial Tribunal System,* Dickens, Jones, Weekes & Hart, 1985, Basil Blackwell.)

It is also necessary to keep its practical impact in perspective. Far less than 1 per cent of employees leaving their jobs make such claims, and each year only one out of 100 firms with fewer than 200 employees is likely to be faced with such application.

The underlying policy of some of the judiciary and tribunals in this respect was enunciated by Phillips J in *Cook* v *Thomas Linnell and Sons Ltd* [1977] ICR 770:

> It is important that the operation of the legislation in relation to unfair dismissal should not impede employers unreasonably in the efficient management of their business, which must be in the interests of all.

While management expectations are thus well recognised and well served, the aspirations of the workforce appear much less to the fore. Further, notwithstanding widespread misconceptions, compensation awards remain low. Awards are rarely even close to the maximum permitted by statute and the maximum award has lagged well behind the rate of inflation.

14 Redundancy Payments

A worker of long standing is now recognised as having an accrued right in his job, and his right gains in value with the years. So much so, that if the job is shut down, he is entitled to compensation for loss of a job — just as a director gets compensation for loss of office. The director gets a golden handshake. The worker gets a redundancy payment. It is not unemployment pay. I repeat 'not'. Even if he gets another job straightaway, he nevertheless is entitled to full redundancy payment. It is, in a real sense, compensation for long service.

(Lord Denning MR in *Lloyd* v *Brassey* (1969) 4 ITR 100.)

Ironically, a major function of redundancy law has changed; from protecting a particular kind of job right for the innocent worker, it has become in part a package for legitimation of his dismissal.

(K. W. Wedderburn, *The Worker and the Law,* 3rd ed., Penguin, 1988.)

14.1 INTRODUCTION

The redundancy payments scheme was introduced under the Redundancy Payments Act 1965 as the first of the substantial statutory individual employment rights. In retrospect its chief significance was that, 'for the first time it turned dismissal into a prima facie compensable event rather than a generally non-compensable event' (Davies and Freedland, *Labour Law: Text and Materials,* op. cit., p. 395).

The current law has been substantially consolidated in the Employment Rights Act 1996. The original structure remains intact and provides a lump sum payment designed to tide an employee over the period of uncertainty and hardship after dismissal or redundancy. Until 1986 the employer could claim a rebate of 41 per cent (later reduced to 35 per cent) from the Redundancy Fund, which consists of employer's national insurance contributions. Under the former Wages Act 1986, however, such recourse was open only to employers of nine or fewer persons, and no rebates at all are available since the Employment Act 1989. If the employer is insolvent the employee can gain his full entitlement directly from the National Insurance Fund. The amount of payment increases, like basic award for unfair dismissal, with the number of years continuous service of the employee. His entitlement is in the bank, as it were, only maturing at dismissal, but payment is denied if the employee unreasonably refuses a suitable alternative offer of employment from his employer, his successor or an associated employer. A measure of the importance of the scheme is that about a quarter of a million people receive such payments each year.

14.1.1 Justifying the scheme

Various justifications of the scheme have been proffered, but few explain all its features. Some have described it as establishing a 'proprietary interest in the job'. Thus, the President of Industrial Tribunals in *Wynes* v *Southrepps Hall Broiler Farm Ltd* (1968) 3 ITR 407, said:

> Just as a property owner has a right in his property and when he is deprived, he is entitled to compensation, so a long-term employee is considered to have a right of property in his job, he has a right to security and his rights gain in value with the years.

It seeks to assist training and resettlement and thus stimulate mobility of labour, the lack of which has been diagnosed as one of the major problems of Britain's economy. However, as P. Elias *et al* have pointed out (*Labour Law (Cases and Materials)*, Butterworth, 1981, p. 646) this is difficult to sustain as a primary function, since the way in which payments are assessed means that 'the most money goes to the older, longer-serving workers who are the least likely, as a group, to be prepared to leave their homes and families in search of new work'.

Other commentators see the payment less idealistically as a bribe to employees to go quietly. In particular, Fryer (1973 2 ILJ 1) has argued that the legislation is a positive inducement to insecurity of work by encouraging abandonment by workers of protective attitudes to job security, often manifested in so-called 'restrictive practices'. It has certainly stimulated the negotiation with unions of redundancy agreements, which were formerly anathema to them. Yet Fryer argues that the scheme is of little use as a cover to employees losing their jobs, since only less than one third of redundant employees actually qualify for statutory payments.

Professor C. Grunfeld has described the scheme more pragmatically as:

> just one lubricant of this particular unavoidable component [loss of employment] in the process of adaptation to the larger changes rolling relentlessly forward in the modern world as countless businesses close down to lighten existing or make way for new enterprises and as heavily-manned, long-established industries drive to sharpen their efficiency and reduce or remove their dead weight in relation to the total economy.

(*Law of Redundancy*, 3rd ed., Sweet & Maxwell, 1989.) The scheme was a product of the 1960s — a decade of hope, relatively full employment and the 'white heat of the technological revolution'. The 1990s are a very different age, as unemployment has become endemic in all the depressed western economies. The numbers of redundancies have risen sharply and all projections suggest that they will continue to rise as the electronic microchip revolution means that machines increasingly replace people, and Britain has a regular unemployment figure of above 2,000,000. In particular, any optimism about redundancy overcoming malutilisation of labour appears to be dashed.

Contradictions in the case law might be identified as arising from the particular viewpoint taken on this by the tribunal in question. Many believe that the scheme achieves none of its manifold objects with any degree of success.

Certainly when unfair dismissal was introduced, 'the RPA was somewhat relegated to a back seat' (Davies and Freedland, op. cit., p. 396), and in *O'Hare and Rutherford* v

Rotaprint Ltd [1980] ICR 94, Kilner Brown J made a rousing call for reform, commenting that: 'It seems that the original intention of the Redundancy Payments Act 1965 has been clouded by a slipshod acceptance of a bottomless purse.'

The case law also demonstrates tension in another rather subtle way. For those seeking to prove redundancy as a reason for dismissal have, in many cases, changed sides. In the beginning, it was in the interests of employers to disprove redundancy since that was the only reason for dismissal which would cost them money, but with the Industrial Relations Act 1971 and its introduction of unfair dismissal, management began to put it forward as a potentially fair reason for dismissal. The battle lines were redrawn; the decisions drew different distinctions; the patchwork became more complicated.

14.2 DEFINITION OF REDUNDANCY

Redundancy is much more strictly defined in the ERA 1996 than the concept as used in ordinary speech. It is not uncommon to hear that a man has been 'made redundant' when in fact he has really been dismissed for misconduct or incapability. The statute uses the same definition for three different purposes:

(a)   determining entitlement to redundancy payments;
(b)   establishing a potentially fair reason for dismissal (para. 13.10); and
(c)   requiring consultation with unions (Chapter 15).

Under s. 139(1) of ERA 1996, an employee is dismissed for redundancy where the dismissal is attributable wholly or mainly to:

(a)   the fact that his employer has ceased, or intends to cease, to carry on the business for the purposes of which the employee was employed by him, or has ceased, or intends to cease, to carry on that business in the place where the employee was so employed; or

(b)   the fact that the requirements of that business for employees to carry out work of a particular kind, or for employees to carry out work of a particular kind in the place where he was so employed, have ceased or diminished or are expected to cease or diminish.

After some doubt, it has been held that an employee dismissed on a transfer of undertaking may be able to claim a redundancy payment (*Gorictree Ltd* v *Jenkinson* [1984] IRLR 391, *Anderson & McAlonie* v *Dalkeith Engineering Ltd* [1984] IRLR 429; for fuller treatment see para. 16.4).

14.2.1   Dismissal and proof

A dismissal is a condition precedent to a redundancy payment just as it is the basis for a claim of unfair dismissal (para. 13.3). Its definition has already been considered and the slight differences in respect of redundancy payments noted. However, it should be here emphasised that the frequently used term 'voluntary redundancies' is apt to be misleading, since for a claim to succeed the initiative must come from the employer; an employee who resigns except in reaction to a fundamental breach of contract is not entitled to a redundancy payment (*Walley* v *Morgan* (1969) 4 ITR 122).

An employee engaged on a succession of fixed-term contracts is dismissed for redundancy on the expiration of each one (*Pfaffinger* v *City of Liverpool Community College* [1996] IRLR 508).

After dismissal has been proved, for the purposes of redundancy payment alone and not unfair dismissal, redundancy is presumed to be the reason 'unless the contrary is proved' (ERA 1996, s. 163(2)).

14.2.2 Total cessation of the employer's business

There are three discrete parts to the definition of redundancy. The first limb applies when a worker's employer completely closes the business in which the applicant was employed. Business, by statute, includes any trade or profession or activity carried on by a body of persons, and it is not necessary to prove that the employer owns the business in question in order to succeed in claiming a payment on its closure, nor is it necessary that it is a commercial venture if it is to fall within the Transfer of Undertakings (Protection of Employment) Regulations 1981. Thus, in *Thomas* v *Jones* [1978] ICR 274, the applicant was hired and fired by a subpostmistress, although the Post Office actually owned the business in which she worked. The EAT held that the former was correctly named as respondent.

Early decisions refused to countenance a redundancy payment where an employee was in effect himself responsible for the redundancy caused (*Marsland* v *Francis Dunn Ltd* (1967) 2 ITR 353). However, this was rejected as authority for any general principle of self-induced redundancy in *Sanders* v *Ernest A. Neale* [1974] ICR 565, where dismissal followed a strike.

14.2.3 Cessation of business at place of employment

If the employee works at a particular factory, office or shop of the employer company or firm which closes, his dismissal then will be on grounds of redundancy notwithstanding that the employer continues to carry on business elsewhere. This will also be the case when the employee ceases the work of a particular kind in the place where the employee was employed. This puts into focus the *place of employment* and, according to the NIRC: 'These words do not mean "where he in fact worked". They mean "where under his contract of employment he could be required to work"'. In the case where this principle was established, *UK Atomic Energy Authority* v *Claydon* [1974] IRLR 6, the employee's conditions reserved to the employing Authority 'the right to require any member of their staff to work at any of their establishments in Great Britain or in posts overseas'. The applicant, a draughtsman, was originally employed at Orford Ness, and was dismissed when the work on which he was engaged moved to Aldermaston and he refused to go with it. The Court upheld the employer's contention that requirements for workers had not ceased 'in the place where he was employed', since he was obliged to work at any place in Great Britain where the employers so chose. In *Bass Leisure Ltd* v *Thomas* [1994] IRLR 104, the EAT held that the 'place' where an employee was employed did not extend to any place where he could *contractually* be required to work. The location and extent of that place must be ascertainable whether or not the employee is in fact to be required to move, i.e. therefore, before any such requirement is made, if it is made, and without knowledge of the terms of any such requirement or of the employee's response, or of whether any conditions upon the making of it have been complied with.

A term of mobility will only rarely be implied (see *United Bank Ltd* v *Akhtar* [1989] IRLR 507). In *O'Brien* v *Associated Fire Alarms Ltd* [1968] ITR 182, the employing company installed fire and burglar alarms throughout the United Kingdom, but the applicant electrician worked for its north western area, which covered a very large area (at least 200 miles long) and was controlled from the Liverpool Office. He lived in Liverpool and generally worked within commutable distance of home. When requirements in that area diminished, the management sought to compel him to work 120 miles away in Barrow-in-Furness claiming that it was implied in his contract that he would work anywhere in the north west. They thus claimed that there was *no* diminution in the place he was required to work. The Court of Appeal would only imply a term that the employee should work within daily travelling distance of his home and no more. His dismissal by reason of the employer's repudiation *was* thus due to a diminution of work in the relevant *place* where he was employed. (See *F. Little* v *Charterhouse Magna Assurance Co. Ltd* [1980] IRLR 19; cf. *Jones* v *Associated Tunnelling Co.* [1981] IRLR 477; see para. 13.3.3.3 for full discussion).

Where there is a clear term of mobility and an employee's refusal to move results in his dismissal the statutory reason will be disobedience to orders, i.e. misconduct, and not because his employer has ceased to carry on business at a place where he is employed, so that he cannot claim redundancy (*Rowbotham* v *Arthur Lee & Sons Ltd* [1974] IRLR 377). (See also *Sutcliffe* v *Hawker Siddeley Aviation Ltd* (1974) 9 ITR 58 DC, express term; *Parry* v *Holst and Co. Ltd* (1968) 3 ITR 317, collective agreement; *Bective Electrical Co. Ltd* v *Warren* (1968) 3 ITR 119, custom.)

14.2.4 Diminution in requirements of the business

The third limb of redundancy comprises a reduction in requirements for *employees* because of, say, a fall off in demand or rationalisation of the business altogether or in the particular place where the employee was employed, or because fewer men and women as opposed to machines or new techniques are necessary, and it is the most difficult to construe. It is important to emphasise that the vital question is not whether less work was required but whether there was less need for *employees* to carry on that work (*McCrea* v *Cullen & Davison Ltd* [1988] IRLR 30). Although the work in question remains to be done, an employee is redundant if the company has so organised its affairs that the work required is done by fewer employees, whether this is achieved by improved mechanisation, automation, other technical advance or reallocation of functions.

Further, the proper question is not the reason *why* the employer's requirement has ceased but the *fact* that it has ceased. The EAT decision in *Association of University Teachers* v *University of Newcastle upon Tyne* [1988] IRLR 10 concerned the dismissal of a temporary lecturer in the training of teachers of the deaf. The teacher had been engaged on a three-year fixed-term contract, which was not renewed because funding for the course had run out. The industrial tribunal held that there was no redundancy but the EAT rebuked them for considering the cause of the cessation of the employer's requirements rather than merely the fact that there was a cessation of need for an employee. (See also *Lamont* v *Fry's Metals Ltd* [1985] ICR 566 and *Macfisheries* v *Findlay* [1985] ICR 160.)

14.2.4.1 Work of a particular kind Only if the requirements for employees to carry out the *particular work* the employee was contracted to perform have ceased or diminished is the employee redundant under this heading. The NIRC declared it to mean 'work which is distinguished from other work of the same general kind by requiring special aptitudes, special skills or knowledge' (*Amos* v *Max-Arc Ltd* [1973] IRLR 285 and *O'Neill* v *Merseyside Plumbing Ltd* [1973] ICR 96). This means that fine lines sometimes have to be drawn to characterise jobs, and the EAT and Court of Appeal have frequently stated that it is a matter of fact and degree for the industrial tribunal (*Murphy* v *Epsom College* [1984] IRLR 271), as the following cases demonstrate:

(a)   In *Vaux and Associated Breweries Ltd* v *Ward* (1968) 3 ITR 385, the employers decided to relaunch one of their hotels by employing young 'bunny girls' in place of older barmaids, and the vital question in deciding whether one of the dismissed middle-aged barmaids was entitled to redundancy payment concerned whether 'the work that the barmaid in the altered premises was going to do was work of a different kind to what the barmaid in the unaltered premises had been doing'. The Divisional Court found that the *work* was not different, even though the type of *person* required to fill the position was, and, therefore, the applicant was not entitled to redundancy payment.

(b)   On the other hand, in *Archibald* v *Rossleigh Commercials Ltd* [1975] IRLR 231, the tribunal held that the work of an emergency unsupervised night mechanic could be distinguished from that of an ordinary mechanic. The test clearly focuses on the characteristics of the job and whether these have gone, rather than the aptitudes of the employee filling it (*Pillinger* v *Manchester AHA* [1979] IRLR 430 EAT).

(c)   To dismiss two plumbers to make way for a heating engineer was a redundancy even though the work done was broadly the same and the total number of employees did not change. The employees, however, had different qualifications and skills (*Murphy* v *Epsom College* (supra)).

The scope and extent of the business in which a redundant employee is employed is also a question of fact for the tribunal to determine. Partners who operate more than one enterprise may be regarded for redundancy purposes as operating a single business. The relevant factors include the similarity of the work done at each establishment, the skilled nature of the work, and the degree of interchangeability between members of staff (*Babar Indian Restaurant* v *Rawat* [1985] IRLR 57; see further para. 14.2.4.4).

The EAT in *Haden* v *Cowen* [1982] IRLR 314 derived from *Nelson* v *BBC* [1977] ICR 649 the principle that the tribunal should focus not on the work that the employee actually did before dismissal, but rather on the work which he could be expected to do under his contract of employment (approved in *Pink* v *White and White & Co. (Earls Barton) Ltd* [1985] IRLR 489).

Johnson v *Peabody Trust* [1996] IRLR 387, represents a further elaboration of this doctrine. The employee claimed that he could not properly be found to have been made redundant since the employer's requirement for carrying out all the multi-trade operations which he could have been asked to perform had not diminished. The EAT held, however, that where an employee is employed to perform a particular, well-recognised and well-defined category of skilled trade — here roofing — it is that basic contractual obligation which has to be considered when deciding whether the employer's requirement has ceased or diminished. The contractual test in the statute should not be read in an over-technical or legalistic way but in a commonsense manner in order to ascertain the basic task which the employee was contracted to perform.

14.2.4.2   Reorganisation of terms or reduction in requirements?   The courts have excluded from redundancy a mere reorganisation of work programme. Thus, where duties are different or hours have been changed, but the overall needs of the persons doing the collection of those duties, i.e. the job, is not less, the courts have not awarded a redundancy payment. The essential question is whether the process 'results in the employee's work being encompassed in other posts and whether the employer's business is such that it no longer has a requirement for a separate and additional employee to carry out the work' (*Sutton* v *Revlon Overseas Corporation Ltd* [1973] IRLR 173). Only in this case is there a redundancy. The employee's skill and qualifications and hours of work are irrelevant. Night shift as opposed to day shift work may, however, be work of a particular kind (*Macfisheries Ltd* v *Findlay* [1985] ICR 160). The distinction between job description and the job itself is sometimes little short of metaphysical. The most that perhaps can be done is to accept Phillips J's statement that: 'In truth all these cases of redundancy claims ultimately raise questions of fact and the decided cases are only of value in enunciating the principles.'

In *Chapman* v *Goonvean and Rostowrack China Clay Ltd* [1973] ICR 310, seven workers used to travel to work each day on a bus provided by the employers. As this became uneconomic it was decided to cut off the service. The employees claimed to be thus constructively dismissed by reason of redundancy and argued that if they had not been dismissed, the employers would be running the business at a loss which would eventually have led to redundancy. Lord Denning, however, held that, 'the requirements of the business — for the work of these seven men — continued just the same as before. After they stopped work the firm had to take on another seven men to replace them . . . it would be necessary to import the words on the existing terms and conditions to justify the employees' arguments'. Redundancy did not cover a change of terms. The Master of the Rolls was pleased to reach this result since it accorded with his view of public policy:

> It is very desirable in the interests of efficiency that employers should be able to propose changes in the terms of a man's employment for such reasons as these so as to get rid of restrictive practices; or to induce higher output by piece work; or to cease to provide free transport at an excessive cost . . . the employers can properly say to the men . . . 'you have lost your job because you live so far away that it is not worth our while paying the costs of bringing you here . . .'

(See also *Lesney Products & Co. Ltd* v *Nolan* [1977] ICR 235.)

The distinction between different terms and different jobs is further illustrated by the important Court of Appeal decision in *Johnson* v *Nottinghamshire Combined Police Authority* [1974] ICR 170. The two applicant women employees had worked as clerks in one of the respondent's police stations for some years, coming in between 9.30 a.m. and 5.30 p.m. or 6 p.m. from Monday to Friday. In 1974 the Authority sought to introduce a shift system of 8 a.m. to 3 p.m. and 1 a.m. to 8 a.m., which both women refused, and they were dismissed. The Court of Appeal decided that the sacking was not by reason of redundancy, since the clerical work for which they were employed had neither ceased nor diminished, even though there was no need for women doing those hours. The NIRC declared: 'Work of a particular kind refers to the task to be performed not to the other elements which go to make up the kind of job which it is.' Moreover, 'an employer is entitled to reorganise his business so as to improve its efficiency'. Since it was 'the same job done to a different time schedule', the dismissal was not attributable to redundancy. (See also, to the same effect, *Blakely* v *Chemetron Ltd* (1972) 7 ITR 224, *Delanair Ltd* v *Mead* [1976] ICR 522, *North Riding Garages Ltd* v *Butterwick* (1967) 2 ITR 229; cf. *Kykot* v *Smith Hartley* [1975] IRLR 372, *Macfisheries Ltd* v *Findlay* (supra); *Overend* v *Perkins Engines Ltd* EAT 479/88).

14.2.4.3 Replacement If an employee is replaced there can be no redundancy. Thus, in *Wren* v *Wiltshire CC* (1969) 4 ITR 251, no payment could be claimed where an unqualified teacher was replaced by one with qualifications; the employers still required employees to do the same kind of work. It is, however, only the requirement of the business for *employees* that need cease or diminish; if they are replaced by self-employed workers, there would probably be a redundancy (*Bromby and Hoare Ltd* v *Evans* [1972] ITR 76, *Amos* v *Max-Arc Ltd* [1973] IRLR 285, *Ladbroke Courage Holidays Ltd* v *Asten* [1981] IRLR 59).

14.2.4.4   Variations on the theme

(a)   It does not matter that the employee knows from the beginning of his job that his work is going to diminish, as shown by *Nottinghamshire CC* v *Lee* [1979] IRLR 294, where the employee was offered a post as a temporary lecturer for one year, at the end of which period the post was extended for another 12 months. He knew that there would be no further extension since the college's requirements had already ceased. Slynn J found that this was not included in the statutory definition since the employer's requirements had not diminished *during* his second period of employment and that it would be unfair in the circumstances if a redundancy payment be required. The Court of Appeal overruled this interpretation, applying the exact words of the statute. The appellant's contract was not renewed because the employer's requirements for employees had diminished. The statute did not mean that the requirement must cease or diminish *during the period of employment*. The case also serves to re-emphasise that fairness has nothing to do with redundancy payment.

(b)   The diminution in requirements must arise in the job being done, so that, as in *North East Coast Ship Repairers Ltd* v *Secretary of State for Employment* [1978] IRLR 149, there is no redundancy where an apprentice is not taken on at the end of his apprenticeship as a journeyman because there is not enough work for him to do.

(c)   There is a redundancy where the employer takes on additional workers in the hope of increased production which never in fact materialises, although in *O'Hare and Rutherford* v *Rotaprint Ltd* [1980] IRLR 47, Kilner Brown J criticised the decision which he felt compelled to reach on the language of the statute. For in his view it outraged common sense that employers should be inhibited from taking justifiable commercial risks by the thought that they would have to make a redundancy payment if things went wrong. This appears more a political than legal point.

(d)   By s. 139(1), (2) of ERA 1996, if the employee is dismissed because of an overall reduction in requirements within a group of associated employers (defined in para. 10.4.2), he can claim a redundancy payment even if there is no redundancy on his particular employer's part. Further, it is enough that redundancy is the main reason where there is more than one cause for dismissal, or that requirements are expected to cease or diminish in the future, so that a claim may be brought before the closure actually takes place.

(e)   'Bumping' is the vivid American terminology describing the situation where, although there is a reduction in the requirements for employees in part A of the business, an employee in that part is transferred to another section B, and an employee there is dismissed. The latter's sacking does fall within the meaning of redundancy according to several decisions, even though there is no less need for *him* and no diminution in his section (*W. Gimber & Sons Ltd* v *Spurrett* (1967) 2 ITR 308, *Gordon* v *Adams (Dalkeith) Ltd* (1972) 7 ITR 81, *Elliott Turbomachinery Ltd* v *Bates* [1981] ICR 218; see also discussion of the concept in *North Yorkshire CC* v *Fay* [1985] IRLR 247).

(f)   It has, however, been questioned whether a dismissal is attributable wholly or mainly to redundancy if the motive for dismissal actually uppermost in the employer's mind is something other than redundancy, notwithstanding that a redundancy situation may exist. In *Hindle* v *Percival Boats Ltd* (1969) 4 ITR 86, the Court of Appeal decided that, provided that the employer honestly believes that dismissal is justified by another reason, here, because the applicant boatbuilder was 'too good and too slow' to adapt to new techniques with fibreglass boats, it did not matter that he was also redundant. At the time, this decision meant that he could claim nothing: now he would be entitled to claim unfair dismissal. Lord Denning MR dissented on the ground that if redundancy was a prominent cause of the dismissal it was not necessary that the employer should have it in mind as his reason, and this, it is submitted, is the better view.

14.3 OFFER OF NEW EMPLOYMENT

14.3.1 The statutory provisions

If the employee accepts the renewal of his contract on the same terms as before, he is not entitled to a redundancy payment, and the same applies if he is re-engaged in a *suitable alternative* position (ERA 1996, s. 138(1)), *Camelo* v *Sheerlyn Productions Ltd* [1976] ICR 531). In either case the offer is also valid if it comes from an associated employer, on transfer of the business, or involves a move to Crown service. A job offer by a company associated with the employee's employer counts as an offer by an associated employer even though at the time of the offer the company making the offer was dormant and had no employees of its own. The EAT so held in construing s. 84 of EPCA 1978 (now ERA 1996, s. 138) in *Lucas* v *Henry Johnson (Packers & Shippers) Ltd* [1986] ICR 384. In the special case of an employee employed in local government service, the offer may come from any other local government employer (see also Redundancy Payments (Local Government) (Modification) Order 1983 (SI 1983 No. 1160) as amended by further Modification Orders (SI 1985 No. 1872 and SI 1988 No. 905; see also to similar effect for the NHS, Redundancy Payments (National Health Service) (Modification) Order 1993 (SI 1993 No. 3167))). Any renewal or re-engagement must, however, take effect either immediately on the end of the previous employment or not more than four weeks thereafter and then his service will be treated as unbroken and continuous. Where the old job ends on a Friday, Saturday or Sunday, it suffices if the new employment begins on the following Monday or within four weeks of that Monday (s. 146(2)).

Section 138 applies only for the purposes of redundancy pay. It does not apply to unfair dismissal (*Hempell* v *W.H. Smith & Sons Ltd* [1986] IRLR 95). The section is merely designed to provide a defence for an employer faced with a claim for a redundancy payment in circumstances where the employee even before dismissal has obtained another job with the same or an associated employer (see *EBAC Ltd* v *Wymer* [1995] ICR 466).

14.3.2 Trial period

14.3.2.1 Application If the proffered new contract differs as to capacity or place of employment, the offer must be made before the redundancy takes effect, and the employee is entitled to a trial period of up to four weeks to test the new terms (ERA 1996, s. 138(4)–(6)). This does not apply where the differences are *de minimis,* for example, where his pay is 5p less (*Rose* v *Henry Trickett & Sons Ltd (No. 2)* (1971) 6 ITR 211), but it does not matter that the new conditions are better than the old (*Baker* v *Gill* (1971) 6 ITR 61). The aim is that during the four weeks the employee can decide whether to take the new position or leave. If he finds it disagreeable and resigns, he can claim a redundancy payment, being treated as dismissed, and the statutory reason for dismissal is the reason for the original dismissal, that is, before the trial period began (see para. 13.3.4.2). Further, the four-week trial period may be extended for such longer period as is agreed between the employer and employee or his representative in writing, provided that the following restrictive conditions are fulfilled:

(a)   the agreement is reached before the employee starts the work;
(b)   the extra time is for training only; and
(c)   the parties specify the date of the end of the longer period and the terms and conditions to apply after it.

The trial period is four *calendar* weeks even though not all days during that period were working days (*Benton* v *Sanderson Kayser Ltd* [1989] ICR 136). Moreover, the employer can end the trial period if he can show a reason connected with or arising out of the change in terms, such as reorganisation or redundancy or the employee's incompetence in the position (s. 138(4)). If the employer takes this step the original dismissal stands and the employee may claim a redundancy payment unless the employer makes a more successful offer of suitable alternative employment at that stage.

14.3.2.2   Resigning after the trial period   If the employee leaves *after* the four-week period of grace he is treated as having resigned in the normal way and cannot claim a redundancy payment or unfair dismissal. The strictness of the rule is shown by *Meek* v *Allen Rubber Co. Ltd and Secretary of State for Employment* [1980] IRLR 21. The employee used to drive a lorry for the first respondent on a shuttle between Lydney and Whitecroft and when the latter depot was closed down, he was offered the alternative of a London to Lydney route. Part of the deal was that he might try it out for at least *six months* and at the end of this period he decided that it was not for him. Notwithstanding the six months offer, it was held that he could not claim a redundancy payment when he then resigned, since he was taken to have accepted the offer of alternative employment, and the four statutory weeks had gone. It was open to the Department of Employment, who were not party to the arrangement, to refuse redundancy rebate. The EAT also rejected a submission that his acceptance of the new route was conditional on his satisfaction.

14.3.2.3   Trial period at common law   If, but only if, the dismissal is a repudiation of contract by the employer's unilateral change in his worker's contractual terms, the employee can claim time to make up his mind in what is effectively a trial period at common law (para. 13.3.4.2). He may say that he never properly accepted the new terms but worked under duress or in order to test them (*Shields Furniture Ltd* v *Goff* [1973] ICR 187), and this doctrine, which was enunciated by the courts before the statutory trial period was introduced (*Marriott* v *Oxford and District Co-op Society Ltd (No. 2)* [1970] 1 QB 186, *Sheet Metal Components Ltd* v *Plumridge* [1974] ICR 373), was set out by Bristow J in *Turvey* v *C. W. Cheyney & Son Ltd* [1979] IRLR 105 EAT, thus:

At common law, where the employer has repudiated the contract, the employee has an option. He can either treat the contract as at an end or he can take a new job with the employer on trial. If he takes the job on trial he has a reasonable period in which to make up his mind whether he will accept the new job before he will be taken to have made a new contract or renewed the old one with variations . . . (*Air Canada* v *Lee* [1978] ICR 1202).

Such a trial period may last even as long as 12 months (*McKindley* v *William Hill (Scotland) Ltd* [1985] IRLR 492).

14.3.3 Acceptance of job offer

If the employee accepts the job offered there is no problem as there is no redundancy. The fact that it may be wildly unsuitable and he is forever dreadfully unhappy about the decision is irrelevant. He retains his continuous service, provided that, if there are changes in conditions, the offer was made before the former redundant employment terminated.

14.3.4 Refusal of job offer

If, on the other hand, the employee refuses the new offer there are two more complicated situations:

(a) Where the new terms do not differ from the old, the tribunal must decide whether his refusal was *reasonable* and it is for the employer to prove that it was not (s. 141(2)).

(b) If the proffered terms do *differ,* the employer must prove that the offer was of *suitable* alternative employment and that the employee was *unreasonable* in refusing it, if he is to avoid liability to make a redundancy payment (s. 141(3)(b)).

We now look at the requirements of a valid offer (para. 14.3.4.1), when the alternative is likely to be found suitable (para. 14.3.4.2) and when the employee will be regarded as reasonable in refusing it (para. 14.3.4.3).

14.3.4.1 The offer The offer of new terms must be sufficiently certain, unconditional and duly communicated (*Havenhand* v *Thomas Black Ltd* (1968) 3 ITR 271, *Rosseyer Motors Ltd* v *Bradshaw* (1972) 1 ITR 3), although it may be addressed to a group of workers (*McCreadie* v *Thomson & MacIntyre (Patternmakers) Ltd* [1971] 2 All ER 1135), rather than solely to the individual. The offer need not be in writing but it must contain specific information about 'the capacity and place and other terms and conditions of employment' (*Roberts* v *Essoldo Circuit (Control) Ltd* (1967) 2 ITR 351).

Moreover, the employer must have a reasonable expectation of fulfilling the offer made (*Kane* v *Raine & Co.* [1974] ICR 300); it is not good enough to pluck a post out of the air in a desperate effort to avoid a redundancy payment.

The Act does not apply where an offer is made by a third party, unless he is a transferee or associated employer of the employer or both are local government employers (*Farquharson* v *Ross* (1966) 1 ITR 335). It is not intended to prevent the award of a redundancy payment simply because the redundant worker gains another job.

14.3.4.2 Suitability This question is one of fact in every case, and Bridge J suggested in *Collier* v *Smith's Dock Ltd* (1969) 4 ITR 338, that appeal bodies should not interfere with the decisions made by industrial tribunals apart from cases where a job is so obviously unsuitable that the tribunal must have misdirected itself in finding to the contrary or where the tribunal has failed to take account of relevant circumstances. In *Carron Company* v *Robertson* (1967) 2 ITR 484 at 489, the Court gave this general survey:

Now suitability is an imprecise term, but I accept that in deciding as to the suitability of employment in relation to an employee, one must consider not only the nature of the work, hours and pay, the employee's strength, training, experience and ability but such matters as status in the premises of the employer.

Neill LJ in *Spencer* v *Gloucestershire CC* [1985] IRLR 393 considered that it was confusing to 'draw too rigid a distinction between' suitability and reasonableness because 'some factors may be common to both aspects of the case'.

This was brought out neatly in the EAT's decision in *Cambridge and District Co-operative Society Ltd* v *Ruse* [1993] IRLR 156, when it held that, even though the tribunal felt that the alternative job offered was suitable, where the employee felt it was not (due to his perceived drop in status), that did not mean that his refusal to accept the offer was unreasonable. Reasonableness did not relate merely to personal factors of the employee which were extraneous to the job.

The effect of the most important factors has emerged in several cases:

(a) *Pay:* the most important criterion of pay concerns what is actually earned in the new position, including bonuses, and not basic wage alone (*F. Kennedy* v *Werneth Ring Mills Ltd* [1977] ICR 206, *Tocher* v *General Motors (Scotland) Ltd* [1981] IRLR 55).

(b) *Hours of work:* a change from day to night work will often render a job offer unsuitable (*Morrison & Poole* v *Ceramic Engineering Co. Ltd* (1966) 1 ITR 404).

(c) *Status:* the leading case is *Taylor* v *Kent CC* (1969) 4 ITR 294, where the headmaster of a boys' secondary school was, on its closure, offered a post in a pool of mobile staff, meaning that he would have to teach in any school where he was required. Although he would still be remunerated on his old scale as a headmaster, the Divisional Court held that this was not suitable because of the large drop in status, and drew a comparison with a company director being expected to work as a navvy.

(d) *Skill:* in *Dutton* v *Hawker Siddeley Aviation Ltd* [1978] IRLR 390, Phillips J said:

Great care has to be exercised before it can be said that an employee who is skilled and with a particular trade can be required to move to some other in a case where his contract does not provide for it.

A patternmaker has been held reasonable in rejecting work as a progress clerk (*Souter* v *Balfour Ltd* (1966) 1 ITR 383), and a gantry cranedriver as an articulated lorry driver (*Watson* v *Bowaters UK Pulp & Paper Mills Ltd* (1967) 2 ITR 278).

(e) *Place of work:* that the new offer involves greater distance to travel from home may render a job offer unsuitable, unless this disadvantage is counterbalanced by higher pay or travel expenses (*Gotch & Partners* v *Guest* (1966) 1 ITR 65; cf. *McIntosh* v *British Rail* (1967) 2 ITR 26).

14.3.4.3 Reasonable refusal   It is for the employer still to go on to show, even if he has established that the alternative offer was suitable, that the employee's rejection of it was unreasonable (*Jones* v *Aston Cabinet Co. Ltd* [1973] ICR 292). Objections on the following grounds have figured in the case law and been held reasonable:

(a) travel difficulties (cf. *Hitchcock* v *St Ann's Hosiery* (1971) 6 ITR 98), although an offer which would maintain the same rate of pay together with nine months' travelling expenses and altered working hours to fit in with travelling times was held unreasonably refused;

(b)   the unsociability of shiftwork (*Silver* v *Jel Group of Companies* (1966) 1 ITR 238);

(c)   bad health and safety conditions (*Denton* v *Neepsend Ltd* [1976] IRLR 164);

(d)   the necessity for the individual to change his skills;

(e)   family problems which make it difficult to travel (*Wilson-Undy* v *Instrument Co. Ltd* [1976] ICR 508);

(f)   the lateness of the offer, especially when the employee has by that time made alternative arrangements (*Barratt* v *Thomas Glover & Co. Ltd* (1970) 5 ITR 95);

(g)   lack of housing in the vicinity of the job (*Bainbridge* v *Westinghouse Brake & Signal Co. Ltd* (1966) 1 ITR 55);

(h)   ill health: in *Daniels Elliott & Hare* v *Thomas Glover Ltd* (1966) 1 ITR 283, an offer to the female applicant was reasonably refused because it entailed heavy physical labour and she had come out of hospital only 10 days before;

(i)   loss of status (*Cambridge and District Co-operative Society Ltd* v *Ruse*, supra).

Tribunals take into account the existence of other local employment (*Laing (John) & Son Ltd* v *Best* (1968) 3 ITR 3), but have held that an offer is not in itself unreasonable because it is in an industry, for example, coal, which is contracting so that the new job in it is unlikely to be permanent (*James and Jones* v *National Coal Board* (1969) 4 ITR 70). This was notwithstanding that the tribunal thought that the applicants had made a wise decision to leave the declining industry and appeared sympathetic to the worker who, having just undergone one trauma, did not wish to uproot himself again. It may be inevitable, however, at a time of recession when so many industries are in sharp decline. For similar reasons the refusal of an offer which 'on any view was to last 12 to 18 months' though not necessarily for ever (*Morganite Crucible* v *Street* [1972] ICR 110), was held unreasonable. It is a matter of degree, so that in *Thomas Wragg & Sons Ltd* v *Wood* [1976] ICR 313, on the other hand, uncertainty of future prospects, combined with the fact that the employee was 56, had accepted a job elsewhere, and that the offer came very late, provided valid grounds for refusal. (See also *Paton Calvert & Co. Ltd* v *Westerside* [1979] IRLR 108.) In *Spencer* v *Gloucestershire CC* (supra), the Court of Appeal disagreed with the proposition of the EAT that it was not legitimate for school cleaners to refuse reduced hours of work on the ground that they did not consider that they could do a satisfactory job in the time and with the numbers available. The EAT thought that this was a matter for the employers alone to decide. The Court of Appeal considered that there was no rule of law that questions of standards are irrelevant to the decision; it was a question of fact and the EAT should not have interfered with the decision of the industrial tribunal that the employees were *not* unreasonable in refusing the offered positions.

Where the Transfer of Undertakings (Protection of Employment) Regulations 1981 apply the transferee must continue the employee's contract exactly as before (see Chapter 16).

14.4   DISQUALIFICATION FROM REDUNDANCY PAYMENT

An employee may lose his entitlement to redundancy payment or part thereof even though he satisfies other requirements so far considered, by reason of:

(a)   misconduct;

(b)   strike action;

(c)   leaving during notice;

(d)   grant of pension.

14.4.1 Misconduct

An employee may not gain a redundancy payment if the employer was entitled to terminate the employment by reason of his misconduct (ERA 1996, s. 140(1)). For this to apply, the contract must be terminated either without notice, or with shorter notice than was contractually necessary. Where the misconduct occurred before notice of redundancy the employer must either sack instantly or give a written statement that he is entitled to dismiss at once.

This is a strange provision, since if the employer dismisses the employee for cause, whether incapability or misconduct, that is not a dismissal for redundancy because it would not fall in the terms of ERA 1996, s. 139. The reason the provision was inserted may have been because the Redundancy Payments Act 1965, in which it is first found in exactly the same form, predated the wider unfair dismissal jurisdiction. Its continuance now is more problematic. *Sanders* v *Ernest A. Neale Ltd* [1974] ICR 565 suggests that the subsection is intended to apply where the employee is dismissed in fact for redundancy when he *could have been* sacked for cause. (See *Bonner* v *Gibert Ltd* [1989] IRLR 475.)

If the dismissal for gross misconduct takes place *during the statutory period of notice*, the employee may apply to a tribunal which can pay all or some of the redundancy payment, and will make such decision on the justice and equity of the case. In *Simmons* v *Hoover Ltd* [1977] ICR 61, the majority of the EAT decided that a strike could be considered misconduct, but went on to say that action in response to deliberate provocation or unreasonable demands by an employer would not prejudice the employee's rights.

14.4.2 Industrial action

There are three further strike specific provisions:

(a) If the employee takes part in a strike within the period of notice of termination which the employer must give, and the employer then terminates the contract for that reason, s. 140(1) does not apply and he remains entitled to a redundancy payment (s. 140(2)).

(b) If the employer dismisses for any other reason during this time, an industrial tribunal may award the whole or part of the redundancy payment to which the employee would have been otherwise entitled if this appears just and equitable (s. 140(3)).

(c) By s. 143(2), where a redundant employee goes on strike the employer may require him by 'notice of extension' to make up the time lost in the strike if he is still to be entitled to redundancy payment. It must warn that the employer will dispute the employee's right to redundancy payment if he does not comply (s. 143(2)(c)).

14.4.3 Early leaving

If the employee is under notice of redundancy and wishes to leave before the notice runs out, for example, to start another job, he may himself give notice. If the employer objects to him leaving early, he can request the employee to withdraw the notice and warn him that he will contest his redundancy payment. The industrial tribunal must then decide whether to award all or part of the redundancy payment, reviewing all the circumstances (s. 142). The provision appears to have been little used.

14.4.4 Pension

By s. 158 of ERA 1996 and the Redundancy Payments Pensions Regulations 1965 (SI 1965 No. 1932), the right to redundancy payment may be excluded if:

(a) the pension rights accrue within one week of the termination of employment;
(b) those rights are worth at least one-third of the employee's annual pay;
(c) the employee's right to the pension/payment is secure; and
(d) the employer gives the recipient a written notice.

Should the pension be worth less than one-third, some redundancy payment must be made but the pension may be offset against it. Further, if the employee is also entitled to compensation for loss of office under another statute, by the Redundancy Payments Statutory Compensation Regulations 1965 (SI 1965 No. 1988) the redundancy payments are made in full, but the other entitlement is abated or reduced by that amount (see *British Telecommunications plc* v *Burwell* [1986] ICR 35 and *Royal Ordnance plc* v *Pilkington* [1989] IRLR 489).

14.5   CALCULATION OF REDUNDANCY PAYMENT

Redundancy pay, like the basic award in unfair dismissal, is based on the week's pay in accordance with ERA 1996, ss. 221–229. Calculation depends first on whether or not the employee has normal working hours and secondly whether he is paid by time, piece or is on shift or rota work. First the vocabulary will be explained, then the mode of calculation (see J. Bowers 79 LSG 325).

14.5.1   Normal working hours

Section 234 of ERA 1996 defines normal working hours as where the contract fixes the number, or the minimum number, of hours in a week, whether or not those hours can be reduced in certain circumstances. The number must be included in the written statement of . terms. The working of overtime involves manifold complications which tribunals have generally resolved in favour of the employer. It is unusual to find hours of overtime expressly fixed by a contract of employment, and the more common situation was examined by the Court of Appeal in *Tarmac Roadstone Holdings Ltd* v *Peacock* (1973) 8 ITR 300. The employee's standard hours were 40, but his contract also stated 'workers shall work overtime in accordance with the demands of the industry', and in fact they regularly laboured 57 hours. The Court considered that the decisive issue was whether the contract not only obliged the employee to work overtime, which it did, but also the employer to provide it, which was not so here. A unilateral obligation on the employer is, in fact, much more frequent. The 'normal working hours' were held to be 40 and the applicant's redundancy pay consequently amounted to less than the amount he normally took home in his pay packet each week. (See also *Fox* v *C. Wright (Farmers) Ltd* [1978] ICR 98, *Lotus Cars Ltd* v *Sutcliffe and Stratton* [1982] IRLR 381, *Pearson* v *William Jones Ltd* (1967) 2 ITR 471, *Minister of Labour* v *Country Bake Ltd* (1968) 3 ITR 379, *Darlington Forge Ltd* v *Sutton* (1968) 3 ITR 196.)

Moreover, the EAT is reluctant to infer a variation of contract by reason of practice (*Friend* v *PMA Holdings Ltd* [1976] ICR 330; cf. *ITT Components (Europe) Ltd* v *Kolah* [1977] ICR 740) although this is not unknown. In *Dean* v *Eastbourne Fishermen's and Boatmen's Protection Society Ltd* [1977] ICR 556, for example, the applicant worked fixed bar sessions and at other times as and when his employer needed him. The regular periods demanded amounted to less than the 21 hours which was then necessary to gain employment protection. The EAT held that in the absence of any express term as to number of hours, the industrial tribunal should have inferred a term from what happened in practice; and that since during the two years necessary to qualify for the redundancy payment he was claiming he had worked for more than the statutory minimum on 86 occasions, he was entitled to claim.

Several cases concern a conflict between the hours of work laid down in national and in local collective agreements. In *Loman and Henderson* v *Merseyside Transport Services Ltd* (1969) 4 ITR 108 the Divisional Court adopted the former.

14.5.2 Remuneration

Having worked out the normal hours it is then necessary to determine the pay for them. For these purposes the week is deemed to end on Saturday, unless pay is calculated on a weekly basis, in which case the week ends on the day on which the employee is regularly paid (s. 235(1)).

(a) The relevant remuneration is by statute '*money paid under the contract of employment by the employer*' (*Lyford* v *Turquand* (1966) 1 ITR 554). A useful definition which gives some flavour of the width of remuneration was found in the Prices and Charges (Notification of Increases and Information) Order 1977 (SI 1977 No. 1281), para. 16(2), including 'any benefit, facility or advantage, whether in money or otherwise, provided by the employer or by some other person under arrangements with the employer whether for the employee or otherwise, by reason of the fact that the employer employs him'.

(b) The concept has always been understood to refer to the *gross* amount of weekly pay. However, the EAT in *Secretary of State for Employment* v *Jobling* [1980] ICR 380, thought it was net of tax in a case which was concerned with calculation of an insolvent employer's debts from the Redundancy Fund. This is generally regarded as an isolated 'rogue decision' and was not followed in *Secretary of State for Employment* v *John Woodrow & Sons (Builders) Ltd* [1983] IRLR 11.

(c) The wage taken is that to which the employee is contractually entitled, even if the employer does not (for example because he is in breach of a Wages Council order) pay that sum (*Cooner* v *P. S. Doal & Sons* [1988] IRLR 338). The week's pay certainly does not include the value of, for example, a company car or free accommodation but does cover bonuses, allowances and commission, if they are provided for by an express or implied term in the contract of employment (e.g. *Lawrence* v *Cooklin Kitchen Fitments Ltd* (1966) 1 ITR 398). This was justified in *Weevsmay Ltd* v *Kings* [1977] ICR 244, on the ground that tribunals must interpret the word in a common sense way.

(d) The remuneration is only that which is paid in respect of hours 'when the employee was actually working', thus excluding that which is apportioned to rest days (*British Coal Corporation* v *Cheesbrough* [1990] ICR 317).

(e) Section 221(3) of ERA 1996 provides that if bonuses are annual payments, or in any other way do not coincide with the periods of normal pay, in effect a proportionate amount is to be included (*J.S. Buckley Ltd* v *Maslin* [1977] ICR 425). The average hourly rate was to be calculated by reference to all hours worked and all remuneration including overtime payments calculated at the rate attributable to normal working hours.

(f) A Christmas bonus payable *ex gratia* is clearly excluded (*Skillen* v *Eastwoods Froy Ltd* (1967) 2 ITR 112), while the treatment of *tips* depends on their precise nature. Where a restaurant levied a compulsory service charge, and shared this each week between its waiters, their right was contractually enforceable and included in the relevant remuneration (*Tsoukka* v *Potomac Restaurants Ltd* (1968) 3 ITR 259), but tips paid direct to the employee, on the other hand, are not reckoned (*S & U Stores Ltd* v *Lee* (1969) 4 ITR 227), since they are not money paid by the employer. (See also *Cofone* v *Spaghetti House* [1980] ICR 155, T. Kibling and W. O'Brien, 'Tips and service charges', *Legal Action*, Dec. 1988, p. 11).

(g) The week's pay includes a site bonus where there was by custom a term that when the main contractor paid such an extra sum to the subcontractor the respondent subcontractor would divide it amongst his employees (*Donelan* v *Kerrby Constructions Ltd* [1983] ICR 237).

(h) For similar reasons *state benefits*, like industrial injuries benefits, are not included (*Wibberley* v *Staveley Iron & Chemical Co. Ltd* (1966) 1 ITR 558), while *holiday pay* is outside the definition since it is referable to weeks of *absence*, not normal working time (*Secretary of State for Employment* v *Haynes* [1980] IRLR 270).

(i) Items described as *expenses* are taken into account only where they represent a profit over actual outlay (*S & U Stores Ltd* v *Wilkes* [1974] ICR 645), but nothing is awarded where the relevant arrangement is illegal as a fraud on the Inland Revenue.

14.5.3 Calculation date

The relevant pay and hours for redundancy payment purposes are those governing at the 'calculation date' as specified in ERA 1996, s. 226. This is generally the last date of working under the employee's contract of employment, but some modification is made to prevent employers escaping liability to pay higher amounts (because of a pay rise) by giving shorter notice than that to which the employee is entitled by contract. The calculation date is then the date on which notice would have expired had the employer given the minimum notice as required by s. 86 of ERA 1996. The proper method is to find the statutory period and work back from the relevant date of termination. Thus, if the employee has worked for 10 years and is dismissed in week 20, the calculation is in week 10 whether or not the necessary 10 weeks has in fact been given. If he has worked two years the calculation date is week 18.

14.5.3.1 Backdated pay awards Doubts surround the treatment of a pay agreement backdated to the calculation date; for example, the agreement is announced in week 25 but starts in week 15 and the employee is dismissed in week 20. Since the vital words are '*is payable*' it is thought that it should be included in the remuneration to be so calculated. This view has been upheld (*obiter*) in *Leyland Vehicles Ltd* v *Reston* [1980] IRLR 376, where there was evidence that wages were annually increased on a particular date, and it may be confined to these special facts. In fact the particular applicant was not entitled since he was not employed on the starting date. If the backdated agreement is announced after the calculation for redundancy payment falls to be made, a new claim may be submitted (*Cowan* v *Pullman Spring Filled Co. Ltd* (1967) 2 ITR 650).

14.5.4 Week's pay of particular workers

It is now possible to apply these general provisions in the concrete situation of particular workers, that is, time workers, piece workers and shift workers.

(a) A *time worker* has normal working hours and his 'remuneration for employment in normal working hours (whether by the hour or week or other period) does not vary with the amount of work done in the period' (ERA 1996, s. 221(2)). His week's pay is that 'payable' under the contract of employment in force on the calculation date.

(b)   A *piece worker* has normal working hours, but his pay varies with the amount of work done; this may take the form of payment for every piece of work he does, an incentive bonus, or a commission related to output. One arrives at his 'week's pay' by multiplying the normal hours worked by the average hourly rate of remuneration in the 12 weeks before the last complete week before the calculation date (ERA 1996, s. 221(3)). It does not matter whether these previous weeks were full working weeks or not (*Sylvester* v *Standard Upholstery Co. Ltd* (1967) 2 ITR 507), although any week in which no pay at all was received in the relevant 12-week period is ignored and an earlier week used. Overtime premium rates are to be excluded even when the hours are counted.

(c)   *Shift and rota workers* are those whose hours 'differ from week to week or over a longer period so that the remuneration payable for . . . any week varies according to the incidence of those days or times' (ERA 1996, 222(1)). Here one multiplies the *average* weekly hours by the average hourly rate of remuneration. Both calculations are again made by taking an average of the 12 weeks preceding the calculation date if that date is the last day of a week, or otherwise ending with the last complete week before the calculation date. The average hourly rate of remuneration is the average pay for the hours actually worked in the 12 weeks preceding the calculation date, if that should be the last day of the week, or in other circumstances the last complete week before the calculation date. Again, the remuneration to be considered is only that paid in respect of hours 'when the employee was actually working', so excluding rest days.

Example   Edward has been employed for 15 years as a shift worker. He is given five weeks' notice in week 30. The calculation date is week 23 because the relevant date of termination is week 35 from which the minimum period of notice, i.e. 12 weeks' maximum, must be taken. The tribunal then looks at the previous 12 week period, thus:

Week	Basic	Overtime
1	45	5
2	40	5
3	35	5
4	45	5
5	40	5
6	35	5
7	45	5
8	40	5
9	35	5
10	45	5
11	40	5
12	35	5

The average weekly hours are 40, notwithstanding that there is regular overtime of five hours, unless there is an obligation on the company to provide it as well as on the employee to work when it is provided.

(d)   *No normal working hours:* some employees have no normal working hours at all, Professor Grunfeld giving the example of university teachers, salesmen on commission, and those employed in a managerial, administrative or professional capacity (*Law of Redundancy*, op. cit. para. 14.1.1, p. 279). None of these is employed on a strict 9 a.m. to 5 p.m. basis. Here again, an average of a 12-week period is taken (ERA 1996, s. 224(2)). There are, however, some cases in which the employee has not been employed in the same job for 12 weeks, yet is still able to claim employment protection rights, because continuity is preserved from a previous employment. If this is so, the weeks of that previous job are taken into account but if this would not be appropriate or is impossible, the industrial tribunal is directed to reach a computation it considers just in all the circumstances.

14.5.5 The method of calculation

The appropriate redundancy payment is reached by multiplying the week's pay by a multiplier depending on age:

(a) $1\frac{1}{2}$ for every year during the whole of which the employee was 41 or over;
(b) 1 for every year during the whole of which the employee was between 22 and 40; and
(c) $1\frac{1}{2}$ for every year below 21.

(ERA 1996, s. 102(2).)

The maximum payable is thus 30 weeks and this would be appropriate where an employee has been working for 20 years' continuous employment over 41. The amount of remuneration to be awarded for redundancy payment, as for unfair dismissal basic award, is subject to a *maximum limit*, and the Secretary of State has a statutory duty to review this sum annually and may do so more often. The present maximum stands at £210 per week, and this clearly reduces the compensation which would otherwise have been awarded to a large section of the workforce.

Between the ages of 64 and 65, in the case of a man, a twelfth was taken from the redundancy payment for every month since his 64th birthday, and the same was true for a woman between 59 and 60. Since 1989, the reduction is made as from the age of 64 in the case of both men and women (ERA 1996, s. 162(4)). The rules of continuity already discussed (see Chapter 10) apply in determining the proper multiplier. The following points should also be noted:

(a) *overseas employment* may be counted only if the employee remained employed for the purposes of social security legislation (s. 215(2)); weeks which do not count for this reason do not, however, break the continuity of employment;
(b) payment of an *earlier redundancy payment* breaks continuity (s. 214(2));
(c) where there is a *gap* of up to four weeks on renewal of employment following a redundancy, and the offer of an alternative job or renewal of the old one, this counts towards continuity.

Just as with ordinary weekly pay (para. 4.1.3), the employer must give the redundant worker a written statement setting out how his amount of redundancy payment has been calculated (ERA 1996, s. 165). This is not required where the computation has been carried out by an industrial tribunal, who might be trusted to get the sums right! An employer in default is liable to a small fine, and if no statement is given the employee may in writing demand it by a specified date giving at least one week to reply (s. 165(3) and (4)).

14.6 CLAIMING A REDUNDANCY PAYMENT

The employer usually offers the correct redundancy payment to his employee without any formal claim being necessary. In the event of dispute the employee should submit a written claim, making it clear to the employer what he is seeking. In this respect, a call for a meeting to 'discuss the position' of the employee who was made redundant while off sick was insufficiently precise (*Hetherington* v *Dependable Products Ltd* (1971) 6 ITR 1). If this does not succeed the next step is to refer the matter to an industrial tribunal within six months of the relevant date of dismissal by submitting an originating application to the Central Office of Industrial Tribunals (ERA 1996, s. 164). This may be combined with a complaint of unfair dismissal, but the claim cannot be made until the dismissal actually takes effect (*Watts* v *Rubery Owen Conveyancer Ltd* [1977] 2 All ER 1, *Pritchard-Rhodes Ltd* v *Boon* [1979] IRLR 19). If the employee fails to take any of these steps within six months he may have an extension of up to six months, but only if the industrial tribunal thinks it to be 'just and equitable that the employee should receive a redundancy payment' (s. 164(2)). A complaint of unfair dismissal presented within six months may entitle the applicant to a redundancy payment if the tribunal decides that the reason for dismissal was redundancy even where there is no claim as such for a redundancy payment (*Duffin* v *Secretary of State for Employment* [1983] ICR 766; see also *Secretary of State for Employment* v *Banks* [1983] ICR 48). If the employee has died in the meantime the right to redundancy payment devolves with his estate, and ERA 1996 allows a special representative to be appointed solely for the purposes of tribunal proceedings. (See J. Bowers, D. Brown and G. Mead, *Industrial Tribunal Practice and Procedure*, FT Law & Tax, 1996.)

14.7 REBATES

The Government's interest in assisting mobility and rationalisation of labour was reflected in the Redundancy Payments Act 1965 by providing a rebate from a government Redundancy Fund to the employer in respect of each redundancy payment made. The rebate was reduced to a standard 50 per cent by the Redundancy Rebates Act 1969, to 41 per cent by regulations in 1977 (Variation of Rebates Order 1977 (SI 1977 No. 1321)) and to 35 per cent as from 1 April 1985. Under the former Wages Act 1986 entitlement to a rebate was limited to an employer who at no time on the appropriate day employed, together with the number employed by any associated employer, more than nine employees. Section 17 of the Employment Act 1989 removed the right of employers of fewer than 10 employees to receive redundancy payment rebates from the Redundancy Fund and the Employment Act 1990 wound up the Redundancy Fund and merged it with the National Insurance Fund. There is thus no longer any government interest to intervene in issues of redundancy payments, save in cases of insolvency.

14.8 INSOLVENCY

14.8.1 Preferential creditor status

A worker whose employer becomes insolvent risks losing all his employment protection rights in the financial wreck of the company, partnership or individual. He does, however, have preferential creditor status in the assets of the insolvent employer under the Companies Act 1985, so that he ranks to be paid out of company funds, along with PAYE tax and VAT, before anything goes into the pool for ordinary creditors. This may mean that the employees are paid in full or pro rata. Employee's preferential debts under the Insolvency Act 1986, s. 175, Sch. 6 are:

(a)   four months' wages or a maximum set by the Secretary of State from time to time by statutory instrument;

(b)   guarantee payment;

(c)   payment for time off for trade union duties or for ante-natal care;

(d)   protective award for failure to consult over redundancies.

Similar provisions are contained in s. 328 of and para. 9 of Sch. 6 to the Insolvency Act 1986. Any other sums due and owing may be claimed as an unsecured debt and proof of debt forms may be gained from the trustee or liquidator, but the process may take a very long time.

In *Nicoll* v *Cutts* [1985] BCLC 322, the plaintiff argued that a receiver appointed under a debenture was himself liable for his wages under s. 492(3) of the Companies Act 1985 which provided that: 'A receiver . . . shall to the same extent as if he had been appointed by an order of a court, be personally liable on any contract entered into by him in the performance of his functions, except in so far as the contract otherwise provides. . .' The Court of Appeal decided that if the receiver had entered into a new contract with the employee he would be personally liable but this had not occurred by the receivership itself. This has been largely reversed by s. 40 of the Insolvency Act 1986.

In the combined appeals of *Powdrill* v *Watson* and *Talbot* v *Cadge*, the House of Lords ([1995] IRLR 267) construed s. 19, Insolvency Act 1986 (inferences similar to s. 40) which provides that:

> Any sums payable [by the administrator] in respect of . . . contracts entered into or contracts of employment adopted by him . . . shall be charged on and paid out . . . in priority. . . . For this purpose, the administrator is not to be taken to have adopted a contract of employment by reason of anything done or omitted to be done within 14 days after his appointment.

There is a similar but not identical provision for administrative receivers by s. 44 of the 1986 Act. The main difference is that administrative receivers become liable for all liabilities 'on' contracts which extend to all liabilities whether incurred before, during or after the receivership. The receivers had in all the conjoined cases sent to employees letters stating that they were not to be taken to have adopted their contracts of employment. Lord Browne-Wilkinson decided that a contract of employment is adopted if the employee is continued in employment for more than 14 days after the appointment of the administrator or receiver and it is not possible to avoid this result or alter its consequences unilaterally by informing employees that he is not adopting the contract or only doing so on terms, but the consequence of adoption is to give priority only to liabilities incurred by the administrator or receiver during his tenure of office.

Immediately after the decision in *Powdrill* in the Court of Appeal, Parliament rushed through the Insolvency Act 1994 by which the liability of receivers and administrative receivers on contracts of employment adopted by them on or after 15 March 1994 is restricted to payment of wages, salary and contributions to a pension scheme in respect of services rendered after the adoption of the contract of employment.

14.8.2   Direct government payment

The Employment Rights Act 1996 builds on earlier legislation to offer three further ways of ensuring that the employee's position is somewhat protected where:

(a)   an individual has been declared bankrupt or has made a composition or arrangement with his creditors;

(b)   an individual's estate is being administered in accordance with an order under s. 421 of the Insolvency Act 1986; or

(c)   a company is wound up by a shareholders' resolution.

The provisions do not go so far as to cover an individual firm or company which is only unable to meet its debts as they fall due (*Pollard* v *Teako (Swiss) Ltd* (1967) 2 ITR 357).

14.8.2.1 National Insurance Fund Speedy and safe recourse may be made to the Government's National Insurance Fund in the case of the following debts (ERA 1996, s. 182):

(a)   up to eight weeks' *wages* including guarantee pay, medical suspension pay, union duties pay, ante-natal care pay, statutory sick pay and protective award (s. 184(1)(a)), up to a maximum of £210 per week (at £1,680 this is higher than the preferential creditor maximum);

(b)   minimum pay during *notice* under s. 86 of ERA 1996 or damages for failure to give such notice (s. 184(1)(b)), but not including the appropriate holiday pay during notice according to the EAT in *Secretary of State for Employment* v *Haynes* [1980] IRLR 270 (see also *Secretary of State for Employment* v *Jobling* [1980] ICR 380);

(c)   up to six weeks' accumulated holiday pay during the last 12 months preceding the relevant date (s. 184(1)(c));

(d)   basic award made by an industrial tribunal for unfair dismissal (s. 184(1)(d));

(e)   reimbursement of premiums or fees paid for *apprenticeship* or articles of clerkship (s. 184(1)(e).

Item (d) may be reclaimed in full, but the other payments are subject to a maximum of £210 per week for, it would appear, each type (s. 186(1)). In the unusual case where the employer has a cross-claim against the employee, for example in respect of a loan, this may be set off (*Secretary of State for Employment* v *Wilson and BCCI* [1996] IRLR 330). This maximum is subject to reduction if the employee earns from another source or receives unemployment or other state benefits during the period of his notice. In *Westwood* v *Secretary of State for Employment* [1984] IRLR 209 the House of Lords also decided that the employee need only account for *net* benefits received during the period of unemployment. This had an important effect in the case of Mr Westwood who had been unemployed for more than a year and was entitled to a refund based on the loss arising from exhaustion of unemployment benefit after a year. This was, however, cleared up by the Social Security (General Benefit) Amendment Regulations 1984 (SI 1984 No. 1259) which provide that days covered by payments made under the insolvency provisions do not count in establishing eligibility to unemployment benefit (see also *Secretary of State for Employment* v *Cooper* [1987] ICR 766).

The Department of Employment may apply the limit before making deductions in respect of income tax and national insurance contributions (*Morris* v *Secretary of State for Employment* [1985] IRLR 297).

The claims arise on the 'relevant date' which is defined as the latest of the following dates: when the employer becomes insolvent; when the employment came to an end; and where the debt is a basic award for unfair dismissal or a protective award for failure to consult the union over redundancies, the date when the award was made.

Gaining these payments involves a mass of form filling. A written application must be first made to the Department of Employment certifying that one of the appropriate debts was owing on the 'relevant date'. The payments are not actually made until a trustee or liquidator is appointed, since he must then submit to the Department of Employment a statement of what is due to each employee as soon as reasonably practicable. If there is no such statement within six months of the submission of the written request, the Department has a discretion to pay without it, but if the Department refuses to pay what the employee claims he is entitled to, he can refer the matter to an industrial tribunal within three months of the alleged default. If the Secretary of State is satisfied that he does not require a statement in order to determine the amount of the debt owed to the employee, he may make a payment without having received such a statement.

14.8.2.2 Pensions The right to unpaid employer's pension contributions from the Department of Employment extends to:

(a)   arrears accrued within 12 months prior to insolvency;

(b)   arrears certified by an actuary to be necessary to pay employee's benefits on dissolution of the scheme;

(c)   10 per cent of the last 12 months' payroll for the employees covered by the scheme.

The maximum is the lowest of these figures. Again, the Department defers until a trustee or liquidator is appointed before paying, and recourse is to an industrial tribunal in the event of dispute.

14.8.2.3 Redundancy payments An employee can claim a redundancy payment direct from the National Insurance Fund where he is entitled to such a payment in the usual way, and he has taken all reasonable steps to obtain payment besides resorting to legal proceedings, or the employer is insolvent as defined in s. 166(5) of ERA 1996. The worker then receives his normal redundancy payment less any payment in fact already made towards it by the employer. The employee's rights and remedies are taken over by (subrogated to) the Secretary of State (s. 167), who may take proceedings against the employer while disputes over these payments may be referred to an industrial tribunal (s. 170).

14.8.2.4 Maternity payments There are similar provisions for a claim from the Maternity Fund save that the employer need not be insolvent (Statutory Maternity Pay (General) Regulations 1986 (SI 1986 No. 196), regs. 9 and 30), and the employee is entitled to her maternity pay even though the employer is put into liquidation in the course of her absence (*Secretary of State for Employment* v *Cox* [1984] IRLR 437).

15 Redundancy Consultation

The consultation may result in new ideas being ventilated which avoid the redundancy situation altogether. Equally it may lead to a lesser number of persons being made redundant than was originally thought necessary. Or it may be that alternative work can be found during a period of consultation.

(Slynn J in *Spillers-French Holdings Ltd* v *USDAW* [1980] ICR 31 at 37D.)

Part IV of the Employment Protection Act 1975 for the first time extended collective bargaining to cover consultation over redundancies. Aptly described by Dr Freedland as a 'Redundancy Procedures Act' in itself, ss. 99 to 107 impose the duty on employers who recognise a trade union to consult with its 'authorised representatives' when even only one employee of the class for which the union is recognised is to be made redundant, and whether or not the worker(s) in question is a member of the union. The sanction on the employer for default is a protective award unless there are special circumstances explaining his omission. The provisions have been consolidated into the Trade Union and Labour Relations (Consolidation) Act (TULR(C)A) 1992.

The legislation has an English mother and European father. The EEC Council Directive 75/129 (see 1976 5 ILJ 24), was the chief European impetus, while the British genesis is found in the Donovan Commission Report. Consultation was embodied in the Code of Industrial Relations Practice but only in an advisory capacity.

These provisions are now contained in TULR(C)A 1992. Yet the legislation remains a sickly child, since on several points the statutory language is so vague that further judicial elucidation is necessary. The main questions concern:

(a) definition of redundancy (para. 15.1);
(b) recognition (para. 15.2);
(c) elected representatives (para. 15.3);
(d) time limits for consultation (para. 15.4);
(e) the extent of an establishment (para. 15.5);
(f) the meaning of consultation (para. 15.6);
(g) special circumstances (para. 15.7);
(h) protective awards (para. 15.8);
(i) the union's authorised representatives (para. 15.9);
(j) special statutory regimes (para. 15.10).

From the same European source derives a parallel obligation to inform representatives of recognised unions about takeovers and mergers, enacted in the Transfer of Undertakings (Protection of Employment) Regulations 1981 (SI 1981 No. 1794) which will be discussed in Chapter 16.

The ECJ in *Commission of the European Communities* v *UK* [1994] ICR 664, held that UK law was not in accordance with EC Directive 75/129 on Collective Redundancies because it contained no provision for information and consultation in a case where the employer refused to accord recognition to a trade union. It is less clear what vehicle must be adopted in order to comply with the Directive, and legislation on this point is expected soon. The UK was held further to be in breach of the Directive in:

(a) its narrow definition of redundancy for these purposes. The ECJ paid particular attention to the failure to cover 'cases where workers have been dismissed as a result of new working arrangements within an undertaking unconnected with its volume of business';

(b) the failure to require consultation 'with a view to reach agreement' and to 'cover ways and means of avoiding collective redundancies or avoiding the number of workers affected or reducing the number of workers affected';

(c) the low penalty by way of protective award.

By the time the ECJ delivered judgment, these points had already been addressed by the wider definition of redundancy for these consultation purposes, the new scope of consultation and the higher ceiling on protective awards introduced by TURERA 1993.

15.1 DEFINITION OF REDUNDANCY

From the introduction of the legislation in 1975 until TURERA 1993, the same definition of redundancy served for the purposes of consultation over redundancy as applied to statutory redundancy payments. Under the impulse of the relevant European Directive, however, the definition has been altered in relation to consultation to 'dismissal for a reason not related to the individual concerned or a number of reasons all of which are not so related' (TULR(C)A 1992, s. 195).

15.2 RECOGNITION

At the forefront stood the issue of what is sufficient recognition by management of a trade union to trigger the consultation requirements. The government in March 1995 published a Consultation Paper about reform of these provisions in order to meet the European case law, and these were belatedly enacted as the Collective Redundancies and Transfer of Undertakings (Protection of Employment) (Amendment) Regulations 1995 (SI 1995 No. 2587). This is a mixed question of fact and law. The only definition of this concept, important though it is throughout modern labour law, is to be found in the statutory recognition provisions of TULR(C)A 1992, s. 178(3). It is self-reflexive, and of no great assistance, citing 'recognition of the union by an employer to any extent for the purpose of collective bargaining'. Collective bargaining is then extensively construed in TULR(C)A 1992 (para. 19.4).

The matter is straightforward in the paradigm case of a written agreement to recognise. At the other end of the scale a right to be consulted about terms and conditions is not enough. Much more problematic is the fact situation arising in the leading case, the Court of Appeal decision in *National Union of Gold, Silver and Allied Trades* v *Albury Brothers*

Ltd [1978] IRLR 504, where the union sought to prove recognition on the ground that the company was a member of the British Jewellers' Association, which had negotiated a series of agreements on terms and conditions with it. The Court of Appeal emphasised the high burden of proof resting on the union since 'recognition was such an important matter involving serious consequences on both sides'. In the absence of an actual agreement, only clear and distinct conduct signifying implied accord would suffice and Eveleigh LJ thought 'a point must be reached where one can use the expression "it goes without saying"'. That position was not reached on the facts.

What more is required is illustrated in *National Union of Tailors and Garment Workers* v *Charles Ingram & Co. Ltd* [1977] IRLR 147, where not only was the employer a member of a bargaining trade association, but the manager of the factory in question had 'over a substantial period of time' discussed terms and conditions of employment, and grievances raised by the shop steward, with the local union official. It was powerful evidence also that the employer had stated on a government form that the union was recognised. In *Joshua Wilson & Bros Ltd* v *USDAW* [1978] IRLR 120, the union qualified as recognised because management followed Joint Industrial Council wage agreements, allowed the shop steward to put up a notice announcing a particular increase and consulted with the shop steward over changes in employees' duties. The company had also talked with an area organiser of the union.

There is no place for automatic recognition to be thrust on an employer by a third party over whom he had no control. In *Cleveland CC* v *Springett* [1985] IRLR 131, the Association of Polytechnic Teachers claimed that they were recognised at Teesside Polytechnic because although they had been refused recognition despite requests over many years, enquiries by union representatives concerning conditions at work were answered and the union was encouraged to send representatives to meetings of the Polytechnic Health and Safety Committee. Further, in 1981 the Secretary of State for Education decided that it should be represented on the Burnham Pay Committee. The EAT thought that the action of the Secretary of State was in no way decisive as the tribunal had thought that it was, and that the other matters did not add up to recognition for the purposes of the statute.

Unions have attempted to cut through the generally restrictive interpretation of recognition by arguing that use of the words 'recognition to any extent' signified acts preliminary to the completed act of recognition. In *Transport and General Workers' Union* v *Dyer* [1977] IRLR 93 this contention was supported by the fact that negotiations about procedure and machinery for collective bargaining (talks about talks), are comprised in the Act's definition of collective bargaining. However, the argument was rejected here as it had been in *NUGSAT* v *Albury Bros* (supra), the EAT holding that the words referred to an employer recognising a union, say, for the purpose of discussing wages but not holidays or pension rights.

The cases make clear that discussion about matters of mutual interest on a 'one-off' basis is not enough. In *NUGSAT* v *Albury* there were a few letters and one meeting, in *TGWU* v *Dyer* there was very limited and unwilling contact over the reinstatement of a union member; in neither case did the events found an inference of recognition. As Lord McDonald put it, there must be *consensus ad idem* on recognition, and this must be without any misapprehension, the employer realising the significance of the step he is taking (*TGWU* v *Courtenham Products Ltd* [1977] IRLR 9). It is not enough that the employer has been wont to negotiate with two employees who happen to be Amalgamated Union of Engineering Workers members but are not accredited stewards (*AUEW* v *Sefton Engineering Co. Ltd* [1976] IRLR 318). That an employer recognised a union did not bind his successor in title to continue the practice according to the EAT in *Union of Construction Allied Trades and Technicians* v *Burrage* [1978] ICR 314, but reg. 9 of the Transfer of Undertakings (Protection of Employment) Regulations 1981 (SI 1981 No. 1794) now changes this position. This applies, however, only 'where after a relevant transfer the undertaking or part of the undertaking transferred maintains an identity distinct from the remainder of the transferee's undertaking'.

Policy considerations appear to lie behind the difficult decision of the EAT in *Union of Shop, Distributive and Allied Workers* v *Sketchley* [1981] IRLR 291. The applicant union had reached a formal 'recognition for representation agreement' with the respondents in May 1978; clause VIII clearly provided that 'this agreement does not confer recognition by the company for negotiation of terms and conditions'. Even so, in January 1980 the company agreed to a meeting to discuss wages, and when it began to select candidates for redundancy, on 28 February, it fully discussed the crisis with the union. This meeting resulted in a memorandum of agreement providing that, *inter alia*, union officials would be given two hours' notice before any redundancy proposal was discussed, one of them would be available for discussion with staff, and that volunteers for redundancy would be encouraged. The EAT upheld the industrial tribunal's decision that the 1978 agreement did not amount to recognition. They saw a clear distinction between, on the one hand, the role of a trade unionist who, under existing grievance procedures, is entitled to make representations on behalf of a worker and, on the other, the brief of another who has the right to negotiate over what the procedures themselves should be. Browne-Wilkinson P was particularly concerned about the cost to orderly industrial relations in the multi-union situation, if every union which obtained the right to represent its own members was thereby considered recognised for the purposes of EPA 1975, s. 99 and other provisions. The EAT, however, concluded by remitting the case for reconsideration by the industrial tribunal as to whether the meeting of 29 February and the subsequent memorandum amounted to recognition. It also commented that an employer who enters into an agreement with a union relating to terms and conditions of employment of union members runs a severe risk that the inference will be drawn that the employer has recognised the union as having negotiating rights in that field.

It is thus sometimes difficult for an employer to know whether he must discuss redundancies. The burden of proof on the union is very high. As Kilner Brown J put it in *Wilson & Bros Ltd* v *USDAW* [1978] IRLR 120), 'in the balance of probabilities the side labelled recognition must go down with a bump, and the scales must not hover and teeter in an indecisive fashion'. These decisions demonstrate the difficulties of making a flexible industrial relations institution like recognition a legal term of art. The reduction of the scope of recognition in many industries has further limited the extent of the redundancy consultation provisions.

In *Griffin and others* v *South West Water Services Ltd* [1994] IRLR 15, Blackburne J had to decide whether the Collective Redundancies Directive was capable of being directly enforced against a state authority by a union which did not enjoy recognition. He said:

> In my view where there is no agreement between employer and employee as to who the employee's representative is for the purpose of consulting over collective redundancies, the Directive requires that the member State should bring into force laws, regulations or administrative provisions . . . to enable the workers' representatives to be identified. Since the Directive gives to the member State such a wide discretion in designating who the 'workers' representatives' are to be, it cannot in my view be said that Article 2 is 'unconditional and sufficiently precise'.

15.3 ELECTED REPRESENTATIVES

The 1995 Amendment Regulations extend the definition of those to be consulted to 'employee representatives elected by the relevant employees'. Such employee representatives must be employees at the time when they were elected, so it is not possible to draft in someone from outside the employing company. There is, however, nothing to require that they be independent of the employer.

Different groups of workers may have different representatives to be consulted, whether elected or union representatives. Should there be both elected representatives and a recognised trade union for employees of a particular description, the employer may choose which representatives he consults. The employer also has a duty to allow appropriate representatives, whether from the recognised union or as elected by employees, 'access to the employees whom it is proposed to dismiss as redundant' and they must be given 'such accommodation and other facilities as may be appropriate'. The representatives need not be elected only for the purposes of consultation about redundancies, but if they may have been elected for other purposes it must be appropriate for the employer to consult them over redundancies. Thus, it would be appropriate for the employer to consult members of a works council, but probably not those elected as canteen representatives.

The elected representative and candidates for such posts have a right not to be subjected to detrimental treatment or to dismissal on the grounds of their functions or activities and to reasonable time off with pay, for the purposes of their activities.

15.4 CONSULTATION AT THE EARLIEST OPPORTUNITY

By TULR(C)A 1992, s. 188, the overriding duty on an employer when he proposed to dismiss employees as redundant, was to begin consultation with the recognised union 'at the earliest opportunity'. The 1995 Regulations now state that consultation shall 'begin in good time', a less exacting test. 'Proposal' means more than a remote possibility of dismissal (*National Union of Public Employees* v *General Cleaning Contractors* [1976] IRLR 362), and requires, as the EAT put it in *Association of Patternmakers and Allied Craftsmen* v *Kirvin Ltd* [1978] IRLR 318, 'a state of mind directed to a planned or proposed course of events'. The employer must thus have formed some view of how many are to be dismissed, when this is to take place and how it is to be arranged. The duty arises only when matters have reached a stage when a specific proposal has been formulated (*Hough* v *Leyland DAF Ltd* [1991] IRLR 194, [1991] ICR 696). That was a later stage than diagnosis of the problem and the realisation that one answer would be redundancies. Section 188 thus does not require consultation about the *reasons* for redundancy, that is whether a plant should close, but rather on the *carrying out* of any redundancy programme which management deems necessary.

There is, however, a strong argument for saying that this approach does not satisfy European obligations. For EEC Council Directive 75/129 requires that where an employer is *contemplating* large-scale redundancies, he should consult with the union to consider at least ways to avoid the redundancies. It may be claimed that a firm proposal is too late in the process of decision-making. This was rejected by the EAT in *Hough* on a matter of linguistic construction. Indeed, the EAT considered the French language version of the Directive before concluding that 'contemplating' did not require a wider construction than they placed on it. In *Re Hartlebury Printers Ltd* [1992] ICR 560, Morritt J held that 'contemplating' in Article 2(1) of Council Directive 75/129/EEC was to be construed in the same sense as 'proposing' in s. 99 of the EPA 1975.

It is instructive to consider *R* v *British Coal Corporation and Secretary of State for Trade and Industry ex parte Price and others* [1994] IRLR 72, although consultation was considered there for the purposes of s. 46(1) of the Coal Industry Nationalisation Act 1946. It was defined as involving:

(a)   consultation when the proposals are still at a formative stage;
(b)   adequate information on which to respond;
(c)   adequate time in which to respond;
(d)   conscientious consideration by the employer of the response to consultation.

In *Green & Son (Castings) Ltd* v *ASTMS & AUEW* [1984] IRLR 135 the employers claimed that they had consulted on the day that redundancy notices were issued, and that this constituted the start of statutory consultations. The EAT reiterated their decision in *National Union of Teachers* v *Avon County Council* [1978] IRLR 55 that this could not constitute consultation in any meaningful sense of the word. It was also insufficient to inform the unions that the criteria for selection would 'be determined in consultation with union representatives'. The employers had to inform the unions of their proposed method before consultation began, and this must be done before notices of dismissal are dispatched, for union representatives must be enabled to properly consider the proposals put to them. In *Transport and General Workers' Union* v *Ledbury Preserves (1928) Ltd* [1985] IRLR 412 dismissal notices were sent out half an hour after a meeting with union representatives at which redundancy proposals were put to them for the first time. The EAT had little difficulty in deciding that this was a sham exercise.

On the other hand, in *NALGO* v *National Travel (Midlands) Ltd* [1978] ICR 598 the EAT stated that, 'This legislation never envisaged a requirement for a trade union to be involved in preliminary policy considerations which are a managerial responsibility.'

Minimum periods of time are laid down by s. 188(2): where 100 or more men are to be made redundant at one establishment within a period of 90 days or less, at least 90 days must be left for consultations, before the first of the dismissals takes effect. Thirty days must be allowed for this process where between 10 and 99 men are to be dismissed within 30 days (Employment Protection (Handling of Redundancies) Variation Order 1979 (SI 1979 No. 958)). Further, the employees need not be union members. The Secretary of State for Employment has power to vary further this provision (s. 197(1)) as long as he does not reduce it to less than 30 days. The workers concerned do not have to be entitled to redundancy pay so that it includes those with less than two years' service and part-timers. It does not, however, apply to employees on fixed-term contracts for 12 weeks or less or those taken on to do a specific task which is not expected to last more than 12 weeks. While there is no statutory minimum where fewer than 10 are dismissed, two or three days has been held to be useless (*Transport and General Workers' Union* v *Nationwide Haulage Ltd* [1978] IRLR 143). The duty arises even if the employees are not actually members of the recognised trade union (*Governing Body of the Northern Ireland Hotel and Catering College* v *NATFHE* [1995] IRLR 83).

Particular difficulty is experienced by building contractors since it is often envisaged almost from the outset of a project that the men will be made redundant. The few tribunal decisions on this question indicate that the proper time to initiate consultation is 'once the tide had turned and the work has actually begun to run out', although each case depends on its own particular facts (*Union of Construction Allied Trades and Technicians* v *G. Ellison*

Carpentry Contractors Ltd [1976] IRLR 398, *Amalgamated Union of Engineering Workers* v *William Press and Son Ltd*, COIT 3126/218; Grunfeld, *Law of Redundancy*, op. cit., para. 14.1.1, p. 50).

15.5 MEANING OF ESTABLISHMENT

The minimum amount of time for consultation depends on the number of persons employed at the 'establishment' in question. This concept derives from the EEC Directive itself and is by no means a term of art in English labour law; *Barratt Developments Ltd* v *UCATT* [1978] ICR 319 yields few clues. The employers were a building company which operated on 14 sites in Lancashire, and made 24 employees at eight of these places redundant at the same time. In deciding the appropriate number in an establishment, the industrial tribunal were advised to consider the matter as an 'industrial jury', using their common sense on the particular facts of the case. Since here the sites were all administered from one base at Bradford, the EAT upheld the industrial tribunal's decision that there was only one establishment.

The courts have sought guidance in the definition of this same word (for the purposes of selective employment tax) which focused on:

(a) the exclusive occupation of premises;
(b) degree of permanence;
(c) organisation of workers;
(d) how administration is organised.

(See *Barley* v *Amey Roadstone Corp. Ltd* [1977] ICR 546, referring to *Secretary of State for Employment and Productivity* v *Vic Hallam Ltd* (1970) 5 ITR 108.)

The EAT had to consider the meaning of 'establishment' for the purposes of what was then s. 99 of EPA 1975 in *USDAW* v *Cooperative Wholesale Society*, 304 IRLIB 15. The Society owned a number of stores in each of its three regions, and proposed to dismiss over 100 employees in one region. The question was whether each store was a separate establishment. The industrial tribunal found that each store had a degree of permanence and separate identity; each was separately rated; and where the store was licensed it had its own licence. The industrial tribunal thought that this suggested that each store was a separate establishment, and the EAT refused to interfere with this decision since it was a question of pure fact.

In *Green & Son (Castings) Ltd* v *ASTMS and AUEW* [1984] IRLR 135 the three appellant companies were all subsidiaries of the same holding company, operated from the same site and shared the same accounting and personnel services. The tribunal sought to decide the number of employees to be made redundant at one establishment by aggregating the numbers employed by the three companies on the one site. Nolan J considered that this approach was misconceived. The first question is the identity of the employer, and only within the one company can numbers at a particular establishment be aggregated.

Establishment must be understood as a matter of European law as designating the unit to which the worker made redundant was assigned to carry out his duties (*Rockfon A/S* v *Specialarbejderdrbundet i Danmark* [1996] IRLR 168).

15.6 INFORMED CONSULTATION

There was no statutory definition of 'consultation' beyond the vague instruction that the employer must consider any representation made by trade unions' representatives and reply to them (TULR(C)A 1992, s. 188(6)) until amendments made by TURERA 1993, s. 34(2). There is still no exhaustive definition but consultation must include consultation about 'ways of (a) avoiding the dismissals; (b) reducing the numbers of employees to be dismissed and (c) mitigating the consequences of the dismissals'. Further the employer must undertake the consultation 'with a view to reaching agreement with trade union representatives'. A breach of this provision is likely to be difficult to substantiate, for it is not clear how far actual bargaining must take place. However, talks must proceed on an informed basis, so that the employer is required at the beginning (s. 188(4)) to disclose in writing to union representatives: the reason for the loss of jobs; the number, although not the names, of those to be dismissed; the total number of workers employed; and the proposed method of selection. The details should also include how much notice the employer intends to give, and whether he will be making any enhanced severance payments. The employer's attempt to comply with the Act in *Electrical and Engineering Association* v *Ashwell-Scott* [1976] IRLR 319, was not enough, since their letter only gave general notification of impending redundancies, and went on 'if there is any further information you should require please communicate...'. Some tribunals have sought guidance on the meaning of consultation in the administrative law case *Rollo* v *Minister of Town and Country Planning* [1947] 2 All ER 488, which decided that it means the communication of a genuine invitation, extended with a receptive mind, to give advice. It was not enough to commence consultation for the union to be sent merely a copy of the notification by the employer of redundancies to the Department of Employment since this did not say anything about which divisions of the company might be affected or in what proportion (*MSF* v *GEC Ferranti (Defence Systems) Ltd (No. 2)* [1994] IRLR 113).

15.7 THE DEFENCE OF 'SPECIAL CIRCUMSTANCES'

An employer may plead 'special circumstances' as a partial exemption from the requirement to consult with a recognised union, although he must still 'take all such steps towards compliance . . . as are reasonably practicable' (TULR(C)A 1992, s. 189(6)). The employer may not, however, rely upon 'a failure on the part of a person controlling the employer (directly or indirectly) . . . to provide information to the employer' (TULR(C)A 1992, s. 188(7) inserted by TURERA 1993, s. 34(2)). The defence reflects the problems which affect particular trades and industries, especially construction. In *Amalgamated Society of Boilermakers* v *George Wimpey Ltd* [1977] IRLR 95, the employers contended that it was not reasonably practicable for them to comply since the building site at Grangemouth, where the redundancies were declared, was subject to resignations, unexpected delays, uncertain weather and design changes. These were precisely the arguments unsuccessfully used in Parliament to justify an amendment excluding the building trade altogether from the scope of the provisions, and the EAT decided that such matters *could* provide an acceptable excuse, but did not in this case, since the employers had not done their best in the circumstances. Yet in denial of the principle that for the breach of a right there exists a remedy, no protective award was granted to the employees. On the other hand, in what may seem a harsh decision, where a builder was wrongly informed by the Department of Employment that he could make a man redundant without first consulting the union, this misleading advice was held not to be a 'special circumstance' (*Union of Construction Allied Trades and Technicians* v *H. Rooke and Son (Cambridge) Ltd* [1978] IRLR 204).

The most common set of special circumstances to come before tribunals concerns the last breaths of a dying business. The employers in *Clarks of Hove Ltd* v *Bakers Union* [1978]

ICR 1076, had carried on business for many years as manufacturers and retailers of confectionery. By the early autumn of 1976 they were in grave financial difficulties, but in October it was apparent that their last hopes had failed. Yet it was only two hours before the night shift came to work on the final day at 7.00 p.m. that a notice was posted on their numerous factory and bakery premises announcing that the workforce were then dismissed. The Court of Appeal confirmed the opinion of the industrial tribunal that *'special'* circumstances must be 'out of the ordinary or uncommon and in this context commercial and financial events such as the destruction of the plant, a general trading boycott or a sudden withdrawal of supplies from the main supplier'. Insolvency *alone* was not 'special' but it might be so if it were proved that the employer had continued trading in the face of adverse economic pointers in the genuine but nonetheless reasonable expectation that redundancies would be avoided. Here, on the other hand, the company's management knew of the closure plans long before the date of dismissal and they ought to have seen that there was little chance that they could ward it off, and thus should have consulted the unions earlier.

In *Association of Patternmakers and Allied Craftsmen* v *Kirvin Ltd* [1978] IRLR 318, Lord Macdonald drew a valuable distinction between a foreseeable insolvency as in *Clarks'* case, which could not be a special circumstance, and carrying on in the reasonable hope that the company would be sold as a going concern, which would obviate the need for redundancies and which might be within the scope of the excuse. The Employment Appeal Tribunal thought *Kirvin's* case was in the latter category. Here, there were potential purchasers in the field, and government subsidies in the background, and it was accepted that consultation would be fatal to delicate negotiations surrounding a 'rescue operation'. It might be thought that this was exactly the sort of circumstances for which the procedures section was envisaged, but Lord Macdonald did warn that an employer will not prove special circumstances 'if he shut his eyes to the obvious'. *Hamish Armour* v *ASTMS* [1979] IRLR 24, applied the same principle and was taken as a precedent in rather less stringent circumstances in *Union of Shop, Distributive and Allied Workers* v *Leancut Bacon Ltd* [1981] IRLR 295. The respondent company's directors had for some time been negotiating for the purchase of its shares by a third party; on the breakdown of these talks, the receiver declared redundancies without the necessary consultations taking place. This was held to be a special circumstance, even though, unlike in *Hamish Armour*, where the future depended on the discretion of a government department, all factors were within the employer's knowledge. It is not sufficient to amount to 'special circumstances' that the business could not be sold and that there were no orders anticipated by the employers (*GMB* v *Rankin and Harrison* [1992] IRLR 514).

Workforce unrest which caused the date of the first sacking to be brought forward is not, however, a special circumstance. It is vital that the policy of consultation about redundancies is not destroyed by a sidewind in the definition of the exception, especially one so elastic.

15.8 SANCTION: THE PROTECTIVE AWARD

15.8.1 Application

The remedy for failure to comply with the duty to consult on any of the procedural requirements of the section lies in the 'protective award' (TULR(C)A 1992, s. 189(3)). This is an unusual hybrid in that it may only be sought in an industrial tribunal by a recognised union, but is in favour of, and can ultimately be enforced by, the individual employee dismissed as redundant. It is an entitlement 'to be paid remuneration by the employer for the protected period' (s. 190(1)), conditional upon, in the main, the employee's being available for work should management wish to use his services. Besides maxima of 90, 30 and 28 days, for dismissals of over 100, 10-99, and below 10, respectively (the Secretary of State having power to vary these by order), the only guidance provided for industrial tribunals is that the award must be 'just and equitable in all the circumstances having regard to the employer's default' (s. 189(4)).

An application must be presented 'before the proposed dismissal takes effect or before the end of the period of three months beginning with a date on which the dismissal takes effect' or within a further period which the tribunal finds it just and equitable to grant, by way of extension. The question of whether an individual employee who may not be a trade union member can force the recognised union to make a claim on his behalf remains unanswered.

15.8.2 The amount

The primary judicial guidance on the size of the award is to be found in *Talke Fashions Ltd v Amalgamated Society of Textile Workers and Kindred Trades* [1977] ICR 833, where the EAT emphasised that it was discretionary and in no way penal. Tribunals should weigh the loss suffered by the employees and the seriousness of the employer's conduct in relation to them. Kilner Brown J called in aid the experience of the penal provisions of the Industrial Relations Act 1971, saying: 'We regard the imposition of penalties for bad behaviour as a retrograde step.' Moreover:

> . . . the seriousness of the default ought to be considered in its relationship to the employees and not in its relationship to the trade union representative who has not been consulted.

In *Barratt Developments Ltd v UCATT* [1978] ICR 319, the EAT thought the appropriate award was the 'amount of money, either by way of wages or in lieu of notice, that the employee would have got if the proper consultation procedures required by the Act had been applied'. This was adopted by Slynn P in *Spillers-French Holdings Ltd v USDAW* [1979] IRLR 339, where the employers argued that they were not liable to make an award to redundant employees at 13 of the bakeries which they had closed, because they had immediately secured jobs with the transferee company. The EAT remitted the case to the industrial tribunal to examine the number of days consultation lost and the seriousness of their default. On the latter, it pointed to a difference of substance between disclosing certain matters orally which should have been in writing and failure to give reasons for the redundancy at all, and went on:

> If the employer has done everything that he can possibly do to ensure that his employees are found other employment . . . a tribunal may well take the view that either there should be no award or if there is an award it should be minimal.

Remuneration paid by another employer during the protected period was to be disregarded (see *GKN Sankey Ltd v National Society of Motor Mechanics* [1980] IRLR 8).

Section 189(4) of TULR(C)A 1992 provides that the protected period for award 'shall be a period beginning with the date on which the first of the dismissals to which the complaint relates takes effect'. In *Transport and General Workers' Union* v *Ledbury Preserves (1928) Ltd* [1986] IRLR 492, the EAT decided that the time runs from the *proposed* date of the first dismissal rather than the actual date. There, 25 employees were given notice of redundancy without consultation with the union. In fact one of the employees left (and was by statute treated as having been dismissed) two months before the proposed date of termination. The maximum protective award would be 30 days and if that time began with the first actual dismissal, his own, the other employees would receive no award. The words 'takes effect' means take effect in accordance with the proposal in s. 188(3).

The employers are no longer entitled to deduct from the protective awards the amount paid to employees at the time of their dismissal since the old s. 190(3) TULR(C)A 1992 which so permitted was repealed by TURERA 1993.

It is open to an industrial tribunal to make a nil award. Thus in *Association of Scientific, Technical and Managerial Staffs* v *Hawker Siddeley Aviation Ltd* [1977] IRLR 418, the parties had already agreed on payment by the employer of wages in lieu of notice so that, even though the first employee left only nine days after the beginning of consultation, the tribunal awarded no compensation. Also, where the breach was only lack of written information this was treated as a technical default, since the workers were kept fully informed; and the EAT made no protective award (*Amalgamated Society of Boilermakers* v *George Wimpey* [1977] IRLR 95). In *Sovereign Distribution* v *TGWU* [1989] IRLR 334, however, the EAT decided that a protective award should be made even though consultation would have been unlikely to have made any difference to the final outcome.

Moreover, the employee loses entitlement to a protective award if during the period covered he:

(a)   is not ready and willing to work;
(b)   goes on strike;
(c)   is fairly dismissed for a reason other than redundancy;
(d)   unreasonably terminates his contract;
(e)   is offered suitable new employment; or
(f)   his old contract is renewed to take effect before or during the protected period.

Protective awards are treated as earnings for social security purposes, and national insurance contributions are taken off.

The employee cannot claim jobseeker's allowance for the period of the protective award. The normal situation is that benefit is paid in the first instance because of uncertainty whether an award will be made but when made it is subject to recoupment as ordered by the industrial tribunal. The award must not be paid to the relevant employees until social security received has been returned to the DSS. They are treated as golden handshakes for tax purposes and are thus usually exempt.

It is not possible to set off in respect of an insolvent employer in relation to failure to consult over redundancies sums not paid for failure to give statutory minimum notice (*Secretary of State for Employment* v *Mann* [1996] IRLR 4).

15.9   WHO ARE THE UNION'S AUTHORISED REPRESENTATIVES?

It is difficult in some cases to decide who are the appropriate representatives of the union who should be consulted, in the absence of a legally created plant-level body such as exists on the continent. Section 196 TULR(C)A 1992 identifies 'an official or other person authorised to carry on collective bargaining with the employer in question by that trade union'. In *General and Municipal Workers' Union* v *Wailes Dove Bitumastic Ltd* [1977] IRLR 45, an industrial tribunal rejected the union's complaint that the employer had not discharged his statutory duty because he had consulted the shop steward with whom he bargained over plant matters, rather than the full-time organiser of the union, since the latter had never carried on collective bargaining with the company.

The autonomy of collective bargains on redundancy consultations is preserved so that where there exists a procedure which is on the whole at least as favourable to employees as that contained in the Act, the Secretary of State may order by statutory instrument that the statute is not to apply. The agreement must be no less favourable to the employer than the statutory provisions (TULR(C)A 1992, s. 198(3)–(5)).

15.10 SPECIAL STATUTORY REGIMES

In some limited cases there is more particular provision protecting employees from dismissal. The Divisional Court decision in *R* v *British Coal Corporation ex parte Vardy* [1993] IRLR 104, concerned the collective agreement between British Coal and the National Union of Mineworkers made pursuant to s. 46(1) of the Coal Industry Nationalisation Act 1946. The court was able to declare the announcement of the closure of 31 collieries unlawful by reason of lack of consultation with the unions. It failed to satisfy the legitimate expectation of the unions.

16 Transfers of Undertakings

The objective of the Directive [77/187 on Acquired Rights] is to ensure as far as possible the continuation without change of the contract of employment or the employment relationship with the transferee in order to avoid the workers concerned being placed in a less favourable position by reason of the transfer alone.

(*Landsorganisationen i Danmark* v *Ny Molle Kro* [1989] IRLR 37 at para. 28.)

The common law considered each contract of employment a discrete unit, and for the best of reasons, since if an employee could be forcibly transferred from one employer to another, they would be 'serfs and transferred as though they were property' (*Nokes* v *Doncaster Amalgamated Collieries Ltd* [1940] AC 1014). This may, however, act against an employee's interest in the context of modern employment rights where continuity of service is important. Under the pressure of European Directive 187 on Acquired Rights, the Transfer of Undertakings (Protection of Employment) Regulations 1981 (SI 1981 No. 1794) (in this chapter called the Regulations) considerably altered the position as from 1 February 1982 (for detailed commentary, see P. Elias and J. Bowers, *Transfer of Undertakings: The Legal Pitfalls*, 5th edn., FT Law and Tax Professional Intelligence Reports, 1996).

Enforcement proceedings against the UK Government were initiated on 21 October 1992 to challenge the following parts of the UK Regulations:

(a) the exclusion of non-commercial ventures;

(b) the limitation of the Regulations to 'situations in which the business transferred is owned by the transferor';

(c) the failure to require the parties to consult with a view to seeking agreement;

(d) the lack of an effective sanction for a breach of the requirement to inform and consult employee representatives; and

(e) the failure to designate employee representatives when there is no voluntary appointment.

The Government reacted to these proceedings with s. 33(2) of TURERA 1993. Of the five matters raised by the EC Commission, the UK Government has in effect conceded on four but not on the compulsory granting of recognition by the transferee employer ((e) above). Infraction proceedings continued and the ECJ held ([1994] ICR 664) that the UK had failed to fulfil its European obligations by:

(a) failing to provide for the designation of employee representatives where an employer did not agree to it (i.e. recognition);

(b) excluding non profit-making undertakings from the Transfer of Undertaking Regulations (the non-commercial ventures principle);

(c) not requiring a transferor or transferee to consult in good time with a view to seeking agreement;

(d) failing to provide effective sanctions for failure to consult and inform.

Further amendments were made by the Collective Redundancies and Transfer of Undertakings (Protection of Employment) (Amendment) Regulations 1995 (SI 1995 No. 2587) to deal with the strictures made on UK law by the ECJ in respect of information and consultation rights on transfer of undertakings. These came into effect on 1 March 1996. Further, the Government took the opportunity to reverse the decision of the EAT in *Milligan v Securicor Cleaning Ltd* [1995] IRLR 288, to the effect that employees need have no period of qualifying service to claim unfair dismissal by reason of a transfer, although ironically that decision was later overruled by the Court of Appeal in *MRS Environmental Services Ltd v Marsh, The Times*, 22 July 1996.

The Government survived its first test on the lawfulness of the Regulations in the Divisional Court in *R v Secretary of State for Trade and Industry ex parte UNISON, GMB and NASUWT* [1996] IRLR 438. The three trade unions launched a series of challenges to the Regulations, which we deal with in turn:

(a) Method of legislating: the court was satisfied that the Secretary of State was entitled to amend domestic primary legislation by reason of s. 2(2) of the European Communities Act 1972 in order to implement the Acquired Rights Directive.

(b) Consultation and election of workers' representatives: it was sufficient compliance with the Directive to invite employees to elect representatives, and no more was required. Otton LJ concluded (at Transcript p. 34) that:

It was open to the Secretary of State to lay down specific requirements concerning the procedures for the election of employee representatives or the definition of constituencies from which the representatives are drawn and the other provisions contended for by the applicants. The fact that he did not make such elaborate and detailed stipulations did not constitute a breach of a community obligation to do so.

16.1 A RELEVANT TRANSFER

16.1.1 Introduction

The Regulations apply only where there is a transfer of an undertaking situated in the UK at the time of transfer. There is no definition of 'an undertaking' as such, but reg. 2 provides that undertakings are to include 'any trade or business'. In general, therefore, the transfer of an undertaking will involve the transfer of a trade or business. The purchaser may simply purchase it to lease or sell (see *Premier Motors (Medway) Ltd v Total Oil (GB) Ltd* [1984] ICR 58). Although in general the transfer will be achieved by sale, reg. 3(2) expressly provides that it may be involuntary, being by operation of law, e.g. on succession, and also that it may be a voluntary transfer activated otherwise than by sale, e.g. by gift or exchange. The Regulations will also apply where there is a change in the identity of the person operating an 'economic entity' which is transferred. It is not necessary for the transferee actually to acquire the ownership of that entity. A series of two or more transactions between the same or different parties may also constitute a transfer of undertaking.

Further, s. 33(3) of TURERA 1993 declares that a transfer 'may take place whether or not any property is transferred to the transferee by the transferor'. It may also 'be effected by a series of two or more transactions'. This reflects the considerable European case law to this effect (e.g. *Bork International* v *Foreningen af Arbejdsledere i Danmark* [1989] IRLR 41; *Foreningen af Arbejdsledere i Danmark* v *Daddys Dance Hall A/S* [1988] IRLR 315).

16.1.2 The essential question

In so far as there is one general formulation derived from the case law, both UK and European, it is as follows: Has there been a change in the legal or natural person responsible for carrying on the business and is there an economic entity which has retained its identity and is transferred from one to another? There is a difference between change in ownership (which is not required for a transfer of undertaking) and change in employer (which is a prerequisite but is not itself sufficient). The question must be answered by reference to the substance of the transaction, not necessarily its form (see *Council of the Isles of Scilly* v *Brintel Helicopters Ltd* [1995] IRLR 6 and *Kelman* v *Care Contract Services Ltd* [1995] ICR 260 ('a change of employer responsible for the activities of an undertaking which continues to be identifiable will usually mean that there has been a relevant transfer' (at 267)).

16.1.3 European authority

The European authority on the meaning of 'transfer' has become ever more important and has influenced the whole approach to the question. The proper starting point is *Spijkers* v *Gebroeders Benedik Abattoir CV* [1986] 2 CMLR 296, which concerned a transferor company which had entirely ceased activity and dissipated its goodwill by the time it had sold its assets (a slaughterhouse and appurtenant premises and goods). The ECJ in this case said that the proper question was whether the entity retained its identity; all the circumstances had to be considered, but the mere sale of the assets of an enterprise did not constitute a transfer. 'That at the time of transfer the business is still active, that machinery is being used, customers supplied, workers employed and that all the physical assets and goodwill are sold are strong indications that a transfer . . . has taken place' (Advocate-General Sir Gordon Slynn, at para. 29). It was not, however, conclusive against a transfer taking place that 'goodwill or existing contracts are not transferred', or that there was a gap before trading was resumed after transfer. This was all a matter of fact to be determined by the national court. The court stated (at para. 303) that:

> To decide whether these conditions [for transfer] are fulfilled it is necessary to take account of all the factual circumstances of the transaction in question, including the type of undertaking or business in question, the transfer or otherwise of tangible assets such as buildings and stocks, the value of intangible assets as at the date of transfer, whether the majority of staff are taken over by the new employer, the transfer or otherwise of the circle of customers, the degree of similarity between activities before and after the transfer and the duration of any interruption in those activities. It should be made clear, however, that each of these factors is only a part of the overall assessment which is required and therefore they cannot be examined independently of each other.

In the cases of *Bork International* v *Foreningen af Arbejdsledere i Danmark* [1989] IRLR 41, *Landsorganisationen i Danmark* v *Ny Molle Kro* [1989] IRLR 37, *Berg and Busschers* v *Besselsen* [1989] IRLR 447 and *Foreningen af Arbejdsledere i Danmark* v *Daddys Dance Hall A/S* [1988] IRLR 315, discussed below, the ECJ has emphasised that the key question is whether there has been a transfer of an economic entity. Although that concept is not wholly clear, it ought to be treated consistently with *Spijkers* (above) as involving the transfer of an operation as a *going concern*. This does not require any permanent change in the ownership of the business, provided that the economic entity is being operated by a different employer. The court of appraisal must assess whether there is a distinct entity in operation at the time when a transfer passes from the transferor to the transferee.

The most influential European decisions are now *Dr Sophie Redmond Stichting* v *Bartol* [1992] IRLR 366 and the later case of *Watson Rask AO* v *ISSS* [1993] IRLR 133, and these must be considered in detail. The basic facts of the *Bartol* case were that the Groningen Kantonrechrter changed its grant from one foundation named Redmond engaged in providing assistance to drug dependents (mainly from Surinam and Antilles) to the Sigma Foundation. It was held that there was a transfer of undertaking, and that employees who worked first for Redmond and later for Sigma could claim continuity of existing terms enjoyed with Redmond when engaged by Sigma. There was a degree of coordination and cooperation which existed between the two foundations. The important features of the case included the facts that:

(a)   the Sigma Foundation partially absorbed the Redmond Foundation;

(b)   the two foundations collaborated to set up the transfer transaction;

(c)   Redmond's knowledge was transferred to Sigma;

(d)   the building originally leased by Redmond was leased then to Sigma; and

(e)   Sigma offered contracts to some but not all former employees of Redmond.

The fact that the foundations were not paid for their services did not exclude this transaction from the scope of the Directive so that the restriction to commercial ventures in the Regulations was unfounded. Rather, the decisive criterion was whether the business in question generally retained its identity, although it did not need to be absolutely *identical* before and after the purported transfer. A transfer occurs where there is a change in the legal or natural person responsible for carrying on business and who incurs the obligations of employer towards employees of the undertaking (ECJ in *Bartol* (supra) at para. 11). The ECJ stated that Article 1(1) of the Directive:

> covers the situation in which a public body decides to terminate a subsidy paid to one legal person, as a result of which the activities of that legal person are fully and definitively terminated, and to transfer it to another legal person with similar aims. (*Bartol* (supra) at para. 21)

The absence of any direct legal transfer between Redmond and Sigma was irrelevant. It was this case which made clear that the fact that the entity was not commercial in nature was quite irrelevant to the operation of the Directive.

Watson Rask (supra) dealt with the particular situation of contracting out of services. In this case, ISS, as catering contractors, had a contract under which they became 'fully and completely responsible for managing Philips' canteens, in particular for planning menus, purchases, preparation, transport, all administrative tasks and also for recruiting and training staff'. The judgment, following *Spijkers* (supra), states (at para. 20) that:

It is appropriate to take into consideration all the circumstances characterising the operation concerned, among which are, namely, the type of business or institution involved, the transfer or otherwise of tangible assets such as buildings or movables, the value of intangible assets at the time the transfer takes place, the taking back or otherwise of the main part of the workforce by the new head of the business, the transfer or otherwise of clients and also the degree of similarity of the activities pursued before and after the transfer and the duration of any possible suspension of those activities.

On this basis, it was held that there *was* a transfer of undertaking on the facts of the instant case. The case is the most directly applicable to the situation of contracting out or 'compulsory competitive tendering' and in most such cases means that there is a transfer of undertaking, although in each case the particular facts must be considered before a view can be expressed. This case established unequivocally that the transfer of a service to be provided at a fixed fee may be the transfer of an undertaking (see, in particular, at para. 17).

The approach taken in *Watson Rask* was further developed by the ECJ in *Schmidt* v *Spar und Lihkasse* [1994] IRLR 302. The appellant was employed by a savings bank to clean the head office of its premises, but was dismissed on account of the refurbishment of the branch because the bank wanted to trust the cleaning to Spiegelblank, the firm which was already responsible for the cleaning of most of the other premises of the bank. This raised, for the first time before the ECJ, the issue of a one-person undertaking. The ECJ repeated its views in *Watson Rask* that 'the fact that in such a case the activity transferred for the transferor is an ancillary activity not necessarily connected with its object cannot have the effect of excluding that operation from the scope of the Directive'. The number of employees engaged in the undertaking was irrelevant (see para. 15). The central question was whether the business retained its identity. The court held that it had and that the retention of that identity was 'indicated *inter alia* by the actual continuation or resumption by the new employer of the same or similar activities' and here it did.

These cases reflect a very broad approach to the question of when there is a transfer, and suggest that in the case of contracting out, mere continuation of the same activity (at least at the same location) will often suffice.

There is a case for saying that the ECJ ironically has reversed itself at the same time that the EAT is extending the boundaries of a transfer, and is now narrowing down the scope of a transfer. This view is, however, mainly based upon the decision in *Ledernes Hovedoeganisation acting on behalf of Ole Rygaard* v *Dansk Arbejdsgiverforening, acting on behalf of Stro Molle Akustik A/S* [1996] IRLR 51, where the ECJ appear for the first time to have pulled back from the ample extent of the concept of transfer in other cases, and stressed that the economic entity to be transferred must be a stable one. The firm had been entrusted by SAS Service Partner with the construction of a canteen, but was informed by the main contractor that part of the work on ceilings and joinery work should be completed by the respondent. The second contractor refunded the first for the cost of materials supplied. The alleged transferor was declared bankrupt and the employee sued the respondent for wrongful dismissal. The Advocate General found that the identity was retained since there were the same or similar economic activities. The Court reiterated that the central test was whether the business in question retained its identity (that is the *Spijkers* test from long ago in 1986), but it interpreted it and applied it to the facts in a way which is somewhat out of line with recent ECJ decisions and may reflect a pulling back from the high water mark of cases such as *Schmidt*. The ECJ rejected the claim because the transfer must 'relate to a *stable* economic entity whose activity is not limited to performing one specific works contract'. It could fall within the terms of the Directive only if it included 'transfer of a body of assets enabling the activities or certain activities of the transferor undertaking to be carried on in a stable way'. That was not the case here.

While the decision in this case may mark the beginning of a more restrictive approach to the scope of a transfer of undertaking, and the issue of 'stability' is an important gloss on existing case law, it is more likely to be confined to its specific facts where a specific building or other contract is to be completed and no assets or goodwill go across. The ECJ decided the case on the basis (at para. 22) that 'the transferor undertaking merely [made] available to the new contractor certain workers and material for carrying out the work in question'. It was noted that no assets or goodwill transferred, and those in contract cleaning want it to mean that the old requirement for goodwill to transfer (as it usually will not in such cases) should be reinstated.

A more orthodox interpretation of the Directive may be seen in *Merckx* v *Ford Motor Co. Belgium SA* (1996) IRLR 467 which concerned the application of the ARD to the transfer of a motor vehicle dealership covering a particular geographical area from one undertaking to another. The employers argued in essence that one undertaking had terminated and another had commenced, so that there was no transfer between them. The ECJ however concluded that the second company had carried on the activity performed by the first without interruption, in the same sector and subject to similar conditions. It had taken on part of the staff of the first company and was recommended to the customers of the first in order to ensure continuity in the operation of the dealership. The ECJ held that neither the transfer of tangible or intangible assets nor the partial preservation of the transferor's undertaking were crucial to the application of the Directive.

The fact that this case is going to be given a narrow interpretation is shown in *BSG Property Services and Mid Beds DC* v *Tuck* [1996] IRLR 134, where the EAT said that *Rygaard* is only intended to apply to short-term contracts.

Surprisingly, the ECJ in *Hencke* v *Gemeinde Schierke* [1996] IRLR 701 decided that there was no transfer of undertaking when a municipal administration was dissolved and its tasks were transferred to a regional authority.

16.1.4 The UK cases

A whole host of UK cases decided between 1993 and 1996 have modified greatly the approach taken to the concept of transfer and gave it a much more European flavour. In *Wren* v *Eastbourne DC* [1993] IRLR 425, the council terminated its existing arrangements for refuse collection and made fresh arrangements by way of contract with the Onyx Company. A major degree of control was retained by the council, of which refuse collection was one of its statutory functions, and the Industrial Tribunal thus held that there was no transfer of undertaking within the Regulations (see especially at para. 32). The EAT overturned the decision and remitted the case for rehearing in accordance with the correct legal principles, in particular to consider:

whether there is a recognisable entity, a going concern (this can include the provision of services), which is run or operated or carried on by the alleged transferor . . . and which is being continued by the alleged transferee . . . One must look at the substance of what has occurred and not the form . . . There is no necessity for the transfer of assets . . . All these questions are questions of fact and degree.

The ECJ's guidance in *Watson Rask* was also influential in the important decision in *Kenny* v *South Manchester College* [1993] IRLR 265. Sir Michael Ogden QC, sitting as a Deputy High Court judge, decided in an application for a preliminary decision under RSC Ord. 14A that there was a transfer within the Directive when the Home Office terminated an arrangement by which a local authority provided education at a young offenders' institution and awarded a new contract to provide those services at a further education college. The judge applied the questions posed in *Watson Rask*, whether 'the education department will retain its identity and its operation will continue' and whether it was a 'going concern'. This decision was reached notwithstanding that the transferee had no intention of taking on any existing staff. The learned judge in *Kenny* emphasised that:

> The prisoners and young offenders who attend, say, a carpentry class next Thursday will, save for those released from the institution, be likely in the main to be those who attended the same class in the same classroom the day before and will doubtless be using exactly the same tools and machinery.

In *Porter and Nanayakkara* v *Queen's Medical Centre* [1993] IRLR 486, Sir Godfray Le Quesne QC, sitting as a deputy High Court judge, held that there was a transfer when paediatric and neo-natal services at Grantham and Kesteven Hospitals were provided initially by the hospital itself and then contracted out to the defendant trust. This was a determination directly on the Directive since both the transferor, the Health Authority, and the transferee, the NHS Trust, were in the public sector. This was, however, expressly so decided on the basis that a 'snapshot' should be taken of the position before and after the contract. It did not matter that there was some difference between the services provided before and after the putative transfer, since it was inevitable in a fast-moving field such as paediatrics that there would be some difference of approach. Further, it was immaterial that an NHS contract is not in itself legally enforceable between the purchaser and provider. All that the words 'legal' contract meant was 'not illegal'.

The decision of the EAT in *Dines* v *Initial Services Ltd* [1993] IRLR 521, however, appeared to be out of line with ECJ decisions. It concerned the provision of cleaning services at Orsett Hospital, Basildon. There was held to be no transfer of any tangible assets because Initial supplied the equipment, the stock and the cleaning material to enable its employees to clean the Hospital. All that was withdrawn at the end of the contract. Under the new contract Pall Mall introduced its own management, equipment, stock and supplies. Thus, the industrial tribunal held that there was no transfer because:

(a)   each operator provided its own equipment; and
(b)   there was no agreement between the two contractors, rather they were in competition for the new contract;

and the EAT upheld that decision. The Court of Appeal ([1994] IRLR 336), overturned the EAT's judgment, however, in the light of the ECJ cases. In particular, the Court decided that there was an error of law in that the industrial tribunal had said:

> when one company enters into competition with a number of other companies to obtain a contract . . . and a different company wins the contract from the company which was previously providing the services that is the cessation of the business of the first contractors on the hospital business and the commencement of a new business by [Pall Mall, the new contractors] who were awarded the contract.

This was unsustainable in the light of the decisions in *Foreningen af Arbejdsledere i Danmark* v *Daddys Dance Hall A/S* [1988] IRLR 315 and *Schmidt* v *Spar und Lihkasse* [1994] IRLR 302. The Court of Appeal stressed that the transaction in such a case might take effect in two stages: the handing back by Initial to the authority of the cleaning services at the hospital; and the grant or handing over by the authority to Pall Mall of those cleaning services. The Court went on to say that the facts of the case pointed to the transfer of an undertaking since 'the cleaning services were to be carried out by (mainly) the same staff on the same premises and for the same Authority'.

An economic entity may just comprise activities and employees and there need be no tangible assets (*Council of the Isles of Scilly* v *Brintel Helicopters Ltd* [1995] IRLR 6). The business may be one for the provision of labour only. The industrial tribunal should ask whether, having regard to all the circumstances, the economic entity identified prior to the transfer can be found after the transfer. The economic activity does not have to be separate and discrete in the sense that it is conducted separately from any other business being carried on by the employer. Morison J stated:

> The decisive criterion for establishing whether there has been a transfer is whether the business in question retains its identity following the events alleged to constitute the transfer. Retention of identity is indicated *inter alia* by examining whether the activities which were carried out before the relevant events are being carried out afterwards in the same or similar manner. In other words one should examine the similarity between the work done before and after the relevant events and the identity of those carrying out the work.

One of the criteria is the number of employees who were actually taken on by the transferee (*Council of the Isles of Scilly* v *Brintel Helicopters Ltd*, supra).

In *Birch* v *Nuneaton Borough Council and Sports and Leisure Management Ltd* [1995], IRLR 518, the EAT adopted a wide view that 'If similar activities are continued in different hands, the identity of the undertaking is retained, a transfer occurs, the employees follow the work and protection is enjoyed by the employees'. It is indicative that recent decisions of the EAT have been increasingly liberal in interpreting the Transfer Regulations. There is a case for saying that the EAT was for many years well behind European thought (in cases such as *Dines* v *Initial Care Services* and *Wren* v *Eastbourne BC*), but now it is well in the vanguard.

In *Betts* v *Brintel Helicopters Ltd* [1996] IRLR 45, there was a change in the provision of transport for men and equipment to Shell's oil rigs in the southern North Sea even though no employees transferred, no assets were taken on, there were different types of helicopter, avionics systems and different maintenance standards, and the base of operations moved from Beccles to Norwich. Scott Baker J eschewed a 'minute examination of detail' and said (at para. 27) that 'there is no change in the basic activity, although some of the details as to how it is provided have changed, e.g. different aircraft, pilots and base'. The absence of any employees actually transferring did not stand against there being a transfer (para. 28). The crucial features pointing towards the maintenance of a stable entity were the facts (specified at para. 34) that:

(a) the service is being provided for the same person;
(b) the destinations are the same;
(c) the journeys, give or take a few kilometres, are the same;

(d)   the same or similar personnel and goods are being carried;

(e)   the mode of transport is the same, albeit with different aircraft and pilots.

The unifying feature of these important authorities is that the central questions now to be posed are:

(a)   Is there an entity?

(b)   Is it stable?

(c)   Is it carried on in different hands before and after putative transfer?

In *Kelman* v *Care Contract Services Ltd* [1995] ICR 260, Mummery J summarised the present position: 'The theme running through all the recent cases is the necessity of viewing the situation from an employment perspective, not from a perspective conditioned by principles of property, company or insolvency law'.

16.1.5   The present position: summary

In essence, the tendency of the case law is readily to find a transfer, at least where the same activities continue at the same location. No factor is decisive — although it is submitted that the absence of goodwill in a traditional sale of a business (as opposed to the contracting out of a function or utility) will be a strong indicator against finding a transfer. Equally, following *Schmidt* and *Dines* (supra) it appears that while a tribunal must look at all relevant factors, the fact that no assets are transferred will, in many cases, be of little significance. Mummery J explained the position thus in *Kelman* v *Care Contract Services Ltd* [1995] ICR 260 at 268:

The theme running through all the recent cases is the necessity of viewing the situation from an employment perspective, not from a perspective conditioned by principles of property, company or insolvency law. The crucial question is whether, taking a realistic view of the activities in which the employees are employed, there exists an economic entity which, despite changes, remains identifiable, though not necessarily identical, after the alleged transfer.

(See also *Charlton* v *Charlton Thermosystems (Romsey) Ltd* [1995] ICR 56.)

In view of the fact that the ground rules have changed so fundamentally, and that contracting out has been brought firmly within the scope of the Directive and the Regulations, it would be unwise to rely upon earlier case law when determining what is a transfer.

The principles which follow are now to be applied:

(a)   The industrial tribunal should take a robust and realistic view of the facts (*Spijkers* [1986] 2 CMLR 296 at 299, *Kenny* v *South Manchester College* [1994] IRLR 336).

(b)   The tribunal should take a snapshot before and after the alleged transfer and see how an ordinary person would consider the circumstances; it is not sufficient that the same activity is going on before and after the putative transfer (*Kenny* v *South Manchester College*, (supra)).

(c)   One approach is to ask whether there is an economic entity which retains its identity and is transferred from one to another (*Rastill* v *Automatic Refreshment Services* [1978] ICR 289 at 295, *Spijkers* (supra)).

(d)   The industrial tribunal should take into consideration all the circumstances characterising the operation concerned (*Dines* v *Initial Services Ltd* [1994] IRLR 336).

(e)   The tribunal should look at the substance and not the form of the transaction (*Spijkers* (supra), *Wren* v *Eastbourne DC* [1993] IRLR 425, *Dines* (supra)).

(f)   The fact that the activity transferred is only an ancillary activity of the transferor not necessarily related to its objects may count against there being a transfer of undertaking.

(g)   The fact that goodwill is not transferred is not a factor telling conclusively against there being a transfer but if no goodwill is transferred this counts as a factor against a transfer being established (*Spijkers* (supra)).

(h)   There is no requirement of a transfer of assets or property (e.g. *Kelman* v *Care Contract Services Ltd* [1995] ICR 260 at 267f).

(i)   There may only be one employee involved in the transfer (*Schmidt* v *Spar* [1995] ICR 237).

(j)   The undertaking may consist only in the provision of or the right to provide services (*Kelman* v *Care Contract Services Ltd* [1995] ICR 260 at 267g).

16.1.6   The *de facto* transfer

There may be a transfer of business even though an envisaged merger which caused an employee to work for another company was subsequently called off. In *Dabell* v *Vale Industrial Services (Nottingham) Ltd* [1988] IRLR 439, the employee had been working for Vale Industrial Services for eight years when discussions started with Nofotec Co. with a view to Vale joining that group. An agreement was reached in principle and Vale's orders, machines and other items and materials were transferred. Twenty-two days after he started being paid by Nofotec, Mr Dabell resigned. Thereafter, the merger was called off. The Court of Appeal decided that whether there had been a transfer of business had to be determined as at the date when the act of which the employee complains occurs, and at this stage there was indeed a transfer of undertaking. The EAT had also erred in determining that there could be no transfer of ownership of a business without a written agreement (*SI (Systems and Instruments) Ltd* v *Grist and Riley* [1983] IRLR 391).

16.1.7   Transfer by way of two or more transactions

Regulation 5(3) provides that, where a transfer is effected by a series of two or more transactions, reg. 5 will bite on the contract of a person employed immediately before any of those transactions. A transaction will only form part of a series for the purposes of reg. 5(3), however, if it is instrumental in effecting the transfer; it is not sufficient that it forms part of a chain of events leading up to the transfer (*Longden* v *Ferrari Limited and another* [1994] IRLR 157). There may be a transfer when a company has been dissolved but the business it conducted is carried on by the main shareholders in the company (*Charlton* v *Charlton Thermosystems (Romsey) Ltd* [1995] ICR 56).

16.1.8   Exclusions and waiver

The Regulations do not cover a sea-going vessel on its own, but do extend to the transfer of part of an undertaking. A transfer of share capital (which account for 40 per cent of British takeovers) is excluded since the identity of the employer remains the same in law. Any agreement to contract out of the Regulations is void (reg. 12; see *Foreningen af*

Arbejdsledere i Danmark v *Daddy's Dance Hall A/S* (supra) on contracting out of the Directive). The Regulations do not apply to an employee who ordinarily works outside the United Kingdom (reg. 13).

16.1.9 Employment by the transferor in the part transferred

The question of who is transferred when only a part of an undertaking is transferred was considered by the ECJ in the case of *Botzen* v *Rotterdamsche Droogdok Maatschappij BV* [1986] 2 CMLR 50. In that case, certain specific departments of a company were sold following a liquidation, and the question arose whether employees employed in general departments (e.g. personnel, porters' services, general maintenance) were also transferred. It was accepted that they carried out certain duties for the benefit of the transferred part of the undertaking, as well as for other departments of the business.

However, the ECJ held that the staff were not transferred merely because they used assets located in the part transferred or carried out work which benefited that part. There had to be more, since they had to be *assigned* to the part transferred. In reaching this conclusion, the ECJ adopted the view of the European Commission who had described the 'decisive criterion' as 'whether or not a transfer takes place of the departments to which they were assigned and which formed the organisational framework within which their employment relationship took effect'.

Sometimes, the contract of employment will expressly define the section or department wherein the employee is required to work; in other cases the answer to that question will have to be implied from all the surrounding facts and circumstances (see *Northern General Hospital NHS Trust* v *Gale* [1994] IRLR 292). In order to be assigned to the part transferred, it is unnecessary for the employee to work exclusively in that part; the question is one of fact to be determined by considering all the relevant circumstances (*Buchanan-Smith* v *Schleicher & Co. International Ltd* [1996] ICR 613).

A related question concerns whether the employee is employed by the transferor. In *Webb (Duncan) Offset (Maidstone) Ltd* v *Cooper* [1995] IRLR 633 the EAT, in considering the case where a person is employed by X to work on Y's business and Y transfers that business to Z, decided that prima facie the Regulations would not apply but that 'Industrial tribunals will be astute to ensure that the provisions of the Regulations are not evaded by devices such as service companies or by complicated group structures which conceal the true position'. Industrial tribunals were advised to 'keep in mind the purpose of the Directive and the need to avoid complicated corporate structures from getting in the way of a result which gives effect to that purpose'. This focuses on evasion and requires the adjudicating body to strip away the veil of incorporation.

An apparently altogether more radical approach was taken by the EAT sitting in Scotland in *Sunley Turriff Holdings Ltd* v *Thomson* [1995] IRLR 184. Mr Thomson was employed as company secretary and chief accountant for Lilley Construction Ltd and Lilley Construction (Scotland) Ltd. His contract was with Lilley Construction Ltd. On 18 January 1993 the business of Lilley Construction (Scotland) Ltd was transferred to Sunley Turriff Holdings Ltd and Mr Thomson was not on the list of employees transferred; in effect he claimed that he should have been. He was dismissed on the grounds of redundancy on 1 March 1993 by the receivers of Lilley Construction Ltd and he claimed against Sunley Turriff Holdings Ltd as transferee. It was held that the Regulations applied since the part transferred included Lilley Construction (Scotland) Ltd for whom Mr Thomson provided services and accordingly Mr Thomson was assigned to the part transferred. The question however was whether the claimant was an employee in that undertaking (para. 13). The tribunal did not focus on that question; an employee may well work in a particular undertaking but not be employed by the transferor or anyone connected with the transferor. We have in mind, in particular, secondees and contractors working within an undertaking but not employed by the transferor.

It was argued by the putative transferees that in any event Mr Thomson had entered into a new contract and was thus retained by the transferor, but this contention was rejected by the industrial tribunal and the EAT because Mr Thomson had been constantly seeking to establish what his employment position was. The EAT thus had to focus on whether he was transferred, notwithstanding that on a purely contractual analysis he was not employed by the transferor. One can see why the EAT wanted to reach the conclusion that he was covered by the transfer principle, but the analysis is unsound and the reasoning is somewhat sparse. The *Peters* case (infra) (which had at that stage been decided but not reported) was not cited to the EAT in *Sunley Turriff*. Further, in *Sunley Turriff,* there was much confusion about the shape of the organisation (see e.g. para. 3). Nevertheless, the purported application of the *Botzen* test to reach the result that Mr Thomson could be said to be assigned to these subsidiary companies is still somewhat surprising since *Botzen* is not a case in which the employee might have been employed by either of two companies, so that the issue now under discussion did not arise in *Botzen.*

The decision in *Peters (Michael) Ltd* v *Farnfield and Peters (Michael) Group plc* [1995] IRLR 190 is altogether more orthodox. Mr Farnfield was chief executive of the Michael Peters Group plc and was responsible for the financial management of all 25 subsidiary companies in the group. The group went into receivership on 27 August and Mr Farnfield on that date was made redundant. Three days later four subsidiary companies were sold to CLK and the subsidiary companies were named as the seller. CLK also acquired part of the assets of the parent company which belonged to the subsidiary companies. Mr Farnfield failed in his claim against the transferee on the ground that he worked for the group as a whole and not exclusively for the subsidiaries sold. He was thus not employed by the transferor. The decision might have been otherwise, however, if Mr Farnfield had been employed by the group company but had worked almost exclusively for the subsidiary.

16.2 EFFECT OF TRANSFER ON THE CONTRACT OF EMPLOYMENT

16.2.1 Rights and duties transferred

The effect of the transfer is in the nature of a statutory novation of the contract of employment so that the purchaser stands in the shoes of the vendor as far as the vendor's employment responsibilities are concerned. More specifically, the transferee of the undertaking takes over all 'rights, powers, duties and liabilities under or in connection with any such contract' (reg. 5). The phrase 'in connection with' is probably ample enough to include statutory continuity rights but it does not include a protective award claimed by a trade union which has not been properly consulted over redundancies under the Employment Protection Act 1975 (*Angus Jowett & Co. Ltd* v *National Union of Tailors and Garment Workers* [1985] IRLR 326). Where an employee was found to have been dismissed unfairly by the vendors before the transfer, was re-engaged after the transfer and then dismissed unfairly by the transferees, the purchasers are potentially liable for two basic awards as unfair dismissal compensation (*Fenton* v *Stablegold Ltd* [1986] IRLR 64). The EAT rejected the argument that such employees did not fall within the Regulations since their employment would not have been terminated by the transfer. (See also *Bullard* v *Marchant* [1986] ICR 389 and *Berg and Busschers* v *Besselsen* [1989] IRLR 447, ECJ.)

The decision of the EAT in *Wilson & Sanders and Wallace* v *St Helens Borough Council* [1996] IRLR 320 sent shock waves through the profession since it suggests that employers and employees cannot vary the contract of employment by agreement at the time of transfer. The orthodox concept of the Regulations is that they hold a mirror at the time of transfer, and anything which could be achieved with the transferor employer with his employees such as a consensual variation, could be done with the transferee. The Appellants were teachers or carers at a school which was formerly owned by Trustees and controlled by Lancashire County Council. The County Council decided to withdraw and St Helens Borough Council agreed to take over the School. The Appellants received an Extraneous Duties Allowance from the County Council, but St Helens Borough Council made it clear that they would not continue to pay this. The Appellants started proceedings under the Wages Act 1986 after the transfer. The Industrial Tribunal rejected the employees' claim on the basis that new contracts of employment were agreed with the St Helens Borough Council which operated to vary the Appellants' terms and conditions as previously enjoyed with the County Council.

The EAT, however, allowed the appeal. The crucial question under the Wages Act was 'what is the total amount of wages properly payable to the employee'. The central point was 'the identity of the reason for the alteration or variation in the terms of the contracts of employment which the [Appellants] had with the transferor County Council'. Mummery J relied on the ECJ decision in *Daddy's Dance Hall* for the proposition that the policy of the Directive, and thus of the 1981 Regulations, precludes even a consensual variation in the terms of that contract if the transfer of the undertaking is the reason for the variation. The parties would, however, be free to vary an agreement if the reason was something else. This is a question of fact in each case. There was no possibility here of relying upon the exception in reg. 8(2) for 'an economic, technical or organisational reason' since the employees had not been dismissed. In summary 'there was no break in the causal link in the variation between the terms and conditions and the transfer of the undertaking. The cause of the variation was the transfer itself. For that reason the variation was ineffective. The terms of the original contracts of employment with the County Council remained in force'. This opens up the prospect of a torrent of litigation in the civil courts from employees whose contracts were varied at the point of transfer. In many cases, it will not be as clearcut on the facts as in *Wilson* that the reason for the variation was indeed the transfer.

There is specific exclusion from the Regulations in respect of the transfer of occupational pensions, and criminal liabilities. In *Perry* v *Intec Colleges Ltd* [1993] IRLR 56, an industrial tribunal decided that the Acquired Rights Directive contemplated something much wider than the limited protection of existing rights contained in the Social Security Acts and that the Regulations must perforce be construed purposively by adding at the end of reg. 7 the words 'but any contract of employment transferred by virtue of regulation 5 shall be deemed to include such rights as are necessary to protect the interests of the employee in respect of rights conferring on him immediate or prospective entitlement to old age benefits including survivors' benefits under supplementary pension schemes'. This approach was, however, disapproved by the EAT in *Walden Engineering Co. Ltd* v *Warrener* [1993] IRLR 420.

The issue was considered more fully by Robert Walker J in *Adams* v *Lancashire CC and BET Catering Services Ltd* [1996] IRLR 154. In that case Lancashire County Council put its school catering service out to tender. BET acquired the contract. It was argued that the Regulations applied to the transfer. BET offered to take the transferred employees into its own pension scheme, but this excluded many of the transferred staff, including the plaintiffs. They sought declarations to the effect that the local authority pension rights were protected on a transfer. Essentially their argument was as follows:

(a) Notwithstanding the different language used in limbs (a) and (b) of Article 3(3) (i.e. all severance rights in limb (a), and rights to immediate or prospective entitlement in limb (b)), the two limbs were intended to cover the same rights.

(b) The primary analysis was that Article 3(3) applies only to accrued rights in both limbs, so that the transferee remained liable for securing future pension provision.

(c) The secondary and alternative submission was that both limbs covered all pension rights, so that although there was no liability on the transferee, the State was responsible for securing both accrued pension rights and future pension rights. It was further contended that if this was indeed the correct analysis, the second limb was directly effective and could be enforced as against the Council in respect of future pension rights.

The judge rejected both arguments. He did not accept that the two limbs were symmetrical, in the sense of covering the same ground. He held that it was an *acte clair* that limb (a) appeared to exclude all pension rights, and that limb (b) merely protected accrued rights. Furthermore, he held that in any event, even if his construction was wrong, it would not be possible so to construe reg. 7 as to give effect to the plaintiffs' construction of Article 3(3). It would, thought the judge, involve an impermissible distortion of the regulation, going beyond the legitimate scope recognised in such cases as *Litster.*

Anything done by the transferor before the transfer in respect of the employee's contract is deemed to have been done by the transferee (reg. 5(2)(b)). Further, there is a right introduced for the first time in 1993 for an employee to object to being transferred (see infra 16.4(b)).

The effect on restrictive covenants was first considered in *Morris Angel Ltd* v *Hollande* [1993] ICR 71, where the court held that if the literal transposition of a term would impose wider obligations than those originally contemplated by the parties, the term in question must be construed purposively, so that it has the same effect post-transfer as it did pre-transfer.

16.2.2 Employment immediately before the transfer

Only persons employed 'immediately before the transfer' are, however, involved. The appeal bodies have been reluctant to give 'immediately' its literal meaning, but just as reluctant to define what leeway is permissible. In *Apex Leisure Hire Ltd* v *Barratt* [1984] ICR 452 the EAT withdrew from this conundrum by suggesting that it was a question of fact in each case. In contrast, in the *Premier Motors'* case, a different division of the EAT appears to have assumed that a dismissal even an instant before the transfer meant that the employee was excluded from the scope of the Regulations. The obligations passed to the transferee where the transferor's employees were given due notice of dismissal which was timed to expire on the date of transfer. The vital date for the purposes of the Regulations was the effective date of termination. Construing the Regulations broadly in the light of the European Directive, as they should be construed, it did not matter in which order the dismissals and transfer occurred if they took effect on the same day (*Secretary of State for Employment* v *Anchor Hotel (Kippford) Ltd* [1985] IRLR 452). An employee dismissed by the transferors after contracts of sale were exchanged but before completion was employed 'immediately before the transfer' (*Kestongate Ltd* v *Miller* [1986] ICR 672). Reading the Regulations as a whole, Wood J thought that there was no difficulty in construing transfer as a period of time rather than a specific point in time.

In *Secretary of State for Employment* v *Spence* [1986] IRLR 248 the employer went into receivership in November 1983. At 11 a.m. on 28 November 1983 all employees were dismissed, and the business was sold three hours later to a company which re-engaged the entire workforce. The transferor then went into liquidation and the litigation arose when the Secretary of State for Employment refused to make a redundancy payment from the Redundancy Fund on the sole ground that such employees were not employed by the transferor immediately before the transfer. The Court of Appeal took a very narrow view of 'immediately before'. The employees were held not to be employed 'immediately before the transfer'. It is important to note that in this case there was an express finding of fact by the industrial tribunal that there was no 'collusion' between transferor and transferee to ensure dismissal by the former before the transfer took place.

The reason why the receivers in *Spence* had decided to dismiss the workforce was that until a contract could be renegotiated with the company's principal customer, there was no prospect of any work for the business. The case was narrowly distinguished by the House of Lords in *Litster* v *Forth Dry Dock & Engineering Co. Ltd* [1989] IRLR 161. The House followed its earlier decision in *Pickstone* v *Freemans plc* [1988] IRLR 357 (an equal value case) to the effect that (in the words of Lord Keith), 'in order that the manifest purpose of the Regulations might be achieved and effect given to the clear but inadequately expressed intention of Parliament certain words must be read in by necessary implication' (see also Lord Templeman at para. 19, Lord Oliver at paras 21, 50). This principle justified not taking a narrow approach to the phrase 'a person employed immediately before the transfer' in the Transfer Regulations. To do so would render the Regulations 'capable of ready evasion through the transferee arranging with the transferor for the latter to dismiss its employees a short time before the transfer becomes operative', said Lord Keith. Lord Oliver (at para. 50) thought it necessary to remember in this regard that the purpose of the Directive and Regulations was to 'safeguard' the rights of employees on transfer and that there was a mandatory obligation to 'provide remedies which are effective and not merely symbolic to which the Regulations are intended to give effect. The remedies . . . in the case of an insolvent transferor are largely illusory unless they can be exerted against the transferee as the Directive contemplates.' It was the duty of the court to give to reg. 5 a construction which accords with the decisions of the European Court on the corresponding provisions of the Directive. Thus reg. 5(3) had to be construed on the 'footing that it applies to a person employed immediately before the transfer or who would have been so employed if he had not been unfairly dismissed before transfer for a reason connected with the transfer' (Lord Templeman at para. 19).

Lord Oliver stated that the sequence of events in this transfer could not be rationally explained otherwise than on the basis that the dismissal of the workforce was engineered to prevent any liability attaching to Forth Estuary Engineering Ltd (the solvent transferee). On the other hand:

Where, before the actual transfer takes place, the employment of an employee is terminated for a reason unconnected with the transfer, I agree that the question of whether he was employed 'immediately' before the transfer cannot sensibly be made to depend on the temporal proximity between the two events, except possibly in a case where they are so closely connected in point of time, that it is, for practical purposes, impossible realistically to say that they are not precisely contemporaneous.

His Lordship (at para. 35) did not consider that the correctness of the *Spence* decision arose for consideration in *Litster*, pointing to the fact that in *Spence* the industrial tribunal found as a matter of fact that there was no collusion. (See also *Macer* v *Aberfast Ltd* [1990] ICR 234, [1990] IRLR 137).

It is the better view that transfer takes place at the moment of completion rather than on exchange of contracts (*Wheeler* v *Patel and J. Golding Group of Companies* [1987] IRLR 211).

16.3 'HIVING DOWN'

Special rules apply to 'hiving down', the practice adopted by the receiver or liquidator of a company of transferring the company's undertaking, or part of it, to a wholly owned subsidiary without also transferring the employees. The aim is to sell the viable part of the business without the incubus of employee responsibilities. By reg. 4 the provisions do not operate until either the subsidiary ceases to be wholly owned by the holding company (whether by share or asset sale and whether by transfer of all or by a majority of the shares) or the business of the subsidiary is transferred. When this occurs, there is deemed to be a transfer of undertaking from parent to subsidiary company. In general it will be possible for the vendor to terminate contracts long before the ultimate sale to the third party, so that the latter has no liabilities to employees. The effect of the Regulations is thus suspended until ultimate sale. Since the House of Lords decision in *Litster and others* v *Forth Dry Dock & Engineering Co. Ltd* (supra) however, the effect of reg. 4 has been much curtailed. Dismissals by the parent company 'immediately before the transfer' under such circumstances will almost certainly be found to be sufficiently connected with the transfer, and so, unless they can be explained by an ETO reason, reg. 5 may still be held to apply.

16.4 THE POSITION OF THE EMPLOYEE

(a) By reg. 5(5) the employee loses the right he would have at common law to resign on a change of identity of his employer. He can only claim constructive dismissal if there is a substantial change in his working conditions. It is likely that this will be construed as on all fours with the test in *Western Excavating Ltd* v *Sharp* [1978] QB 761.

(b) In *Katsikas* v *Konstantinidis* [1993] IRLR 179, the ECJ decided that the Acquired Rights Directive did not prevent an employee from refusing the transfer to a transferee of his contract of employment or employment relationship. The Directive does not require member States to provide that the contract of employment should be maintained with the transferor in the event that the employee freely decides not to continue the contract of employment with the transferor. The ECJ said that 'Such an obligation would undermine the fundamental rights of the employee who must be free to choose his employer and cannot be obliged to work for an employer'. Further it leaves to member States the right to determine the fate of the contract in the event of a transfer. On the basis of this doctrine, TURERA 1993 introduced a new reg. 5(4A) into the Regulations. This disapplies the automatic transfer principle 'if the employee informs the transferor or transferee that he objects to becoming employed by the transferee' in which case, by reg. 5(4B), the transfer operates 'to terminate his contract of employment with the transferor' but he 'shall not be treated, for any purpose, as having been dismissed by the transferor'.

The ECJ has subsequently held that where the contract is terminated by the employee on account of a substantial detrimental change in his or her working conditions, the Member

State must provide that the employer is to be regarded as responsible for the termination (*Merckx* v *Ford Motor Co. Belgium SA* [1996] IRLR 467).

In *Photostatic Copiers (Southern) Ltd* v *Okuda and Japan Office Equipment Ltd* [1995] IRLR 11, the EAT held that reg. 5(1) does not take effect in relation to an employee's contract of employment unless and until the employee is given notice of both the fact of the transfer and the identity of the transferee.

(c) It is not, however, possible to gain an injunction to prevent a transfer of undertaking taking place. In *Newns* v *British Airways plc* [1992] IRLR 575, British Airways decided to hive off part of its business to a subsidiary, but employees were told only on 11 June that this would occur on 26 June. Notwithstanding this, the appellant did not have an arguable case on an application for an injunction that the transfer of a contract of employment or a proposal to so transfer was a repudiatory breach by the employer when the employee was entitled to restrain. (see to the same effect, *Betts* v *Brintel Helicopters* [1996] IRLR 45.)

16.5 DISMISSAL ON TRANSFER OF UNDERTAKING

The Regulations render a dismissal automatically unfair if the transfer or a reason connected with it is the reason or principal reason for dismissal. The only escape for the employer is where the reason or principal reason was 'an economic, technical or organisational reason *entailing changes in the workforce of either the transferor or transferee* before or after a relevant transfer'. In such a case, the reason is treated as some other substantial reason for dismissal.

A pivotal question is whether the dismissal must be by reason of a specific transfer or whether a dismissal designed to enhance the prospects of any transfer being effected will suffice. In *Harrison Bowden Ltd* v *Bowden* [1994] ICR 186, the EAT held that a dismissal was unfair if it was to facilitate a transfer, even though the identity of the employer was not known at the time. A later EAT decision (*Ibex Trading Ltd* v *Walton* [1994] ICR 907) has chosen not to follow the *Bowden* case and has held that the dismissal must be by reason of a specific transfer to qualify. Morison J said:

> . . . A transfer is not just a single event: it extends over a period of time culminating in a completion. However, here the employees were dismissed before any offer had been made for the business. Whilst it could properly be said that they were dismissed for a reason connected with a possible transfer of the business, on the facts here we are not satisfied that they were dismissed by reason of *the* transfer or for a reason connected with *the* transfer. A transfer was, at the stage of the dismissal, a mere twinkle in the eye and might well never have occurred.

In *Meikle* v *McPhail* [1983] IRLR 351, the purchaser established an economic reason for dismissal when it made some employees redundant shortly after the transfer when it realised that the pub transferred could not be run economically with so many staff. In *Wheeler* v *Patel and J. Golding Group of Companies* (supra), the EAT indicated that an economic reason must be connected with the conduct or running of the business and not merely a dismissal to achieve a better price for the entity transferred (see to the same effect *Wendelboe* v *LJ Music ApS* [1985] ECR 457, *Gateway Hotels Ltd* v *Stewart* [1988] IRLR 287).

In *Trafford* v *Sharpe & Fisher (Building Supplies) Ltd* [1994] IRLR 325, the EAT held that the rights of workers not to be dismissed on the transfer of an undertaking may be outweighed by economic reasons.

An organisational reason may be established if the transferee can show that a change in the way the business is run creates a need for new skills which the employee does not possess (*Porter and Nanayakkara* v *Queen's Medical Centre (Nottingham University Hospital)* [1993] IRLR 486).

A significant limitation on the scope of this exception to automatic unfairness was revealed by the Court of Appeal's judgment in *Berriman* v *Delabole Slate Ltd* [1984] ICR 636. The employee was constructively dismissed since he would not accept new disadvantageous terms required by the transferee employer who sought to standardise his contract with that of other existing employees. This neither had the object of effecting nor did it bring about a change in the workforce as required by the Regulations to fall within the relevant exception. Changes in the identity of individuals who make up the workforce do not constitute changes in the workforce itself if the overall numbers and functions of the employees as a whole remain unchanged. Their Lordships thought, however, that a change in the *function* of the workforce would suffice and the consequences of this dictum have still to be worked out.

'Workforce' means the workforce as an entity separate from the individuals who make up that workforce. The issue under the Regulations is whether the reason for dismissal involved a change in that workforce. There could be such a change even if the same people were retained but were given different jobs by the transferee (*Crawford* v *Swinton Insurance Brokers Ltd* [1990] ICR 85).

Doubt has been placed on the economic, technical or organisational reason exception in reg. 8(2) by the Advocate-General's opinion for the ECJ's decision in *D'Urso* v *Ercole Marelli Elettromeccanica General SpA* [1992] IRLR 136. Referring to the 1977 Directive which the Regulations seek to implement, he argued that the exception should apply only where there would have been dismissals for an economic, technical or organisational reason in any event, and not where such reasons are consequent on the transfer. This makes sense in that in such circumstances there would seem to be no reason why what would be fair dismissals but for the transfer should be converted into unfair dismissals. However, as Rubenstein has pointed out, this means that there is a major flaw in the way the Regulations implement the Directive (see [1992] IRLR 107). It was not followed by the EAT in *Trafford* v *Sharpe & Fisher Ltd* [1994] IRLR 325.

Where there is a relevant reason entailing changes in the workforce, the tribunal must decide in the normal way whether the dismissal is fair within the rubric of s. 98 of ERA 1996 (see *McGrath* v *Rank Leisure Ltd* [1985] ICR 527). The EAT has seen little difference between this and the conclusions reached on 'some other substantial reason' on business reorganisation (*Richmond Precision Engineering Ltd* v *Pearce* [1985] IRLR 179). One vital issue concerns dismissal by the vendor at the behest of the purchaser. In *Anderson & McAlonie* v *Dalkeith Engineering Ltd* [1984] IRLR 429 the Scottish EAT decided that this was an 'economic, technical or organisational reason' and that the motives of the purchaser in requiring the dismissals were irrelevant. The mere fact that it was under his pressure rendered the dismissal by the vendor fair. If this decision stands, it may drive a coach and horses through the unfair dismissal provisions in the Regulations (cf. *Gateway Hotels Ltd* v *Stewart* [1988] IRLR 287).

BSG Property Services & Mid Beds DC v *Tuck* [1996] IRLR 134 raised many issues of everyday concern on dismissals in compulsory competitive tendering cases. The employees were all employed by the Mid Bedfordshire District Council in the Housing Maintenance Direct Services Organisation ('DSO') in bricklaying, carpentry and plumbing work. The Council contracted with their own DSO for a five-year period. The DSO board, however, decided to terminate the contract and not put in a bid for a further contract since they had failed to make the required 5 per cent return on capital and thus were in breach of the appropriate regulations. They were given notice by the Council on 12 February 1993 to expire on 15 May 1993. One day before the expiry of the notice, the Council concluded a contract with BSG for the provision of day-to-day jobbing maintenance work by self-employed tradesmen. The Council and BSG argued that there was no transfer of undertaking, but the EAT upheld the decision of the industrial tribunal that the relevant economic entity was 'the provision of maintenance services to Council tenants in the Area concerned' and that there was a transfer.

The industrial tribunal had also decided that the reason for dismissal was an economic or organisational reason and the dismissals were fair in all the circumstances. Several issues arose for consideration on appeal:

(a)   The first point was what was the appropriate date for determining the reason for dismissal in the circumstances, whether the date when notice was given, when the applicants were engaged by the Council, or the date of expiry of the notice when they had transferred (briefly) to the service of BSG. The EAT held that the crucial question was the Council's reason for dismissal as at the date when notice was given.

(b)   As a result, the Council could not have any economic or organisational reasons since they did not believe that the TUPE Regulations applied. BSG, the transferee, inherited the liabilities of the Council and were deemed to have given the notice of termination already given by the Council, but did nothing in relation to the dismissals 'because they did not believe that they had to do anything about the dismissal of the Applicants'.

(c)   If BSG are liable for dismissing them it is for a reason fixed by the deeming effect of the Regulations, not because they (BSG) dismissed for *their own reason*. BSG were therefore stuck with the reason of the Council. Thus, there was no economic or organisational reason for dismissal on the part of the Council, and there was no valid reason for dismissal and the dismissals were automatically unfair.

(d)   The EAT thus did not need to address another point of general importance as to whether the fact that BSG only employed persons under contracts for services *could* amount to an economic or organisational reason for dismissal.

One other dubious interpretation of the Regulations has now been laid to rest. There was initially doubt whether an employee could claim a redundancy payment on a transfer dismissal (*Canning* v *Niaz* [1983] IRLR 431, *Meikle* v *McPhail* (supra)), but the EAT has now decided that he can if s. 135 of ERA 1996 is in the normal way satisfied (*Gorictree Ltd* v *Jenkinson* [1984] IRLR 391, *Anderson & McAlonie* v *Dalkeith Engineering Ltd* (supra)).

Where the purchaser takes over the vendor's employees with the intention of dismissing some of them, he faces a difficulty; whether he can select those to be dismissed simply from the employees transferred by the vendor. A dismissal may be unfair because the selection is unreasonable (see e.g. *Williams* v *Compair Maxam* [1982] ICR 156). It may be considered unreasonable simply to select from a pool of employees of the vendor. On the other hand, it could damage the morale of the purchaser's own original employees if they are dismissed. Indeed, this possibility might lead them to oppose the transfer. Case law is awaited.

One of the greatest surprises of interpretation of the Regulations (which sent many solicitors to check their professional indemnity cover!) came in this area, in the case of *Milligan* v *Securicor Cleaning Ltd* [1995] IRLR 288. This sent shockwaves through the legal profession which had always assumed (as had earlier editions of this book) that an employee had to be employed for two years to claim unfair dismissal on transfer. The employee, Mr Milligan, was dismissed for a transfer-connected reason within two years of commencement of employment. The EAT decided that he could, nevertheless, bring a claim because:

(a) Article 4 of the Acquired Rights Directive provided that the transfer of an undertaking 'shall not in itself constitute ground for dismissal';
(b) to form an exemption from this principle, the Member State must make provision for 'certain specific categories of employees' but reg. 8(1) did not do so;
(c) Article 4 was enacted into English law by way of reg. 8(1) by which the employee shall be *treated* for the purposes of Part V of the [Employment Protection (Consolidation) Act 1978] as unfairly dismissed. This gave a separate right to that found generally in the 1978 Act. It did not import each and every restriction found in that statute.

The Collective Redundancies and Transfer of Undertakings (Protection of Employment) (Amendment) Regulations 1995 (SI 1995 No. 2587) amended this, but only in respect of cases where dismissals are effected on or after 26 October 1995. This provision itself is currently being challenged in judicial review proceedings against the UK Government. Although the 1995 Regulations make the point largely academic, the Court of Appeal in *MRS Environmental Services Ltd* v *Marsh, The Times,* 22 July 1996 decided that *Milligan* was incorrect.

16.6 CONSULTATION WITH THE RECOGNISED UNIONS

Recognised trade unions and elected representatives have similar rights to consultation over transfers of undertakings as on redundancies. The transferor has a duty to inform such union or unions, where members thereof may be affected by the transfer or by 'measures' to be taken in connection with it, of:

(a) the fact that the relevant transfer is to take place;
(b) when, approximately, the transfer is to take place;
(c) the reasons for the transfer;
(d) the legal, economic, and social implications for affected employees;
(e) the measures which he envisages the transferor or the transferee will take or if there will be no such measures, that fact.

In *Institution of Professional Civil Servants* v *Secretary of State for Defence* [1987] IRLR 373, Millett J construed s. 1 of the Dockyard Services Act 1986, which re-enacted reg. 10 of the Transfer of Undertakings Regulations for the special purpose of the 'privatisation' of the naval dockyards. He considered that 'measures' was a word of wide import, including 'any action, step or arrangement'. 'Envisages' meant 'visualises' or 'foresees'. Whilst manpower projections were not measures, reductions in the level of manpower would be. Where information to be divulged under the equivalent of reg. 10(2) is not factual but is based on appraisal or judgment, such as manpower forecasts, the employer need only divulge the result of his deliberations; the union may not demand information on the calculations or assumptions on which the appraisal or judgment is based.

The relevant information must be given to a 'union representative . . . long enough before a relevant transfer to enable consultations to begin'. The employers need only actually consult if any 'measures' are to be taken, in which case management must consider any representations which the union may make (see generally on construction of these provisions, *NATTKE* v *Rank Leisure Ltd,* COIT 1388/134).

The only defence for the employer is where he is faced by 'special circumstances rendering it not reasonably practicable' for him to conform. This exception is likely to be construed in much the same restrictive manner as under the Employment Protection Act 1975. In *Angus Jowett & Co. Ltd* v *NUTGW* [1985] IRLR 326, the financial circumstances which gave rise to the appointment of a receiver were neither sudden in onset nor unforeseeable and the industrial tribunal had correctly decided that there was no special circumstance. Regulation 10(3) provides that 'the transferee shall give the transferor such information at such time as will enable the transferor to perform the duty imposed on him . . .'.

Any complaint of default must be made to the industrial tribunal within three months or such longer period as the tribunal considers reasonable. Subject to the low maximum limit of four weeks' pay, the tribunal should award such compensation for breach of the consultation provisions as 'the tribunal considers just and equitable having regard to the seriousness of the failure of the employer to comply with his duty'. The amount is a question of fact with which the EAT is unlikely to interfere *(Angus Jowett* case).

This whole requirement for consultation only with recognised unions was thrown into doubt following the decision by the ECJ in *Commission of European Communities* v *UK* [1994] ICR 664 (see full discussion in Chapter 15).

A new reg. 9(4) was introduced to widen those to be informed and consulted from representatives of a recognised independent trade union to 'employee representatives elected by' the employees or, if both are present, then either representatives of a recognised independent trade union or elected employee representatives 'as the employer chooses'. Whether the employer consults elected representatives or representatives of a recognised union is entirely a matter for the employer. It is possible that an employer may consult a recognised trade union for one group of employees and elected representatives for another.

There are no criteria of independence for the elected representatives, so that they might be representatives of a body which is dependent on the employer. The only rule as to eligibility is that the elected representatives must be employed by the employer at the time that they are elected.

The elected representatives are defined by the new reg. 11A as having been elected 'for the specific purpose of being informed or consulted' under the Transfer Regulations, or persons who have been 'elected by employees otherwise than for that specific purpose' but whom 'it is appropriate (having regard to the purposes for which they were elected) for their employer to inform and consult' under the Transfer Regulations.

A representative might be an elected member of an existing works or staff council or joint consultative committee. Alternatively, he might be a person who is elected for handling redundancy consultations. The DTI has put out some non-statutory guidance to the effect that it would not be sufficient to consult members of a committee specifically established to run the staff canteen, but it might well be appropriate to consult a committee which is regularly informed or consulted more generally about the company's financial position and personnel matters (para. 9 of the guidance).

There is no express provision about, or restriction on, the mode of election of the elected representatives, and no provision as to when the election of the elected representatives must take place. The DTI's guidance on the subject, however, states that where an employer chooses to consult through elected representatives rather than the union, it must take steps to ensure that they are elected in proper time for consultation to be undertaken. The Government has left unaddressed the avoidance of undue employer influence on the conduct of the election. Further, there is no provision to cover the possible scenario when the employer calls for an election but no one puts himself forward. It is, however, conceivable. that the industrial tribunal might see this as a special circumstance excusing the employer from carrying out what would otherwise be his obligations.

The DTI guidance is thus weak as could be, avoiding prescriptions and merely stating that the employer will 'wish to consider' such matters as whether:

(a)   employees have sufficient time to nominate and consider candidates;

(b)   employees (including any who are absent from work at the relevant time) can freely choose for whom they wish to vote;

(c)   there may be some normal company custom and practice for similar elections.

This is the other end of the spectrum from the tight conditions applied by the law to trade union ballots for industrial action or elections for the principal executive committees.

There are certain rights which go with the post of elected representative. The elected representative and union representative are accorded the right not to suffer detriment as a consequence of carrying out the functions or activities of an employee representative or a candidate for such elections, and time off for such purposes (ERA 1996, ss. 47(1), 61(1)). A dismissal will be automatically unfair if the reason or principal reason is that the employee performed or proposed to perform any functions as an employee representative.

Further, the employer must provide elected representatives or trade union representatives with access to the affected employees (reg. 10(6A)), such as by use of the telephone. The DTI guidance states that 'what is appropriate will vary according to the circumstances' (para. 17).

16.7   TRADE UNION RIGHTS

Regulation 6 requires that rights and duties arising under a collective bargain should be transferred to the transferee but this is expressly without prejudice to the non-binding nature of such agreements (TULR(C)A 1992, s. 179). Further, a transferee is obliged to succeed to and honour the transferor's union recognition arrangements but only 'where after a relevant transfer the undertaking or part of the undertaking maintains an identity distinct from the remainder of the transferee undertaking' (reg. 9).

17   Trade Unions

Current union boundaries are historical deposits and repositories of history.

(R. Hyman, *Industrial Relations: a Marxist Introduction*, Macmillan, 1975.)

Trade unions today face increasing pressures from a fragmented labour market and hostile Government. Trade union membership has fallen to just over 8,000,000, whilst the increasingly restrictive legislation, typified by TURERA 1993, has presented trade unions with an organisational headache. In particular, the difficulties in obtaining the written consent of union members to the deduction of union subscriptions (to comply with the new legislation on check off arrangements) has diverted valuable union resources to simply retaining existing membership. These circumstances have encouraged the merger of trade unions into ever larger organisations so that the trade union world is now dominated by about five major super unions.

17.1   DEFINITION OF TRADE UNION

Although most people reckon they know a trade union when they see one, it is like the elephant — a good deal easier to recognise than to define. However, a statutory definition is necessary to determine what organisations are eligible for the various privileges accorded such bodies. Thus s. 1 of TULR(C)A 1992 characterises as a union, 'an organisation (whether permanent or temporary) which . . . (a) consists wholly or mainly of workers of one or more descriptions and is an organisation whose principal purposes include the regulation of relations between workers of that description or those descriptions and employers or employers' associations'. It is a constitutional formality which distinguishes an organisation from a collection of individuals, so it cannot just be all workers at a particular factory. Moreover, the *principal purposes* of the organisation must be within the scope of the section, so that in *Midland Cold Storage* v *Turner* [1972] ICR 230, although a shop stewards' committee drawn from the members of various unions in London docks was an organisation of workers, it was not a trade union since its main objects did not include regulating industrial relations between employers and employees. Rather the court found that, 'its most apparent activity seems to be recommending the taking or abandonment of industrial action'. It did not take part in negotiation of terms on the resumption of work, but instead ceded that role to the official union's structure. A group engaged in political activities which may indirectly influence industrial relations is not thereby a trade union. In *BAALPE* v *NUT* [1986] IRLR 497 the Court of Appeal stated that an Association which, due to its size and constitution, was not able to carry out all of the functions of a bigger trade union could still be a trade union. The fact that it demonstrated that it had a principal purpose of regulating industrial relations between employers and its members was sufficient.

A committee of workers in a branch, a section of a union or a coordinating committee in a particular area may be defined as a trade union.

In *News Group Newspapers Ltd v Society of Graphical and Allied Trades (SOGAT 1982)* [1986] ICR 716, CA, the question to be determined was whether assets in the name of branches of the SOGAT 1982 trade union belonged to the trade union or to the individual branches. Glidewell LJ (p. 726 at E) distinguished two types of union branches — those in a federal union (such as the National Union of Mineworkers), in which each regional or local organisation is a separate trade union and the national trade union is a federation of local trade unions, and a centralised trade union, in which the branch has no more status than as an agency of the national union.

The Court of Appeal distinguished a third type of branch — that of an unincorporated association of members, similar to a social club. In this case, the members paid their union dues, 40 per cent of which was deducted by the branch, at source, for its own use. The national and local union rules allowed the legal ownership of these funds to be held for the benefit of the members of the branches. Consequently, these funds were not union property.

So whilst each branch was not a separate trade union, the fact that it had the status of an unincorporated association meant that its fund belonged to the branch rather than the union.

While it was never argued that each branch was a separate trade union, in the above-mentioned case, this was done in *News Group Newspapers v SOGAT 82 (No. 2)* [1987] ICR 181. Stuart Smith J (at p. 224) held that each branch of SOGAT 82 was a trade union in itself. In his view, each branch was an organisation consisting wholly or mainly of workers of which one of the principal purposes was the regulation of relations between workers and employers.

Stuart Smith J cited the *BAALPE v NUT* case (supra) as supporting his view. As mentioned above, the fact is that BAALPE did not have the resources of the much larger NUT. This did not prevent it being a trade union.

The definition of 'workers' has already been considered (para. 2.4), but it is particularly important that it includes, in addition to employees, all those who agree to perform personally any service for another, except where the relationship is that of professional and client. This serves to exclude from the definition of trade unions solicitors' organisations (*Carter v Law Society* [1973] ICR 113) because they are professionals; and authors (*Writers' Guild of Great Britain v BBC* [1974] ICR 234) since they are under no obligation to provide services. Policemen are expressly excluded (TULR(C)A 1992, s. 280) but health service employees are included (TULR(C)A 1992, s. 279). In *Home Office v Evans, The Times,* 18 November 1993, May J decided that the Prison Officers Association was not a trade union since it did not consist wholly or mainly of *workers.* This was amended by the Criminal Justice Act 1994, but, in so far as it affects the Prison Officers Association itself, it did not otherwise affect the definition (see also *Boddington v Lawton* [1994] ICR 478).

The statutory definition also expressly includes federations or confederations of unions, such as (i) the International Transport Workers Federation (see *NWL Ltd v Woods* [1979] 3 All ER 614, *Universe Tankships Inc. of Monrovia v ITWF* [1980] IRLR 363), (ii) the Trades Union Congress itself, which represented some 7.3 million unionised workers as at 1 January 1994, (iii) unions (such as the National Union of Mineworkers) which are made up of separate regional unions, e.g. South Wales, Yorkshire, (iv) unions which have merged but have kept separate sections (such as MSF with the Health Visitors Association and the GMB with APEX).

17.2 EMPLOYERS' ASSOCIATIONS

There are several hundred employers' associations in various sectors of the economy, performing functions as diverse as pay bargaining, tribunal representation, and supervising disputes procedures (see H.A. Clegg, *The Changing System of Industrial Relations in Great Britain*, Basil Blackwell, 1979, pp. 62-100). They are entitled to certain statutory privileges, as unions are, and are defined as: 'an organisation which comprises wholly or mainly of employers or individual proprietors . . . and whose principal purposes include the regulation of relations between employers . . . and workers' (TULR(C)A 1992, s. 122(1)). This is the mirror image of the definition of trade unions, but an employers' association must also be 'responsible to members who associated themselves for such purpose'. It was on this ground that, in *Greig* v *Insole* [1978] 1 WLR 302, the international cricket conference was held not to be an employers' association, as it was responsible to the cricket council and not to its members.

An employers' association, unlike a trade union, may be an incorporated or an unincorporated association, but if it is the latter, it has the same quasi-corporate benefits as does a trade union. It may also have more than 20 members without having to be incorporated as is normally required under s. 716 of the Companies Act 1985.

17.3 SPECIAL REGISTER ORGANISATIONS

The Special Register is a leftover from the Industrial Relations Act 1971, s. 34, where it provided a home for bodies active in industrial relations, and even collective bargaining, but among whose *principal* objects could not be said to fall regulation of relations between employers and employees. They include the British Medical Association and the Royal College of Nursing, and are usually incorporated. The list is now closed, although the advantage of such registration remains that such bodies obtain the same immunity from restraint of trade as do trade unions, but only in so far as their activities are concerned with the regulation of labour-management relations.

17.4 THE LEGAL STATUS OF TRADE UNIONS AND EMPLOYERS' ASSOCIATIONS

The birth of the industrial revolution was also the birth of organised labour. The realisation of this, coupled with the hysteria amongst Britain's aristocracy caused by the French Revolution, made for a very twitchy ruling class in the last century. Coercive measures were used to stamp out Britain's fledgling trade unions. Ordinary working people, such as the Tolpuddle Martyrs, were exiled abroad for organising workers. Trade unions were held to be unlawful associations because they restricted the terms on which each member would sell his labour (*Hornby* v *Close* (1867) 2 LR QB 153).

A trade union is an unincorporated association at common law, which means prima facie that it is not a separate entity from its members, and its property must rest in the hands of trustees. It is in this respect more like a members' club than a company, although several cases have suggested that it has a quasi-corporate status and it may be sued as such by reason of s. 10(1) of TULR(C)A 1992. The most notorious was the decision in *Taff Vale Railway Company* v *Amalgamated Society of Railway Servants* [1901] AC 426, which concluded from the fact that they were registered under the Trade Union Acts 1871 and 1876 that unions could be sued in tort in their registered name, although only Lord Brampton went as far as ascribing to it full corporate status.

The issue next arose in the rather different context of deciding whether an employee could sue for breach of rules by its officers. In *Bonsor v Musicians' Union* [1956] AC 104, Lord Morton said that a union was 'a body distinct from the individuals who from time to time compose it'; Lord Parker thought it 'an entity, a body, a "near corporation"'. As part of its aim to make unions pay for the consequences of their industrial action, the Industrial Relations Act 1971 went further and imposed corporate status on all unions. This was, however, reversed by the Trade Union and Labour Relations Act 1974.

Although the legal form is different from corporate entities, the reality underneath is not, since s. 10(1) of TULR(C)A 1992 confers on unions many of the characteristics of legal corporate status, as indeed did the pre-1971 Acts. Thus:

(a)   A union is capable of making contracts in its own name.

(b)   All union property must be vested in trustees who hold it in trust for the trade union; if they were ordinary unincorporated associations it would be in trust for the members or otherwise void as a purpose trust and perpetual.

(c)   A union is capable of suing or being sued in its own name.

(d)   Proceedings may be brought against a union for a criminal offence.

(e)   A union is liable for enforcement of judgments as though it were a body corporate.

There are, however, some residual consequences of the unincorporated structure. Thus a trade union does not have the necessary legal personality to suffer injury to its reputation and thus cannot sue for libel (*Electrical, Electronic, Telecommunication and Plumbing Union v Times Newspapers* [1980] 1 All ER 1097).

17.5   LIABILITY IN TORT

A union is now fully liable in tort except where it acts in contemplation or furtherance of a trade dispute, but this immunity, already diminished by the Employment Act 1980 was further reduced by the 1982 Act. There is, however, a maximum level of damages to be awarded under s. 22 of TULR(C)A 1992 depending on the membership of the union as follows: £10,000 when the union has fewer than 5,000 members; £50,000 where it has between 5,000 and 25,000; £125,000 between 25,000 and 100,000 members; and £250,000 where more than 100,000 belong. Interest may be awarded in addition to the appropriate sum (*Boxfoldia Ltd v National Graphical Association (1982)* [1988] ICR 752). For the union to be liable the action must have been authorised or endorsed by a responsible person, and this is defined as: the principal executive committee; any person empowered by the rules to give endorsement; the president or general secretary; any employed official; or a union committee to whom an employed official regularly reports; any committee of the union (whether employed by it or not); or a group of persons, the purposes of which include organising or co-ordinating industrial action. (TULR(C)A 1992, s. 20).

Unions, however, have power to repudiate actions purported to be taken on their behalf, if they do so 'as soon as reasonably practicable after it has come to [their] knowledge' and if the person who takes the action 'has been notified in writing and without delay'. The principal executive committee or president or general secretary must not, however, thereafter 'behave in a manner which is inconsistent with the purported repudiation' (TULR(C)A 1992, s. 21(5)) (see *Express & Star Ltd v NGA* [1986] IRLR 222, *Thomas v National Union of Mineworkers (South Wales Area)* [1985] IRLR 136, *News Group Newspapers v SOGAT 82* [1986] IRLR 337; see also para. 17.9.1).

The union can only repudiate action by going through a detailed procedure with which many unions may find it unpalatable, if not impossible, to comply. Written notice must be given to the official or committee who is or which has authorised or endorsed the relevant action without delay. Further, the union must 'do its best to give individual written notice of the fact and date of repudiation without delay (i) to every member of the union who the union has reason to believe is taking part, or might otherwise take part, in industrial action as a result of the act and (ii) to the employer of every such member'. Such a notice must include a 'health warning' in the following terms:

> Your union has repudiated any call for industrial action to which this notice relates and will give no support to such action. If you are dismissed while taking unofficial action, you will have no right to complain of unfair dismissal (TULR(C)A 1992, s. 21(2)).

The union will also confirm such repudiation on any request which is made to the union's principal executive committee, president or general secretary within six months of the repudiation by 'a party to a commercial contract whose performance has been or may be interfered with as a result of the act in question'.

Where damages are awarded no execution may be levied against:

(a)   property belonging to union trustees or members otherwise than on behalf of the union;
(b)   the union's political fund or provident benefit funds (TULR(C)A 1992, s. 23).

17.6   RESTRAINT OF TRADE

At common law trade unionism itself is in unreasonable restraint of trade, since unions restrict the freedom of contract between employer and employee, most particularly in the taking of strike action and the closed shop (*Hornby* v *Close* (1867) 2 LR QB 153). The consequence is that the contract of union membership is void and unenforceable. This potentially severe brake on union development was alleviated initially by the Trade Union Act 1871, and TULR(C)A 1992, s. 11 now provides that no trade union *purposes or rules* should be unlawful or unenforceable on this ground of restraint of trade. The provision legalising specifically union *rules* was added in 1974 by the Trade Union and Labour Relations Act because of the potential restriction of the word 'purposes' in *Edwards* v *SOGAT* [1970] 3 All ER 689, where Sachs LJ said that if a rule was 'capricious or oppressive' it might not be made pursuant to the proper purposes of the union. The same immunities also apply for similar reasons to employers' associations (TULR(C)A 1992, s. 128); see discussion in *Goring* v *British Actors' Equity Association* [1987] IRLR 122).

17.7   LISTING

By TULR(C)A 1992, s. 2, the Certification Officer is charged with the duty of keeping a voluntary list of trade unions and employers' associations. The following unions are automatically listed:

(a)   any union registered under the Trade Union Act 1871 on the day of the coming into force of the Industrial Relations Act;

(b)   unions registered under the Industrial Relations Act; and

(c)   TUC affiliated unions.

Outside of this rubric the Certification Officer grants a listing if he is satisfied that the organisation comes within the appropriate definition. He retains a copy of the rules, a list of officers, and its address; and the union pays the prescribed fee. Further, to be registered a union's name must not be too similar to an existing union's appellation nor likely to deceive the public (TULR(C)A 1992, s. 3(4)).

The Certification Officer may remove a union from the list, which is open to public view, if it ceases to fall within the definition or to exist altogether (TULR(C)A 1992, s. 4). An appeal against either refusal to register or against removal from the register lies to the EAT on a point of fact or law (TULR(C)A 1992, s. 9).

There are only minor differences between listed and non-listed unions, in that listing provides:

(a)   a precondition for a certificate of *independence* which itself confers many additional benefits (para. 17.8);

(b)   entitlement to *tax relief* on income and chargeable gains applied for provident benefits (Income and Corporation Taxes Act 1988, s. 467); and

(c)   prima facie *evidence* that the organisation is a trade union, should the matter arise in any legal proceedings (TULR(C)A 1992, s. 2(4)).

17.8   INDEPENDENCE OF TRADE UNIONS

What Parliament will not tolerate is the recognised and certificated existence of a band of people claiming to be an independent trade union when in reality they are unable to offer a vigorous challenge to the employers on behalf of their members whether collectively or individually.

(Kilner Brown J in *Association of HSD (Hatfield) Employees* v *Certification Officer* [1978] ICR 21 at 23H.)

17.8.1   Purpose

An employer who fears that a union is about to gain strength among his employees has several cards up his sleeve to resist it. He may pay more than the union rates in order to convince his workers that there is no need for outside intervention, or he can stimulate and nurture a staff association (a quasi-union active solely within his firm). The latter is often controlled by middle management who do not wish to blot their copy book with senior executives. Such a 'house union' often represents its members only feebly, being rather more of a sophisticated tool of personnel management. This is a frequently adopted tactic in the USA and has been often attempted here. There is no law prohibiting the existence of such weak associations. However, the consequence of their dependence is that they cannot now claim the advantages of important statutory rights.

This idea that such groups of workers do not merit the privileges accorded to unions, derives originally from the ILO Convention Number 98 of 1951, and now under ss. 5 to 9 of TULR(C)A 1992, the characterisation rests with the Certification Officer, with a right of appeal by the union to the Employment Appeal Tribunal on both law *and fact*. It is a vital criterion for conferring the following rights:

(a)   to take part in trade union activities;
(b)   to gain information for collective bargaining purposes (TULR(C)A 1992, s. 181);
(c)   to secure consultation over redundancies and transfers of undertakings;
(d)   time off for trade union duties and activities;
(e)   to appoint health and safety representatives.

17.8.2   Definition of independence

By s. 5 of TULR(C)A 1992 a union is independent if it is:

(a)   not under the domination or control of an employer; and
(b)   not liable to interference by an employer (arising out of provision of financial or material support or by any other means tending towards such control).

The second limitation is the more difficult to apply since it demands a subjective approach and a good deal of speculation about the union's likely future performance. In *Squibb UK Staff Association* v *Certification Officer* [1979] ICR 235, the Court of Appeal determined that the proper question was whether the union was 'exposed to, vulnerable to, or at the risk of, interference'. Shaw LJ continued (at para. 20):

> If the facts present a possibility of interference tending towards control, and it is a possibility which cannot be dismissed as trivial or fanciful or illusory, then it can properly be asserted that the union is at risk of, and therefore liable to, such interference. The risk need be no more than one which is recognisable and capable in the ordinary course of human affairs of becoming an actuality.

There is no statutory requirement that a union be *effective* in its activities to be independent and many trade unions have criticised the Certification Officer for his liberality in granting certificates.

17.8.3   Criteria of independence

Although each case must ultimately depend on its own facts, this 'critique calls for a subtle assessment', and the main criteria are most helpfully set out in the Certification Officer's Report for 1976. This was approved by the EAT in *Blue Circle Staff Association* v *Certification Officer* [1977] ICR 224, and will provide the basis for treatment of the subject here.

(a)   *History:* where the union was set up at the behest of management, the more recent the connection with the employer's coat tails, the less likely it is that the union is genuinely independent therefrom. Thus in the *Blue Circle SA* case (supra) it was important to the EAT's decision refusing independence that the Association had been formed only six months earlier with complete employer control; the change of rules since then was treated as a mere facade. The Certification Officer did, however, state that 'it was not unusual for a staff association to start as a creature of management and grow into something independent' (at 231).

(b)   *Membership base:* a single-company union is more vulnerable to employer interference than one which draws its membership from many sources. This cannot be taken too far, however, since the members of the National Union of Mineworkers derive from a single employer, yet no one would doubt its sturdy independence and effectiveness.

(c) *Finance:* a low bank balance may make a union dependent, while a direct employer subsidy would probably be decisive against independence.

(d) *Employer-provided facilities:* a major influence in the refusal of a certificate in the *Squibb* case (a decision ultimately approved by the Court of Appeal), was the fact that the employer accorded, *inter alia*, time off with pay for its officials; free use of office accommodation; free stationery; and internal mailing facilities. This suggested dependence on the employer, yet the irony is that when a union *has* established its independence, the employer is actively encouraged to make provision of this sort. Generally, the Certification Officer should enquire what would be the effects of the removal of employer-provided facilities from a small organisation.

(e) *Collective bargaining record:* although the Certification Officer has stated that 'a robust attitude in negotiation is regarded as an item on the credit side', yet in *Blue Circle,* the EAT 'deplored any suggestion that a record of bad relations is an index of freedom from domination or control.'

(f) *Organisation and structure:* one of the major elements arguing against independence in *Blue Circle* was the limited role which ordinary members might play in the union. Only employees of three years or more service were eligible for election as area committee representatives; the employer could insist on the withdrawal of credentials of a union representative on the Joint Central Council, the chairman of which was always nominated by the employer. The EAT said:

> The main requirement is that the union should be organised in a way which enables the members to play a full part in the decision-making process and excludes any form of employer involvement or influence in the union's internal affairs.

(See *A. Monk and Co. Staff Association* v *Certification Officer* [1980] IRLR 431.)

The Government Communications Staff Federation which was formed at GCHQ after the infamous ban on union membership instituted by the Thatcher Government was held not to be independent by a five-member EAT in *Government Communications Staff Federation* v *Certification Officer* [1993] IRLR 260. The Federation was determined to be vulnerable to or exposed to the risk of interference by the employer because its continued existence was dependent on the approval of the Director of GCHQ. Further, it was a condition of service that staff were not allowed to be members of other unions and any attempt to affiliate with another union would probably lead to derecognition.

17.8.4 Procedure for determining independence

In deciding on independence the Certification Officer may make such enquiries as he thinks fit and should take into account any relevant information submitted to him by any person including, it appears, the comments of rival unions. At least a month must elapse between application and his decision thereon, to allow proper soundings. While the burden lies on the union to prove its independence (*Association of HSD Employees* v *Certification Officer* [1978] ICR 21) the Certification Officer often helpfully recommends changes which will increase the union's prospects of being considered independent at a later date. However, as the EAT said in *Blue Circle SA* (supra):

There must be a heavy onus on such a body to show that it has shaken off the material control which brought it into existence, and fostered its growth and which finally joined in drafting the very rules by which the control appears to be relaxed.

Although they can make representations to the Certification Officer, rival unions do not have a right of appeal to the EAT against his decisions, however much the characterisation may affect them indirectly (*General and Municipal Workers' Union* v *Certification Officer* [1977] ICR 183).

The Certification Officer also makes periodic checks that a union is maintaining its independence since he may withdraw certificates if the characterisation of the union changes. If doing so, he must notify the union concerned and receive any appropriate representations.

An appeal from the Certification Officer to the EAT takes the form of a full re-hearing and 'the parties are not limited to the material presented to or considered by the Certification Officer in the course of his enquiries. The tribunal considers the facts as they are at the date of the hearing before it' (*Blue Circle Staff Association* v *Certification Officer* [1977] ICR 224). The Certification Officer's position is then very delicate; he is not to be cross-examined on appeal as to the reasons for reaching his decision: rather the Treasury Solicitor should represent his interest as *amicus curiae*.

In order to preserve the single channel of adjudication in the Certification Officer, if the question of independence arises in any legal proceedings (whether at an industrial tribunal, the Employment Appeal Tribunal, the Central Arbitration Committee or the Advisory Conciliation and Arbitration Service), those proceedings must be stayed until the Certification Officer has decided whether or not to issue a certificate of independence (TULR(C)A 1992, s. 8(4)). The certificate is conclusive evidence that the union is independent (s. 8(1)).

17.9   INTERNAL UNION AFFAIRS

17.9.1   Liability for officials

A union can only work through its officials, and the question frequently arises whether it is liable for their actions. They may be employees, independent contractors or mere office holders, and this has the usual consequences concerning unfair dismissal, other statutory rights and the operation of the rules of vicarious liability. The most important question has been how far a union is liable for its shop stewards who purport to act on its behalf. Some unions do not mention their existence in their rule book and the ambit of their authority is rarely defined with precision. A union is a hydra-headed body, and shop stewards often use its name in actions which would be anathema to the central leadership. This issue was particularly vital during the currency of the Industrial Relations Act 1971, when severe sanctions were placed on unions for engaging in certain forms of industrial action, and which sought, in particular, to curb the excesses of unofficial strikes conducted by shop stewards without official backing. In *Heaton's Transport Ltd* v *TGWU* [1973] AC 15, the major test case, although the Court of Appeal thought the respondent union was generally liable for its officials, the House of Lords saw the steward's authority as depending on the rule book and custom and practice. In this case he possessed no authority to call a strike. (See also *General Aviation Services (UK)* v *TGWU* [1976] IRLR 224.) The issue has again become of importance since the Employment Act 1982 withdrew the immunity from union funds (para. 17.5; see now TULR(C)A 1992, ss. 22 and 23).

Although both terms are often used interchangeably, TULR(C)A 1992, s. 119 makes a distinction: an 'officer' is defined as a member of either the governing body of the union or any trustee of any union fund; an 'official' is an officer of the union or of a branch or section of the union, or a person elected within the rules of the union. Therefore, every officer is also an official but not *vice versa*. A union must lodge a list of 'officers' when it applies to have its name entered on the Certification Officer's list (s. 8(4)). If the union does not keep a proper financial record, as required by law, any responsible officer must be prosecuted (s. 12(2)). An 'officer' is the holder of an office created by the union rules, such as president, treasurer, etc. The union's national executive committee and trustees are also included. An 'official' includes any other representative, elected or appointed, whether the position is part of the union's formal constitution or not.

17.9.2 Union accounts

17.9.2.1 Duty to maintain accounts TULR(C)A 1992 lays down detailed rules for the carrying on of unions' and employers' associations' financial affairs, and these have close similarities to the obligations imposed on limited companies and the same end in view, that of protecting their membership.

Primarily the union must make annual returns to the Certification Officer (TULR(C)A 1992, s. 32), including a profit and loss account, a balance sheet, an auditor's report and any other documents or particulars he may require. All must be approved by auditors who should be, as in companies, independent and professionally qualified. Their overriding obligation is to present figures which are a 'true and fair view of the state of the affairs of the trade union and explain its transactions' (TULR(C)A 1992, s. 28(2)).

The union must include in the return a statement of the number of names on the register of names at the end of the period to which the return relates (TULR(C)A 1992, s. 32(3)(d), inserted by TURERA 1993).

17.9.2.2 Members' right of access to their trade union's accounts Many union rule books give members the right to examine the union's books of account, and where there is such a right, the member has a right to be accompanied by an accountant in so inspecting them (*Taylor v National Union of Mineworkers (Derbyshire Area)* [1985] IRLR 65).

The Conservative Government in 1988 were concerned that trade union members had only a right to inspect post-audit accounts, whereas it felt there was a legitimate interest in the current state of the union's financial affairs. The Employment Act 1988 therefore placed upon unions the duty to allow their accounts to be inspected for at least a six-year period following their creation (see now TULR(C)A 1992, ss. 29–31, 45). The right to inspect is given to a member of the union who may be accompanied by a qualified accountant (s. 30(4)). The member, and any accountant who may accompany him, must be allowed to see the records within a 28-day period running from the date the request was made for an inspection. In default, the court may make such order as is necessary for compliance, which will usually be a declaration, but may be an injunction.

A union must provide a summary of the union accounts for individual members (s. 32A). This must include, for example, a statement of the total income and expenditure of the union for the period of the annual return, specify the amount of income gained from membership subscription, state the salary and benefits paid to the general secretary, president and national executive, detail the income and expenditure of the political fund and set out the auditors' report.

The union may publish the statement by printing it in the union journal, or by sending a copy of the statement to each individual member (s. 32A(2)). The union has eight weeks to print this information following the day the annual return is sent to the Certification Officer (s. 32A(1)).

Under TURERA 1993, a union must also include in the annual return details of the salary paid to and other benefits provided to or in respect of:

(a)   each member of the executive (and this includes any person who under the rules or practice of the union may attend and speak at some or all of the meetings, whether that person in fact does so or not, other than persons who attend to provide the executive with factual or professional advice: Sch. 8, para. 42, which inserts TULR(C)A 1992, s. 32(7));

(b)   the president; and

(c)   the general secretary.

17.9.2.3   Access to register of members   The union must also provide a statement of the number of names on the union's register as at the end of the period covered by the return and the number of names not accompanied by the member's address (TULR(C)A 1992, s. 32(3)(d)). The independent scrutineer may either inspect the register of names and addresses of the members of the union or examine a copy of the register, whenever it appears appropriate to do so (TULR(C)A 1992, new s. 49(3)(aa)). The new duty should be performed, in particular, when there is a request to inspect the register or the copy from a union member or candidate within the 'appropriate period' who suspects, on well founded grounds, that the register is not, or at the 'relevant date' was not, accurate and up to date (TULR(C)A 1992, new s. 49(3A)). The appropriate period, defined in a new s. 49(3B), begins with the first day on which a person may become a candidate in the election or, if later, the day on which the scrutineer is appointed, and ends with the day before the day on which the scrutineer makes the report to the union.

17.9.2.4   Pension funds   Specially strict rules apply to union superannuation schemes, in particular to ensure that they are run on actuarily sound bases and are dealt with as separate funds from the general monies of the union (TULR(C)A 1992, s. 38). Thus every union must have its plan examined by an actuary at least every five years (TULR(C)A 1992, s. 40), and the Certification Officer must receive a copy of his report relating to matters set out in s. 40 to TULR(C)A 1992. The most difficult legal problems with funds surround unions' expenditure on political activities.

The duty of trustees of a union pension fund is to act in the best interests of their beneficiaries whatever their political beliefs. A power of investment has to be exercised so that the funds yield the best return by way of income and capital appreciation judged in relation to the risks being considered. This must pay no regard to the trustees' personal views of the companies to be invested in or their moral reservations about the most suitable investments (*Cowan* v *Scargill* [1984] ICR 646).

17.9.2.5   Investigatory powers of the Certification Officer   The Certification Officer may require the production of any relevant documents at any time (TULR(C)A 1992, s. 37A(1)). Further, the Certification Officer may appoint inspectors where either (s. 37B(2)):

(a)   there is evidence to suggest fraud or unlawful use of finance; or

(b)   persons in charge of the union's finances have been convicted of fraud or misconduct in relation to such management; or

(c) the union has not observed the statutory requirements in relation to finances; or

(d) there has been breach of a union rule in relation to finance.

The inspectors must produce a final report to the Certification Officer (s. 37C(1)(b)). This report must be made available to the union, the auditor of the union and to any complaining member. Non-cooperation or hindrance of the investigation is punishable by a fine or six months' imprisonment (s. 45).

17.10 CONTROL OF UNION FUNDS AND PROPERTY

17.10.1 Indemnification by unions of individuals

It was a matter of some controversy before 1988 how far a trade union might use its funds to indemnify members for their criminal conduct, typically such activity as occurs in the course of strike action. In *Drake* v *Morgan* [1978] ICR 56, Park J refused an application for an injunction to restrain the National Union of Journalists from implementing a resolution of its National Executive Committee to pay the fines of certain members who had committed picketing offences during a long-running industrial dispute. The application was refused because the resolution was passed *after* the offences had been committed. The judge said that a *general* prospective indemnity would, however, probably be unlawful. As with other areas of regulation of trade union affairs, the present Conservative Government has put beyond doubt by statute the common law position which was unclear.

Section 15 of TULR(C)A 1992 now renders it unlawful for a union's property to be applied for the purposes of indemnifying individuals for any penalty imposed by a court for:

(a) contempt of court, or

(b) a criminal offence other than an offence which is excepted by order.

If the property of a union is so applied, the union may recover its value from the individual indemnified (s. 15(2)). Since the union itself may have no interest in taking such proceedings and indeed may be controlled by the very persons whose actions have been indemnified, any member who claims that the union is unreasonably refusing to take steps towards recovery may apply to the court for authority to take such proceedings on behalf of the union (s. 15(3)). Such proceedings may be ordered to be taken by the member at the expense of the union. This provision is without prejudice to any other enactment, trade union rule or provision which would otherwise make it unlawful for trade union property to be used in a particular way (s. 15(6)).

17.10.2 Trustees of unions

Union officials in general owe a fiduciary duty to their union. By s. 16 of TULR(C)A 1992, members of trade unions have powers to act against trustees of the union's property in respect of unlawful application of such assets, or trustees who comply with any unlawful direction given to them under the rules of the union. A direction may be unlawful even though it is apparently in strict accordance with the rules. In *Clarke* v *Heathfield (No. 2)* [1985] ICR 606, the NUM ordered its trustees to transfer funds abroad rather than pay a fine for contempt of court. Although this order was given in accordance with the union rules, the trustees were obliged to obey only *lawful* instructions given in accordance with the rules. Consequently, the trustees were removed from office.

In formulating this provision, the Government had in mind the experience of the 1984–5 miners' strike, when a receiver was appointed by the court to, and the union trustees removed from, the National Union of Mineworkers. To bring a claim, the person must have been a member of the union at such time as the relevant property was misapplied or the unlawful direction complied with (s. 16(1)). The court has power to make such orders as it considers appropriate, including:

(a)   requiring that the trustees take all steps specified to protect or recover the union's property;
(b)   appointing a receiver, or in Scotland a judicial factor, of the union's property;
(c)   removing one or more of the trustees (s. 16(3)(c)).

The discretion of the court is circumscribed where the property of the union has been applied, or the trustees are proposing to apply the union's property:

(a)   in contravention of the order of any court; or
(b)   in compliance with any direction given in contravention of a court order.

In such a case, the court must remove all trustees except a trustee who satisfies the court that there is good reason for allowing him to remain as a trustee.

17.11   POLITICAL FUND

17.11.1   Background

The nascent Labour Movement saw as one of the foremost ways of solidifying its power the election for the first time of working-class MPs and representatives on orthodox official bodies. The only way workers could afford this was by union subsidy. In *Amalgamated Society of Railway Servants* v *Osborne* [1910] AC 87, however, the House of Lords decided that the use of union funds for political purposes was illegal, since they were only empowered to pursue those objects permitted in the Trade Union Act 1871 and this was not one of them. This put a significant brake on the development of the Labour Party, but three years later their allies in the Liberal Government secured the passage of the Trade Union Act 1913, which is now consolidated into Part I TULR(C)A 1992. Section 71 permits unions to pursue any object sanctioned by their constitution, although it places restrictions on the funds which may be used for political purposes. Substantial amendments were introduced by the Trade Union Act 1984 and the Employment Act 1988. The Government had threatened to reintroduce the contracting-in system but this was shelved in favour of a requirement that unions must ballot their members every 10 years as to whether they wished to maintain a political fund. So far, all unions which have balloted have returned majorities (usually large ones) in favour of the continuance of the fund. Moreover, some new funds have been established.

17.11.2   Political purposes from the political fund

The most fundamental rule relating to the political fund (TULR(C)A 1992, s. 82(1)(a)) is 'that payments in the furtherance of the political objects to which this chapter applies' can only be made from a separate political fund. Political objects are then defined by TULR(C)A

1992, s. 72(1). The definition covers: contributions to the funds and expenses of a political party; provision of any service or property for a political party; expenditure in connection with the registration of electors; the candidature of any person or the selection of any candidate; the maintenance of any holder of a political office (including an MP, MEP, local councillor or party office holder) and holding a party political conference or meeting (including sending observers or other non-participants). Every form of political advertising is covered. The definition extends to 'the production, publication or distribution of any literature, document, film, sound recording or advertising the main purpose of which is to persuade people to vote' for or against a political party or candidate (TULR(C)A 1992, s. 72(1)(f)). This would probably include a special election edition of a union's journal (cf. *McCarthy* v *APEX* [1980] IRLR 335) and a campaign at election time emphasising the importance of public services, while seeking to persuade people not to vote Conservative (*Paul and Fraser* v *NALGO* [1987] IRLR 413).

The Certification Officer had taken a narrow view of the meaning of 'political' in *Coleman* v *Post Office Engineering Union* [1981] IRLR 427. A member of the respondent union sought to restrain his union branch from affiliating to the Canterbury and District Trades Council Campaign against the Cuts with money out of its general rather than political fund. The Certification Officer, however, thought this was not a political activity since the adjective required expenditure on literature or meetings held by a political party which has or seeks members in Parliament, or directly and expressly in support of such party. It was not enough here that the Committee distributed literature and held meetings at which views on matters of public concern were expressed, and those opinions were of one particular persuasion. The factors weighing against political status included the heterogeneous nature of the Campaign's constituents, and its active support from unions not affiliated to the Labour Party. The overall approach may be contrasted with *Richards* v *NUM* [1981] IRLR 247, where the Certification Officer held that money spent on a march and Parliamentary lobby against Government cuts should have come from the union's *political* fund. Contributions to the funding of the Labour Party Headquarters also had to be borne out of the political fund since this was a political rather than a commercial investment (*Association of Scientific, Technical and Managerial Staffs* v *Parkin* [1984] ICR 127, *Richards* v *NUM* (supra). See also *Paul and Fraser* v *NALGO* [1987] IRLR 413).

Traditionally, unions have been affiliated to the Labour Party even though many members clearly support other parties. In *Parkin* v *ASTMS* [1980] IRLR 188 Woolf J found that there was nothing in principle nor in the respondent union's rules to restrain branches from contributing to the Conservative Party. In the instant case, the branch's request that the money go 'to ensure the help and cooperation of Conservative union MPs' was not an object within the statute.

17.11.3 Establishing the fund

The 1992 Act contains strict safeguards for those who oppose the idea of a union political fund. A resolution to establish the fund must be passed strictly in accordance with the union's own procedure for rule changes, or by a majority of members or of delegates at a meeting called for the purpose. A ballot of members must then be held under rules approved by the Certification Officer and under the scrutiny of an independent scrutineer; he should be satisfied that 'every member has an equal right, and if reasonably possible a fair opportunity of voting and that the secrecy of the ballot is properly secured' (TULR(C)A 1992, s. 74).

The Certification Officer must sanction the political fund rules themselves and his stringent requirements, in particular, protect those who contract out of contribution. Section 82(1) provides that:

(a)   A member may be exempted from the obligation to contribute if he gives due notice, and he must be told of this right.

(b)   The contribution to the political fund shall not be a condition of admission to the union.

There must also be provision for independent scrutineers of the ballot as provided for by TULR(C)A 1992, s. 75.

If the political levy is not kept separate from the general union subscription, each member has a right to know how much of his contribution goes to that purpose (*McCarthy* v *APEX* [1979] IRLR 255, *Reeves* v *TGWU* [1980] IRLR 307).

Under TULR(C)A 1992, s. 73(3), the union must ballot its members at least every 10 years on whether they wish to retain the union's political fund. If it fails so to do, or the resolution is defeated in the ballot, the fund lapses. The union must not confine the voting constituency to those who presently contribute to the fund. Only overseas members may be excluded. All members must furthermore be free to vote without interference or constraint by the union or any of its members, officials or employees. The voter must be supplied with a voting paper 'immediately before, immediately after or during his working hours, and at his place of work or at a place which is more convenient'. He must be given the opportunity to vote by post, and must not incur any cost to himself (TULR(C)A 1992, s. 77).

Section 75 of TULR(C)A 1992 applies to the conduct of political fund ballots, requirements similar to those for union executive elections as inserted by TURERA 1993, so that the ballot must be postal. An independent person is required to store, distribute and count the votes. The scrutineer is required to inspect the register of names and addresses of union members or to examine the copy of the register whenever appropriate and, in particular, when a request has been made by a union member who suspects that the register is not or was not accurate during the 'appropriate period', or by a member who suspects that the register is not or was not accurate and up to date. The union is under an obligation to ensure that nothing in the independent person's appointment would make it reasonable for anyone to call into question that person's independence in relation to the union. The union must respond to all reasonable requests made in carrying out his or her function and ensure that there is no interference with that performance that would make it reasonable for anyone to call into question the independence of the person. The scrutineer's report must include a statement of the name of the person, or persons, appointed as the independent person and, if no one was so appointed, then that fact.

If the political fund lapses because of a contrary vote or no vote being held, the union must at once discontinue the political levy on its members, and any sum collected after that date must be refunded to the member concerned. No property may be added to the fund other than that which accrues to the fund in the course of administering its assets, and the union may, whatever its rules or trust provides, transfer the whole or part of the fund to another union fund.

17.11.4   Protection of the non-contributor

A member who does not contribute to the political fund must not suffer any disadvantage compared to other members save that the rules may exclude him from the control or management of the political fund itself (TULR(C)A 1992, s. 82(1)(c)(ii)). The extent of this exception fell to be considered in *Birch* v *NUR* [1950] Ch 602. The respondent union's rules provided that a non-contributor 'should be ineligible to occupy any office or representative position *involving* any such control or management' of the political fund. When the union's national executive declared invalid on this ground the election of a branch chairman who was a non-contributor, Dankwerts J found this unlawful discrimination, since 'an exempted member might find himself excluded from practically all activities of his branch'. On the other hand, some detriments are too trifling to amount to discrimination. This includes a refund of the political funds contributions in arrears (*Reeves* v *TGWU* [1980] IRLR 307), and a requirement that the employee had to forward his union money himself rather than having the subscription automatically deducted by computer, as it would have been had he contracted in (*Cleminson* v *POEU* [1980] IRLR 1, cf. *Richards* v *NUM* [1981] IRLR 247). On the other hand, in *McCarthy* v *APEX* [1979] IRLR 255, the Certification Officer thought it was illegal that the plaintiff was expected to pay $\frac{5}{13}$ of a penny per week to the fund which was only returned at the end of the quarter. It appears that the general rule extends to non-contributors in non-political matters also, so that when the union attempted to charge exempt members a higher subscription, the rules were broken (*Griffiths* v *NUGMW*, Report of Registrar 1928).

There has been considerable criticism that unions do not make clear to their members their rights not to contribute to the political fund. Indeed, the Government has made threats that it would legislate further in this area. The TUC thus issued guidance to unions that they should each produce an information sheet about the reasons for the fund. The sheet should show how much of a member's subscriptions went to the fund, indicate that the member might contract out of the levy without discrimination and explain how he could do so. Further, unions should not place any obstacle in the way of one who wishes to contract out and should keep exemption forms readily available.

In the event of a successful complaint under these provisions the Certification Officer may order the repayment of political levy improperly demanded and that the member in question be treated as exempt from the levy (TULR(C)A 1992, s. 80). He may make 'such order as he thinks just under the circumstances', which can then be enforced as though an order of the county court (TULR(C)A 1992, s. 82(2), (3) and (4)). An appeal may be made on a question of law to the EAT; in *Reeves*'s case, however, the EAT said it had no jurisdiction to decide that fund rules were in breach of the statute as *ultra vires*, which is a matter for declaration by the civil courts, especially the Divisional Court of Queen's Bench.

17.11.5 Political fund and 'check off'

Section 68 of TULR(C)A 1992 deals with those union members whose subscriptions are collected by their employers under the 'check off' system. The employer must not deduct any part of the political levy from the pay of a member who gives the appropriate certificate in writing that he is exempt from the political levy or that he has sent to the union a notice of objection to paying the levy. Further, the employer must not discriminate between exempt and non-exempt members of the union by operating a check off for the latter whilst denying the facilities to the former. If the employer fails to live up to these duties, the relevant employee may apply to the industrial tribunal for a declaration and an order requiring the employer to take such steps within a specified time to prevent a repetition of such default (s. 68A).

17.11.6   Remedy for breach of rules on political fund ballots

Since the enactment of the Employment Act 1988 a complaint of breach of the political ballot rules may be made to the Certification Officer or the High Court. An application may also be made in the case of a *proposed* ballot which it is claimed will contravene the provisions. A person bringing an application must have been a member at the time of the ballot and must still be a member when he makes such an application (TULR(C)A 1992, s. 79(2)). He has a year in which to bring the application from the date on which the ballot is announced by the relevant trade union (TULR(C)A 1992, s. 79(3)). The provisions of ss. 54 to 56 of TULR(C)A 1992 are also applicable to political fund ballots. This means the following requirements apply:

(a)   A declaration by the Certification Officer or court must specify the provisions with which the union has failed to comply.

(b)   The Certification Officer or court may make an enforcement order requiring that:

(i)   a ballot be held;
(ii)   other steps be taken to remedy the declared failure;
(iii) the union abstain from any acts.

17.12   THE BRIDLINGTON RULES AND INTER-UNION DISPUTES

17.12.1   Status of the rules

The Bridlington Agreement was first adopted by the TUC in 1939 to govern inter-union disputes and curtail 'poaching' of members.

The agreement is binding in honour only. It states:

These Principles, Procedures and accompanying paragraphs . . . are not intended by organisations or the TUC to be a legally enforceable contract.

This follows an extension of the 1939 agreement in 1969. Further amendments were made in 1979 and 1985. A code of practice in single union agreements was also introduced in 1988.

Until recently disputes concerning breaches of the rules were referred to the TUC Disputes Committee consisting of three senior union officials. This would normally be done by the General Secretary following informal conciliation by a senior officer of the TUC. However, Regulation G of the new rules allows the General Secretary to appoint a legally qualified individual as Chair of the Committee. This reflects the increasing complexity and legal regulation of this area.

The general principles of Bridlington needed updating for a number of reasons. The primary reason is TURERA 1993, s. 14 (substituting s. 174 of TULR(C)A 1992), which allows an individual to choose which union he or she wished to join, whether or not that union seeks to recruit members in that area (provided that the individual qualifies to join under the rules of the union). So, for example, a factory worker could insist on joining the GMB despite the TGWU being the recognised union in the factory. However, that individual could not insist on joining, for example, the National Union of Mineworkers, since he or she would not qualify under the union rules to join.

The Bridlington Agreement had also been under strain from the increased tendency of certain unions to negotiate 'single union deals'. The most important impact of this amendment is to make unlawful any decisions of the Disputes Committee for unions to exclude members in breach of the Bridlington agreement.

Principle 1 of the agreement remains largely the same. Unions are encouraged to develop joint working agreements, where appropriate, with other unions.

Principle 2 has been revised to prohibit union campaigns for active recruitment of individuals in an area in which another union is organised. The Principle states:

> All affiliates . . . accept as a binding commitment to their continued affiliation to the TUC that they will not knowingly and actively seek to take into membership the present or 'recent' members of another union by making recruitment approaches, either directly or indirectly, without the agreement of that organisation.

If a union breaches the above principle it will be under a 'normal obligation . . . to offer compensation to the complainant union'.

Principle 3 states:

> No union shall commence organising activities at any establishment or undertaking in respect of any grade or grades of workers on which another union has the majority of workers employed and negotiates terms and conditions, unless by arrangement with that union.

Principle 4 concerns the avoidance of inter-union disputes. It was initially introduced in 1969 as Principles 7 and 8. This establishes a requirement that unions involve the TUC before any industrial action is taken.

A Disputes Committee may make an award with which the parties are obliged to comply with (TUC Rule 12(b)). As mentioned under Principle 2 above, financial compensation may be awarded to the complainant union. A ceiling of two years' loss of contributions is used. In addition, a Disputes Committee may issue a censure against a union. It may require this to be printed in a prominent place in the union's journal.

17.12.2 The Rules and the courts

As noted above, the rules are not legally binding. Consequently, a union cannot legally enforce or appeal against an award made by a Disputes Committee. However, where a Disputes Committee acts *ultra vires* in making a decision this may allow a legal challenge (*Rothwell* v *APEX* [1976] ICR 211). However, in *Cheall* v *APEX* [1983] ICR 398, the Lords rejected the view that any form of self-regulation of competition by trade unions was contrary to public policy.

17.13 TRADE UNION AMALGAMATIONS

17.13.1 The background

As we saw in the historical introduction, the early British unions were mainly organised among skilled craft workers before the general unions began to operate at the turn of the century. This distinction still remains, and a third type of union, the white collar sector, has emerged to add to the multiplicity of unions and the illogicality of their structure. This presents a different picture from that elsewhere in the European Union, where unions are generally organised on industrial lines, with one union per industry and one industry per union. The closest to that degree of exclusive jurisdiction over every occupational group was the National Union of Mineworkers, but even they have competition from the National Association of Colliery Overmen, Deputies and Shotfirers (NACODS) and now the breakaway Union of Democratic Mineworkers. On the other hand, a large company may have to negotiate with 20 or more unions.

Many argue that much better industrial relations would result from the elimination of multi-unionism and a movement towards industrial unions. In recent years this has spurred the development of single-union deals which have been especially favoured by the AEEU.

There have been two major periods of amalgamation; the first was after the easing of the process by the Trade Union (Amalgamations) Act 1917, and saw the formation of the enormous Transport and General Workers Union in 1921 and the General and Municipal Workers Union in 1924. In recent years the second wave has seen giant unions fast absorbing some of their smaller brethren and the 'mega-merger', producing such unions as the Manufacturing, Science and Finance Union out of ASTMS and TASS, and the GMB has solidified its presence in white collar areas by amalgamating with APEX. The hostile environment in which trade unions have found themselves has made merger an increasingly popular option. In 1993, COHSE, NUPE and NALGO merged to form the huge UNISON trade union. Similarly, the NUS and NUR merged to form the RMT, and the EETPU and the AEU formed the AEEU. Further mergers are a distinct possibility in the short to medium term. Whilst these large amalgamations have occurred with increasing frequency, smaller unions have also been more prepared to become part of larger unions. This will reduce a wasteful duplication of resources and help such organisations gain from economies of scale.

This process has, however, done little to create industrial unions, partly because the unions best able to invite mergers have been those with a trade group structure, that is, separate conferences and staffs for different interest groups, so that the concerns of little fish transferors are not submerged in the larger pond of the transferee. These have tended to be the general unions; the TGWU is the best example, and has had more unions join it than any other. The AEEU has allowed its affiliates virtual independence in control of rule making and funds while under its umbrella.

17.13.2   The Trade Union and Labour Relations (Consolidation) Act 1992

There are two ways of proceeding under the 1992 Act, which also applies to unincorporated employers' associations (s. 133), either:

(a)   by *amalgamation* which must be supported by a separate ballot of both transferor and transferee union; or
(b)   a *transfer of engagements* which requires approval only by a vote of the transferor's membership.

Prior to the ballot, each merging union must agree to an instrument of transfer. The Certification Officer must approve the instrument (s. 98(1)). This instrument must comply with Sch. 1 of the Trade Union and Employers' Associations (Amalgamations etc). Regulations 1975 (SI 1975 No. 536) (reg. 4). It must, for example, set out the rules of the new union and give details of the new union, such as the name, purposes, conditions of membership (including members' contributions), structure and procedure for altering the rules. A draft of this document is then usually sent to the Certification Officer for his preliminary views. This document should be accompanied by the current rules of the merging unions.

The draft must be formally approved by the Certification Officer before a ballot can take place. The Certification Officer checks to see that the statutory requirements have been met (s. 98(2)). If so, the draft instrument must be approved (*R* v *Certification Officer ex parte AUEW (Engineering Section)* [1983] ICR 125, CA).

The Act ensures the full and informed participation of union members in that each amalgamating organisation must hold a ballot (s. 97).

In addition to the above, the merging unions must also send a notice of the proposed amalgamation to each union member (s. 99(1)). This must be sent at least seven days before voting begins. Full details of the proposed amalgamation must be given. Approval must be obtained from the Certification Officer before the notice can be sent out (s. 99(5)). This notice must not urge members to vote one way or another (s. 99(5A)). However, this does not stop the union expressing a viewpoint on the proposed merger elsewhere. This is commonly done through the union members' journal. Each member is entitled to vote and the ballot must be fair (s. 100).

The Certification Officer is 'likely to approve' a notice which:

(a) is clearly set out (stating that the document is a Notice to Members under TULR(C)A 1992);

(b) sets out the relevant parts of the instrument of amalgamation;

(c) states that a ballot is required to be held and the majority necessary for the instrument of amalgamation to be approved; and

(d) states that the instrument and notice have been approved by the Certification Officer.

There is a full guide to the above in 'Mergers: A Guide to the Statutory Requirements for Transfers of Engagements and Amalgamations of Trade Unions and Employers Associations', produced by the Certification Officer.

The notice to members must accompany the ballot paper in an amalgamation of unions (s. 99(1)). Every member is entitled to vote (s. 100B). This includes those in arrears and potentially those with a restricted form of membership (such as a student or unemployed members) provided they have an interest in the union.

The ballot in either case must conform strictly to guidelines laid down in statutory regulations. Moreover, any alteration in rules to smooth the progress of the merger must be passed in accordance with the existing provisions for change, so that if the union rule book requires an 80 per cent majority before the negotiations for merger can take place then an 80 per cent majority must be gained.

Where there is a transfer of engagements of a union, the rules of the transferee may, so far as necessary to give effect to the proposed transfer, be altered by the executive committee by memorandum in writing (s. 102(1)) and all its members must be sent a copy of a notice approved by the Certification Officer at least a clear week before voting (ss. 98 and 99) fairly setting out the issues at stake.

17.13.3 Hearing objections

Objections may be made to the Certification Officer by any member of the organisations concerned that the ballot was improperly conducted, or that a vote to reject amalgamation has been construed as in fact favouring it. The Certification Officer must ensure that the rules of the new union are in line with the instrument of transfer, and cannot register it until he has considered such complaint (ss. 101 and 102), allowing six weeks to elapse so that any challenge may be formulated. This requirement is, however, directory only and does not avoid an amalgamation if not followed (*Rothwell* v *APEX* [1976] ICR 211; see also *R* v *Certification Officer ex parte AUEW (Engineering Section)* [1983] IRLR 113).

If the Certification Officer finds a complaint justified, he must so declare and may order steps to remedy the defect. The Certification Officer has a wide discretion as to any order he makes (s. 103(4)). However, he must give reasons for the decision reached (s. 103(4)). One *cause célèbre* concerned a proposed merger between the Association of Cinematograph Television and Allied Technicians and the Association of Broadcasting Staffs, which did not proceed because of allegations that the membership had not been properly informed of the consequences in preparation for the ballot. There is an appeal from the Certification Officer's determination on a point of law to the EAT (s. 104) but, if all goes smoothly, the property of the old union(s) is automatically vested in the new organisation as from the date of registration (s. 105(1)).

By s. 107(1) of the 1992 Act a union may change its name even if there is no provision to this effect in its rule book.

17.14   SECESSION FROM A UNION

Every member of a union has a statutory right to terminate his membership (TULR(C)A 1992, s. 69). In practice, most union rule books expressly allow this. There is an increasing tendency for larger unions to take over smaller ones but allow them to act as an autonomous group within the union. This may involve them in having control of their own resources and budget. In this situation members of the autonomous section may feel that they can secede without too much difficulty. However, AUEW (TASS) (one of the unions which amalgamated into MSF) found that this was not necessarily so (*AUEW (TASS)* v *AUEW (Engineers)* [1983] IRLR 108). The central union rules bind its constituent autonomous affiliates. Consequently, if the central rules do not allow for secession, or only on terms which the autonomous section cannot meet, there is no legal avenue which the autonomous section may have recourse to. However, even if the rules allow a secession, the question of property may in practice stop such a move. The union rules may be important in determining who actually owns certain property. As seen earlier, the smaller union may own assets which are often perceived to be owned by the larger (*News Group Newspapers Ltd* v *SOGAT '82* [1986] ICR 716, CA). Potentially, a seceding section of a union could leave with nothing (*Burnley Nelson Rossendale and District Textile Workers' Union* v *Amalgamated Textile Workers' Union* [1987] ICR 69).

18 The Union and its Members

Is it possible to leave the control over their own membership to the unfettered discretion of the unions themselves without encroaching upon that freedom of the individual worker to be a member of a union which is, and must be, the foundation of any system of industrial relations in a democratic society? Is it, on the other hand, possible to restrict this control without depriving the unions of that autonomy without which they cannot perform their vital role in industrial relations?

(O. Kahn-Freund, *Labour and the Law*, 3rd ed., op. cit. para. 3.1, p. 223.)

18.1 THE RULE BOOK

18.1.1 The rule book and the judges

The basis for legal control within unions is the rule book, on the terms of which the contract of membership is made, although increasingly statute has intervened to make requirements as to the contents of that rule book. The process of incorporation of the rule book into the contract of membership is analogous to the way in which the law implies into the contract of employment any relevant collective bargain. The similarity goes further in that neither contract is an equal agreement, so that the law has often intervened to protect the individual. The vital question in the trade union case is whether in doing so the courts have ignored the need of a properly functioning union for solidarity in collective actions. Lawyers trained in a *laissez-faire* individualism often find this aim difficult to understand and this perhaps explains some of the deep antipathy felt towards judges by the trade union movement and vice versa. Indeed, Professor Kahn-Freund commented, 'the trade unions are entitled to claim, especially in this country, that their norms and institutions express a subculture and that the courts have in the past shown their inability to understand it' (1970 33 MLR 241). For the court's general reluctance to intervene in the affairs of voluntary associations, in particular not enjoining 'mere irregularity in the form of [their] conduct' (*Edwards* v *Halliwell* [1950] 2 All ER 1064 at 1066), does not extend to trade unions because of the powers they are thought to possess. The stereotype of the closed shop has often been referred to and thus Lord Denning saw the rules of the unions not as agreements whose terms the law allows the members to determine, but instead as by-laws, that is:

. . . a legislative code laid down by some members of the union to be imposed on all members of the union. In those circumstances the rules are to be construed not only against the makers of them, but, further, if it should find that if any of those rules is contrary to natural justice . . . the courts would hold them to be invalid.

(See also *Bonsor* v *Musicians' Union* [1956] AC 104.) These can thus be controlled if unreasonable, as in the administrative law of public bodies, and his Lordship went on to suggest that unions wield powers as great as, if not greater than, those exercised by the courts of law: 'They can deprive a man of his livelihood. They can bar him from the trade in which he has spent his life and which is the only trade he knows.' The height of judicial intervention was reached during the prolonged miners' strike of 1984/5, and concerned the rules of the National Union of Mineworkers, but much of the judicial law-making in that dispute has now been codified into, and taken further by, the provisions of the Employment Act 1988 (now TULR(C)A 1992).

The right of action of union members is somewhat restricted by the fitful application to trade unions of the rule in *Foss* v *Harbottle* (1843) 2 Hare 461, well known in company law. This provides that the proper plaintiff in a wrong done to a corporate organisation is the corporation itself, that is, the company and not individual members thereof (see *Cotter* v *National Union of Seamen* [1929] 2 Ch 58). Even if it should be applied to unincorporated associations like unions, its scope is restricted in the trade union area because most union litigation is to restrain *ultra vires* action or infringement of the personal rights of members, both of which are exclusions from the general rule (*Edwards* v *Halliwell* (supra); *Wise* v *USDAW* [1996] ICR 691).

18.1.2 Contents of the rule book

An initial problem in construing union rule books is that they, again like the contract of employment, are often little more than the sum of accretions of custom and practice. Kahn-Freund described them as 'no more than the tip of the iceberg' (*Labour and the Law*, p. 214). Many are ill-drafted. They rarely have the precision beloved by lawyers and Lord Wilberforce judicially acknowledged this in *Heaton's Transport Ltd* v *TGWU* [1973] AC 15:

> Trade unions rule books are not drafted by parliamentary draftsmen. Courts of law must resist the temptation to construe them as if they were; for that is not how they would be understood by the members who are the parties to the agreement of which the terms, or some of them, are set out in the rule book, or how they would be and in fact were understood by the experienced members of the court.

(Cf. *British Actors' Equity Association* v *Goring* [1978] ICR 791.) Custom and practice could thus supplement the written rules 'particularly as respects the discretion conferred by the members upon committees or officials of the union as to the way in which they may act on the union's behalf'. It would also take into consideration in this respect statements made by union officials, committee minutes, agreements with employees and union shop stewards' handbooks. Lord Denning also recognised in *Marley Tile Ltd* v *Shaw* [1980] ICR 72 that, 'the rules of a trade union are not to be construed like a statute. They grow by addition and amendment'. In *Hamlet* v *GMB* [1986] IRLR 293, Harman J said, 'one must not look at them with an eye accustomed to Income Taxes Acts; one must construe them in a more benign and loose way of reading' (see also *Jacques* v *AUEW (Engineering Section)* [1987] 1 All ER 621).

18.1.3 Legal control over the rule book

18.1.3.1 Statute The only rule now specifically guaranteed by statute is that:

In every contract of membership of a trade union, whether made before or after the passing of this Act, a term conferring a right on a member, on giving reasonable notice and complying with any reasonable conditions, to terminate his membership of the union shall be implied.

(TULR(C)A 1992, s. 69)

More generally, the discrimination statutes have some effect on rule books, rendering it unlawful to discriminate on the grounds of race or sex in membership applications, access to benefits, or by subjecting members to any other detriment (RRA 1976, s. 11, SDA 1975, s. 12). A union must not discriminate against EU nationals. A union can, however, put on special training for members of a particular racial group (RRA 1976, s. 38(3)) and reserve positions on elected bodies for members of one sex (SDA 1975, s. 49).

18.1.3.2 Common law Union rules must not be illegal at common law. The following cases illustrate the principles to be applied:

(a) In *Drake v Morgan* [1978] ICR 56, the House of Lords thought that a general union policy to pay the fines of members who were convicted of unlawful picketing would be unlawful, although on the facts they did not declare void an NUJ resolution to indemnify members since it had been passed after one particular event, and did not encourage an assumption that future breaches of the law would be treated in the same way (see now TULR(C)A 1992, s. 15, para. 17.10.1).

(b) In *Porter v NUJ* [1980] IRLR 404, the House of Lords held that a union can validly provide for its members to take strike or other industrial action even though it is in breach of their contracts of employment.

(c) In *Thomas v National Union of Mineworkers (South Wales Area)* [1985] IRLR 136, Scott J decided that while it would be *ultra vires* the rules of the union for its officials to embark upon and finance a form of picketing that would be *bound* to involve criminal acts, it was not *ultra vires* if the picketing was merely *capable* of involving criminal acts. In the instant case a resolution that 'any subsequent fines would be paid by the union' was declared void. The union did, however, have power to provide assistance to members arrested for picket line offences in individual cases, if it thought that this was in the interests of the union and its membership as a whole. In such a case, the court would only intervene if the decision of the union was so perverse that no reasonable person could suppose that it was indeed in the interests of the union.

(d) In *Goring v British Actors' Equity Association* [1987] IRLR 122, an instruction to actors not to work in South Africa was declared *ultra vires* the objects of Equity, the actors' trade union.

18.1.4 Implied terms (in contract of membership)

Like other contracts, the common law implies into union contracts of membership constituted by the rule book terms to which any bystander, asked whether they formed part of it, would say, 'of course'. Thus the courts have required:

(a) reasonable notice to be given of important meetings (*MacLelland v NUJ* [1975] ICR 116);

(b)   that a right to demand a referendum of the union's membership in respect of a general meeting resolution should be exercised in reasonable time (*British Actors' Equity Association* v *Goring* [1978] ICR 791);

(c)   a right for a union disciplinary body to re-open or re-hear a disciplinary matter, not only in the light of fresh evidence but whenever in all the circumstances justice required it (*McKenzie* v *National Union of Public Employees* [1991] ICR 155);

(d)   by way of an implied term, UNISON had power to discipline its members in relation to events before its creation out of a merger of three trade unions (*McVitae* v *UNISON* [1996] IRLR 33).

On the other hand, they have refused to imply:

(e)   that members be entitled to vote by proxy (*Goring's* case);

(f)   that a member should abide by all reasonable directions of the union (*Radford* v *NATSOPA* [1972] ICR 484).

Many unions provide legal advice and representation for members. *Bourne* v *Colodense Ltd* [1985] IRLR 339 raised the novel point on the union's responsibilities to the other party in the event that a union-supported plaintiff is unsuccessful. NATSOPA supported a test case for damages for personal injuries against the defendants who employed one of the union's members. The defendants were successful and secured a costs order of over £50,000. Since the individual plaintiff could not afford such a sum, the defendants sought the appointment of a receiver by way of equitable execution to take proceedings in the plaintiff's name against his union for an indemnity by way of costs. The Court of Appeal considered that this was a proper application. Although no one on behalf of the union had expressly told the plaintiff that the union would give him an indemnity against any costs he might be ordered to pay, the court should have regard to the surrounding circumstances including general practice over many years in such claims. This showed an understanding, amounting to a contract, that the union would discharge any liability for costs which the plaintiff might incur.

A union does *not* owe a duty to individual members to take reasonable care to protect their employment and to safeguard the conditions under which they work. The Court of Appeal thus upheld the striking out of such a claim in *Iwanuszezak* v *GMB* [1988] IRLR 219. The plaintiff had complained that the union was negligent and in breach of contract in that a new shift system introduced by his employer did not suit him. Where the collective interests of the union conflict with the interests of an individual member, the collective interests should prevail.

18.2   TRADE UNION GOVERNMENT

The union rule book, like the articles of association of a company, provides for institutions to govern the union, and often several bodies with conflicting and co-ordinate jurisdiction. The courts must sometimes restrain a union organ which acts *ultra vires*. Conferences and national executives are frequently at daggers drawn, and in a series of cases the courts have been concerned to ensure that the correct union body takes the relevant decision. *Hodgson* v *NALGO* [1972] 1 All ER 15, is a good example of conflicting jurisdictions. NALGO's annual conference resolved against Britain's entry to the EEC, but the union's NEC did a *volte face* and instructed its delegates to the forthcoming TUC to vote *for* entry. Goulding

J granted an injunction to prevent such a vote since this was a matter which the rule book placed in the hands of an annual conference. The court excluded the operation of the rule in *Foss* v *Harbottle* (1843) 2 Hare 461, because the decision had to be taken as a matter of urgency. (See also *National Union of Miners (Kent)* v *Gormley, The Times*, 20 October 1977.)

Other cases have decided that:

(a)   The member has a right to insist that the rules relating to calling meetings and holding ballots are carried out to the letter (e.g. *Young* v *Ladies Imperial Club* [1920] 2 KB 523).

(b)   A strike must be called in proper form. In *Porter* v *NUJ* [1980] IRLR 404, the NUJ was in protracted dispute with provincial newspapers and called a strike of its 8,500 members, and 200 at the Press Association. Some journalists who refused to strike were expelled. The plaintiff succeeded in having this declared void on the ground that while the National Executive had the exclusive right to call a strike, it was obliged to ballot its members if there was to be 'a withdrawal from employment affecting a majority of the members of the union.' Although there were only 8,500 provincial journalists out of 30,000 members, the House of Lords held that the strike affected other members, both those whose earnings would be reduced by the strike, and those who would have to break their contracts of employment in the secondary blacking of local papers. Although it was not clear how many members would be affected, since it was quite likely to be at least half the members, an interlocutory injunction against expulsion was granted on the grounds of the balance of convenience (see now TULR(C)A 1992, s. 62, and para. 21.10.9).

(c)   If the rules of the union provide expressly that strike benefit will be paid to members on an *official* strike called in accordance with union procedures, it is a misapplication of union funds and *ultra vires* the union that funds be paid to those on *unofficial* strike. The decision in *Taylor* v *National Union of Mineworkers (Derbyshire Area)* [1985] IRLR 99 was that union members were entitled not to strike or to cross picket lines without being disciplined. Past custom and practice could not override such a clear rule. The plaintiffs obtained a declaration that the miners' strike called by the NUM was in breach of the Derbyshire Union's rules and went on to seek damages against the union's secretary and treasurer for breach of contract and/or breach of trust for misapplying the union's funds. The rule in *Foss* v *Harbottle* did not apply since the transaction was *ultra vires* the union and could not be ratified by it. Any member of the union had an interest in preserving the funds of the union and was entitled to insist that the union's funds be used exclusively in furthering the objects within its constitution. The defendant union officers had sanctioned payments of over £1.7 million to unofficial strikers and were liable to reimburse the union. Vinelott J refused to give summary judgment, however, since a majority of the members, if they thought it right in the interests of the union to do so, could resolve that no action should be taken to redress the wrong thus done to the union. He took note that 85 per cent of the members of the union were indeed then on strike and that the payments had not been made in conscious breach of the rules or for the personal private benefit of the defendants.

See also *Clarke* v *Chadburn* [1984] IRLR 350, *Hopkins* v *National Union of Seamen* [1985] IRLR 157, *Taylor* v *NUM (Yorkshire Area)* [1984] IRLR 445.

18.3   UNION ELECTIONS AND BALLOTS

Two types of ballots, concerning amalgamations and the political fund, have, for some time, been under statutory control, and have already been described (paras 17.11 and 17.13). The attitude of the law to other instances has changed over time. The Donovan Report rejected compulsory *strike* ballots on the ground that experience in North America showed that they almost always favoured strikes and they gave negotiators less room for manoeuvre. Even so the Industrial Relations Act 1971 sought to use them as a means of mobilising moderate trade unionists. The NIRC could direct that no steps be taken in calling specified industrial action until a ballot of the workers affected had been held, where there were reasons for doubting whether the workers concerned wanted to strike or the effect of the strike would be very serious. This procedure was repealed by the Trade Union and Labour Relations Act 1974. The Conservative Government elected in 1979 sought again to encourage trade union ballots, providing subsidies from public funds by s. 1 of the Employment Act 1980.

The Trade Union Act 1984 went much further and required ballots before industrial action, for the principal executive committee, and on retaining the political fund. The Employment Act 1988 refined and modified these requirements and also introduced the office of Commissioner for the Rights of Trade Union Members to assist ordinary members to enforce the sanctions available (now TULR(C)A 1992, ss. 266 to 271). Further modifications were made by TURERA 1993. We will consider in turn:

(a)   state funds for ballots;
(b)   ballots for the principal executive committee of a union;
(c)   election addresses;
(d)   the independent scrutiny of ballots;
(e)   conduct of the ballot;
(f)   enforcement;
(g)   the right to hold workplace ballots.

18.3.1 State funds for union postal ballots

Money is available to independent unions for secret ballots on the following issues:

(a)   the calling of strikes or other industrial action;
(b)   elections under the union rules or elections to the national executive as required by TULR(C)A 1992;
(c)   elections of work-place representatives;
(d)   amendment to the union rules, although the ballot in itself does not directly have to effect the change of rules (*R* v *Certification Officer for Trade Unions and Employers Associations ex parte Royal College of Nursing of the United Kingdom* [1991] IRLR 258). As in many unions, the ballot in the RCN acted by way of a mandate for change rather than itself *effecting* the rule change without more;
(e)   amalgamations under the 1992 Act;
(f)   the continuation of political funds under TULR(C)A 1992;
(g)   such other purposes as may be specified by the Secretary of State.

The Secretary of State added by statutory instrument in 1982 ballots on an employer's proposal about terms and conditions of employment. The ballot on such a proposal must be confined to union members who are 'affected by' the proposal. The details are worked out in statutory instruments (now Funds for Trade Union Ballots Regulations 1984 (SI 1984 No. 1654) as amended by the Funds for Trade Union Ballots (Amendment) Regulations 1988 (SI 1988 No. 1123) and (Amendment No. 2) Regulations 1988 (SI 1988 No. 2116) and the 1990 Amendment Regulations (SI 1990 No. 2379)). With transitional effect from 1 April

1993, the Funds for Trade Union Ballots Regulations (Revocation) Regulations 1993 (SI 1993 No. 233) revoked the 1988 and 1990 Regulations. On 1 April 1996, state funding for these ballots ceased. Between 1993 and 1996 there was a staged reduction in the payments made to unions:

(a)   by a quarter, if the date of the ballot fell after 31 March 1993 but before 1 April 1994;
(b)   by a half, if the date of the ballot fell after 31 March 1994 but before 1 April 1995; and
(c)   by three-quarters, if the date of the ballot fell after 31 March 1995.

There is no provision for state funds in respect of the election of work-place representatives. The Regulations cover only the election of the president, secretary or treasurer or any other position where the officer will be an employee of the union. Moreover, the ballot does not qualify for payment unless the issues to be decided fall *exclusively* within the named purposes and cover no other matters. The ballot must be returnable by post. The Certification Officer can assume that these stringent conditions have been met unless the contrary is shown. He may also seek the union's assurance to that effect.

If the requirements are satisfied the union may claim to be reimbursed for reasonable costs of stationery and printing for ballot papers, envelopes, explanatory material, and the postal costs of sending them out and their return. Application for payment must be made to the Certification Officer, itemising all expenditure, but the union cannot receive the money until six weeks after the result of the ballot becomes known. This period provides an opportunity for the making of objections that the appropriate conditions have not been met, and the Certification Officer must also himself ensure that:

(a)   The ballot was properly conducted under the union rules unless the breach had no significant effect.

(b)   Where it is a strike ballot, that all participants or likely participants in the industrial action were entitled to vote.

(c)   It was a free and fair ballot, that is, without interference or constraint.

(d)   Every voter had a fair opportunity to vote.

(e)   Any decision not to count the vote was a result of a material change in circumstances during the ballot.

(f)   The count was fair.

(g)   The ballot was conducted so as to secure that the result was indicated solely by counting the number of votes cast directly by those voting.

A union may challenge a refusal by the Certification Officer to make a payment required by the Regulations by seeking judicial review of his decision (e.g. *R* v *Certification Officer ex parte EPEA* [1990] IRLR 398).

Most TUC unions at first refused to accept government funds, even for qualifying ballots which they had held. The Electrical, Electronic, Telecommunication and Plumbing Union and Amalgamated Union of Engineering Workers were exceptions and were threatened with TUC discipline for doing so. All unions have now accepted such funds.

18.3.2   Elections of principal executive committees: the scope of the provisions

By s. 46 of TULR(C)A 1992, every *voting* member of the principal executive committee of a trade union has to be elected every five years by all members of the union. This refers to the main executive body, whatever its name might be (s. 119). The Act overrides anything in the rule book of the union, and a union in default may face an enforcement order in the High Court. The Act also overcomes any provision to the contrary in a contract of employment of an executive committee member about his tenure of that office. There is, however, a special exemption for older, long-serving members, and:

(a)   unions which are solely federations of other unions, e.g. the TUC (TULR(C)A 1992, s. 118(6)(a));

(b)   a union which consists of other unions but with certain individual members who are merchant seamen and a majority of whom are ordinarily resident outside the UK, e.g. International Transport Workers' Federation (TULR(C)A 1992, s. 118(6)(b)).

Section 46 includes:

(a)   the voting members of the principal executive committee and;

(b)   non-voting members of the principal executive committee who attend and speak at some or all of its meetings;

(c)   a union's general secretary and president or any equivalent position.

The rules do not, however, apply to:

(a)   a special register body (see para. 17.3);

(b)   persons who attend a principal executive committee merely to provide:

(i)   factual information, such as members of the union's research department;

(ii)   technical advice;

(iii)   professional advice, such as the union's solicitors and accountants;

(c)   a president or general secretary who:

(i)   is neither a voting member of the principal executive committee nor an employee of the union;

(ii)   holds the position for no more than 13 months;

(iii)   has not held his position within the previous 12 months before he took up the position;

(d)   a person who is a full-time employee of the union, is entitled under the union rules to hold the position until retiring age, will reach retirement age within two years and has been an employee for at least 10 years. He can only be required to stand for re-election in so far as he continues to hold office after reaching retiring age. Thus, if the union retirement age is 65, and the full-time employee was aged 63 years and two months when the Act came into force on 26 July 1988, he will not have to face re-election unless he continues in office after his 65th birthday.

TULR(C)A 1992, s. 57 makes provisions in the case of amalgamated unions.

18.3.3   Conduct of the ballot

The Trade Union and Labour Relations (Consolidation) Act 1992 defines the franchise of voters in such ballots with the broad aim of ensuring that all union members may vote save for 'overseas members' that is, those 'outside Great Britain throughout the period during which the votes may be cast' (s. 60(2)). Within this general principle the union may formulate various constituencies for its executive as it chooses. The executive may thus consist of representatives of particular areas, industries or trade groups, but such representatives may not be indirectly elected by the regional trade group or industry conference as often happened in the past.

The following ground rules are prescribed for such elections. The voter must:

(a)   mark the voting paper in secret;

(b)   vote without interference from or constraint by 'the union or any of its members, officials or employees';

(c)   not be put to any direct cost to himself 'so far as is reasonably practicable';

(d)   be sent by the union a list of candidates and be given a 'convenient opportunity of voting by post'.

As an alternative to a postal vote, a union used to be able to conduct a semi-postal ballot or work-place ballot if the union was satisfied that there were no reasonable grounds to believe that this would not result in a free election as required by ss. 2 and 3 of the Trade Union Act 1984. The Employment Act 1988 ensured that such ballots were to be held by postal voting only. This was achieved by amendment of s. 4 of TUA 1913 (which had itself been amended by TUA 1984) for political fund ballots and the repeal of s. 3 of TUA 1984 (EA 1988, s. 14). Ballot papers must now be both sent out and returned by post. The result of the election must in all cases be 'determined solely by counting the number of votes cast directly for each candidate' (TULR(C)A 1992, s. 51(6)). A single transferable vote system is, however, permitted (TULR(C)A 1992, s. 51(7)).

A union member does not have a right of access to union records of balloting of branches other than his own. Vinelott J held in *Hughes* v *TGWU* [1985] IRLR 382 that there was no provision in the defendant union's rules to this effect and no inherent right outside the rules. The plaintiff's argument that as a union member, he belonged to an unincorporated body and had a proprietary interest in the assets of the union including its documents could not be accepted since s. 2(1)(b) of TULRA 1974 (now TULR(C)A 1992, s. 12(1)) provided that a union's property was to be treated as corporate property. The only right of the member was to know the result of the local ballot.

It is essential to the election process that the union maintain a register of the proper names and addresses of its members, and keep it up to date. This is required by s. 24 of TULR(C)A 1992. The following classes of membership may be excluded from the right to vote: the unemployed, those in arrears with their subscriptions, apprentices, trainees, students or new members of the union. If these categories *are* excluded, all such persons must be left out; it is not lawful to pick and choose, for example between those unemployed members who can and those who cannot vote. The votes must be fairly and accurately counted, but the court may disregard any inaccuracy in counting if it is accidental and insufficient to affect the result of the election.

The union member has a right not to be unreasonably excluded as a candidate for election, and must not be required to join a political party in order to stand. A rule excluding particular groups of members (e.g. Communists or National Front members) is not outlawed (TULR(C)A 1992, s. 47).

A union has no implied power to set aside the result of an election ballot after the result has been declared (*Douglas* v *GPMU* [1995] IRLR 426).

18.3.4   Election addresses

Voting may be influenced if some candidates are given the opportunity to send well-prepared election addresses to members, but other candidates are less well favoured in this matter. By reason of s. 48 of TULR(C)A 1992 the union must:

(a)   give every candidate in the election the right to have an election address in his own words distributed to members entitled to vote; and

(b)   secure so far as is reasonably practicable that a copy of each election address is distributed by post to each voter at his proper address.

No candidate need pay for this privilege, and no modification of any election address submitted by a candidate must be made by the union save:

(a)   at the request of or with the consent of the candidate;

(b)   where modification is necessarily incidental to the method adopted for producing that copy.

The same method of producing copies must be applied to each election address and no facility or information should be given to one candidate but not to others in respect of:

(a)   the method by which copies of the election addresses are produced (for example by photocopying or printing); or

(b)   the modifications which are necessarily incidental to that method (TULR(C)A 1992, s. 48(5)(b)).

The union should also as far as is reasonably practicable secure the same facilities and restrictions for all candidates in relation to:

(a)   preparation of election addresses;

(b)   submission of election addresses;

(c)   length of election addresses;

(d)   modification of election addresses (for example, in order that they follow a standard format); and

(e)   the incorporation of a photograph or any other matter not in words (TULR(C)A 1992, s. 48(6)).

There may be restrictions, so long as they are applied equally to all candidates, in respect of:

(a)   the length of the address, subject to a minimum of 100 words; and

(b)   photographs and other non-verbal material (such as diagrams or drawings) (TULR(C)A 1992, s. 48(3)).

The time for submission of election addresses must be no later than the time for submitting candidatures (TULR(C)A 1992, s. 48(2)).

Only the candidate who formulates the election address will be subject to civil or criminal liability in respect of its publication.

18.3.5 Independent scrutiny of ballots

Several cases of alleged malpractice in union elections were taken up by the Press in the mid-1980s. Concern was expressed at cases of completion of voting papers by the wrong person, manipulation of the membership register and copying ballot papers.

By ss. 49 and 75 of TULR(C)A 1992, both political fund ballots and principal executive committee ballots must be independently scrutinised.

18.3.5.1 Duties of independent scrutineer Each union must appoint a qualified independent scrutineer, and give him the duties set out in s. 49(3) or s. 75(3). He may be given 'additional functions'. The union should ensure that it would be unreasonable for any person to call the scrutineer's independence into question by reason of:

(a) anything in the terms of the scrutineer's appointment;
(b) interference with the carrying out of his function.

Further, the union must comply with all reasonable requests made by the scrutineer for the purposes of or in connection with the carrying out of his functions (s. 49(7) or s. 75(7)).

The scrutineer must satisfy conditions set down in an order made by the Secretary of State for Employment by statutory instrument subject to annulment by resolution of either House of Parliament (s. 49(2) or s. 75(2)). The following may be scrutineers:

(a) solicitors or accountants qualified to be an auditor; or
(b) the Electoral Reform Ballot Services Ltd, the Industrial Society or Unity Security Balloting Services Ltd (Trade Union Ballots and Elections (Independent Scrutineer Qualifications) Order 1993 (SI 1993 No. 1909).

The scrutineer must:

(a) supervise the production and distribution of all voting papers;
(b) be the person to whom the voting papers are to be returned;
(c) retain custody of all voting papers:

(i) for one year beginning with the announcement by the union of the result of the ballot or election; and
(ii) if an application is made under s. 79 of TULR(C)A 1992 or ss. 25 and/or 26 of TULR(C)A 1992, for the period after the end of that year until the Certification Officer or the High Court authorises disposal of the papers (TULR(C)A 1992, s. 49(3)(d)(ii) or s. 75(3)(d)(ii)).

18.3.5.2 Independent scrutineer's report The scrutineer's report must state:

(a) the number of voting papers distributed;
(b) the number of voting papers returned;
(c) the number of valid votes cast for each proposition or candidate, as the case may be;
(d) the number of spoiled or otherwise invalid voting papers.

He must state whether he is satisfied that:

(a)   there are no reasonable grounds for believing that there was any contravention of a requirement imposed by statute;

(b)   there were proper security arrangements for production, storage, distribution, return or other handling of the voting papers and the counting of votes; he must be satisfied that the arrangements were all that was reasonably practicable for the purpose of minimising the risk of unfairness or malpractice;

(c)   he has been able to carry out his functions without interference (TULR(C)A 1992, s. 52(2)(c) or s. 78(2)(c)).

The union must not publish the result of the ballot or election before it has received the scrutineer's report. That report must also be sent within three months to every member of the union to whom it is reasonably practicable to send such a copy. Alternatively, the union must take such other steps for notifying members of the contents of the report as is their practice when matters of general interest to all members need to be brought to their attention (TULR(C)A 1992, s. 52(4) or s. 78(4)). If the union does not send a copy of the report to each member, it must include a statement that the union will on request supply any member with a copy of the report either free of charge or on payment of a reasonable fee.

18.3.6   Enforcement

To have *locus standi* to complain, whether in the court or before the Certification Officer, where an election has been improperly held, the complainant must have been a member on the date of the election and when he makes his application to the court. When the complaint is that an election has *not* been held, the vital date is when the application is made. In any event, the action must be taken within a year from the default. The declaration should specify the provisions with which the union has failed to comply, and the court may make an enforcement order unless it considers it inappropriate to do so. Such an order will require the union to hold an election, to 'take such other steps to remedy the declared failure as may be so specified within a certain time', or to abstain from certain acts in the future. The order may be enforced by contempt proceedings (TULR(C)A 1992, s. 54(1)).

The procedure before the Certification Officer is less formal. He has express power to regulate his own procedure, but should 'ensure so far as is reasonably practicable that every application . . . is determined within six months' (TULR(C)A 1992, s. 55(6)). If the Certification Officer requests information from any person and it is not forthcoming, he may determine the application without it. The making of an application to the Certification Officer does not 'prevent the applicant or any other person, from making a subsequent application to the court . . . in respect of the same matter'. If he does so, the court shall 'have due regard to any declaration, reasons or observations of the Certification Officer' (TULR(C)A 1992, s. 56(2)). On the interrelationship between applications to the court and to the Certification Officer, see *Lenahan* v *UCATT* [1991] ICR 378.

An executive committee member who fails to gain re-election is allowed a period of grace up to six months so that effect may be given to the results of the election (TULR(C)A 1992, s. 59). Nothing in Chapter IV of the Act affects the validity of anything done by the Executive (TULR(C)A 1992, s. 61(2); see also s. 46(2)).

18.3.7   Judicial review of union elections

The courts have often intervened to ensure that elections for union offices are properly held and that candidates are not deprived of their rights to stand for office. The most serious instance of corruption was the systematic ballot rigging by Communists in the Electricians Trade Union in the late 1950s, culminating in a protracted fraud case (*Byrne* v *Chappell,* unreported). More commonly the civil courts have intervened to prevent breaches of: (a) the statutory requirements concerning the political fund; (b) the union rule book; or (c) the rules of natural justice (e.g. *Birch* v *NUR* [1950] Ch 602).

In *Leigh* v *NUR* [1970] Ch 326, for example, the general secretary of the respondent union used a rule which stated that 'no circular will be authorised for distribution until the nomination has been received and approved' to give himself power to reject the applicant's nomination altogether. The court decided that the rule concerned only administrative tasks, and avoided the prohibition.

A whole election is likely to be declared void only if it was not 'conducted substantially in accordance with the procedure laid down in the rules'. The fact that 600 out of 29,000 members were without papers was not sufficient to overturn the election in *Brown* v *AUEW* [1976] ICR 147.

The only remedy for breach of the obligation to allow a trade union official to take up his position for reasons of economics is damages for breach of his notice rights in the contract of employment. There is no requirement of natural justice. The position of a trade union as prospective employer is no different from that of any other employer (*Meacham* v *Amalgamated Engineering and Electrical Union* [1994] IRLR 218).

18.4 THE RIGHT TO JOIN A TRADE UNION

Unions are in essence voluntary associations like the Boy Scouts or a youth club and in few such organisations is there an automatic right to join. However, in the case of unions, many urge that different considerations should obtain, particularly in the case of a pre-entry closed shop, since failure to be admitted into the appropriate union may mean inability to get a particular job at all. We will consider common law and then statutory attempts to subject this power to legal control.

18.4.1 The common law and the 'right to work'

In controlling admission the difficulty for the ordinary common law is that the prospective union member cannot claim that any contract has been broken by reason of refusal of his application. His grudge is rather that there *is no* contract of membership and he wants one. He complains of deprival of an expectation for which, in the absence of a previous relationship or tort, there is normally no legal remedy. In an Irish case on this point, the judge commented appositely (*Tierney* v *Amalgamated Society of Woodworkers* [1959] IR 254 at 258):

> He is certainly not deprived of any right of property nor is he deprived of any other right, be it work or otherwise, which he had before. He is, at most, only deprived of acquiring a right.

The Court of Appeal, and in particular Lord Denning MR, have, however, in several cases suggested that the so-called *'right to work'* provides a basis for judicial control of the admission process and that natural justice applies to such dashing of legitimate expectations.

The genesis of this principle can be traced to the case of *Nagle* v *Feilden* [1966] 2 QB 633. The plaintiff claimed that she had been refused a trainer's licence by the Jockey Club solely because she was a woman, notwithstanding her experience in the sport and the fact that her head lad was accorded such permission. The power of the defendant resides in the rule that no horse may be entered for a race on the flat unless the Club has licensed its trainer. The Court of Appeal would not accept that the plaintiff's claim was grounded in contract as she had contended, but called in aid the unruly horse of public policy. The Master of the Rolls' dicta, relying *inter alia* on the seventeenth-century decision in the *Tailors & Co. of Ipswich* 1614 11 Co Rep 53a, ranged wider than the facts before him when he said (at p. 646g):

> When an association, who have the governance of a trade, take it upon themselves to licence persons to take part in it, then it is at least arguable that they are not at liberty to withdraw a man's licence — and thus put him out of business — without hearing him. Nor can they refuse a man a licence — and thus prevent him from carrying on his business — in their uncontrolled discretion. If they reject him arbitrarily or capriciously, there is ground for thinking that the courts can intervene.

The limitations of the *Nagle* case as authority for closed shops should be noted: the decision related only to failure to strike out the plaintiff's pleadings as disclosing no cause of action. The facts did not concern a trade union, although dicta did dwell on this area. It appears to run contrary to the House of Lords decision in *Weinberger* v *Inglis* [1919] AC 606, which held it lawful for the Stock Exchange to refuse membership to a broker on the grounds of his German origins, and also fails to deal with the proper remedial structure. (See also *Boulting* v *ACTT* [1963] 2 QB 606, and *Faramus* v *Film Artistes' Association* [1964] AC 925.)

Lord Denning repeated his remarks in *Edwards* v *SOGAT* [1971] Ch 354, a trade union expulsion case, and addressed himself specifically to a closed shop where a union has power to ensure that a man does not work in a particular trade. He said (at 376B):

> I do not think that the trade union or any other trade union can give itself by its rules an unfettered discretion to expel a man or withdraw his membership. The reason lies in a man's right to work . . . The courts of this country will not allow so great a power to be exercised arbitrarily or capriciously or with unfair discrimination, neither in the making of rules nor in the enforcement of them . . . A man's right to work at his trade or profession is just as important to him as, perhaps more important than, his rights to property.

Such a decision would be capricious if based on personal animosity, spite or pure prejudice, but might be legitimate if it seeks to cut down the number of entrants to a trade or industry for valid reasons. Again, this was strictly *obiter* since the only issue before their Lordships was the amount of damages for an admittedly unlawful *expulsion*. It did, however, serve to clarify somewhat the character of the action. Lord Denning thought the union could not rely on its immunity from restraint of trade claims since the union's action was *ultra vires* in destroying the right of the individual to earn his living. Sachs LJ drew a distinction that 'a rule that enabled such capricious and despotic action [cannot be said to be] proper to the "purposes" of this or indeed of any trade union'. This argument is now unavailable by reason of the widening of the restraint of trade immunity to include rules specifically. (See also *Greig* v *Insole* [1978] 3 All ER 449.)

The 'right to work' doctrine has never been applied as ratio to prevent unreasonable refusal of admission to a union which has a closed shop. This is probably only a matter of time since there are weighty *obiter dicta* available for a judge so inclined to draw on. It would have to meet the objection raised by Megarry V-C in *McInnes* v *Onslow Fane* [1978] 3 All ER 211 (not a trade union case), that, 'the right to work can hardly mean that a man has a "right" to work at whatever employment he chooses, however unsuitable he is for it'. Further, Professor Hepple (1981 10 ILJ 84) has directed trenchant criticism at the whole concept. The provisions of what is now TULR(C)A 1992, s. 174 (see below) mean that it is less likely to be pressed into service, although the statute expressly does *not* exclude the development of the common law (see discussion in *Goring* v *British Actors' Equity Association* [1987] IRLR 122).

18.4.2 Statute

The Trade Union and Labour Relations (Consolidation) Act 1992 accords the employee a right not to be *unreasonably* refused, or excluded from, membership of a trade union. This right remains alongside the more general provisions on unjustifiable discipline by trade unions. *Unreasonable delay* by the union in determining an application to a union is deemed to be tantamount to refusal of an application, but it is a nice point as to what delay is unreasonable.

There is, however, no doctrine of 'constructive expulsion'. In *McGhee* v *TGWU* [1985] IRLR 198, the applicant argued that this was similar in concept to constructive *dismissal*. He had resigned his membership as a consequence of being treated as in arrears when he had not paid a fine imposed for criticising the union's leadership, but was not entitled to claim under what was then s. 4 of the Employment Act 1980. The applicant can, however, also claim if he is offered membership only of a particular, unfavourable, class of membership, according to *Kirkham* v *NATSOPA* [1981] IRLR 244, but the refusal of a union to allow a member additional shifts in the printing industry did not mean that he had thereby been refused membership of a branch or section of the union (*Goodfellow* v *NATSOPA* [1985] IRLR 3). Exclusion does not include suspension from the benefits of union membership (*NACODS* v *Gluchowski* [1996] IRLR 252). A claim may fall within TULR(C)A 1992, s. 174 even if the applicant has no specific job in view but is merely seeking employment in a closed shop industry (*Clark* v *NATSOPA* [1985] IRLR 494).

'Unreasonableness' is not defined by statute, so that tribunals use their expertise in construing the same word as for unfair dismissal purposes. They are, indeed, instructed in the same way to examine each case in accordance with 'equity and the substantial merits' (TULR(C)A 1992, s. 174(6)). The Act provides that it is not necessarily reasonable action for the union to abide by its own rules, nor necessarily unreasonable to break them.

Any contracting out of the section is void (TULR(C)A 1992, s. 288(1) and (2)), although the services of an ACAS Conciliation Officer are available, and a settlement reached with his aid is binding. Both provisions have their counterparts in the unfair dismissal jurisdiction. It is not necessary to exhaust all the union's internal procedures to use the tribunal.

The remedial mechanism is of some complexity and has more stages than in unfair dismissal. It begins with a declaration of unreasonableness. The award made by the industrial tribunal at this stage serves to compensate for the loss sustained by the union's earlier refusal subject to the usual duty of the worker to mitigate his damage, and to reduction if the complainant caused or contributed to the union's action (TULR(C)A 1992, s. 176(5)). The maximum award is 30 weeks' pay plus the maximum compensatory award for the time being in respect of unfair dismissal (TULR(C)A 1992, s. 176(6)).

If the union refuses to abide by the tribunal's initial declaration of unreasonableness, having been given four weeks to put matters right, the sanction becomes more severe. The complainant may now go straight to the EAT, within six months of the original refusal giving what is usually an appeal body its only original jurisdiction (TULR(C)A 1992, s. 176(2)). The judge and two laymen may then award whatever sum they consider just and equitable in all the circumstances and this is likely to be measured by the loss of future earnings caused by the employee losing a job in a closed shop employment. The maximum is now 52 weeks' pay in addition to the highest award available in an industrial tribunal (TULR(C)A 1992, s. 176(6)) and in the case of an award by the EAT shall not be less than £5,000. There are four potential heads of compensation: loss of earnings during the period of unemployment; net loss of earnings resulting from the dismissal; loss of earning opportunity generally as a result of being denied union membership; and non-pecuniary loss. In *Howard* v *NGA* [1985] ICR 101 the EAT reduced the award by 15 per cent because the applicant had contributed to the refusal of membership by the union when he took a job with a company which he knew subscribed to the closed shop agreement whilst his application for union membership was under consideration (see also *Saunders* v *Bakers, Food and Allied Workers' Union* [1986] IRLR 16, *Day* v *SOGAT (1982)* [1986] ICR 640). Unusually, there is an appeal on questions of both *fact and law* to the EAT.

The Trade Union and Labour Relations (Consolidation) Act 1992 provides in this respect that the rights it confers are in addition to and not in substitution for any other right whether by statute or at common law. Three other statutes incidentally impinge on the right of admission. The Race Relations Act 1976, the Sex Discrimination Act 1975 and the Disability Discrimination Act 1995 make it illegal to discriminate against an applicant for a trade union or employers' association on the ground of race, sex or disability. In addition, the 1992 Act states that if a union has a political fund, it must not make contribution thereto a condition of admission nor discriminate against a non-contributor (para. 17.11.4). Sections 64 to 67 provide a general prohibition of unjustifiable discipline of trade union members (para. 18.5.5).

18.4.3 Invalid admissions

The courts have insisted that any admission be made in accordance with the union's rule book, and have tended to construe rules strictly. Thus in *Faramus* v *Film Artistes' Association* [1964] AC 925, the union had a rule that no person who had committed a criminal offence was eligible for membership. The House of Lords thus decided that the plaintiff, who had been convicted of two offences in the Channel Islands, was not, and never had been, a member, even though he was treated as such for eight years. Similarly in *Martin* v *Scottish Transport and General Workers Union* [1952] 1 All ER 691, it was held that the plaintiff's 'temporary membership' was illegal since there was no such status contemplated by the rule book. More procedural protection is available for one admitted who seeks readmission, since he has a contractual right to the observance of the rule book in any procedure that may be applied to him and these form the next part of the discussion.

18.5 DISCIPLINE AND THE RULE BOOK

18.5.1 Construing union disciplinary rules

All unions have some provision for disciplining members. This is no different from most organisations but is especially necessary to maintain union solidarity, and to ensure that the union can 'deliver' on industrial agreements it has entered into. Any such disciplinary action must be carried out in accordance with the union's own rule book, and these are read restrictively in order to protect the member. Breaches are usually restrained by way of an injunction or a declaration that an offending action is void, and damages are occasionally awarded. Most cases arise in connection with expulsion, the most serious disciplinary step which in the closed shop in the past entailed loss of job, and which is likely in other cases to have serious consequences.

The judges are reluctant to allow a domestic union tribunal to be final arbiters of legal questions of *construction* of its constitution, and also intervene if there is no evidence to support a finding of fact found by any disciplinary committee (*Lee v Showmen's Guild* [1952] 2 QB 329, also *Partington v NALGO* [1981] IRLR 533). Thus in *MacLelland v NUJ* [1975] ICR 116, where the appellant was disciplined for failing to 'attend' a union meeting as required by its rule book, the court avoided this result on the ground that 'attend' meant only that the member should sign on, and not that he remain glued to his chair for the whole assembly. (On the construction of the union rule book as to appeals, see *Loosley v National Union of Teachers* [1988] IRLR 157.)

In *Kelly v NATSOPA* (1915) 31 TLR 632, the court held that taking a part-time job could not constitute 'conduct prejudicial to the union's interests', which the union's own tribunal had decided it was. Similarly, general rules providing discipline for conduct injurious to the union do not extend, for example, to a refusal to do overtime which was persisted in after the member had been censured once.

18.5.2 Natural justice

18.5.2.1 General Trade union bodies must comply with the rules of natural justice because 'although the jurisdiction of a domestic tribunal is founded on contract, express or implied, nevertheless the parties are not free to make any contract they like' (*Breen v AEU* [1971] 2 QB 175). It is thus impossible to exclude, even by an express and unambiguous rule, the right of a member to be heard in his defence before disciplinary action is taken against him, and Lord Denning MR made this general statement about a domestic union tribunal in *Breen:*

> Even though its functions are not judicial or quasi-judicial but only administrative, still it must act fairly. Should it not do so the courts can review its decisions just as they can review the decisions of a statutory body. The courts cannot grant the prerogative writs such as *certiorari* and mandamus against domestic bodies, but they can grant declarations and injunctions which are the modern machinery for enforcing administrative law.

This applies not only to the deprival of rights of members, but also when their legitimate expectations are dashed (*Schmidt v Home Secretary* [1969] 2 Ch 149, *McInnes v Onslow Fane* [1978] 3 All ER 211).

The content of natural justice 'depend[s] on the circumstances of the case, the nature of the enquiry, the rules under which the tribunal is acting, the subject matter that is being dealt with and so forth' (*Russell v Duke of Norfolk* [1949] 1 All ER 109 at 118). Professor Kahn-Freund thought natural justice was no more than 'elementary rules of decency'. The principles were codified in the Industrial Relations Act 1971 which also accorded the right to an aggrieved member to apply to an industrial tribunal for redress.

The common law requires the following elements which cannot be excluded by union rules (*Radford v NATSOPA* [1972] ICR 484 at 491). The withdrawal by a union of nomination for the position of delegate to a Labour Party Regional Conference without a hearing was not, however, a breach of natural justice (*Hudson* v *GMB* [1990] IRLR 67).

18.5.2.2 Notice A member must be given *notice of any charge* he has to meet and the potential penalties. In *Annamunthodo* v *Oilfield Workers Trade Union* [1961] AC 945, the plaintiff's expulsion from the defendant union was declared void because he had no knowledge of the precise charge on which it was based. Such notice must also be specific except where the case is simple and already well known to all (*Stevenson* v *URTU* [1977] ICR 893), and even then the member should have sufficient time to prepare his defence.

18.5.2.3 Opportunity to be heard The member must be given the chance to reply to any allegations against him even though the case may superficially appear unanswerable. The hearing must thus be held at a time reasonably convenient to him, although if the member decides not to take the opportunity offered that is his misfortune (*Annamunthodo*'s case). The hearing should normally be conducted orally (see e.g. *University of Ceylon* v *Fernando* [1960] 1 All ER 631, *R* v *Hull Prison Board of Visitors ex parte St Germain (No. 2)* [1979] 3 All ER 545) and allow the member to call evidence on his own behalf and cross-examine witnesses for the 'prosecution'.

18.5.2.4 The rule against bias The normally very strict rules against bias in judicial or quasi-judicial proceedings are modified in the case of domestic tribunals, since often the roles of prosecutor and judge are expressly and necessarily combined under the rule book. The rather less stringent principle which applies in this situation was summarised by Viscount Simon in *White* v *Kuzych* [1951] AC 585:

> What those who considered the charge against the respondent and decided that he was guilty ought to bring to their task was a will to reach an honest conclusion after hearing what was urged on the other side and a resolve not to make their minds up beforehand on his personal guilt, however firmly held their conviction as to union policy and however strongly they had joined in previous adverse criticism of the respondent's conduct.

Here the plaintiff was expelled from the union because of his vehement opposition to its closed shop policy, but the fact that those hearing the complaint against him had already spoken out in favour of the principle did not disqualify them. They were not expected to have 'the icy impartiality of Rhadamanthus'. The member must instead 'put up with the fact that, as members of the union, and as officers, the members of the tribunal itself are rightly and properly concerned to uphold the union and its officers'.

On the other hand, blatant instances of prejudgment should be avoided. In particular, justice must be seen to be done. In *Roebuck* v *NUM (Yorkshire Area)* [1977] ICR 573, the bystander would not have thought it was. The plaintiff was disciplined for allegedly misleading the respondent union's solicitors in a case involving its area president, Arthur Scargill. Yet it was the latter who presided over both the initial disciplinary process and the confirming Area Council after he had already condemned the parties. This action was held to break the general requirement to act fairly and it made no difference that the union rules generally required the president to chair the meeting since he could vacate it in special circumstances and should have done so here. Moreover, in *Taylor* v *National Union of Seamen* [1967] 1 All ER 767, where the union's general secretary dismissed an official and then presided at his appeal, his decision was quashed (see also *Hamlet* v *GMB* [1986] IRLR 293, *Longley* v *NUJ* [1987] IRLR 109).

18.5.2.5 Legal representation The cases on whether natural justice requires the individual to have the right to legal representation before union and other voluntary association organs are somewhat difficult to reconcile. There is authority for the following propositions:

(a) An accused has no absolute right to be represented before a domestic tribunal (*Enderby Town FC* v *Football Association* [1971] 1 Ch 591, *R* v *Secretary of State for the Home Department ex parte Tarrant* [1984] 1 All ER 799).

(b) He may have a qualified right to representation where an adverse decision may ruin him (*Pett* v *Greyhound Racing Association Ltd (No. 1)* [1969] 1 QB 125).

(c) Even that qualified right may be taken away by the rules of the union or association (*Enderby Town*).

(d) The fact that difficult points of law are involved is no ground for seeking representation before a tribunal because the matter can be referred to the court instead.

18.5.2.6 Miscellaneous Internal union tribunals are not generally required to give reasons for decisions in the ordinary case (*Weinberger* v *Inglis* [1919] AC 606). It is unlikely that a fair appeal can remedy an unfair procedure at first instance (*Leary* v *NUVB* [1971] Ch 34 at 49; see *Calvin* v *Carr* [1979] 2 All ER 440).

18.5.3 Ousting the jurisdiction of the court at common law

All the above rules would be futile if the union could ensure by its own rules that its members did not pursue the legal redress given by them. The courts have thus been vigilant to preserve recourse to themselves and to ensure that a union rule ousting their jurisdiction has no effect (this is now supplemented by TULR(C)A 1992, see para. 18.5.4). Lord Denning MR put this very clearly in *Lee* v *Showmen's Guild* [1952] 2 QB 329:

If the parties should seek by agreement to take the law out of the hands of the courts and put it into the hands of a private tribunal without any recourse at all to the courts in case of error of law then the agreement is to that extent contrary to public policy and void.

(See also *Leigh* v *NUR* [1970] Ch 326, *Lawlor* v *UPW* [1965] Ch 712 at 733.)

Less clear-cut is the validity of a rule that the union's internal disciplinary procedures must be exhausted before the member can apply to the court. For the courts recognise that there are many advantages in encouraging voluntary bodies to develop fair internal procedures and that they would be rendered nugatory if too easily by-passed. Thus, in *Leigh* v *NUR* [1970] Ch 326, Goff J said that while the court 'is not absolutely bound by it', the plaintiff would have to show cause why a court should interfere with such a provision in the rule book. He continued that even if the rules do not *require* that domestic procedures be used as a preliminary, the court might choose to stay proceedings to see whether the matter could be dealt with internally, unless: the domestic proceedings were irretrievably biased (*White* v *Kuzych* [1951] AC 581); there is a serious point of law (*Radford* v *NATSOPA* [1972] ICR 484) or fraud at issue; or the internal procedures would involve excessive delay. The Chancery Division went further in *Esterman* v *NALGO* [1974] ICR 626 to hold that a plaintiff may bring an action in the court to stop *impending* disciplinary proceedings if he can show that there is no lawful basis for them. The strength of internal procedures lies in fact-finding and discretion-exercising; those on the spot are in a better position to perform these functions than High Court judges.

18.5.4   Access to the courts

Section 63 of TULR(C)A 1992 provides a new right for union members not to be denied access to the court to pursue a grievance against their union. Where court proceedings relate to a grievance which a member began to pursue against his union more than six months before applying to court, the court must not: (a) dismiss, (b) stay or sist, or (c) adjourn, the proceedings on the ground that further proceedings for resolving the grievance are available under the union's rules. Determination or conciliation in the section extends to any steps for the purpose of or in connection with any: (a) appeal, (b) review, or (c) reconsideration of a decision, under the rules of the union. The union cannot circumvent the principle by declaring the member's complaint to be invalid and by sitting on it. If the application to the union for determination or conciliation is invalid, the union must so inform the member, within 28 days of its having received such application, of all respects in which the application contravened the requirements of those rules.

18.5.5   Unjustifiable discipline of members by a union

A union is prohibited from disciplining a member for not taking part in industrial action notwithstanding that a majority of that member's colleagues voted in favour of the action in a properly held ballot, and this is naturally seen by the unions as a threat to traditional union concepts of solidarity.

18.5.5.1   The grounds   The most important grounds (TULR(C)A 1992, s. 65(2)) on which discipline of a trade union member is to be taken as unjustifiable are:

(a)   failure to support a strike or industrial action by members of his own trade union or any other;

(b)   failure to participate in a strike or industrial action by members of his own trade union or any other (on the definition of 'industrial action', see *Fire Brigades Union* v *Knowles* [1996] IRLR 617);

(c)   indication of opposition to a strike or industrial action by members of his own trade union or any other;

(d)   indication of lack of support for a strike or industrial action by members of his own trade union or any other;

(e)   failure to contravene a contract of employment or any other agreement between the member and 'a person for whom he normally works' (this is a concept wider than 'employee', see para 2.4);

(f)   the making of an assertion that the union, or any official, representative or trustee thereof, has contravened or is proposing to contravene a requirement imposed by the union rules;

(g)   consulting the Commissioner for the Rights of Trade Union Members or Certification Officer or asking them to provide advice or assistance;

(h)   failure to agree to the making of a deduction of subscriptions arrangement;

(i)   resigning from one union to join another (thus rendering the Bridlington principles effectively unenforceable);

(j)   working with individuals who are not members of that union or another union;

(k)   working for an employer who employs or has employed individuals who are not members of that union or another union; or

(l)   requiring the union to do an act which the union is, pursuant to TULR(C)A 1992, required to do on the requisition of a member.

'Discipline' is widely defined and includes advice that another trade union or branch or section of another trade union should be encouraged or advised not to accept that individual as a member and subjecting the individual to any detriment (*Medhurst* v *Dental Estimates Board Branch of NALGO and NALGO* [1990] IRLR 459). Detriment may take the form of the publication of her name in a circular or newsletter circulated to all branch members (*NALGO* v *Killorn and Simm* [1990] IRLR 459).

18.5.5.2   Exclusion   The section does not apply to discipline for criticism of the union's leadership if the relevant assertion was false and the person making it or attempting to vindicate it acted:

(a)   in the belief that it was false; or
(b)   otherwise in bad faith,

and there was no other reason for disciplining him which was within the grounds of unjustifiable discipline.

18.5.5.3   Procedure for claiming unjustifiable discipline   In order to claim there must be a determination. To qualify as a 'determination' the decision has to dispose of the issue of discipline once and for all and not, as in *TGWU* v *Webber* [1990] IRLR 462, merely be a recommendation of a Regional Council to the General Executive Council of the union, when the latter body was the only one which could decide on implementation of it. A union member may complain of unjustifiable discipline to an industrial tribunal within three months of the unjustifiable discipline being imposed. The industrial tribunal has a power to extend this period if it considers it reasonable to do so if it was not reasonably practicable to present the application within that period and the delay is wholly or partly attributable to any reasonable attempt to appeal against such determination. All references in this section are to TULR(C)A 1992 unless otherwise stated.

Any provision in an agreement is void if it purports to exclude or limit an individual's right to complain under s. 288(1) unless it is an agreement reached through an ACAS Conciliation Officer pursuant to s. 18 of the Industrial Tribunals Act 1992 (s. 288(2)) just as in the unfair dismissal jurisdiction. A member whose complaint is upheld by the industrial tribunal may claim compensation; such an application is to be made to:

(a)   the industrial tribunal if the union has already revoked its disciplinary decision and done what is necessary to reverse such penalty as was imposed; or
(b)   the EAT in all other cases (s. 67(2)).

The application for compensation must be presented between four weeks and six months after the declaration has been made by the industrial tribunal (s. 67(3)). There is a right of appeal on a point of law only to the EAT (s. 291(2)). The industrial tribunal or EAT as appropriate may make such an award of compensation as it considers 'just and equitable in all the circumstances' (s. 67(5)).

The following principles, however, apply, which are similar to those relevant to the unfair dismissal compensatory award:

(a) the common law rules of mitigation of loss (s. 67(6));

(b) contributory fault by the applicant, in which case the relevant body should 'reduce the amount of the compensation by such proportion as it considers just and equitable' having regard to such conduct (s. 67(7)).

Compensation may be awarded for injury to feelings (*Bradley* v *NALGO* [1991] IRLR 159, ICR 359), but within a reasonable bracket and not where the injury arose not from the discipline itself but from the calculated behaviour of certain members after the applicants had been expelled in that they wrote articles criticising the applicants. (See on remedy, *NALGO* v *Courteney-Dunn* [1992] IRLR 114).

The maximum special award is 30 times a week's pay, that is, at present, 30 x £210 = £6,300 together with the maximum compensatory award currently available, that is £11,300. Thus the grand total at present is £17,600. Where the application is to the EAT because the union has not complied with the declaration made by the EAT, there is a minimum award, which is the same as the minimum amount in trade union membership or activities dismissals where the employer has failed to comply with an order for reinstatement or re-engagement, at present £2,700 (s. 67(8)).

Moreover, if an individual is unjustifiably disciplined under these provisions, no one may enforce:

(a) the payment of any sums; or

(b) the performance of any other obligation.

18.5.6 Review of internal disciplinary hearings

The courts insist that meetings to dispense discipline must be properly called, so that an expulsion has been held void because two members of the branch committee who decided to expel the plaintiff did not receive the papers relating to his case (*Leary* v *NUVB* [1971] Ch 34), and a similar result was reached where a meeting was called with only a few minutes' notice (*MacLelland* v *NUJ* [1975] ICR 116).

The courts will not normally, however, review the facts as found by the internal tribunal (*Weinberger* v *Inglis* [1919] AC 606), as long as it acts honestly, in good faith and in accordance with its rules (*Maclean* v *Workers Union* [1929] 1 Ch 602), although there is no presumption to this effect. The exception is where the tribunal reaches a decision at which no reasonable tribunal could arrive. *Radford* v *NATSOPA* [1972] ICR 484, provides a good example. The employers and unions in the printing industry agreed to a scheme under which those made redundant could choose between alternative employment in the industry in which case they would lose their right to a redundancy payment, and departure from printing whereby they would receive a larger award. The plaintiff sought to stay in the industry *and* claim his payment. He was thus charged with 'taking action against the union', and expelled. Plowman J, dismissing the interests of union solidarity, held that there was no evidence to support the charge and declared the expulsion void. (See also *Esterman* v *NALGO* (supra).)

18.6 COMMISSIONER FOR THE RIGHTS OF TRADE UNION MEMBERS

Since the Employment Act 1988 there has existed the post of Commissioner for the Rights of Trade Union Members, first filled by Mrs G. Rowlands. This role is modelled on the part played by the Commission for Racial Equality in race discrimination cases and the Equal Opportunities Commission in relation to sex discrimination cases. An individual may apply to the Commissioner for assistance as an actual or prospective party to proceedings. The Commissioner must notify such an applicant of his or her decision as soon as reasonably practicable, and may if he or she thinks fit give the reasons for refusal of assistance, but does not have to do so (TULR(C)A 1992, s. 110(5)).

Assistance could as first enacted take one or more of the following forms:

(a)   bearing the costs of advice by a solicitor or counsel;

(b)   making arrangements for the giving of such advice;

(c)   making arrangements for representation of the applicant;

(d)   bearing the costs of representation of the applicant;

(e)   arranging for or paying the costs incurred in arriving at or giving effect to a compromise of proceedings.

In exercising his or her discretion, the Commissioner may have regard to the following considerations:

(a)   whether the case raises a question of principle;

(b)   whether it is unreasonable in view of the complexity of the case to expect the applicant to proceed unaided (TULR(C)A 1992, s. 110(2)(b));

(c)   whether the case involves a matter of substantial public interest.

The discretion of the Commissioner is fettered only in the case of an application under:

(a)   TULR(C)A 1992, s. 46 (requirements of union elections); or

(b)   TULR(C)A 1992, s. 64 (unjustifiable discipline).

In those cases where the Certification Officer has already made a declaration and it appears that the applicant would have a reasonable prospect of securing the making of an order, then the Commissioner *must* grant assistance (TULR(C)A 1992, s. 110(3)). The Commissioner may not, however, provide assistance to an applicant to the Certification Officer. The aim is that such proceedings should be informal and free from lawyers.

The remit of the Commissioner extended originally to the following proceedings:

(a)   right of trade union member to require a ballot before industrial action (s. 62);

(b)   right of member to inspect union accounts (s. 30);

(c)   remedy against trade union trustees for unlawful use of property (s. 16);

(d)   remedy with respect to political fund;

(e)   application to court for remedy for unlawful use of funds for indemnifying for unlawful conduct;

(f)   remedy for failure to hold valid principal executive committee elections (s. 56);

(g)   unlawful application of trade union political funds (s. 71);

(h)   any other proceedings against:

(i)   a trade union;

(ii)   a trade union official;

(iii) trustees of a trade union's property;

as specified in an order made by the Secretary of State for Employment. Such an order is made by statutory instrument and must be approved by resolution of each House of Parliament (TULR(C)A 1992, s. 109(3)).

The Employment Act 1990, s. 10 (now TULR(C)A 1992, s. 109(2)) added to the above list a breach or threatened breach of certain union rules in respect of:

(a) appointment or election to or removal of a person from any office;
(b) disciplinary proceedings by the union (including expulsion);
(c) the authorising or endorsing of industrial action;
(d) balloting of members;
(e) application of the union's funds or property;
(f) imposition, collection or distribution of any industrial action levy;
(g) the constitution or proceedings of any committee, conference or other body.

The only criteria for giving funding are that the breach in question affects or may affect other members than the applicant or that 'similar breaches of the rules have been or may be committed in relation to other members of the union'.

The Commissioner is protected from misuse of the funds he or she provides by the fact that he or she may recover any amount expended by him or her for a person who has made a statement which he knew to be 'false in a material particular' or was reckless whether it was true or false (TULR(C)A 1992, s. 113(1)). Further, the other party to proceedings must be informed that the Commissioner is providing assistance in the same way as the other party in a legally aided case (TULR(C)A 1992, s. 111(4)). Where the Commissioner decides to assist in the conduct of any proceedings, he or she must, unless he or she notifies the applicant to the contrary, indemnify the applicant for any costs order made against him in those proceedings (TULR(C)A 1992, s. 111(3)). Where the applicant is given assistance by the Commissioner and the applicant recovers costs against another party in proceedings, those costs and expenses constitute a first charge for the benefit of the Commissioner. This also applies to any sum payable to the applicant under any compromise or settlement.

As a matter of procedure, a claim sponsored by the Commissioner for the Rights of Trade Union Members may contain in the title the words '(assisted by the Commissioner for the Rights of Trade Union Members)'.

18.7 PROCEDURE BEFORE CERTIFICATION OFFICER

Various jurisdictions are given by statute to the Certification Officer in respect of trade union affairs. In particular, he exercises an adjudicative role on the political fund, trade union amalgamations and principal executive committee elections.

Save where express provision is otherwise made, the Certification Officer is given specific power to regulate his own procedure.

He may, somewhat unusually, restrict the circumstances in which the identity of an applicant is disclosed to any person. The provision is designed to restrict the risk of intimidation of applicants who bring a complaint against their own unions. The Certification Officer may now make provision for expenses to be paid for the purpose of or in conjunction with their attendance at hearings before the Certification Officer. The money comes from a fund held by ACAS.

18.8 DEDUCTION OF TRADE UNION SUBSCRIPTIONS BY EMPLOYER AND RESIGNATION FROM UNION

The Trade Union and Labour Relations (Consolidation) Act 1992, as amended by TURERA 1993, seeks to ensure that members who leave their union do not continue to pay subscriptions under a check-off system operated by their employer. Where an employee certifies to his employer that he:

(a)   has terminated his membership of a trade union to the union's knowledge, or

(b)   intends to resign from his union on a particular date,

the employer must stop deducting union subscriptions from his pay as from the date of termination (TULR(C)A 1992, s. 68(1)).

If the employer continues to deduct subscriptions, the employee may apply to an industrial tribunal for:

(a)   a declaration; and

(b)   an order requiring the employer to repay the amount deducted.

This is similar to the remedies provided under s. 13(1) of the ERA 1996 (formerly the Wages Act 1986) (TULR(C)A 1992, s. 68A(4)(b), see Chapter 5).

19 Collective Bargaining

19.1 THE BRITISH SYSTEM

As we have already seen, collective bargaining grew up in the nineteenth century to replace customary rates of pay set by the masters in each particular district and industry. With the impulse of the 'new model unions', and then the unskilled general unions, national bodies emerged as the forum for negotiations (usually annual) between a union or several unions and the appropriate employers' association. This practice was given a major boost following the First World War when a Committee of Inquiry under Whiteley, then Deputy Speaker of the House of Commons, recommended the establishment of joint industrial councils as a way of improving productivity by handling bargaining over pay and conditions throughout industry. By 1921 there were 73 such bodies; many still remain in existence but are of declining importance.

There has, in recent years, been a decline in the scope of collective bargaining as many employers have de-recognised trade unions, or set up greenfield sites without any degree of union recognition. A well-known example of the latter is the Wapping printing plant owned by News International plc. Indeed, it has been public policy during the period in office of the present Conservative Government to *discourage* collective bargaining. The most celebrated example of de-recognition was by the Government itself at the Government Communications Headquarters at Cheltenham (which went further, in that employees were not permitted to be members of trade unions at all and could only join a staff association which was subsequently held by the EAT not to qualify as an independent trade union).

19.2 ENFORCEMENT OF COLLECTIVE BARGAINS

The central legal question raised by collective bargaining is whether agreements can be enforced in the courts. Most controversy has surrounded whether the employer can sue the union for taking strike action before the procedure for settling disputes laid down in the collective bargain has been pursued. There is no problem with privity here; the vital question is instead whether they are intended to have legal effect.

Collective agreements are not drafted with the precision to which a lawyer is accustomed, rarely covering all eventualities and this is particularly so at local level. It was primarily for these reasons that, in the leading case at common law, *Ford Motor Co.* v *AEU* [1969] 2 QB 302, Lane J found that the Ford Motor Company's collective agreement was not intended to create legal relations, and therefore not open to construction and enforcement by the courts. He also referred to 'the general climate of opinion on both sides of industry' and 'the vague aspirational wording' of the agreement before him (see B. Hepple, 1970 CLJ 124), and went on: 'Agreements such as these, composed largely of optimistic aspirations, presenting grave practical problems of enforcement and reached against a background of opinion adverse to enforceability are, in my judgment, not contracts in the legal sense.' He said, on the general issue of intention:

If one applies the subjective test and asks what the intentions of the various parties were, the answer is that so far as they had any express intentions they were certainly not to make the agreement enforceable at law. If one applies an objective test and asks what intention must be imputed from all the circumstances of the case the result is the same.

(See also *Edwards* v *Skyways Ltd* [1964] 1 WLR 349.) In *Monterosso Shipping Ltd* v *International Transport Workers' Federation* [1982] ICR 675 the Court of Appeal decided that the collective bargain was not a contract at all for the purposes of private international law.

The nature of the collective bargain was further explored in *National Coal Board* v *National Union of Mineworkers* [1986] IRLR 439. The NCB agreed in 1946 with the NUM for reference of disputes to a national reference tribunal. In 1985 following the miners' strike, the NCB gave six months' notice of its intention to terminate the agreement. The NUM did not accept that this was valid, arguing that the agreement was legally binding since it actually stated that the parties were 'bound'. Scott J thought that this was insufficient to replace the presumption in what was then s. 18 of the Trade Union and Labour Relations Act 1974 (now TULR(C)A 1992, s. 179) that collective bargains are *not* intended to be legally binding. The union also sought to argue that the agreement was incorporated into the contracts of employment of individuals. This was rejected on the basis that such incorporation refers to substantive terms such as wages and conditions and not to collective procedural matters such as arose in this case.

Notwithstanding this lack of direct legal enforcement, reg. 6 of the Transfer of Undertakings (Protection of Employment) Regulations 1981 (SI 1981 No. 1794) provides that on a transfer of undertaking, 'any collective bargain agreed by the transferor shall have effect as if made by the transferee' (see para. 16.7).

19.3 THE AUXILIARY ROLE OF THE LAW

The general duties laid on ACAS by TULR(C)A 1992 (s. 209) as amended by TURERA 1993 are 'the improvement of industrial relations, in particular, by exercising its functions in relation to the settlement of trade disputes . . .'. The legislation introduced by Labour Governments also recognised that successful bargaining can only be carried out when employees achieve a sufficient degree of organisation. Thus TULRA 1974 and EPCA 1978 sought to enhance union strength and cohesion by such provisions as time off for union activities, banning discrimination against members (Chapter 20) and upholding the integrity of the closed shop. This has been limited by later statutory interventions. The Employment Act 1989 was the first statute to focus on the subject of negotiation in respect of which the union is recognised, since by s. 14 (now TULR(C)A 1992, s. 168) an official of a union henceforth had a right to time off only in respect of duties concerned with negotiations related to or connected with any matters within TULR(C)A 1992, s. 178(2) and 'in relation to which the trade union is recognised by the employer'.

We look in turn at the following statutory provisions and common law developments:

(a) recognition of trade unions (para. 19.4);
(b) the closed shop (para. 19.5);
(c) rights to information (para. 19.6);
(d) ACAS (para. 19.7);
(e) Central Arbitration Committee (para. 19.8);
(f) low pay (para. 19.9);
(g) Codes of Practice (para. 19.10);
(h) health and safety (para. 19.11);
(i) the right of public sector employees to be consulted before changes in terms (para. 19.12).

19.4 RECOGNITION

Recognition entails accepting a trade union to some extent as the representative of the employees for the purpose of carrying on negotiations in relation to or connected with one of the matters set out in [s. 178(2) of TULR(C)A 1992]. Thus it entails not merely a willingness to discuss but also to negotiate in relation to one or more such matters. That is to say, to negotiate with a view to striking a bargain upon an issue and this involves a positive mental decision.

(Eveleigh LJ in *National Union of Gold, Silver and Allied Trades* v *Albury* [1978] IRLR 504.)

The treatment of trade union recognition is in many ways a case study of the approach of the law to collective bargaining at various stages of development. Until 1971, recognition of unions by management so that bargaining could take place, was, like most industrial relations issues, one which the parties thought the law should leave well alone. Recognition spread mainly by custom and practice, although increasingly comprehensive management-union agreements were drawn up. These were valuable in that they specified in detail who the employer would negotiate with, where, and over what issues, and also such subsidiary questions as trade union facilities on the employer's premises, and the automatic deduction of union subscriptions from the employee's pay packet (the 'check off').

The only statutory provision for recognition is the Transfer of Undertakings (Employment Protection) Regulations 1981 (SI 1981 No. 1794). Where there is a transfer of undertaking 'whether by sale or by some other disposition or by operation of law', the transferee must continue to recognise any trade union recognised by the transferor, provided that 'the undertaking or part of the undertaking transferred maintains an identity distinct from the remainder of the transferee's undertaking' (reg. 9). There is, however, no specific enforcement provision and it may thus remain rather a pious exhortation (see Chapter 16). (See also the discussion of the decision of the ECJ in *Commission of the European Communities* v *UK* [1994] ICR 664, in Chapter 15).

It is unlawful on the ground of a requirement of union membership to (TULR(C)A 1992, s. 145):

(a) fail to include any person or company on a list of approved suppliers of goods or services;
(b) terminate a contract for the supply of goods or services;
(c) exclude anyone from the list on which tenders are invited;
(d) fail to permit a person to submit a tender;

(e)   otherwise determine not to enter into a contract with a person for the supply of goods or services.

The Act also outlaws a requirement that another party to a contract recognise a trade union or negotiate or consult with it. Sections 186 to 187 of TULR(C)A 1992 provides an action for breach of statutory duty to a person damnified by such a condition. That may be any other party to the contract or 'any other person who may be adversely affected by its contravention'. There is no trade dispute immunity under s. 219 of TULR(C)A 1992 for the union which seeks to enforce the union membership requirement (see para. 21.11).

Recognition is a prerequisite for some rights such as consultation over redundancies and about a transfer of an undertaking with a trade union, but elected representatives now have similar rights.

19.5   RIGHT OF TRADE UNIONS TO INFORMATION

A vital factor in facilitating collective bargaining is the provision of information so that discussion may proceed on an informed basis. The Industrial Relations Act 1971 made provision for the disclosure of information but the appropriate section was not actually brought into force. It was only with EPA 1975 (now TULR(C)A 1992, ss. 181 to 185) that the disclosure of information so long advocated in trade union circles became a reality, and then arguably in a most attenuated form. One major defect is that, based as it is on a threshold of recognition, an employer can resist the disclosure of information on a particular subject by refusing to bargain on that issue (*General and Municipal Workers' Union et al & BL Cars Ltd,* CAC Award No. 80/65). Difficulties in reconciling rights to confidentiality on the one hand, and rights to know, on the other, are also responsible for the unacceptable vagueness of the provisions as enacted.

19.5.1   Trade Union and Labour Relations (Consolidation) Act 1992

19.5.1.1   What must be disclosed   The employer must disclose to any recognised union, information:

(a)   without which the trade union representative would be to a material extent impeded in carrying on with him . . . collective bargaining; and
(b)   which it would be in accordance with good industrial relations practice that he should disclose to them for the purposes of collective bargaining (TULR(C)A 1992, s. 181(2)). Collective bargaining is defined by s. 178 of TULR(C)A 1992 as concerned with:

(i)   terms and conditions of employment, or the physical conditions in which any workers are required to work;
(ii)   engagement or non-engagement, or termination or suspension of employment or the duties of employment of one or more workers;
(iii)   allocation of work or the duties of employment between workers or groups of workers;
(iv)   matters of discipline;
(v)   a worker's membership or non-membership of a trade union;
(vi)   facilities for officials of trade unions;
(vii)   machinery for negotiation or consultation, and other procedures, relating to any of the above matters, including the recognition by employers or employers' associations of

the right of a trade union to represent workers in such negotiation or consultation or in the carrying out of such procedures.

The CAC has itself commented on the difficulty in applying the second test (b), since:

> there is a very weak consensus as to current practice. Information which is commonly disclosed in one sector of industry may be regarded as a tightly guarded secret in another.

(Annual Report 1978, para. 2(11)). Moreover, it may be difficult for a union to say it is impeded in collective bargaining through lack of information when it has *ex hypothesi* managed without it for many years past. The general test was stated in CAC Award No. 78/353 para. 20: 'Is the information sought in this case relevant and important in general terms?' Later, in its Annual Report for 1979, the CAC said: 'As a general point, the relevance of information under any of the categories . . . increases when jobs are at risk.'

The relevant ACAS Code of Practice directs negotiators to:

> take account of the subject-matter of the negotiations and the issues raised during them; the level at which negotiations take place (department, plant, division, or company level); the size of the company; and the type of business the company is engaged in.

Joint understandings are especially encouraged. The Code sets out the following list of subjects but they are not the only evidence of good practice; they serve neither as a checklist nor are they intended to be exhaustive:

(a) *pay and benefits:* principles and structure of payment systems;

(b) *conditions of service:* policies on recruitment, redeployment, redundancy, training, equal opportunity and promotion; appraisal systems; health, welfare and safety matters;

(c) *manpower:* numbers employed analysed according to grade, department, location, age and sex; labour turnover; absenteeism; overtime and short-time; manning standards; planned changes in work methods, materials, equipment or organisation; available manpower plans; investment plans;

(d) *performance:* productivity and efficiency data;

(e) *financial:* cost structures; gross and net profits; sources of earnings; assets; liabilities; allocation of profits; details of government financial assistance; transfer prices; loans to parent and subsidiary companies and interest charged.

This does not extend to commercial information about market share of products, cash flow and government assistance, and in a survey it was shown that few applications for information about profits, non-labour costs and redundancy plans have met with success.

The details sought must be relevant for the description of workers in which the union is recognised, and the application must be made in writing by a representative of the union, defined as: 'an official or other person authorised by the trade union to carry on such collective bargaining' (TULR(C)A 1992, s. 181(1)), thus including a shop steward. It is not, however, sufficient to disclose material to representatives only on condition of its not being available to full-time officers of the union or denying access to individual members (*IPC Ltd and the National Union of Journalists,* CAC Award Nos. 80/4, 78/711, 80/73). The union may require the information to be given in writing but not that any particular documents be produced. It is possible that the employer could be sued for negligent mis-statement in the event of false information.

19.5.1.2 Restrictions on disclosure There is a list of exceptions from the right to information which must normally be proved by the employer (TULR(C)A 1992, s. 182). They relate to cases where:

(a) Disclosure would contravene a prohibition imposed by *statute*. This served, for example, to exclude a survey of earnings in an industry since the copyright was in the surveying company (*Joint Credit Card Co. & NUBE,* CAC Award No. 78/2/2).

(b) Information has been communicated to the employer *in confidence* or where he has obtained it in consequence of the confidence reposed in him by another person. In *Civil Service Union v CAC* [1980] IRLR 274 QB, the cost of transferring cleaning operations to outside contractors had been conveyed on a form marked 'in confidence', and this suggested that the person communicating it was relying on its remaining secret.

(c) Information which relates to an *individual*, unless that person has consented to its disclosure. This arises particularly where grading schemes are in issue. While the CAC in *Rolls Royce Ltd & ASTMS,* CAC Award No. 80/30 said that such information should be given even where it might enable an individual to be identified, in No. 79/121 an application for information about a directors' pension scheme was refused since it related only to individuals.

(d) Disclosure would cause *substantial injury* to the employers' undertaking. The Code of Practice suggests as examples where the employer might lose customers to competitors, where suppliers will refuse to supply necessary materials, and where the ability to raise funds to finance the company would be seriously impeded. It does not, however, allow the argument that the use of the information in negotiations would harm the company.

(e) The information has been obtained for the purpose of bringing or defending any *legal proceedings* (TULR(C)A 1992, s. 182(1)(f)).

(f) The compilation or assembly of the information would involve an amount of work or expenditure out of all reasonable proportion to the value of the information in the conduct of collective bargaining (TULR(C)A 1992, s. 182(2)(b)).

(g) Disclosure would involve a breach of *national security* and a certificate to this effect signed by the Minister is conclusive evidence that the information must be withheld (TULR(C)A 1992, s. 182(1)(a)).

19.5.1.3 Remedies for failure to disclose collective bargaining information To gain a remedy for failure to provide information is a curious, complicated and lengthy process. Like the right itself, it is a hybrid between the collective and individual enforcement (TULR(C)A 1992, s. 183) and consists of these stages:

(a) The union applicant makes a *complaint* to the Central Arbitration Committee.

(b) The CAC may refer the matter to ACAS for settlement by *conciliation,* failing which —

(c) The CAC conducts a *hearing* at which anyone whom it considers to have a proper interest in the matter may be heard and the CAC must give reasons for its findings.

(d) If the committee upholds the complaint it may make a *declaration* of the information which ought to be disclosed and a final date by which this must be done.

(e) If the employer still fails to comply, the union may make *a further complaint,* and also seek changes in those parts of the individual contract in respect of which the union is recognised (s. 184).

The Act merely states that the Committee may award the terms claimed or others as it considers appropriate. There is no appeal from this finding, and it does not apply to the Crown.

The policy appears to be that if the union does not have information to achieve meaningful collective bargaining, the CAC will arbitrate the bargaining for it. The employer may render the whole remedial process meaningless, however, if he complies with the statute even at the last minute. The stages may move like a tortoise and the remedy will be effective only long after collective bargaining for the year has been completed. The CAC itself has commented that this remedy, 'is unlikely to be attractive to either party except in very special cases'. This partly explains why less use has been made of the provisions thus far than was originally anticipated.

There are also two other duties of disclosure, to which we now turn.

19.5.2 Health and safety

Provided that a safety representative gives the employer reasonable notice, he may inspect and take copies of any document which the employer is required to keep by virtue of statutory health and safety provisions. There is also the more general duty on the employer to make available to him information which is within his knowledge and which is necessary for the safety representative to fulfil his functions. The 'Health and Safety Commission Code of Practice: Safety Representatives and Safety Committees (1978)', reg. 6 exemplifies:

(a)   plans and performance of the undertaking, and any changes affecting the health and safety at work of the employees;

(b)   technical data about hazards and necessary precautions; and

(c)   accident records.

Such information may also be revealed by an inspector.

19.5.3 Pensions

Schedule 2 to the Social Security Act 1985 introduced 12 new sections into the Social Security Pensions Act 1975 giving the Secretary of State for Social Services the power to make provisions for disclosure by trustees to members of a pension scheme and to a register of pensions schemes. They also prescribe the contents of a scheme's annual report and require schemes to obtain reports from qualified auditors and actuaries.

The Occupational Pension Schemes (Disclosure of Information) Regulations 1986 (SI 1986 No. 1046) provide, *inter alia,* that documents containing the constitution of an occupational pension scheme must be made available by the trustees for inspection by members and prospective members, spouses, beneficiaries and independent trade unions recognised in respect of members or prospective members. Copies of the actuarial valuation of the scheme (which must be carried out at least once every three and a half years) must also be open to inspection by the same persons and bodies.

19.6 THE ADVISORY, CONCILIATION AND ARBITRATION SERVICE (ACAS)

The policy of the statutes is to exclude 'trade disputes' . . . from judicial review of the courts . . . There is substituted for judicial review of trade disputes an advisory conciliation and arbitration process with ACAS as the statutory body to operate it.

(Court of inquiry into a dispute between Grunwick Processing Laboratories Ltd and members of APEX, Cmnd 6922, 1977.)

It is in the interests of everyone, above all the general public, that industrial disputes are resolved peacefully and quickly. From earliest times government services have therefore been made available to assist independently warring industrial parties. The role used to be filled mainly by the Ministry of Labour but its functions were transferred in 1969 to the quasi-autonomous Commission for Industrial Relations, the brainchild of the Donovan Commission. The Advisory Conciliation and Arbitration Service (ACAS) took over all the CIR's functions in 1974, originally on a non-statutory basis, although its constitution was soon laid down by EPA 1975 and it was given the duty:

of promoting the improvement of industrial relations, and in particular of encouraging the extension of collective bargaining and the development, and where necessary, the reform of collective bargaining machinery.

Lord Scarman in *ACAS* v *United Kingdom Association of Professional Engineers* [1980] IRLR 124 at para. 29, thought that:

The subsection [s. 1(2)] formulated the various objectives of statutory policy which it is for ACAS to implement as in the exercise of its independent and expert judgment it thinks best in individual cases.

Its main strength in this respect lies in its doughty independence from both of the two sides of industry and of the Government. The TULR(C)A 1992 clearly provides that it is not to be 'subject to directions of any kind from any Minister of the Crown as to the manner in which it is to exercise any of its functions under any enactment' (s. 247(3)). The Service is instead controlled by a Council which is responsible for policy matters and consists of nine members serving part-time, and the chairman who is full-time and holds office for five years. All are appointed by the Secretary of State for Employment — three after consultation with employers and three on the recommendation of the unions, while the rest sit as independents. The Council was thus intended, like ACAS itself, to reflect whatever consensus existed in British industrial relations, and to be the constructive side of dispute management.

The chief functions of ACAS under the Employment Protection Act include:

(a)   assistance in the settlement of complaints to *industrial tribunals* for which purpose it employs about 200 conciliation officers;
(b)   *arbitration* before CAC or independent arbitrators;
(c)   *general advice* on industrial relations;
(d)   *holding inquiries* into questions relating to industrial relations generally or in a particular industry;
(e)   controlling the CAC and choosing its members (para. 19.7);
(f)   responsibility for various pieces of collective bargaining, usually in the public sector, like the Police Arbitration Tribunal and the Railway Staff National Tribunal;
(g)   issuing *codes of practice* (para. 19.9).

The most important role of ACAS is its peace-keeping and fire-fighting function trying to prevent industrial action at the very first stages. It must strike a fine balance between intervening too readily in disputes and yet being available if the parties desire its assistance. It thus has power where a *trade dispute* (as defined) exists 'by way of conciliation or by other means to offer assistance to the parties to the dispute with a view to bringing about a settlement'. The following methods, which are selected according to the circumstances of each particular dispute, will be considered in turn:

(a)   conciliation (para. 19.6.1);
(b)   mediation (para. 19.6.2);
(c)   advice (para. 19.6.3);
(d)   inquiry (para. 19.6.4);
(e)   arbitration (para. 19.6.5).

19.6.1   Conciliation

There is a long history to the independent conciliatory approach now provided by ACAS. The Conciliation Act 1896 gave power to the Board of Trade to inquire into the causes of any dispute and 'take such steps as to the Board may seem expedient'. These were extended, after the experience of wartime and the Whitley Report, by the Industrial Courts Act 1919; and this function duly passed to ACAS in 1975. Conciliation involves not so much making suggestions to the two parties, but rather providing a forum for discussion and procedural guidance to bring them together. Thus the Service does not involve itself unless both sides agree, and not until internal procedures under the collective bargain have been exhausted (TULR(C)A 1992 s. 210(1)). The hope is that it can then flexibly react to particular problems involved.

This process of conciliation requires considerable reserves of psychological analysis, and Phelps Brown has described the conciliator's role thus (*The Growth of British Industrial Relations*, 1960, p. 127):

When the parties lose their tempers with one another too easily to be able to talk face to face he can go backwards and forwards between them. He may be able to devise proposals new in form or substance, which go some way to reconcile conflicting claims, or provide a rough compromise, or make it easier to give ground without losing face ... Especially when both sides have stuck fast, thinking it a sign of weakness to be the first to climb down, he can get them to make concessions because he can tell them what the other will do in return.

Sometimes the Government itself intervenes in particularly contentious disputes.

ACAS conciliation officers are also involved in conciliation on an individual level, since every complaint to an industrial tribunal, other than one claiming only redundancy pay, is examined by them to see whether a settlement is feasible.

19.6.2   Mediation

Mediation is a more intrusive and active process than conciliation, for the mediator, who may or may not come from the ACAS staff, makes recommendations of his own for a way out of an industrial dispute, and the parties then consider his suggestions.

19.6.3 Advice

ACAS not only offers advice on particular matters as exemplified in TULR(C)A 1992, s. 213, but also on aspects of industrial relations in general. Included are a telephone advice service and a comprehensive industrial relations handbook.

19.6.4 Inquiry

The offer of a far-ranging independent inquiry can sometimes defuse an apparently intractable industrial dispute by providing a calmer atmosphere in which to review all the underlying issues involved (TULR(C)A 1992, s. 214). The generally held convention is that the parties call off their strike or lock-out pending the results of the inquiry. The TULR(C)A 1992 accords power to the Secretary of State for Employment to refer any matter connected with a trade dispute to a court of inquiry conducted either by one person or a board. Such 'courts' have been set up to consider some of the most damaging industrial disputes; thus Lord Wilberforce's court investigated the miners' strike of 1972 and Lord Scarman attempted to untangle the events in the Grunwick affair. There have been few inquiries of this nature in recent years. The hearing before the court is invariably formal in procedure and it has power to compel witnesses, whose evidence may be heard on oath. It may otherwise generally regulate its own procedure, but it must lay a report before Parliament (s. 215(3)).

Less formal Departmental Committees of Inquiry may be set up when appropriate: the Houghton Report on all issues of teachers' pay is a good example. They are established under general ministerial powers but are independent of the Government once appointed. ACAS itself has conducted several wide investigations under s. 214 of TULR(C)A 1992, including inquiries into the newspaper industry. It may act in this regard on its own initiative, but if its findings are to be published, a draft report must be sent to the parties for their comments.

19.6.5 Arbitration

Whereas the conciliator is a builder of bridges, an arbitrator is an umpire; he decides the extent to which a claim should succeed.

(J.G. Riddall, *Law of Industrial Relations*, Butterworth, 1981, p. 213.)

Arbitration is a much stronger step for the parties in dispute since it in effect delegates the autonomy of both sides to a third party over whom they can have no control. As a Department of Employment Paper comments: 'It is argued not only that such a commitment involves an unacceptable renunciation of responsibility [but] weakens the incentive to reach an agreed settlement and distorts the negotiating process by directing the attention and tactics of the parties to a possible arbitration hearing rather than to possible agreement' (Department of Employment Manpower Paper No. 14, *Industrial Relations Procedures*, para. 185).

A trade dispute may be referred to arbitration by ACAS with the consent of all parties and provided that internal bargaining procedures have already been adopted, unless there is a 'special reason' for by-passing such procedures. Further, ACAS must have considered the likelihood of the dispute being settled by conciliation (TULR(C)A 1992, s. 212(2)). The

Service may itself appoint an arbitrator or a board of arbitrators but none of them should be on the ACAS staff, so that the independence of the institution is not compromised (s. 212(1)(a)). Alternatively, the case may be referred to the CAC. The latter's chairman appoints a panel consisting of one member from each of the three lists of employers' representatives, employees' representatives and independent persons. ACAS looks on arbitration as a matter of last resort, urging the parties not to abdicate responsibilities but to reach agreement between themselves (ACAS Annual Report 1978). Little use has been made of these facilities. Compulsory arbitration by the State has been enacted during wartime and in EPA 1975 and its predecessors, but is now of little importance.

19.7 CENTRAL ARBITRATION COMMITTEE (CAC)

The Central Arbitration Committee replaced the Industrial Arbitration Board in 1975 but it traces its descent to the Industrial Court set up in 1919 and continues to act as an independent focus for arbitration, along with the following limited statutory jurisdictions (TULR(C)A 1992, s. 259(1), Sch. 3, para. 7):

(a) review of collective agreements and pay structures which contain terms 'applying specifically to men only or women only' under the Equal Pay Act 1970 (para. 7.6);
(b) adjudication on complaints of failure to disclose information to a recognised trade union for the purposes of collective bargaining (TULR(C)A 1992, ss. 183 to 185) (para. 19.5).

Like industrial tribunals, the CAC consists of a chairman sitting with 'wingmen' who are representatives of employers and employees; they seek to reach unanimous decisions, and where this is impossible the chairman acts as an umpire, his decision counting even if outvoted by the wingmen. As befits a body well versed in industrial relations, its procedure is flexible, and the Arbitration Acts do not apply (TULR(C)A 1992, s. 263(6); *Imperial Metal Industries (Kynoch) Ltd* v *AUEW* [1978] IRLR 407). It has no power to summon witnesses nor to punish for contempt and usually first considers written representations which are then amplified at a formal hearing, normally held in public. While there is no appeal, its decisions are subject to judicial review by the Divisional Court of the Queen's Bench Division where there is an error of law or procedure. The judges have refrained from intervening in the CAC as they have to correct ACAS. Lord Widgery CJ inferred, from the lack of any appeal that 'Parliament intended these matters to be dealt with without too much assistance from the lawyers' (*R* v *CAC ex parte TI Tube Divisional Services Ltd* [1978] IRLR 183).
Like most administrative bodies, it is not obliged to give reasons for its decisions (except when upholding a complaint of failure to disclose information for collective bargaining purposes) (TULR(C)A 1992, ss. 183(3) and 184(2)), but it has now broken from the practice of the Industrial Court and sets out the 'general considerations' behind its awards. They are, however, to 'be read by the parties as a guide — not as a precise legal judgment' (CAC Report 1977).

19.8 LOW PAY

There is no minimum wage in Britain, unlike many continental countries. Generally, *laissez-faire* and the free market rule, while the union's seek free collective bargaining without legislative intervention.

Until 1986 over three million workers had their earnings protected by some 43 wages councils and the Agricultural Wages Board. All were regulated by the Wages Councils Act 1979. Under the Wages Act 1986, which repealed the Wages Councils Act 1979, wages councils ceased to have any functions in relation to workers under the age of 21. For those over 21, the scope of wages councils orders was restricted, but these were abolished by TURERA 1993, s. 35, with effect from 30 August 1993.

19.9 CODES OF PRACTICE

Codes of practice are a fertile source of quasi-law and confusion in the industrial relations area. A distinction must be now drawn in procedure and effect between codes promulgated by ACAS and the Department of Employment. Section 199 of TULR(C)A 1992 requires that ACAS provide guidance by codes of practice on disclosure of information and time off for trade union duties and activities, both of which were only generally defined in the statute. In the exercise of its discretion it has also published a code on disciplinary practice and procedures. All these are intended as authoritative statements of proper practice and supersede the relevant parts of the Industrial Relation Code issued at the time of the Industrial Relations Act 1971 and revoked in June 1991. They are first issued in draft form for comment, and come into effect unless either House of Parliament objects within 14 days.

The TULR(C)A 1992, s. 203, now gives coordinate power to the Department of Employment also to issue codes of practice. The procedure here requires the Secretary of State to consult ACAS, issue a draft, consider representations, if necessary amend the draft, and then lay it before Parliament for approval. The codes of practice so far promulgated in this manner on the closed shop, picketing and industrial action ballots concern controversial issues on which the tripartite ACAS Council was not likely to reach meaningful agreement; indeed they refused to even comment on them when before Parliament. Perhaps significantly, the statutory aim of the codes is stated by TULR(C)A 1992, s. 203(1)(a), to be the improvement of industrial relations and there is no parallel duty as for ACAS to promote the extension of collective bargaining.

Section 207(1) of TULR(C)A 1992 clearly states that:

a failure on the part of any person to observe any provision of a Code of Practice shall not of itself render him liable to any proceedings

but any such code is admissible in evidence, with the same persuasive but not decisive authority as the Highway Code has in road traffic cases. An important difference between ACAS and Secretary of State codes is that the latter may be referred to in the courts as well as industrial tribunals and the CAC. This may be particularly important with regard to picketing, which often strays into the criminal area (see use of the code in *Thomas* v *NUM (South Wales Area)* [1985] IRLR 136). Moreover, a code issued by the Secretary of State may expressly supersede one put out by ACAS.

Section 203(1)(b) of TULR(C)A 1992 gives the Secretary of State for Employment the power to issue codes of practice for the purpose of 'promoting what appear to him to be desirable practices in relation to the conduct by trade unions of ballots and elections' (see para. 21.10). The EOC, CRE and Health and Safety Executive also have similar powers under their respective enabling Acts.

19.10   HEALTH AND SAFETY AND COLLECTIVE BARGAINING

Health and safety matters were not considered issues for joint industry-management regulation before 1975. The impulse to change came with the Committee of Inquiry under Lord Robens which reported in 1972 (Cmnd 5034), and sought to make it central to collective bargaining. The Health and Safety at Work etc. Act 1974 provided for the election of safety representatives by all employees at the appropriate work place but this was soon repealed by EPA 1975, which channelled their appointment through recognised unions. The detail is contained in the Safety Representatives and Committees Regulations 1977 (SI 1977 No. 1500 as amended by SI 1992 No. 2051), which provide for their appointment where one or more workers are employed by the employer which recognises the union. They are empowered to inspect the work place, to investigate potential hazards and complaints and to make representations to management. To enable them to do these tasks effectively, they must be provided with relevant documents and information by management, and, like union officials, they can take time off with pay to perform their statutory duties (Health and Safety at Work etc. Act 1974, s. 2(7) (para. 20.9).

Safety committees are plant level institutions and must be formed when at least two safety representatives make such a written request to the employer. Guidance on all these issues is provided by a Health and Safety Commission Code of Practice, breach of which has the same effect as that of other such codes. Otherwise there is no sanction on the employer for failure to carry out these responsibilities.

Consistent with the changes made to consultation over transfers of undertakings and redundancy, the Health and Safety (Consultation with Employees) Regulations 1996 (SI 1996 No. 1513) provide that where there are no union safety representatives, consultation must take place with employees directly or 'one or more persons in the group who were elected . . . to represent that group for the purposes of such consultation' (reg. 4(1)). They are given the somewhat clumsy title of 'representatives of employee safety'. They have the same rights to time off and protection against victimisation as other employee representatives. What is particularly noticeable about this structure is that the employer may consult employees individually should he so choose.

19.11   THE RIGHT OF PUBLIC SECTOR EMPLOYEES TO BE CONSULTED ABOUT CHANGES IN TERMS OF EMPLOYMENT

The House of Lords decision in *Council of Civil Service Unions* v *Minister for the Civil Service* [1985] IRLR 28 raises fundamental questions about the right of Crown employees to be consulted about changes in their terms. The case concerned a challenge by the unions represented at Government Communications Headquarters to the Government's decision without consulting them to remove the right of employees to join unions of their choice. Instead they were allowed only to join an approved staff association. The House of Lords decided that since the Crown might at any time change the conditions of service of civil servants, they and their unions had no *right* to prior consultation when there were changes. They would, however, have a *legitimate expectation* to be so consulted because of the practice to this effect ever since the establishment of GCHQ. The courts would protect this right in a proper case by an application for judicial review. Lord Diplock indicated that there were three grounds for judicial review: illegality, irrationality (where the decision is so outrageous that no sensible person could reach it), and procedural impropriety. Here, however, the interests of national security overrode the normal right in this regard. Their

Lordships made clear that these rights did not relate to employees in the private sector. Lord Fraser said that 'if no question of national security arose, the decision-making process in this case would have been unfair' but 'the judicial process is unsuitable for reaching decisions on national security'.

In *Re NUPE and COHSE's Application* [1989] IRLR 202, the Northern Ireland High Court decided that representative trade unions have a legitimate expectation of 'proper consultation' prior to a public sector body making a decision which affects the employment of their members, The material furnished by a hospital board should contain sufficient information to enable it to tender 'helpful advice'.

20 Protection of Trade Union and Cognate Activities

Workers shall enjoy adequate protection against acts of anti-union discrimination in respect of their employment.

(Article 1(1), ILO Convention Concerning Application of the Principles of the Right to Organise and Bargain Collectively, No. 88.)

Workers without distinction whatever shall have the right to establish and subject only to the rules of the organisation to join organisations of their own choosing without previous authorisation.

(Article 2, ILO Convention Concerning Freedom of Association and Protection of Right to Organise, No. 87.)

20.1 THE RIGHTS

The rights of an employee to join an independent trade union and take part in its activities are safeguarded in many countries by their constitutions (e.g. France, Germany). In Britain the rights were enacted only in 1971 and are protected in three important ways by the Trade Union and Labour Relations (Consolidation) Act 1992:

(a)   By s. 146, he has 'the right not to have action (short of dismissal) taken against him', so that there must be no discrimination against him on this ground any more than by reason of race or sex (para. 20.4). Section 14 of EA 1980 and s. 10 of EA 1982 also outlawed acts short of dismissal designed to compel an employee to join a union.

(b)   Under s. 152, dismissal is regarded as automatically unfair, and is an inadmissible reason in selecting an employee for redundancy (s. 153, TULR(C)A) if the reason was that the employee:

(i)   was, or proposed to become, a member of an independent trade union;

(ii)   had taken, or proposed to take, part at any appropriate time in the activities of an independent trade union; or

(iii)   had refused, or proposed to refuse, to become or remain a member of a trade union which was not an independent trade union.

The rights have been extended to cover employees with particular functions cognate to trade union duties, that is those involved in health and safety activities, whether on behalf of a trade union or not, employee representatives (for consultation purposes) and occupational pension fund trustees.

An employee so dismissed can claim statutory remedies even though he does not have the length of service normally necessary to apply, or even though he is over normal retiring age. Moreover, 'interim relief (under s. 161) in the form of reinstatement or suspension on full pay until final determination of the complaint, is available to him (para. 20.11.3).

(c) Officials and members of recognised unions are given the right to reasonable time off without pay to participate in these activities (s. 168) (para. 20.6), while union officials may take time off *with* pay to carry out their *duties* in connection with collective bargaining, but this was restricted in scope by the Employment Act 1989.

We first examine the definitions of trade union activity (para. 20.2) and appropriate time (para. 20.3), which are central to all three rights. Independence of trade unions (para. 17.8) has already been considered. It should, however, be emphasised that while the employee need not usually belong to a union *recognised* for the purposes of collective bargaining where there is a closed shop in operation, only members of the specified trade union(s) have the rights. Moreover, the general provisions do not apply to the police and armed forces (Police Act 1996, s. 64 and ERA 1996, ss. 192, 200).

20.2 ACTIVITIES

20.2.1 Scope

The interpretation of the phrase 'activities of an independent trade union at any appropriate time' is of the utmost importance to s. 146 and s. 152 rights. It is also necessary to construe the words 'had refused or proposed to refuse to become or remain a member' of a trade union. The underlying tension in the case law was well expressed by Phillips J in *Lyon* v *St James Press* [1976] ICR 413 (a dismissal case):

> The special protection afforded to trade union activities must not be allowed to operate as a cloak or an excuse for conduct which may ordinarily justify dismissal; equally the right to take part in the affairs of a trade union must not be obstructed by too easily finding acts done for that purpose to be a justification for dismissal.

In *Dixon and Shaw* v *West Ella Developments Ltd* [1978] IRLR 151, the same learned judge said:

> [Section 58 EPCA 1978 now TULR(C)A 1992, s. 152] was intended, and must have been intended, to discourage employers from penalising participation in activities of a fairly varied kind . . . and should be reasonably, and not too restrictively, interpreted.

He gave little guidance to expand this statement and few hints can be gleaned from the ACAS Code of Practice on Time Off for Trade Union Duties. This defines activities rather restrictively in paras 21 and 22, where it details attendance at executive meetings or annual conferences, and voting in union elections.

The cases have established that the following activities are protected: collecting union subscriptions; discussing union affairs (*Zucker* v *Astrid Jewels Ltd* [1978] IRLR 385); seeking advice from union representatives on industrial issues (*Stokes and Roberts* v *Wheeler-Green Ltd* [1979] IRLR 211); posting union notices (*Post Office* v *Crouch* [1974] 1 WLR 89); speaking at a recruitment forum (*Bass Taverns Ltd* v *Burgess* [1995] IRLR 596; and seeking recognition for a union (*Taylor* v *Butler Machine Tool Ltd* [1976] IRLR 133). The protection extends to criticism of the union itself (*British Airways Engine Overhaul Ltd* v *Francis* [1981] IRLR 9), and union recruiting activities even where, as in *Lyon* v *St James Press Ltd* (supra), the employees went about their attempt to start a union chapel with utmost secrecy, and thus caused considerable ill feeling in the small respondent firm. The EAT did say, however, that:

> unreasonable and malicious acts done in support of trade union activities might be a valid ground for dismissal.

It would not extend to strike action. It may, however, extend to the enlisting by a member of the help of a union official to elucidate and negotiate the terms and conditions of her employment since this was 'to use a prayer book expression the outward and visible manifestation of trade union membership' (*Discount Tobacco Ltd* v *Armitage* [1990] IRLR 14). In *Speciality Care plc* v *Pachella* [1996] IRLR 248, the EAT supported *Armitage* and held that the industrial tribunal may consider whether the introduction of a union representative into the employment relationship had led to the employer dismissing the employee.

The industrial tribunal, in deciding whether the dismissal was on the grounds of trade union activities, must consider why the employee was not considered for alternative work (*Driver* v *Cleveland Structural Engineering Co. Ltd* [1994] ICR 372) as well as the reason for the dismissal itself. A discriminatory motive is not required, however (*Dundon* v *GPT Ltd* [1995] IRLR 403).

In *O'Dea* v *ISC Chemicals Ltd* [1995] IRLR 599, Mr O'Dea spent half of his time on union activities and the remainder working as a packaging operator. He claimed under s. 153 TULR(C)A 1992, that 'the circumstances constituting the redundancy applied equally to one or more employees . . . who held similar positions held by him and who have not been dismissed by the employer' and that the reason for differentiation was on the grounds of his trade union activities. In order to construe the subsection properly it was necessary to ignore the trade union activities of Mr O'Dea.

A controversial issue concerns the holding of union meetings in company time, with consequent loss of production. On one view, this is tantamount to a strike, yet an employer should give reasonable time to his employees to attend union meetings necessary for the proper functioning of collective bargaining. In *Marley Tile Co. Ltd* v *Shaw* [1980] ICR 72, Goff LJ was 'inclined to doubt' whether this was a protected activity, where the caller of the assembly in question was an unaccredited shop steward. Eveleigh LJ, however, thought that nothing should be done to 'fetter the judgment of members of industrial tribunals'. All their Lordships agreed that the question should 'not be dressed up as a point of law'. However, it is difficult for industrial tribunals to decide this issue, since the Court of Appeal gave no guidance as to criteria, even though in the instant case their Lordships criticised the 'industrial jury' for their 'broad brush approach'. The ACAS Code advises that meetings are protected where to hold the meeting is 'reasonable because of the urgency of the matter or where to do so would not adversely affect production or services'.

20.2.2 Limitations

20.2.2.1 Activities of trade union or trade unionist An assault has been made on the generality of 'activities of a trade union' from five directions. The first, a distinction between the activities of a *union* and a trade *unionist,* owes its provenance to *Gardner* v *Peaks Retail Ltd* [1975] IRLR 244 but this was criticised in *Palmer* and *Wilson* (see below para. 20.4). The applicant was there dismissed for having made various complaints to management about the unsatisfactory state of the staff room. She was not protected since 'individual complaints may be of a trouble-making kind . . . if supported by a union this provides some guarantee that they have substance'. Kilner Brown J made the point forcefully in *Chant* v *Aquaboats Ltd* [1978] 3 All ER 102:

> The mere fact that one or two employees making representations happen to be trade unionists and the mere fact that the spokesman happens to be a trade unionist does not make such representations a trade union activity.

In this case a round-robin petition protesting against unsafe machinery was held not to be a trade union activity.

What authorisation must proceed from the union for the activities, and in what form, is left unclear. It is not enough, however, that the applicants are trade union officers and considered a course of conduct to be in the interests of their members (*Stokes and Roberts* v *Wheeler-Green Ltd* (supra)). A difficult case arises where there may be a union policy, contained in a conference resolution, to resist a particular management decision on the ground that such is inimical to employers' obligations regarding health and safety. If the union member wrongly takes that as a sanction for resisting management, is his action included? In *Drew* v *St Edmundsbury BC* [1980] ICR 513, a parks gardener was dismissed because of his refusal to clear snow during an official go-slow and his long-standing one-man campaign against the council's health and safety record. The EAT rejected his contention that he had been sacked for an inadmissible reason, firstly because the industrial tribunal had no jurisdiction where he was dismissed during industrial action even though this constituted a continuation of his own campaign. The second ground was that he had no official standing in the union. It is submitted that a more suitable interpretation is that the protection should cover activities of the sort carried out by a trade union, even if in the particular circumstances, the precise *modus operandi* has not been referred to, nor received express approval from, the official union hierarchy. This would at once recognise the independent power of shop stewards, and deal more satisfactorily with the facts in *Chant* for example.

20.2.2.2 Activities before employment Secondly, the sections have been held not to extend to activities *before* the applicant's employment began, even though this may put Britain in breach of its international obligations. In *City of Birmingham* v *Beyer* [1977] IRLR 211, a blacklisted trade unionist had to resort to a false name to get a job with the appellants and was sacked when recognised. Kilner Brown J said that union activity protected by the section,

> could not conceivably refer to activities outside and before the employment began . . . There is nothing in the legislation . . . which lays down that an employer may not refuse to employ a man unless he has reasonable grounds for refusing. Until there is work available for all, obviously the employer must have a vested right to pick and choose.

Beyer's case gave a *carte blanche* for the keeping of blacklists of trade union activists and reflected the failure of English law, outside race and sex discrimination, to control the employer's power to hire.

Although the same conclusion was reached by the EAT in *Fitzpatrick* v *British Railways Board* [1990] ICR 674, this was overturned by the Court of Appeal ([1992] ICR 221). The Court of Appeal distinguished *Beyer* as dealing with a case where the reason for dismissal was obtaining employment by deceit. It was, however, perfectly possible for what happened in a previous employment [to] form the reason for the dismissal in subsequent employment' (per Woolf LJ at para. 18). It is also unnecessary to identify precise activities (para. 22). The political activities of the applicant were subsidiary to her trade union activities so that the dismissal was on trade union grounds.

20.2.2.3   Activities contrary to union rules   The third potential restriction on trade union activity relates to the position where the union activity is contrary to a particular union rule. This was accepted as a principle in *Marley Tile* v *Shaw* (supra), although, on the facts, the court held that the action did not infringe rule 13 of the rules of the Amalgamated Union of Engineering Workers. Moreover, the point was made by Goff LJ that rule books of this sort were not to be construed like statutes. In *McQuade* v *Scotbeef Ltd* [1975] IRLR 332, the industrial tribunal went so far as to say that activities were not protected under this rubric if they were in breach of a union management procedure agreement, while a shop steward who advised his members to strike was held not engaged in trade union activity since this was contrary to union policy as laid down in the Shop Stewards Handbook (*Fortune* v *Thames Water Authority,* IDS Brief 161, p. 7).

20.2.2.4   Claim to recognition   The Court of Appeal in *Therm-A-Stor Ltd* v *Atkins* [1983] IRLR 78 narrowly construed the provision so that it did not apply to employees dismissed because the employer objected to the *recognition* of their union. Rather the section was concerned only with the *individual* employee's activities in the trade union.

20.2.2.5   Strikes   In no sense can trade union activities comprise strike action. Even so this phrase may prove difficult to construe. One possibility is anything in breach of contract, but does a refusal to work voluntary overtime, which may not involve breach of contract, come within it? Is it confined to collective union action, or does it comprise individual protests? Would a demonstration to protest at government policy be included? An argument was raised in *Winnett* v *Seamarks Bros* [1978] ICR 1240, a case on the old EPCA 1978, s. 23, that the strike is a well-recognised activity of an independent trade union, but this was summarily rejected. Two rationales have been put forward for this result:

(a)   In *Brennan* v *W. Ellward (Lancs) Ltd* [1976] IRLR 378, it was held that the activity was not at 'an appropriate time: The Employment Protection Act cannot extend to . . . suddenly downing tools and leaving the premises, in order to consult their union officials elsewhere'.

(b)   In *Drew* v *St Edmundsbury BC* [1980] ICR 513, the EAT based their *obiter* conclusion on the fact there is a different provision in the legislation for strike dismissals.

The fact that an employee does acts preparatory to a strike may constitute trade union activities according to the EAT in *Britool* v *Roberts* [1993] IRLR 481.

In *Rath* v *Cruden Construction Ltd* [1982] IRLR 9, the EAT held that the protection against dismissal on grounds of trade union membership did not extend to inter-union disputes.

20.2.2.6 Proposal to refuse to remain a member of a trade union As we have seen, the Employment Act 1988 removed the limited remaining protection for the closed shop, and placed dismissal on the ground that an employee is not a member of any trade union or of one of a number of particular trade unions or has refused or proposes to refuse to become or remain a member, on exactly the same footing as dismissal on the grounds of trade union membership or activities whether or not there is a union membership agreement.

In *Crosville Motor Services Ltd* v *Ashfield* [1986] IRLR 475, the applicant made it clear that unless there were changes in union policy and organisation, he would leave the union. The EAT held that the words in what was then s. 58 of EPCA 1978 (now TULR(C)A 1992, s. 152) rendering unfair a dismissal where an employee 'proposed to refuse to . . . remain a member [of a trade union]' covered such a contingent event. Garland J said that the subsection 'is saying that if somebody refuses to remain a member of a union he can do it now; he can do it with effect from next week, or next month, or in six months' time . . .. That is something which can be conditional or contingent on something occuring or not occurring as the case may be'.

20.2.2.7 Refusal of employment on trade union grounds Following the policy outlined in the 1989 Green Paper, the Employment Act 1990 outlawed the last remnants of the closed shop by rendering unlawful the pre-entry closed shop. It is unlawful to refuse a person employment on the ground that:

(a) he is a member of a trade union; or
(b) he is not a member of a trade union; or
(c) he will not agree to become a member of a trade union; or
(d) he will not cease to be a member of a trade union (now TULR(C)A 1992, s. 137).

This includes refusal of employment on the grounds that an employee had been engaged in trade union activities (*Harrison* v *Kent County Council* [1995] ICR 434). Where an advertisement indicates that employment is open only to a member of a trade union or a person who is not a member, a person who applied for but was refused employment is conclusively presumed to have been refused unlawfully. 'Advertisement' is widely defined.

The provisions specifically tackle informal practices which were still common in some industries. Thus it is unlawful where there is an arrangement or practice under which employment is offered only to persons put forward or approved by a trade union, and where the trade union puts forward or approves only persons who are members of the union, a person who is not a member of the union and who is refused employment in pursuance of the arrangement or practice is treated unlawfully. Refusal of employment extends to a person who is made a 'spurious offer of employment which he does not accept', that is when 'the terms are such as no reasonable employer who wished to fill the post would offer'. These prohibitions extend to an employment agency, and anyone refused the services of that agency may complain in a similar way. Throughout these provisions, employment extends only to employees.

A person refused employment for that reason may only complain to an industrial tribunal. A complaint must be presented 'before the end of the period of three months beginning with the date of the conduct to which the complaint relates' subject to an extension if such complaint is not reasonably practicable (TULR(C)A 1992, s. 139). Compensation is to be 'assessed on the same basis as damages for breach of statutory duty and may include compensation for injury to feelings' (TULR(C)A 1992, s. 140(2)), but the total is subject to the limit for the compensatory award, at present £11,300 (s. 140(4)). The tribunal may make a recommendation of action which 'appears practicable for the purpose of obviating or reducing the adverse effect on the complainant' and if the respondent fails to comply with this further compensation may be granted (s. 140(1)(b)). Relief may be directed against a trade union which puts pressure on an employer to act in breach of the above sections (s. 142(1)). The appeal provisions and restrictions on contracting out found in the unfair dismissal area will apply to the new jurisdiction, and there are similar exclusions for Crown employees, those in police service, employees ordinarily working outside Great Britain, mariners and offshore employees.

20.3 WHAT TIME IS APPROPRIATE FOR TRADE UNION ACTIVITIES?

The appropriate time for trade union activities is defined as not only occasions 'outside the employee's working hours' but also time 'within working hours at which, in accordance with arrangements agreed with, or consent given by his employer, it is permissible for him to take part in those activities' (TULR(C)A 1992, s. 146(2), 152(2), 170(2)). In *Post Office v UPW* [1974] ICR 378, Lord Reid declared that, 'it does not include periods when in accordance with his contract the worker is on his employer's premises, but not actually working'. He went on to cut down the scope of his judgment by saying that 'the incursion of these rights on the employer's rights . . . must be reasonable' and the employer must not be caused substantial inconvenience. He continued: 'It is a very different matter to use facilities which are normally available to the employer's workers or to ask him to submit to some trifling inconvenience'. He went on:

> Discrimination against a man's trade union generally affects him personally. The prejudice to the man himself may be so small as to be negligible. But where it is substantial and a necessary consequence of the discrimination against the trade union and this must have been known to the employer the employer has in fact so acted as to worsen the man's position in comparison with that of a man in another union against which there has been no discrimination.

Interpreting 'arrangement' and 'consent' in the definition was central to the ratio in *Marley Tile Co. Ltd v Shaw* [1980] ICR 72. The EAT had held that a meeting of maintenance men to protest about the shop steward's lack of credentials during working hours was 'at an appropriate time', because the legislation had to be construed in the light of 'actual industrial practice'. The higher court, however, disapproving of this 'broad brush approach', viewed the issue more narrowly. While consent might be implied, it could not arise by way of extension from other factories, custom and practice at the plant in question, nor the employer's silence. The EAT and industrial tribunal were overruled because they 'considered too much the reasonableness of the behaviour and the reactions of the employees'. Yet it is submitted that this view ignores the fundamental importance of informal works rules, of which there was here adequate evidence. It takes the sort of strict contractual rights position which the House of Lords found unsatisfactory in the *Post Office* case and leaves unclear what are the circumstances from which consent might be inferred outside the obvious cases.

20.4 ACTION SHORT OF DISMISSAL

The protection of trade unionists and their activities extends to action short of dismissal, since otherwise the employer could make life miserable for the trade unionist without going as far as sacking him. Statute thus prohibits action against a trade unionist because he is a trade unionist by preventing him or deterring him from being or seeking to become a member or penalising him for doing so, or for participating in its activities, whether by means of the 'velvet glove of bribery . . . or the mailed fist of coercion' (B. Bercusson, *Current Law Statutes Annotated* 1978, vol. 2, Sweet & Maxwell/Stevens). Section 146, TULR(C)A 1992 made it clear that the only complaint is about treatment as an *individual*. The phrase 'action *short of* dismissal' cannot include a failure to renew a fixed-term contract on its expiry since this in fact amounts to a dismissal (*Johnstone* v *BBC Enterprises Ltd* [1994] ICR 180).

Valuable guidance on the scope of the remedy was given by the Court of Appeal in *Ridgway and Fairbrother* v *National Coal Board* [1987] IRLR 70. At Ellistown Colliery, the National Coal Board decided to pay increased wages to members of the Union of Democratic Mineworkers but not to members of the National Union of Mineworkers. The EAT decided against the employees on the ground that the remedy applied only to discrimination against persons for being members of any trade union whatsoever, rather than to discrimination for membership of one union as opposed to another. According to Bingham LJ, however, what was then s. 23 was concerned with employees' rights and a general right to be an active trade unionist would not be of much value to an employee if he could not join and take part in the activities of his chosen union. The EAT had also erred in deciding that the appellants had not had action 'taken against them *as individuals*'. To fall within s. 23(1)(a) the action must affect the employee otherwise than merely as a member or officer of the union. Nicholls LJ found it difficult to think of an action short of dismissal which could be taken by an employer against an employee which would more obviously qualify as action taken against him as an individual than a reduction in, or failure to increase, pay. May LJ, however, dissented on the ground that the action complained of must be directed against the employee *personally* to be taken against him 'as an employee', whereas in the present case it was directed against the NUM itself. The Court of Appeal unanimously rejected the NCB's argument that 'omission' does not mean merely failure to act.

It is provided by statute that 'action' includes refusal to confer a benefit on an employee, but doubt has surrounded the question of whether it also comprises a threat. In *Brassington* v *Cauldon Wholesale Ltd* [1977] IRLR 479, the EAT by way of *obiter dicta* (since the only question was the assessment of damages) doubted whether a threat to close down a factory, sack the workforce and open under a different name if the workers joined a union, sufficed. In *Carter* v *Wiltshire CC* [1979] IRLR 331, however, a tribunal decided that a threat was included; here it consisted of sending employees before a disciplinary tribunal for holding a union meeting on the premises.

In *Carlson* v *Post Office* [1981] IRLR 158, the EAT held that a failure to give a member of a small union a car parking permit at his place of work because its allocation was determined between the employers and the Council of Post Office Unions, of which his union was not a member, *could* amount to action penalising him. Slynn J thus overturned the industrial tribunal's holding that this was *de minimis*, and said that the provision was not restricted to 'the imposition of what may be called a positive punishment on to a financial penalty'.

In *Gallagher* v *Department of Transport* [1994] IRLR 231, the employee spent effectively the whole of his time on trade union activities. He put his name forward for consideration for the higher grade of senior executive officer but was turned down by reason of doubts about his managerial ability. The Court of Appeal decided that the industrial tribunal erred in deciding that the Department's comments about his managerial ability were intended to deter him from continuing with full-time union activities. The words 'for the purpose of' in TULR(C)A 1992, s. 146 connoted an object which the employer desires or seeks to achieve; it was not to be confused with its effect.

In *Palmer* v *Associated British Ports* and *Wilson* v *Associated Newspapers Ltd*, employers offered financial inducements to those employees who were prepared to sign new contracts in the context of derecognition of trade unions. These contracts were 'personal' contracts, in that they contained no reference to collective bargaining in the setting of terms and conditions. In both cases the employees claimed that they had been subjected to action short of dismissal with the purpose of preventing or deterring membership of a trade union. The key issue which fell to be determined in both cases was whether the payment of money to individuals who accepted new individual contracts which excluded union negotiation of terms and conditions, could give rise to a claim that those who did not sign — and so did not receive any money — had been subjected to action short of dismissal on the grounds of trade union membership.

The Court of Appeal [1994] ICR 97 decided that the applicants had proved their case. In *Palmer* the employers had argued that their purpose was to achieve greater flexibility in their business through being able to reward individuals on the basis of merit, and they pointed out that those who did not accept the new terms still had their pay determined through the union. The Court of Appeal disagreed. In its view, the aim of offering extra money to those who signed personal contracts was to ensure that as many employees as possible abandoned union membership and that the union would eventually 'wither on the vine'. Similarly, in the *Wilson* case the Court of Appeal upheld the tribunal's decision that the employer's ultimate purpose fell within the definition of deterring or penalising the membership of a trade union.

However, on 16 March 1995 ([1995] IRLR 258) the House of Lords overruled the decision of the Court of Appeal on the basis that the action did not include an omission in the context of the subsection. This point was not open to the tribunals, EAT or Court of Appeal because of the decision in *Ridgway*, which had relied on the fact that by s. 153(1) 'In this Act . . . except so far as the context otherwise requires — ''act'' or ''action'' shall include omissions . . .'. Here their Lordships decided that 'the context otherwise required'. Lord Bridge rejected the suggestion in *Armitage* that there was a 'general proposition of law that . . . membership of a union is to be equated with using the ''essential'' services [because] at best it puts an unnecessary and imprecise gloss on the statutory language, at worst it is liable to distort the meaning of those provisions which protect union membership as such'. Lord Browne-Wilkinson agreed with regret because 'it leaves an undesirable lacuna in the legislation protecting employees against victimisation'. Lords Slynn and Lloyd dissented on the omission point but agreed in the overall result.

The Government responded within a week of the decisions of the Court of Appeal in *Wilson* and *Palmer* by inserting in the Trade Union Reform and Employment Rights Bill (which by that stage had technically completed consideration by the House of Lords committee and thus very unusually had to be called back thereto) what became s. 13 of the TURERA 1993. This was designed to deal specifically with the employer who derecognised a union (the facts of those cases), but it may have a somewhat wider impact. It adds to

TULR(C)A 1992, s. 148, an exemption from liability for the employer whose purpose included the furthering of 'a change in his relationship with all or any class of his employees' unless the industrial tribunal considers that the employer's action was 'such as no reasonable employer would take having regard to the purpose'. 'Class' for these purposes is defined as meaning 'those employed at a particular place of work, those employees of a particular grade, category or description or those of a particular grade, category or description employed at a particular place of work'.

20.5 PROOF

Discrimination, whether on the grounds of race, sex or trade union activities, is, as we have already seen, most difficult to prove. Unless the employer blatantly says, 'no trade unionists here', the evidence is likely to take the form of inferences, nods and winks. This helps to explain the low success rate of applicants for all three types of discriminatory treatment, and why there is a case for placing the burden of proof on the employer since he knows the grounds for dismissal or action short of dismissal. Lord Denning MR was attracted to this view, when, dissenting in *Smith* v *Hayle Town Council* [1978] IRLR 413, he said that the weight of the burden at least must depend 'on the opportunities and knowledge with respect to the facts to be proved which may be possessed by the parties respectively'. The other two Lord Justices took the orthodox approach, confirming *Goodwin Ltd* v *Fitzmaurice* [1977] IRLR 393, that the burden fell squarely on the applicant. The latter case also stands as authority for the rule that a tribunal must first decide whether the dismissal was for trade union activities before examining whether it was redundancy or some other ground. (See also *Maund* v *Penwith DC* [1982] IRLR 399.)

Another problem concerns collective decisions. In *Smith* v *Hayle Town Council* (supra), the employee was dismissed by a one vote majority of the respondent Council. Although he proved that at least one councillor was motivated by his dislike of trade unionists, this did not prove that it was the principal reason for the decision to dismiss. (On time limits, see *Williams* v *Monsanto plc*, EAT 183/89.)

20.6 PAID TIME OFF FOR TRADE UNION DUTIES

Where his union is recognised, an official is entitled to time off with pay 'to carry out those duties . . . which are concerned with industrial relations between his employer and any associated employer and their employees' (s. 168(1), TULR(C)A 1992), and this is in accordance with ILO Convention No. 135. This is restricted to those duties concerned with negotiations about matters within s. 244, TULR(C)A 1992 'in relation to which the trade union is recognised by the employer' or 'any functions related to or connected with any [such] matters . . . and the employer has agreed may be so performed by the trade union' (see para. 21.8.2 for discussion of s. 244, TULR(C)A 1992). If the employer refuses, the official can complain to the industrial tribunal and seek a declaration and compensation. 'Official' is defined as any officer of the union or branch and any other person elected under the union rules to represent the members or some of them (TULR(C)A 1992, s. 119), thus clearly including a shop steward. The right to paid time off does not include time off between the hours of 7 p.m. and 11 p.m. when these are not normal hours of work (*Hairsine* v *Kingston upon Hull CC* [1992] ICR 212).

The ACAS Code of Practice on Time Off gives some indication of the duties for which time off should be granted:

(a)   collective bargaining with the appropriate level of management;
(b)   informing constituents about negotiations or consultations with management;
(c)   meetings with other lay officials or with full-time officials;
(d)   interviews with and on behalf of constituents on grievance and disciplinary matters;
(e)   appearing on behalf of constituents before an outside body;
(f)   explanations to new employees whom he or she will represent of the role of the union.

Paragraph 32 of the Code further suggests that where an official is not himself engaged on industrial action being taken by his constituents, he should be allowed time off to represent them. We will consider first the meaning of duties and then the reasonableness of the time taken off.

20.6.1   Meaning of industrial relations duties

The central problem with the section is that the essential terms 'industrial relations' and 'duties' are nowhere defined, nor does the Code of Practice grasp this nettle. Moreover, there is an inevitable tension in that what is phrased as a right is, in reality, a privilege, since employers retain a significant degree of control over what time off is reasonable and when it should be taken (see the Code of Practice).

In three EAT decisions these ambiguities surfaced and difficulties, especially in relation to unions organising in a group of companies, became apparent. In *Sood* v *GEC Elliott Process Automation Ltd* [1979] IRLR 416, an official of ASTMS claimed that he should be granted time off with pay to attend a meeting of his union's Telecommunications, Electronics and Automation Product Advisory Committee (PAC). This was a collection of representatives from GEC plants where the appropriate products were manufactured. It had no powers to represent anyone or negotiate with any GEC companies. Its brief was, instead, threefold:

(a)   to exchange information and experience;
(b)   to supply information to the ASTMS National Executive Committee;
(c)   to coordinate activities in relation to the affairs of members working with the relevant products.

Virtually the only matter which united all members of the Industrial and Employment Appeal Tribunals was the view that this was 'a useful body,' so that by attending its meetings the members became 'better representatives.' The EAT's judgment, given by Slynn J, first rejected various contentions made by the employers against the claim, thus making it clear that the section did not only cover those areas of collective bargaining for which the union was recognised. Further, the right was not only concerned with meetings with representatives of management; it also comprised planning, strategy and discussion with other workers who were negotiating with their employers. Yet the EAT went on to refuse the instant application. Slynn J drew two distinctions in the crucial section of the judgment (author's italics):

> Although it was no doubt *beneficial* to the union members that their representatives should attend such meetings, attendance was *not required* in order to enable the official to carry out his duties . . . We do not consider that the mere exchange of information between trade union officials themselves necessarily qualifies.

It is submitted that 'duties' in s. 168, TULR(C)A 1992 is used in the layman's sense of 'business, office or function' (*Shorter Oxford Dictionary*), rather than in the sense of distinguishing between what an official was and was not obliged to do. Thus, the adoption of the employee's contention that any meetings reasonably likely to be relevant to industrial relations are covered by the section, would be closer to the intention of Parliament.

That was the view which appears to be taken in the industrial tribunal decision in *Duncan* v *Weir Pacific Valves Ltd* [1978] IRLR 523. A union official claimed time off to attend a joint meeting with shop stewards from other plants in his group of companies to discuss a united approach to the Weir Group to 'negotiate pay policy on a group-wide basis'. The tribunal allowed the claim, referring in particular to para. 8 of the Code of Practice, that the purpose of the section 'is to aid and improve the conduct of industrial relations'.

In *Sood*, Slynn J also takes a narrow definition of 'industrial relations'. Having said that 'industrial relations is capable of covering many matters', he then applied it to collective bargaining and nothing else. This causes particular problems in groups like RHP or GEC with autonomous bargaining units. In *RHP Bearings Ltd* v *Brookes* [1979] IRLR 452, we are informed that 'each unit conducts its own negotiations . . . though subject to the policy of and financial control by the holding company . . .'. Unions would surely be failing the best interests of their members if they did not also coordinate policy and information on a group basis. As the union's letter to RHP Joint Shop Stewards Group members said: 'Meetings of this character are . . . essential if the wages and conditions of the group are to be improved.' If 'industrial relations' is analogised to 'collective bargaining', union officials will never succeed in getting paid time off for such important meetings.

Indeed, a wider approach to industrial relations duties was evident in the case of *Young* v *Carr Fasteners Ltd* [1979] IRLR 420, decided by the same EAT panel. It concerned the analogous training subsection of s. 168, which for these purposes uses the same concepts. Mrs Young, a GMWU shop steward, attended a course at the union's college called 'Pensions and Participation.' The EAT, reversing the view of the industrial tribunal held that she was, indeed, entitled to paid time off for this purpose. It was irrelevant that there were no negotiations in progress about pensions at the company. The learned judge thought that: 'Employees may well wish to consider making representations to the company . . .'. It was, further, not a conclusive objection that the pension scheme was administered in such a way that no employee could at that time be a trustee, or that the scheme was substantially administered in accordance with the advice of an insurance company. On the narrow view in *Sood* it might be thought that for these reasons pensions were hardly within the duties of Mrs Young as a shop steward; a broader approach was clearly taken.

The enormous problems with Slynn J's twofold distinction were also clearly demonstrated in *RHP Bearings Ltd* v *Brookes* (supra). The RHP joint shop stewards' committee decided in 1978 to change its former practice and henceforth meet in working time. As a test case, Mr Brookes, a committee member, claimed paid time off in connection with the first such meeting. The industrial tribunal allowed the application, but was criticised by the EAT, since it had not looked in detail at what took place at the meeting. In remitting the case to a differently constituted industrial tribunal, Bristow J said that:

The approach of the new tribunal should be to examine each item discussed in the minutes and to consider, in its capacity as 'an industrial jury', whether it is a matter in which Mr Brookes was doing his duty as a union official concerned with industrial relations between the company and other employers in the group and the group work force.

The EAT expressed confidence that the industrial tribunal would reach a 'sensible answer' in drawing the distinction outlined in *Sood* between 'exchange of information' and 'negotiating with companies'. This approach puts a premium on well-kept and unslanted minutes. Even with them, the difficulties are enormous. Take the agenda item of Trade Union Contribution (Check Off) discussed at the meeting in question. Does the industrial tribunal's decision depend on the wording of the final resolution, or the (probably) incomplete record of the discussion leading thereto? The judgment goes on to give guidance without authority in statute, or hint in the Code of Practice, that if 'only a proportion of time was spent on s. 168 matters the Industrial Tribunal will probably think that only a proportion of the time should reasonably be paid for'.

A wider view was taken by the EAT in *Beal v Beecham Group Ltd* [1982] ICR 460. The ASTMS National Advisory Committee for the Beecham Group organised two subgroups on Products and Pharmaceuticals, and members sought time off to attend such meetings claiming they were trade union duties. The EAT thought that the subsection was not restricted to the actual transaction of industrial relations business; it was more generally concerned with industrial relations, but not, as such, a mere exchange of information. The test was not whether the meeting was essential. Here, 'a coordinated approach in industrial relations is a legitimate objective even though the negotiating groups comprise disparate groups of employees who might in the end achieve varied settlements'. The Court of Appeal agreed with this analysis. Moreover, the time off could not be made subject to a condition that it should be unpaid (*Beecham Ltd v Beal (No. 2)* [1983] IRLR 317).

Unless the recognised union expressly or impliedly requires the attendance of an official at a meeting, his attendance at the meeting cannot be a duty 'as such an official' within the statutory language. The right does not extend to functions which the shop steward as opposed to the union considers desirable (*Ashley v Ministry of Defence* [1984] IRLR 57). In *Adlington v British Bakeries (Northern) Ltd* [1989] IRLR 218 attendance at a union workshop on the implications of the proposed repeal of the Baking Industry (Hours of Work) Act 1954 was held to be within 'industrial relations duties'. The question was whether the meeting was 'sufficiently proximate' to actual negotiations with the employers to constitute 'industrial relations'. In this case there was a very close connection between repeal of the legislation and employees' working conditions.

This may include meetings prior to negotiations, provided that there is sufficient nexus between the collective bargaining and the duty involving the preparation for that particular issue (*London Ambulance Service v Charlton* [1992] ICR 773).

20.6.2 Reasonableness of the time off sought

The time taken off must be reasonable as to amount and the circumstances when it is taken. The Code of Practice directs attention to, *inter alia*, the exigencies of production, services and shifts in process industries, the size of the enterprise and the size of the workforce. An employer may also properly consider the occasions on which an applicant had previously enjoyed time off in assessing the reasonableness of a further request. In *Wignall v British Gas Corporation* [1984] IRLR 493 the applicant had already been granted 12 weeks' leave for union business when he sought a further 10 days for the preparation of a union district monthly magazine. The EAT upheld the tribunal's decision that it was reasonable for the employers to refuse the further time.

In *Thomas Scott & Sons (Bakers) Ltd v Allen* [1983] IRLR 329, the Court of Appeal emphasised that the question of the reasonableness of the time off sought was a matter of fact for the industrial tribunal, and the Court of Appeal would accordingly not interfere with the tribunal's view that it was unreasonable to seek leave for all 11 shop stewards at the same time. Moreover, May LJ appeared to suggest that the tribunal had to decide not only whether it was reasonable for them to attend the meeting, but also whether it was reasonable that they should be paid for so doing. This analysis is difficult to square with the wording of the section.

20.7 UNPAID TIME OFF FOR TRADE UNION ACTIVITIES

By s. 170 of TULR(C)A 1992, a trade union member is to be allowed reasonable time off during working hours *without pay* to take part in the *activities* of an independent trade union recognised by the employer for the purposes of collective bargaining. These activities need have nothing to do with industrial relations, providing they are reasonable. As the ACAS Code of Practice No. 3 (Time off for trade union duties and activities) (para. 21) states: 'To operate effectively and democratically, trade unions need the active participation of members in certain union activities.'

The issue is one of fact for the industrial tribunal. The EAT held in *Luce* v *London Borough of Bexley* [1990] IRLR 422 [1990] ICR 159, that whilst the words 'any activity of an independent trade union' should not be construed restrictively, it was not the intention of Parliament to include *any* activity at all. Rather, it had to be within the ambit of the relationship between employer and employee and that trade union. It must be linked with the employment relationship. The EAT thus upheld an industrial tribunal decision that the applicant, the Honorary Treasurer of the Bexley Branch of the National Union of Teachers, was not allowed time off as a matter of right to attend a Trades Union Congress lobby of Parliament in connection with the Education Reform Bill which was then under consideration by Parliament. A lobby intended to convey only political or ideological objections to proposed legislation could not qualify under the relevant section. The Bexley Schools Subcommittee recommended that the Authority should refuse requests for trade union members to attend any Parliamentary lobbies arranged by their trade unions. The EAT held that the resolution of the Bexley Schools Subcommittee was far too sweeping without considering the details of each case; some activities directed at Parliament might fall within the scope of s. 170(1), such as those of a trade union which had developed specialist technical knowledge relevant to a measure before Parliament concerned with health and safety. In such a case representations arising out of such expertise might well satisfy s. 170(1).

20.8 TIME OFF FOR INDUSTRIAL RELATIONS TRAINING

Reasonable time off must also be given to a trade union *official* for training which is relevant to industrial relations duties and which is approved by the TUC or the applicant's own union (on relevance see *Ministry of Defence* v *Crook and Irving* [1982] IRLR 488). However, approval by the union alone is not sufficient and this was the important message demonstrated by *Menzies* v *Smith & McLaurin Ltd* [1980] IRLR 180. The EAT decided that an employee had been properly refused time off to attend a union course on redundancy because its syllabus was not relevant to industrial relations duties, being far too general in scope. It covered issues like North Sea Oil, import controls and responses to the EEC and the employee had failed to establish that anything he learned on the course would be of direct value to him in negotiations with the company. He was allowed time off as a union activity but he had no right to be paid for it.

20.9　TIME OFF FOR HEALTH AND SAFETY REPRESENTATIVES

A duly appointed health and safety representative has a right to reasonable time off with pay to perform his function and to train therefor (Safety Representatives and Safety Committee Regulations 1977 (SI 1977 No. 1500) reg. 4, para. 2). Where the employer provides an adequate internal course it is not necessarily reasonable to seek time off also to attend a TUC sponsored school (*White* v *Pressed Steel Fisher Ltd* [1980] IRLR 176).

The Code of Practice issued by the Health and Safety Commission states that safety representatives should be given basic training as soon as possible after appointment and such further training thereafter as may be appropriate.

There are several exclusions from the above rights to time off:

(a)　police service;
(b)　share fishermen;
(c)　employees who ordinarily work outside Great Britain.

20.10　PROTECTION OF HEALTH AND SAFETY ACTIVITIES

Section 44 to ERA 1996 gives an employee 'the right not to be subjected to any detriment by any act, or any deliberate failure to act, by his employer' on the ground that:

(a)　having been designated by the employer to carry out activities in connection with preventing or reducing risks to the health and safety of employees at work, he carried out or proposed to carry out any such activities;

(b)　if a representative of employees on matters of health and safety at work, he performed or proposed to perform any functions as such;

(c)　if a member of a safety committee formed in accordance with any enactment or acknowledged as such by the employer, he performed or proposed to perform any functions as such;

(d)　he left or proposed to leave his place of work or any dangerous part of his place of work in circumstances of danger which was serious and imminent and which he could not reasonably have been expected to avert; or

(e)　he took or proposed to take appropriate steps to protect himself or other employees from danger in circumstances of serious and imminent danger.

In a case where there is no safety representative or safety committee, or it was not reasonably practicable for the employee to raise a health and safety issue with those persons, the employee is protected if he brings to the employer's attention, by reasonable means, circumstances connected with his work which he reasonably believes were harmful or protentially harmful to health and safety.

The appropriateness of such steps must be judged by reference to all the circumstances including his knowledge and the facilities available to him at the time (s. 44(2)). There is no protection for an employee 'if the employer shows that it was (or would have been) so negligent for the employee to take the steps which he took (or proposed to take) that a reasonable employer might have treated him as the employer did' (s. 44(3)).

This right derives from an EC Directive to the effect that the employer 'should take action and give instructions to enable workers in the event of serious, imminent and unavoidable danger to stop work and/or immediately to leave the workplace and proceed to a place of safety'.

The right is given to a worker to complain to an industrial tribunal, and the onus is on the employer to show the ground on which any act or failure to act was done (s. 48(2) of ERA 1996). Any such complaint must be presented before the end of three months beginning with the date of the act or failure to act to which the complaint relates, or where the act or failure is part of a series of similar acts or failures, the last of them (s. 48(3)(a)). There is the normal extension power found in applications, for example, for unfair dismissal, where it was not reasonably practicable for the complaint to be presented within the three-month period, in which case it must be presented within such further period as the industrial tribunal considers reasonable (s. 48(3)(b)). A deliberate failure to act is treated as done when it was decided upon (s. 48(4)(b)) that is, when he does an act inconsistent with doing the failed act or if he does no such inconsistent act when the period expires within which it might reasonably have been expected to do the failed act if it was to be done.

An industrial tribunal has power to award compensation and this award of compensation is on a similar basis to compensation for unfair dismissal, that is, what the tribunal considers just and equitable in all the circumstances having regard to the infringement complained of and to any loss which is attributable to the act or failure which infringed his right (s. 49(2)). That loss includes any expenses incurred and the loss of any benefit which the applicant 'might reasonably be expected to have had but for that failure' (s. 49(3)). The principles of mitigation and contributory fault apply just as they do in analogous unfair dismissal proceedings (s. 49(4) and (5)).

There is a new species of automatically unfair dismissal to go alongside the remedies for dismissal on trade union grounds if dismissal is by reason of some of the circumstances that give rise to the right not to suffer detriment in health and safety cases. A selection for redundancy on these grounds is also automatically unfair (s. 105 of ERA 1996). This is achieved in respect of dismissal by a new s. 100 of ERA 1996, but there is an exception in that the dismissal is not to be regarded as unfair if the employer shows that it was or would have been so negligent for the employee to take the steps which he took or proposed to take that a reasonable employer might have dismissed him for taking or proposing to take them (s. 100(3)). There is no qualifying period to make a claim (s. 108). The law is neutral in the sense that such representatives have no right to positive discrimination in their favour, so that in *Smiths Industries Aerospace and Defence Systems v Rawlings* [1996] IRLR 656, the EAT overturned a decision of the industrial tribunal that in deciding on selection for redundancy the employer should have taken into account the skills and qualities shown by the employee in performing his representative duties.

The award to be made in the case of such an automatically unfair dismissal is a special award such as is made in trade union cases, that is, at present 104 weeks' pay (without the normal cap on the week's pay) or £13,775 whichever is the greater but not exceeding £27,500 (s. 125(1)). The amount may be even higher where the industrial tribunal has made an order for reinstatement but the employer does not comply with the order, save where the employer satisfies the industrial tribunal that it was not practicable so to comply. In such a case the special award is increased to one week's pay multiplied by 156, or £20,600 whichever is the greater (s. 125(2)). This award may be reduced on the ground of any conduct of the complainant when the tribunal considers it just and equitable to do so (s. 125(4)).

The similarity with trade union dismissal cases is taken further by the ability of a person dismissed on these health and safety grounds to apply for interim relief (s. 128(1)). (See the Health and Safety (Consultation with Employees) Regulations 1996 (SI No. 1513).)

20.11 RIGHTS OF PENSION FUND TRUSTEES

Pension fund trustees have protection from any detriment by any act or any deliberate failure to act by the employer done on the grounds that he was a trustee of a relevant occupational pension scheme (s. 46(1) of ERA 1996). A dismissal on those grounds is automatically unfair (s. 102).

Pension fund trustees have similar rights to time off to perform their duties and to undergo training. In determining the reasonableness of the time off sought, the industrial tribunal must consider 'the circumstances of the employer's business and the effect of the employee's absence on the running of that business' (ss. 58–60).

20.12 REMEDIES

If the applicant has mounted the foregoing hurdles, the remedies available to him are several, depending on the way in which his rights to participate in union activities have been infringed.

20.12.1 Action short of dismissal

A declaration may be granted and compensation which is 'just and equitable in all the circumstances having regard to the infringement of the complainant's rights' (TULR(C)A 1992, s. 149(2)). *Brassington* v *Cauldon Wholesale Ltd* [1978] IRLR 479, determined that 'compensation for the employee, not a fine on the employer, however tactfully wrapped up, is the basis of the award'. The applicants could thus recover their expenses in going to the industrial tribunal, and also non-pecuniary losses such as 'the stress engendered by such a situation' and compensation if a 'deep and sincere wish to join a union . . . had been frustrated' with all the benefits of help and advice which that might entail. In *Cheall* v *Vauxhall Motors* [1979] IRLR 253, the applicant could show no financial loss but the tribunal awarded him £50 on account of his frustration and stress for not being allowed to have his case presented by his own representative while he was still a member of one trade union. The normal provision for reasonable mitigation of loss applies, and the remedy can be sought by complaint within three months to an industrial tribunal (see *Adlam* v *Salisbury and Wells Theological College* [1985] ICR 786). The employer or employee may reclaim such compensation by joining in proceedings any union or person pressurising him to take such action (TULR(C)A 1992, s. 150(1)).

20.12.2 Failure to permit time off

Breach of this provision similarly entitles the complainant to a declaration and just and equitable compensation (TULR(C)A 1992, s. 172). A trade union official cannot, however, be held to have been refused time off if the employer did not know of the request for that time off to be taken (*Ryford Ltd* v *Drinkwater* [1996] IRLR 16).

20.12.3 Dismissal: compensation

The usual remedies of compensation up to £11,300 (plus the basic award), reinstatement and re-engagement used to be available on a dismissal for trade union membership or activities. There are the same provisions for enhanced payments as apply to dismissals for refusal to join a trade union, that is, a basic award minimum of £2,700 and a special award of 104 weeks' pay or £13,775 up to a maximum of £27,500. Even greater sums of 156 weeks' pay or £20,600 are available if an order of reinstatement is not carried out (ERA 1996, s. 125).

In assessing compensation, by TULR(C)A 1992, s. 155(2), the tribunal must ignore any breach of or refusal to comply or objection to a requirement to be a member of any trade union or a particular trade union, or to cease membership or not to take part in such activities. In *TGWU* v *Howard* [1992] ICR 106, the applicant was employed by and was a member of the TGWU. She resigned and joined another union and was dismissed. The tribunal found that the dismissal was automatically unfair within TULR(C)A 1992, s. 152 and that the applicant had contributed to her dismissal in that her conduct in resigning was unreasonable but that TULR(C)A 1992, s. 155(2) required the tribunal to disregard that conduct. The EAT upheld appeals by the TGWU on the ground that there was a distinction between what was done by the applicant and the way in which it was done, and that if the conduct of the applicant prior to dismissal deserved to be criticised, the tribunal could make an appropriate deduction.

20.12.4 Interim relief

The applicant may also claim interim relief, a special emergency interlocutory procedure which reflects the serious industrial relations consequences that often ensue, especially from the dismissal of a shop steward' (ERA 1996, s. 128). It does not, however, apply to selection for redundancy for an inadmissible reason. It also applies to an employee dismissed for refusing to join a union and to those dismissed for health and safety activities, as trustees of occupational pension schemes and as employee representatives.

An application must be made to the industrial tribunal within seven days of the effective date of termination, supported by a written certificate signed by an official of the employee's union who is specifically so authorised. This should contain the reasons why the particulars fall within the scope of interim relief (*Stone* v *Charrington & Co.* [1977] ICR 248), although tribunals have eschewed technicalities in its interpretation. Thus it was accepted that a union regional organiser was an authorised official notwithstanding he had no such express appointment (cf. *Farmeary* v *Veterinary Drug Co. Ltd* [1976] IRLR 322). Moreover, the tribunal may read together an application lodged within the time limit which does not comply with s. 161(2) of TULR(C)A 1992 and a letter presented after the period has expired which does so comply (*Barley* v *Amey Roadstone Ltd* [1977] ICR 546). Where, however, the authority of the official to give such a certificate is challenged by the employers before the tribunal, the onus lies on him to prove that he has actual or implied authority to sign the certificate, and if he had not, the certificate is defective and the claim must fail (*Sulemany* v *Habib Bank Ltd* [1983] ICR 60).

The tribunal must hear an interim relief application as quickly as possible (TULR(C)A 1992, s. 162(1)), and to expedite matters, its chairman may sit alone. The crucial issue is whether it is 'likely' that the tribunal will, at the end of the day, make a finding of unfair dismissal on account of an inadmissible reason. If so, it should at this stage order a reinstatement or re-engagement pending final determination (TULR(C)A 1992, s. 164). 'Likely' has been interpreted as demanding more than a reasonable chance of success; the prospects must be 'pretty good' (*Taplin* v *C. Shippam Ltd* [1978] IRLR 450). On the other hand, Slynn J did not 'think it right in a case of this kind to ask whether the applicant has proved his case on a balance of probabilities'.

An employer or employee may apply for the revocation or variation of an order once made (TULR(C)A 1992, s. 165). Such an application may be determined by a different industrial tribunal from that which made the original order (*British Coal Corporation* v *McGinty* [1988] IRLR 7).

21 Strikes and Other Industrial Action

[The period since 1906 has seen] a shifting pattern of Parliamentary assertions and judicial responses, a legal point counterpoint which has been more productive of excitement than of harmony.

(Lord Scarman in *NWL Ltd* v *Woods* [1979] 3 All ER 614 at 630.)

The strike is . . . the equivalent of the managerial prerogative, the factual power of management, unilaterally to change the conditions of work. Experience has shown in many countries that whatever the law may say it cannot suppress spontaneous action in response to unilateral change.

(O. Kahn-Freund and R.A. Hepple, *Laws Against Strikes*, Fabian Research Series 305, 1973.)

21.1 A RIGHT TO STRIKE?

21.1.1 History

There is no general right to strike in Britain, unlike several other countries where industrial action is protected by Constitutions. Strikes are discouraged by criminal, civil and administrative means, and social security benefits are withheld from strikers. Such liberty as exists to take industrial action has been established by way of statutory immunity from the law of tort and its extent has been a constant political football, not only between the political parties, but also between the legislature and the courts (see generally John Bowers and Michael Duggan, *The Modern Law of Strikes*, Financial Training Ltd, 1987, Supplement 1989; John Bowers and Simon Auerbach, *The Employment Act 1988*, Blackstone Press, 1988).

21.1.2 Justification of freedom to strike

It is worth briefly examining what are the arguments for a right or freedom to strike. Professors Kahn-Freund and Hepple have isolated four rationales (*Laws Against Strikes*, op. cit., pp. 5–8):

(a) the *equilibrium argument:* that labour needs a sanction to resist the otherwise total prerogative of management;

(b)   the need for *autonomous sanctions* to enforce collective bargains, self-help being stronger than legal enforcement could be;

(c)   the *voluntary labour argument*, that compulsion to work is tantamount to serfdom;

(d)   the *psychological argument*, which sees strikes as a necessary release of tension.

The authors conclude that, 'the imperative need for a social power countervailing that of property overshadows everything else'.

21.1.3   Legal liabilities

You cannot make a strike effective without doing more than is lawful.

(Lindley LJ in *Allen* v *Flood* [1898] AC 1.)

There are eight ways in which common law and statute now regulate and control strikes and other industrial action:

(a)   breach of the worker's contract of employment;

(b)   liability for economic torts of inducing breach of contract, interference with contract, or trade or business intimidation and conspiracy;

(c)   government emergency powers;

(d)   residual criminal liability mainly concerned with conspiracy and control of picketing;

(e)   a union member's right to remove authorisation by the union for strikes and industrial action held without a proper ballot;

(f)   the right of a member to complain against his union about unjustifiable discipline (TULR(C)A 1992, ss. 64 to 67; see para. 18.5.5);

(g)   the right of a member to complain of indemnification by his union of individuals (TULR(C)A 1992, s. 15; see para. 17.10.1);

(h)   the right of a member to complain of unlawful application of union assets by trustees of unions (TULR(C)A 1992, s. 16; see para. 17.10.2).

Moreover, separate Codes of Practice promulgated by the Department of Employment now cover strike ballots and the conduct of picketing.

The potential legal liabilities will be considered in turn and then the 'golden formula' which gives an individual immunity from torts when acting 'in contemplation or furtherance of a trade dispute'.

21.2   INDUSTRIAL ACTION AND THE INDIVIDUAL CONTRACT

The effect of strikes and other industrial action on the individual contract of employment is, paradoxically, rarely of direct importance. Employers normally do not wish to disturb post-strike calm by resorting to the courts to sue individual workers, although this has changed to some extent (e.g. *Boxfoldia* v *NGA* [1988] IRLR 383). On the contract of employment the effect of industrial action is still vital indirectly, for it provides the illegality central to the economic torts of intimidation, inducing breach of contract, and conspiracy. In this way management may seek redress from strike leaders and unions unless they are acting in contemplation or furtherance of a trade dispute as defined. The most valuable remedy is an injunction to prevent a strike taking place. Basically the law is still as stated in *Allen* v *Flood* [1898] AC 1:

A strike may be legal if due notice is given, that is, if the employee gives the minimum he must give to terminate his employment.

21.2.1 Notice to terminate

There is now a statutory minimum of one week for an employee's notice but longer periods are usually demanded by the individual contract. If such notice is given in a strike by each employee, the effect is that the employee has resigned, although this rarely happens in practice, since the object of industrial action is not to sever relations with the employer, but to impose different terms on which that relationship is to be carried on. As Donovan LJ said in *Rookes* v *Barnard* [1963] 1 QB 623, in the Court of Appeal:

It would, however, be affectation not to recognise that in the majority of strikes no such notice to terminate the contract is either given or expected. The strikers do not want to give up their jobs; they simply want to be paid more for it or to secure some other advantage in connection with it. The employer does not want to lose his labour force; he simply wants to resist the claim. Not till the strike has lasted some time, and no settlement is in sight, does one usually read that the employers have given notice that unless the men return to work their contracts will be terminated and they will be dismissed.

Lord Denning MR recognised that:

The strike notice is nothing more nor less than a notice that the men will not come to work. In short, they will break their contract . . .

(*Stratford* v *Lindley* [1965] AC 269.)

Moreover, there might be difficulties in a union giving notice to terminate on behalf of its members, not only because it is not their agent but also because employee A may have to give eight weeks under his contract, B three weeks and C one week. Davies LJ, dissatisfied with the ramifications of the notice idea, saw strike notices as notices to terminate the present contractual conditions coupled with an offer to work on new terms (*Morgan* v *Fry* [1968] 2 QB 710). Thus the striker does not intend to put an end to the employment altogether, Only if the employee is subject to a non-strike agreement between his employer and union, would he then be acting in breach of contract. There is no rule that notice of a strike is to be construed as giving notice of a breach of contract rather than terminating the contract, but in the particular case the union had no authority from its members to act as their agents to terminate their contracts of employment (*Boxfoldia Ltd* v *NGA (1982)* [1988] ICR 752; see also *Solihull Metropolitan Borough* v *National Union of Teachers* [1985] IRLR 211).

21.2.2 Suspension of contract

Another contention which has at times attracted the courts is that a strike suspends the contract of employment. This focuses on the fact that there is clearly no right to pay during a strike. Thus, in *Morgan* v *Fry* (supra), Lord Denning MR held that there was an implied term that each side to a contract agreed to its suspension by strike action after the giving of notice which could determine the contract. He said (at p. 728): 'if a strike takes place the contract of employment is not terminated. It is suspended during the strike and revives again when the strike is over.' The Donovan Commission rejected the general adoption of this idea on the ground of 'considerable technical difficulty', including problems over its application to unofficial, unconstitutional strikes and other forms of industrial action like a go-slow and work-to-rule. It is also unclear what would happen if a strike were never settled, or if the employer sought to dismiss all the strikers.

21.2.3 Repudiatory breach

The courts thus generally see a strike without proper contractual notice as a repudiation of their contracts by the strikers. The EAT in *Simmons* v *Hoover Ltd* [1977] ICR 61 at 76, said, 'It seems to us to be plain that it was a [repudiation] for here there was a settled, confirmed and continued intention on the part of the employee not to do any of the work which under his contract he had been engaged to do; which was the whole purpose of his contract.' Phillips J thought that *Morgan* v *Fry* was not 'intended to revolutionise the law on this subject' and held to the view that a strike is a repudiatory breach, citing *Bowes & Partners* v *Press* [1894] 1 QB 202, for it is a failure by the employee to perform the most fundamental duty under his contract — to work.

The employer has a choice whether or not to accept the repudiation by the strikers; if he does, he reacts by dismissing them and this counts as a termination of contract by the employer. Those cases which suggested that a strike, and indeed any other repudiatory breach, automatically brings the contract to an end as a form of 'constructive resignation' are now regarded as unsound (*London Transport Executive* v *Clarke* [1981] IRLR 166; see para. 12.3.2). Striking employees can thus claim unfair dismissal since they have been dismissed, but will only succeed if the employer has discriminated between them or they have failed to respond to a properly given warning notice (TULR(C)A 1992, ss. 237 to 239).

The other major consequence of the breach theory is that the employer is not obliged to pay during a strike; the employee must prove that he is ready and willing to work (*Henthorn and Taylor* v *CEGB* [1980] IRLR 361) (see para. 4.1.2.5). The situation was not affected by the old Wages Act 1986 (now ss. 13–20 of ERA 1996). The general principle is that deductions from pay are regulated by agreement between the parties. There is, however, an exception by ERA 1996, s. 14(5): 'where the worker has taken part in a strike or other industrial action and the deduction is made by the employer on account of the worker's having taken part in that strike or other action'. Strikers may not gain an injunction to prevent their employers dismissing them since they do not come to equity with clean hands (*Chappell* v *Times Newspapers Ltd* [1975] ICR 145).

21.2.4 Damages

The employer may also sue strikers for damages; but a major difficulty arises in their calculation. The courts have rejected an aliquot share of overhead expenses during lost days as the appropriate measure (*Ebbw Vale Steel, Iron and Coal Co.* v *Tew* (1935) 79 SJ 593). In *National Coal Board* v *Galley* [1958] 1 WLR 16, the Court of Appeal ignored the breaches of contract by other employees, and awarded the employers of the defendant, a colliery deputy engaged on safety work, only the cost of hiring a substitute — the princely sum of £3 18s 2d — and not a proportional amount of the whole loss as they had claimed.

If the factory were running at a loss only nominal damages could be secured, and sometimes strikes may even enhance a company's chance of profitability by reducing wage costs at a time of slack demand. In reality very few employers take the risk of further exacerbating industrial relations by suing for damages after the end of a dispute. As the CBI said in evidence to the Donovan Commission (para. 413 of the Report): 'The main interest of the employer is in the resumption of work and the preservation of good will.'

21.2.5 Other forms of industrial action

'The strike is not the only method of bringing industrial pressure to bear on the employer, and indeed it is the most expensive from the employees' viewpoint' (see H. Clegg, *The Changing System of Industrial Relations in Great Britain*, Basil Blackwell, 1979, pp. 258–60). These forms of action do not lead to full loss of wages for the individuals involved:

(a)   The *work-to-rule* and *go-slow* are particularly common on the railways. Employees follow work rules meticulously. Forms may be completed in great detail, and usually ignored safety provisions activated. All this slows down the rate of work progress and the Court of Appeal have held that this withdrawal of cooperation can amount to a breach of contract (*Secretary of State for Employment* v *ASLEF (No. 2)* [1972] 2 All ER 949, *British Telecommunications plc* v *Ticehurst* [1992] ICR 383; on go-slow see *General Engineering Services Ltd* v *Kingston and St Andrew Corporation* [1988] 3 All ER 867).

(b)   Overtime bans have traditionally occurred most frequently in the newspaper and electricity supply industries and on the railways and are only a breach of contract if overtime is compulsory, which is rarely the case. This tactic is often combined with a ban on shift working.

(c)   Employees may work normally but refuse to perform the particular duty about which they are protesting. Thus, bus drivers on one-man buses may refuse to collect fares, and teachers may refrain from dinner duties (*Gorse* v *Durham CC* [1971] 2 All ER 666), or refuse to cover for absent colleagues (*Sim* v *Rotherham Metropolitan Borough Council* [1986] IRLR 391).

(d)   Sit-ins, which normally take place after the termination of the contract of employment in order to preserve a factory, constitute the tort of trespass and can be restrained by injunction. In general, an employee is not entitled to remain on his employer's property without the employer's consent (*City and Hackney Health Authority* v *NUPE* [1985] IRLR 252).

In *Miles* v *Wakefield Metropolitan District Council* [1987] ICR 368, Lord Templeman stated that any form of industrial action by a worker is repudiatory, since it is a breach of contract intentionally to harm the employer's business.

21.2.6 Industrial action by the employer

The employer does not often have to resort to overt industrial action, since he retains the prerogative to make whatever changes he wishes in his business. Thus, until a few years ago, the employer's main offensive tactic against his workforce, the lock-out, was little used in Britain. In the last two decades it has, however, achieved some notoriety, particularly in the newspaper and printing industry, with the long *Times* dispute in 1979 the leading example.

21.3 THE LEGALITY OF INDUSTRIAL ACTION: THE QUESTIONS FOR THE COURT

The court must ask itself three questions to test the legality of most industrial action. The stages were first adumbrated as such by Brightman LJ in *Merkur Island Shipping Corporation v Laughton* [1983] IRLR 218 and approved by Lord Diplock and repeated in *Dimbleby & Sons Ltd v NUJ* [1984] 1 WLR 427 at 434F. The questions are:

(a)   Whether the plaintiff employers have a cause of action at common law.

(b)   Whether the defendants are acting in contemplation or furtherance of a trade dispute against the plaintiff. If so, s. 219 of TULR(C)A 1992 gives immunity from action which:

(i)   induces a person to break a contract of employment;
(ii)   threatens that a contract of employment will be broken;
(iii) interferes with the trade, business or employment of a person; or
(iv)   constitutes an agreement by two or more persons to procure the doing of any such act.

(c)   Whether the immunity is removed. In order to retain the immunity from certain torts, there must be an affirmative ballot amongst those likely to be called out in the action, and if the industrial action is to take place at different workplaces, the complex requirements of s. 228 of TULR(C)A 1992 must be satisfied. Action to enforce union membership is also unlawful. The liability of trade unions in tort has already been discussed (para. 17.5). We will first consider the main economic torts used in strike claims, and then turn to the immunities.

21.4 INDUCING BREACH OF CONTRACT

21.4.1 Importance of the tort

This centrally important tort is committed where a person directly or indirectly induces a party to a contract to break it without legal justification. It will be almost always committed in a strike which breaches not only the contracts of employment of the strikers, but also commercial contracts entered into by the employer struck against. The tort has thus always been at the forefront of regulation of strikes and it was appropriate that it should form the basis for the short-lived concept of unfair industrial practice introduced by the Industrial Relations Act 1971.

In the first authority on inducement *Lumley v Gye* (1853) 2 E & B 216, the defendant theatre owner persuaded an opera singer to sing for him at Her Majesty's Theatre, thus inducing breach of her exclusive engagement for three months to the plaintiff at the rival Queen's Theatre. The court held that there was a cause of action and thus generalised the existing action for enticement of a servant. Since then it has been applied to all manner of agreements. Lord Watson later stated the principle in *Allen v Flood* [1898] AC 1 at 107, that:

> He who wilfully induces another to do an unlawful act which, but for his persuasion, would or might never have been committed, is rightly held to be responsible for the wrong which he procured.

21.4.2 Different modes of committing the tort

There are several different ways of committing this tort in a strike, and although nomenclature varies and the categories are by no means watertight, they will be dealt with under the headings:

(a)   direct inducement (para. 21.4.3);
(b)   indirect inducement by unlawful means (para. 21.4.4);
(c)   procuring breach of contract by unlawful means (para. 21.4.5).

In the following diagrams the *dramatis personae* are:

Union organiser — Bill
Employer in dispute — Slim Trousers
Employee of Slim — Joan
Suppliers to Slim Trousers — Bright Buttons
Employee of Bright Buttons — Kevin

(a)   *Direct inducement*

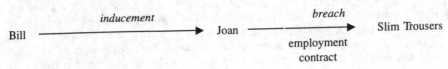

Bill pressures Joan to break her contract of employment with Slim Trousers.

(b)   *Indirect inducement*

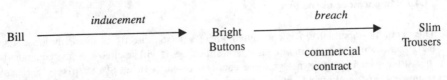

Bill induces Bright Buttons to breach its commercial contracts to supply Slim Trousers.

(c)   *Procuring breach*

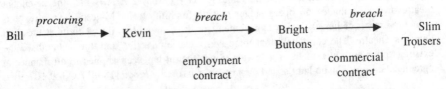

Bill tells Kevin not to switch on the machine which makes buttons which will be supplied to Slim Trousers. This prevents Bright Buttons from performing its contract to supply buttons to Slim Trousers. Slim will lose profits and is likely to seek an early settlement of the dispute. Here two contracts are broken: the employment contract between Bright and Kevin and the commercial contract between Bright and Slim. Bill has *induced* breach of the former by persuasion of Kevin, but only indirectly *procured* breach of the latter.

21.4.3 Direct inducement

Most commonly in strikes, the tort is committed when a shop steward directly operates on an employee and persuades him to breach his contract of employment.

21.4.4 Indirect inducement

Another common fact-situation is the case of a boycott or 'blacking' where union organisers take action against suppliers or distributors of the employer with whom it is in dispute and so induce breach of the employer's commercial contracts. This is an essential feature of solidarity action and *Torquay Hotel Co. Ltd* v *Cousins* [1969] 2 Ch 106, is a good example. The owner of the plaintiff hotel company had criticised the defendant union's action in an inter-union dispute already affecting other hotels in the area. The defendants thus contacted the drivers for Esso Ltd, which supplied the plaintiff hotel with fuel, and stated that they would prevent all oil supplies. The non-delivery of oil was a result of the employees' inducement and a majority of the Court of Appeal held there was a breach of contract. The inducement was, however, indirect and for it to be illegal required unlawful means. There were unlawful means, however, in the information conveyed to Esso Ltd that if they did not cut off oil supplies, the union would be calling on its members in that company to break their contracts of employment.

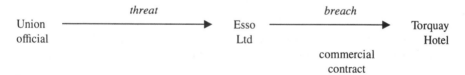

21.4.5 Procuring breach of contract

The tort is also committed if the strikers unlawfully interfere with any contract by actually preventing performance by, for example, removing essential tools, or kidnapping an employee (examples given in *Thomson (D.C) & Co.* v *Deakin* [1952] Ch 646, *GWK* v *Dunlop* (1926) 42 TLR 376), or switching off the lights at a theatre to prevent the production of a play. This, again, requires unlawful means. Blacking the goods of a particular employer is the example *par excellence* of procurement, and often two contracts will thereby be broken: that of the employee who procures it, and the employer's agreement with the outside party. *Stratford (J.T.) and Son* v *Lindley* [1965] AC 269, provides a good illustration of this *modus operandi*. The plaintiff was the chairman of companies A and B. A owned Thames motor barges while B hired them out to firms which employed their own crews. Forty-five of A's employees were members of the Transport and General Workers Union, while three belonged to the much smaller Watermen's Union. Both organisations sought negotiating rights with Stratford for A & Co. When the TGWU made a breakthrough by negotiations, the WU sought to use whatever industrial muscle they had to compel the same end. They had no power to attack Company A directly since they had very few members there, and instead they put pressure on B by calling on their members in companies to which B's barges were hired not to return them to the moorings when the contracts ended. The breaches of these agreements were thus achieved indirectly but were no less successful in achieving their end. The High Court granted an injunction, since the union had induced the hirers' employees to act in breach of their contracts of employment in order to procure a breach of contract between their employers and Company B on whom the union was seeking to exert pressure. Procuring breach of contract most commonly constitutes secondary action, the restriction on which is considered later (para. 21.9).

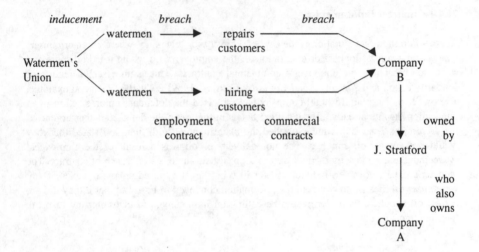

In *Thomson* v *Deakin* [1952] Ch 646 at 697, Jenkins LJ essayed a statement of general principle that for this variant of the tort to be committed it must be shown (author's italics):

> first, that the person charged with actionable interference *knew* of the existence of the contract and intended to procure its breach; secondly that the person so charged did *definitely and unequivocally* persuade, induce or procure the employees to breach their contracts of employment with the intent mentioned; thirdly, that the employees so persuaded, induced or procured did *in fact break* their contracts of employment, and fourthly, that the breach of the contract forming the alleged subject of interference ensued as a *necessary consequence* of the breach of the employees concerned of their contracts of employment.

This dictum has been approved by the House of Lords in *Merkur Island Shipping Corporation* v *Laughton* [1983] AC 570.

The four elements will now be considered in order and then we will look at unlawful means, justification and the statutory immunity.

21.4.6   Knowledge of contract

Economic torts require intention by the defendant, which means that he must foresee the possibility of a breach of contract and desire that result. The older cases demanded that the defendant have *actual knowledge* of the contract breached and some cognisance of its terms (*Thomson* v *Deakin* [1952] Ch 646, also *Long* v *Smithson* (1918) 88 LJ KB 223 at 225, and *Smithies* v *National Association of Operative Plasterers* [1909] 1 KB 310), but the threshold has been reduced over time. Ignorance may be bliss but it will not always excuse liability for inducement. Thus in *Cunard SS Co. Ltd* v *Stacey* [1955] 2 Lloyd's Rep 247, strike organisers were taken to know that, on their calling a strike, union members would thereby break their articles as seamen. Similarly, the Master of the Rolls took the more objective view in his wide statement of principle:

Even if [the Defendants] did not know of the actual terms of the contract, but had the means of knowledge which they deliberately disregarded — that would be enough.

Diplock LJ thought that the defendant is liable if he intends to have the contract ended by breach if it cannot be ended lawfully; again, motive enters the field. He could not 'turn a blind eye to it', and Russell LJ agreed. Here they found that the defendants did intend a breach, for even though the defendants said they assumed that the contracts could be terminated lawfully, they were in the end indifferent whether they did so or not. (See also *British Industrial Plastics Ltd* v *Ferguson* [1938] 4 All ER 504, *Emerald Construction Co. Ltd* v *Lowthian* [1966] 1 WLR 691, *Merkur's* case (supra).) In *Greig* v *Insole* [1978] 3 All ER 449 at 488, Slade J said:

It will suffice for the plaintiff to prove that the defendant knew of the *existence* of the contract, provided that he can prove also that the defendant intended to procure the breach of it . . . ignorance of the precise terms may in particular circumstances enable him to satisfy the court that he did not have such intent; ignorance of this nature, however, does not alone suffice to show absence of intent to procure a breach.

(See also *Solihull Metropolitan Borough* v *NUT* [1985] IRLR 211.)

21.4.7 Inducement

Although inducement must be carefully distinguished from the giving of friendly advice the line of distinction is difficult to draw. It is not enough that a union official tells employees that the boss is going to cut overtime payments from next week, and they immediately strike in protest. The Court of Appeal thus held that there was no inducement in *Thomson* v *Deakin* (supra) because the defendants simply stated the facts as they knew them. In *Torquay Hotel Co. Ltd* v *Cousins* [1969] 2 Ch 106 Winn LJ, however, thought that mere advice could be an inducement, going on to say:

A man who writes to his mother-in-law telling her that the central heating in his house has broken down may thereby induce her to cancel an intended visit.

In *Stratford* v *Lindley* [1965] AC 269 at 333, Lord Pearce abstracted from the case law the proposition that:

The fact that an inducement to break a contract is couched as an irresistible embargo rather than in terms of seduction does not make it any the less an inducement.

It would be enough if the union members were threatened with loss of their union membership if they did not take part in particular action.

It does not matter that the recipient of information is willing to break the contract. In *Camellia Tanker SA* v *ITF* [1976] ICR 274, it was held that the defendants, in informing their members of negotiations with the plaintiff, did not induce them to break their contract in support, since there was no 'pressure, persuasion or procuration'. The breach of the commercial contract was not the *necessary* result of the union's action, only being reasonably likely, and this was not sufficient.

Section 127, Criminal Justice and Public Order Act 1994 creates a new statutory tort of inducing a prison officer to withhold his services or to commit a breach of discipline.

21.4.8 Breach of contract

A *breach* of contract is a fundamental requirement for the commission of this tort, although there is a wider tort of interference which does not require breach. Thus in *Allen* v *Flood* [1898] AC 1, the defendant boilermakers' action in informing management that they would 'knock off work if the plaintiff shipwrights were not dismissed' was not unlawful since they were free to leave at any time without breaking their contracts. The fact that the motive for their leaving was to injure the plaintiffs was irrelevant. The tort has no application where the term of the contract breached is itself void for illegality, nor is there 'a tort of wrongfully inducing a person not to enter into a contract'. (See Megarry J in *Midland Cold Storage* v *Steer* [1972] Ch 630, *Solihull Metropolitan Borough* v *NUT* (supra), *Hadmor Productions Ltd* v *Hamilton* [1983] 1 AC 191.) Breach of an equitable duty suffices, so that in *Prudential Assurance Co.* v *Lorenz* (1971) 11 KIR 78, trade union members who refused to submit insurance premiums they had collected to their head office were enjoined from this course of action, since it was inducing breach of their equitable duty to account, which they owed as agents to their principal, the plaintiff.

21.4.9 Causation

Thomson v *Deakin* [1952] Ch 646, shows the need for a chain of causation between inducement and breach of contract. The plaintiff printers had a policy of refusing to employ trade unionists and they required workers to sign a written undertaking that they would not join one. This was challenged by NATSOPA, who called out on strike their 75 secret members at the company and asked other unions to disrupt the company's activities as a sign of solidarity. TGWU members at Bowaters responded by stating that they would not deliver paper to Thomson and another union refused to load it. In fact, the threats never materialised into a breach of contract by the employees, although there was a breach of the contract to supply between Bowaters and Thomsons. This was held not to be due to any inducement of the employees but to Bowater's decision not to supply, for it could not be proved conclusively that this had been caused by messages from the union. Lord Evershed said (at p. 686): 'The links in the chain which connect the defendants with the plaintiffs are . . . very insubstantial.' In any event, the employees were not in breach of their contracts so that the necessary unlawful means were not present. Jenkins LJ said (at p. 697):

A person who advocates the objects without advocating the means is [not] to be taken to have advocated recourse to unlawful means.

The fact that the contracted party may be perfectly willing to break the contract does not mean that the inducement is not effective.

```
                          no breach              breach
NATSOPA  ──────────▶  Bowater's  ─ ─ ─ ─ ─▶ Bowater  ──────────▶  Thomson
                      employees
                                                     commercial
                                                      contract

                                              Breach of contract to
                                              supply paper due not
                                              to Bowater's employees
                                              but to decision of Bowater
                                              not to deliver paper.
```

21.4.10 Unlawful means

Unlawful means are necessary in the tort variants of indirect inducement and procuring breach of contract. To return to the diagrammatic example in para. 21.4.2, if Bill had simply stood peacefully outside Bright Buttons factory with a placard stating 'Employers are rogues', there would be no tort, since there Bill would not be adopting any unlawful means to put his point across. His protest would have been well within his lawful rights. In the example, the unlawful means for procuring the breach of the commercial contract is provided by the inducing of the breach of the employment contract by Kevin. Unlawful means may be by way of tort, breach of contract or any other form of civil liability. This is a vital restriction because of the enormous potential width of this tort if it were not observed. Otherwise, for example, a wholesaler's action in persuading a retailer to cancel his supply contract with a competitor because of its lower prices might be illegal, yet this is generally considered fair in a free market economy.

Lord Denning suggested that there was a tort even if lawful means were adopted, in *Daily Mirror Newspapers* v *Gardner* [1968] 2 QB 762, but he retracted this view a year later in *Torquay Hotel Co. Ltd* v *Cousins* [1969] 2 Ch 106 at 138, with the salient comment that the 'distinction [between lawful and unlawful means] must be maintained, else we should take away the right to strike altogether'. He went on to explain:

> Nearly every trade union official who calls a strike . . . knows that it may prevent the employers from performing their contracts. He may be taken even to intend it. Yet no one has supposed hitherto that it was unlawful; and we should not render it unlawful today. A trade union official is only in the wrong when he procures a contracting party directly to break his contract or when he does it indirectly by unlawful means.

Unlawful means in the indirect inducement of breach of commercial contracts may be found in the direct inducement of breach of employment contracts, as *Emerald Construction Co. Ltd* v *Lowthian* [1966] 1 WLR 691 shows. The main contractors for a CEGB power station had entered into a lump labour contract with the plaintiffs, but this was not to the liking of the union's officers, who were opposed to such arrangements in principle. The union called its bricklayer members out on strike, and as a result the work fell behind, which put the plaintiffs in breach of their contract with the main contractors. The Court of Appeal held that there was a prima facie case that the union's action was intended to procure a breach of contract; the unlawful means used were the inducement of the employees' breaches. Moreover, there was no statutory protection at the time, since the breach induced was not of a contract of employment.

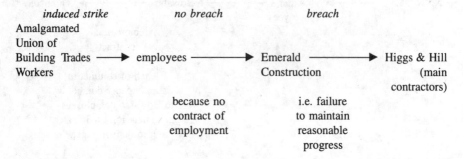

induced strike   *no breach*   *breach*

Amalgamated Union of Building Trades Workers ⟶ employees ⟶ Emerald Construction ⟶ Higgs & Hill (main contractors)

because no contract of employment

i.e. failure to maintain reasonable progress

21.4.11 Justification

Justification is more narrowly circumscribed as a defence to inducement than to the other economic torts. Indeed, it has succeeded only in *Brimelow* v *Casson* [1924] 1 Ch 302, and there in very special circumstances. Chorus girls employed by the defendant, a notorious impresario at the time, were paid so little that they had to resort to immorality to make ends meet. A strike in protest at these conditions was held justified in the circumstances, even though it induced breach of the employer's contract to perform his 'King Wu Tut Tut' review for the good burghers of Dudley.

The wider argument that the defence is available where there is no ill-will towards the employer (thus attempting to generalise from *Brimelow*'s case), was scotched in *South Wales Miners' Federation* v *Glamorgan Coal Co. Ltd* [1905] AC 239. (See *British Motor Trades Association* v *Salvadori* [1949] Ch 556, *Camden Nominees Ltd* v *Forcey* [1940] Ch 352.) Moreover, in *Greig* v *Insole* [1978] 3 All ER 449, where the International Cricket Council were found to have induced breach of cricketers' contracts with the Kerry Packer World Cricket Series, Slade J held that the Council's contention that they had acted from 'disinterested and impersonal motives' did not amount to justification.

21.4.12 Immunity

The original immunity was enacted in the Trade Disputes Act 1906 for inducement to breach a contract in contemplation or furtherance of a trade dispute but applied only in the case of *employment* contracts. It endured until 1971 when the Industrial Relations Act converted certain methods of inducing breach of contract into unfair industrial practices, e.g. where a person was acting outside the scope of authority and calling a strike without notice, and only gave immunity to registered unions (s. 96). The 1906 position was restored by the Trade Union and Labour Relations (Amendment) Act 1976 which inserted s. 13(1)(a) into TULRA 1974 (now TULR(C)A 1992, s. 219). This provided that an act done by a person in contemplation or furtherance of a trade dispute shall not be actionable in tort on the ground only:

(a)   that it induces another person to break a contract or interferes or induces any other person to interfere with its performance; or

(b)   that it consists of his threatening that a contract (whether one to which he is a party or not) will be broken or its performance interfered with, or that he will induce another person to break or to interfere with its performance.

The Employment Act 1980 reduced its scope by excluding from protection certain secondary action, that is, to bring pressure to bear on a party not in dispute, and also declared that any act of picketing leading to inducement of breach of contract was not lawful unless conforming to the now stricter immunity for picketing (TULR(C)A 1992, s. 220) (para. 21.9 and see Chapter 22 on picketing).

Example   Slim Trousers' workers strike and in order to exert pressure on him his workers picket Bright Buttons Ltd and persuade its workers not to make buttons required by Slim. They have induced breach of the workers' contracts of employment, and since the picketing does not meet the conditions of s. 15 of the 1974 Act as amended by the 1980 Act because the picketing is not of Slim's premises, they are not protected from the tort of inducing breach of contract.

21.5   INTERFERENCE WITH CONTRACT

21.5.1   The tort

Lord Denning MR has, on several occasions, stated that a wide tort exists of interference with contract by unlawful means, of which inducement of breach and intimidation are but two examples. This opens a much wider liability — there need be no breach of contract and the plaintiff need not be a party to the contract broken, but need only have an interest capable of protection. It may also extend to the prevention of an *expectation* that a contract would be made (*Brekkes Ltd* v *Cattel* [1972] Ch 105). In *Barretts & Baird (Wholesale) Ltd* v *IPCS* [1987] IRLR 3, Henry J stated the basic elements of the tort as follows:

first that there should be interference with the plaintiffs' trade or business . . . ; secondly, that there should be the unlawful means . . . ; thirdly, that that should be with the intention to injure the plaintiffs . . . ; and, fourthly, that the action should in fact injure [the plaintiffs].

The central significance of such a development for labour law is that it lies altogether *outside* the trade dispute immunity. In *Merkur Island Shipping Corporation* v *Laughton* [1983] 2 AC 570 at 609 Lord Diplock regarded the tort of 'interfering with the trade or business of another person by doing unlawful acts' as a 'genus of torts' of which procuring breach of contract is a 'species'.

The history of the tort is a complex one and its definition is still imprecise. The House of Lords in *Allen* v *Flood* [1898] AC 1, said that an individual was not liable *per se* for intentionally inflicting economic loss on another, if the means used were otherwise lawful. The presence of malice or bad motive did not constitute the border post between lawfulness and unlawfulness. Thus the defendant union official could with impunity threaten to call on the boilermakers who worked for the plaintiff to strike unless shipwrights also so employed were dismissed. Neither action was in breach of contract and so was quite legal even though the reason was to punish the shipwrights. This was always difficult to reconcile with *Quinn* v *Leathem* [1901] AC 495, also a decision of the House of Lords, and there were some straws in the wind before Lord Denning's series of pronouncements. For example, in *Stratford* v *Lindley* [1965] AC 269, Lord Reid doubted whether breach of contract was essential to constitute a tort, although Lord Donovan thought this argument 'as novel and surprising as I think the members of this House who decided *Crofter Handwoven Harris Tweed Co. Ltd* v *Veitch* would have done'.

The issue arose directly in *Torquay Hotel Co. Ltd* v *Cousins* [1969] 2 Ch 106, the facts of which have already been given (para. 21.4.4). There was a clause in the agreement between the fuel suppliers and the hotel that the former, Esso, would not be liable in contract for failure to supply should that be due to industrial dispute. Russell LJ narrowly interpreted this as 'an exception from liability for non-performance' (so that there was a breach of contract) and considered it as an ordinary inducement of breach of contract. Winn LJ suggested that if the contract allowed performance in mode A or mode B it would be tortious to prevent performance in mode A even if it could still be performed in mode B. (See also *Greig* v *Insole* [1978] 3 All ER 449). However, Lord Denning MR, disagreeing, made an ample formulation that ([1969] 2 Ch at p. 130):

> . . . if one person deliberately interferes with the trade or business of another, and does so by unlawful means, that is, by an act which he is not at liberty to commit, then he is acting unlawfully.

He thought this was the properly understood basis of *Stratford* v *Lindley* (supra) and *Rookes* v *Barnard* [1963] 1 QB 623, and defined the requirements of the tort of interference in some detail (at p. 139):

> First, there must be interference in the execution of a contract. The interference is not confined to the procurement of a *breach* of contract. It extends to a case where a third person prevents or *hinders* one party from performing his contract, even though it be not a breach. Second, the interference must be deliberate. The person must know of the contract, or, at any rate, turn a blind eye to it and intend to interfere with it: see *Emerald Construction Co. Ltd* v *Lowthian* [1966] 1 WLR 691. Third, the interference must be *direct*. Indirect interference will not do.

The existence of the tort was affirmed by the House of Lords in *Hadmor Productions Ltd* v *Hamilton* [1983] 1 AC 191, where the plaintiff alleged that ACTT (Association of Cinematograph Television and Allied Technicians) officials threatened to persuade union members to refuse to transmit television programmes produced by the plaintiff. They claimed that this was interference with the plaintiff's business by unlawful means. Thames TV had acquired a licence to transmit the programmes but was not contractually *bound* to do so. The House of Lords accepted the plaintiff's proposition that it could complain since the company's commercial *expectation* that the programmes would be broadcast was 'shattered' by the 'blacking'. (For a fuller version of the facts of this case, see para. 21.8.1).

The tort was rationalised in *Merkur Island Shipping Corporation* v *Laughton* [1983] 2 AC 570. The facts followed the familiar pattern in shipping cases. The International Transport Workers Federation organised blacking of the plaintiff's Liberian registered ship after a crew member complained of low wages. When the ship sought to leave the port of Liverpool, tugmen and lock-keepers refused to assist its free passage. The House of Lords agreed with Parker J that the tort of 'interfering by unlawful means' consisted of 'procuring the tugmen and the lockmen to break their contracts of employment by refusing to carry out operations on the part of the tugmen and the port authorities that were necessary to enable the ship to leave the dock'. The contractual duty under the charter was to 'prosecute voyages with the utmost dispatch'. The plaintiff could not rely on procurement of breach of contract since there was a *force majeure* clause. This provided an exclusion from liability, *inter alia,* 'in the event of loss of time due to boycott of the vessel in any port or place by shore labour or others'. Lord Diplock distinguished for these purposes between the primary obligations of the parties to perform under the contract, and their secondary obligations, to pay damages for breach, and said (at p. 608B):

> All prevention of due performance of a primary obligation under a contract was intended to be included [in the definition of interference] even though no secondary obligation to make monetary compensation thereupon came into existence, because the second obligation was excluded by some *force majeure* clause.

As to knowledge of the contract breached, Lord Diplock thought that there 'can hardly be anyone better informed than the International Transport Workers Federation as to the terms of the sort of contracts under which ships are employed'. (See also *Dimbleby & Sons Ltd v NUJ* [1984] 1 WLR 427, *Thomas v NUM (South Wales Area)* [1985] 2 WLR 1081, *Messenger Newspaper Group v NGA* [1984] IRLR 397.)

The tort of interference may also cover interference with future contracts not yet in existence (*Stratford (J.T.) & Son Ltd v Lindley* [1965] AC 269 at p. 339, *Union Traffic Ltd v TGWU* [1989] ICR 98 at p. 105). This was not constituted by the distribution of leaflets outside supermarkets urging members of the public to boycott the employer's mushrooms (*Middlebrook Mushrooms Ltd v TGWU* [1993] ICR 612). The plaintiff was not able to prove a causal connection between the defendant's action and a contract breaker. Since the leaflet was directed at the public and not the management of the supermarkets, any pressure or inducement to act in breach of contract would come from the public and only indirectly from the defendants, so that the action was not tortious at all. To be tortious the persuasion had to be directed at one of the parties to the commercial contract in issue.

The case of *Falconer v ASLEF & NUR* [1986] IRLR 331 is potentially very important throughout the law of economic torts and particularly interference, notwithstanding that it was decided at Sheffield County Court and concerned only £153. The plaintiff successfully sued the defendant unions in respect of his inability to travel by train from Doncaster to London because of a rail strike which they had called in January 1985 without a ballot. The defendants argued that their action was aimed at British Rail and that they did not know of any inconvenience to the plaintiff, still less did they intend to harm him. Judge Henham considered that it was sufficient that the plaintiff was 'one of a definite and identifiable group of people in contractual relationship with the British Railways Board'. It was indeed the intention of the unions in calling the strike to direct its effect on the plaintiff and people like him, and in so doing create pressure on the Board. The judge awarded special damages of £53 and general damages for inconvenience of £100. The decision has not had the far-reaching consequences predicted by some commentators, but may have inspired the notion of claims which may be made by affected members of the public in respect of industrial action affecting the supply of goods or services under TULR(C)A 1992. s. 235A.

21.5.2 Unlawful means

Indirect interference can only be restrained if unlawful means are adopted. Interference appears to include any hindrance upon the freedom of either party to perform the contract (see also *Acrow (Automation) Ltd v Rex Chain Belts Inc.* [1971] WLR 1676 at 1682). In

Torquay Hotel Co. v *Cousins* (supra) the majority held that they were breaches of contract (Megarry J was less sure in *Midland Cold Storage Ltd* v *Steer* [1972] Ch 630), but Lord Denning MR returned to a similar theme in *BBC* v *Hearn* [1978] 1 All ER 111 and *Beaverbrook Newspapers Ltd* v *Keys* [1978] IRLR 34, where he said that coercive interference with another's freedom of action was unlawful. In *Associated Newspapers* v *Wade* [1979] ICR 664, he widened the principle still further by suggesting that some matters (here interference with freedom of the press) could be so contrary to public policy that they could themselves amount to unlawful means. Thus the National Graphical Association's blacking of advertisements in a local newspaper with which it was in dispute was held to be unlawful means, partly because it prevented some public authorities and local councils from complying with their statutory duties to publish formal notice of proposed actions. It did not matter that neither party could enforce the unlawfulness by independent cause of action. An act contrary to the Restrictive Practices Act 1956 has also been held, albeit *obiter*, to suffice (*Daily Mirror Ltd* v *Gardner* [1968] 2 QB 762).

The Court Appeal has indicated that inducing breach of statutory duty may constitute unlawful means (*Meade* v *Haringey LBC* [1979] 2 All ER 1016), notwithstanding that some such breaches are only technical and almost incidental to the strike action. In *Associated Newspapers Ltd* v *Wade* (supra), the defendant and the Executive of the National Graphical Association ordered the blacking of all advertisements of advertisers who continued to use the Nottingham Evening Post with which the union was engaged in a bitter industrial dispute. This incidentally made it difficult for many public bodies to fulfil their statutory duties to make public announcements, and provided the unlawful means for indirect inducement. Further, Lord Denning MR thought the action would anyway have been unlawful as an infringement of Article 10 of the European Convention of Human Rights, which secures freedom of expression. Inducing such a breach of statutory duty lies outside the trade dispute immunity which refers only to inducing breach of *contract*. The presence of unlawful means depends on the true construction of the appropriate statute (*Lonrho* v *Shell Petroleum Co. Ltd (No. 2)* [1982] AC 173).

Inducing a breach of statutory duty may thus constitute unlawful means, but that was not the case in:

(a) *Barretts & Baird (Wholesale) Ltd* v *IPCS* [1987] IRLR 3, since there was nothing in the relevant statutes which imposed a statutory duty that the Meat and Livestock Commission should produce a strike-free system.

(b) *Associated British Ports* v *TGWU* [1989] IRLR 399, since there was, properly construed, no statutory obligation by clause 8(1)(b) of the National Dock Labour Scheme 1967 requiring registered dock workers to work. It provided that: 'A permanent worker ... shall ... (b) work for such periods as are reasonable in his particular case.' The House of Lords upheld the judgment of Millett J (which had been overturned by the Court of Appeal) and decided that this was not a statutory obligation but rather a condition of applicability of the scheme to registered dock workers.

This finding by the House of Lords that clause 8(5)(b) did not impose a statutory duty meant that they did not have to consider the judgments of the Court of Appeal as to the scope of the tort. The Court of Appeal thought it was at least arguable that the breach of statutory duty relied upon did not have to be actionable at the suit of the plaintiff in order to constitute unlawful means. The union argued that this was the result compelled by the decision of the House of Lords in *Lonrho Ltd* v *Shell Petroleum Co. Ltd (No. 2)* [1982] AC 173 (see also *CBS Songs Ltd* v *Amstrad Consumer Electronics plc (No. 2)* [1988] Ch 61,

Lonrho plc v *Fayed* [1989] 2 All ER 65, *Rickless* v *United Artists Corporation* [1986] FSR 502, *RCA* v *Pollard* [1983] Ch 135).

In *Barretts & Baird Wholesale Ltd* v *IPCS* (supra), Henry J determined that there was an arguable case that a striker's own breach of his contract of employment constituted unlawful means.

In order to render an individual striker liable in tort to any third party damaged by that strike, it is necessary that his predominant purpose be injury to the plaintiff rather than his own self-interest.

21.5.3 Immunity

There was an immunity from a species of this tort which dated back to the Trade Disputes Act 1906. Section 13(2) of TULRA 1974 provided:

> For the avoidance of doubt it is hereby declared that an act done in contemplation or furtherance of a trade dispute is not actionable in tort on the ground only that it is an interference with the trade, business or employment of another person or with the right of another person to dispose of his capital or his labour as he will.

This was, however, repealed by s. 19(1) of the EA 1982.

21.6 INTIMIDATION

21.6.1 The tort

In 1793 the master of a slave trading ship (A) in the Cameroons fired at a canoe which was about to do business with another vessel (B), and the natives in panic ceased to trade with B as a result of the volley. On an action by vessel B the Court of Common Pleas held that the defendant, the master of ship (A), was liable in damages for intimidation since the plaintiff had lost financially as the result of a threat of violence (*Tarleton* v *McGawley* (1793) 1 Peake 270). This may seem far removed from the modern industrial dispute, but in *Rookes* v *Barnard* [1964] AC 1129, the House of Lords developed this tort to include threat of a breach of contract or other unlawful act as well as threats of violence. This was one of the most controversial cases of the century and the result was reached notwithstanding that Pearson LJ in the Court of Appeal had described the tort as 'obscure, unfamiliar and peculiar' ([1963] 1 QB 623 at 695). The Association of Engineering and Shipbuilding Draughtsmen threatened to withdraw their labour if a non-unionist was not removed by BOAC within three days, in order to preserve their informal closed shop. Inducement of breach of contract was not here available as a cause of action, since the employee was lawfully dismissed with notice, but the House of Lords held that this anyway constituted the tort of intimidation and awarded exemplary damages to the employee concerned. The unlawful threat was contained in threatening to act in breach of contract, since it had been conceded by counsel for the union that a no-strike clause of a collective agreement had been incorporated into the contracts of individual workers. More generally, Lord Devlin commented that (at p. 1209):

> I find nothing to differentiate a threat of breach of contract from a threat of physical violence or any other illegal threat. All that matters to the plaintiff is that, metaphorically

speaking, a club has been used. It does not matter to the plaintiff what the club is made of — whether it is a physical club or an economic club or tortious club or an otherwise illegal club.

The objection that allowing breach of contract to be a threat enabled a person not a party to a contract to sue on it was summarily rejected by the House of Lords. The principle seems to be that the plaintiff can sue the defendant for intimidation if he could succeed in an action for breach of contract had the defendant carried out the threat. Liability in *Rookes* was for an unlawful threat against BOAC, a third party which indirectly but unintentionally caused the plaintiff loss. The decision gave rise to much controversy, both academic (e.g. 1964 CLJ 159, 81 LQR 116), and political.

The most salient criticisms from the legal point of view concerned the following questions:

(a)   Why was the defendant 'Silverthorne' a full-time union official, held liable when he was not the employee of BOAC and could thus not have threatened a breach of contract?
(b)   What was the unlawful act? If individuals had threatened to withdraw labour that was not a threat likely to have made BOAC dismiss the plaintiff.
(c)   If the union members had actually gone on strike, they would not have been liable in tort, so that the decision portended a greater liability for threats than for carrying out the action itself.

There must be proof of loss to constitute the tort. Thus, referring back to our earlier example, if Bill says to Slim that unless it shuts its factory he will break all its windows, and Slim keeps the factory open and Bill does not carry out his threat, Slim has no cause of action. There must be a threat and damage resulting therefrom — if a union organiser says to the employer that if he does not concede higher wages he will paralyse the company's operations, and the employer does not give an increase and the union leader finds his fierce words not backed up by his members' actions, the employer has no cause of action in intimidation. *Hodges* v *Webb* [1920] Ch 70, defined a threat as 'an intimation by one to another that unless the latter does or does not do something, the former will do something which the latter will not like'. The difficulty is to distinguish between a threat and a warning or mere advice.

It has also been suggested that the party who submits to a threat may claim the loss flowing therefrom (*DC Builders* v *Rees* [1966] 2 QB 617 at 625). This is known as two party intimidation. It is probably necessary that the defendant must then have the plaintiff directly in mind when making the threat. However, the threat must be 'of sufficient consequence to induce the other to submit' (Lord Denning in *Morgan* v *Fry* [1968] 2 QB 710 at 724).

21.6.2   Immunity

The development of the tort of intimidation caused an outcry in the trade union movement as it threatened to make every strike illegal. Thus the Trade Disputes Act 1965 soon afterwards extended trade dispute immunity to the newly coined tort where the person acted 'in contemplation or furtherance of a trade dispute'. Section 13(1)(b) of TULRA 1974 (now s. 219(1)(b) of TULR(C)A 1992) continued that policy by granting immunity to action 'where it consists in threatening that a contract (whether one to which he is a party or not) will be broken or its performance interfered with, or that he will induce another person to break a contract or interfere with its performance'. The provision was further widened in 1976 to cover breaches of commercial as well as employment contracts, but there is no protection against intimidation for secondary action (para. 21.9).

21.7 CONSPIRACY

21.7.1 The tort

It was only a few years after the abolition of the criminality of trade unions for conspiracies (Conspiracy and Protection of Property Act 1875, s. 3) that the courts developed a *tort* of conspiracy with precisely similar components. Since injunctions were granted freely its effects were also similar. It was described by Willes J in *Mulcahy v R* (1868) LR 3 HL 306 at 317, as consisting 'in the agreement of two or more to do an unlawful act, or to do a lawful act by unlawful means'. A conspiracy to commit a crime or a tort is clearly included in this class whereas whether it includes agreement to commit a breach of contract is less certain (see *Rookes v Barnard* [1964] AC 1129, Lord Devlin at p. 1210.)

It is, however, the second part of the definition — 'unlawful means' conspiracy — which is the most difficult and invidious, because it makes unlawful when done by two or more what would have been quite lawful when performed by an individual, e.g. *Kamara v DPP* [1974] AC 104. A conspiracy to injure is an agreement to cause deliberate loss to another without cause or excuse with the intention of injuring the plaintiff (e.g. *Huntley v Thornton* [1957] 1 All ER 234). The unlawful means of pursuing the strike must, however, be integral to the aims of the conspirators and not peripheral. Similarly it would not make it unlawful that the strike organiser broke the speed limit as he raced to a mass meeting. The scope of the tort appeared to have been cut down by the House of Lords in *Lonrho Ltd v Shell Petroleum Ltd (No. 2)* [1982] AC 173 (see also *Metall und Rohstoff AG v Donaldson Lufkin & Jenrette Inc.* [1989] 3 All ER 14) insofar as Lord Diplock was taken to have suggested that even in an unlawful means conspiracy, the court had to determine that the predominant purpose of the defendants was to injure the plaintiffs. In the case of *Lonrho plc v Fayed* [1992] AC 448, the House of Lords clarified that this was requisite only in a lawful means conspiracy.

In *Quinn v Leathem* [1901] AC 495 officials of the union asked the respondent to dismiss a non-unionist, and on his refusal to do so told him that an important customer would be warned to cease dealing with him under threat of strike if he persisted in denying their request. The matter went before a jury which found that the union's motive was to *injure* the respondent and not to promote the interests of the union. On appeal, five members of the House of Lords decided that this was actionable as a tortious conspiracy notwithstanding that the defendants had not committed any otherwise unlawful act in inducing the butcher no longer to trade with the plaintiff, there had been no crime, tort or breach of contract. This decision was also reached notwithstanding that *Allen v Flood* [1898] AC 1 showed that action done with the desire to injure was not in itself necessarily tortious. In *Mogul Steamship Co. v McGregor, Gow and Co.* [1892] AC 25, the House of Lords delineated the three-fold requirements of the tort as:

(a) *combination* by at least two persons;
(b) intentionally causing *loss;* with
(c) the *predominant purpose* not to further a legitimate interest.

(See an attempted reconciliation in *Thomas* v *NUM (South Wales Area)* [1985] 2 WLR 1081.)

The plaintiff must thus always prove an agreement between the parties, not merely coincidental action on their part.

21.7.2 Justification

Traders often combine in an attempt to create a monopoly and this has received the blessing of the common law in, for example, the *Mogul Steamship* case, where it was said that 'otherwise most commercial men would be at risk of legal liability in their legitimate trading practices and competition would be dead'. The most important justification case involving trade unions is *Crofter Handwoven Harris Tweed Co.* v *Veitch* [1942] AC 435, where the TGWU combined with Stornaway dockers to prevent yarn imports from the mainland in order to achieve a closed shop. The House of Lords found this conspiracy to injure justified since the predominant purpose was the promotion of the combiners' legitimate interest, for they wished to secure the elimination of price competition which was holding down wages at the largest spinning mill where their members were employed. (See also *Reynolds* v *Shipping Federation* [1924] 1 Ch 28.) Lord Wright said that: 'The true contrast is between the case where the object is the legitimate benefit of the combiners and the case where the object is deliberate damage without any such just cause.'

Courts have also held legitimate: attempts to force an employer to abandon a policy of refusing to employ trade unionists (*D. C. Thomson & Co. Ltd* v *Deakin* [1952] Ch 646); a campaign against a colour bar in a club (*Scala Ballroom (Wolverhampton) Ltd* v *Ratcliffe* [1958] 3 All ER 220); and the enforcement of a closed shop (*Reynolds* v *Shipping Federation* [1924] 1 Ch 28). *Huntley* v *Thornton* [1957] 1 All ER 234, was an exception, since most members of a union district committee who expelled the plaintiff, a fellow member, acted merely out of personal grudge and a desire for vengeance, although two were acquitted of such motivations and thus were not liable for the tort. The bitterness arose because he had not complied with union instructions to stop work some 24 hours before.

21.7.3 Immunity

In most cases in the trade union area, an immunity against liability for conspiracy is superfluous since the motivation with which it is carried on would amount to justification at common law. Out of an abundance of caution immunity is provided generally by what is now TULR(C)A 1992, s. 219(2) (replacing the Trade Disputes Act 1906), so that:

> An agreement or combination by two or more persons to do or procure the doing of any act in contemplation or furtherance of a trade dispute shall not be actionable in tort if the act is one which, if done without any such agreement or combination, would not be actionable in tort.

21.7.4 Criminal conspiracy

The law of criminal conspiracy was the most potent weapon against the early trade unions, both as in restraint of trade and for strike action. Section 3 of the Conspiracy and Protection of Property Act 1875 provided a first small step towards the modern immunities when it excluded criminal liability for acts in contemplation or furtherance of a trade dispute which would not be punishable as a crime if done by an individual. It also removed liability for conspiracy to injure committed without use of unlawful means. This was repeated by the Criminal Law Act 1977, a general statute reforming criminal conspiracy which provides a specific statutory form of conspiracy (s. 1(3)), normally biting on actions which would be crimes by individuals.

It is, however, specifically provided for trade unionists that where the acts agreed upon are to be done in contemplation or furtherance of a trade dispute any offence that would be committed shall be disregarded so long as it is a summary offence which is not punishable with imprisonment.

There is, indeed, now little incentive to bring a charge of conspiracy since the maximum sentence is the same as that for the substantive offence. Section 3 of the 1977 Act takes the sting out of the furore over the Shrewsbury Pickets case where two 'flying pickets' received three years' imprisonment for conspiracy to intimidate even though the substantive offence carried only a maximum of three months' imprisonment. Further, where the substantive crime is triable only summarily, proceedings for conspiracy may be brought only with the approval of the Director of Public Prosecutions. The 1977 Act does, however. enact two offences which might be used against factory work-ins which became an aspect of worker militancy in the 1970s; they consist of threatening violence to persons or property to gain entry to premises (s. 6) and being a trespasser on any premises with a weapon of offence (s. 8).

21.8 TRADE DISPUTE IMMUNITY

21.8.1 The section

When Parliament granted immunities to the leaders of trade unions, it did not give them any rights. It did not give them a right to break the law or to do wrong by inducing people to break their contracts. It only gave them immunity if they did . . . such statutes are to be construed with due limitations so as to keep the immunity within reasonable bounds.

(*Express Newspapers Ltd* v *McShane* [1980] ICR 42.)

We have already considered how immunity safeguards trade unionists against liability for each individual tort, but must return to the overall structure of s. 19 of TULR(C)A 1992. It begins: 'An act done by a person in contemplation or furtherance of a trade dispute shall *not be actionable in tort on the ground only*' — and then sets out the torts immunised against. Every word counts. The section protects a defendant against a claim for an injunction as well as an action in damages (*Torquay Hotel Co. Ltd* v *Cousins* [1969] 2 Ch 106 at 141, 144–6).

21.8.1.1 The meaning of 'not actionable' The words only render the strike '*not actionable*' and do not make it lawful for all purposes. Thus, for example, in *Stratford* v *Lindley* [1965] AC 269, the plaintiff could not sue for the direct inducement by the union of the employee's breach of contract of employment since that clearly fell within the immunity. However, that illegality provided the *unlawful means* for procuring breach of commercial contract and the strike could be restrained on that ground. To remedy this anomaly, s. 13(3)(b) of TULRA 1974 provided that a tort involving breach of contract within the 'golden formula' (see para. 21.8.2), 'shall not be regarded as the doing of an unlawful act or as the use of unlawful means for the purpose of establishing liability in tort'.

The subsection was, however, repealed by the Employment Act 1980, and the effect of the repeal arose in *Hadmor Productions Ltd* v *Hamilton* [1983] 1 AC 191. The plaintiff company produced a series of programmes ironically called 'Unforgettable' featuring pop musicians. Their *modus operandi* involved hiring freelance members of the Association of Cinematograph Television and Allied Technicians (ACTT), rather than direct employment, and was viewed with suspicion by the union. This hostility had led in the past to a complete blacking of programmes made by facility companies (as they were called), but by the time of Hadmor's foundation in August 1979 this stance had softened somewhat, as was confirmed in a letter from the union. As a result, Thames TV informally undertook to purchase the relevant series, but the ACTT shop stewards at Thames were not amused, threatened to black the series and consequently the company withdrew its transmission. As we have seen, the House of Lords held that the defendant shop stewards had interfered with the plaintiff's business by unlawful means. They disagreed with Lord Denning MR, who thought that due to the repeal of s. 13(3) of TULRA, the blacking in breach of the technicians' contracts constituted unlawful means.

21.8.1.2   Other torts   There are certain torts such as trespass and inducement of breach of statutory duty against which no statutory protection is given by the 'golden formula' (para. 21.8.2). Another possible flanking movement is an action in restitution for duress. This was canvassed without success in *Universe Tankships Inc. of Monrovia* v *ITWF* [1983] AC 366. The plaintiff claimed to recover money paid to the defendant Federation's Welfare Fund on the ground that it had been paid under duress. The action was framed in restitution rather than tort, but the House of Lords paid regard to the intention of TULRA 1974 to exempt all forms of industrial action from liability. Thus where there were alternative remedies of restitution and damages available, the plaintiff should not be allowed to circumnavigate the Act by recovering by a restitutionary remedy what he could not gain as damages.

Dimskal Shipping Co. SA v *International Transport Workers Federation* [1992] ICR 37, [1992] IRLR 78, concerned the blacking of the vessel 'Evia Luck' at Uddevalla, Sweden, in pursuance of the ITF's campaign against the registration of vessels under flags of convenience. Under pressure, the plaintiffs paid over US$110,000 to the ITF, and thereafter sought restitution thereof, and damages for the torts of intimidation and interference with contractual rights. The judge found that the industrial action was lawful under Swedish law. The House of Lords, with Lord Templeman dissenting, held that the material or essential validity of the contract was governed by its proper law, which in this case was English law, and that illegitimate economic pressure, including blacking of a ship, was duress, which avoided the contract made between the ITF and the shipowners.

21.8.2   Trade dispute

To be protected, the individual must be acting in contemplation or furtherance of *a trade dispute*, and by s. 244(1) of TULR(C)A 1992, this means: 'A dispute between workers and their employer, that is to say, which relates wholly or mainly to one of the following:

(a)   terms and conditions of employment, or the physical conditions in which any workers are required to work;

(b)   engagement or non-engagement, or termination or suspension of employment or the duties of employment, of one or more workers;

(c)   allocation of work or the duties of employment as between workers or groups of workers;

(d) matters of discipline;

(e) the membership or non-membership of a trade union on the part of a worker;

(f) facilities for officials of trade unions; and

(g) machinery for negotiation or consultation, and other procedures, relating to any of the foregoing matters, including the recognition by employers or employers' associations of the right of a trade union to represent workers in any such negotiation or consultation or in the carrying out of such procedures.'

This is commonly termed the 'golden formula' and dates back to the Conspiracy and Protection of Property Act 1875, although in that statute it dealt with picketing alone. It was extended in the Trade Disputes Act 1906, passed by the Liberal Government to give protection to trade unionists specifically against the decision sanctioning tortious conspiracy, *Quinn* v *Leathem* [1901] AC 495, since this case threatened to make most strike action unlawful.

The Industrial Relations Act 1971 altered the nomenclature to 'industrial dispute' and restricted the scope of the immunity to exclude disputes between groups of workers. After this short-lived experiment the substance of the 1906 provisions was re-enacted with some extensions in TULRA 1974, amended by the Trade Union and Labour Relations (Amendment) Act 1976, and then again restricted by the Employment Acts 1980 and 1982 and Trade Union Act 1984. All this material is now consolidated by TULR(C)A 1992. It does not add up to a general right to strike, as the numerous injunctions granted in recent years testify. The economic torts reign supreme where the variant of tort committed is not precisely within those granted immunity and where the act is not in contemplation or furtherance of a trade dispute, as defined. This has left the judges much room for manoeuvre, and A.W.R. Carothers has described the area as exhibiting 'a sea-saw vendetta between the courts and the legislature' (*Collective Bargaining Law in Canada*, p. 57). The discussion of trade disputes is divided into the definition of:

(a) parties (para. 21.8.3);

(b) dispute (para. 21.8.4);

(c) subject-matter (para. 21.8.5);

(d) 'relates wholly or mainly to' (para. 21.8.6);

(e) in contemplation or furtherance of (para. 21.8.7).

We then turn to:

(f) secondary action (para. 21.9);

(g) strike ballots (para. 21.10);

(h) union recruitment strikes (para. 21.11);

(i) statutory restrictions on industrial action (para. 21.12).

As a matter of terminology, 'secondary action' means action directed against an employer's suppliers or customers, i.e. those in a business relationship with him, rather than at the employer himself, which is primary action (TULR(C)A 1992, s. 224).

21.8.3 Parties

The freedom to strike afforded by the 'golden formula' used to extend to a dispute between employers and workers or between workers and workers and thus protected demarcation disputes or arguments over union recognition. This was restricted by s. 18(2) of EA 1982 to disputes between 'workers and their employer'. The operative word is 'workers' and this used to include those who seek to work, and those reinstated after dismissal. Section 244(5) of TULR(C)A 1992 now excludes a person who has ceased to be employed unless:

(a) his employment was terminated in connection with the dispute; or
(b) was one of the circumstances giving rise to it.

It is irrelevant that the employer may change his business identity during the course of the conflict. Thus Lord Denning said 'the words "employers" and "workers" in [s. 244(5)] apply to employers whatever the particular hat those particular employers may wear from time to time' (*Examite Ltd* v *Whittaker* [1977] IRLR 312, *The Marabu Porr* [1979] 2 Lloyd's Rep 331). The veil will not, however, be lifted as between separate companies in respect of secondary action (*Dimbleby & Sons Ltd* v *NUJ* [1984] 1 WLR 427; see para. 21.9).

Before 1982 where an employers' association was involved in a dispute, its constituent employers were deemed also to be parties, and a dispute to which the trade union is a party was deemed to be a dispute to which workers were privy (TULRA 1974, s. 29(4)) (see *Camellia Tanker SA* v *ITF* [1976] ICR 274). This meant that a trade union might initiate a trade dispute, notwithstanding that the workers it purported to be fighting for were at best lukewarm about the cause. This was repealed by s. 18(5) of EA 1982 (see *Mercury Communications Ltd* v *Scott-Garner* [1984] Ch 37). The employees, by voting in favour of action in a ballot, will, however, thereby adopt the demands made by the union (*R* v *National Arbitration Tribunal ex parte Keable Press Ltd* [1943] 2 All ER 633).

The immunity may be claimed by any person sued when acting in contemplation or furtherance of a trade dispute, whether or not he is an officer of the union, and there is thus no distinction at all between official and unofficial action save in respect to the ballot provisions which apply only to official action. Disputes between employer and employer are not granted immunity (*Larkin* v *Long* [1915] AC 814), so that union activity to support one side or another is not protected.

21.8.4 The dispute

Lord Denning has said that a dispute 'exists whenever a difference exists, and a difference can exist long before the parties become locked in combat . . . It is sufficient that they should be sparring for an opening' (*Beetham* v *Trinidad Cement Ltd* [1960] AC 132). A dispute need not be in existence to provide immunity. According to *Conway* v *Wade* [1909] AC 506, it may be 'an objective event or situation . . . likely to occur' (Lord Atkinson at p. 517) or 'a real thing imminent' (Lord Shaw at p. 512) (see now *Associated British Ports plc* v *TGWU* [1989] IRLR 399). There may also be a dispute even if the employers concede to the demands of the union. For s. 244(4) of TULR(C)A 1992 provides that 'an act, threat or demand done or made by one person or organisation against another which, if resisted, would have led to a trade dispute with that other, shall, notwithstanding that because that other submits . . . [and] no dispute arises, be treated as being done . . . in contemplation of a trade dispute with that other'. This provision reverses the decision in *Cory Lighterage Ltd* v *TGWU* [1973] ICR 339, where the employers were at one with the union in seeking to preserve a closed shop, but could not get permission from the National Dock Labour Board to dismiss the employee whose sacking the union sought. Buckley LJ decided (at p. 362):

If someone threatens me with physical injury unless I hand over my wallet and I hand it over without demur, no one could, in my opinion, sensibly say that there had been any dispute about my handing over my wallet.

Thus, there was no immunity for the union's action since there was no dispute, but this is now changed by s. 244(4) and a clear illustration of the effect of the statute was provided in *Hadmor Productions Ltd* v *Hamilton* [1983] AC 191, where Thames TV submitted without a fight to the union's demand not to show a series made by a facility company. There is, however, no immunity for any action taken after a dispute has been settled (*Stewart* v *AUEW* [1973] ICR 128).

21.8.5 Subject matter

A trade dispute must relate wholly or mainly to one or more of the matters set out in s. 244 of TULR(C)A 1992 (para. 21.8.2), a list which is intended to separate the sheep of industrial grievances, which it is legitimate for trade unions to pursue, from the goats of political or personal grievances with which, according to the policy of statute, they should not concern themselves. The 1906 immunity was restricted to disputes 'connected with the employment or non-employment, terms of employment or conditions of labour of any person'. This was then greatly extended in several directions, but EA 1982 restricted it again, especially by requiring that the dispute relate *wholly or mainly* to the listed matters rather than merely being connected therewith, the lesser requirement under s. 29(1) of TULRA 1974 as originally enacted. The 1982 Act also removed immunity from pressure to impose an unlawful union membership only requirement, and this itself was modified by the Employment Act 1988 (see para. 21.11).

The fact of the strike itself cannot be a dispute; it must be the manifestation of a grievance over something comprised within the definition of trade dispute. This was clearly demonstrated in *BBC* v *Hearn* [1977] IRLR 273. The BBC sought to enjoin television technicians who were threatening to prevent transmission of the FA Cup Final to South Africa because of the policy of the Association of Broadcasting Staffs (of which the defendant was General Secretary) to oppose racial discrimination in that country. The Court of Appeal rejected the union's claim that this in itself amounted to a dispute about whether there should be a condition that employees should not be compelled to transmit to South Africa while its Government practised apartheid. There had been no such demand before the strike was called and accordingly no trade dispute existed. Lord Denning described the union's actions as 'coercive interference', and not within s. 29(1), even though he thought the definition included 'not only the contractual terms and conditions but those terms which are understood and applied by the parties in practice, or habitually or by common consent, without ever being incorporated into the contract. If the union had only asked: "We would like you to consider putting a clause in the contract by which our members are not bound to take part in any broadcast which may be viewed in South Africa", and the BBC had refused, they *would* then have been cloaked with the immunity.' Lord Diplock confirmed in *NWL Ltd* v *Woods* [1979] 3 All ER 614 (at pp. 633–34), that the ratio of *Hearn*'s case would be strictly construed (cf. also *Hadmor Productions Ltd* v *Hamilton* [1983] 1 AC 191 at 227). There are *dicta* that the dispute must be about the current contract and that the claims of a union may be so preposterous as not to be genuine. One of the defendant unions' arguments in *Dimbleby & Sons Ltd* v *NUJ* [1984] 1 WLR 427 (at p. 433) was that there was a dispute over terms and conditions in that there was an implied term in the journalists' contracts entitling them to refuse to comply with instructions given to them by the employers to provide copy of the kind they were employed to obtain if the NUJ gave them an instruction to the contrary. Lord Diplock stated that 'it passes beyond the bounds of credibility that any responsible newspaper proprietor would agree to such a term in contracts of employment with his journalists'. (See also para. 21.9 and *Universe Tankships Inc. of Monrovia* v *ITF* [1983] AC 366 at 388, *London Borough of Wandsworth* v *National Association of Schoolmasters/Union of Women Teachers* [1993] IRLR 344.)

We will now consider the following strikes which fall *outside* the definition of trade dispute:

(a) disputes motivated by personal malice (para. 21.8.5.1);
(b) political strikes (para. 21.8.5.2);
(c) foreign disputes (para. 21.8.5.3).

21.8.5.1 Personal disputes   It may be a matter of some difficulty to identify properly what a strike is connected with, especially when it is called for a variety of different reasons. However, in some cases the reasons for action clearly have nothing to do with pursuing a trade dispute. In *Conway* v *Wade* [1909] AC 506 at 512, Lord Loreburn said:

> If, however, some meddler sought to use the trade dispute as a cloak beneath which to interfere with impunity in other people's work or business, a jury would be entirely justified in saying that what he did was done in contemplation or in furtherance, not of a trade dispute, but of his own designs, sectarian, political or purely mischievous as the case might be.

Huntley v *Thornton* [1957] 1 All ER 234 was a strong case falling outside of protection. As a result of the plaintiff's refusal to take part in a one-day strike, his workmates declined to work with him and the Hartlepool District Committee of his union attempted to ensure that he did not get another job in the area. They threatened to organise strikes to secure the success of this policy. The atmosphere was poisonous and Harman J decided that even if there had been a trade dispute in the first place, the union was now acting merely out of ruffled dignity in a personal vendetta. Similarly, in *Torquay Hotel Co. Ltd* v *Cousins* [1969] 2 Ch 106, the court found that the blacking of the plaintiff's hotel by the defendant union was motivated by a desire to suppress criticism by its manager of their existing dispute; there was no trade dispute between the defendant and plaintiff so that there was no immunity. In *Stratford (J.T.) & Son Ltd* v *Lindley* [1965] AC 269, the House of Lords held that there was no trade dispute because the union's contentions were really not about terms and conditions, but because the Watermen's Union was annoyed with the employer in the course of rivalry with the TGWU (see para. 21.4.5).

21.8.5.2 Political strikes   The distinguishing features of a political strike are by no means easy to delineate. As Roskill LJ commented in *Sherard* v *AUEW* [1973] IRLR 188 (at para. 20):

> It is all too easy for someone to talk of a strike as being a political strike when what that person really means is that the object of the strike is something of which, as an individual, he objectively disapproves.

There is also great force in Kahn-Freund's questions (*Labour and the Law*, op. cit., para. 3.1, p. 317):

Is not every major industrial problem a problem of governmental economic policy? Is it not true that, not only in publicly owned industries, governmental decisions on wages policies — whether statutory or not — on credits and on subsidies, on the distribution of industry and on housing and town planning, and on a thousand other things, affect the terms and conditions of employment at least as much as decisions of individual firms?

The most famous determination of political dispute was the General Strike of 1926 which was thus deprived of immunity by Astbury J (*National Sailors and Firemen's Union of GB and Ireland* v *Reed* [1926] 1 Ch 536). (See Goodhart (1927) 36 Yale LJ 464.)

Strikes held to protest against government policies have received the same treatment, whether called, as in *Associated Newspapers Group Ltd* v *Flynn* (1970) 10 KIR 17, to protest against the Industrial Relations Bill, or whether as in *Beaverbrook Newspapers Ltd* v *Keys* [1978] IRLR 34, part of the unions' collective 'day of action' against the Conservative Government's economic policies. One outstanding characteristic of these disputes is that the employer is in no position to concede the demands of those taking the industrial action. Thus, in *Gouriet* v *UPW* [1978] AC 435, the Post Office, whose employees threatened to stop mail to South Africa, could have no direct effect on the racialist government there. Similarly, there is no immunity where employees strike with the aim of bringing about a change in their employer's policy, e.g. objecting to the contribution of the employer to the Conservative Party, local government workers protesting about their employer council's policy of investing in South Africa, or hospital workers rejecting the principle of pay beds. On the other hand, in *Sherard*'s case the Court of Appeal would not enjoin a one-day strike against the Government's wage freeze, for the union had some members who were employed by the Government and objected to their pay being restrained in this way, and this was a typical industrial grievance. Further, union members are protected if they are directly affected by the government policies protested against in other ways, for example, concerning denationalisation as in *General Aviation Services UK Ltd* v *TGWU* [1974] ICR 35, since this might lead to redundancies (see also *Hadmor Productions Ltd* v *Hamilton* [1983] 1 AC 191, *Associated British Ports plc* v *TGWU* [1989] IRLR 399).

It is necessary in this area to distinguish the role of government as national guardian and employer. The 'golden formula' does not cover the former but in the latter capacity it is no different from any other management. Moreover, a dispute between a Minister and workers may be a trade dispute, even where he is not the employer, if he must approve a settlement (TULR(C)A 1992, s. 244(2)). Examples closer to the line include road workers striking against a decision not to build a motorway, or prison officers against any increase in prison numbers which they fear may lead to violent confrontation. Action designed above all to change the policies of the union's own executive is outside the scope of the immunity (*PBDS National Carriers* v *Filkins* [1979] IRLR 356). The more stringent test introduced by s. 18(2) of EA 1982, that the dispute relate *wholly or mainly* to the s. 244(1) (TULR(C)A 1992) list rather than merely being connected thereto, has meant that strikes are more often held to fall outside the golden formula (see *Mercury Communications Ltd* v *Scott-Garner* [1984] Ch 37; para. 21.8.6).

21.8.5.3 Foreign disputes By s. 244 of TULR(C)A a trade dispute existed 'even though it relates to matters occurring outside the United Kingdom' provided that 'the person or persons whose actions in the United Kingdom are said to be in contemplation or furtherance of a trade dispute relating to matters outside the United Kingdom are likely to be affected in respect of one or more of the matters specified in s. 244 [of TULR(C)A] . . . by the outcome of that dispute' (s. 244(3)). This sanctions the taking of action in solidarity with colleagues working for the same multi-national abroad, but only if their pay is likely to have an effect on that in the UK. The utility of the provision is thus likely to be minimal.

21.8.6 'Relate wholly or mainly'

Until 1982 a dispute need only be 'connected with' the acceptable subjects of the 'golden formula'. The provision of the 1982 Act that it must 'relate wholly or mainly' to one or more such subjects is among the most important reforms ushered in by that legislation. This restriction sought to deal with the wide connotation given to 'connected with' in *NWL Ltd* v *Woods* [1979] 1 WLR 1294, where the House of Lords considered that there need be only a genuine connection between the dispute and the relevant subject matter. The industrial issue need not be predominant in the minds of the strikers.

The significance of the reform arose first in *Mercury Communications Ltd* v *Scott-Garner* [1984] Ch 37, although the Court of Appeal gave little firm guidance on the matter for the future. The union objected to the Government's liberalisation of telecommunications from which the plaintiff as one of the first licensed operators besides British Telecom stood to gain. The plaintiff planned to establish a digital communications network partly using the BT network. The National Executive Committee of the Post Office Engineers Union instructed its members, the vast majority of whom were employed by BT, not to connect Project Mercury to the BT system. The Court of Appeal decided that the dispute was wholly or mainly about government policy. Although the union honestly and fervently believed that their campaign was in the best interests of the jobs and conditions of service of employees in the industry, it did not follow that industrial action in the course of that campaign constituted a dispute 'wholly or mainly' about the threat of redundancy if the monopoly were not maintained.

Sir John Donaldson MR thought that (at p. 79):

> In context the phrase 'wholly or mainly relates to' directs attention to what the dispute is about and, if it is about more than one matter, what it is mainly about. What it does *not* direct attention to is the reason why the parties are in dispute. . . . A contributory cause of the dispute and possibly the main cause is the belief that redundancy ('termination . . . of employment' in the words of the section) is just around the corner, but the dispute is not about that or, if it be preferred, relates wholly or mainly to pay . . .

He thought that Parliament 'intended a relatively restricted meaning to be given to the phrase "relates wholly or mainly to"' and that the most obvious way to find out what a particular dispute is wholly or mainly about 'is to inquire what the men concerned . . . said to management at the time'. Here it was fatal that the union at no stage referred to the job security agreement, which it would have done had the dispute been truly about redundancies.

May LJ commended an 'ordinary common-sense approach' analogous to that which is adopted when a court has before it a question of causation. He saw the present action as springing from 'a political and ideological campaign seeking to maintain the concept of public monopoly against private competition' (see also *Associated British Ports plc* v *TGWU* [1989] IRLR 291).

21.8.7 Contemplation or furtherance of a trade dispute

21.8.7.1 Contemplating a dispute As we have seen, there must be a starting point to the coverage of the immunity; simply anticipating a fight as a future possibility is not enough. The words meant, according to Lord Loreburn in *Conway* v *Wade* [1909] AC 506, 'that either a dispute is imminent and the act is done in expectation of and with a view to it, or that the dispute is already existing and the act is done in support of one side to it'. (See also *Bent's Brewery Co. Ltd* v *Hogan* [1945] 2 All ER 570.) On the other hand, in *Health Computing Ltd* v *Meek* [1980] IRLR 437, NALGO sought, as a matter of policy, to ensure that its members in the National Health Service had nothing to do with the plaintiff, a private company which sought to supply computer systems. Goulding J upheld the union leaders' contention that a dispute was contemplated as likely to arise between its members and any Health Service employers who engaged the plaintiff's services, notwithstanding that there was apparently no original demand made to management (cf. *Stratford (J.T.) & Son* v *Lindley* [1965] AC 269 and *BBC* v *Hearn* [1977] IRLR 273).

21.8.7.2 A remoteness test for secondary action The words 'in contemplation or further-ance' were fashioned by the Court of Appeal into a 'remoteness' test to enjoin secondary action but this was struck down several times by the House of Lords. In several cases the Court of Appeal held that a union could not properly claim immunity for such secondary action because it found, objectively reviewing the evidence before it, that it was not furthering their trade dispute, but was too remote from it (*Star Sea Transport Corp of Monrovia* v *Slater* [1978] IRLR 507 CA, *Express Newspapers Ltd* v *McShane* [1979] 2 All ER 760, *Associated Newspapers Ltd* v *Wade* [1979] 1 WLR 697, *PBDS* v *Filkins* [1979] IRLR 356, *Beaverbrook Newspapers Ltd* v *Keys* [1978] ICR 582). The House of Lords, however, decided that the only proper consideration was whether the defendant honestly and genuinely believed the action he was taking would contribute in the disputes (*NWL Ltd* v *Woods* [1979] 3 All ER 614, *Express Newspapers* v *McShane* [1980] AC 672, and *Duport Steels Ltd* v *Sirs* [1980] 1 All ER 529).

In *NWL Ltd* v *Woods* (supra) the International Transport Workers Federation threatened to black the *Nawala,* a ship owned by the plaintiff company, in pursuance of their longstanding protest against flags of convenience. They wanted to force the owners to pay higher wages in line with the ITF norm, but the Court of Appeal decided that this was not connected with matters listed in s. 29 of TULRA 1974 (now s. 244 of TULR(C)A) because the employers *could not* accede to the union's demands. The House of Lords overruled this and Lord Diplock stated (at p. 624A):

> If a demand on an employer by the union is about terms and conditions of employment the fact that it appears to the court to be unreasonable because compliance with it is so difficult as to be commercially impracticable or will bankrupt the employer or drive him out of business, does not prevent its being a dispute connected with terms and conditions of employment. Immunity under s. 13 [of TULRA 1974] is not forfeited by being stubborn or pig-headed.

(See also *Norbrook Laboratories Ltd* v *King* [1984] IRLR 200.)

The amendments made by s. 18 of EA 1982 expressly 'do not affect the question whether an act done by a person is done by him in contemplation or furtherance of a dispute, whether he is a party to the dispute or not'.

21.9 STATUTORY CONTROL OF SECONDARY ACTION

The Conservative Government resolved to cut down what these cases had shown to be the wide scope of the trade dispute immunity, by the popularly called 'secondary action' provisions of the Employment Act 1980. The sections made an exception to the immunity; they made strikers liable for action which causes breach of commercial contracts against other employers besides their own. This was subject to restricted exceptions which were still cloaked with the immunity, and constituted permitted secondary action.

Section 17(2) of EA 1980 first defined 'secondary action' as:

When, and only when, a person—

(a)   induces another to break a contract of employment or interferes or induces another to interfere with its performance, or

(b)   threatens that a contract of employment under which he or another is employed will be broken or its performance interfered with, or that he will induce another to break a contract of employment or to interfere with its performance,

if the employer under the contract of employment is not a party to the trade dispute.

Section 4 of the Employment Act 1990 finally removed all immunity for secondary action other than secondary picketing which is peaceful. This swept away all the complex 'gateway' provisions under the Employment Act 1982 of first supplier and first distributor (now TULR(C)A 1992, s. 244(1)).

Secondary action is defined as occurring where there would normally be immunity under TULR(C)A 1992, s. 219, but the employer under the contract of employment in question (where there is inducement to break etc.) is not the party to the trade dispute. A contract of employment for these purposes includes work done by independent contractors who undertake to perform the work personally.

By the Education (Modification of Enactments Relating to Employment) Order 1989 (SI 1989 No. 901) there is no immunity from actions in tort when 'the inducement, interference or threat . . . relates to a contract the performance of which does not affect directly or indirectly the school or institution over which the governing body in question exercises its functions' (reg. 5).

21.10 STRIKE BALLOTS

Part II of the Trade Union Act 1984 (now s. 226–234, TULR(C)A 1992) removed the immunity of unions and individual strike organisers from certain actions in tort unless a majority of union members likely to be called out in industrial action have approved that action in a properly held ballot. The section applies, however, only to the torts of: inducing an employee to break his contract of employment; inducing an employee to interfere with the performance of his own contract of employment; and indirectly procuring a breach of or interference in a commercial contract by the unlawful means of inducing a breach of a contract of employment. It does not apply to intimidation or conspiracy to injure.

21.10.1 When a ballot is required

A ballot is required only in respect of 'an act done by a trade union'; that is, if it is authorised or endorsed by the principal executive committee, the president or general secretary or some other person in accordance with the rules of the union. This is the same codification as governs the vicarious liability of a union in tort actions under TULR(C)A 1992 (see para. 17.5).

The first authorisation or endorsement of the strike or other industrial action must be given within four weeks from the date the ballot is taken. The union does not have the flexibility to hold a ballot at the start of negotiations and then wait until the result is known six weeks later before putting it into effect. In the event that unofficial action is later given official backing (i.e. endorsed), the ballot must be held before but not more than four weeks before the union declares it official.

The time limits focus on a 'relevant act' being within four weeks. This is defined in TULR(C)A 1992, s. 226 as an act of inducing a person to breach his contract of employment or interfere with its performance. There is, however, no need that the inducement of members should be successful. The Court of Session in *Secretary of State for Scotland* v *Scottish Prison Officers' Association* [1991] IRLR 371, had to consider whether the instruction by the Association's executive to hold meetings of members during working hours without permission was a relevant act. It was held to be so even though in the event no breach of contract occurred in fact because the meetings called by the POA were authorised by the employers.

Authorising or endorsing does not extend to communicating the decision to authorise a ballot with a view to more extensive industrial action, and it was entitled to be partisan in this respect (*Newham London Borough Council* v *NALGO* [1993] ICR 189). The union was demonstrating that it wanted industrial action to be extended to members in addition to those already on strike but it was not calling on them to strike.

In the docks dispute in 1989 the TGWU were prevented from calling industrial action during this period because of an injunction. In similar circumstances the union may now apply for an extension of time, but no application may be made more than eight weeks after the ballot (TULR(C)A 1992, s. 234). If the ballot no longer appears to represent the views of the members, the court may not grant the extension. This means that the courts will be drawn into the merits of the dispute and into hypothetical areas.

In *Monsanto plc* v *TGWU* [1987] ICR 269, the union held a proper ballot and received a mandate for a strike, which took place. After some weeks, however, the union suspended the action while it negotiated with the employers, but then reimposed the action when the negotiations failed. The Court of Appeal held that the union did not have to hold a further ballot since the resumption of action was in connection with the original trade dispute (cf. *Boxfoldia Ltd* v *NGA (1982)* [1988] ICR 752).

New action requires the support of a fresh ballot, but a single ballot may provide the necessary support for a long campaign of action provided that it was sufficiently continuous and self-contained. Whether it is or is not is a question of fact in each case (*Post Office* v *Union of Communications Workers* [1990] IRLR 143). The union may call out members who had joined since the date of a ballot, and to do so does not lose the union immunity which it would otherwise have (*London Underground Ltd* v *RMT* [1996] ICR 170). The Court of Appeal so decided on the basis that it was the industrial action which required to be supported by a ballot, not industrial action in which a particular person has been induced to take part. Their Lordships rejected the proposition that the industrial action which had been called was thus different from that on which the ballot had been held. They disapproved some comments of Lord Donaldson MR in *Post Office* v *UCW*.

The union must give the right to vote to 'all those members of the trade union who it is reasonable at the time of the ballot for the union to believe will be called upon in the strike or other industrial action'. Each such person must have one and only one vote. No one else may be permitted to vote, not even those who will be subject to lay-off as a result. The ballot is required even if there are no individual members of the union and the rules do not make any provision for a ballot (*Shipping Company Uniform Inc.* v *ITWF* [1985] ICR 245).

Until 1990 the ballot requirements applied only to persons engaged in industrial action who were employees. Section 5 of the 1990 Act rendered the provisions of s. 10 of the Trade Union Act 1984 (no immunity in tort for industrial action without a ballot) and s. 1 of the Employment Act 1988 equally applicable to those who work pursuant to contracts for services.

21.10.2 Industrial action at different workplaces

A union intending to organise industrial action must conduct separate ballots for each place of work. Industrial action may not be taken at a particular workplace unless the union has obtained a majority vote for the action at that workplace.

Section 17 of the Employment Act 1988 addressed this question and introduced a new s. 11(1A) and (1B) into the Trade Union Act 1984 (now TULR(C)A 1992, s. 228)). In so far as the union believes, and it is a reasonable belief, that the persons to be induced to take part in a strike or other industrial action are engaged at different places of work, it must hold a ballot at each such place of work.

This provision does not apply where there is some factor:

(a)   which relates to the terms, conditions, or occupational description of each member entitled to vote;
(b)   which that member has in common with some or all members of the union who have the same employer.

Similarly, if all members would have the same place of work if overseas members were excluded, then only one ballot need be held. The High Court has held, in *University of Central England* v *NALGO* [1993] IRLR 81 that it is not necessary for entitlement to vote in a ballot to be restricted to employees of one employer. It would have been easy for reference to be made to a restriction to one employer in TULR(C)A 1992, s. 288, but none was made.

In order to retain immunity from action in tort, a majority at the workplace at which the strike or other industrial action takes place must have voted in favour of such action in a separate ballot (TULR(C)A 1992, s. 228(1)).

'Place of work' means the premises occupied by his employer at or from which that person works. If he works from more than one set of premises, the ballot is to be held at the place with which his employment has the closest connection.

If the union fails to comply with these provisions, it will:

(a)   lose its immunity from action in pursuance of a trade dispute;
(b)   be open to an action by a member of the union under s. 235A(1) of TULR(C)A 1992.

21.10.3 The ballot paper

Under the Trade Union Act 1984, the question on the ballot paper had to require the voter to answer a somewhat loaded question; that is, 'whether he is prepared to take part, or as the case may be to continue to take part in a strike involving him in a breach of his contract of employment . . .' or other industrial action in breach of contract as the case may be. This was amended by the Employment Act 1988, after which the ballot paper must:

(a) contain the specific statement 'If you take part in a strike or other industrial action, you may be in breach of your contract of employment';

(b) ask the relevant members (using whatever words) whether they are willing to take part in a strike (if a strike is proposed by the union) or other industrial action (if that is recommended) or, separately, both questions (if action of both kinds is proposed); and

(c) make no comment or qualification upon the statement required by (a) (TULR(C)A 1992, s. 229(2), (4)).

In *London Underground Ltd* v *NUR* [1989] IRLR 341, Simon Brown J held that an act could not be taken to have been done with the support of a ballot if the ballot posed a question which, either in whole or part, asked whether the member was prepared to participate in a strike by reference to issues other than trade disputes (cf. *Associated British Ports plc* v *TGWU* [1989] IRLR 291).

21.10.4 Protection of the voter

There appears to be nothing to prevent the union from including tendentious campaigning material with the ballot. It may not however, merely ask whether the members agree with the union's negotiating position. Rather it must put the member on the spot as to whether *he* is prepared to *participate* in the action proposed.

There are provisions protecting the voter similar to those found in Part I of the 1984 Act (now Part I, TULR(C)A 1992), relating to the election for the principal executive committee. He must not be interfered with or constrained in exercising his rights to vote, nor should he have to bear any costs in so doing (TULR(C)A 1992, s. 230(1)).

The ballot paper should be available so far as reasonably practicable to the potential striker before, immediately after or during his working hours. Again, subject to the reasonable practicability defence, the voting must be in secret.

A majority of the voters must be in favour of the action in question for the union to have immunity. Thus spoiled votes in effect count *against* the action. The union must take reasonably practicable steps to inform those entitled to vote of the complete result of the ballot, although here again it can exempt overseas members. Any inaccuracy in counting the votes is to be disregarded if it is accidental and on a scale which could not affect the result of the ballot (TULR(C)A 1992, s. 230(4)).

In *British Railways Board* v *National Union of Railwaymen* [1989] IRLR 349, Lord Donaldson MR indicated that there is a profound difference between denial of a right to vote and inadvertently failing to give a member an opportunity to vote. The latter is governed by s. 230(2) of TULR(C)A 1992, which provides that the opportunity must be given 'as far as reasonably practicable'. Where, as in the instant case, the trade union does its best in good faith to comply with the balloting provisions, the mere fact that some members are missed out does not in itself mean that s. 230 is not satisfied.

21.10.5 Call before the ballot

The industrial action will not be treated as supported by the ballot if there has been a call for such action before the date of the ballot (TULR(C)A 1992, s. 233(3)). However, the

Court of Appeal held in *Newham London Borough Council* v *National and Local Government Officers Association* [1993] ICR 189 that s. 233(3) does not require the union to take a neutral stance. A union can indicate its desire for industrial action to be held without that amounting to a call for, or authorisation or endorsement of, such action.

21.10.6 Notice of the ballot

A further important requirement for the validity of a ballot was added by TURERA 1993, s. 18, substituting a new s. 226A into TULR(C)A 1992. The trade union must 'take such steps as are reasonably necessary to ensure that not less than the seventh day before the opening day of the ballot' there is received, by every person whom it is reasonable for the union to believe will be the employer of those persons who will be entitled to vote in the ballot, a written notice to the effect that the union intends to hold a ballot, specifying the opening date of the ballot and describing the employees who will be entitled to vote therein.

It is not sufficient for the union to indicate that it was to ballot 'all its members employed by your institution'; rather it must specify a category or name individuals, or by a combination of the two enable the employer readily to ascertain which of the employees are to be balloted and subsequently to be called upon to take the relevant action. It is a question of fact in each particular case whether the notice gives the employer the requisite knowledge or not. It did not do so in *Blackpool and Fylde College* v *NATFHE* [1994] IRLR 227, because although the employers were aware that 288 of the 872 lecturers at the College were members of the union and they knew who 109 of those were because they had their union dues debited directly from their salaries, they did not know who of the other 760 lecturers made up the remaining 179 members.

Further, such an employer must be sent not later than the third day before the opening date of the ballot a sampled voting paper. The employer must be informed of the ballot result (TULR(C)A 1992, new s. 231A).

21.10.7 Notice of industrial action

One of the most important features of the TURERA 1993 was the introduction by s. 21 (adding s. 234A to TULR(C)A 1992) of a requirement to give advance notice of industrial action to the affected employer(s). The trade union must 'take such steps as are reasonably necessary to ensure that the employer receives' a specified notice of industrial action. This must describe 'the employees of the employer who the union intends to induce or has induced to take part or continue to take part in the industrial action, specify whether the industrial action is intended to be continuous or discontinuous and specify where it is to be continuous the intended date for any of the affected employees to begin to take part in the action and where it is to be discontinuous the intended dates for any of the affected employees to take part in the action'.

21.10.8 Balance of convenience on interlocutory injunctions when there has been no ballot

The weighing of the balance of convenience in giving an injunction when there has been no ballot may be seen in *Solihull Metropolitan Borough* v *National Union of Teachers* [1985] IRLR 211. The NUT issued guidelines to its members to refuse to cover for absences of colleagues known in advance and various other tasks. No ballot had been held and Warner

J granted an injunction that the union must rescind its instructions. Whilst he saw detriment to the plaintiff in the harm done to the children in their schools, which could not be remedied in damages, there would be little inconvenience to the union. It was merely a matter for the union of choosing between holding a ballot and accepting arbitration.

21.10.9 Member's right to remove authorisation for strikes and industrial action

When the obligations to have a ballot before strike action were introduced in 1984, the only enforcement mechanism was in the hands of the employer, in that the union's immunity from action was taken away. There was much criticism that it should not be the employer who was able to restrain strikes without the support of a ballot. Section 1 of the Employment Act 1988 introduced the right of the ordinary member not to have his union make official a strike or other industrial action which is not supported by a ballot. Alternatively, it covers the situation where a ballot has been held but its terms infringe the requirements of TULR(C)A 1992, ss. 226 to 232 (see paras 21.10.3 and 21.10.4).

21.10.9.1 Application Section 1 applies where a trade union authorises or endorses strike or industrial action. This is defined in the same way as for other acts of authorisation, and bites on an inducement by the union even though such a 'call to arms' has not succeeded in its object of calling employees out on strike or to participate in other industrial action: it may be one which would be ineffective because the member was 'unwilling to be influenced by it or for any other reason'. 'Strike' is specifically defined as 'any concerted stoppage of work'.

A member of the relevant union may apply to the High Court Queen's Bench or Chancery Division for an order that the union withdraw any authorisation or endorsement for the strike or other industrial action in the event that a proper ballot has not been held. To apply, the member must be a person who is likely to be or has been induced by the union to take part in the action. The action called for need not have actually commenced for an order to be made.

21.10.9.2 The court order On such an application, the court may make such order as it considers appropriate to require the union to take steps to ensure that there is no, or no further, inducement of members to take part in such action. The statute specifically mentions in this respect an order for 'the withdrawal of any relevant authorisation or endorsement'. The order may not, however, require the union expressly and positively to hold a ballot. It might restrain the union from paying strike pay to those taking part in a strike not supported by a ballot. The court may grant interlocutory relief and it is likely that most cases will come before the courts by way of an application for an interlocutory injunction, as was the first application brought unsuccessfully by members of the NUR supported by the Commissioner for the Rights of Trade Union Members in July 1989 on behalf of NUR members. It did not succeed.

21.10.10 Persons authorised to call industrial action

By TULR(C)A 1992, s. 229(3)) an industrial action ballot paper must specify who is authorised for the purposes of calling members to take part or continue to take part in industrial action. There will be no immunity for the trade union if action supported by a ballot is not in fact called by the person named in the ballot paper. Further, there must be no call by the trade union to take part or to continue to take part in industrial action before the date of the ballot.

Action was called by the specified person when the general secretary of the union gave authority for industrial action to take place should a meeting the following day between the employers and local union officials prove unsuccessful. Section 7(3)(b) does not require an unequivocal call by the specified person which is free of all conditions. Some matters must be left for the judgment of those on the ground who must decide how and when as a matter of common sense the call for action should be put into operation. On the other hand, it is not consistent with the purpose of the Act for a specified person to give blanket authority for a local union official to go ahead with negotiations on the basis that a strike could then be treated as authorised if things did not go well (*Tank & Drums Ltd* v *TGWU* [1992] ICR 1).

The Code of Practice on Trade Union Ballots on Industrial Action was issued by the Department of Employment pursuant to the Employment Act 1988 and draws together the threads of the TULR(C)A 1992 on industrial action together with various non-statutory guidance. The 'purpose of this Code' is proclaimed in para. 1 to be 'to provide practical guidance to promote the improvement of industrial relations and desirable practices in relation to the conduct by trade unions of ballots about industrial action'. The most noteworthy provisions of this Code, which go beyond existing statutory provisions, are that:

(a)   an industrial action ballot should not take place before agreed procedures which might lead to the resolution of a dispute without the need for industrial action have been completed (para. 8);

(b)   a ballot should be held only if the union is contemplating industrial action and it would be lawful to organise it (para. 9);

(c)   a union should inform every employer whose workers may be given entitlement to vote of its intention to hold the ballot (para. 11);

(d)   fully postal ballots should be chosen in the normal case, save where only a few members are entitled to vote or the speed of obtaining the response is of the essence (para. 20);

(e)   voters should not be misled or confused by the framing of the question and should not, for example, be led to believe that they are being asked to agree to an opinion about the union's view of the merits of a dispute (para. 28);

(f)   steps should be taken to maintain the security of the balloting process (para. 30);

(g)   a union should tell its members information relevant to the ballot, such as the turnout or size of majority vote required and the potential consequences of workers taking industrial action (para. 33);

(h)   the union should respond positively (and in writing when so requested) to a request from any employer whose workers participate in the industrial action ballot for such details of the ballot result, as the law requires a union to provide to those entitled to vote in the ballot.

21.11   UNION RECRUITMENT STRIKES

Section 225(1) of TULR(C)A 1992 limits immunity from actions in tort in relation to disputes over the closed shop or to promote trade union membership. Neither a union nor its officials are to have a trade dispute immunity where the reason or one of the reasons for the act of the union is the fact or belief that an employer is employing, has employed or might employ a person:

(a) who is not a member of any trade union;

(b) who is not a member of a particular trade union; or

(c) who is not a member of one of a number of trade unions.

Alternatively, the pressure may be brought because the employer is failing, has failed or might fail to discriminate against any such person in that he treats: (a) employees; (b) applicants for employment, differently according to whether or not those persons are such members and is more favourable to such people who *are* members of trade unions in general or a particular trade union. Membership of a trade union in this context may mean membership of a particular branch or section of a trade union.

21.12 STATUTORY RESTRICTIONS ON INDUSTRIAL ACTION

21.12.1 Restrictions on classes of workers

There is nothing in Britain like the wide restrictions on strikes by *Beamter*, established public servants, in West Germany. There are, however, several statutory limitations on the right to withdraw labour for various classes of workers, and these generally concern the public sector:

(a) *Armed forces* Any member of the armed forces who engages in disruptive activity in order to redress a grievance can be disciplined under the Army Act 1955, Airforce Act 1955 or Naval Discipline Act 1953; and s. 1 of the Incitement to Disaffection Act 1934 also makes it an offence 'if any person maliciously and advisedly endeavours to seduce any member of her Majesty's forces from his duty or allegiance to her Majesty'.

(b) *Police* Section 53 of the Police Act 1964 enacts the offence of causing disaffection or inducing a policeman to withhold his services or commit breaches of discipline.

(c) *Merchant seamen* were severely restricted in calling strikes since they had to give at least 48 hours' notice to the ship's master of their intention to terminate their employment so long as the ship is safely moored in the UK (s. 42 of the Merchant Shipping Act 1970). The provision has now been repealed and replaced by s. 32 of the Merchant Shipping Act 1988, which makes it a crime to endanger a ship, life or limb in breach of duty.

(d) *Postal workers* The Post Office Act 1953, ss. 58, 68 and Telegraph Act 1863, s. 45 render it an offence wilfully to delay or procure the delay of any post packet or message (*Gouriet* v *UPW* [1978] AC 435; see also Telecommunications Act 1984, ss. 44 and 45).

(e) *Aliens* The Aliens Restriction (Amendment) Act 1919, s. 3(2) makes it a crime punishable by three months' imprisonment for an alien to promote industrial unrest unless engaged *bona fide* in the same industry for at least two years. This measure was passed to seek to insulate Britain from the shockwaves of the Russian revolution.

(f) *Endangering life* Section 240(1) of TULR(C)A 1992 states, 'where any person wilfully and maliciously breaks a contract of service or of hiring, knowing or having reasonable cause to believe that the probable consequences of his so doing, either alone or in combination with others, will be to endanger human life or cause serious bodily injury, or to expose valuable property whether real or personal to destruction or serious injury', he is guilty of an offence punishable by fine up to £500 or imprisonment for three months (Criminal Justice Act 1991, s. 17(2)). This includes doctors, firemen, nurses and also lorry drivers, within its scope. There is no record of prosecution under this section, but it may be a ground for an injunction. The Industrial Relations Act 1971 finally repealed the anomalous provision making it a crime for gas, electricity or water workers to go on strike in breach of contract.

21.12.2 Emergencies

In the event of a national emergency the Government retains very wide powers under the Emergency Powers Act 1920 as amended by the 1964 Act of the same name. It can proclaim a state of emergency lasting one month where there have occurred 'events of such a nature as to be calculated by interfering with the supply and distribution of food, water, fuel or light, or with the means of locomotion, to deprive the community of a substantial proportion of the community's essentials of life'. It may then make regulations 'for securing the essentials of life to the community' but these must not, *inter alia*, make it an offence to take part in a strike or peacefully persuade others to do so. A state of emergency has been declared on 12 occasions as a response to a particularly damaging strike action, including the seamen's strike in 1966, the dock strike in 1970 and the miners' strike in 1972. It was under this power that during the miners' strike of 1974 there were rota power cuts and workers were put on a three-day week. The Army has been called in to assist in several disputes, including the power strike of 1977, pursuant to the Defence (Armed Forces) Regulations 1939, now rendered permanent by s. 2 of the Emergency Powers Act 1964. (See G. Morris, *Strikes in Essential Services*, Mansell Publishing, 1986.)

21.12.3 Support of industrial action by public bodies

In *R v London Borough of Ealing ex parte Times Newspapers Ltd* [1987] IRLR 129, a ban by local authorities on newspapers owned by News International plc, which was then involved in the Wapping dispute, was held to be unlawful as an abuse of discretion. The ban was imposed for an ulterior object, to assist the dismissed print workers. Watkins LJ said (at para. 49): 'I would go so far as to say that no rational local authority would for a moment have thought that such a ban was open to it to impose in discharge of its duty to service libraries.'

21.13 CONSUMER ACTIONS

Consumers are given statutory rights to pursue trade unions in respect of unlawful industrial action by TURERA 1993, s. 22, which inserted a new s. 235A into TULR(C)A 1992. An individual may apply to the High Court where he claims that any trade union or other person has done, or is likely to do, an unlawful act to induce any person to take part, or to continue to take part, in industrial action, and an effect, or a likely effect, of that industrial action is or will be to prevent or delay the supply of goods or services, or reduce the quality of goods or services supplied to that individual. That individual need not actually have an entitlement, contractual or otherwise, to be supplied with the particular goods or services in question (s. 235A(3)). The normal remedy will be an interlocutory injunction to restrain such action, and it appears that such an application may be considered by the court even if an application is also made by an employer. The union may have to fight at very short notice on two separate fronts.

A new official is also created to assist the individual litigant with his claim. The Commissioner for Protection against Unlawful Industrial Action may provide assistance to an individual pursuing such a claim (TULR(C)A 1992, s. 235B)).

21.14 INJUNCTIONS

21.14.1 Use of injunctions in strikes

Most employers are not concerned to claim damages from striking employees. The employer wants them back to work to prevent any further losses of production, rather than to claim monetary judgments which would be difficult to enforce. He thus turns to the equitable remedies. As we have seen, it is only in very exceptional circumstances that the courts have countenanced specific performance of a contract of employment; it savours too much of forced labour (para. 12.5.1). TULR(C)A 1992, s. 236 now provides that no court may by an order for specific performance of a contract of employment or by an injunction to restrain breach thereof compel an employee to work (see also *Barretts & Baird (Wholesale) Ltd* v *IPCS* [1987] IRLR 3).

The courts have no compunction about granting injunctions to prevent torts and these have very much the same effect. The Rules of the Supreme Court generally provide, by ord. 29, r. 1(1), that injunctions may be sought at any stage of proceedings 'in all cases in which it appears to the court to be just and convenient to do so'. Application may be speedily made by motion to the Chancery Division in open court or by summons to the judge in chambers in the Queen's Bench Division. Although the plaintiff must in most circumstances give two days' notice, this may be dispensed with and an application may even predate the issue of a writ or originating summons in the action. If an *ex parte* interlocutory injunction (that is, one without notice) is granted, the absent defendants will be given leave to apply to discharge it on short notice. Actions in trade disputes differ from most (though not all) other areas of law in which injunctions are sought, since they rarely go for trial, although they may be more likely to do so now that the union itself is liable in damages. The need for special rules here to reflect this fact was confirmed in particular by a change in the principles governing the granting of interlocutory injunctions. (On presentation of further evidence, see *London Underground Ltd* v *NUR* [1989] IRLR 341.)

21.14.2 Principles determining whether injunctions are to be granted

21.14.2.1 The balance of convenience Before 1975, the plaintiff had to establish a prima facie case before he was entitled to injunctive relief (*Stratford and Son Ltd* v *Lindley* [1965] AC 269), so that the merits of the case were at least partially aired in court at this early stage. What is now the leading case arose in the completely different jurisdiction of patent law. For in *American Cyanamid Ltd* v *Ethicon* [1975] AC 396, the House of Lords postulated that it was only necessary that the plaintiff have an arguable case, and that there was a serious issue to be tried. Then the only other consideration was the balance of convenience of giving or refusing the injunction. The court was thus not justified in embarking on anything resembling a trial of the action on conflicting affidavits in order to evaluate the strength of each party's case. The court should not express a concluded opinion as to the law unless it is reasonably clear (*Associated British Ports plc* v *TGWU* [1989] IRLR 305). This makes it considerably easier for a plaintiff employer to gain an interlocutory injunction against a strike not covered by immunity. It is balanced only to some degree by the plaintiff having to give an undertaking in damages, promising to compensate the defendant if he has suffered loss as a result of its issue and the trial court determines, on reviewing all the evidence, that the injunction should not in fact have been granted. This is, however, of little use in dispute cases to a union enjoined because, firstly full trials are very few and far between and, secondly, because the loss which the union could prove it has suffered by not being able to strike is likely to be nominal in money terms, save that it may be able to recover the costs incurred in holding a ballot (cf. *Cayne* v *Global Natural Resources plc* [1984] 1 All ER 225).

For the same reason the balance of convenience frequently sways in favour of preserving the status quo, which, in the case of a trade dispute, means maintaining production. The particular union concern here is that it is easy to portray the employer losing immediately and irretrievably by a strike, and the union as suffering little tangible hardship. The general principle is that if there is only a risk of unquantifiable damage to the defendant yet a certainty of unquantifiable damage to the plaintiff, an injunction should be issued (*John Walker & Sons Ltd* v *Rothmans International Ltd* [1978] FSR 357). The industrial reality is that the impetus of the workers' case is lost when it is restrained; once postponed it is difficult to revive. Further, the employer can organise to defeat a subsequent strike, including making alternative arrangements for supplies or subcontracting his work to other firms. Lord Diplock realised this when he said in *NWL Ltd* v *Woods* [1979] 3 All ER 64:

> It is in the nature of industrial action that it can be promoted effectively only so long as it is possible to strike while the iron is hot; once postponed it is unlikely to be revived.

In *Associated British Ports plc* v *TGWU* [1989] IRLR 305, the Court of Appeal stated that the status quo was to be understood in the sense that work was still proceeding at the time the writ was issued. In the High Court, Millett J had decided that the court had to balance the status quo of the union's position in negotiations (especially given that their declared aim was to preserve the existing contractual position after the abolition of the National Dock Labour Scheme).

The Labour Government reacted to the judicial developments in *American Cyanamid* by enacting TULRA 1974, s. 17(1) (now TULR(C)A 1992, s. 221), which provided that if there might be a 'trade dispute' defence to an injunction, the court must not grant *ex parte* relief unless all reasonable steps have been taken: (a) to notify the other side of the application; and (b) to give them an opportunity of putting their side of the story. Further, subsection (2) stated that on an application for an interim injunction the court must 'have regard' to the fact that the defendant would succeed at trial with a trade dispute defence. Employers have since raised the argument that the court may consider it, yet find that it was outweighed by the damaging consequences of the dispute in question. The House of Lords in *NWL* v *Woods* (supra), however, indicated that if the defendant had shown that it was *more likely than not* that he could prove he was within the trade dispute definition the injunction should be refused, except where the seriousness of the consequences for the employer, a third party or the general public, demanded a higher degree of probability. Lord Diplock thought the subsection was a reminder to judges that:

> they should in exercising their discretion whether or not to grant an interlocutory injunction put into the balance of convenience in favour of the defendant those countervailing practical realities, and in particular that the grant of an injunction is tantamount to giving final judgment against the defendant.

Lord Wedderburn has lamented that:

> The land of the interlocutory injunction was little more disturbed by TULRA s. 17(2) than a pond by a pebble. A central issue of British labour law reform is whether Parliament

can assert control over the civil remedies and court procedures. In labour relations a positive right is of limited value to a defendant if the plaintiff can obtain an injunction . . .

(*The Worker and the Law*, 3rd ed., p. 812.)

In cases outside the trade dispute defence, the ordinary principles of *Cyanamid* apply. This was determined by the House of Lords in *Dimbleby & Sons Ltd v NUJ* [1984] 1 WLR 427 at 431–2 (see also *Associated British Ports plc v TGWU* [1989] IRLR 288 HL, [1989] IRLR 305 CA).

21.14.2.2 Public interest Immediate threats to health and safety if a strike went ahead would override s. 17(2) of TULRA 1974 (*Beaverbrook Newspapers Ltd v Keys* [1980] IRLR 34). Lord Scarman applied this to a dispute by journalists in *Express Newspapers Ltd v MacShane* [1980] IRLR 35, thus:

> In a case where action alleged to be in contemplation or furtherance of a trade dispute endangers the nation or puts at risk such fundamental rights as the right of the public to be informed and the freedom of the press, it could well be a proper exercise of the court's discretion to restrain the industrial action pending trial of the action.

This is open to a good deal of subjective judgment and in *Duport Steel Ltd v Sirs* [1980] IRLR 116, Lord Scarman took the opposite view on the facts in relation to the 1980 national steel strike, commenting:

> The economic damage threatened by the extension of the strike to the private sector, though very serious, is not so immediate as to justify intervention by the court granting relief to which it is probable that the plaintiff was not entitled.

In *Associated British Ports plc v TGWU* [1989] IRLR 305, the Court of Appeal criticised Millett J for not considering that 'a dock strike at the [National Dock Labour] Scheme ports would have a grave effect on the public interest' in weighing the balance of convenience. Neill LJ said that: 'It was a factor of such importance as to require express mention and evaluation.'

The balance of convenience where no strike ballot has been held was considered in *Solihull Metropolitan Borough v NUT* [1985] IRLR 211 (see para. 21.10; see also in a picketing case *Union Traffic Ltd v TGWU* [1989] ICR 98).

21.14.3 Injunctions to restrain criminal offences

Where a strike constitutes a crime it may also be restrained by injunction, but the private citizen does not usually have *locus standi* to maintain an action. Instead he must ask the Attorney-General to proceed for a relator action. The House of Lords declared this still to be the law in the notorious case of *Gouriet v UPW* [1978] AC 435. The Post Office unions were there alleged to be about to commit offences under the Post Office Act 1953 if they implemented plans to boycott mail to South Africa. The Attorney-General's refusal to bring a relator action was upheld by the House of Lords.

21.15 BREACH OF INJUNCTIONS: ENFORCEMENT

The primary methods of enforcement on the breach of injunctive orders are committal for contempt (para. 21.15.1), and sequestration of assets (para. 21.15.2).

21.15.1   Committal for contempt

21.15.1.1   The application and hearing   The plaintiff may apply for committal of the trade union or one or more of its officers for contempt. This may lead to a fine or imprisonment. Not surprisingly, courts insist that all procedural aspects of a committal for contempt are fully complied with. The injunction must be served personally on the defendant save in the most exceptional circumstances (see *Bernstein* v *Bernstein* [1960] 1 Ch 128). In *Express Newspapers Ltd* v *Mitchell* [1982] IRLR 465, however, personal service was dispensed with since it was proved that the injunction had been served on the defendant's wife and had been widely announced in the news media. It was highly unlikely that the defendant had failed to hear of it.

Two clear days' notice must be given to the other side of the application to commit. There is no direct authority that a court has power to take action against parties in contempt of its own accord. Sir Robert Megarry V-C, however, boldly stated during the course of the miners' strike, in *Clarke* v *Chadburn* [1985] 1 WLR 78 at 83, that the court may feel it necessary to act of its own accord when orders were openly flouted and the administration of justice was thereby brought into disrepute.

The allegations in the motion to commit must be proved 'with all the strictness that is necessary in such a proceeding as this when you are going to deprive people of their liberty' (*Churchman* v *Joint Shop Stewards Committee* [1972] 1 WLR 1094). A defendant is not, however, excused on the ground that he did as much as he could unless the order merely required this standard. Sir John Donaldson said in *Howitt Transport* v *TGWU* [1973] ICR 1:

> It is not sufficient by way of an answer to an allegation that a court order has not been complied with, for the person concerned to say he 'did his best'. The only exception to that proposition is where the court order itself only orders the person concerned to 'do his best'. But if a court order requires a certain state of affairs to be achieved, the only way in which the order can be complied with is by achieving that state of affairs.

When it is alleged that the respondent failed to take a positive step required by an injunction, the applicant must prove that there was something the respondent *could* reasonably have done but failed to do to secure its enforcement. This was the central issue in *Express Newspapers* v *Mitchell* (supra). The plaintiffs gained an injunction against unlawful secondary action by electricians in Fleet Street in support of the TUC's 'day of action' for the health service workers then on national strike. The order restrained, among others, Sean Geraghty, leader of the Fleet Street electricians from inducing workers to breach their contracts, and required him to withdraw the strike call. The strike went ahead. Geraghty argued that there was nothing he could do to withdraw the strike call since he had not made it in the first place. Leonard J thought, however, that he could have done more in the time available to encourage compliance with the injunction granted and thus fined him £350.

In *Austin Rover Group Ltd* v *AUEW (TASS)* [1985] IRLR 162, the union TASS sought to avoid liability with the argument that the act of calling a strike which the order said should be reversed was that of a larger body of which it was part, namely the staff side of the Joint Negotiating Committee and not the action of the union alone. The union had authorised industrial action without a ballot and the plaintiff obtained an order that the union should 'withdraw and cancel any instruction, direction or decision' to take strike action. Hodgson J said (at para. 29) that: 'In a proper case it may be permissible in the face of a mandatory injunction for someone to sit back and do absolutely nothing but it is obviously highly dangerous because by definition, the court has been satisfied by evidence that there is something he can do.' His Lordship thought that it was obvious here what was required and condemned the attitude of the union's general secretary that because he did not consider that the order should have been made there was no need to obey it. It was not possible for the union, which had not appeared when the order was made, to claim at this late stage that the injunction should not have been granted.

When an order is to be obeyed 'forthwith', this is taken to mean forthwith after proper notice is given to the defendants. Proper notice may not be avoided by the defendants refusing access to the process server and it was no excuse that the proper constitutional machinery of the union could not be enforced forthwith (*Kent Free Press Ltd* v *NGA* [1987] IRLR 267).

21.15.1.2 Vicarious liability The union may be in contempt of court if it does not prevent its officials from acting in contempt of court. The code of responsibility for authorising or endorsing industrial action set out in the Employment Act 1982 does not apply to contempt proceedings (*Express & Star Ltd* v *NGA* [1985] IRLR 455) so that one has to go back to the general principles of vicarious liability (*Heaton's Transport (St Helens) Ltd* v *TGWU* [1972] ICR 308 at 404). A plea that the union had not authorised breach of an injunction was the central issue in *Richard Read (Transport) Ltd* v *NUM (South Wales Area)* [1985] IRLR 67, and the court took a typically robust response to the claim. The plaintiff companies were independent road hauliers whose businesses had been affected by mass picketing by striking miners at the Port Talbot Steel Works to which they regularly delivered. The companies gained an order restraining the union by its servants or agents from 'continuing to instruct or otherwise encourage its members from stopping approaching or in any other way interfering with the free passage of the plaintiffs' vehicles into or out of the Port Talbot Works . . . or abusing or threatening the drivers thereof'. The defendants were obliged to 'withdraw any such instruction or encouragement already given'. The defendants did not appear at the hearing, holding to the NUM's resolute refusal to do so during most of their 1984/5 strike. The union did, however, write a letter to the court assuring the court that it would comply with the order, but stressing the difficulty of so doing, since the plaintiffs' vehicles travelled in a long convoy of between 50 and 130 vehicles with those of other companies which did not have the protection of any such order. The vehicles of the plaintiffs were still stoned after the injunction was granted just as before. On the committal application, Park J thought it was an insufficient response by the defendants to say that they had not committed breaches of the injunction *knowingly*. There was evidence that the conduct of the pickets towards the drivers had been authorised or endorsed by responsible people in the union who appeared completely indifferent to the consequences of the pickets' violent behaviour. The defendants' letter was silent about any instructions given to the pickets to cease violence against the plaintiffs' vehicles. The union was thus fined £25,000 in each case, making a total of £50,000.

The union is liable for the acts of its officials if it gives them discretion as to their response to a court order and there is no evidence that the union hierarchy was displeased with its officials' defiance of the order (*Kent Free Press Ltd* v *NGA* [1987] IRLR 267; see also para. 17.5).

21.15.1.3 Punishment The court may imprison the contemnor for up to two years (Contempt of Court Act 1981, s. 14), fine or order him to give security for good behaviour. In *Austin Rover Group Ltd* v *AUEW* (supra) the judge did not decree any punishment since the contempt was not serious and the union might have taken sufficiently vigorous steps to dissociate themselves from the industrial action had they taken legal advice at an earlier stage, whilst in the *Richard Read* case the NUM (South Wales Area) was fined £50,000. The largest fine so far is on the National Union of Mineworkers in 1984 of £250,000.

21.15.2 Sequestration

Sequestration is the remedy of last resort to enforce a judgment requiring a person to do an act within a specified time or to abstain from doing a specified act. It operates by sequestrating all the real and personal property of the union or person subject to the order, and is cumulative to other methods of enforcing an order such as committal. The writ is addressed to not less than four commissioners, of whom at least two must act. In recent strike cases, they have tended to be chartered accountants. The writ binds all property of the person sequestered from the date of its issue, and the sequestrators enter at once to take possession of his real and personal estate.

The sequestrators act as officers of the court, and may from time to time be given directions by the judge. Any resistance or interference by any person with the sequestrators carrying out their proper duties is in itself a contempt of court. Where there is, however, a dispute about the ownership of property, a party may apply to the court by summons or motion to direct an enquiry as to the precise nature of the respective interests in the property.

A party seeking sequestration as a mode of enforcement must issue a writ and requires leave of the court to do so. The court must also be satisfied that disobedience to the order has been more than casual, accidental or unintentional, save in the event that disobedience is repeated (*Worthington* v *Ad-Lib Club Ltd* [1965] Ch 236). The remedy is in the discretion of the court. In *Richard Read (Transport) Ltd* v *NUM (South Wales Area)* [1985] IRLR 67, the judge ordered sequestration of the defendant area union's assets 'because from a report in the *Daily Express* . . . it would appear that the defendant may be seeking to avoid payment of any fines imposed by this court by the device of transferring its funds into the private bank accounts of its leaders' (para. 26). The funds of the Society of Graphical and Allied Trades 1982 (SOGAT) were sequestrated in February 1986 because of the union's defiance of an injunction restraining the blacking of newspapers owned by subsidiaries of News International plc during the 'Wapping dispute'. The Court of Appeal in *News Group Newspapers Ltd* v *SOGAT 1982* [1986] ICR 716 determined that this order did not entitle the sequestrators to seize the considerable funds of the unions' branches and chapels. In construing the rules, their Lordships decided that branch funds were to be used solely for the benefit of their members and not for the union as a whole.

A third party is prohibited from knowingly assisting in a breach of the sequestration order (*Eckman* v *Midland Bank Ltd* [1973] ICR 71). The defendant union's accountant must give full cooperation. This sensitive issue was explored in *Messenger Newspapers Group Ltd* v *NGA* [1984] 1 All ER 293. The assets of the NGA were sequestered in order to ensure that the union pay substantial fines imposed on it for contempt in failing to desist from picketing the Warrington premises of the plaintiff. The union's auditors, mindful of their duty of confidentiality, refused to disclose details of the union's assets. The Court of Appeal decided that the accountants must not obstruct the sequestrators' investigations, even though they did not hold any property belonging to the union. Sir John Donaldson MR thought that: 'A sequestration would be quite impossible if it required the consent of, for example, the officers of the company against whom the writ of sequestration is issued.' In *Clarke* v *Heathfield (No. 2)* [1985] ICR 606, the court went further and removed the trustees of the National Union of Mineworkers who had sought to frustrate the efforts of the sequestrators by sending money abroad.

22　Picketing

There is no legal right to picket as such, but peaceful picketing has long been recognised as being lawful.

(Department of Employment Code of Practice on Picketing, para. 2.)

22.1　INDUSTRIAL BACKGROUND

Picketing is an ill-defined term which covers various methods of strengthening strike action by employees standing at the factory gate. It has over time subtly changed its function. At the beginning of the century, the picket was mainly concerned to prevent blackleg labour being taken in to replace strikers. Later it became a medium of protest, while the 1970s witnessed a growth in 'secondary picketing' broadly aimed at parties extraneous to the actual trade dispute to bring pressure on the employer in dispute. By this means union members seek to prevent goods leaving their employer's factory and to stop him moving his production elsewhere. The target may be fellow workers who have not joined the strike or substitute labour. The modern phenomenon is also a recognition that employers are increasingly organised on a multi-plant, if not multi-national basis, and that such solidarity action by strong unions is of particular value to weakly organised sectors.

The tactic was used to particular effect during the two miners' strikes of the 1970s, when picketing by various groups of workers prevented the delivery of replacement oil to power stations, and made the strike much more effective in bringing almost the whole of industry to a halt. During the bitter Grunwick dispute 300 arrests were made between June 1977 and January 1978. A useful corrective to this scene is to consider the words of the Chief Constable of South Wales giving evidence to the House of Commons Select Committee on Employment, 27 February 1980 (p. 39):

You must not assume that on every occasion there is a mass picket there is going to be trouble. You sometimes get a very jaundiced picture from the news media who tend to highlight the occasions when things go wrong, but this is by no means the norm because there are many other incidents which pass off day by day without any difficulty whatever.

There was, however, unprecedented picket-line violence during the miners' strike in 1984/5; 10,372 criminal charges were brought (*The Times*, 20 March 1985). There was also violent picketing and many arrests in 1986 outside the News International plc printing plant at Wapping, and mostly peaceful picketing at Dover during the seafarers' dispute of 1988/9.

The central justification of peaceful picketing lies in the right to freedom of speech and peaceful protest, and in many countries it is protected by the Constitution. Typically, in Britain what freedom exists is found in the interstices of a narrow immunity from several general and particular prohibitions of common law and statute by way of crimes and torts. Unlike other areas of trade disputes, this is phrased as a 'right'. Much depends on the practice of police on the spot in controlling pickets, with relatively little guidance from the case law. The Employment Act 1980, however, restricted the right to picket to the workers' own place of work. There is a Department of Employment Code of Practice on picketing which supplements this body of law and which was found to be persuasive in *Thomas* v *NUM (South Wales Area)* [1985] IRLR 136.

22.2   OFFENCES AND PICKETING

Pickets may commit the following crimes:

(a)   obstruction of the highway (para. 22.2.1);
(b)   obstructing a police constable in the execution of his duty (para. 22.2.2);
(c)   assault (para. 22.2.3);
(d)   Public Order Act offences (para. 22.2.4);
(e)   unlawful assembly (para. 22.2.5);
(f)   affray and riot (para. 22.2.6);
(g)   public nuisance (para. 22.2.7);
(h)   offences under the Conspiracy and Protection of Property Act 1875 (para. 22.2.8);
(i)   refusing to obey conditions imposed on public assembly (para. 22.2.9).

We will then consider the bail conditions which may be attached to the granting of bail (para. 22.2.10).

22.2.1   Obstruction of the highway

By s. 137 of the Highways Act 1980, 'if a person without lawful authority or excuse in any way wilfully obstructs the free passage along the highway, he shall be guilty of an offence . . .'. This is a charge frequently brought against pickets. The illegality of an obstruction is in all cases a question of fact, and depends on, *inter alia*, 'the length of time the obstruction continues, the place where it occurs, the purpose for which it is done, and of course whether it does in fact cause an actual obstruction as opposed to a potential obstruction' (*Nagy* v *Weston* [1965] 1 WLR 280 at 284 per Lord Parker CJ). In *Lowdens* v *Keaveney* [1903] 2 IR 82, the judge said: 'No body of men has a right to appropriate the highway and exclude citizens from using it. The question whether use is reasonable or not is a question of fact to be determined by common sense with regard to ordinary experience.' *Mens rea* is not, however, a requirement of the offence (*Arrowsmith* v *Jenkins* [1963] 2 QB 561), which is committed by anyone freely causing an obstruction; it is irrelevant that he *bona fide* believes he has a right to picket or demonstrate. (See also *Broome* v *DPP* [1974] AC 587.) There is statutory control of processions and assemblies under ss. 11 to 16 of the Public Order Act 1986 (see para. 22.2.9).

22.2.2   Obstructing a police constable

Section 51(3) of the Police Act 1964 makes it criminal to obstruct a police constable in the execution of his duty and that duty is to prevent trouble where he reasonably apprehends a breach of the peace as a 'real possibility'. Very few magistrates' courts *ex post facto* doubt the policeman's opinion at the time, and this provides an enormous discretion for the police to control picketing. It allows a constable to tell demonstrators to all go home or reduce their number and visit any resistance to these instructions with prosecution for the Police Act offence. Thus, in *Kavanagh* v *Hiscock* [1974] QB 600, a policeman claimed he had reason to believe there would be a breach of the peace if an exit from a hospital was not completely clear of pickets, and he thus proceeded to remove those who were waiting to harangue 'blacklegs' being transported to work by bus. The court held that the offence of breach of the peace had been committed and the pickets had no legal right to stop a vehicle without the consent of the driver.

In *Piddington* v *Bates* [1960] 3 All ER 660, the defendant was prevented from reaching a factory entrance by a constable who told him that two pickets were enough, The report quaintly states that he 'pushed gently past the policeman and was gently arrested'. Although this occurred without obstruction or threats of violence, Lord Parker held that a policeman was entitled to 'take such steps as he thinks proper', including limiting the number of pickets. He continued (at p. 663B):

> . . . it is not enough that his contemplation is that there is a remote possibility but there must be a real possibility of a breach of the peace. Accordingly in every case it becomes a question whether on the particular facts there were reasonable grounds on which a constable charged with this duty reasonably anticipated that a breach of the peace might occur.

It is immaterial whether the breach of the peace is likely to be caused by the pickets themselves, the picketed or bystanders (*Kavanagh* v *Hiscock* (supra)).

In *Moss* v *McLachlan* [1985] IRLR 76 the Divisional Court determined that the offence might be committed when pickets ignore police orders some distance from the site to be picketed if the policeman in question honestly and reasonably fears an imminent breach of the peace if the accused continues with his journey. This sanctioned the police practice during the 1984/5 miners' strike of stopping people on the way to picket in the Midlands coalfields, but far away from the picket at the time of arrest — including one famous incident at the Dartford Tunnel.

A constable can arrest without warrant in the case of obstruction if that obstruction was such that it actually caused or was likely to cause a breach of the peace (*Wershof* v *Metropolitan Police Commissioner* [1978] 3 All ER 540).

22.2.3 Assaults

While assaults may be committed on a picket-line, there is no such crime or tort unless the capacity to carry into effect the intention to commit a battery is present at the time of the overt act indicating an immediate intention to commit a battery. There was thus no liability in *Thomas* v *NUM (South Wales Area)* [1985] IRLR 136 since the threats uttered by the picketing striking miners were made from the side of the road to working miners who were in vehicles which the pickets could not reach.

22.2.4 Public Order Act 1986

Section 5 of the Public Order Act 1936 (as amended by the Race Relations Act 1965, s. 7) made it an offence for any person in any public place or at any public meeting to (a) use threatening, abusive or insulting words or behaviour, or (b) distribute or display any writing, sign or visible representation which was threatening, abusive or insulting, with intent to provoke a breach of the peace or whereby a breach of the peace is likely to be occasioned. The words are to be defined by the standards of the ordinary man (*Cozens* v *Brutus* [1972] AC 854).

The Public Order Act 1986 repealed s. 5 and replaced it with two new offences. By s. 4 of the 1986 Act a person is guilty of an offence if he:

(a)   uses towards another person threatening, abusive or insulting words or behaviour, or

(b)   distributes or displays to another person any writing, sign or other visible representation which is threatening, abusive or insulting with intent to cause that person to believe that immediate unlawful violence will be used against him or another by any person, or to provoke the immediate use of unlawful violence by that person or another or whereby that person is likely to believe that such violence will be used or it is likely that such violence will be provoked.

By s. 5 of the Act a person commits an offence if he:

(a)   uses threatening, abusive or insulting words or behaviour, or disorderly behaviour, or

(b)   displays any writing, sign or other visible representation which is threatening, abusive or insulting,

within the hearing or sight of a person likely to be caused harrassment, alarm or distress thereby.

The requirement that another person must be present is intended as a safeguard, although it is not necessary for the prosecution to show that that person was actually alarmed, harassed or distressed.

By s. 4A of the Public Order Act 1986, introduced by the Criminal Justice and Public Order Act 1994 as from 3 February 1995, a person is guilty of an offence if he with intent, causes another person harassment, alarm or distress by using threatening, abusive or insulting words or behaviour or disorderly conduct or by displaying any writing, sign or other visible representation which is threatening, abusive or insulting. It is a defence for an accused person to prove that his conduct was reasonable in the circumstances of the case. The offence carries a maximum penalty of six months' imprisonment or a fine not exceeding £5,000. It is an arrestable offence.

22.2.5   Unlawful assembly

An unlawful assembly consists of the assembly of three or more persons with the intention of fulfilling a common purpose in such a manner as to endanger the public peace. It was one of the charges on which the defendants were convicted in the Shrewsbury pickets case (*R* v *Jones* [1974] ICR 310) in which two 'flying pickets' were goaled for substantial terms. By s. 2 of the Public Order Act 1986 there is a new offence based on unlawful assembly:

Where three or more persons who are present together use or threaten violence and the conduct of them (taken together) is such as would cause a person of reasonable fitness present at the scene to fear for his personal safety, each of the persons using or threatening violence is guilty of violent disorder.

22.2.6 Affray and riot

Affray and riot are other possible charges. The former at common law meant unlawful fighting by one or more persons in a public place in such manner that reasonable people might be frightened or intimidated. Section 3 of the Public Order Act 1986 clarifies this offence.

Riot was the collection of at least three people with a common purpose, and an intent to help one another by force, if necessary, in the execution of that object, against anyone who may oppose them. Further, force or violence had to be displayed in such a manner as to alarm at least one person of reasonable firmness. (See e.g. *Field* v *Receiver of Metropolitan Police* [1907] 2 KB 853.) By s. 1(1) of the Public Order Act 1986:

> Where 12 or more persons who are present together use or threaten violence for a common purpose and the conduct of them (taken together) is such as would cause a person of reasonable firmness present at the scene to fear for his personal safety, each of the persons using unlawful violence for the common purpose is guilty of riot.

22.2.7 Public nuisance

It is an offence at common law to obstruct the public in the exercise or enjoyment of rights common to all, including free passage along the highway. Picketing often falls foul of this prohibition, but picketing in itself probably does not constitute nuisance. In *J. Lyons & Sons* v *Wilkins* [1899] 1 Ch 255 Lindley LJ thought it did, since it constituted an attempt to persuade, regardless of any obstruction. But Lord Denning MR in *Hubbard* v *Pitt* [1975] ICR 308, considered that this view 'has not stood the test of time . . .'. He was concerned not to restrict free speech and assembly by restricting picketing. He decided, dissenting, that a group of non-industrial protesters standing on the pavement outside an estate agents, in reasonable numbers and orderly manner, to protest against the 'gentrification' of Islington was quite lawful and not a nuisance. The majority of the Court of Appeal, on the other hand, merely affirmed the use by Forbes J of his discretion in deciding to grant an interlocutory injunction to the plaintiffs, and said little on the general principle. The Master of the Rolls commented (at 318H):

> There was no obstruction, no violence, no intimidation, no molestation, no noise, no smells, nothing except a group of six or seven people standing about with placards and leaflets outside the plaintiff's premises, all quite orderly and well-behaved. That cannot be said to be a nuisance at common law.

He considered that, in any case, the real grievance of the plaintiff concerned the defendant's placards and leaflets and that to enjoin these would be an interference with free speech: 'These are rights which it is in the public interest that individuals should possess: and indeed that they should exercise without impediment so long as no wrongful act is done . . . As long as all is done peaceably and in good order, without threats or incitement to violence or obstruction to traffic, it is not prohibited.' He saw no reason to distinguish between picketing connected with a strike and other purposes. (See also *Mersey Dock and Harbour*

Co. v *Verrinder* [1982] IRLR 152; *News Group Newspapers Ltd* v *Sogat 82 (No. 2)* [1987] ICR 181).

In *Tynan* v *Balmer* [1967] 1 QB 91 40 people walking in a circle was held unreasonable, and a nuisance: that a passer-by might avoid the obstruction by a detour, did not make it lawful. Further, the pickets were held not to be protected by the precursor of the TULRA 1974 immunity because they were doing more than was absolutely necessary for conveying information about their own cause. In *Thomas* v *NUM (South Wales Area)* [1985] IRLR 136 Scott J decided that regular picketing of a person's home would in itself be a common law nuisance.

Public nuisance is a tort as well as a crime but civil proceedings may be brought only with the consent of the Attorney-General on a relator action. He has, however, complete discretion (*Gouriet* v *UPW* [1978] AC 435) whether or not to allow it, and a private individual can only act if he can show that he has suffered damage greater than that borne by the general public.

22.2.8   Conspiracy and Protection of Property Act 1875

It was originally an offence under the Combination Act 1825 'by threat or intimidation or by molesting or in any way obstructing another, to endeavour to force any workman or other person not being employed from accepting employment'. This very general prohibition was abolished by the Conspiracy and Protection of Property Act 1875, but re-enacted therein as specific offences, which are still on the statute book. Section 7 makes it a criminal offence if a person 'wilfully and without legal authority':

(a)   uses violence or intimidates another;

(b)   persistently follows another from place to place (see *Smith* v *Thomasson* (1890) 62 LT 68);

(c)   hides any tools, clothes or other property owned or used by such other person, or deprives him of or hinders him in the use thereof;

(d)   watches or besets the house or other place where such other person resides, or works, or carries on business or happens to be, or the approach to such house or place;

(e)   follows such other person with two or more other persons in a disorderly manner in or through any street or road.

In each case the action must be without legal authority.

J. Lyons and Sons v *Wilkins* [1896] 1 Ch 811, decided that the wrongful action might consist solely of the trespassing of the provisions of s. 7 in itself, whereas *Ward Lock & Co.* v *Operative Printers' Assistants Society* (1906) 22 TLR 327, suggests that they must be independently unlawful. Fletcher Moulton LJ summed up the provision thus: 'It legalises nothing and it renders nothing wrongful that was not so before. Its object is solely to visit certain selected classes of acts which were previously wrongful, i.e. were at least civil torts, with penal consequences.' Scott J decided in *Thomas* v *NUM (South Wales Area)* (supra) that conduct must first be tortious in order to constitute an offence under s. 7. The purpose of the Act was merely to render certain acts unlawful in the *criminal* sense.

Most of the subsections add little to common law nuisance but subsection (a) is of importance, especially since James LJ in *R* v *Jones* [1974] ICR 310 extended 'intimidate' to include 'putting persons in fear by the exhibition of force or violence or the threat of violence, and there is no limitation restricting the meaning to cases of violence or threats of violence to the person'. Hence violence against buildings was sufficient and even 'harsh words'. (See also *Gibson* v *Lawson* [1891] 2 QB 545, *Elsey* v *Smith* [1983] IRLR 292.) Occupying property as a 'sit-in' may amount to 'watching and besetting'.

The fact that the respondents' actions are protected from civil liability within the meaning of s. 219 of TULR(C)A 1992 does not mean that they could not be done 'wrongfully and without legal authority' for the purposes of criminal proceedings. There is nothing in the language of s. 13 which can convert what was a wrongful act into one which is legally innocent (*Galt* v *Philp* [1984] IRLR 156).

Large numbers of pickets during the miners' strike of 1984/5 were charged with these offences even though they had lain dormant for many years. The Public Order Act 1986, Sch. 2 para. 1 makes the maximum sentence six months' imprisonment or a fine not exceeding level 5 on the standard scale or both (at present the fine is up to £5,000, Criminal Justice Act, s. 17(2), Sch. 12 para. 6). Further, a police constable may arrest without warrant anyone whom he reasonably suspects is committing an offence under the section.

22.2.9 Public processions and assemblies

The Public Order Act 1986 gave the police new powers to impose conditions on public processions and assemblies under threat of criminal sanctions for failure to obey these conditions. Since pickets are usually stationary, only the latter powers are considered here. Section 14 applies if the senior police officer present at an assembly '. . . having regard to the time or place at which and the circumstances in which any public assembly is being held or is intended to be held, reasonably believes that:

(a)   it may result in serious public disorder, serious damage to property or serious disruption to the life of the community, or

(b)   the purpose of the persons organising it is the intimidation of others with a view to compelling them not to do an act they have a right to do, or to do an act they have a right not to do.'

He may then give directions imposing on the person organising or taking part in the assembly such conditions as to the place at which the assembly may be (or continue to be) held, its maximum duration, or the maximum number of persons who may constitute it as appears to him necessary to prevent such disorder, damage, disruption or intimidation.' Failure to obey such conditions is a criminal offence. The intimidation leg of the section was clearly drafted with picketing in mind. The effect has been watered down, however, by the addition of a definition of public assembly, in s. 16, as being an assembly of more than 20 persons in a public place.

22.2.10 Bail conditions

Where there is a likelihood of further offences being committed whilst the accused is on bail on a charge connected with picketing, magistrates may properly grant bail subject to a condition that the accused shall not participate in picketing in connection with the industrial dispute in the course of which he was arrested (*R* v *Mansfield Justices ex parte Sharkey* [1984] IRLR 496). The magistrates' court merely had to ask the question: 'Is this condition necessary for the prevention of the commission of an offence by the defendant when on bail?' It is enough if they perceive a real and not a fanciful risk of an offence being committed.

22.3 CIVIL LIABILITY

Picketing is not actionable *per se* but only if a tort is committed by the pickets (*News Group Newspapers Ltd* v *SOGAT 1982* [1986] IRLR 337). Civil liability is important in relation to picketing, just as in strike cases, not because damages are often awarded, but due to the availability of injunctive relief, particularly of an interlocutory nature.

22.3.1 Private nuisance

Private nuisance is an unlawful interference with an individual's enjoyment or use of his land. To sue for the tort, the plaintiff must have some proprietary interest in land and this action is most likely where pickets block an access route. Picketing accompanied by violence, or even merely noise, may be a private nuisance. Scott J in *Thomas* v *NUM (South Wales Area)* [1985] IRLR 136 held that mass picketing at the gates of five collieries in South Wales during the miners' strike of 1984/5 was tortious and could be restrained at the suit of the plaintiffs who were working miners. The picketing was of a nature and was carried out in such a manner that it represented an unreasonable harassment of the plaintiffs in the exercise of the right to use the highway in order to go to work. While picketing of itself was not a nuisance, this was different since by sheer weight of numbers it blocked the entrance to premises or prevented the entry thereto of vehicles or people. Where feelings ran high, the presence of substantial numbers of pickets was almost bound to have an intimidatory effect on those going to work especially as here some 50 to 70 striking miners attended at the gates each day. Even if nothing was said, the action could not fail to be highly intimidatory. Scott J held that the public right to use the highway was a sufficient proprietary interest to support an action in nuisance. This was, however, doubted by Stuart Smith J in *News Group Newspapers Ltd* v *SOGAT 82* (supra).

In *Mersey Dock and Harbour Co.* v *Verrinder* [1982] IRLR 152 the picketing was entirely peaceful. Judge McHugh nevertheless decided that there was a nuisance since the pickets had mounted 'an attempt . . . to regulate and control the container traffic to and from the company's terminals' and so their intention was not merely to obtain or communicate information. This rather puts the cart of determining the scope of the immunity before the horse of establishing the tort committed. (See also *Messenger Newspaper Group Ltd* v *NGA* [1984] IRLR 397, *British Airports Authority* v *Ashton* [1983] 1 WLR 1079, *News Group Newspapers Ltd* v *SOGAT 1982 (No. 2)* [1987] ICR 181.)

22.3.2 Trespass to the highway

A person commits a tort if he uses the highway 'otherwise than reasonably for passage and repassage and for any other purpose reasonably incidental thereto' (*Hickman* v *Maisey* [1900] 1 QB 752; see also *Hubbard* v *Pitt* [1976] QB 142), and pickets may trespass even though moving around in a circle (*Tynan* v *Balmer* [1967] 1 QB 91). The proper plaintiff is the owner of the soil beneath the relevant highway — usually abutting landowners have such rights up to midpoint in the road, or the local authority. The liability is more apparent than real since few such landowners would be able to show special damage from the picketing. There was no right to sue in tort for obstruction to the highway for working miners since no special damage was caused to them (*Thomas* v *NUM (South Wales Area)* (supra)).

22.3.3 Interference with contracts

The existence of a picket-line may be sufficient in itself to induce another person to break his contract of employment and not attend for work (*Union Traffic Ltd* v *TGWU* [1989] ICR 98). Alternatively, it may be an interference with a commercial contract but it is then necessary that a primary obligation under the contract is interfered with (see *Thomas* v *NUM (South Wales Area)* (supra)).

Where there is such evidence, in order for the defendant to be immune, the action must fall within the limited immunity for 'secondary action' (see para. 21.9) even if it takes place at the pickets' own place of work. This is achieved by s. 224 of TULR(C)A 1992, which provides that secondary action 'done in the course of attendance declared lawful by s. 220 of the 1992 Act' retains the protection of s. 219 of TULR(C)A 1992 if done by a worker employed by a party to the trade dispute or by a trade union official whose attendance is lawful.

22.4 IMMUNITY

The immunity for picketing is found in s. 220 of TULR(C)A 1992, which reads:

It shall be lawful for a person in contemplation or furtherance of a trade dispute to attend

(a)   at or near his own place of work, or
(b)   if he is an official of a trade union, at or near the place of work of a member of that union whom he is accompanying and whom he represents,

for the purpose only of peacefully obtaining or communicating information, or peacefully persuading any person to work or abstain from working.

22.4.1 History

The provision derives in part from the protection against the watching and besetting offence in the Conspiracy and Protection of Property Act 1875. It offered immunity for attendance 'merely to obtain or communicate information', and since the early case of *J. Lyons & Sons* v *Wilkins* [1896] 1 Ch 811, which held that it did not include the persuasion of men not to go into work, it has been narrowly defined. The Trade Disputes Act 1906 added the proviso that picketing be carried on 'peacefully' and restricted it to action 'in contemplation or furtherance of a trade dispute' (for the definition of which, see para. 21.8). It thus does not extend to picketing for non-industrial purposes, e.g. to protest against the practices of a shopkeeper or estate agents (as in *Hubbard* v *Pitt* [1976] QB 142), and this fact has led to claims that trade unionists have privileges beyond those open to other members of the community. The Industrial Relations Act 1971 was similar in its terms except that it removed protection for picketing outside an individual's home, and this was undisturbed by TULRA 1974.

22.4.2 Secondary picketing

A secondary picket is not liable for economic torts, like inducing breach of contract, where he pickets his own place of work and his employer is:

(a)   an immediate supplier or customer of the employer in dispute, *and* the aim is to disrupt services between them; or

(b)   an associated employer of the employer in dispute and the aim is to cut off substitute goods or services which would normally have been provided to or by the employer in dispute (TULR(C)A 1992, s. 224).

22.4.3   Place of work

Even if he fulfils all the other requirements of secondary action, the picket must be at or near his *place of work* to attract immunity (see *Mersey Dock and Harbour Co.* v *Verrinder* [1982] IRLR 152). According to the Code of Practice on Picketing, 'place of work' means 'an entrance to or an exit from the factory, site or office at which the picket works'. There are some statutory elaborations:

(a)   If an employee works at *more than one place* or it is impossible to attend that place, he can picket the administrative headquarters of his employer (for example, if it is a North Sea oil rig or a pit) (TULR(C)A 1992, s. 220(2)).

(b)   A person *dismissed* during an industrial dispute in question may picket his former place of work (s. 220(3)).

(c)   A *union official* appointed or elected for a section of union members may lawfully protest at property other than his own place of work but he must be representing members for whom he is responsible (s. 220(1)(b), (4)); thus national officials have 'licence' to picket any place where their members are working, but a regional union officer may only accompany members of a branch within his region. It is not apparently necessary that the member accompanied should be a lawful picket. There is, however, no recognition of support by one union of another.

(d)   The previous location restriction against picketing at an employer's home, which was added by the Industrial Relations Act 1971, remains.

Where the place from or at which employees used to work has been closed down, pickets may have nowhere where they can lawfully picket. The place of work must be the person's principal place of work or base (see *News Group Newspapers Ltd* v *SOGAT 1982* [1986] IRLR 337, *Union Traffic Ltd* v *TGWU* [1989] ICR 98). In *Rayware Ltd* v *TGWU* [1989] IRLR 134, the plaintiffs carried on business on a private trading estate along with 20 other companies. As part of the dispute between the plaintiff and its employees, pickets stood at the gate from the road into the trading estate, about seven-tenths of a mile away. The Court of Appeal held that this was 'at or near' their place of work within what is now s. 220(1)(a) of TULR(C)A 1992. The phrase was to be understood in a geographical sense in accordance with the intent and purpose of the legislation, although it was a question of fact and degree in each case.

22.4.4   Limitations of the immunity

The immunity has also been severely limited by case law. It legalises only the *attendance* of the pickets for peaceful communication and not their activities while so attending. As Lord Salmon said in *Broome* v *DPP* [1974] ICR 84: 'The section gives no protection in relation to anything the pickets may say or do whilst they are attending if what they say or do is itself unlawful . . . The section therefore gives a narrow but nevertheless real immunity to pickets. It clearly does no more.' Lord Reid said, at 89F:

I see no ground for implying any right to require the person whom it is sought to persuade to submit to any kind of constraint or restriction of his personal freedom . . . But if a picket has a purpose beyond those set out in the section, then his presence becomes unlawful and in many cases such as I have supposed it would not be difficult to infer as a matter of fact that pickets who assemble in unreasonably large numbers do have the purpose of preventing free passage. If that were the proper inference then their presence on the highway would become unlawful.

The section offers no immunity from criminal or tortious activities of pickets as opposed to their mere attendance. For example, the immunity does not prevent a picket being liable in trespass whether at common law or under British Airports by-laws at Heathrow (*Larkin* v *Belfast Harbour Commissioners* [1908] 2 IR 214, *British Airports Authority* v *Ashton* [1983] IRLR 287; see also *Elsey* v *Smith* [1983] IRLR 292). Moreover, it covers only the purposes stated and not, for instance, where the pickets go further and also seek to prevent access to the gates by vehicles (*Tynan* v *Balmer* [1967] 1 QB 91). 'Peacefully' in this context means without a breach of the peace (*Charnock* v *Court* [1899] 2 Ch 35).

It is important to identify who is and who is not a picket for the purposes of the immunity. There is no statutory definition, and references in the case law were scant until *News Group Newspapers Ltd* v *SOGAT 1982* [1986] IRLR 337. There, the word 'picket' was held to comprehend both the six official union pickets who stood each day by the entrance to News International's Wapping printing plant and also the 50 to 200 demonstrators who stood each day some 80 yards away behind barriers. It would not include the 700 to 7,000 who marched twice a week to hold a protest meeting addressed by speakers. In so far as some of these broke ranks and attempted to rush the main gates, it was arguable that they too were pickets.

22.4.5 Number of pickets

The statute contains no specific restriction on the number of pickets, but clearly large numbers may intimidate more easily than the actions of the few. Lord Reid's opinion has already been reviewed. The Code of Practice describes mass picketing as 'obstruction if not intimidation' and para. 31 recommends ensuring that 'in general the number of pickets does not exceed six at any entrance to a workplace: frequently a smaller number will be appropriate'.

In *Thomas* v *NUM (South Wales Area)* [1985] IRLR 136 Scott J decided that the attendance of between 50 and 70 striking miners at colliery gates could not fall within the scope of the immunity. He could not understand the need for so many people to attend if the aim was merely peaceful persuasion: threats of violence and intimidatory language were inconsistent in any event with such peaceful persuasion. Insults were not in themselves against the peace but here the language was carried to extremes and persisted in over a long period. The learned judge thought that the Code of Practice provided a sensible guide as to the maximum number of pickets, beyond which, simply by weight of numbers, pickets will commit intimidation (*News Group Newspapers Ltd* v *SOGAT 82 (No. 2)* [1987] ICR 181).

22.4.6 Right to stop vehicles?

Much controversy has surrounded the claim of pickets to stop vehicles in order to convey their message, often somewhat forcefully, to drivers who may be bringing in supplies in order to keep the plant open, and which it is the aim of the pickets to prevent. This was obviously not relevant as an issue when the immunity was substantially formulated in 1875 and 1906. It is now vital, since picketing may otherwise be wholly ineffective. As J.G. Riddall enquires (*The Law of Industrial Relations,* op. cit. para. 19.6.5, p. 130): 'What effect will the shouts of the pickets have on a lorry driver, high up in his cab, with the window closed and the radio on?' In *Broome* v *DPP* [1974] ICR 84, the House of Lords put a decisive brake on any flexibility in the current law. The defendant stood with a poster in front of a lorry trying to enter a factory and was convicted for his temerity even though there was no violence, and the whole incident lasted only nine minutes. Lord Reid could see:

> no ground for implying any right to require the person whom it is sought to persuade to submit to any kind of constraint or restriction of his personal freedom. One is familiar with persons at the side of the road signalling to a driver requesting him to stop. It is then for the driver to decide whether he will stop or not. That, in my view, a picket is entitled to do. If the driver stops, the picket can talk to him but only for as long as the driver is willing to listen.

22.5   THE CODE OF PRACTICE

Trade unions have accepted that some actions of pickets have not been in the interests of the wider trade union movement. The TUC thus advised that official pickets wear distinctive armbands and consider restriction of numbers. The Department of Employment's Code of Practice includes this advice but goes considerably further, including the following 'guidance':

(a) 'Mass picketing . . . is not picketing in its lawful sense of an attempt at peaceful persuasion and may well result in a breach of the peace or other criminal offence. Moreover, anyone seeking to demonstrate support for those in dispute should keep well away from any picket-line so as not to create the risk of a breach of the peace . . .' (para. 30).

(b) 'Large numbers . . . exacerbate disputes and sour relations not only between management and employees but between pickets and their fellow employees.'

(c) An experienced person should be in charge of the picket-line with a letter of authority from the union (para. 32).

(d) Pickets should maintain close contact with the police by advance consultation and accepting directions as to reasonable numbers (para. 33).

(e) There should be cooperation where several unions are picketing.

The Code is also concerned to maintain essential services and supplies: this is a direct response to picketing associated with widespread strikes in the public sector and especially among health service manual workers. It includes under this rubric medical and pharmaceutical products, supplies essential to health and welfare institutions, heating for schools, etc., 'other supplies for which there is a crucial need during a crisis in the interests of public health and safety (e.g. chlorine, lime and other agents for water purification) . . . and the operation of essential services, such as police, fire, ambulance, medical and nursing services . . .'.

The Code seeks to influence union discipline by providing that: 'Disciplinary action should not be taken against a member on the ground that he crossed a picket-line which it had not authorised or which was not at the member's place of work.' An exclusion or expulsion, therefore, is likely to be unlawful.

The Code is 'admissible in evidence' and must be 'taken into account'. These phrases do not, however, indicate the weight to be attached to its provisions nor to what is relevant. Unlike the ACAS codes, many of its provisions go considerably further than previous legislation and judicial determinations, and there must remain a serious question as to whether it is constitutionally legitimate for subdelegated legislation which is not extensively debated before Parliament to do so. Scott J in *Thomas* v *NUM (South Wales Area)* (supra) relied on the Code for the proposition that no more than six pickets should be allowed at each entrance to the workplace. He said that: 'This paragraph simply provides a guide as to a sensible number for a picket-line in order that the weight of numbers should not intimidate those who wish to get to work.'

The Government has issued a new Code of Practice which adds the following recommendations:

(a)   pickets on an entrance also used by workers of other companies should not call on them to join the dispute;

(b)   where possible, picketing should take place as near as feasible to the workplace;

(c)   pickets should not assert that they are official unless organised and endorsed by the union;

(d)   pickets should not jeopardise activities essential to maintenance of important plant and machinery.

Index